Hershman & McFarlane
Children Act Handbook

Hershman & McFarlane
Children Act Handbook

Family Law

Published by
Jordan Publishing Limited
21 St Thomas Street
Bristol BS1 6JS

© Jordan Publishing Limited 2010

All rights reserved. No part of this publication may be reproduced, stored in a retrieval system, or transmitted in any way or by any means, including photocopying or recording, without the written permission of the copyright holder, application for which should be addressed to the publisher.

Crown Copyright material is reproduced with the permission of the Controller of Her Majesty's Stationery Office.

British Library Cataloguing-in-Publication Data

A catalogue record for this book is available from the British Library.

ISBN   978 1 84661 233 6.

Typeset by Letterpart Ltd, Reigate, Surrey

Printed and bound in Great Britain by CPI Antony Rowe, Chippenham, Wilts

PREFACE TO THE FIRST EDITION

In the ten years since the publication of *Children Law and Practice*, one drawback of the layout of the text has been that, in order to have both the commentary and the statutory material at court, it has been necessary for users to carry both volumes of the work with them. This modestly sized handbook is being published in order to ease the physical burden on users by providing core statutory material in a portable supplement.

We hope that this handbook will be a useful addition to the family law library and that the selection that we have made is sufficient to meet both the need for portability and the need to provide essential core material. Any suggestions for additional material are welcome.

The *Children Act Handbook* will be updated each year and issued as part of the subscription package to all *Children Law and Practice* subscribers. In addition, the *Handbook* will be available for sale separately to non-subscribers.

David Hershman and
Andrew McFarlane
August 2001

CONTENTS

Preface to the First Edition   v

Part I – Statutes
Adoption and Children Act 2002   3
   ss 1, 18–29, 52   3
Children Act 1989   15

Part II – Statutory Instruments
Allocation and Transfer of Proceedings Order 2008   281
Family Proceedings Rules 1991   304
   Pt I; Pt II, rr 2.38–2.40, 2.57; Pts III–XI; Apps 1, 3, 4   304
Family Proceedings Courts (Children Act 1989) Rules 1991   480

Part III – Practice Directions and Guidance
President's Direction (Human Rights Act 1998) (24 July 2000)   561
President's Direction (Family Proceedings: Court Bundles (Universal Practice to be Applied in All Courts other than the Family Proceedings Court)) (27 July 2006)   562
Practice Direction (Experts In Family Proceedings Relating To Children) (1 April 2008)   569
Practice Direction (Allocation and Transfer of Proceedings) (3 November 2008)   585
Practice Direction (Residence and Contact Orders: Domestic Violence and Harm) (14 January 2009)   592
Family Proceedings (Allocation to Judiciary) Directions 2009   599
Practice Direction (Attendance of Media Representatives at Hearings in Family Proceedings (High Court and county courts)) (20 April 2009)   603
Practice Direction (Attendance of Media Representatives at Hearings in Family Proceedings (Family Proceedings Court)) (20 April 2009)   608

President's Guidance (Applications Consequent upon the
    Attendance of the Media in Family Proceedings) (22 April
    2009)   613
The Revised Private Law Programme (1 April 2010)   618
The Public Law Outline (April 2010)   626

Part IV – Miscellaneous
Calendars 2008–2011   659
Weights and Measures Conversion Tables   661

Part I

STATUTES

ADOPTION AND CHILDREN ACT 2002

ARRANGEMENT OF SECTIONS

PART 1
ADOPTION

Chapter 1
Introductory

Section		Page
1	Considerations applying to the exercise of powers	3

Chapter 3
Placement for Adoption and Adoption Orders

Placement of children by adoption agency for adoption

18	Placement for adoption by agencies	5
19	Placing children with parental consent	5
20	Advance consent to adoption	6
21	Placement orders	7
22	Applications for placement orders	7
23	Varying placement orders	9
24	Revoking placement orders	9
25	Parental responsibility	9
26	Contact	9
27	Contact: supplementary	10
28	Further consequences of placement	11
29	Further consequences of placement orders	12

Placement and adoption: general

52	Parental etc consent	13

PART 1
ADOPTION

Chapter 1
Introductory

1 Considerations applying to the exercise of powers

(1) This section applies whenever a court or adoption agency is coming to a decision relating to the adoption of a child.

(2) The paramount consideration of the court or adoption agency must be the child's welfare, throughout his life.

(3) The court or adoption agency must at all times bear in mind that, in general, any delay in coming to the decision is likely to prejudice the child's welfare.

(4) The court or adoption agency must have regard to the following matters (among others) –

(a) the child's ascertainable wishes and feelings regarding the decision (considered in the light of the child's age and understanding),
(b) the child's particular needs,
(c) the likely effect on the child (throughout his life) of having ceased to be a member of the original family and become an adopted person,
(d) the child's age, sex, background and any of the child's characteristics which the court or agency considers relevant,
(e) any harm (within the meaning of the Children Act 1989) which the child has suffered or is at risk of suffering,
(f) the relationship which the child has with relatives, and with any other person in relation to whom the court or agency considers the relationship to be relevant, including –
  (i) the likelihood of any such relationship continuing and the value to the child of its doing so,
  (ii) the ability and willingness of any of the child's relatives, or of any such person, to provide the child with a secure environment in which the child can develop, and otherwise to meet the child's needs,
  (iii) the wishes and feelings of any of the child's relatives, or of any such person, regarding the child.

(5) In placing the child for adoption, the adoption agency must give due consideration to the child's religious persuasion, racial origin and cultural and linguistic background.

(6) The court or adoption agency must always consider the whole range of powers available to it in the child's case (whether under this Act or the Children Act 1989); and the court must not make any order under this Act unless it considers that making the order would be better for the child than not doing so.

(7) In this section, "coming to a decision relating to the adoption of a child", in relation to a court, includes –

(a) coming to a decision in any proceedings where the orders that might be made by the court include an adoption order (or the revocation of such an order), a placement order (or the revocation of such an order) or an order under section 26 (or the revocation or variation of such an order),
(b) coming to a decision about granting leave in respect of any action (other than the initiation of proceedings in any court) which may be taken by an adoption agency or individual under this Act,

but does not include coming to a decision about granting leave in any other circumstances.

(8) For the purposes of this section –

(a) references to relationships are not confined to legal relationships,
(b) references to a relative, in relation to a child, include the child's mother and father.

****

Chapter 3
Placement for Adoption and Adoption Orders

Placement of children by adoption agency for adoption

18 Placement for adoption by agencies

(1) An adoption agency may –

(a) place a child for adoption with prospective adopters, or
(b) where it has placed a child with any persons (whether under this Part or not), leave the child with them as prospective adopters,

but, except in the case of a child who is less than six weeks old, may only do so under section 19 or a placement order.

(2) An adoption agency may only place a child for adoption with prospective adopters if the agency is satisfied that the child ought to be placed for adoption.

(3) A child who is placed or authorised to be placed for adoption with prospective adopters by a local authority is looked after by the authority.

(4) If an application for an adoption order has been made by any persons in respect of a child and has not been disposed of –

(a) an adoption agency which placed the child with those persons may leave the child with them until the application is disposed of, but
(b) apart from that, the child may not be placed for adoption with any prospective adopters.

"Adoption order" includes a Scottish or Northern Irish adoption order.

(5) References in this Act (apart from this section) to an adoption agency placing a child for adoption –

(a) are to its placing a child for adoption with prospective adopters, and
(b) include, where it has placed a child with any persons (whether under this Act or not), leaving the child with them as prospective adopters;

and references in this Act (apart from this section) to a child who is placed for adoption by an adoption agency are to be interpreted accordingly.

(6) References in this Chapter to an adoption agency being, or not being, authorised to place a child for adoption are to the agency being or (as the case may be) not being authorised to do so under section 19 or a placement order.

(7) This section is subject to sections 30 to 35 (removal of children placed by adoption agencies).

19 Placing children with parental consent

(1) Where an adoption agency is satisfied that each parent or guardian of a child has consented to the child –

(a) being placed for adoption with prospective adopters identified in the consent, or
(b) being placed for adoption with any prospective adopters who may be chosen by the agency,

and has not withdrawn the consent, the agency is authorised to place the child for adoption accordingly.

(2) Consent to a child being placed for adoption with prospective adopters identified in the consent may be combined with consent to the child subsequently being placed for adoption with any prospective adopters who may be chosen by the agency in circumstances where the child is removed from or returned by the identified prospective adopters.

(3) Subsection (1) does not apply where –

(a) an application has been made on which a care order might be made and the application has not been disposed of, or
(b) a care order or placement order has been made after the consent was given.

(4) References in this Act to a child placed for adoption under this section include a child who was placed under this section with prospective adopters and continues to be placed with them, whether or not consent to the placement has been withdrawn.

(5) This section is subject to section 52 (parental etc consent).

20 Advance consent to adoption

(1) A parent or guardian of a child who consents to the child being placed for adoption by an adoption agency under section 19 may, at the same or any subsequent time, consent to the making of a future adoption order.

(2) Consent under this section –

(a) where the parent or guardian has consented to the child being placed for adoption with prospective adopters identified in the consent, may be consent to adoption by them, or
(b) may be consent to adoption by any prospective adopters who may be chosen by the agency.

(3) A person may withdraw any consent given under this section.

(4) A person who gives consent under this section may, at the same or any subsequent time, by notice given to the adoption agency –

(a) state that he does not wish to be informed of any application for an adoption order, or
(b) withdraw such a statement.

(5) A notice under subsection (4) has effect from the time when it is received by the adoption agency but has no effect if the person concerned has withdrawn his consent.

(6) This section is subject to section 52 (parental etc consent).

21 Placement orders

(1) A placement order is an order made by the court authorising a local authority to place a child for adoption with any prospective adopters who may be chosen by the authority.

(2) The court may not make a placement order in respect of a child unless –

- (a) the child is subject to a care order,
- (b) the court is satisfied that the conditions in section 31(2) of the 1989 Act (conditions for making a care order) are met, or
- (c) the child has no parent or guardian.

(3) The court may only make a placement order if, in the case of each parent or guardian of the child, the court is satisfied –

- (a) that the parent or guardian has consented to the child being placed for adoption with any prospective adopters who may be chosen by the local authority and has not withdrawn the consent, or
- (b) that the parent's or guardian's consent should be dispensed with.

This subsection is subject to section 52 (parental etc consent).

(4) A placement order continues in force until –

- (a) it is revoked under section 24,
- (b) an adoption order is made in respect of the child, or
- (c) the child marries[, forms a civil partnership]¹ or attains the age of 18 years.

"Adoption order" includes a Scottish or Northern Irish adoption order.

NOTES

Amendments.¹ Words inserted: Civil Partnership Act 2004, s 79(1), (2).

22 Applications for placement orders

(1) A local authority must apply to the court for a placement order in respect of a child if –

- (a) the child is placed for adoption by them or is being provided with accommodation by them,
- (b) no adoption agency is authorised to place the child for adoption,
- (c) the child has no parent or guardian or the authority consider that the conditions in section 31(2) of the 1989 Act are met, and
- (d) the authority are satisfied that the child ought to be placed for adoption.

(2) If –

- (a) an application has been made (and has not been disposed of) on which a care order might be made in respect of a child, or

(b) a child is subject to a care order and the appropriate local authority are not authorised to place the child for adoption,

the appropriate local authority must apply to the court for a placement order if they are satisfied that the child ought to be placed for adoption.

(3) If –

(a) a child is subject to a care order, and
(b) the appropriate local authority are authorised to place the child for adoption under section 19,

the authority may apply to the court for a placement order.

(4) If a local authority –

(a) are under a duty to apply to the court for a placement order in respect of a child, or
(b) have applied for a placement order in respect of a child and the application has not been disposed of,

the child is looked after by the authority.

(5) Subsections (1) to (3) do not apply in respect of a child –

(a) if any persons have given notice of intention to adopt, unless the period of four months beginning with the giving of the notice has expired without them applying for an adoption order or their application for such an order has been withdrawn or refused, or
(b) if an application for an adoption order has been made and has not been disposed of.

"Adoption order" includes a Scottish or Northern Irish adoption order.

(6) Where –

(a) an application for a placement order in respect of a child has been made and has not been disposed of, and
(b) no interim care order is in force,

the court may give any directions it considers appropriate for the medical or psychiatric examination or other assessment of the child; but a child who is of sufficient understanding to make an informed decision may refuse to submit to the examination or other assessment.

(7) The appropriate local authority –

(a) in relation to a care order, is the local authority in whose care the child is placed by the order, and
(b) in relation to an application on which a care order might be made, is the local authority which makes the application.

23 Varying placement orders

(1) The court may vary a placement order so as to substitute another local authority for the local authority authorised by the order to place the child for adoption.

(2) The variation may only be made on the joint application of both authorities.

24 Revoking placement orders

(1) The court may revoke a placement order on the application of any person.

(2) But an application may not be made by a person other than the child or the local authority authorised by the order to place the child for adoption unless –

(a) the court has given leave to apply, and
(b) the child is not placed for adoption by the authority.

(3) The court cannot give leave under subsection (2)(*a*) unless satisfied that there has been a change in circumstances since the order was made.

(4) If the court determines, on an application for an adoption order, not to make the order, it may revoke any placement order in respect of the child.

(5) Where –

(a) an application for the revocation of a placement order has been made and has not been disposed of, and
(b) the child is not placed for adoption by the authority,

the child may not without the court's leave be placed for adoption under the order.

25 Parental responsibility

(1) This section applies while –

(a) a child is placed for adoption under section 19 or an adoption agency is authorised to place a child for adoption under that section, or
(b) a placement order is in force in respect of a child.

(2) Parental responsibility for the child is given to the agency concerned.

(3) While the child is placed with prospective adopters, parental responsibility is given to them.

(4) The agency may determine that the parental responsibility of any parent or guardian, or of prospective adopters, is to be restricted to the extent specified in the determination.

26 Contact

(1) On an adoption agency being authorised to place a child for adoption, or placing a child for adoption who is less than six weeks old, any provision for contact under the 1989 Act ceases to have effect.

Part I Statutes

(2) While an adoption agency is so authorised or a child is placed for adoption –

   (a) no application may be made for any provision for contact under that Act, but
   (b) the court may make an order under this section requiring the person with whom the child lives, or is to live, to allow the child to visit or stay with the person named in the order, or for the person named in the order and the child otherwise to have contact with each other.

(3) An application for an order under this section may be made by –

   (a) the child or the agency,
   (b) any parent, guardian or relative,
   (c) any person in whose favour there was provision for contact under the 1989 Act which ceased to have effect by virtue of subsection (1),
   (d) if a residence order was in force immediately before the adoption agency was authorised to place the child for adoption or (as the case may be) placed the child for adoption at a time when he was less than six weeks old, the person in whose favour the order was made,
   (e) if a person had care of the child immediately before that time by virtue of an order made in the exercise of the High Court's inherent jurisdiction with respect to children, that person,
   (f) any person who has obtained the court's leave to make the application.

(4) When making a placement order, the court may on its own initiative make an order under this section.

(5) This section does not prevent an application for a contact order under section 8 of the 1989 Act being made where the application is to be heard together with an application for an adoption order in respect of the child.

(6) In this section, "provision for contact under the 1989 Act" means a contact order under section 8 of that Act or an order under section 34 of that Act (parental contact with children in care).

27 Contact: supplementary

(1) An order under section 26 –

   (a) has effect while the adoption agency is authorised to place the child for adoption or the child is placed for adoption, but
   (b) may be varied or revoked by the court on an application by the child, the agency or a person named in the order.

(2) The agency may refuse to allow the contact that would otherwise be required by virtue of an order under that section if –

   (a) it is satisfied that it is necessary to do so in order to safeguard or promote the child's welfare, and
   (b) the refusal is decided upon as a matter of urgency and does not last for more than seven days.

(3) Regulations may make provision as to –

(a) the steps to be taken by an agency which has exercised its power under subsection (2),
(b) the circumstances in which, and conditions subject to which, the terms of any order under section 26 may be departed from by agreement between the agency and any person for whose contact with the child the order provides,
(c) notification by an agency of any variation or suspension of arrangements made (otherwise than under an order under that section) with a view to allowing any person contact with the child.

(4) Before making a placement order the court must –

(a) consider the arrangements which the adoption agency has made, or proposes to make, for allowing any person contact with the child, and
(b) invite the parties to the proceedings to comment on those arrangements.

(5) An order under section 26 may provide for contact on any conditions the court considers appropriate.

28 Further consequences of placement

(1) Where a child is placed for adoption under section 19 or an adoption agency is authorised to place a child for adoption under that section –

(a) a parent or guardian of the child may not apply for a residence order unless an application for an adoption order has been made and the parent or guardian has obtained the court's leave under subsection (3) or (5) of section 47,
(b) if an application has been made for an adoption order, a guardian of the child may not apply for a special guardianship order unless he has obtained the court's leave under subsection (3) or (5) of that section.

(2) Where –

(a) a child is placed for adoption under section 19 or an adoption agency is authorised to place a child for adoption under that section, or
(b) a placement order is in force in respect of a child,

then (whether or not the child is in England and Wales) a person may not do either of the following things, unless the court gives leave or each parent or guardian of the child gives written consent.

(3) Those things are –

(a) causing the child to be known by a new surname, or
(b) removing the child from the United Kingdom.

(4) Subsection (3) does not prevent the removal of a child from the United Kingdom for a period of less than one month by a person who provides the child's home.

29 Further consequences of placement orders

(1) Where a placement order is made in respect of a child and either –

    (a)   the child is subject to a care order, or
    (b)   the court at the same time makes a care order in respect of the child,

the care order does not have effect at any time when the placement order is in force.

(2) On the making of a placement order in respect of a child, any order mentioned in section 8(1) of the 1989 Act, and any supervision order in respect of the child, ceases to have effect.

(3) Where a placement order is in force –

    (a)   no prohibited steps order, residence order or specific issue order, and
    (b)   no supervision order or child assessment order,

may be made in respect of the child.

(4) Subsection (3)(*a*) does not apply in respect of a residence order if –

    (a)   an application for an adoption order has been made in respect of the child, and
    (b)   the residence order is applied for by a parent or guardian who has obtained the court's leave under subsection (3) or (5) of section 47 or by any other person who has obtained the court's leave under this subsection.

(5) Where a placement order is in force, no special guardianship order may be made in respect of the child unless –

    (a)   an application has been made for an adoption order, and
    (b)   the person applying for the special guardianship order has obtained the court's leave under this subsection or, if he is a guardian of the child, has obtained the court's leave under section 47(5).

(6) Section 14A(7) of the 1989 Act applies in respect of an application for a special guardianship order for which leave has been given as mentioned in subsection (5)(*b*) with the omission of the words "the beginning of the period of three months ending with".

(7) Where a placement order is in force –

    (a)   section 14C(1)(b) of the 1989 Act (special guardianship: parental responsibility) has effect subject to any determination under section 25(4) of this Act,
    (b)   section 14C(3) and (4) of the 1989 Act (special guardianship: removal of child from UK etc) does not apply.

****

Placement and adoption: general

52 Parental etc consent

(1) The court cannot dispense with the consent of any parent or guardian of a child to the child being placed for adoption or to the making of an adoption order in respect of the child unless the court is satisfied that –

   (a)   the parent or guardian cannot be found or [lacks capacity (within the meaning of the Mental Capacity Act 2005) to give consent][1], or

   (b)   the welfare of the child requires the consent to be dispensed with.

(2) The following provisions apply to references in this Chapter to any parent or guardian of a child giving or withdrawing –

   (a)   consent to the placement of a child for adoption, or

   (b)   consent to the making of an adoption order (including a future adoption order).

(3) Any consent given by the mother to the making of an adoption order is ineffective if it is given less than six weeks after the child's birth.

(4) The withdrawal of any consent to the placement of a child for adoption, or of any consent given under section 20, is ineffective if it is given after an application for an adoption order is made.

(5) "Consent" means consent given unconditionally and with full understanding of what is involved; but a person may consent to adoption without knowing the identity of the persons in whose favour the order will be made.

(6) "Parent" (except in subsections (9) and (10) below) means a parent having parental responsibility.

(7) Consent under section 19 or 20 must be given in the form prescribed by rules, and the rules may prescribe forms in which a person giving consent under any other provision of this Part may do so (if he wishes).

(8) Consent given under section 19 or 20 must be withdrawn –

   (a)   in the form prescribed by rules, or

   (b)   by notice given to the agency.

(9) Subsection (10) applies if –

   (a)   an agency has placed a child for adoption under section 19 in pursuance of consent given by a parent of the child, and

   (b)   at a later time, the other parent of the child acquires parental responsibility for the child.

(10) The other parent is to be treated as having at that time given consent in accordance with this section in the same terms as those in which the first parent gave consent.

Part I Statutes

NOTES

Amendments.[1] Words substituted: Mental Capacity Act 2005, s 67(1), Sch 6, para 45.

****

CHILDREN ACT 1989

ARRANGEMENT OF SECTIONS

PART I
INTRODUCTORY

Section		Page
1	Welfare of the child	21
2	Parental responsibility for children	22
3	Meaning of 'parental responsibility'	23
4	Acquisition of parental responsibility by father	24
4ZA	Acquisition of parental responsibility by second female parent	25
4A	Acquisition of parental responsibility by step-parent	26
5	Appointment of guardians	26
6	Guardians: revocation and disclaimer	28
7	Welfare reports	29

PART II
ORDERS WITH RESPECT TO CHILDREN IN FAMILY AND OTHER PROCEEDINGS

General

8	Residence, contact and other orders with respect to children	30
9	Restrictions on making section 8 orders	31
10	Power of court to make section 8 orders	32
11	General principles and supplementary provisions	34
11A	Contact activity directions	35
11B	Contact activity directions: further provision	36
11C	Contact activity conditions	37
11D	Contact activity conditions: further provision	38
11E	Contact activity directions and conditions: making	38
11F	Contact activity directions and conditions: financial assistance	39
11G	Contact activity directions and conditions: monitoring	40
11H	Monitoring contact	41
11I	Contact orders: warning notices	42
11J	Enforcement orders	42
11K	Enforcement orders: further provision	43
11L	Enforcement orders: making	43
11M	Enforcement orders: monitoring	44
11N	Enforcement orders: warning notices	45
11O	Compensation for financial loss	45
11P	Orders under section 11O(2): further provision	46
12	Residence orders and parental responsibility	46
13	Change of child's name or removal from jurisdiction	47
14	Enforcement of residence orders	48

Special guardianship

14A	Special guardianship orders	48
14B	Special guardianship orders: making	50
14C	Special guardianship orders: effect	50
14D	Special guardianship orders: variation and discharge	51
14E	Special guardianship orders: supplementary	52
14F	Special guardianship support services	52
14G		54

Financial relief

15	Orders for financial relief with respect to children	54

Family assistance orders

16	Family assistance orders	55
16A	Risk assessments	56

PART III
LOCAL AUTHORITY SUPPORT FOR CHILDREN AND FAMILIES

Provision of services for children and their families

17	Provision of services for children in need, their families and others	57
17A	Direct payments	59
18	Day care for pre-school and other children	60
19		61

Provision of accommodation for children

20	Provision of accommodation for children: general	61
21	Provision of accommodation for children in police protection or detention or on remand, etc	62

Duties of local authorities in relation to children looked after by them

22	General duty of local authority in relation to children looked after by them	64
22C	Ways in which looked after children are to be accommodated and maintained	65
22F	Regulations as to children looked after by local authorities	66
23	Provision of accommodation and maintenance by local authority for children whom they are looking after	67

Visiting

23ZA	Duty of local authority to ensure visits to, and contact with, looked after children and others	68
23ZB	Independent visitors for children looked after by a local authority	69

Advice and assistance for certain children and young persons

23A	The responsible authority and relevant children	70
23B	Additional functions of the responsible authority in respect of relevant children	71
23C	Continuing functions in respect of former relevant children	72

Personal advisers and pathway plans

23D	Personal advisers	74
23E	Pathway plans	74
24	Persons qualifying for advice and assistance	75
24A	Advice and assistance	76
24B	Employment, education and training	77
24C	Information	78
24D	Representations: sections 23A to 24B	79

Secure accommodation

25	Use of accommodation for restricting liberty	79

Independent reviewing officers

25A	Appointment of independent reviewing officer	80

25B	Functions of the independent reviewing officer	81

Supplemental

26	Review of cases and inquiries into representations	82
26ZB	Representations: further consideration (Wales)	85
26A	Advocacy services	86
27	Co-operation between authorities	87
28	Consultation with local education authorities	88
29	Recoupment of cost of providing services etc	88
30	Miscellaneous	90
30A	Meaning of appropriate national authority	91

PART IV
CARE AND SUPERVISION

General

31	Care and supervision orders	91
31A	Care orders: care plans	93
32	Period within which application for order under this Part must be disposed of	93

Care orders

33	Effect of care order	94
34	Parental contact etc with children in care	95

Supervision orders

35	Supervision orders	97
36	Education supervision orders	97

Powers of court

37	Powers of court in certain family proceedings	99
38	Interim orders	100
38A	Power to include exclusion requirement in interim care order	101
38B	Undertakings relating to interim care orders	103
39	Discharge and variation etc of care orders and supervision orders	103
40	Orders pending appeals in cases about care or supervision orders	104

Representation of child

41	Representation of child and of his interests in certain proceedings	105
42	Right of officer of the Service to have access to local authority records	107

PART V
PROTECTION OF CHILDREN

43	Child assessment orders	108
44	Orders for emergency protection of children	109
44A	Power to include exclusion requirement in emergency protection order	112
44B	Undertakings relating to emergency protection orders	114
45	Duration of emergency protection orders and other supplemental provisions	114
46	Removal and accommodation of children by police in cases of emergency	116
47	Local authority's duty to investigate	118
48	Powers to assist in discovery of children who may be in need of emergency protection	121

49	Abduction of children in care etc	123
50	Recovery of abducted children etc	123
51	Refuges for children at risk	125
52	Rules and regulations	126

PART VI
COMMUNITY HOMES

53	Provision of community homes by local authorities	127
54		128
55	Determination of disputes relating to controlled and assisted community homes	128
56	Discontinuance by voluntary organisation of controlled or assisted community home	129
57	Closure by local authority of controlled or assisted community home	130
58	Financial provisions applicable on cessation of controlled or assisted community home or disposal etc of premises	131

PART VII
VOLUNTARY HOMES AND VOLUNTARY ORGANISATIONS

59	Provision of accommodation by voluntary organisations	133
60	Voluntary homes	134
61	Duties of voluntary organisations	134
62	Duties of local authorities	135

PART VIII
REGISTERED CHILDREN'S HOMES

63	Private children's homes etc	137
64	Welfare of children in children's homes	137
65	Persons disqualified from carrying on, or being employed in, children's homes	138
65A	Appeal against refusal of authority to give consent under section 65	139

PART IX
PRIVATE ARRANGEMENTS FOR FOSTERING CHILDREN

66	Privately fostered children	139
67	Welfare of privately fostered children	140
68	Persons disqualified from being private foster parents	141
69	Power to prohibit private fostering	142
70	Offences	143

PART X
CHILD MINDING AND DAY CARE FOR YOUNG CHILDREN

PART XA
CHILD MINDING AND DAY CARE FOR CHILDREN IN ... WALES

Introductory

79A	Child minders and day care providers	145
79B	Other definitions, etc	146

Regulations

79C	Regulations etc governing child minders and day care providers	147

Registration

79D	Requirement to register	148

Children Act 1989

79E	Applications for registration	149
79F	Grant or refusal of registration	149
79G	Cancellation of registration	150
79H	Suspension of registration	151
79J	Resignation of registration	151
79K	Protection of children in an emergency	152
79L	Notice of intention to take steps	152
79M	Appeals	153

Inspection: England

79N	General functions of the Chief Inspector	154
79P		154
79Q	Inspection of provision of child minding and day care in England	154
79R	Reports of inspections	154

Inspection: Wales

79S	General functions of the Assembly	154
79T	Inspection: Wales	154

Supplementary

79U	Rights of entry etc	155
79V	Function of local authorities	156

Checks on suitability of persons working with children over the age of seven

79W	Requirement for certificate of suitability	156

Time limit for proceedings

79X	Time limit for proceedings	157

PART XI
SECRETARY OF STATE'S SUPERVISORY FUNCTIONS AND RESPONSIBILITIES

80	Inspection of children's homes etc by persons authorised by Secretary of State	158
81		160
82	Financial support by Secretary of State	161
83	Research and returns of information	162
84	Local authority failure to comply with statutory duty: default power of Secretary of State	164

PART XII
MISCELLANEOUS AND GENERAL

Notification of children accommodated in certain establishments

85	Children accommodated by health authorities and local education authorities	164
86	Children accommodated in care homes or independent hospitals	165
86A	Visitors for children notified to local authority under section 85 or 86	166
87	Welfare of children in boarding schools and colleges	167
87A	Suspension of duty under section 87(3)	169
87B	Duties of inspectors under section 87A	170
87C	Boarding schools: national minimum standards	171
87D	Annual fee for boarding school inspections	171

Part I Statutes

Adoption

88	Amendments of adoption legislation	172
89		172

Criminal care and supervision orders

90	Care and supervision orders in criminal proceedings	172

Effect and duration of orders etc

91	Effect and duration of orders etc	172

Jurisdiction and procedure etc

92	Jurisdiction of courts	174
93	Rules of Court	176
94	Appeals	177
95	Attendance of child at hearing under Part IV or V	178
96	Evidence given by, or with respect to, children	179
97	Privacy for children involved in certain proceedings	180
98	Self-incrimination	181
99		181
100	Restrictions on use of wardship jurisdiction	181
101	Effect of orders as between England and Wales and Northern Ireland, the Channel Islands or the Isle of Man	182

Search warrants

102	Power of constable to assist in exercise of certain powers to search for children or inspect premises	183

General

103	Offences by bodies corporate	184
104	Regulations and orders	185
104A	Regulations and orders made by the Welsh Ministers under Part 3 etc	186
105	Interpretation	186
106	Financial provisions	191
107	Application to the Channel Islands	191
108	Short title, commencement, extent, etc	191
	Schedule A1 – Enforcement Orders	193
	Part 1 – Unpaid Work Requirement	193
	Part 2 – Revocation, Amendment or Breach of Enforcement Order	194
	Schedule 1 – Financial Provision for Children	199
	Schedule 2 – Local Authority Support for Children and Families	213
	Part I – Provision of Services for Families	213
	Part II – Children Looked After by Local Authorities	217
	Part III – Contributions Towards Maintenance of Children	225
	Schedule 3 – Supervision Orders	230
	Part I – General	230
	Part II – Miscellaneous	233
	Part III – Education Supervision Orders	234
	Schedule 4 – Management and Conduct of Community Homes	238
	Part I – Instruments of Management	238
	Part II – Management of Controlled and Assisted Community Homes	240
	Part III – Regulations	241
	Schedule 5 – Voluntary Homes and Voluntary Organisations	242
	Part I – Registration of Voluntary Homes	242
	Part II – Regulations as to Voluntary Homes	242
	Schedule 6 – Private Children's Homes	242
	Part I – Registration	242

Part II – Regulations	242
Schedule 7 – Foster Parents: Limits on Number of Foster Children	243
Schedule 8 – Privately Fostered Children	245
Schedule 9A – Child Minding and Day Care for Young Children in Wales	250
Schedule 10 – Amendments of Adoption Legislation	256
Schedule 11 – Jurisdiction	256
Part I – General	256
Part II – consequential amendments	259
Schedule 12 – Minor Amendments	259
Schedule 13 – Consequential Amendments	259
Schedule 14 – Transitionals and Savings	259

An Act to reform the law relating to children; to provide for local authority services for children in need and others; to amend the law with respect to children's homes, community homes, voluntary homes and voluntary organisations; to make provision with respect to fostering, child minding and day care for young children and adoption; and for connected purposes.
[16 November 1989]

PART I
INTRODUCTORY

1 Welfare of the child

(1) When a court determines any question with respect to –

(a) the upbringing of a child; or
(b) the administration of a child's property or the application of any income arising from it,

the child's welfare shall be the court's paramount consideration.

(2) In any proceedings in which any question with respect to the upbringing of a child arises, the court shall have regard to the general principle that any delay in determining the question is likely to prejudice the welfare of the child.

(3) In the circumstances mentioned in subsection (4), a court shall have regard in particular to –

(a) the ascertainable wishes and feelings of the child concerned (considered in the light of his age and understanding);
(b) his physical, emotional and educational needs;
(c) the likely effect on him of any change in his circumstances;
(d) his age, sex, background and any characteristics of his which the court considers relevant;
(e) any harm which he has suffered or is at risk of suffering;
(f) how capable each of his parents, and any other person in relation to whom the court considers the question to be relevant, is of meeting his needs;
(g) the range of powers available to the court under this Act in the proceedings in question.

(4) The circumstances are that –

(a) the court is considering whether to make, vary or discharge a section 8 order, and the making, variation or discharge of the order is opposed by any party to the proceedings; or

(b) the court is considering whether to make, vary or discharge [a special guardianship order or]¹ an order under Part IV.

(5) Where a court is considering whether or not to make one or more orders under this Act with respect to a child, it shall not make the order or any of the orders unless it considers that doing so would be better for the child than making no order at all.

NOTES

Amendments. ¹ Words inserted: Adoption and Children Act 2002, s 115(2), (3).

Definitions. 'A section 8 order': s 8(2); 'child': s 105(1); 'harm': ss 31(9), 105(1); 'the court': s 92(7); 'upbringing': s 105(1).

2 Parental responsibility for children

(1) Where a child's father and mother were married to each other at the time of his birth, they shall each have parental responsibility for the child.

[(1A) Where a child –

(a) has a parent by virtue of section 42 of the Human Fertilisation and Embryology Act 2008; or

(b) has a parent by virtue of section 43 of that Act and is a person to whom section 1(3) of the Family Law Reform Act 1987 applies,

the child's mother and the other parent shall each have parental responsibility for the child.]²

(2) Where a child's father and mother were not married to each other at the time of his birth –

(a) the mother shall have parental responsibility for the child;

(b) the father [shall have parental responsibility for the child if he has acquired it (and has not ceased to have it)]¹ in accordance with the provisions of this Act.

[(2A) Where a child has a parent by virtue of section 43 of the Human Fertilisation and Embryology Act 2008 and is not a person to whom section 1(3) of the Family Law Reform Act 1987 applies –

(a) the mother shall have parental responsibility for the child;

(b) the other parent shall have parental responsibility for the child if she has acquired it (and has not ceased to have it) in accordance with the provisions of this Act.]²

(3) References in this Act to a child whose father and mother were, or (as the case may be) were not, married to each other at the time of his birth must be read with section 1 of the Family Law Reform Act 1987 (which extends their meaning).

(4) The rule of law that a father is the natural guardian of his legitimate child is abolished.

(5) More than one person may have parental responsibility for the same child at the same time.

(6) A person who has parental responsibility for a child at any time shall not cease to have that responsibility solely because some other person subsequently acquires parental responsibility for the child.

(7) Where more than one person has parental responsibility for a child, each of them may act alone and without the other (or others) in meeting that responsibility; but nothing in this Part shall be taken to affect the operation of any enactment which requires the consent of more than one person in a matter affecting the child.

(8) The fact that a person has parental responsibility for a child shall not entitle him to act in any way which would be incompatible with any order made with respect to the child under this Act.

(9) A person who has parental responsibility for a child may not surrender or transfer any part of that responsibility to another but may arrange for some or all of it to be met by one or more persons acting on his behalf.

(10) The person with whom any such arrangement is made may himself be a person who already has parental responsibility for the child concerned.

(11) The making of any such arrangement shall not affect any liability of the person making it which may arise from any failure to meet any part of his parental responsibility for the child concerned.

NOTES

Amendment. [1] Words substituted: Adoption and Children Act 2002, s 111(5). [2] Subsections inserted: SI 2009/479.

Definitions. 'Child': s 105(1); 'married ... at the time of his birth': s 2(3); 'parental responsibility': s 3.

3 Meaning of 'parental responsibility'

(1) In this Act 'parental responsibility' means all the rights, duties, powers, responsibilities and authority which by law a parent of a child has in relation to the child and his property.

(2) It also includes the rights, powers and duties which a guardian of the child's estate (appointed, before the commencement of section 5, to act generally) would have had in relation to the child and his property.

(3) The rights referred to in subsection (2) include, in particular, the right of the guardian to receive or recover in his own name, for the benefit of the child, property of whatever description and wherever situated which the child is entitled to receive or recover.

(4) The fact that a person has, or does not have, parental responsibility for a child shall not affect –

Part I Statutes

(a) any obligation which he may have in relation to the child (such as a statutory duty to maintain the child); or
(b) any rights which, in the event of the child's death, he (or any other person) may have in relation to the child's property.

(5) A person who –

(a) does not have parental responsibility for a particular child; but
(b) has care of the child,

may (subject to the provisions of this Act) do what is reasonable in all the circumstances of the case for the purpose of safeguarding or promoting the child's welfare.

NOTES
Definitions. 'Child': s 105(1); 'parental responsibility': s 3.

4 Acquisition of parental responsibility by father

(1) Where a child's father and mother were not married to each other at the time of his birth [, the father shall acquire parental responsibility for the child if –

(a) he becomes registered as the child's father under any of the enactments specified in subsection (1A);
(b) he and the child's mother make an agreement (a 'parental responsibility agreement') providing for him to have parental responsibility for the child; or
(c) the court, on his application, orders that he shall have parental responsibility for the child.]¹

[(1A) The enactments referred to in subsection (1)(a) are –

(a) paragraphs (a), (b) and (c) of section 10(1) and of section 10A(1) of the Births and Deaths Registration Act 1953;
(b) paragraphs (a), (b)(i) and (c) of section 18(1), and sections 18(2)(b) and 20(1)(a) of the Registration of Births, Deaths and Marriages (Scotland) Act 1965; and
(c) sub-paragraphs (a), (b) and (c) of Article 14(3) of the Births and Deaths Registration (Northern Ireland) Order 1976.

(1B) The [Secretary of State]⁴ may by order amend subsection (1A) so as to add further enactments to the list in that subsection.]²

(2) No parental responsibility agreement shall have effect for the purposes of this Act unless –

(a) it is made in the form prescribed by regulations made by the Lord Chancellor; and
(b) where regulations are made by the Lord Chancellor prescribing the manner in which such agreements must be recorded, it is recorded in the prescribed manner.

[(2A) A person who has acquired parental responsibility under subsection (1) shall cease to have that responsibility only if the court so orders.

(3) The court may make an order under subsection (2A) on the application –

(a) of any person who has parental responsibility for the child, or
(b) with leave of the court, of the child himself,

subject, in the case of parental responsibility acquired under subsection (1)(c), to section 12(4).][3]

(4) The court may only grant leave under subsection (3)(b) if it is satisfied that the child has sufficient understanding to make the proposed application.

NOTES

Amendments.[1] Words substituted: Adoption and Children Act 2002, s 111(1), (2). [2] Subsections (1A), (1B) inserted: Adoption and Children Act 2002, s 111(1), (3). [3] Subsections (2A), (3) inserted: Adoption and Children Act 2002, s 111(1), (4). [4] Words substituted: SI 2003/3191, arts 3(a), 6, Sch, para 1.

Definitions. 'Child': s 105(1); 'parental responsibility': s 3; 'parental responsibility agreement': s 4(1)(b); 'prescribed': s 105(1); 'the court': s 92(7).

[4ZA Acquisition of parental responsibility by second female parent

(1) Where a child has a parent by virtue of section 43 of the Human Fertilisation and Embryology Act 2008 and is not a person to whom section 1(3) of the Family Law Reform Act 1987 applies, that parent shall acquire parental responsibility for the child if –

(a) she becomes registered as a parent of the child under any of the enactments specified in subsection (2);
(b) she and the child's mother make an agreement providing for her to have parental responsibility for the child; or
(c) the court, on her application, orders that she shall have parental responsibility for the child.

(2) The enactments referred to in subsection (1)(a) are –

(a) paragraphs (a), (b) and (c) of section 10(1B) and of section 10A(1B) of the Births and Deaths Registration Act 1953;
(b) paragraphs (a), (b) and (d) of section 18B(1) and sections 18B(3)(a) and 20(1)(a) of the Registration of Births, Deaths and Marriages (Scotland) Act 1965; and
(c) sub-paragraphs (a), (b) and (c) of Article 14ZA(3) of the Births and Deaths Registration (Northern Ireland) Order 1976.

(3) The Secretary of State may by order amend subsection (2) so as to add further enactments to the list in that subsection.

(4) An agreement under subsection (1)(b) is also a "parental responsibility agreement", and section 4(2) applies in relation to such an agreement as it applies in relation to parental responsibility agreements under section 4.

Part I Statutes

(5) A person who has acquired parental responsibility under subsection (1) shall cease to have that responsibility only if the court so orders.

(6) The court may make an order under subsection (5) on the application –

(a) of any person who has parental responsibility for the child; or
(b) with the leave of the court, of the child himself,

subject, in the case of parental responsibility acquired under subsection (1)(c), to section 12(4).

(7) The court may only grant leave under subsection (6)(b) if it is satisfied that the child has sufficient understanding to make the proposed application.][1]

NOTES

Amendments.[1] Section inserted: Human Fertilisation and Embryology Act 2008, s 56, Sch 6, Pt 1, para 27.

[4A Acquisition of parental responsibility by step-parent

(1) Where a child's parent ('parent A') who has parental responsibility for the child is married to[, or a civil partner of,][2] a person who is not the child's parent ('the step-parent') –

(a) parent A or, if the other parent of the child also has parental responsibility for the child, both parents may by agreement with the step-parent provide for the step-parent to have parental responsibility for the child; or
(b) the court may, on the application of the step-parent, order that the step-parent shall have parental responsibility for the child.

(2) An agreement under subsection (1)(a) is also a 'parental responsibility agreement', and section 4(2) applies in relation to such agreements as it applies in relation to parental responsibility agreements under section 4.

(3) A parental responsibility agreement under subsection (1)(a), or an order under subsection (1)(b), may only be brought to an end by an order of the court made on the application –

(a) of any person who has parental responsibility for the child; or
(b) with the leave of the court, of the child himself.

(4) The court may only grant leave under subsection (3)(b) if it is satisfied that the child has sufficient understanding to make the proposed application.][1]

NOTES

Amendments.[1] Section inserted: Adoption and Children Act 2002, s 112.[2] Words inserted: Civil Partnership Act 2004, s 75(1), (2).

5 Appointment of guardians

(1) Where an application with respect to a child is made to the court by any individual, the court may by order appoint that individual to be the child's guardian if –

(a) the child has no parent with parental responsibility for him; or
(b) a residence order has been made with respect to the child in favour of a parent [, guardian or special guardian]¹ of his who has died while the order was in force[; or
(c) paragraph (b) does not apply, and the child's only or last surviving special guardian dies.]²

(2) The power conferred by subsection (1) may also be exercised in any family proceedings if the court considers that the order should be made even though no application has been made for it.

(3) A parent who has parental responsibility for his child may appoint another individual to be the child's guardian in the event of his death.

(4) A guardian of a child may appoint another individual to take his place as the child's guardian in the event of his death[; and a special guardian of a child may appoint another individual to be the child's guardian in the event of his death]².

(5) An appointment under subsection (3) or (4) shall not have effect unless it is made in writing, is dated and is signed by the person making the appointment or –

(a) in the case of an appointment made by a will which is not signed by the testator, is signed at the direction of the testator in accordance with the requirements of section 9 of the Wills Act 1837; or
(b) in any other case, is signed at the direction of the person making the appointment, in his presence and in the presence of two witnesses who each attest the signature.

(6) A person appointed as a child's guardian under this section shall have parental responsibility for the child concerned.

(7) Where –

(a) on the death of any person making an appointment under subsection (3) or (4), the child concerned has no parent with parental responsibility for him; or
(b) immediately before the death of any person making such an appointment, a residence order in his favour was in force with respect to the child,[or he was the child's only (or last surviving) special guardian]²

the appointment shall take effect on the death of that person.

(8) Where, on the death of any person making an appointment under subsection (3) or (4) –

(a) the child concerned has a parent with parental responsibility for him; and
(b) subsection (7)(b) does not apply,

the appointment shall take effect when the child no longer has a parent who has parental responsibility for him.

Part I Statutes

(9) Subsections (1) and (7) do not apply if the residence order referred to in paragraph (b) of those subsections was also made in favour of a surviving parent of the child.

(10) Nothing in this section shall be taken to prevent an appointment under subsection (3) or (4) being made by two or more persons acting jointly.

(11) Subject to any provision made by rules of court, no court shall exercise the High Court's inherent jurisdiction to appoint a guardian of the estate of any child.

(12) Where the rules of court are made under subsection (11) they may prescribe the circumstances in which, and conditions subject to which, an appointment of such a guardian may be made.

(13) A guardian of a child may only be appointed in accordance with the provisions of this section.

NOTES

Amendments. [1] Words substituted: Adoption and Children Act 2002, s 115(2), (4)(a)(i). [2] Words inserted: Adoption and Children Act 2002, s 115(2), (4)(a)(ii), (b), (c).

Definitions. 'Child': s 105(1); 'family proceedings': s 8(3); 'guardian of a child': s 105(1); 'parental responsibility': s 3; 'residence order': s 8(1); 'signed': s 105(1); 'the court': s 92(7).

6 Guardians: revocation and disclaimer

(1) An appointment under section 5(3) or (4) revokes an earlier such appointment (including one made in an unrevoked will or codicil) made by the same person in respect of the same child, unless it is clear (whether as the result of an express provision in the later appointment or by any necessary implication) that the purpose of the later appointment is to appoint an additional guardian.

(2) An appointment under section 5(3) or (4) (including one made in an unrevoked will or codicil) is revoked if the person who made the appointment revokes it by a written and dated instrument which is signed –

    (a)   by him; or
    (b)   at his direction, in his presence and in the presence of two witnesses who each attest the signature.

(3) An appointment under section 5(3) or (4) (other than one made in a will or codicil) is revoked if, with the intention of revoking the appointment, the person who made it –

    (a)   destroys the instrument by which it was made; or
    (b)   has some other person destroy that instrument in his presence.

[(3A) An appointment under section 5(3) or (4) (including one made in an unrevoked will or codicil) is revoked if the person appointed is the spouse of the person who made the appointment and either –

    (a)   a decree of a court of civil jurisdiction in England and Wales dissolves or annuls the marriage, or

(b) the marriage is dissolved or annulled and the divorce or annulment is entitled to recognition in England and Wales by virtue of Part II of the Family Law Act 1986,

unless a contrary intention appears by the appointment.][1]

[(3B) An appointment under section 5(3) or (4) (including one made in an unrevoked will or codicil) is revoked if the person appointed is the civil partner of the person who made the appointment and either –

(a) an order of a court of civil jurisdiction in England and Wales dissolves or annuls the civil partnership, or
(b) the civil partnership is dissolved or annulled and the dissolution or annulment is entitled to recognition in England and Wales by virtue of Chapter 3 of Part 5 of the Civil Partnership Act 2004,

unless a contrary intention appears by the appointment.][2]

(4) For the avoidance of doubt, an appointment under section 5(3) or (4) made in a will or codicil is revoked if the will or codicil is revoked.

(5) A person who is appointed as a guardian under section 5(3) or (4) may disclaim his appointment by an instrument in writing signed by him and made within a reasonable time of his first knowing that the appointment has taken effect.

(6) Where regulations are made by the Lord Chancellor prescribing the manner in which such disclaimers must be recorded, no such disclaimer shall have effect unless it is recorded in the prescribed manner.

(7) Any appointment of a guardian under section 5 may be brought to an end at any time by order of the court –

(a) on the application of any person who has parental responsibility for the child;
(b) on the application of the child concerned, with leave of the court; or
(c) in any family proceedings, if the court considers that it should be brought to an end even though no application has been made.

NOTES

Amendments.[1] Subsection inserted: Law Reform (Succession) Act 1995, s 4(1). [2] Subsection inserted: Civil Partnership Act 2004, s 76.

Definitions. 'Child': s 105(1); 'family proceedings': s 8(3); 'parental responsibility': s 3; 'signed': s 105(1); 'the court': s 92(7).

7 Welfare reports

(1) A court considering any question with respect to a child under this Act may –

(a) ask [an officer of the Service][1] [or a Welsh family proceedings officer][2]; or
(b) ask a local authority to arrange for –
  (i) an officer of the authority; or

Part I   Statutes

> (ii) such other person (other than a probation officer) as the authority considers appropriate,

to report to the court on such matters relating to the welfare of that child as are required to be dealt with in the report.

(2) The Lord Chancellor may[, after consulting the Lord Chief Justice,]³ make regulations specifying matters which, unless the court orders otherwise, must be dealt with in any report under this section.

(3) The report may be made in writing, or orally, as the court requires.

(4) Regardless of any enactment or rule of law which would otherwise prevent it from doing so, the court may take account of –

> (a) any statement contained in the report; and
> (b) any evidence given in respect of the matters referred to in the report,

in so far as the statement or evidence is, in the opinion of the court, relevant to the question which it is considering.

(5) It shall be the duty of the authority or [an officer of the Service]¹ [or a Welsh family proceedings officer]² to comply with any request for a report under this section.

[(6) The Lord Chief Justice may nominate a judicial office holder (as defined in section 109(4) of the Constitutional Reform Act 2005) to exercise his functions under subsection (2).]⁴

NOTES

Amendments.¹ Words substituted: Criminal Justice and Court Services Act 2000, s 74, Sch 7, paras 87, 88.² Words inserted: Children Act 2004, s 40, Sch 3, paras 5, 6.³ Words inserted: Constitutional Reform Act 2005, s 15(1), Sch 4, Pt 1, paras 203, 204(1), (2).⁴ Subsection inserted: Constitutional Reform Act 2005, s 15(1), Sch 4, Pt 1, paras 203, 204(1), (3).

Definitions. 'Child': s 105(1); 'local authority': s 105(1); 'the court': s 92(7).

PART II
ORDERS WITH RESPECT TO CHILDREN IN FAMILY AND OTHER PROCEEDINGS

General

8 Residence, contact and other orders with respect to children

(1) In this Act –

> 'a contact order' means an order requiring the person with whom a child lives, or is to live, to allow the child to visit or stay with the person named in the order, or for that person and the child otherwise to have contact with each other;
> 'a prohibited steps order' means an order that no step which could be taken by a parent in meeting his parental responsibility for a child, and which is of a kind specified in the order, shall be taken by any person without the consent of the court;

'a residence order' means an order settling the arrangements to be made as to the person with whom a child is to live; and

'a specific issue order' means an order giving directions for the purpose of determining a specific question which has arisen, or which may arise, in connection with any aspect of parental responsibility for a child.

(2) In this Act 'a section 8 order' means any of the orders mentioned in subsection (1) and any order varying or discharging such an order.

(3) For the purposes of this Act 'family proceedings' means any proceedings –

(a) under the inherent jurisdiction of the High Court in relation to children; and
(b) under the enactments mentioned in subsection (4),

but does not include proceedings on an application for leave under section 100(3).

(4) The enactments are –

(a) Parts I, II and IV of this Act;
(b) the Matrimonial Causes Act 1973;
[(ba) Schedule 5 to the Civil Partnership Act 2004;][4]
(c) ...[1]
[(d) the Adoption and Children Act 2002;][3]
(e) the Domestic Proceedings and Magistrates' Courts Act 1978;
[(ea) Schedule 6 to the Civil Partnership Act 2004;][4]
(f) ...[1]
(g) Part III of the Matrimonial and Family Proceedings Act 1984;
[(h) the Family Law Act 1996][1];
[(i) sections 11 and 12 of the Crime and Disorder Act 1998.][2]

NOTES

Amendments.[1] Paragraphs inserted or repealed: Family Law Act 1996, s 66(1), Sch 8, Pt III, para 60.[2] Paragraph inserted: Crime and Disorder Act 1998, s 119, Sch 8, para 68.[3] Paragraph substituted: Adoption and Children Act 2002, s 139(1), Sch 3, paras 54, 55.[4] Paragraphs inserted: Civil Partnership Act 2004, s 261(1), Sch 27, para 129(1)–(3).

Definitions. 'A section 8 order': s 8(2); 'child': s 105(1); 'contact order': s 8(1); 'family proceedings': s 8(3); 'parental responsibility': s 3; 'prohibited steps order': s 8(1); 'residence order': s 8(1); 'specific issue order': s 8(1).

9 Restrictions on making section 8 orders

(1) No court shall make any section 8 order, other than a residence order, with respect to a child who is in the care of a local authority.

(2) No application may be made by a local authority for a residence order or contact order and no court shall make such an order in favour of a local authority.

(3) A person who is, or was at any time within the last six months, a local authority foster parent of a child may not apply for leave to apply for a section 8 order with respect to the child unless –

Part I Statutes

   (a) he has the consent of the authority;
   (b) he is relative of the child; or
   (c) the child has lived with him for at least [one year]¹ preceding the application.

(4) ...²

(5) No court shall exercise its powers to make a specific issue order or prohibited steps order –

   (a) with a view to achieving a result which could be achieved by making a residence or contact order; or
   (b) in any way which is denied to the High Court (by section 100(2)) in the exercise of its inherent jurisdiction with respect to children.

(6) [No court shall make a specific issue order, contact order or prohibited steps order]⁴ is to have effect for a period which will end after the child has reached the age of sixteen unless it is satisfied that the circumstances of the case are exceptional.

(7) No court shall make any section 8 order, other than one varying or discharging such an order, with respect to a child who has reached the age of sixteen unless it is satisfied that the circumstances of the case are exceptional.

NOTES

Amendments.¹ Words substituted: Adoption and Children Act 2002, s 113(a).² Subsection repealed: Adoption and Children Act 2002, s 113(b), 139(3), Sch 5.³ Words inserted: Adoption and Children Act 2002, s 114(2). ⁴ Words substituted: Children and Young Persons Act 2008, s 37(1).

Definitions. 'A section 8 order': s 8(2); 'child': s 105(1); 'contact order': s 8(1); 'local authority': s 105(1); 'local authority foster parent': s 23(3); 'prohibited steps order': s 8(1); 'relative': s 105(1); 'residence order': s 8(1); 'specific issue order': s 8(1); 'the court': s 92(7).

10 Power of court to make section 8 orders

(1) In any family proceedings in which a question arises with respect to the welfare of any child, the court may make a section 8 order with respect to the child if –

   (a) an application for the order has been made by a person who –
       (i) is entitled to apply for a section 8 order with respect to the child; or
       (ii) has obtained the leave of the court to make the application; or
   (b) the court considers that the order should be made even though no such application has been made.

(2) The court may also make a section 8 order with respect to any child on the application of a person who –

   (a) is entitled to apply for a section 8 order with respect to the child; or
   (b) has obtained the leave of the court to make the application.

(3) This section is subject to the restrictions imposed by section 9.

(4) The following persons are entitled to apply to the court for any section 8 order with respect to a child –

(a) any parent[, guardian or special guardian][1] of the child;
[(aa) any person who by virtue of section 4A has parental responsibility for the child;][2]
(b) any person in whose favour a residence order is in force with respect to the child.

(5) The following persons are entitled to apply for a residence or contact order with respect to a child –

(a) any party to a marriage (whether or not subsisting) in relation to whom the child is a child of the family;
[(aa) any civil partner in a civil partnership (whether or not subsisting) in relation to whom the child is a child of the family;][4]
(b) any person with whom the child has lived for a period of at least three years;
(c) any person who –
   (i) in any case where a residence order is in force with respect to the child, has the consent of each of the persons in whose favour the order was made;
   (ii) in any case where the child is in the care of a local authority, has the consent of that authority; or
   (iii) in any other case, has the consent of each of those (if any) who have parental responsibility for the child.

[(5A) A local authority foster parent is entitled to apply for a residence order with respect to a child if the child has lived with him for a period of at least one year immediately preceding the application.][3]

[(5B) A relative of a child is entitled to apply for a residence order with respect to the child if the child has lived with the relative for a period of at least one year immediately preceding the application.][5]

(6) A person who would not otherwise be entitled (under the previous provisions of this section) to apply for the variation or discharge of a section 8 order shall be entitled to do so if –

(a) the order was made on his application; or
(b) in the case of a contact order, he is named in the order.

(7) Any person who falls within a category of person prescribed by rules of court is entitled to apply for any such section 8 order as may be prescribed in relation to that category of person.

[(7A) If a special guardianship order is in force with respect to a child, an application for a residence order may only be made with respect to him, if apart from this subsection the leave of the court is not required, with such leave.][3]

(8) Where the person applying for leave to make an application for a section 8 order is the child concerned, the court may only grant leave if it is satisfied that he has sufficient understanding to make the proposed application for the section 8 order.

(9) Where the person applying for leave to make an application for a section 8 order is not the child concerned, the court shall, in deciding whether or not to grant leave, have particular regard to –

(a) the nature of the proposed application for the section 8 order;
(b) the applicant's connection with the child;
(c) any risk there might be of that proposed application disrupting the child's life to such an extent that he would be harmed by it; and
(d) where the child is being looked after by a local authority –
 (i) the authority's plans for the child's future; and
 (ii) the wishes and feelings of the child's parents.

(10) The period of three years mentioned in subsection (5)(b) need not be continuous but must not have begun more than five years before, or ended more than three months before, the making of the application.

NOTES

Amendments.[1] Words substituted: Adoption and Children Act 2002, s 139(1), Sch 3, paras 54, 56(a).[2] Paragraph inserted: Adoption and Children Act 2002, s 139(1), Sch 3, paras 54, 56(b).[3] Subsection inserted: Adoption and Children Act 2002, s 139(1), Sch 3, paras 54, 56(c), (d).[4] Paragraph inserted: Civil Partnership Act 2004, s 77. [5] Subsection inserted: Children and Young Persons Act 2008, s 36.

Definitions. 'A section 8 order': s 8(2); 'child': s 105(1); 'child who is looked after by a local authority': s 22(1); 'child of the family': s 105(1); 'contact order': s 8(1); 'family proceedings': s 8(3); 'guardian of a child': s 105(1); 'harm': ss 31(a), 105(1); 'local authority': s 105(1); 'parental responsibility': s 3; 'residence order': s 8(1); 'the court': s 92(7).

11 General principles and supplementary provisions

(1) In proceedings in which any question of making a section 8 order, or any other question with respect to such an order, arises, the court shall (in the light of any rules made by virtue of subsection (2)) –

(a) draw up a timetable with a view to determining the question without delay; and
(b) give such directions as it considers appropriate for the purpose of ensuring, so far as is reasonably practicable, that that timetable is adhered to.

(2) Rules of court may –

(a) specify periods within which specified steps must be taken in relation to proceedings in which such questions arise; and
(b) make other provision with respect to such proceedings for the purpose of ensuring, so far as is reasonably practicable, that such questions are determined without delay.

(3) Where a court has power to make a section 8 order, it may do so at any time during the course of the proceedings in question even though it is not in a position to dispose finally of those proceedings.

(4) Where a residence order is made in favour of two or more persons who do not themselves all live together, the order may specify the periods during which the child is to live in the different households concerned.

(5) Where –
   (a) a residence order has been made with respect to a child; and
   (b) as a result of the order the child lives, or is to live, with one of two parents who each have parental responsibility for him,

the residence order shall cease to have effect if the parents live together for a continuous period of more than six months.

(6) A contact order which requires the parent with whom a child lives to allow the child to visit, or otherwise have contact with, his other parent shall cease to have effect if the parents live together for a continuous period of more than six months.

(7) A section 8 order may –
   (a) contain directions about how it is to be carried into effect;
   (b) impose conditions which must be complied with by any person –
      (i) in whose favour the order is made;
      (ii) who is a parent of the child concerned;
      (iii) who is not a parent of his but who has parental responsibility for him; or
      (iv) with whom the child is living,
      and to whom the conditions are expressed to apply;
   (c) be made to have effect for a specified period, or contain provisions which are to have effect for a specified period;
   (d) make such incidental, supplemental or consequential provision as the court thinks fit.

NOTES

Definitions. 'A section 8 order': s 8(2); 'child': s 105(1); 'contact order': s 8(1); 'parental responsibility': s 3; 'residence order': s 8(1); 'the court': s 92(7).

[11A Contact activity directions

(1) This section applies in proceedings in which the court is considering whether to make provision about contact with a child by making –

   (a) a contact order with respect to the child, or
   (b) an order varying or discharging a contact order with respect to the child.

(2) The court may make a contact activity direction in connection with that provision about contact.

(3) A contact activity direction is a direction requiring an individual who is a party to the proceedings to take part in an activity that promotes contact with the child concerned.

(4) The direction is to specify the activity and the person providing the activity.

(5) The activities that may be so required include, in particular –

    (a) programmes, classes and counselling or guidance sessions of a kind that –
        (i) may assist a person as regards establishing, maintaining or improving contact with a child;
        (ii) may, by addressing a person's violent behaviour, enable or facilitate contact with a child;
    (b) sessions in which information or advice is given as regards making or operating arrangements for contact with a child, including making arrangements by means of mediation.

(6) No individual may be required by a contact activity direction –

    (a) to undergo medical or psychiatric examination, assessment or treatment;
    (b) to take part in mediation.

(7) A court may not on the same occasion –

    (a) make a contact activity direction, and
    (b) dispose finally of the proceedings as they relate to contact with the child concerned.

(8) Subsection (2) has effect subject to the restrictions in sections 11B and 11E.

(9) In considering whether to make a contact activity direction, the welfare of the child concerned is to be the court's paramount consideration.][1]

NOTES

Amendment.[1] Section inserted: Children and Adoption Act 2006, s 1.

[11B Contact activity directions: further provision

(1) A court may not make a contact activity direction in any proceedings unless there is a dispute as regards the provision about contact that the court is considering whether to make in the proceedings.

(2) A court may not make a contact activity direction requiring an individual who is a child to take part in an activity unless the individual is a parent of the child in relation to whom the court is considering provision about contact.

(3) A court may not make a contact activity direction in connection with the making, variation or discharge of a contact order, if the contact order is, or would if made be, an excepted order.

(4) A contact order with respect to a child is an excepted order if –

(a) it is made in proceedings that include proceedings on an application for a relevant adoption order in respect of the child; or
(b) it makes provision as regards contact between the child and a person who would be a parent or relative of the child but for the child's adoption by an order falling within subsection (5).

(5) An order falls within this subsection if it is –

(a) a relevant adoption order;
(b) an adoption order, within the meaning of section 72(1) of the Adoption Act 1976, other than an order made by virtue of section 14 of that Act on the application of a married couple one of whom is the mother or the father of the child;
(c) a Scottish adoption order, within the meaning of the Adoption and Children Act 2002, other than an order made –
 (i) by virtue of section 14 of the Adoption (Scotland) Act 1978 on the application of a married couple one of whom is the mother or the father of the child, or
 (ii) by virtue of section 15(1)(aa) of that Act; or
(d) a Northern Irish adoption order, within the meaning of the Adoption and Children Act 2002, other than an order made by virtue of Article 14 of the Adoption (Northern Ireland) Order 1987 on the application of a married couple one of whom is the mother or the father of the child.

(6) A relevant adoption order is an adoption order, within the meaning of section 46(1) of the Adoption and Children Act 2002, other than an order made –

(a) on an application under section 50 of that Act by a couple (within the meaning of that Act) one of whom is the mother or the father of the person to be adopted, or
(b) on an application under section 51(2) of that Act.

(7) A court may not make a contact activity direction in relation to an individual unless the individual is habitually resident in England and Wales; and a direction ceases to have effect if the individual subject to the direction ceases to be habitually resident in England and Wales.][1]

NOTES

Amendment.[1] Section inserted: Children and Adoption Act 2006, s 1.

[11C Contact activity conditions

(1) This section applies if in any family proceedings the court makes –

(a) a contact order with respect to a child, or
(b) an order varying a contact order with respect to a child.

(2) The contact order may impose, or the contact order may be varied so as to impose, a condition (a 'contact activity condition') requiring an individual falling within subsection (3) to take part in an activity that promotes contact with the child concerned.

(3) An individual falls within this subsection if he is –

(a) for the purposes of the contact order so made or varied, the person with whom the child concerned lives or is to live;
(b) the person whose contact with the child concerned is provided for in that order; or
(c) a person upon whom that order imposes a condition under section 11(7)(b).

(4) The condition is to specify the activity and the person providing the activity.

(5) Subsections (5) and (6) of section 11A have effect as regards the activities that may be required by a contact activity condition as they have effect as regards the activities that may be required by a contact activity direction.

(6) Subsection (2) has effect subject to the restrictions in sections 11D and 11E.][1]

NOTES

Amendment.[1] Section inserted: Children and Adoption Act 2006, s 1.

[11D Contact activity conditions: further provision

(1) A contact order may not impose a contact activity condition on an individual who is a child unless the individual is a parent of the child concerned.

(2) If a contact order is an excepted order (within the meaning given by section 11B(4)), it may not impose (and it may not be varied so as to impose) a contact activity condition.

(3) A contact order may not impose a contact activity condition on an individual unless the individual is habitually resident in England and Wales; and a condition ceases to have effect if the individual subject to the condition ceases to be habitually resident in England and Wales.][1]

NOTES

Amendment.[1] Section inserted: Children and Adoption Act 2006, s 1.

[11E Contact activity directions and conditions: making

(1) Before making a contact activity direction (or imposing a contact activity condition by means of a contact order), the court must satisfy itself as to the matters falling within subsections (2) to (4).

(2) The first matter is that the activity proposed to be specified is appropriate in the circumstances of the case.

(3) The second matter is that the person proposed to be specified as the provider of the activity is suitable to provide the activity.

(4) The third matter is that the activity proposed to be specified is provided in a place to which the individual who would be subject to the direction (or the condition) can reasonably be expected to travel.

(5) Before making such a direction (or such an order), the court must obtain and consider information about the individual who would be subject to the direction (or the condition) and the likely effect of the direction (or the condition) on him.

(6) Information about the likely effect of the direction (or the condition) may, in particular, include information as to –

   (a)   any conflict with the individual's religious beliefs;
   (b)   any interference with the times (if any) at which he normally works or attends an educational establishment.

(7) The court may ask an officer of the Service or a Welsh family proceedings officer to provide the court with information as to the matters in subsections (2) to (5); and it shall be the duty of the officer of the Service or Welsh family proceedings officer to comply with any such request.

(8) In this section 'specified' means specified in a contact activity direction (or in a contact activity condition).][1]

NOTES

Amendment.[1] Section inserted: Children and Adoption Act 2006, s 1.

[11F Contact activity directions and conditions: financial assistance

(1) The Secretary of State may by regulations make provision authorising him to make payments to assist individuals falling within subsection (2) in paying relevant charges or fees.

(2) An individual falls within this subsection if he is required by a contact activity direction or condition to take part in an activity that promotes contact with a child, not being a child ordinarily resident in Wales.

(3) The National Assembly for Wales may by regulations make provision authorising it to make payments to assist individuals falling within subsection (4) in paying relevant charges or fees.

(4) An individual falls within this subsection if he is required by a contact activity direction or condition to take part in an activity that promotes contact with a child who is ordinarily resident in Wales.

(5) A relevant charge or fee, in relation to an activity required by a contact activity direction or condition, is a charge or fee in respect of the activity payable to the person providing the activity.

(6) Regulations under this section may provide that no assistance is available to an individual unless –

(a) the individual satisfies such conditions as regards his financial resources as may be set out in the regulations;
(b) the activity in which the individual is required by a contact activity direction or condition to take part is provided to him in England or Wales;
(c) where the activity in which the individual is required to take part is provided to him in England, it is provided by a person who is for the time being approved by the Secretary of State as a provider of activities required by a contact activity direction or condition;
(d) where the activity in which the individual is required to take part is provided to him in Wales, it is provided by a person who is for the time being approved by the National Assembly for Wales as a provider of activities required by a contact activity direction or condition.

(7) Regulations under this section may make provision –

(a) as to the maximum amount of assistance that may be paid to or in respect of an individual as regards an activity in which he is required by a contact activity direction or condition to take part;
(b) where the amount may vary according to an individual's financial resources, as to the method by which the amount is to be determined;
(c) authorising payments by way of assistance to be made directly to persons providing activities required by a contact activity direction or condition.][1]

NOTES

Amendment.[1] Section inserted: Children and Adoption Act 2006, s 1.

[11G Contact activity directions and conditions: monitoring

(1) This section applies if in any family proceedings the court –

(a) makes a contact activity direction in relation to an individual, or
(b) makes a contact order that imposes, or varies a contact order so as to impose, a contact activity condition on an individual.

(2) The court may on making the direction (or imposing the condition by means of a contact order) ask an officer of the Service or a Welsh family proceedings officer –

(a) to monitor, or arrange for the monitoring of, the individual's compliance with the direction (or the condition);
(b) to report to the court on any failure by the individual to comply with the direction (or the condition).

(3) It shall be the duty of the officer of the Service or Welsh family proceedings officer to comply with any request under subsection (2).][1]

NOTES

Amendment.[1] Section inserted: Children and Adoption Act 2006, s 1.

[11H Monitoring contact

(1) This section applies if in any family proceedings the court makes –

(a) a contact order with respect to a child in favour of a person, or
(b) an order varying such a contact order.

(2) The court may ask an officer of the Service or a Welsh family proceedings officer –

(a) to monitor whether an individual falling within subsection (3) complies with the contact order (or the contact order as varied);
(b) to report to the court on such matters relating to the individual's compliance as the court may specify in the request.

(3) An individual falls within this subsection if the contact order so made (or the contact order as so varied) –

(a) requires the individual to allow contact with the child concerned;
(b) names the individual as having contact with the child concerned; or
(c) imposes a condition under section 11(7)(b) on the individual.

(4) If the contact order (or the contact order as varied) includes a contact activity condition, a request under subsection (2) is to be treated as relating to the provisions of the order other than the contact activity condition.

(5) The court may make a request under subsection (2) –

(a) on making the contact order (or the order varying the contact order), or
(b) at any time during the subsequent course of the proceedings as they relate to contact with the child concerned.

(6) In making a request under subsection (2), the court is to specify the period for which the officer of the Service or Welsh family proceedings officer is to monitor compliance with the order; and the period specified may not exceed twelve months.

(7) It shall be the duty of the officer of the Service or Welsh family proceedings officer to comply with any request under subsection (2).

(8) The court may order any individual falling within subsection (3) to take such steps as may be specified in the order with a view to enabling the officer of the Service or Welsh family proceedings officer to comply with the court's request under subsection (2).

(9) But the court may not make an order under subsection (8) with respect to an individual who is a child unless he is a parent of the child with respect to whom the order falling within subsection (1) was made.

(10) A court may not make a request under subsection (2) in relation to a contact order that is an excepted order (within the meaning given by section 11B(4)).][1]

NOTES

Amendment.[1] Section inserted: Children and Adoption Act 2006, s 2.

[11I Contact orders: warning notices

Where the court makes (or varies) a contact order, it is to attach to the contact order (or the order varying the contact order) a notice warning of the consequences of failing to comply with the contact order.][1]

NOTES

Amendment.[1] Section inserted: Children and Adoption Act 2006, s 3.

[11J Enforcement orders

(1) This section applies if a contact order with respect to a child has been made.

(2) If the court is satisfied beyond reasonable doubt that a person has failed to comply with the contact order, it may make an order (an 'enforcement order') imposing on the person an unpaid work requirement.

(3) But the court may not make an enforcement order if it is satisfied that the person had a reasonable excuse for failing to comply with the contact order.

(4) The burden of proof as to the matter mentioned in subsection (3) lies on the person claiming to have had a reasonable excuse, and the standard of proof is the balance of probabilities.

(5) The court may make an enforcement order in relation to the contact order only on the application of –

- (a) the person who is, for the purposes of the contact order, the person with whom the child concerned lives or is to live;
- (b) the person whose contact with the child concerned is provided for in the contact order;
- (c) any individual subject to a condition under section 11(7)(b) or a contact activity condition imposed by the contact order; or
- (d) the child concerned.

(6) Where the person proposing to apply for an enforcement order in relation to a contact order is the child concerned, the child must obtain the leave of the court before making such an application.

(7) The court may grant leave to the child concerned only if it is satisfied that he has sufficient understanding to make the proposed application.

(8) Subsection (2) has effect subject to the restrictions in sections 11K and 11L.

(9) The court may suspend an enforcement order for such period as it thinks fit.

(10) Nothing in this section prevents a court from making more than one enforcement order in relation to the same person on the same occasion.

(11) Proceedings in which any question of making an enforcement order, or any other question with respect to such an order, arises are to be regarded for the purposes of section 11(1) and (2) as proceedings in which a question arises with respect to a section 8 order.

(12) In Schedule A1 –
- (a) Part 1 makes provision as regards an unpaid work requirement;
- (b) Part 2 makes provision in relation to the revocation and amendment of enforcement orders and failure to comply with such orders.

(13) This section is without prejudice to section 63(3) of the Magistrates' Courts Act 1980 as it applies in relation to contact orders.][1]

NOTES

Amendment.[1] Section inserted: Children and Adoption Act 2006, s 4(1).

[11K Enforcement orders: further provision

(1) A court may not make an enforcement order against a person in respect of a failure to comply with a contact order unless it is satisfied that before the failure occurred the person had been given (in accordance with rules of court) a copy of, or otherwise informed of the terms of –

- (a) in the case of a failure to comply with a contact order that was varied before the failure occurred, a notice under section 11I relating to the order varying the contact order or, where more than one such order has been made, the last order preceding the failure in question;
- (b) in any other case, a notice under section 11I relating to the contact order.

(2) A court may not make an enforcement order against a person in respect of any failure to comply with a contact order occurring before the person attained the age of 18.

(3) A court may not make an enforcement order against a person in respect of a failure to comply with a contact order that is an excepted order (within the meaning given by section 11B(4)).

(4) A court may not make an enforcement order against a person unless the person is habitually resident in England and Wales; and an enforcement order ceases to have effect if the person subject to the order ceases to be habitually resident in England and Wales.][1]

NOTES

Amendment.[1] Section inserted: Children and Adoption Act 2006, s 4(1).

[11L Enforcement orders: making

(1) Before making an enforcement order as regards a person in breach of a contact order, the court must be satisfied that –

(a) making the enforcement order proposed is necessary to secure the person's compliance with the contact order or any contact order that has effect in its place;
(b) the likely effect on the person of the enforcement order proposed to be made is proportionate to the seriousness of the breach of the contact order.

(2) Before making an enforcement order, the court must satisfy itself that provision for the person to work under an unpaid work requirement imposed by an enforcement order can be made in the local justice area in which the person in breach resides or will reside.

(3) Before making an enforcement order as regards a person in breach of a contact order, the court must obtain and consider information about the person and the likely effect of the enforcement order on him.

(4) Information about the likely effect of the enforcement order may, in particular, include information as to –

(a) any conflict with the person's religious beliefs;
(b) any interference with the times (if any) at which he normally works or attends an educational establishment.

(5) A court that proposes to make an enforcement order may ask an officer of the Service or a Welsh family proceedings officer to provide the court with information as to the matters in subsections (2) and (3).

(6) It shall be the duty of the officer of the Service or Welsh family proceedings officer to comply with any request under this section.

(7) In making an enforcement order in relation to a contact order, a court must take into account the welfare of the child who is the subject of the contact order.][1]

NOTES
Amendment.[1] Section inserted: Children and Adoption Act 2006, s 4(1).

[11M Enforcement orders: monitoring

(1) On making an enforcement order in relation to a person, the court is to ask an officer of the Service or a Welsh family proceedings officer –

(a) to monitor, or arrange for the monitoring of, the person's compliance with the unpaid work requirement imposed by the order;
(b) to report to the court if a report under paragraph 8 of Schedule A1 is made in relation to the person;
(c) to report to the court on such other matters relating to the person's compliance as may be specified in the request;
(d) to report to the court if the person is, or becomes, unsuitable to perform work under the requirement.

(2) It shall be the duty of the officer of the Service or Welsh family proceedings officer to comply with any request under this section.][1]

NOTES

Amendment.[1] Section inserted: Children and Adoption Act 2006, s 4(1).

[11N Enforcement orders: warning notices

Where the court makes an enforcement order, it is to attach to the order a notice warning of the consequences of failing to comply with the order.][1]

NOTES

Amendment.[1] Section inserted: Children and Adoption Act 2006, s 4(1).

[11O Compensation for financial loss

(1) This section applies if a contact order with respect to a child has been made.

(2) If the court is satisfied that –

   (a)   an individual has failed to comply with the contact order, and
   (b)   a person falling within subsection (6) has suffered financial loss by reason of the breach,

it may make an order requiring the individual in breach to pay the person compensation in respect of his financial loss.

(3) But the court may not make an order under subsection (2) if it is satisfied that the individual in breach had a reasonable excuse for failing to comply with the contact order.

(4) The burden of proof as to the matter mentioned in subsection (3) lies on the individual claiming to have had a reasonable excuse.

(5) An order under subsection (2) may be made only on an application by the person who claims to have suffered financial loss.

(6) A person falls within this subsection if he is –

   (a)   the person who is, for the purposes of the contact order, the person with whom the child concerned lives or is to live;
   (b)   the person whose contact with the child concerned is provided for in the contact order;
   (c)   an individual subject to a condition under section 11(7)(b) or a contact activity condition imposed by the contact order; or
   (d)   the child concerned.

(7) Where the person proposing to apply for an order under subsection (2) is the child concerned, the child must obtain the leave of the court before making such an application.

(8) The court may grant leave to the child concerned only if it is satisfied that he has sufficient understanding to make the proposed application.

(9) The amount of compensation is to be determined by the court, but may not exceed the amount of the applicant's financial loss.

(10) In determining the amount of compensation payable by the individual in breach, the court must take into account the individual's financial circumstances.

(11) An amount ordered to be paid as compensation may be recovered by the applicant as a civil debt due to him.

(12) Subsection (2) has effect subject to the restrictions in section 11P.

(13) Proceedings in which any question of making an order under subsection (2) arises are to be regarded for the purposes of section 11(1) and (2) as proceedings in which a question arises with respect to a section 8 order.

(14) In exercising its powers under this section, a court is to take into account the welfare of the child concerned.][1]

NOTES

Amendment.[1] Section inserted: Children and Adoption Act 2006, s 5.

[11P Orders under section 11O(2): further provision

(1) A court may not make an order under section 11O(2) requiring an individual to pay compensation in respect of a failure by him to comply with a contact order unless it is satisfied that before the failure occurred the individual had been given (in accordance with rules of court) a copy of, or otherwise informed of the terms of –

  (a) in the case of a failure to comply with a contact order that was varied before the failure occurred, a notice under section 11I relating to the order varying the contact order or, where more than one such order has been made, the last order preceding the failure in question;

  (b) in any other case, a notice under section 11I relating to the contact order.

(2) A court may not make an order under section 11O(2) requiring an individual to pay compensation in respect of a failure by him to comply with a contact order where the failure occurred before the individual attained the age of 18.

(3) A court may not make an order under section 11O(2) requiring an individual to pay compensation in respect of a failure by him to comply with a contact order that is an excepted order (within the meaning given by section 11B(4)).][1]

NOTES

Amendment.[1] Section inserted: Children and Adoption Act 2006, s 5.

12 Residence orders and parental responsibility

(1) Where the court makes a residence order in favour of the father of a child it shall, if the father would not otherwise have parental responsibility for the child, also make an order under section 4 giving him that responsibility.

[(1A) Where the court makes a residence order in favour of a woman who is a parent of a child by virtue of section 43 of the Human Fertilisation and Embryology Act 2008 it shall, if that woman would not otherwise have parental responsibility for the child, also make an order under section 4ZA giving her that responsibility.][4]

(2) Where the court makes a residence order in favour of any person who is not the parent or guardian of the child concerned that person shall have parental responsibility for the child while the residence order remains in force.

(3) Where a person has parental responsibility for a child as a result of subsection (2), he shall not have the right –

(a) ...[1]
(b) to agree, or refuse to agree, to the making of an adoption order, or an order under [section 84 of the Adoption and Children Act 2002][2], with respect to the child; or
(c) to appoint a guardian for the child.

(4) Where subsection (1) [or (1A)][4] requires the court to make an order under section 4 [or 4ZA][4] in respect of the [parent][4] of a child, the court shall not bring that order to an end at any time while the residence order concerned remains in force.

[(5) ...[5]

(6) ...[5]][3]

NOTES

Amendments.[1] Paragraph repealed: Adoption and Children Act 2002, s 139(1), (3), Sch 3, paras 54, 57(a), Sch 5.[2] Words substituted: Adoption and Children Act 2002, s 139(1), (3), Sch 3, paras 54, 57(b).[3] Subsections inserted: Adoption and Children Act 2002, s 114(1). [4] Subsection inserted, words inserted and word substituted: Human Fertilisation and Embryology Act 2008, s 56, Sch 6, Pt 1, para 28. [5] Subsections repealed: Children and Young Persons Act 2008, s 36.

Definitions. 'Child': s 105(1); 'guardian of a child': s 105(1); 'parental responsibility': s 3; 'residence order': s 8(1); 'the court': s 92(7).

13 Change of child's name or removal from jurisdiction

(1) Where a residence order is in force with respect to a child, no person may –

(a) cause the child to be known by a new surname; or
(b) remove him from the United Kingdom;

without either the written consent of every person who has parental responsibility for the child or the leave of the court.

(2) Subsection (1)(b) does not prevent the removal of a child, for a period of less than one month, by the person in whose favour the residence order is made.

(3) In making a residence order with respect to a child the court may grant the leave required by subsection (1)(b), either generally or for specified purposes.

NOTES

Definitions. 'Child': s 105(1); 'parental responsibility': s 3; 'residence order': s 8(1); 'the court': s 92(7).

14 Enforcement of residence orders

(1) Where –

(a) a residence order is in force with respect to a child in favour of any person; and
(b) any other person (including one in whose favour the order is also in force) is in breach of the arrangements settled by that order,

the person mentioned in paragraph (a) may, as soon as the requirement in subsection (2) is complied with, enforce the order under section 63(3) of the Magistrates' Courts Act 1980 as if it were an order requiring the other person to produce the child to him.

(2) The requirement is that a copy of the residence order has been served on the other person.

(3) Subsection (1) is without prejudice to any other remedy open to the person in whose favour the residence order is in force.

NOTES

Definitions. 'Child': s 105(1); 'residence order': s 8(1).

[Special guardianship

14A Special guardianship orders

(1) A 'special guardianship order' is an order appointing one or more individuals to be a child's 'special guardian' (or special guardians).

(2) A special guardian –

(a) must be aged eighteen or over; and
(b) must not be a parent of the child in question,

and subsections (3) to (6) are to be read in that light.

(3) The court may make a special guardianship order with respect to any child on the application of an individual who –

(a) is entitled to make such an application with respect to the child; or
(b) has obtained the leave of the court to make the application,

or on the joint application of more than one such individual.

(4) Section 9(3) applies in relation to an application for leave to apply for a special guardianship order as it applies in relation to an application for leave to apply for a section 8 order.

(5) The individuals who are entitled to apply for a special guardianship order with respect to a child are –

(a) any guardian of the child;
(b) any individual in whose favour a residence order is in force with respect to the child;
(c) any individual listed in subsection (5)(b) or (c) of section 10 (as read with subsection (10) of that section);
(d) a local authority foster parent with whom the child has lived for a period of at least one year immediately preceding the application[;
(e) a relative with whom the child has lived for a period of at least one year immediately preceding the application]².

(6) The court may also make a special guardianship order with respect to a child in any family proceedings in which a question arises with respect to the welfare of the child if –

(a) an application for the order has been made by an individual who falls within subsection (3)(a) or (b) (or more than one such individual jointly); or
(b) the court considers that a special guardianship order should be made even though no such application has been made.

(7) No individual may make an application under subsection (3) or (6)(a) unless, before the beginning of the period of three months ending with the date of the application, he has given written notice of his intention to make the application –

(a) if the child in question is being looked after by a local authority, to that local authority, or
(b) otherwise, to the local authority in whose area the individual is ordinarily resident.

(8) On receipt of such a notice, the local authority must investigate the matter and prepare a report for the court dealing with –

(a) the suitability of the applicant to be a special guardian;
(b) such matters (if any) as may be prescribed by the Secretary of State; and
(c) any other matter which the local authority consider to be relevant.

(9) The court may itself ask a local authority to conduct such an investigation and prepare such a report, and the local authority must do so.

(10) The local authority may make such arrangements as they see fit for any person to act on their behalf in connection with conducting an investigation or preparing a report referred to in subsection (8) or (9).

(11) The court may not make a special guardianship order unless it has received a report dealing with the matters referred to in subsection (8).

(12) Subsections (8) and (9) of section 10 apply in relation to special guardianship orders as they apply in relation to section 8 orders.

(13) This section is subject to section 29(5) and (6) of the Adoption and Children Act 2002.]¹

Part I   Statutes

NOTES

Amendments.[1] Section inserted: Adoption and Children Act 2002, s 115(1). [2] Paragraph inserted: Children and Young Persons Act 2008, s 38.

[14B Special guardianship orders: making

(1) Before making a special guardianship order, the court must consider whether, if the order were made –

- (a) a contact order should also be made with respect to the child, ...[2]
- (b) any section 8 order in force with respect to the child should be varied or discharged.
- [(c) where a contact order made with respect to the child is not discharged, any enforcement order relating to that contact order should be revoked, and
- (d) where a contact activity direction has been made as regards contact with the child and is in force, that contact activity direction should be discharged][2]

(2) On making a special guardianship order, the court may also –

- (a) give leave for the child to be known by a new surname;
- (b) grant the leave required by section 14C(3)(b), either generally or for specified purposes.][1]

NOTES

Amendments.[1] Section inserted: Adoption and Children Act 2002, s 115(1).[2] Word repealed and paragraphs inserted: Children and Adoption Act 2006, s 15, Sch 2, paras 7, 8, Sch 3.

[14C Special guardianship orders: effect

(1) The effect of a special guardianship order is that while the order remains in force –

- (a) a special guardian appointed by the order has parental responsibility for the child in respect of whom it is made; and
- (b) subject to any other order in force with respect to the child under this Act, a special guardian is entitled to exercise parental responsibility to the exclusion of any other person with parental responsibility for the child (apart from another special guardian).

(2) Subsection (1) does not affect –

- (a) the operation of any enactment or rule of law which requires the consent of more than one person with parental responsibility in a matter affecting the child; or
- (b) any rights which a parent of the child has in relation to the child's adoption or placement for adoption.

(3) While a special guardianship order is in force with respect to a child, no person may –

- (a) cause the child to be known by a new surname; or
- (b) remove him from the United Kingdom,

without either the written consent of every person who has parental responsibility for the child or the leave of the court.

(4) Subsection (3)(b) does not prevent the removal of a child, for a period of less than three months, by a special guardian of his.

(5) If the child with respect to whom a special guardianship order is in force dies, his special guardian must take reasonable steps to give notice of that fact to –

(a) each parent of the child with parental responsibility; and
(b) each guardian of the child,

but if the child has more than one special guardian, and one of them has taken such steps in relation to a particular parent or guardian, any other special guardian need not do so as respects that parent or guardian.

(6) This section is subject to section 29(7) of the Adoption and Children Act 2002.]¹

NOTES

Amendments.¹ Section inserted: Adoption and Children Act 2002, s 115(1).

[14D Special guardianship orders: variation and discharge

(1) The court may vary or discharge a special guardianship order on the application of –

(a) the special guardian (or any of them, if there are more than one);
(b) any parent or guardian of the child concerned;
(c) any individual in whose favour a residence order is in force with respect to the child;
(d) any individual not falling within any of paragraphs (a) to (c) who has, or immediately before the making of the special guardianship order had, parental responsibility for the child;
(e) the child himself; or
(f) a local authority designated in a care order with respect to the child.

(2) In any family proceedings in which a question arises with respect to the welfare of a child with respect to whom a special guardianship order is in force, the court may also vary or discharge the special guardianship order if it considers that the order should be varied or discharged, even though no application has been made under subsection (1).

(3) The following must obtain the leave of the court before making an application under subsection (1) –

(a) the child;
(b) any parent or guardian of his;
(c) any step-parent of his who has acquired, and has not lost, parental responsibility for him by virtue of section 4A;

(d) any individual falling within subsection (1)(d) who immediately before the making of the special guardianship order had, but no longer has, parental responsibility for him.

(4) Where the person applying for leave to make an application under subsection (1) is the child, the court may only grant leave if it is satisfied that he has sufficient understanding to make the proposed application under subsection (1).

(5) The court may not grant leave to a person falling within subsection (3)(b)(c) or (d) unless it is satisfied that there has been a significant change in circumstances since the making of the special guardianship order.]¹

NOTES

Amendments.¹ Section inserted: Adoption and Children Act 2002, s 115(1).

[14E Special guardianship orders: supplementary

(1) In proceedings in which any question of making, varying or discharging a special guardianship order arises, the court shall (in the light of any rules made by virtue of subsection (3)) –

(a) draw up a timetable with a view to determining the question without delay; and
(b) give such directions as it considers appropriate for the purpose of ensuring, so far as is reasonably practicable, that the timetable is adhered to.

(2) Subsection (1) applies also in relation to proceedings in which any other question with respect to a special guardianship order arises.

(3) The power to make rules in subsection (2) of section 11 applies for the purposes of this section as it applies for the purposes of that.

(4) A special guardianship order, or an order varying one, may contain provisions which are to have effect for a specified period.

(5) Section 11(7) (apart from paragraph (c)) applies in relation to special guardianship orders and orders varying them as it applies in relation to section 8 orders.]¹

NOTES

Amendments.¹ Section inserted: Adoption and Children Act 2002, s 115(1).

[14F Special guardianship support services

(1) Each local authority must make arrangements for the provision within their area of special guardianship support services, which means –

(a) counselling, advice and information; and
(b) such other services as are prescribed,

in relation to special guardianship.

(2) The power to make regulations under subsection (1)(b) is to be exercised so as to secure that local authorities provide financial support.

(3) At the request of any of the following persons –

(a) a child with respect to whom a special guardianship order is in force;
(b) a special guardian;
(c) a parent;
(d) any other person who falls within a prescribed description,

a local authority may carry out an assessment of that person's needs for special guardianship support services (but, if the Secretary of State so provides in regulations, they must do so if he is a person of a prescribed description, or if his case falls within a prescribed description, or if both he and his case fall within prescribed descriptions).

(4) A local authority may, at the request of any other person, carry out an assessment of that person's needs for special guardianship support services.

(5) Where, as a result of an assessment, a local authority decide that a person has needs for special guardianship support services, they must then decide whether to provide any such services to that person.

(6) If –

(a) a local authority decide to provide any special guardianship support services to a person, and
(b) the circumstances fall within a prescribed description,

the local authority must prepare a plan in accordance with which special guardianship support services are to be provided to him, and keep the plan under review.

(7) The Secretary of State may by regulations make provision about assessments, preparing and reviewing plans, the provision of special guardianship support services in accordance with plans and reviewing the provision of special guardianship support services.

(8) The regulations may in particular make provision –

(a) about the type of assessment which is to be carried out, or the way in which an assessment is to be carried out;
(b) about the way in which a plan is to be prepared;
(c) about the way in which, and the time at which, a plan or the provision of special guardianship support services is to be reviewed;
(d) about the considerations to which a local authority are to have regard in carrying out an assessment or review or preparing a plan;
(e) as to the circumstances in which a local authority may provide special guardianship support services subject to conditions (including conditions as to payment for the support or the repayment of financial support);
(f) as to the consequences of conditions imposed by virtue of paragraph (e) not being met (including the recovery of any financial support provided);

(g) as to the circumstances in which this section may apply to a local authority in respect of persons who are outside that local authority's area;

(h) as to the circumstances in which a local authority may recover from another local authority the expenses of providing special guardianship support services to any person.

(9) A local authority may provide special guardianship support services (or any part of them) by securing their provision by –

(a) another local authority; or
(b) a person within a description prescribed in regulations of persons who may provide special guardianship support services,

and may also arrange with any such authority or person for that other authority or that person to carry out the local authority's functions in relation to assessments under this section.

(10) A local authority may carry out an assessment of the needs of any person for the purposes of this section at the same time as an assessment of his needs is made under any other provision of this Act or under any other enactment.

(11) Section 27 (co-operation between authorities) applies in relation to the exercise of functions of a local authority under this section as it applies in relation to the exercise of functions of a local authority under Part 3.]¹

NOTES

Amendments.¹ Section inserted: Adoption and Children Act 2002, s 115(1).

[14G

...²]¹

NOTES

Amendments.¹ Section inserted: Adoption and Children Act 2002, s 115(1).² Section repealed: Health and Social Care (Community Health and Standards) Act 2003, ss 117(2), 196, Sch 14, Pt 2.

Financial relief

15 Orders for financial relief with respect to children

(1) Schedule 1 (which consists primarily of the re-enactment, with consequential amendments and minor modifications, of provisions of [section 6 of the Family Law Reform Act 1969]¹, the Guardianship of Minors Acts 1971 and 1973, the Children Act 1975 and of sections 15 and 16 of the Family Law Reform Act 1987) makes provision in relation to financial relief for children.

(2) The powers of a magistrates' court under section 60 of the Magistrates' Courts Act 1980 to revoke, revive or vary an order for the periodical payment of money [and the power of a clerk of a magistrates' court to vary such an order]² shall not apply in relation to an order made under Schedule 1.

NOTES

Amendments.[1] Words inserted: Courts and Legal Services Act 1990, s 116, Sch 16, para 10(1). [2] Words inserted: Maintenance Enforcement Act 1991, s 11(1), Sch 2, para 10.

Family assistance orders

16 Family assistance orders

(1) Where, in any family proceedings, the court has power to make an order under this Part with respect to any child, it may (whether or not it makes such an order) make an order requiring –

- (a) [an officer of the Service][1] [or a Welsh family proceedings officer][2] to be made available; or
- (b) a local authority to make an officer of the authority available,

to advise, assist and (where appropriate) befriend any person named in the order.

(2) The persons who may be named in an order under this section ('a family assistance order') are –

- (a) any parent [, guardian or special guardian][3] of the child;
- (b) any person with whom the child is living or in whose favour a contact order is in force with respect to the child;
- (c) the child himself.

(3) No court may make a family assistance order unless –

- (a) ...[4]
- (b) it has obtained the consent of every person to be named in the order other than the child.

(4) A family assistance order may direct –

- (a) the person named in the order; or
- (b) such of the persons named in the order as may be specified in the order,

to take such steps as may be so specified with a view to enabling the officer concerned to be kept informed of the address of any person named in the order and to be allowed to visit any such person.

[(4A) If the court makes a family assistance order with respect to a child and the order is to be in force at the same time as a contact order made with respect to the child, the family assistance order may direct the officer concerned to give advice and assistance as regards establishing, improving and maintaining contact to such of the persons named in the order as may be specified in the order.][4]

(5) Unless it specifies a shorter period, a family assistance order shall have effect for a period of [twelve months][4] beginning with the day on which it is made.

[(6) If the court makes a family assistance order with respect to a child and the order is to be in force at the same time as a section 8 order made with respect to the child, the family assistance order may direct the officer concerned to report to the court on such matters relating to the section 8 order as the court may require (including the question whether the section 8 order ought to be varied or discharged).][4]

(7) A family assistance order shall not be made so as to require a local authority to make an officer of theirs available unless –

- (a) the authority agree; or
- (b) the child concerned lives or will live within their area.

(8), (9) ...[1]

NOTES

Amendments.[1] Words substituted or subsections omitted: Criminal Justice and Court Services Act 2000, s 74, Sch 7, paras 87, 89, Sch 8.[2] Words inserted: Children Act 2004, s 40, Sch 3, paras 5, 7.[3] Words substituted: Adoption and Children Act 2002, s 139(1), Sch 3, paras 54, 58.[4] Paragraph repealed, subsections inserted and substituted, and words substituted: Children and Adoption Act 2006, ss 6(1)–(5), 15(2), Sch 3.

Definitions. 'A section 8 order': s 8(2); 'child': s 105(1); 'contact order': s 8(1); 'family assistance order': s 16(2); 'family proceedings': s 8(3); 'guardian of a child': s 105(1); 'local authority': s 105(1); 'the court': s 92(7).

[16A Risk assessments

(1) This section applies to the following functions of officers of the Service or Welsh family proceedings officers –

- (a) any function in connection with family proceedings in which the court has power to make an order under this Part with respect to a child or in which a question with respect to such an order arises;
- (b) any function in connection with an order made by the court in such proceedings.

(2) If, in carrying out any function to which this section applies, an officer of the Service or a Welsh family proceedings officer is given cause to suspect that the child concerned is at risk of harm, he must –

- (a) make a risk assessment in relation to the child, and
- (b) provide the risk assessment to the court.

(3) A risk assessment, in relation to a child who is at risk of suffering harm of a particular sort, is an assessment of the risk of that harm being suffered by the child.][1]

NOTES

Amendments.[1] Section inserted: Children and Adoption Act 2006, s 7.

PART III
LOCAL AUTHORITY SUPPORT FOR CHILDREN AND FAMILIES

Provision of services for children and their families

17 Provision of services for children in need, their families and others

(1) It shall be the general duty of every local authority (in addition to the other duties imposed on them by this Part) –

   (a) to safeguard and promote the welfare of children within their area who are in need; and
   (b) so far as is consistent with that duty, to promote the upbringing of such children by their families,

by providing a range and level of services appropriate to those children's needs.

(2) For the purpose principally of facilitating the discharge of their general duty under this section, every local authority shall have the specific duties and powers set out in Part 1 of Schedule 2.

(3) Any service provided by an authority in the exercise of functions conferred on them by this section may be provided for the family of a particular child in need or for any member of his family, if it is provided with a view to safeguarding or promoting the child's welfare.

(4) The [appropriate national authority][7] may by order amend any provision of Part I of Schedule 2 or add any further duty or power to those for the time being mentioned there.

[(4A) Before determining what (if any) services to provide for a particular child in need in the exercise of functions conferred on them by this section, a local authority shall, so far as is reasonably practicable and consistent with the child's welfare –

   (a) ascertain the child's wishes and feelings regarding the provision of those services; and
   (b) give due consideration (having regard to his age and understanding) to such wishes and feelings of the child as they have been able to ascertain.][6]

(5) Every local authority –

   (a) shall facilitate the provision by others (including in particular voluntary organisations) of services which the authority have power to provide by virtue of this section, or section 18, 20, [23, 23B to 23D, 24A or 24B][3]; and
   (b) may make such arrangements as they see fit for any person to act on their behalf in the provision of any such service.

(6) The services provided by a local authority in the exercise of functions conferred on them by this section may include [providing accommodation and][4] giving assistance in kind or, in exceptional circumstances, in cash.

(7) Assistance may be unconditional or subject to conditions as to the repayment of the assistance or of its value (in whole or in part).

(8) Before giving any assistance or imposing any conditions, a local authority shall have regard to the means of the child concerned and of each of his parents.

(9) No person shall be liable to make any repayment of assistance or of its value at any time when he is in receipt of income support [under][5] [Part VII of the Social Security Contributions and Benefits Act 1992][1][, of any element of child tax credit other than the family element, of working tax credit][5] [or of an income-based jobseeker's allowance][2].

(10) For the purposes of this Part a child shall be taken to be in need if –

(a) he is unlikely to achieve or maintain, or to have the opportunity of achieving or maintaining, a reasonable standard of health or development without the provision for him of services by a local authority under this Part;
(b) his health or development is likely to be significantly impaired, or further impaired, without the provision for him of such services; or
(c) he is disabled,

and 'family', in relation to such a child, includes any person who has parental responsibility for the child and any other person with whom he has been living.

(11) For the purposes of this Part, a child is disabled if he is blind, deaf or dumb or suffers from mental disorder of any kind or is substantially and permanently handicapped by illness, injury or congenital deformity or such other disability as may be prescribed; and in this Part –

'development' means physical, intellectual, emotional, social or behavioural development; and
'health' means physical or mental health.

[(12) The Treasury may by regulations prescribe circumstances in which a person is to be treated for the purposes of this Part (or for such of those purposes as are prescribed) as in receipt of any element of child tax credit other than the family element or of working tax credit][, of an income-based jobseeker's allowance or of an income-related employment and support allowance][8].

NOTES

Amendments.[1] Words substituted: Disability Living Allowance and Disability Working Allowance Act 1991, s 7(2), Sch 3, Pt II, para 13.[2] Words substituted: Social Security (Consequential Provisions) Act 1992, s 4, Sch 2, para 108.[3] Words substituted: Children (Leaving Care) Act 2000, s 7(1), (2).[4] Words inserted: Adoption and Children Act 2002, s 116(1).[5] Words substituted and subsection inserted: Tax Credits Act 2002, s 47, Sch 3, paras 15 and 16.[6] Subsection inserted: Children Act 2004, s 53(1).[7] Words substituted: Children and Young Persons Act 2008, s 39, Sch 3, paras 1, 2.[8] Words inserted: Welfare Reform Act 2007, s 28(1), Sch 3, para 6(1), (2).

Definitions. 'Child': s 105(1); 'child in need': s 17(10); 'development': s 17(11); 'disabled': s 17(11); 'family': s 17(10); 'functions': s 105(1); 'health': s 17(11); 'local authority': s 105(1); 'parental responsibility': s 3; 'prescribed': s 105(1); 'service': s 105(1); 'upbringing': s 105(1); 'voluntary organisation': s 105(1).

[17A Direct payments

(1) The [appropriate national authority]³ may by regulations make provision for and in connection with requiring or authorising the responsible authority in the case of a person of a prescribed description who falls within subsection (2) to make, with that person's consent, such payments to him as they may determine in accordance with the regulations in respect of his securing the provision of the service mentioned in that subsection.

(2) A person falls within this subsection if he is –

(a) a person with parental responsibility for a disabled child,
(b) a disabled person with parental responsibility for a child, or
(c) a disabled child aged 16 or 17,

and a local authority ('the responsible authority') have decided for the purposes of section 17 that the child's needs (or, if he is such a disabled child, his needs) call for the provision by them of a service in exercise of functions conferred on them under that section.

(3) Subsections (3) to (5) and (7) of section 57 of the 2001 Act shall apply, with any necessary modifications, in relation to regulations under this section as they apply in relation to regulations under that section.

(4) Regulations under this section shall provide that, where payments are made under the regulations to a person falling within subsection (5) –

(a) the payments shall be made at the rate mentioned in subsection (4)(a) of section 57 of the 2001 Act (as applied by subsection (3)); and
(b) subsection (4)(b) of that section shall not apply.

(5) A person falls within this subsection if he is –

(a) a person falling within subsection (2)(a) or (b) and the child in question is aged 16 or 17, or
(b) a person who is in receipt of income support, …² under Part 7 of the Social Security Contributions and Benefits Act 1992[, of any element of child tax credit other than the family element, of working tax credit]² [, of an income-based jobseeker's allowance or of an income-related employment and support allowance]³.

(6) In this section –

'the 2001 Act' means the Health and Social Care Act 2001;
'disabled' in relation to an adult has the same meaning as that given by section 17(11) in relation to a child;

'prescribed' means specified in or determined in accordance with regulations under this section (and has the same meaning in the provisions of the 2001 Act mentioned in subsection (3) as they apply by virtue of that subsection).]¹

NOTES

Amendments.¹ Section inserted: Carers and Disabled Children Act 2000, s 7(1); and subsequently substituted: Health and Social Care Act 2001, s 58 (applies to England only).² Words repealed or inserted: Tax Credits Act 2002, s 47, Sch 3, s 60, paras 15, 17, Sch 6.³ Words substituted: Children and Young Persons Act 2008, ss 28(1), 39, Sch 3, paras 1, 3, 6(1), (3).

18 Day care for pre-school and other children

(1) Every local authority shall provide such day care for children in need within their area who are –

    (a)   aged five or under; and
    (b)   not yet attending schools,

as is appropriate.

(2) A local authority [in Wales]¹ may provide day care for children within their area who satisfy the conditions mentioned in subsection (1)(a) and (b) even though they are not in need.

(3) A local authority may provide facilities (including training, advice, guidance and counselling) for those –

    (a)   caring for children in day care; or
    (b)   who at any time accompany such children while they are in day care.

(4) In this section 'day care' means any form of care or supervised activity provided for children during the day (whether or not it is provided on a regular basis).

(5) Every local authority shall provide for children in need within their area who are attending any school such care or supervised activities as is appropriate –

    (a)   outside school hours; or
    (b)   during school holidays.

(6) A local authority [in Wales]¹ may provide such care or supervised activities for children within their area who are attending any school even though those children are not in need.

(7) In this section 'supervised activity' means an activity supervised by a responsible person.

NOTES

Amendments. Words inserted: Childcare Act 2006, s 103(1), Sch 2, para 4.

Definitions. 'Child': s 105(1); 'child in need': s 17(10); 'day care': s 18(4); 'local authority': s 105(1); 'school': s 105(1); 'supervised activity': s 18(7).

19

...[1]

NOTES

Amendments.[1] Section repealed: Education Act 2002, s 149(2).

Definitions. 'Child': s 105(1); 'childminder': s 71(2); 'day care': s 18(4); 'health authority': s 105(1); 'local authority': s 105(1); 'local education authority': s 105(1); 'relevant establishment': s 19(5); 'review period': s 19(5).

Provision of accommodation for children

20 Provision of accommodation for children: general

(1) Every local authority shall provide accommodation for any child in need within their area who appears to them to require accommodation as a result of –

(a) there being no person who has parental responsibility for him;
(b) his being lost or having been abandoned; or
(c) the person who has been caring for him being prevented (whether or not permanently, and for whatever reason) from providing him with suitable accommodation or care.

(2) Where a local authority provide accommodation under subsection (1) for a child who is ordinarily resident in the area of another local authority, that other local authority may take over the provision of accommodation for the child within –

(a) three months of being notified in writing that the child is being provided with accommodation; or
(b) such other longer period as may be prescribed.

(3) Every local authority shall provide accommodation for any child in need within their area who has reached the age of sixteen and whose welfare the authority consider is likely to be seriously prejudiced if they do not provide him with accommodation.

(4) A local authority may provide accommodation for any child within their area (even though a person who has parental responsibility for him is able to provide him with accommodation) if they consider that to do so would safeguard or promote the child's welfare.

(5) A local authority may provide accommodation for any person who has reached the age of sixteen but is under twenty-one in any community home which takes children who have reached the age of sixteen if they consider that to do so would safeguard or promote his welfare.

(6) Before providing accommodation under this section, a local authority shall, so far as is reasonably practicable and consistent with the child's welfare –

(a) ascertain the child's wishes [and feelings][1] regarding the provision of accommodation; and

Part I   Statutes

(b) give due consideration (having regard to his age and understanding) to such wishes [and feelings]¹ of the child as they have been able to ascertain.

(7) A local authority may not provide accommodation under this section for any child if any person who –

(a) has parental responsibility for him; and
(b) is willing and able to –
  (i) provide accommodation for him; or
  (ii) arrange for accommodation to be provided for him,

objects.

(8) Any person who has parental responsibility for a child may at any time remove the child from accommodation provided by or on behalf of the local authority under this section.

(9) Subsections (7) and (8) do not apply while any person –

(a) in whose favour a residence order is in force with respect to the child; ...²
[(aa) who is a special guardian of the child; or]³
(b) who has care of the child by virtue of an order made in the exercise of the High Court's inherent jurisdiction with respect to children,

agrees to the child being looked after in accommodation provided by or on behalf of the local authority.

(10) Where there is more than one such person as is mentioned in subsection (9), all of them must agree.

(11) Subsections (7) and (8) do not apply where a child who has reached the age of sixteen agrees to being provided with accommodation under this section.

NOTES

Amendments.¹ Words inserted: Children Act 2004, s 53(2).² Word repealed: Adoption and Children Act 2002, s 139(1), (3), Sch 3, paras 54, 59, Sch 5.³ Paragraph inserted: Adoption and Children Act 2002, s 139(1), (3), Sch 3, paras 54, 59.

Definitions. 'Child': s 105(1); 'child in need': s 17(10); 'community home': s 53(1); 'local authority': s 105(1); 'ordinary residence': s 105(6); 'parental responsibility': s 3; 'prescribed': s 105(1); 'residence order': s 8(1).

21 Provision of accommodation for children in police protection or detention or on remand, etc

(1) Every local authority shall make provision for the reception and accommodation of children who are removed or kept away from home under Part V.

(2) Every local authority shall receive, and provide accommodation for, children –

(a) in police protection whom they are requested to receive under section 46(3)(f);

(b) whom they are requested to receive under section 38(6) of the Police and Criminal Evidence Act 1984;
(c) who are –
  (i) on remand under [...[8] section][4] 23(1) of the Children and Young Persons Act 1969; ...[8]
  [(ia) remanded to accommodation provided by or on behalf of a local authority by virtue of paragraph 4 of Schedule 1 or paragraph 6 of Schedule 8 to the Powers of Criminal Courts (Sentencing) Act 2000 (breach etc of referral orders and reparation orders);][8]
  [(ii) remanded to accommodation provided by or on behalf of a local authority by virtue of paragraph 21 of Schedule 2 to the Criminal Justice and Immigration Act 2008 (breach etc of youth rehabilitation orders); or
  (iii) the subject of a youth rehabilitation order imposing a local authority residence requirement or a youth rehabilitation order with fostering,][8]
and with respect to whom they are the designated authority.

[(2A) In subsection (2)(c)(iii), the following terms have the same meanings as in Part 1 of the Criminal Justice and Immigration Act 2008 (see section 7 of that Act) –

'local authority residence requirement';
'youth rehabilitation order';
'youth rehabilitation order with fostering'.][8]

(3) Where a child has been –
  (a) removed under Part V; or
  (b) detained under section 38 of the Police and Criminal Evidence Act 1984,

and he is not being provided with accommodation by a local authority or in a hospital vested in the Secretary of State[, the Welsh Ministers][7] [or a Primary Care Trust][3] [or otherwise made available pursuant to arrangements made by a [[Local Health Board][6]][2]][1] [or a Primary Care Trust][3], any reasonable expenses of accommodating him shall be recoverable from the local authority in whose area he is ordinarily resident.

NOTES

Amendments.[1] Words inserted: National Health Service and Community Care Act 1990, s 66(1), Sch 36, para 1.[2] Words substituted: Health Authorities Act 1995, s 2(1), Sch 1, Pt III, para 118(1), (3).[3] Words inserted: Health Act 1999 (Supplementary, Consequential etc Provisions) Order 2000, SI 2000/90.[4] Words substituted: Powers of Criminal Courts (Sentencing) Act 2000, s 165(1), Sch 9, para 126.[5] Words inserted: Anti-social Behaviour Act 2003, s 88, Sch 2, para 5.[6] Words substituted: SI 2007/961.[7] Children and Young Persons Act 2008, s 39, Sch 3, paras 1, 5. [8] Words repealed, paragraphs inserted and substituted, and subsection inserted: Criminal Justice and Immigration Act 2008, ss 6(2), (3), 149, Sch 4, Pt 1, paras 33, 34(1)–(3), Pt 2, para 105, Sch 28, Pt 1.

Definitions. 'Child': s 105(1); 'hospital': s 105(1); 'local authority': s 105(1); 'police protection': s 46(2); 'supervision order': s 31(11).

Part I   Statutes

Duties of local authorities in relation to children looked after by them

22   General duty of local authority in relation to children looked after by them

(1) In this Act, any reference to a child who is looked after by a local authority is a reference to a child who is –

- (a) in their care; or
- (b) provided with accommodation by the authority in the exercise of any functions (in particular those under this Act) which [are social services functions within the meaning of][1] the Local Authority Social Services Act 1970 [, apart from functions under sections [17][3] 23B and 24B][2].

(2) In subsection (1) 'accommodation' means accommodation which is provided for a continuous period of more than 24 hours.

(3) It shall be the duty of a local authority looking after any child –

- (a) to safeguard and promote his welfare; and
- (b) to make such use of services available for children cared for by their own parents as appears to the authority reasonable in his case.

[(3A) The duty of a local authority under subsection (3)(a) to safeguard and promote the welfare of a child looked after by them includes in particular a duty to promote the child's educational achievement.][4]

(4) Before making any decision with respect to a child whom they are looking after, or proposing to look after, a local authority shall, so far as is reasonably practicable, ascertain the wishes and feelings of –

- (a) the child;
- (b) his parents;
- (c) any person who is not a parent of his but who has parental responsibility for him; and
- (d) any other person whose wishes and feelings the authority consider to be relevant,

regarding the matter to be decided.

(5) In making any such decision a local authority shall give due consideration –

- (a) having regard to his age and understanding, to such wishes and feelings of the child as they have been able to ascertain;
- (b) to such wishes and feelings of any person mentioned in subsection (4)(b) to (d) as they have been able to ascertain; and
- (c) to the child's religious persuasion, racial origin and cultural and linguistic background.

(6) If it appears to a local authority that it is necessary, for the purposes of protecting members of the public from serious injury, to exercise their powers with respect to a child whom they are looking after in a manner which may not be consistent with their duties under this section, they may do so.

(7) If the [appropriate national authority][5] considers it necessary, for the purpose of protecting members of the public from serious injury, to give

directions to a local authority with respect to the exercise of their powers with respect to a child whom they are looking after, he may give such directions to [the local authority][5].

(8) Where any such directions are given to an authority they shall comply with them even though doing so is inconsistent with their duties under this section.

NOTES

Amendments.[1] Words substituted: Local Government Act 2000, s 107, Sch 5, para 19.[2] Words inserted: Children (Leaving Care) Act 2000, s 2(2).[3] Reference inserted: Adoption and Children Act 2002, s 116(2).[4] Subsection inserted: Children Act 2004, s 52.[5] Words substituted: Children and Young Persons Act 2008, s 39, Sch 3, paras 1, 6.

Definitions. 'Accommodation': s 22(2); 'child': s 105(1); 'child who is looked after by a local authority': s 22(1); 'functions': s 105(1); 'local authority': s 105(1); 'parental responsibility': s 3; 'service': s 105(1).

[22C Ways in which looked after children are to be accommodated and maintained

(1) This section applies where a local authority are looking after a child ('C').

(2) The local authority must make arrangements for C to live with a person who falls within subsection (3) (but subject to subsection (4)).

(3) A person ('P') falls within this subsection if –

    (a)   P is a parent of C;
    (b)   P is not a parent of C but has parental responsibility for C; or
    (c)   in a case where C is in the care of the local authority and there was a residence order in force with respect to C immediately before the care order was made, P was a person in whose favour the residence order was made.

(4) Subsection (2) does not require the local authority to make arrangements of the kind mentioned in that subsection if doing so –

    (a)   would not be consistent with C's welfare; or
    (b)   would not be reasonably practicable.

(5) If the local authority are unable to make arrangements under subsection (2), they must place C in the placement which is, in their opinion, the most appropriate placement available.

(6) In subsection (5) 'placement' means –

    (a)   placement with an individual who is a relative, friend or other person connected with C and who is also a local authority foster parent;
    (b)   placement with a local authority foster parent who does not fall within paragraph (a);
    (c)   placement in a children's home in respect of which a person is registered under Part 2 of the Care Standards Act 2000; or
    (d)   subject to section 22D, placement in accordance with other arrangements which comply with any regulations made for the purposes of this section.

(7) In determining the most appropriate placement for C, the local authority must, subject to the other provisions of this Part (in particular, to their duties under section 22) –

(a) give preference to a placement falling within paragraph (a) of subsection (6) over placements falling within the other paragraphs of that subsection;
(b) comply, so far as is reasonably practicable in all the circumstances of C's case, with the requirements of subsection (8); and
(c) comply with subsection (9) unless that is not reasonably practicable.

(8) The local authority must ensure that the placement is such that –

(a) it allows C to live near C's home;
(b) it does not disrupt C's education or training;
(c) if C has a sibling for whom the local authority are also providing accommodation, it enables C and the sibling to live together;
(d) if C is disabled, the accommodation provided is suitable to C's particular needs.

(9) The placement must be such that C is provided with accommodation within the local authority's area.

(10) The local authority may determine –

(a) the terms of any arrangements they make under subsection (2) in relation to C (including terms as to payment); and
(b) the terms on which they place C with a local authority foster parent (including terms as to payment but subject to any order made under section 49 of the Children Act 2004).

(11) The appropriate national authority may make regulations for, and in connection with, the purposes of this section.

(12) In this Act 'local authority foster parent' means a person who is approved as a local authority foster parent in accordance with regulations made by virtue of paragraph 12F of Schedule 2.][1]

NOTES

Amendments. [1] Section substituted for s 23 for certain purposes: Children and Young Persons Act 2008, s 8(1).

[22F Regulations as to children looked after by local authorities

Part 2 of Schedule 2 has effect for the purposes of making further provision as to children looked after by local authorities and in particular as to the regulations which may be made under section 22C(11).][1]

NOTES

Amendments. [1] Section substituted for s 23 for certain purposes: Children and Young Persons Act 2008, s 8(1).

23 Provision of accommodation and maintenance by local authority for children whom they are looking after

(1) It shall be the duty of any local authority looking after a child –

(a) when he is in their care, to provide accommodation for him; and
(b) to maintain him in other respects apart from providing accommodation for him.

(2) A local authority shall provide accommodation and maintenance for any child whom they are looking after by –

(a) placing him (subject to subsection (5) and any regulations made by the [appropriate national authority][4]) with –
   (i) a family;
   (ii) a relative of his; or
   (iii) any other suitable person,
   on such terms as to payment by the authority and otherwise as the authority may determine [(subject to section 49 of the Children Act 2004)][3];
[(aa) maintaining him in an appropriate children's home;

(b)–(e) ...][2]

(f) making such other arrangements as –
   (i) seem appropriate to them; and
   (ii) comply with any regulations made by the [appropriate national authority][4].

[(2A) Where under subsection (2)(aa) a local authority maintains a child in a home provided, equipped and maintained by the [appropriate national authority][4] under section 82(5), it shall do so on such terms as [that national authority][4] may from time to time determine.][2]

(3) Any person with whom a child has been placed under subsection (2)(a) is referred to in this Act as a local authority foster parent unless he falls within subsection (4).

(4) A person falls within this subsection if he is –

(a) a parent of the child;
(b) a person who is not a parent of the child but who has parental responsibility for him; or
(c) where the child is in care and there was a residence order in force with respect to him immediately before the care order was made, a person in whose favour the residence order was made.

(5) Where a child is in the care of a local authority, the authority may only allow him to live with a person who falls within subsection (4) in accordance with regulations made by the [appropriate national authority][4].

[(5A) For the purposes of subsection (5) a child shall be regarded living with a person if he stays with that person for a continuous period of more than 24 hours.][1]

(6) Subject to any regulations made by the [appropriate national authority][4] for the purposes of this subsection, any local authority looking after a child shall make arrangements to enable him to live with –

(a) a person falling within subsection (4); or
(b) a relative, friend or other person connected with him,

unless that would not be reasonably practicable or consistent with his welfare.

(7) Where a local authority provide accommodation for a child whom they are looking after, they shall, subject to the provisions of this Part and so far as is reasonably practicable and consistent with his welfare, secure that –

(a) the accommodation is near his home; and
(b) where the authority are also providing accommodation for a sibling of his, they are accommodated together.

(8) Where a local authority provide accommodation for a child whom they are looking after and who is disabled, they shall, so far as is reasonably practicable, secure that the accommodation is not unsuitable to his particular needs.

(9) Part II of Schedule 2 shall have effect for the purposes of making further provision as to children looked after by local authorities and in particular as to the regulations that may be made under subsections (2)(a) and (f) and (5).

[(10) In this Act –

'appropriate children's home' means a children's home in respect of which a person is registered under Part II of the Care Standards Act 2000; and
'children's home' has the same meaning as in that Act.][2]

NOTES

Amendments.[1] Subsection inserted: Courts and Legal Services Act 1990, s 116, Sch 16, para 12(2).[2] Paragraph (aa) substituted for paras (b)–(e) and subsections inserted: Care Standards Act 2000, s 116, Sch 4, para 14(3).[3] Words inserted: Children Act 2004, s 49(3).[4] Words substituted: Children and Young Persons Act 2008, s 39, Sch 3, paras 1, 7.

Definitions. 'Care order': s 8(1); 'child': s 105(1); 'child who is looked after by a local authority': s 22(1); 'community home': s 53(1); 'disabled': s 17(11); 'family': s 17(10); 'local authority': s 105(1); 'local authority foster parent': s 23(3); 'parental responsibility': s 3; 'registered children's home': s 63(8); 'relative': s 105(1); 'residence order': s 8(1); 'voluntary home': s 60(3).

[Visiting

23ZA Duty of local authority to ensure visits to, and contact with, looked after children and others

(1) This section applies to –

(a) a child looked after by a local authority;
(b) a child who was looked after by a local authority but who has ceased to be looked after by them as a result of prescribed circumstances.

(2) It is the duty of the local authority –

(a) to ensure that a person to whom this section applies is visited by a representative of the authority ('a representative');
(b) to arrange for appropriate advice, support and assistance to be available to a person to whom this section applies who seeks it from them.

(3) The duties imposed by subsection (2) –

(a) are to be discharged in accordance with any regulations made for the purposes of this section by the appropriate national authority;
(b) are subject to any requirement imposed by or under an enactment applicable to the place in which the person to whom this section applies is accommodated.

(4) Regulations under this section for the purposes of subsection (3)(a) may make provision about –

(a) the frequency of visits;
(b) circumstances in which a person to whom this section applies must be visited by a representative; and
(c) the functions of a representative.

(5) In choosing a representative a local authority must satisfy themselves that the person chosen has the necessary skills and experience to perform the functions of a representative.][1]

NOTES

Amendments. [1] Section and preceding cross-heading inserted for certain purposes: Children and Young Persons Act 2008, s 15.

[23ZB Independent visitors for children looked after by a local authority

(1) A local authority looking after a child must appoint an independent person to be the child's visitor if –

(a) the child falls within a description prescribed in regulations made by the appropriate national authority; or
(b) in any other case, it appears to them that it would be in the child's interests to do so.

(2) A person appointed under this section must visit, befriend and advise the child.

(3) A person appointed under this section is entitled to recover from the appointing authority any reasonable expenses incurred by that person for the purposes of that person's functions under this section.

(4) A person's appointment as a visitor in pursuance of this section comes to an end if –

(a) the child ceases to be looked after by the local authority;
(b) the person resigns the appointment by giving notice in writing to the appointing authority; or
(c) the authority give him notice in writing that they have terminated it.

(5) The ending of such an appointment does not affect any duty under this section to make a further appointment.

(6) Where a local authority propose to appoint a visitor for a child under this section, the appointment shall not be made if –

(a) the child objects to it; and
(b) the authority are satisfied that the child has sufficient understanding to make an informed decision.

(7) Where a visitor has been appointed for a child under this section, the local authority shall terminate the appointment if –

(a) the child objects to its continuing; and
(b) the authority are satisfied that the child has sufficient understanding to make an informed decision.

(8) If the local authority give effect to a child's objection under subsection (6) or (7) and the objection is to having anyone as the child's visitor, the authority does not have to propose to appoint another person under subsection (1) until the objection is withdrawn.

(9) The appropriate national authority may make regulations as to the circumstances in which a person is to be regarded for the purposes of this section as independent of the appointing authority.]¹

NOTES

Amendments. ¹ Section and preceding cross-heading inserted for certain purposes: Children and Young Persons Act 2008, s 16(1).

Advice and assistance for certain children [and young persons]¹

[23A The responsible authority and relevant children

(1) The responsible local authority shall have the functions set out in section 23B in respect of a relevant child.

(2) In subsection (1) 'relevant child' means (subject to subsection (3)) a child who –

(a) is not being looked after by any local authority;
(b) was, before last ceasing to be looked after, an eligible child for the purposes of paragraph 19B of Schedule 2; and
(c) is aged sixteen or seventeen.

(3) The [appropriate national authority]² may prescribe –

(a) additional categories of relevant children; and
(b) categories of children who are not to be relevant children despite falling within subsection (2).

(4) In subsection (1) the 'responsible local authority' is the one which last looked after the child.

(5) If under subsection (3)(a) the [appropriate national authority]² prescribes a category of relevant children which includes children who do not fall within subsection (2)(b) (for example, because they were being looked after by a local authority in Scotland), [the appropriate national authority]² may in the regulations also provide for which local authority is to be the responsible local authority for those children.]¹

NOTES

Amendments.¹ Section inserted: Children (Leaving Care) Act 2000, s 2(4). ² Words substituted: Children and Young Persons Act 2008, s 39, Sch 3, paras 1, 8.

[23B Additional functions of the responsible authority in respect of relevant children

(1) It is the duty of each local authority to take reasonable steps to keep in touch with a relevant child for whom they are the responsible authority, whether he is within their area or not.

(2) It is the duty of each local authority to appoint a personal adviser for each relevant child (if they have not already done so under paragraph 19C of Schedule 2).

(3) It is the duty of each local authority, in relation to any relevant child who does not already have a pathway plan prepared for the purposes of paragraph 19B of Schedule 2 –

(a) to carry out an assessment of his needs with a view to determining what advice, assistance and support it would be appropriate for them to provide him under this Part; and
(b) to prepare a pathway plan for him.

(4) The local authority may carry out such an assessment at the same time as any assessment of his needs is made under any enactment referred to in sub-paragraphs (a) to (c) of paragraph 3 of Schedule 2, or under any other enactment.

(5) The [appropriate national authority]² may by regulations make provision as to assessments for the purposes of subsection (3).

(6) The regulations may in particular make provision about –

(a) who is to be consulted in relation to an assessment;
(b) the way in which an assessment is to be carried out, by whom and when;
(c) the recording of the results of an assessment;
(d) the considerations to which the local authority are to have regard in carrying out an assessment.

(7) [The local authority]² shall keep the pathway plan under regular review.

(8) The responsible local authority shall safeguard and promote the child's welfare and, unless they are satisfied that his welfare does not require it, support him by –

(a) maintaining him;
(b) providing him with or maintaining him in suitable accommodation; and
(c) providing support of such other descriptions as may be prescribed.

(9) Support under subsection (8) may be in cash.

(10) The [appropriate national authority][2] may by regulations make provision about the meaning of 'suitable accommodation' and in particular about the suitability of landlords or other providers of accommodation.

(11) If the local authority have lost touch with a relevant child, despite taking reasonable steps to keep in touch, they must without delay –

(*a*) consider how to re-establish contact; and
(*b*) take reasonable steps to do so,

and while the child is still a relevant child must continue to take such steps until they succeed.

(12) Subsections (7) to (9) of section 17 apply in relation to support given under this section as they apply in relation to assistance given under that section.

(13) Subsections (4) and (5) of section 22 apply in relation to any decision by a local authority for the purposes of this section as they apply in relation to the decisions referred to in that section.][1]

NOTES

Amendments.[1] Section inserted: Children (Leaving Care) Act 2000, s 2(4).[2] Words substituted: Children and Young Persons Act 2008, s 39, Sch 3, paras 1, 9.

[23C Continuing functions in respect of former relevant children

(1) Each local authority shall have the duties provided for in this section towards –

(a) a person who has been a relevant child for the purposes of section 23A (and would be one if he were under eighteen), and in relation to whom they were the last responsible authority; and
(b) a person who was being looked after by them when he attained the age of eighteen, and immediately before ceasing to be looked after was an eligible child,

and in this section such a person is referred to as a 'former relevant child'.

(2) It is the duty of the local authority to take reasonable steps –

(a) to keep in touch with a former relevant child whether he is within their area or not; and
(b) if they lose touch with him, to re-establish contact.

(3) It is the duty of the local authority –

(a) to continue the appointment of a personal adviser for a former relevant child; and

(b) to continue to keep his pathway plan under regular review.

(4) It is the duty of the local authority to give a former relevant child –

(a) assistance of the kind referred to in section 24B(1), to the extent that his welfare requires it;
(b) assistance of the kind referred to in section 24B(2), to the extent that his welfare and his educational or training needs require it;
(c) other assistance, to the extent that his welfare requires it.

(5) The assistance given under subsection (4)(c) may be in kind or, in exceptional circumstances, in cash.

[(5A) It is the duty of the local authority to pay the relevant amount to a former relevant child who pursues higher education in accordance with a pathway plan prepared for that person.

(5B) The appropriate national authority may by regulations –

(a) prescribe the relevant amount for the purposes of subsection (5A);
(b) prescribe the meaning of 'higher education' for those purposes;
(c) make provision as to the payment of the relevant amount;
(d) make provision as to the circumstances in which the relevant amount (or any part of it) may be recovered by the local authority from a former relevant child to whom a payment has been made.

(5C) The duty set out in subsection (5A) is without prejudice to that set out in subsection (4)(b).][2]

(6) Subject to subsection (7), the duties set out in subsections (2), (3) and (4) subsist until the former relevant child reaches the age of twenty-one.

(7) If the former relevant child's pathway plan sets out a programme of education or training which extends beyond his twenty-first birthday –

(a) the duty set out in subsection (4)(b) continues to subsist for so long as the former relevant child continues to pursue that programme; and
(b) the duties set out in subsections (2) and (3) continue to subsist concurrently with that duty.

(8) For the purposes of subsection (7)(a) there shall be disregarded any interruption in a former relevant child's pursuance of a programme of education or training if the local authority are satisfied that he will resume it as soon as is reasonably practicable.

(9) Section 24B(5) applies in relation to a person being given assistance under subsection (4)(b) as it applies in relation to a person to whom section 24B(3) applies.

(10) Subsections (7) to (9) of section 17 apply in relation to assistance given under this section as they apply in relation to assistance given under that section.][1]

Part I Statutes

NOTES

Amendments.[1] Section inserted: Children (Leaving Care) Act 2000, s 2(4). [2] Subsections inserted: Children and Young Persons Act 2008, s 21(1), (2).

[Personal advisers and pathway plans

23D Personal advisers

(1) The [appropriate national authority][2] may by regulations require local authorities to appoint a personal adviser for children or young persons of a prescribed description who have reached the age of sixteen but not the age of [twenty-five][3] who are not –

(a) children who are relevant children for the purposes of section 23A;
(b) the young persons referred to in section 23C; or
(c) the children referred to in paragraph 19C of Schedule 2[; or
(d) persons to whom section 23CA applies][3].

(2) Personal advisers appointed under or by virtue of this Part shall (in addition to any other functions) have such functions as the [appropriate national authority][2] prescribes.][1]

NOTES

Amendments.[1] Cross-heading and section inserted: Children (Leaving Care) Act 2000, s 3. [2] Words substituted: Children and Young Persons Act 2008, s 39, Sch 3, paras 1, 10. [3] Words substituted, and paragraph and preceding word inserted: Children and Young Persons Act 2008, s 23(1).

[23E Pathway plans

(1) In this Part, a reference to a 'pathway plan' is to a plan setting out –

(a) in the case of a plan prepared under paragraph 19B of Schedule 2 –
  (i) the advice, assistance and support which the local authority intend to provide a child under this Part, both while they are looking after him and later; and
  (ii) when they might cease to look after him; and
(b) in the case of a plan prepared under section 23B, the advice, assistance and support which the local authority intend to provide under this Part,

and dealing with such other matters (if any) as may be prescribed.

[(1A) A local authority may carry out an assessment under section 23B(3) or 23CA(3) of a person's needs at the same time as any assessment of his needs is made under –

(a) the Chronically Sick and Disabled Persons Act 1970;
(b) Part 4 of the Education Act 1996 (in the case of an assessment under section 23B(3));
(c) the Disabled Persons (Services, Consultation and Representation) Act 1986; or
(d) any other enactment.

(1B) The appropriate national authority may by regulations make provision as to assessments for the purposes of section 23B(3) or 23CA.

(1C) Regulations under subsection (1B) may in particular make provision about –
- (a) who is to be consulted in relation to an assessment;
- (b) the way in which an assessment is to be carried out, by whom and when;
- (c) the recording of the results of an assessment;
- (d) the considerations to which a local authority are to have regard in carrying out an assessment.

(1D) A local authority shall keep each pathway plan prepared by them under section 23B or 23CA under review.]³

(2) The [appropriate national authority]² may by regulations make provision about pathway plans and their review.]¹

NOTES

Amendments.¹ Section inserted: Children (Leaving Care) Act 2000, s 3. ² Words in square brackets substituted: Children and Young Persons Act 2008, s 39, Sch 3, paras 1, 11. ³ Subsections inserted for certain purposes: Children and Young Persons Act 2008, s 22(3), (5).

[24 Persons qualifying for advice and assistance

[(1) In this Part 'a person qualifying for advice and assistance' means a person to whom subsection (1A) or (1B) applies.

(1A) This subsection applies to a person –
- (a) who has reached the age of sixteen but not the age of twenty-one;
- (b) with respect to whom a special guardianship order is in force (or, if he has reached the age of eighteen, was in force when he reached that age); and
- (c) who was, immediately before the making of that order, looked after by a local authority.

(1B) This subsection applies to a person to whom subsection (1A) does not apply, and who –
- (a) is under twenty-one; and
- (b) at any time after reaching the age of sixteen but while still a child was, but is no longer, looked after, accommodated or fostered.]³

(2) In [subsection (1B)(b)]⁴, 'looked after, accommodated or fostered' means –
- (a) looked after by a local authority;
- (b) accommodated by or on behalf of a voluntary organisation;
- (c) accommodated in a private children's home;
- (d) accommodated for a consecutive period of at least three months –
  - (i) by any [Local Health Board]⁶, Special Health Authority [or Primary Care Trust or by a local authority in the exercise of education functions]⁸, or

(ii) in any care home or independent hospital or in any accommodation provided by a National Health Service trust [or an NHS foundation trust]²; or
(e) privately fostered.

(3) Subsection (2)(d) applies even if the period of three months mentioned there began before the child reached the age of sixteen.

(4) In the case of a person qualifying for advice and assistance by virtue of subsection (2)(a), it is the duty of the local authority which last looked after him to take such steps as they think appropriate to contact him at such times as they think appropriate with a view to discharging their functions under sections 24A and 24B.

(5) In each of sections 24A and 24B, the local authority under the duty or having the power mentioned there ('the relevant authority') is –

[(za) in the case of a person to whom subsection (1A) applies, a local authority determined in accordance with regulations made by the [appropriate national authority]⁷;]⁵
(a) in the case of a person qualifying for advice and assistance by virtue of subsection (2)(a), the local authority which last looked after him; or
(b) in the case of any other person qualifying for advice and assistance, the local authority within whose area the person is (if he has asked for help of a kind which can be given under section 24A or 24B).]¹

NOTES

Amendments.¹ Section and words in cross-heading inserted: Children (Leaving Care) Act 2000, ss 2(3), 4(1). ² Words inserted: Health and Social Care (Community Health and Standards) Act 2003, s 34, Sch 4, paras 75, 76.³ Subsection substituted: Adoption and Children Act 2002, s 139(1), Sch 3, paras 54, 60(a).⁴ Words substituted: Adoption and Children Act 2002, s 139(1), Sch 3, paras 54, 60(b).⁵ Paragraph inserted: Adoption and Children Act 2002, s 139(1), Sch 3, paras 54, 60(c).⁶ Words substituted: SI 2007/961.⁷ Words substituted: Children and Young Persons Act 2008, s 39, Sch 3, paras 1, 12. ⁸ Words substituted: SI 2010/1158.

[24A Advice and assistance

(1) The relevant authority shall consider whether the conditions in subsection (2) are satisfied in relation to a person qualifying for advice and assistance.

(2) The conditions are that –

(a) he needs help of a kind which they can give under this section or section 24B; and
(b) in the case of a person [to whom section 24(1A) applies, or to whom section 24(1B) applies and]³ who was not being looked after by any local authority, they are satisfied that the person by whom he was being looked after does not have the necessary facilities for advising or befriending him.

(3) If the conditions are satisfied –

(a) they shall advise and befriend him if [he is a person to whom section 24(1A) applies, or he is a person to whom section 24(1B) applies and]⁴ he was being looked after by a local authority or was accommodated by or on behalf of a voluntary organisation; and

(b) in any other case they may do so.

(4) Where as a result of this section a local authority are under a duty, or are empowered, to advise and befriend a person, they may also give him assistance.

(5) The assistance may be in kind [and, in exceptional circumstances, assistance may be given –

  (a) by providing accommodation, if in the circumstances assistance may not be given in respect of the accommodation under section 24B, or
  (b) in cash]².

(6) Subsections (7) to (9) of section 17 apply in relation to assistance given under this section or section 24B as they apply in relation to assistance given under that section.]¹

NOTES

Amendments.¹ Section inserted: Children (Leaving Care) Act 2000, s 4(1).² Words substituted: Adoption and Children Act 2002, s 116(3).³ Words inserted: Adoption and Children Act 2002, s 139(1), Sch 3, paras 54, 61(a).⁴ Words inserted: Adoption and Children Act 2002, s 139(1), Sch 3, paras 54, 61(b).

[24B Employment, education and training

(1) The relevant local authority may give assistance to any person who qualifies for advice and assistance by virtue of [section 24(1A) or]² section 24(2)(a) by contributing to expenses incurred by him in living near the place where he is, or will be, employed or seeking employment.

(2) The relevant local authority may give assistance to a person to whom subsection (3) applies by –

  (a) contributing to expenses incurred by the person in question in living near the place where he is, or will be, receiving education or training; or
  (b) making a grant to enable him to meet expenses connected with his education or training.

(3) This subsection applies to any person who –

  (a) is under twenty-four; and
  (b) qualifies for advice and assistance by virtue of [section 24(1A) or]² section 24(2)(a), or would have done so if he were under twenty-one.

(4) Where a local authority are assisting a person under subsection (2) they may disregard any interruption in his attendance on the course if he resumes it as soon as is reasonably practicable.

(5) Where the local authority are satisfied that a person to whom subsection (3) applies who is in full-time further or higher education needs accommodation during a vacation because his term-time accommodation is not available to him then, they shall give him assistance by –

Part I Statutes

    (a)   providing him with suitable accommodation during the vacation; or
    (b)   paying him enough to enable him to secure such accommodation himself.

(6) The [appropriate national authority][3] may prescribe the meaning of 'full-time', 'further education', 'higher education' and 'vacation' for the purposes of subsection (5).][1]

NOTES

Amendments.[1] Section inserted: Children (Leaving Care) Act 2000, s 4(1). [2] Words inserted: Adoption and Children Act 2002, s 139(1), Sch 3, paras 54, 62. [3] Words substituted: Children and Young Persons Act 2008, s 39, Sch 3, paras 1, 13.

[24C Information

(1) Where it appears to a local authority that a person –

    (a)   with whom they are under a duty to keep in touch under section 23B, 23C or 24; or
    (b)   whom they have been advising and befriending under section 24A; or
    (c)   to whom they have been giving assistance under section 24B,

proposes to live, or is living, in the area of another local authority, they must inform that other authority.

(2) Where a child who is accommodated –

    (a)   by a voluntary organisation or in a private children's home;
    (b)   by any [Local Health Board][3], Special Health Authority [or Primary Care Trust or by a local authority in the exercise of education functions][4]; or
    (c)   in any care home or independent hospital or any accommodation provided by a National Health Service trust [or an NHS foundation trust][2],

ceases to be so accommodated, after reaching the age of sixteen, the organisation, authority or (as the case may be) person carrying on the home shall inform the local authority within whose area the child proposes to live.

(3) Subsection (2) only applies, by virtue of paragraph (*b*) or (*c*), if the accommodation has been provided for a consecutive period of at least three months.

[(4) In a case where a child was accommodated by a local authority in the exercise of education functions, subsection (2) applies only if the local authority who accommodated the child are different from the local authority within whose area the child proposes to live.][4]][1]

NOTES

Amendments.[1] Section inserted: Children (Leaving Care) Act 2000, s 4(1). [2] Words inserted: Health and Social Care (Community Health and Standards) Act 2003, s 34, Sch 4, paras 75, 77. [3] Words substituted: SI 2007/961. [4] Words substituted and subsection inserted: SI 2010/1158.

[24D Representations: sections 23A to 24B

(1) Every local authority shall establish a procedure for considering representations (including complaints) made to them by –

(a) a relevant child for the purposes of section 23A or a young person falling within section 23C;
(b) a person qualifying for advice and assistance; or
(c) a person falling within section 24B(2),

about the discharge of their functions under this Part in relation to him.

[(1A) Regulations may be made by the [appropriate national authority][3] imposing time limits on the making of representations under subsection (1).][2]

(2) In considering representations under subsection (1), a local authority shall comply with regulations (if any) made by the [appropriate national authority][3] for the purposes of this subsection.][1]

NOTES
Amendments.[1] Section inserted: Children (Leaving Care) Act 2000, s 5.[2] Subsection inserted: Adoption and Children Act 2002, s 117(1).[3] Words substituted: Children and Young Persons Act 2008, s 39, Sch 3, paras 1, 14.

Secure accommodation

25 Use of accommodation for restricting liberty

(1) Subject to the following provisions of this section, a child who is being looked after by a local authority may not be placed, and, if placed, may not be kept, in accommodation provided for the purpose of restricting liberty ('secure accommodation') unless it appears –

(a) that –
  (i) he has a history of absconding and is likely to abscond from any other description of accommodation; and
  (ii) if he absconds, he is likely to suffer significant harm; or
(b) that if he is kept in any other description of accommodation he is likely to injure himself or other persons.

(2) The [appropriate national authority][2] may by regulations –

(a) specify a maximum period –
  (i) beyond which a child may not be kept in secure accommodation without the authority of the court; and
  (ii) for which the court may authorise a child to be kept in secure accommodation;
(b) empower the court from time to time to authorise a child to be kept in secure accommodation for such further period as the regulations may specify; and
(c) provide that applications to the court under this section shall be made only by local authorities.

Part I Statutes

(3) It shall be the duty of a court hearing an application under this section to determine whether any relevant criteria for keeping a child in secure accommodation are satisfied in his case.

(4) If a court determines that any such criteria are satisfied, it shall make an order authorising the child to be kept in secure accommodation and specifying the maximum period for which he may be so kept.

(5) On any adjournment of the hearing of an application under this section, a court may make an interim order permitting the child to be kept during the period of the adjournment in secure accommodation.

(6) No court shall exercise the powers conferred by this section in respect of a child who is not legally represented in that court unless, having been informed of his right to apply for [representation funded by the Legal Services Commission as part of the Community Legal Service or Criminal Defence Service][1] and having had the opportunity to do so, he refused or failed to apply.

(7) The [appropriate national authority][2] may by regulations provide that –

- (a) this section shall or shall not apply to any description of children specified in the regulations;
- (b) this section shall have effect in relation to children of a description specified in the regulations subject to such modifications as may be so specified;
- (c) such other provisions as may be so specified shall have effect for the purpose of determining whether a child of a description specified in the regulations may be placed or kept in secure accommodation.

(8) The giving of an authorisation under this section shall not prejudice any power of any court in England and Wales or Scotland to give directions relating to the child to whom the authorisation relates.

(9) This section is subject to section 20(8).

NOTES

Amendments.[1] Words substituted: Access to Justice 1999, s 24, Sch 4, para 45.[2] Words substituted: Children and Young Persons Act 2008, s 39, Sch 3, paras 1, 15.

Definitions. 'Child': s 105(1); 'child who is looked after by a local authority': s 22(1); 'harm': ss 31(9), 105(1); 'local authority': s 105(1); 'secure accommodation': s 25(1); 'significant harm': ss 31(9), (10), 105(1); 'the court': s 92(7).

[Independent reviewing officers

25A Appointment of independent reviewing officer

(1) If a local authority are looking after a child, they must appoint an individual as the independent reviewing officer for that child's case.

(2) The initial appointment under subsection (1) must be made before the child's case is first reviewed in accordance with regulations made under section 26.

(3) If a vacancy arises in respect of a child's case, the local authority must make another appointment under subsection (1) as soon as is practicable.

(4) An appointee must be of a description prescribed in regulations made by the appropriate national authority.]

NOTES

Amendment. [1] Section and preceding cross-heading inserted for purpose of making regulations under subs (4): Children and Young Persons Act 2008, s 10(1).

[25B Functions of the independent reviewing officer

(1) The independent reviewing officer must –

(a) monitor the performance by the local authority of their functions in relation to the child's case;
(b) participate, in accordance with regulations made by the appropriate national authority, in any review of the child's case;
(c) ensure that any ascertained wishes and feelings of the child concerning the case are given due consideration by the local authority;
(d) perform any other function which is prescribed in regulations made by the appropriate national authority.

(2) An independent reviewing officer's functions must be performed –

(a) in such manner (if any) as may be prescribed in regulations made by the appropriate national authority; and
(b) having regard to such guidance as that authority may issue in relation to the discharge of those functions.

(3) If the independent reviewing officer considers it appropriate to do so, the child's case may be referred by that officer to –

(a) an officer of the Children and Family Court Advisory and Support Service; or
(b) a Welsh family proceedings officer.

(4) If the independent reviewing officer is not an officer of the local authority, it is the duty of the authority –

(a) to co-operate with that individual; and
(b) to take all such reasonable steps as that individual may require of them to enable that individual's functions under this section to be performed satisfactorily.]

NOTES

Amendment. [1] Section and preceding cross-heading inserted for purpose of making regulations under subss (1)(b), (d), (2)(a): Children and Young Persons Act 2008, s 10(1).

Supplemental

26 Review of cases and inquiries into representations

(1) The [appropriate national authority][6] may make regulations requiring the case of each child who is being looked after by a local authority to be reviewed in accordance with the provisions of the regulations.

(2) The regulations may, in particular, make provision –

- (a) as to the manner in which each case is to be reviewed;
- (b) as to the considerations to which the local authority are to have regard in reviewing each case;
- (c) as to the time when each case is first to be reviewed and the frequency of subsequent reviews;
- (d) requiring the authority, before conducting any review, to seek the views of –
   - (i) the child;
   - (ii) his parents;
   - (iii) any person who is not a parent of his but who has parental responsibility for him; and
   - (iv) any other person whose views the authority consider to be relevant,

   including, in particular, the views of those persons in relation to any particular matter which is to be considered in the course of the review;
- (e) requiring the authority ...[1], in the case of a child who is in their care [–
   - (i) to keep the section 31A plan for the child under review and, if they are of the opinion that some change is required, to revise the plan, or make a new plan, accordingly;
   - (ii) to consider][1] whether an application should be made to discharge the care order;
- (f) requiring the authority ...[1], in the case of a child in accommodation provided by the authority [–
   - (i) if there is no plan for the future care of the child, to prepare one,
   - (ii) if there is such a plan for the child, to keep it under review and, if they are of the opinion that some change is required, to revise the plan or make a new plan, accordingly,
   - (iii) to consider][1] whether the accommodation accords with the requirements of this Part;
- (g) requiring the authority to inform the child, so far as is reasonably practicable, of any steps he may take under this Act;
- (h) requiring the authority to make arrangements, including arrangements with such other bodies providing services as it considers appropriate, to implement any decision which they propose to make in the course, or as a result, of the review;
- (i) requiring the authority to notify details of the result of the review and of any decision taken by them in consequence of the review to –
   - (i) the child;
   - (ii) his parents;

Children Act 1989, s 26

       (iii) any person who is not a parent of his but who has had parental responsibility for him; and

       (iv) any other person whom they consider ought to be notified;

(j) requiring the authority to monitor the arrangements which they have made with a view to ensuring that they comply with the regulations;

[(k) for the authority to appoint a person in respect of each case to carry out in the prescribed manner the functions mentioned in subsection (2A) and any prescribed function]¹.

[(2A) The functions referred to in subsection (2)(k) are –

(a) participating in the review of the case in question,
(b) monitoring the performance of the authority's functions in respect of the review,
(c) referring the case to an officer of the Children and Family Court Advisory and Support Service [or a Welsh family proceedings officer]², if the person appointed under subsection (2)(k) considers it appropriate to do so.

(2B) A person appointed under subsection (2)(k) must be a person of a prescribed description.

(2C) In relation to children whose cases are referred to officers under subsection (2A)(c), the Lord Chancellor may by regulations –

(a) extend the functions of the officers in respect of family proceedings (within the meaning of section 12 of the Criminal Justice and Court Services Act 2000) to other proceedings;
(b) require any functions of the officers to be performed in the manner prescribed by the regulations.]¹

[(2D) The power to make regulations in subsection (2C) is exercisable in relation to functions of Welsh family proceedings officers only with the consent of the [Welsh Ministers]⁶.]²

(3) Every local authority shall establish a procedure for considering any representations (including any complaint) made to them by –

(a) any child who is being looked after by them or who is not being looked after by them but is in need;
(b) a parent of his;
(c) any person who is not a parent of his but who has parental responsibility for him;
(d) any local authority foster parent;
(e) such other person as the authority consider has a sufficient interest in the child's welfare to warrant his representations being considered by them,

about the discharge by the authority of any of their [qualifying functions]³ in relation to the child.

[(3A) The following are qualifying functions for the purposes of subsection (3) –

(a) functions under this Part,
(b) such functions under Part 4 or 5 as are specified by the [appropriate national authority]⁶ in regulations.

(3B) The duty under subsection (3) extends to representations (including complaints) made to the authority by –

(a) any person mentioned in section 3(1) of the Adoption and Children Act 2002 (persons for whose needs provision is made by the Adoption Service) and any other person to whom arrangements for the provision of adoption support services (within the meaning of that Act) extend,
(b) such other person as the authority consider has sufficient interest in a child who is or may be adopted to warrant his representations being considered by them,

about the discharge by the authority of such functions under the Adoption and Children Act 2002 as are specified by the [appropriate national authority]⁶ in regulations.]⁴

[(3C) The duty under subsection (3) extends to any representations (including complaints) which are made to the authority by –

(a) a child with respect to whom a special guardianship order is in force,
(b) a special guardian or a parent of such a child,
(c) any other person the authority consider has a sufficient interest in the welfare of such a child to warrant his representations being considered by them, or
(d) any person who has applied for an assessment under section 14F(3) or (4),

about the discharge by the authority of such functions under section 14F as may be specified by the [appropriate national authority]⁶ in regulations.]⁵

(4) The procedure shall ensure that at least one person who is not a member or officer of the authority takes part in –

(a) the consideration; and
(b) any discussions which are held by the authority about the action (if any) to be taken in relation to the child in the light of the consideration.

[but this subsection is subject to subsection (5A).]⁴

[(4A) Regulations may be made by the [appropriate national authority]⁶ imposing time limits on the making of representations under this section.]⁴

(5) In carrying out any consideration of representations under this section a local authority shall comply with any regulations made by the [appropriate national authority]⁶ for the purpose of regulating the procedure to be followed.

[(5A) Regulations under subsection (5) may provide that subsection (4) does not apply in relation to any consideration or discussion which takes place as part of a procedure for which provision is made by the regulations for the purpose of resolving informally the matters raised in the representations.]⁴

(6) The [appropriate national authority]⁶ may make regulations requiring local authorities to monitor the arrangements that they have made with a view to ensuring that they comply with any regulations made for the purposes of subsection (5).

(7) Where any representation has been considered under the procedure established by a local authority under this section, the authority shall –

 (a) have due regard to the findings of those considering the representation; and
 (b) take such steps as are reasonably practicable to notify (in writing) –
   (i) the person making the representation;
   (ii) the child (if the authority consider that he has sufficient understanding); and
   (iii) such other persons (if any) as appear to the authority to be likely to be affected,
  of the authority's decision in the matter and their reasons for taking that decision and of any action which they have taken, or propose to take.

(8) Every local authority shall give such publicity to their procedure for considering representations under this section as they consider appropriate.

NOTES

Amendments.¹ Subsections and paragraph inserted, and words inserted or repealed: Adoption and Children Act 2002, s 118.² Words and subsection inserted: Children Act 2004, s 40, Sch 3, paras 5, 8.³ Words substituted: Adoption and Children Act 2002, s 117(2), (3).⁴ Subsections and words inserted: Adoption and Children Act 2002, s 117(2), (4), (5).⁵ Subsection inserted: Health and Social Care (Community Health and Standards) Act 2003, s 117(1).⁶ Words substituted: Children and Young Persons Act 2008, s 39, Sch 3, paras 1, 16.

Definitions. 'Accommodation': s 22(2); 'care order': s 31(11); 'child': s 105(1); 'child in need': s 17(10); 'child who is looked after by the local authority': s 22(1); 'functions': s 105(1); 'local authority': s 105(1); 'local authority foster parent': s 23(3); 'parental responsibility': s 3.

[...²]¹

NOTES

Amendments.¹ Section prospectively inserted: Health and Social Care (Community Health and Standards) Act 2003, s 116(1), from a date to be appointed.² Section repealed: Education and Inspections Act 2006, ss 157, 184, Sch 14, paras 9, 10, Sch 18, Pt 5.

[26ZB Representations: further consideration (Wales)

(1) The [Welsh Ministers]² may by regulations make provision for the further consideration of representations which have been considered by a local authority in Wales under section 24D or section 26.

(2) The regulations may in particular make provision –

 (a) for the further consideration of a representation by an independent panel established under the regulations;
 (b) about the procedure to be followed on the further consideration of a representation;

Part I Statutes

  (c) for the making of recommendations about the action to be taken as the result of a representation;
  (d) about the making of reports about a representation;
  (e) about the action to be taken by the local authority concerned as a result of the further consideration of a representation;
  (f) for a representation to be referred back to the local authority concerned for reconsideration by the authority.

(3) The regulations may require –

  (a) the making of a payment, in relation to the further consideration of a representation under this section, by any local authority in respect of whose functions the representation is made;
  (b) any such payment to be –
    (i) made to such person or body as may be specified in the regulations;
    (ii) of such amount as may be specified in, or calculated or determined under, the regulations; and
  (c) for an independent panel to review the amount chargeable under paragraph (a) in any particular case and, if the panel thinks fit, to substitute a lesser amount.

(4) The regulations may also –

  (a) provide for different parts or aspects of a representation to be treated differently;
  (b) require the production of information or documents in order to enable a representation to be properly considered;
  (c) authorise the disclosure of information or documents relevant to a representation to a person or body who is further considering a representation under the regulations;

and any such disclosure may be authorised notwithstanding any rule of common law that would otherwise prohibit or restrict the disclosure.][1]

NOTES

Amendments.[1] Section inserted: Health and Social Care (Community Health and Standards) Act 2003, s 116(2).[2] Words substituted: Children and Young Persons Act 2008, s 39, Sch 3, paras 1, 17.

[26A Advocacy services

(1) Every local authority shall make arrangements for the provision of assistance to –

  (a) persons who make or intend to make representations under section 24D; and
  (b) children who make or intend to make representations under section 26.

(2) The assistance provided under the arrangements shall include assistance by way of representation.

[(2A) The duty under subsection (1) includes a duty to make arrangements for the provision of assistance where representations under section 24D or 26 are further considered under section ...³ 26ZB.]²

(3) The arrangements –

(a) shall secure that a person may not provide assistance if he is a person who is prevented from doing so by regulations made by the [appropriate national authority]⁴; and
(b) shall comply with any other provision made by the regulations in relation to the arrangements.

(4) The [appropriate national authority]⁴ may make regulations requiring local authorities to monitor the steps that they have taken with a view to ensuring that they comply with regulations made for the purposes of subsection (3).

(5) Every local authority shall give such publicity to their arrangements for the provision of assistance under this section as they consider appropriate.]¹

NOTES

Amendments.¹ Section inserted: Adoption and Children Act 2002, s 119.² Subsection inserted in relation to Wales: Health and Social Care (Community Health and Standards) Act 2003, s 116(3).³ Words repealed: Education and Inspections Act 2006, ss 157, 184, Sch 14, paras 9, 11, Sch 18, Pt 5.⁴ Words substituted: Children and Young Persons Act 2008, s 39, Sch 3, paras 1, 18.

27 Co-operation between authorities

(1) Where it appears to a local authority that any authority ...¹ mentioned in subsection (3) could, by taking any specified action, help in the exercise of any of their functions under this Part, they may request the help of that other authority ...¹, specifying the action in question.

(2) An authority whose help is so requested shall comply with the request if it is compatible with their own statutory or other duties and obligations and does not unduly prejudice the discharge of any of their functions.

(3) The [authorities]² are –

(a) any local authority;
(b) ...⁹
(c) any local housing authority;
(d) any [[Local Health Board]⁷, Special Health Authority]⁴ [, Primary Care Trust]⁵ [, National Health Service trust or NHS foundation trust]⁶; and
(e) any person authorised by the [appropriate national authority]⁸ for the purposes of this section.

(4) ...³

NOTES

Amendments.¹ Words repealed: Courts and Legal Services Act 1990, ss 116, 125(7), Sch 16, para 14(a), Sch 20.² Words substituted or inserted: Courts and Legal Services Act 1990, s 116, Sch 16, para 14(b).³ Subsection repealed: Education Act 1993, s 307, Sch 19, para 147.⁴ Words substituted: Health Authorities Act 1995, s 2(1), Sch 1, Pt III, para 118(1), (5).⁵ Words inserted: Health Act 1999 (Supplementary, Consequential etc Provisions) Order 2000, SI 2000/90.⁶ Words inserted: Health and Social Care (Community Health and Standards) Act 2003, s 34, Sch 4,

Part I   Statutes

paras 75, 78.⁷ Words substituted: SI 2007/961.⁸ Words substituted: Children and Young Persons Act 2008, s 39, Sch 3, paras 1, 19. ⁹ Paragraph repealed: SI 2010/1158.

Definitions. 'Child'; 'functions'; 'health authority'; 'local authority'; 'local education authority'; 'local housing authority'; 'Primary Care Trust'; 'special educational needs': s 105(1).

28   Consultation with local education authorities

…¹

NOTES

Amendments.¹ Section repealed: SI 2010/1158.

Definitions. 'Appropriate local education authority': s 28(4); 'child': s 105(1); 'child who is looked after by a local authority': s 22(1); 'local authority': s 105(1); 'local education authority': s 105(1); 'special educational needs': s 105(1).

29   Recoupment of cost of providing services etc

(1) Where a local authority provide any service under section 17 or 18, other than advice, guidance or counselling, they may recover from a person specified in subsection (4) such charge for the service as they consider reasonable.

(2) Where the authority are satisfied that that person's means are insufficient for it to be reasonably practicable for him to pay the charge, they shall not require him to pay more than he can reasonably be expected to pay.

(3) No person shall be liable to pay any charge under subsection (1) [for a service provided under section 17 or section 18(1) or (5)]⁸ at any time when he is in receipt of income support [under]¹⁰ [Part VII of the Social Security Contributions and Benefits Act 1992]³[, of any element of child tax credit other than the family element, of working tax credit]¹⁰[, of an income-based jobseeker's allowance or of an income-related employment and support allowance]¹⁴.

[(3A) No person shall be liable to pay any charge under subsection (1) for a service provided under section 18(2) or (6) at any time when he is in receipt of income support under Part VII of the Social Security and Benefits Act 1992[, of an income-based jobseeker's allowance or of an income-related employment and support allowance]¹⁴.]⁷

[(3B) No person shall be liable to pay any charge under subsection (1) for a service provided under section 18(2) or (6) at any time when –

(a) he is in receipt of guarantee state pension credit under section 1(3)(a) of the State Pension Credit Act 2002, or
(b) he is a member of a [couple]¹² (within the meaning of that Act) the other member of which is in receipt of guarantee state pension credit.]¹¹

(4) The persons are –

(a) where the service is provided for a child under sixteen, each of his parents;

(b) where it is provided for a child who has reached the age of sixteen, the child himself; and
(c) where it is provided for a member of the child's family, that member.

(5) Any charge under subsection (1) may, without prejudice to any other method of recovery, be recovered summarily as a civil debt.

(6) Part III of Schedule 2 makes provision in connection with contributions towards the maintenance of children who are being looked after by local authorities and consists of the re-enactment with modifications of provisions in Part V of the Child Care Act 1980.

(7) Where a local authority provide any accommodation under section 20(1) for a child who was (immediately before they began to look after him) ordinarily resident within the area of another local authority, they may recover from that other authority any reasonable expenses incurred by them in providing the accommodation and maintaining him.

(8) Where a local authority provide accommodation under section 21(1) or (2)(a) or (b) for a child who is ordinarily resident within the area of another local authority and they are not maintaining him in –

(a) a community home provided by them;
(b) a controlled community home; or
(c) a hospital vested in the Secretary of State[, the Welsh Ministers][15] [or a Primary Care Trust][6], [or any other hospital made available pursuant to arrangements made by [a Strategic Health Authority,][9] a [[Local Health Board][13]][4]][1] [or a Primary Care Trust][6],

they may recover from that other authority any reasonable expenses incurred by them in providing the accommodation and maintaining him.

(9) [Except where subsection (10) applies,][8] where a local authority comply with any request under section 27(2) in relation to a child or other person who is not ordinarily resident within their area, they may recover from the local authority in whose area the child or person is ordinarily resident any [reasonable expenses][2] incurred by them in respect of that person.

[(10) Where a local authority ('authority A') comply with any request under section 27(2) from another local authority ('authority B') in relation to a child or other person –

(a) whose responsible authority is authority B for the purposes of section 23B or 23C; or
(b) whom authority B are advising or befriending or to whom they are giving assistance by virtue of section 24(5)(a),

authority A may recover from authority B any reasonable expenses incurred by them in respect of that person.][8]

NOTES

Amendments.[1] Words inserted: National Health Service and Community Care Act 1990, s 66(1), Sch 9, para 36(3).[2] Words substituted: Courts and Legal Services Act 1990, s 116, Sch 16, para 15.[3] Words substituted: Social Security (Consequential Provisions) Act 1992, s 4, Sch 2, para 108.[4]

Words substituted: Health Authorities Act 1995, s 2(1), Sch 1, Pt III, para 118(1), (6).[5] Words inserted: Jobseekers Act 1995, s 41(4), Sch 2, para 19.[6] Words inserted: Health Act 1999 (Supplementary, Consequential etc Provisions) Order 2000, SI 2000/90.[7] Words and subsection inserted: Local Government Act 2000, s 103.[8] Words and subsection inserted: Children (Leaving Care) Act 2000, s 7(3).[9] Words inserted: National Health Service Reform and Health Care Professions Act 2002 (Supplementary, Consequential etc Provisions) Regulations 2002, SI 2002/2469, reg 4, Sch 1, para 16(1), (2).[10] Word substituted: Tax Credits Act 2002, s 47, Sch 3, paras 15, 18.[11] Subsection inserted: State Pension Credit Act 2002, s 14, Sch 2, Pt 3, para 30.[12] Word substituted: Civil Partnership Act 2004 (Overseas Relationships and Consequential, etc Amendments) Order 2005, SI 2005/3129, art 4(4), Sch 4, para 9.[13] Words substituted: SI 2007/961.[14] Words substituted: Welfare Reform Act 2007, s 28(1), Sch 3, para 6(1), (4).[15] Words inserted: Children and Young Persons Act 2008, s 39, Sch 3, paras 1, 20.

Definitions. 'Child': s 105(1); 'child who is looked after by a local authority': s 22(1); 'community home': s 53(1); 'controlled community home': s 53(4); 'hospital': s 105(1); 'local authority': s 105(1); 'ordinary residence': s 105(6); 'service': s 105(1).

30 Miscellaneous

(1) Nothing in this Part shall affect any duty imposed on a local authority by or under any other enactment.

(2) Any question arising under section 20(2), 21(3) or 29(7) to (9) as to the ordinary residence of a child shall be determined by agreement between the local authorities concerned or, in default of agreement, by the [determining authority][1].

[(2A) For the purposes of subsection (2) 'the determining authority' is –

(a) in a case where all the local authorities concerned are in Wales, the Welsh Ministers;

(b) in any other case, the Secretary of State.

(2B) In a case where –

(a) the determining authority is the Secretary of State, and
(b) one or more of the local authorities concerned are in Wales,

the Secretary of State must consult the Welsh Ministers before making a determination for the purposes of subsection (2).][1]

(3) ...[2]

(4) The [appropriate national authority][1] may make regulations for determining, as respects any [education][2] functions specified in the regulations, whether a child who is being looked after by a local authority is to be treated, for purposes so specified, as a child of parents of sufficient resources or as a child of parents without resources.

NOTES

Amendments.[1] Words substituted and subsections inserted: Children and Young Persons Act 2008, s 39, Sch 3, paras 1, 21. [2] Subsection repealed and word substituted: SI 2010/1158.

Definitions. 'Child who is looked after by a local authority': s 22(1); 'functions': s 105(1); 'local authority': s 105(1); 'local education authority': s 105(1); 'ordinary residence': s 105(6).

[30A Meaning of appropriate national authority

In this Part 'the appropriate national authority' means –

(a) in relation to England, the Secretary of State; and
(b) in relation to Wales, the Welsh Ministers.][1]

NOTES

Amendment.[1] Section inserted: Children and Young Persons Act 2008, s 39, Sch 3, paras 1, 22.

PART IV
CARE AND SUPERVISION

General

31 Care and supervision orders

(1) On the application of any local authority or authorised person, the court may make an order –

(a) placing the child with respect to whom the application is made in the care of a designated local authority; or
(b) putting him under the supervision of a designated local authority ...[2].

(2) A court may only make a care order or supervision order if it is satisfied –

(a) that the child concerned is suffering, or is likely to suffer, significant harm; and
(b) that the harm, or likelihood of harm, is attributable to –
 (i) the care given to the child, or likely to be given to him if the order were not made, not being what it would be reasonable to expect a parent to give to him; or
 (ii) the child's being beyond parental control.

(3) No care order or supervision order may be made with respect to a child who has reached the age of seventeen (or sixteen, in the case of a child who is married).

[(3A) No care order may be made with respect to a child until the court has considered a section 31A plan.][4]

(4) An application under this section may be made on its own or in any other family proceedings.

(5) The court may –

(a) on an application for a care order, make a supervision order;
(b) on an application for a supervision order, make a care order.

(6) Where an authorised person proposes to make an application under this section he shall –

(a) if it is reasonably practicable to do so; and
(b) before making the application,

consult the local authority appearing to him to be the authority in whose area the child concerned is ordinarily resident.

(7) An application made by an authorised person shall not be entertained by the court if, at the time when it is made, the child concerned is –

(a) the subject of an earlier application for a care order, or supervision order, which has not been disposed of; or
(b) subject to –
  (i) a care order or supervision order;
  [(ii) a youth rehabilitation order within the meaning of Part 1 of the Criminal Justice and Immigration Act 2008; or][5]
  (iii) a supervision requirement within the meaning of [Part II of the Children (Scotland) Act 1995][1].

(8) The local authority designated in a care order must be –

(a) the authority within whose area the child is ordinarily resident; or
(b) where the child does not reside in the area of a local authority, the authority within whose area any circumstances arose in consequence of which the order is being made.

(9) In this section –

'authorised person' means –
  (a) the National Society for the Prevention of Cruelty to Children and any of its officers; and
  (b) any person authorised by order of the Secretary of State to bring proceedings under this section and any officer of a body which is so authorised;
'harm' means ill-treatment or the impairment of health or development [including, for example, impairment suffered from seeing or hearing the ill-treatment of another][3];
'development' means physical, intellectual, emotional, social or behavioural development;
'health' means physical or mental health; and
'ill-treatment' includes sexual abuse and forms of ill-treatment which are not physical.

(10) Where the question of whether harm suffered by a child is significant turns on the child's health or development, his health or development shall be compared with that which could reasonably be expected of a similar child.

(11) In this Act –

'a care order' means (subject to section 105(1)) an order under subsection (1)(a) and (except where express provision to the contrary is made) includes an interim care order made under section 38; and
'a supervision order' means an order under subsection (1)(b) and (except where express provision to the contrary is made) includes an interim supervision order made under section 38.

NOTES

Amendments.[1] Words substituted: Children (Scotland) Act 1995, s 105(4), Sch 4, para 48(1), (2). [2] Words omitted: Criminal Justice and Court Services Act 2000, ss 74, 75, Sch 7, paras 87, 90, Sch 8. [3] Words inserted: Adoption and Children Act 2002, s 120. [4] Subsection inserted: Adoption and Children Act 2002, s 121(1). [5] Paragraph substituted: Criminal Justice and Immigration Act 2008, s 6(2), Sch 4, Pt 1, paras 33, 35.

Definitions. 'Authorised person': s 31(9); 'care order': ss 31(11), 105(1); 'child': s 105(1); 'designated local authority': s 31(8); 'development': s 31(9); 'family proceedings': s 8(3); 'harm': s 31(9); 'health': s 31(9); 'ill-treatment': s 31(9); 'local authority': s 105(1); 'ordinary residence': s 105(6); 'significant harm': s 31(10); 'supervision order': s 31(11); 'the court': s 92(7).

[31A Care orders: care plans

(1) Where an application is made on which a care order might be made with respect to a child, the appropriate local authority must, within such time as the court may direct, prepare a plan ('a care plan') for the future care of the child.

(2) While the application is pending, the authority must keep any care plan prepared by them under review and, if they are of the opinion some change is required, revise the plan, or make a new plan, accordingly.

(3) A care plan must give any prescribed information and do so in the prescribed manner.

(4) For the purposes of this section, the appropriate local authority, in relation to a child in respect of whom a care order might be made, is the local authority proposed to be designated in the order.

(5) In section 31(3A) and this section, references to a care order do not include an interim care order.

(6) A plan prepared, or treated as prepared, under this section is referred to in this Act as a 'section 31A plan'.][1]

Amendments.[1] Section inserted: Adoption and Children Act 2002, s 121(2).

32 Period within which application for order under this Part must be disposed of

(1) A court hearing an application for an order under this Part shall (in the light of any rules made by virtue of subsection (2)) –

   (a) draw up a timetable with a view to disposing of the application without delay; and
   (b) give such directions as it considers appropriate for the purpose of ensuring, so far as is reasonably practicable, that that timetable is adhered to.

(2) Rules of court may –

   (a) specify periods within which specified steps must be taken in relation to such proceedings; and

Part I   Statutes

(b) make other provision with respect to such proceedings for the purpose of ensuring, so far as is reasonably practicable, that they are disposed of without delay.

NOTES
Definition. 'The court': s 92(7).

Care orders

33 Effect of care order

(1) Where a care order is made with respect to a child it shall be the duty of the local authority designated by the order to receive the child into their care and to keep him in their care while the order remains in force.

(2) Where –

(a) a care order has been made with respect to a child on the application of an authorised person; but
(b) the local authority designated by the order was not informed that that person proposed to make the application,

the child may be kept in the care of that person until received into the care of the authority.

(3) While a care order is in force with respect to a child, the local authority designated by the order shall –

(a) have parental responsibility for the child; and
(b) have the power (subject to the following provisions of this section) to determine the extent to which [a parent or guardian of the child]
   [(i) a parent, guardian or special guardian of the child; or
   (ii) a person who by virtue of section 4A has parental responsibility for the child,][1]
   may meet his parental responsibility for him.

(4) The authority may not exercise the power in subsection (3)(b) unless they are satisfied that it is necessary to do so in order to safeguard or promote the child's welfare.

(5) Nothing in subsection (3)(b) shall prevent [a person mentioned in that provision who has care of the child][1] from doing what is reasonable in all the circumstances of the case for the purpose of safeguarding or promoting his welfare.

(6) While a care order is in force with respect to a child, the local authority designated by the order shall not –

(a) cause the child to be brought up in any religious persuasion other than that in which he would have been brought up if the order had not been made; or
(b) have the right –

[(i) to consent or refuse to consent to the making of an application with respect to the child under section 18 of the Adoption Act 1976;]²

(ii) to agree or refuse to agree to the making of an adoption order, or an order under [section 84 of the Adoption and Children Act 2002]³, with respect to the child; or

(iii) to appoint a guardian for the child.

(7) While a care order is in force with respect to a child, no person may –

(a) cause the child to be known by a new surname; or

(b) remove him from the United Kingdom,

without either the written consent of every person who has parental responsibility for the child or the leave of the court.

(8) Subsection (7)(b) does not –

(a) prevent the removal of such a child, for a period of less than one month, by the authority in whose care he is; or

(b) apply to arrangements for such a child to live outside England and Wales (which are governed by paragraph 19 of Schedule 2).

(9) The power in subsection (3)(b) is subject (in addition to being subject to the provisions of this section) to any right, duty, power, responsibility or authority which [a person mentioned in that provision]³ has in relation to the child and his property by virtue of any other enactment.

NOTES

Amendments.¹ Words substituted: Adoption and Children Act 2002, s 139(1), Sch 3, paras 54, 63(a), (b).² Subparagraph repealed: Adoption and Children Act 2002, s 139(1), Sch 3, paras 54, 63(c)(i).³ Words substituted: Adoption and Children Act 2002, s 139(1), Sch 3, paras 54, 63(c)(ii), (d).

Definitions. 'Authorised person': s 31(9); 'care order': ss 31(11), 105(1); 'designated local authority': s 31(8); 'guardian of the child': s 105(1); 'local authority': s 105(1); 'parental responsibility': s 3; 'the court': s 92(7).

34 Parental contact etc with children in care

(1) Where a child is in the care of a local authority, the authority shall (subject to the provisions of this section) allow the child reasonable contact with –

(a) his parents;

(b) any guardian [or special guardian]¹ of his;

[(ba) any person who by virtue of section 4A has parental responsibility for him;]¹

(c) where there was a residence order in force with respect to the child immediately before the care order was made, the person in whose favour the order was made; and

(d) where, immediately before the care order was made, a person had care of the child by virtue of an order made in the exercise of the High Court's inherent jurisdiction with respect to children, that person.

(2) On an application made by the authority or the child, the court may make such order as it considers appropriate with respect to the contact which is to be allowed between the child and any named person.

(3) On an application made by –

(a) any person mentioned in paragraphs (a) to (d) of subsection (1); or
(b) any person who has obtained the leave of the court to make the application,

the court may make such order as it considers appropriate with respect to the contact which is to be allowed between the child and that person.

(4) On an application made by the authority or the child, the court may make an order authorising the authority to refuse to allow contact between the child and any person who is mentioned in paragraphs (a) to (d) of subsection (1) and named in the order.

(5) When making a care order with respect to a child, or in any family proceedings in connection with a child who is in the care of a local authority, the court may make an order under this section, even though no application for such an order has been made with respect to the child, if it considers that the order should be made.

(6) An authority may refuse to allow the contact that would otherwise be required by virtue of subsection (1) or an order under this section if –

(a) they are satisfied that it is necessary to do so in order to safeguard or promote the child's welfare; and
(b) the refusal –
   (i) is decided upon as a matter of urgency; and
   (ii) does not last for more than seven days.

(7) An order under this section may impose such conditions as the court considers appropriate.

(8) The Secretary of State may by regulations make provision as to –

(a) the steps to be taken by a local authority who have exercised their powers under subsection (6);
(b) the circumstances in which, and conditions subject to which, the terms of any order under this section may be departed from by agreement between the local authority and the person in relation to whom the order is made;
(c) notification by a local authority of any variation or suspension of arrangements made (otherwise than under an order under this section) with a view to affording any person contact with a child to whom this section applies.

(9) The court may vary or discharge any order made under this section on the application of the authority, the child concerned or the person named in the order.

(10) An order under this section may be made either at the same time as the care order itself or later.

(11) Before making a care order with respect to any child the court shall –

(a) consider the arrangements which the authority have made, or propose to make, for affording any person contact with a child to whom this section applies; and
(b) invite the parties to the proceedings to comment on those arrangements.

NOTES

Amendments.[1] Words and paragraph inserted: Adoption and Children Act 2002, s 139(1), Sch 3, paras 54, 64(a), (b).

Definitions. 'Care order': ss 31(11), 105(1); 'child': s 105(1); 'family proceedings': s 8(3); 'guardian of a child': s 105(1); 'local authority': s 105(1); 'residence order': s 8(1); 'the court': s 92(7).

Supervision orders

35 Supervision orders

(1) While a supervision order is in force it shall be the duty of the supervisor –

(a) to advise, assist and befriend the supervised child;
(b) to take such steps as are reasonably necessary to give effect to the order; and
(c) where –
 (i) the order is not wholly complied with; or
 (ii) the supervisor considers that the order may no longer be necessary,

to consider whether or not to apply to the court for its variation or discharge.

(2) Parts I and II of Schedule 3 make further provision with respect to supervision orders.

NOTES

Definitions. 'Supervised child', 'supervisor': s 105(1); 'supervision order': s 31(11); 'the court': s 92(7).

36 Education supervision orders

(1) On the application of any [local authority][4], the court may make an order putting the child with respect to whom the application is made under the supervision of a designated [local authority][4].

(2) In this Act 'an education supervision order' means an order under subsection (1).

(3) A court may only make an education supervision order if it is satisfied that the child concerned is of compulsory school age and is not being properly educated.

(4) For the purposes of this section, a child is being properly educated only if he is receiving efficient full-time education suitable to his age, ability and aptitude and any special educational needs he may have.

(5) Where a child is –

(a) the subject of a school attendance order which is in force under [section 437 of the Education Act 1996]² and which has not been complied with; or

[(b) is not attending regularly within the meaning of section 444 of that Act –
  (i) a school at which he is a registered pupil,
  (ii) any place at which education is provided for him in the circumstances mentioned in subsection (1) of section 444ZA of that Act, or
  (iii) any place which he is required to attend in the circumstances mentioned in subsection (2) of that section]³,

then, unless it is proved that he is being properly educated, it shall be assumed that he is not.

(6) An education supervision order may not be made with respect to a child who is in the care of a local authority.

(7) The [local authority]⁴ designated in an education supervision order must be –

(a) the authority within whose area the child concerned is living or will live; or
(b) where –
  (i) the child is a registered pupil at a school; and
  (ii) the authority mentioned in paragraph (a) and the authority within whose area the school is situated agree,
  the latter authority.

(8) Where a [local authority]⁴ propose to make an application for an education supervision order they shall, before making the application, consult the ...¹ appropriate local authority [if different]⁴.

(9) The appropriate local authority is –

(a) in the case of a child who is being provided with accommodation by, or on behalf of, a local authority, that authority; and
(b) in any other case, the local authority within whose area the child concerned lives, or will live.

(10) Part III of Schedule 3 makes further provision with respect to education supervision orders.

NOTES

Amendments.¹ Words repealed: Education Act 1993, s 307, Sch 19, para 149, Sch 21, Part II.² Words substituted: Education Act 1996, s 582(1), Sch 37, para 85.³ Paragraph substituted: Education Act 2005, s 117, Sch 18, para 1. ⁴ Words substituted and inserted: SI 2010/1158.

Definitions. 'Appropriate local authority': s 36(9); 'child': s 105(1); 'education supervision order': s 36(2); 'local authority': s 105(1); 'local education authority': s 105(1); 'properly educated': s 36(4); 'registered pupil': s 105(1); 'school': s 105(1); 'special educational needs': s 105(1); 'the court': s 92(7).

Powers of court

37 Powers of court in certain family proceedings

(1) Where, in any family proceedings in which a question arises with respect to the welfare of any child, it appears to the court that it may be appropriate for a care or supervision order to be made with respect to him, the court may direct the appropriate authority to undertake an investigation of the child's circumstances.

(2) Where the court gives a direction under this section the local authority concerned shall, when undertaking the investigation, consider whether they should –

(a) apply for a care order or for a supervision order with respect to the child;
(b) provide services or assistance for the child or his family; or
(c) take any other action with respect to the child.

(3) Where a local authority undertake an investigation under this section, and decide not to apply for a care order or supervision order with respect to the child concerned, they shall inform the court of –

(a) their reasons for so deciding;
(b) any service or assistance which they have provided, or intend to provide, for the child and his family; and
(c) any other action which they have taken, or propose to take, with respect to the child.

(4) The information shall be given to the court before the end of the period of eight weeks beginning with the date of the direction, unless the court otherwise directs.

(5) The local authority named in a direction under subsection (1) must be –

(a) the authority in whose area the child is ordinarily resident; or
(b) where the child [is not ordinarily resident][1] in the area of a local authority, the authority within whose area any circumstances arose in consequence of which the direction is being given.

(6) If, on the conclusion of any investigation or review under this section, the authority decide not to apply for a care order or supervision order with respect to the child –

(a) they shall consider whether it would be appropriate to review the case at a later date; and
(b) if they decide that it would be, they shall determine the date on which that review is to begin.

NOTES

Amendments.[1] Words substituted: Courts and Legal Services Act 1990, s 116, Sch 16, para 16.

Definitions. 'Appropriate authority': s 37(5); 'care order': ss 31(11), 105(1); 'child': s 105(1); 'family proceedings': s 8(3); 'local authority': s 105(1); 'ordinary residence': s 105(6); 'supervision order': s 31(11); 'the court': s 92(7).

38 Interim orders

(1) Where –

(a) in any proceedings on an application for a care order or supervision order, the proceedings are adjourned; or

(b) the court gives a direction under section 37(1),

the court may make an interim care order or an interim supervision order with respect to the child concerned.

(2) A court shall not make an interim care order or interim supervision order under this section unless it is satisfied that there are reasonable grounds for believing that the circumstances with respect to the child are as mentioned in section 31(2).

(3) Where, in any proceedings on an application for a care order or supervision order, a court makes a residence order with respect to the child concerned, it shall also make an interim supervision order with respect to him unless satisfied that his welfare will be satisfactorily safeguarded without an interim order being made.

(4) An interim order made under or by virtue of this section shall have effect for such period as may be specified in the order, but shall in any event cease to have effect on whichever of the following events first occurs –

(a) the expiry of the period of eight weeks beginning with the date on which the order is made;

(b) if the order is the second or subsequent such order made with respect to the same child in the same proceedings, the expiry of the relevant period;

(c) in a case which falls within subsection (1)(a), the disposal of the application;

(d) in a case which falls within subsection (1)(b), the disposal of an application for a care order or supervision order made by the authority with respect to the child;

(e) in a case which falls within subsection (1)(b) and in which –

(i) the court has given a direction under section 37(4), but

(ii) no application for a care order or supervision order has been made with respect to the child,

the expiry of the period fixed by that direction.

(5) In subsection (4)(b) 'the relevant period' means –

(a) the period of four weeks beginning with the date on which the order in question is made; or

(b) the period of eight weeks beginning with the date on which the first order was made if that period ends later than the period mentioned in paragraph (a).

(6) Where the court makes an interim care order, or interim supervision order, it may give such directions (if any) as it considers appropriate with regard to the medical or psychiatric examination or other assessment of the child; but if the child is of sufficient understanding to make an informed decision he may refuse to submit to the examination or other assessment.

(7) A direction under subsection (6) may be to the effect that there is to be –

(a) no such examination or assessment; or
(b) no such examination or assessment unless the court directs otherwise.

(8) A direction under subsection (6) may be –

(a) given when the interim order is made or at any time while it is in force; and
(b) varied at any time on the application of any person falling within any class of person prescribed by rules of court for the purposes of this subsection.

(9) Paragraphs 4 and 5 of Schedule 3 shall not apply in relation to an interim supervision order.

(10) Where a court makes an order under or by virtue of this section it shall, in determining the period for which the order is to be in force, consider whether any party who was, or might have been, opposed to the making of the order was in a position to argue his case against the order in full.

NOTES

Definitions. 'Care order': s 31(11); 'child': s 105(1); 'relevant period': s 38(5); 'residence order': s 8(1); 'supervision order': s 31(11); 'the court': s 92(7).

[38A Power to include exclusion requirement in interim care order

(1) Where –

(a) on being satisfied that there are reasonable grounds for believing that the circumstances with respect to a child are as mentioned in section 31(2)(a) and (b)(i), the court makes an interim care order with respect to a child, and
(b) the conditions mentioned in subsection (2) are satisfied,

the court may include an exclusion requirement in the interim care order.

(2) The conditions are –

(a) that there is reasonable cause to believe that, if a person ('the relevant person') is excluded from a dwelling-house in which the child lives, the child will cease to suffer, or cease to be likely to suffer, significant harm, and
(b) that another person living in the dwelling-house (whether a parent of the child or some other person) –

Part I Statutes

> (i) is able and willing to give to the child the care which it would be reasonable to expect a parent to give him, and
>
> (ii) consents to the inclusion of the exclusion requirement.

(3) For the purposes of this section an exclusion requirement is any one or more of the following –

> (a) a provision requiring the relevant person to leave a dwelling-house in which he is living with the child,
>
> (b) a provision prohibiting the relevant person from entering a dwelling-house in which the child lives, and
>
> (c) a provision excluding the relevant person from a defined area in which a dwelling-house in which the child lives is situated.

(4) The court may provide that the exclusion requirement is to have effect for a shorter period than the other provisions of the interim care order.

(5) Where the court makes an interim care order containing an exclusion requirement, the court may attach a power of arrest to the exclusion requirement.

(6) Where the court attaches a power of arrest to an exclusion requirement of an interim care order, it may provide that the power of arrest is to have effect for a shorter period than the exclusion requirement.

(7) Any period specified for the purposes of subsection (4) or (6) may be extended by the court (on one or more occasions) on an application to vary or discharge the interim care order.

(8) Where a power of arrest is attached to an exclusion requirement of an interim care order by virtue of subsection (5), a constable may arrest without warrant any person whom he has reasonable cause to believe to be in breach of the requirement.

(9) Sections 47(7), (11) and (12) and 48 of, and Schedule 5 to, the Family Law Act 1996 shall have effect in relation to a person arrested under subsection (8) of this section as they have effect in relation to a person arrested under section 47(6) of that Act.

(10) If, while an interim care order containing an exclusion requirement is in force, the local authority have removed the child from the dwelling-house from which the relevant person is excluded to other accommodation for a continuous period of more than 24 hours, the interim care order shall cease to have effect in so far as it imposes the exclusion requirement.][1]

NOTES

Amendments.[1] Section inserted: Family Law Act 1996, s 52, Sch 6, para 1.

[38B Undertakings relating to interim care orders

(1) In any case where the court has power to include an exclusion requirement in an interim care order, the court may accept an undertaking from the relevant person.

(2) No power of arrest may be attached to any undertaking given under subsection (1).

(3) An undertaking given to a court under subsection (1) –

(a) shall be enforceable as if it were an order of the court, and
(b) shall cease to have effect if, while it is in force, the local authority have removed the child from the dwelling-house from which the relevant person is excluded to other accommodation for a continuous period of more than 24 hours.

(4) This section has effect without prejudice to the powers of the High Court and county court apart from this section.

(5) In this section 'exclusion requirement' and 'relevant person' have the same meaning as in section 38A.][1]

NOTES

Amendments.[1] Section inserted: Family Law Act 1996, s 52, Sch 6, para 1.

39 Discharge and variation etc of care orders and supervision orders

(1) A care order may be discharged by the court on the application of –

(a) any person who has parental responsibility for the child;
(b) the child himself; or
(c) the local authority designated by the order.

(2) A supervision order may be varied or discharged by the court on the application of –

(a) any person who has parental responsibility for the child;
(b) the child himself; or
(c) the supervisor.

(3) On the application of a person who is not entitled to apply for the order to be discharged, but who is a person with whom the child is living, a supervision order may be varied by the court in so far as it imposes a requirement which affects that person.

[(3A) On the application of a person who is not entitled to apply for the order to be discharged, but who is a person to whom an exclusion requirement contained in the order applies, an interim care order may be varied or discharged by the court in so far as it imposes the exclusion requirement.

(3B) Where a power of arrest has been attached to an exclusion requirement of an interim care order, the court may, on the application of any person entitled to apply for the discharge of the order so far as it imposes the exclusion requirement, vary or discharge the order in so far as it confers a power of arrest (whether or not any application has been made to vary or discharge any other provision of the order).][1]

(4) Where a care order is in force with respect to a child the court may, on the application of any person entitled to apply for the order to be discharged, substitute a supervision order for the care order.

(5) When a court is considering whether to substitute one order for another under subsection (4) any provision of this Act which would otherwise require section 31(2) to be satisfied at the time when the proposed order is substituted or made shall be disregarded.

NOTES

Amendments.[1] Subsections inserted: Family Law Act 1996, s 52, Sch 6, para 2.

Definitions. 'Care order': ss 31(11), 105(1); 'child': s 105(1); 'local authority': s 105(1); 'supervision order': s 31(11); 'supervisor': s 105(1); 'the court': s 92(7).

40 Orders pending appeals in cases about care or supervision orders

(1) Where –

   (a)   a court dismisses an application for a care order; and
   (b)   at the time when the court dismisses the application, the child concerned is the subject of an interim care order,

the court may make a care order with respect to the child to have effect subject to such directions (if any) as the court may see fit to include in the order.

(2) Where –

   (a)   a court dismisses an application for a care order, or an application for a supervision order; and
   (b)   at the time when the court dismisses the application, the child concerned is the subject of an interim supervision order,

the court may make a supervision order with respect to the child to have effect subject to such directions (if any) as the court may see fit to include in the order.

(3) Where a court grants an application to discharge a care order or supervision order, it may order that –

   (a)   its decision is not to have effect; or
   (b)   the care order, or supervision order, is to continue to have effect but subject to such directions as the court sees fit to include in the order.

(4) An order made under this section shall only have effect for such period, not exceeding the appeal period, as may be specified in the order.

(5) Where –

   (a)   an appeal is made against any decision of a court under this section; or
   (b)   any application is made to the appellate court in connection with a proposed appeal against that decision,

the appellate court may extend the period for which the order in question is to have effect, but not so as to extend it beyond the end of the appeal period.

(6) In this section 'the appeal period' means –

(a) where an appeal is made against the decision in question, the period between the making of that decision and the determination of the appeal; and
(b) otherwise, the period during which an appeal may be made against the decision.

NOTES

Definitions. 'Appeal period': s 40(6); 'care order': ss 31(11), 105(1); 'child': s 105(1); 'the court': s 92(7).

*[Representation of child]*²

41 Representation of child and of his interests in certain proceedings

(1) For the purpose of any specified proceedings, the court shall appoint [an officer of the Service]² [or a Welsh family proceedings officer]³ for the child concerned unless satisfied that it is not necessary to do so in order to safeguard his interests.

(2) The [officer of the Service]² [or Welsh family proceedings officer]³ shall –

(a) be appointed in accordance with rules of court; and
(b) be under a duty to safeguard the interests of the child in the manner prescribed by such rules.

(3) Where –

(a) the child concerned is not represented by a solicitor; and
(b) any of the conditions mentioned in subsection (4) is satisfied,

the court may appoint a solicitor to represent him.

(4) The conditions are that –

(a) no [officer of the Service]² [or Welsh family proceedings officer]³ has been appointed for the child;
(b) the child has sufficient understanding to instruct a solicitor and wishes to do so;
(c) it appears to the court that it would be in the child's best interests for him to be represented by a solicitor.

(5) Any solicitor appointed under or by virtue of this section shall be appointed, and shall represent the child, in accordance with rules of court.

(6) In this section 'specified proceedings' means any proceedings –

(a) on an application for a care order or supervision order;
(b) in which the court has given a direction under section 37(1) and has made, or is considering whether to make, an interim care order;
(c) on an application for the discharge of a care order or the variation or discharge of a supervision order;
(d) on an application under section 39(4);

(e) in which the court is considering whether to make a residence order with respect to a child who is the subject of a care order;
(f) with respect to contact between a child who is the subject of a care order and any other person;
(g) under Part V;
(h) on an appeal against –
   (i) the making of, or refusal to make, a care order, supervision order or any order under section 34;
   (ii) the making of, or refusal to make, a residence order with respect to a child who is the subject of a care order; or
   (iii) the variation or discharge, or refusal of an application to vary or discharge, an order of a kind mentioned in sub-paragraph (i) or (ii);
   (iv) the refusal of an application under section 39(4);
   (v) the making of, or refusal to make, an order under Part V; or
[(hh) on an application for the making or revocation of a placement order (within the meaning of section 21 of the Adoption and Children Act 2002);][5]
(i) which are specified for the time being, for the purposes of this section, by rules of court.

[(6A) The proceedings which may be specified under subsection (6)(i) include (for example) proceedings for the making, varying or discharging of a section 8 order.][4]

(7)–(9) ...[2]

(10) Rules of court may make provision as to –

(a) the assistance which any [officer of the Service][2] [or Welsh family proceedings officer][3] may be required by the court to give to it;
(b) the consideration to be given by any [officer of the Service][2] [or Welsh family proceedings officer][3], where an order of a specified kind has been made in the proceedings in question, as to whether to apply for the variation or discharge of the order;
(c) the participation of [officers of the Service][2] [or Welsh family proceedings officers][3] in reviews, of a kind specified in the rules, which are conducted by the court.

(11) Regardless of any enactment or rule of law which would otherwise prevent it from doing so, the court may take account of –

(a) any statement contained in a report made by [an officer of the Service][2] [or a Welsh family proceedings officer][3] who is appointed under this section for the purpose of the proceedings in question; and
(b) any evidence given in respect of the matters referred to in the report,

in so far as the statement or evidence is, in the opinion of the court, relevant to the question which the court is considering.

[(12) ...[2]][1]

NOTES

Amendments.[1] Subsection inserted: Courts and Legal Services Act 1990, s 116, Sch 16, para 17. [2] Words substituted or omitted: Criminal Justice and Court Services Act 2000, ss 74, 75, Sch 7, paras 87, 91, Sch 8. [3] Words inserted: Children Act 2004, s 40, Sch 3, paras 5, 9. [4] Subsection inserted: Adoption and Children Act 2002, s 122(1)(b). [5] Paragraph inserted: Adoption and Children Act 2002, s 122(1)(a).

Definitions. 'Care order': ss 31(11), 105(1); 'child': s 105(1); 'local authority': s 105(1); 'residence order': s 8(1); 'specified proceedings': s 41(6); 'supervision order': s 31(11); 'the court': s 92(7).

42 [Right of officer of the Service to have access to local authority records][5]

(1) Where [an officer of the Service][5] [or Welsh family proceedings officer][7] has been appointed [under section 41][5] he shall have the right at all reasonable times to examine and take copies of –

(a) any records of, or held by, a local authority [or an authorised person][1] which were compiled in connection with the making, or proposed making, by any person of any application under this Act with respect to the child concerned; ...[2]

(b) any ...[2] records of, or held by, a local authority which were compiled in connection with any functions which [are social services functions within the meaning of][6] the Local Authority Social Services Act 1970, so far as those records relate to that child [; or

(c) any records of, or held by, an authorised person which were compiled in connection with the activities of that person, so far as those records relate to that child.][3]

(2) Where [an officer of the Service][5] [or Welsh family proceedings officer][7] takes a copy of any record which he is entitled to examine under this section, that copy or any part of it shall be admissible as evidence of any matter referred to in any –

(a) report which he makes to the court in the proceedings in question; or
(b) evidence which he gives in those proceedings.

(3) Subsection (2) has effect regardless of any enactment or rule of law which would otherwise prevent the record in question being admissible in evidence.

[(4) In this section 'authorised person' has the same meaning as in section 31.][4]

NOTES

Amendments.[1] Words inserted: Courts and Legal Services Act 1990, s 116, Sch 16, para 18(2). [2] Words repealed: Courts and Legal Services Act 1990, s 125(7), Sch 20. [3] Words inserted: Courts and Legal Services Act 1990, s 116, Sch 16, para 18(3). [4] Words inserted: Courts and Legal Services Act 1990, s 116, Sch 16, para 18(4). [5] Words substituted: Criminal Justice and Court Services Act 2000, s 74, Sch 7, paras 87, 92. [6] Words substituted: Local Government Act 2000, s 107, Sch 5, para 20. [7] Words inserted: Children Act 2004, s 40, Sch 3, paras 5, 10.

Definitions. 'Child': s 105(1); 'functions': s 105(1); 'local authority': s 105(1).

PART V
PROTECTION OF CHILDREN

43 Child assessment orders

(1) On the application of a local authority or authorised person for an order to be made under this section with respect to a child, the court may make the order if, but only if, it is satisfied that –

- (a) the applicant has reasonable cause to suspect that the child is suffering, or is likely to suffer, significant harm;
- (b) an assessment of the state of the child's health or development, or of the way in which he has been treated, is required to enable the applicant to determine whether or not the child is suffering, or is likely to suffer, significant harm; and
- (c) it is unlikely that such an assessment will be made, or be satisfactory, in the absence of an order under this section.

(2) In this Act 'a child assessment order' means an order under this section.

(3) A court may treat an application under this section as an application for an emergency protection order.

(4) No court shall make a child assessment order if it is satisfied –

- (a) that there are grounds for making an emergency protection order with respect to the child; and
- (b) that it ought to make such an order rather than a child assessment order.

(5) A child assessment order shall –

- (a) specify the date by which the assessment is to begin; and
- (b) have effect for such period, not exceeding 7 days beginning with that date, as may be specified in the order.

(6) Where a child assessment order is in force with respect to a child it shall be the duty of any person who is in a position to produce the child –

- (a) to produce him to such person as may be named in the order; and
- (b) to comply with such directions relating to the assessment of the child as the court thinks fit to specify in the order.

(7) A child assessment order authorises any person carrying out the assessment, or any part of the assessment, to do so in accordance with the terms of the order.

(8) Regardless of subsection (7), if the child is of sufficient understanding to make an informed decision he may refuse to submit to a medical or psychiatric examination or other assessment.

(9) The child may only be kept away from home –

- (a) in accordance with directions specified in the order;
- (b) if it is necessary for the purposes of the assessment; and

(c) for such period or periods as may be specified in the order.

(10) Where the child is to be kept away from home, the order shall contain such directions as the court thinks fit with regard to the contact that he must be allowed to have with other persons while away from home.

(11) Any person making an application for a child assessment order shall take such steps as are reasonably practicable to ensure that notice of the application is given to –

- (a) the child's parents;
- (b) any person who is not a parent of his but who has parental responsibility for him;
- (c) any other person caring for the child;
- (d) any person in whose favour a contact order is in force with respect to the child;
- (e) any person who is allowed to have contact with the child by virtue of an order under section 34; and
- (f) the child,

before the hearing of the application.

(12) Rules of court may make provision as to the circumstances in which –

- (a) any of the persons mentioned in subsection (11); or
- (b) such other person as may be specified in the rules,

may apply to the court for a child assessment order to be varied or discharged.

(13) In this section 'authorised person' means a person who is an authorised person for the purposes of section 31.

NOTES

Definitions. 'Authorised person': s 43(13); 'child': s 105(1); 'child assessment order': s 43(2); 'contact order': s 8(1); 'emergency protection order': s 44(4); 'harm': s 31(9); 'local authority': s 105(1); 'parental responsibility': s 3; 'significant harm': s 31(10); 'the court': s 92(7).

44 Orders for emergency protection of children

(1) Where any person ('the applicant') applies to the court for an order to be made under this section with respect to a child, the court may make the order if, but only if, it is satisfied that –

- (a) there is reasonable cause to believe that the child is likely to suffer significant harm if –
  - (i) he is not removed to accommodation provided by or on behalf of the applicant; or
  - (ii) he does not remain in the place in which he is then being accommodated;
- (b) in the case of an application made by a local authority –
  - (i) enquiries are being made with respect to the child under section 47(1)(b); and
  - (ii) those enquiries are being frustrated by access to the child being unreasonably refused to a person authorised to seek access and

that the applicant has reasonable cause to believe that access to the child is required as a matter of urgency; or
(c) in the case of an application made by an authorised person –
  (i) the applicant has reasonable cause to suspect that a child is suffering, or is likely to suffer, significant harm;
  (ii) the applicant is making enquiries with respect to the child's welfare; and
  (iii) those enquiries are being frustrated by access to the child being unreasonably refused to a person authorised to seek access and the applicant has reasonable cause to believe that access to the child is required as a matter of urgency.

(2) In this section –

(a) 'authorised person' means a person who is an authorised person for the purposes of section 31; and
(b) 'a person authorised to seek access' means –
  (i) in the case of an application by a local authority, an officer of the local authority or a person authorised by the authority to act on their behalf in connection with the enquiries; or
  (ii) in the case of an application by an authorised person, that person.

(3) Any person –

(a) seeking access to a child in connection with enquiries of a kind mentioned in subsection (1); and
(b) purporting to be a person authorised to do so,

shall, on being asked to do so, produce some duly authenticated document as evidence that he is such a person.

(4) While an order under this section ('an emergency protection order') is in force it –

(a) operates as a direction to any person who is in a position to do so to comply with any request to produce the child to the applicant;
(b) authorises –
  (i) the removal of the child at any time to accommodation provided by or on behalf of the applicant and his being kept there; or
  (ii) the prevention of the child's removal from any hospital, or other place, in which he was being accommodated immediately before the making of the order; and
(c) gives the applicant parental responsibility for the child.

(5) Where an emergency protection order is in force with respect to a child, the applicant –

(a) shall only exercise the power given by virtue of subsection (4)(b) in order to safeguard the welfare of the child;

(b) shall take, and shall only take, such action in meeting his parental responsibility for the child as is reasonably required to safeguard or promote the welfare of the child (having regard in particular to the duration of the order); and

(c) shall comply with the requirements of any regulations made by the Secretary of State for the purposes of this subsection.

(6) Where the court makes an emergency protection order, it may give such directions (if any) as it considers appropriate with respect to –

(a) the contact which is, or is not, to be allowed between the child and any named person;

(b) the medical or psychiatric examination or other assessment of the child.

(7) Where any direction is given under subsection (6)(b), the child may, if he is of sufficient understanding to make an informed decision, refuse to submit to the examination or other assessment.

(8) A direction under subsection (6)(a) may impose conditions and one under subsection (6)(b) may be to the effect that there is to be –

(a) no such examination or assessment; or

(b) no such examination or assessment unless the court directs otherwise.

(9) A direction under subsection (6) may be –

(a) given when the emergency protection order is made or at any time while it is in force; and

(b) varied at any time on the application of any person falling within any class of person prescribed by rules of court for the purposes of this subsection.

(10) Where an emergency protection order is in force with respect to a child and –

(a) the applicant has exercised the power given by subsection (4)(b)(i) but it appears to him that it is safe for the child to be returned; or

(b) the applicant has exercised the power given by subsection (4)(b)(ii) but it appears to him that it is safe for the child to be allowed to be removed from the place in question,

he shall return the child or (as the case may be) allow him to be removed.

(11) Where he is required by subsection (10) to return the child the applicant shall –

(a) return him to the care of the person from whose care he was removed; or

(b) if that is not reasonably practicable, return him to the care of –
   (i) a parent of his;
   (ii) any person who is not a parent of his but who has parental responsibility for him; or

Part I Statutes

(iii) such other person as the applicant (with the agreement of the court) considers appropriate.

(12) Where the applicant has been required by subsection (10) to return the child, or to allow him to be removed, he may again exercise his powers with respect to the child (at any time while the emergency protection order remains in force) if it appears to him that a change in the circumstances of the case makes it necessary for him to do so.

(13) Where an emergency protection order has been made with respect to a child, the applicant shall, subject to any direction given under subsection (6), allow the child reasonable contact with –

- (a) his parents;
- (b) any person who is not a parent of his but who has parental responsibility for him;
- (c) any person with whom he was living immediately before the making of the order;
- (d) any person in whose favour a contact order is in force with respect to him;
- (e) any person who is allowed to have contact with the child by virtue of an order under section 34; and
- (f) any person acting on behalf of any of those persons.

(14) Wherever it is reasonably practicable to do so, an emergency protection order shall name the child; and where it does not name him it shall describe him as clearly as possible.

(15) A person shall be guilty of an offence if he intentionally obstructs any person exercising the power under subsection (4)(b) to remove, or prevent the removal of, a child.

(16) A person guilty of an offence under subsection (15) shall be liable on summary conviction to a fine not exceeding level 3 on the standard scale.

NOTES

Definitions. 'Authorised person': s 44(2); 'child': s 105(1); 'contact order': s 8(1); 'emergency protection order': s 44(4); 'harm': s 31(9); 'hospital': s 105(1); 'local authority': s 105(1); 'parental responsibility': s 3; 'person authorised to seek access': s 44(2); 'significant harm': s 31(10); 'the applicant': s 44(1); 'the court': s 92(7).

[44A Power to include exclusion requirement in emergency protection order

(1) Where –

- (a) on being satisfied as mentioned in section 44(1)(a), (b) or (c), the court makes an emergency protection order with respect to a child, and
- (b) the conditions mentioned in subsection (2) are satisfied,

the court may include an exclusion requirement in the emergency protection order.

(2) The conditions are –

(a) that there is reasonable cause to believe that, if a person ('the relevant person') is excluded from a dwelling-house in which the child lives, then –
  (i) in the case of an order made on the ground mentioned in section 44(1)(a), the child will not be likely to suffer significant harm, even though the child is not removed as mentioned in section 44(1)(a)(i) or does not remain as mentioned in section 44(1)(a)(ii), or
  (ii) in the case of an order made on the ground mentioned in paragraph (b) or (c) of section 44(1), the enquiries referred to in that paragraph will cease to be frustrated, and
(b) that another person living in the dwelling-house (whether a parent of the child or some other person) –
  (i) is able and willing to give to the child the care which it would be reasonable to expect a parent to give him, and
  (ii) consents to the inclusion of the exclusion requirement.

(3) For the purposes of this section an exclusion requirement is any one or more of the following –

(a) a provision requiring the relevant person to leave a dwelling-house in which he is living with the child,
(b) a provision prohibiting the relevant person from entering a dwelling-house in which the child lives, and
(c) a provision excluding the relevant person from a defined area in which a dwelling-house in which the child lives is situated.

(4) The court may provide that the exclusion requirement is to have effect for a shorter period than the other provisions of the order.

(5) Where the court makes an emergency protection order containing an exclusion requirement, the court may attach a power of arrest to the exclusion requirement.

(6) Where the court attaches a power of arrest to an exclusion requirement of an emergency protection order, it may provide that the power of arrest is to have effect for a shorter period than the exclusion requirement.

(7) Any period specified for the purposes of subsection (4) or (6) may be extended by the court (on one or more occasions) on an application to vary or discharge the emergency protection order.

(8) Where a power of arrest is attached to an exclusion requirement of an emergency protection order by virtue of subsection (5), a constable may arrest without warrant any person whom he has reasonable cause to believe to be in breach of the requirement.

(9) Sections 47(7), (11) and (12) and 48 of, and Schedule 5 to, the Family Law Act 1996 shall have effect in relation to a person arrested under subsection (8) of this section as they have effect in relation to a person arrested under section 47(6) of that Act.

Part I Statutes

(10) If, while an emergency protection order containing an exclusion requirement is in force, the applicant has removed the child from the dwelling-house from which the relevant person is excluded to other accommodation for a continuous period of more than 24 hours, the order shall cease to have effect in so far as it imposes the exclusion requirement.]¹

NOTES

Amendments.¹ Section inserted: Family Law Act 1996, s 52, Sch 6, para 3.

[44B Undertakings relating to emergency protection orders

(1) In any case where the court has power to include an exclusion requirement in an emergency protection order, the court may accept an undertaking from the relevant person.

(2) No power of arrest may be attached to any undertaking given under subsection (1).

(3) An undertaking given to a court under subsection (1) –

(a) shall be enforceable as if it were an order of the court, and
(b) shall cease to have effect if, while it is in force, the applicant has removed the child from the dwelling-house from which the relevant person is excluded to other accommodation for a continuous period of more than 24 hours.

(4) This section has effect without prejudice to the powers of the High Court and county court apart from this section.

(5) In this section 'exclusion requirement' and 'relevant person' have the same meaning as in section 44A.]¹

NOTES

Amendments.¹ Section inserted: Family Law Act 1996, s 52, Sch 6, para 3.

45 Duration of emergency protection orders and other supplemental provisions

(1) An emergency protection order shall have effect for such period, not exceeding eight days, as may be specified in the order.

(2) Where –

(a) the court making an emergency protection order would, but for this subsection, specify a period of eight days as the period for which the order is to have effect; but
(b) the last of those eight days is a public holiday (that is to say, Christmas Day, Good Friday, a bank holiday or a Sunday),

the court may specify a period which ends at noon on the first later day which is not such a holiday.

(3) Where an emergency protection order is made on an application under section 46(7), the period of eight days mentioned in subsection (1) shall begin with the first day on which the child was taken into police protection under section 46.

(4) Any person who –

(a) has parental responsibility for a child as the result of an emergency protection order; and
(b) is entitled to apply for a care order with respect to the child,

may apply to the court for the period during which the emergency protection order is to have effect to be extended.

(5) On an application under subsection (4) the court may extend the period during which the order is to have effect by such period, not exceeding seven days, as it thinks fit, but may do so only if it has reasonable cause to believe that the child concerned is likely to suffer significant harm if the order is not extended.

(6) An emergency protection order may only be extended once.

(7) Regardless of any enactment or rule of law which would otherwise prevent it from doing so, a court hearing an application for, or with respect to, an emergency protection order may take account of –

(a) any statement contained in any report made to the court in the course of, or in connection with, the hearing; or
(b) any evidence given during the hearing,

which is, in the opinion of the court, relevant to the application.

(8) Any of the following may apply to the court for an emergency protection order to be discharged –

(a) the child;
(b) a parent of his;
(c) any person who is not a parent of his but who has parental responsibility for him; or
(d) any person with whom he was living immediately before the making of the order.

[(8A) On the application of a person who is not entitled to apply for the order to be discharged, but who is a person to whom an exclusion requirement contained in the order applies, an emergency protection order may be varied or discharged by the court in so far as it imposes the exclusion requirement.

(8B) Where a power of arrest has been attached to an exclusion requirement of an emergency protection order, the court may, on the application of any person entitled to apply for the discharge of the order so far as it imposes the exclusion requirement, vary or discharge the order in so far as it confers a power of arrest (whether or not any application has been made to vary or discharge any other provision of the order).][2]

(9) ...[5]

Part I Statutes

[(10) No appeal may be made against –
(a) the making of, or refusal to make, an emergency protection order;
(b) the extension of, or refusal to extend, the period during which such an order is to have effect;
(c) the discharge of, or refusal to discharge, such an order; or
(d) the giving of, or refusal to give, any direction in connection with such an order.][1]

(11) Subsection (8) does not apply –
(a) where the person who would otherwise be entitled to apply for the emergency protection order to be discharged –
  (i) was given notice (in accordance with rules of court) of the hearing at which the order was made; and
  (ii) was present at that hearing; or
(b) to any emergency protection order the effective period of which has been extended under subsection (5).

(12) A court making an emergency protection order may direct that the applicant may, in exercising any powers which he has by virtue of the order, be accompanied by a registered medical practitioner, registered nurse or [registered midwife][4], if he so chooses.

[(13) The reference in subsection (12) to a registered midwife is to such a midwife who is also registered in the Specialist Community Public Health Nurses' Part of the register maintained under article 5 of the Nursing and Midwifery Order 2001.][3]

NOTES

Amendments.[1] Words substituted: Courts and Legal Services Act 1990, s 116, Sch 16, para 19.[2] Subsections inserted: Family Law Act 1996, s 52, Sch 6, para 4.[3] Subsection inserted: SI 2004/1771.[4] Words substituted: Nursing and Midwifery Order 2001 [sic], SI 2002/253, art 54(3), Sch 5, para 10(a).[5] Subsection repealed: Children and Young Persons Act 2008, ss 30, 42, Sch 4.

Definitions. 'Bank holiday': s 105(1); 'care order': ss 31(11), 105(1); 'child': s 105(1); 'emergency protection order': s 44(4); 'harm': s 31(9); 'parental responsibility': s 3; 'significant harm': s 31(10); 'the court': s 92(7).

46 Removal and accommodation of children by police in cases of emergency

(1) Where a constable has reasonable cause to believe that a child would otherwise be likely to suffer significant harm, he may –
(a) remove the child to suitable accommodation and keep him there; or
(b) take such steps as are reasonable to ensure that the child's removal from any hospital, or other place, in which he is then being accommodated is prevented.

(2) For the purposes of this Act, a child with respect to whom a constable has exercised his powers under this section is referred to as having been taken into police protection.

Children Act 1989, s 46

(3) As soon as is reasonably practicable after taking a child into police protection, the constable concerned shall –

(a) inform the local authority within whose area the child was found of the steps that have been, and are proposed to be, taken with respect to the child under this section and the reasons for taking them;

(b) give details to the authority within whose area the child is ordinarily resident ('the appropriate authority') of the place at which the child is being accommodated;

(c) inform the child (if he appears capable of understanding) –
  (i) of the steps that have been taken with respect to him under this section and of the reasons for taking them; and
  (ii) of the further steps that may be taken with respect to him under this section;

(d) take such steps as are reasonably practicable to discover the wishes and feelings of the child;

(e) secure that the case is inquired into by an officer designated for the purposes of this section by the chief officer of the police area concerned; and

(f) where the child was taken into police protection by being removed to accommodation which is not provided –
  (i) by or on behalf of a local authority; or
  (ii) as a refuge, in compliance with the requirements of section 51,
  secure that he is moved to accommodation which is so provided.

(4) As soon as is reasonably practicable after taking a child into police protection, the constable concerned shall take such steps as are reasonably practicable to inform –

(a) the child's parents;

(b) every person who is not a parent of his but who has parental responsibility for him; and

(c) any other person with whom the child was living immediately before being taken into police protection,

of the steps that he has taken under this section with respect to the child, the reasons for taking them and the further steps that may be taken with respect to him under this section.

(5) On completing any inquiry under subsection (3)(e), the officer conducting it shall release the child from police protection unless he considers that there is still reasonable cause for believing that the child would be likely to suffer significant harm if released.

(6) No child may be kept in police protection for more than 72 hours.

(7) While a child is being kept in police protection, the designated officer may apply on behalf of the appropriate authority for an emergency protection order to be made under section 44 with respect to the child.

(8) An application may be made under subsection (7) whether or not the authority know of it or agree to its being made.

Part I   Statutes

(9) While a child is being kept in police protection –

(a) neither the constable concerned nor the designated officer shall have parental responsibility for him; but
(b) the designated officer shall do what is reasonable in all the circumstances of the case for the purpose of safeguarding or promoting the child's welfare (having regard in particular to the length of the period during which the child will be so protected).

(10) Where a child has been taken into police protection, the designated officer shall allow –

(a) the child's parents;
(b) any person who is not a parent of the child but who has parental responsibility for him;
(c) any person with whom the child was living immediately before he was taken into police protection;
(d) any person in whose favour a contact order is in force with respect to the child;
(e) any person who is allowed to have contact with the child by virtue of an order under section 34; and
(f) any person acting on behalf of any of those persons,

to have such contact (if any) with the child as, in the opinion of the designated officer, is both reasonable and in the child's best interests.

(11) Where a child who has been taken into police protection is in accommodation provided by, or on behalf of, the appropriate authority, subsection (10) shall have effect as if it referred to the authority rather than to the designated officer.

NOTES

Definitions. 'Appropriate authority': s 46(3)(b); 'child': s 105(1); 'contact order': s 8(1); 'designated officer': s 46(3)(e); 'emergency protection order': s 44(4); 'harm': s 31(9); 'hospital': s 105(1); 'local authority': s 105(1); 'ordinary residence': s 105(6); 'police protection': s 46(2); 'significant harm': s 31(10).

47 Local authority's duty to investigate

(1) Where a local authority –

(a) are informed that a child who lives, or is found, in their area –
   (i) is the subject of an emergency protection order; or
   (ii) is in police protection; …[8]
   [(iii) …[8]][2]
(b) have reasonable cause to suspect that a child who lives, or is found, in their area is suffering, or is likely to suffer, significant harm,

the authority shall make, or cause to be made, such enquiries as they consider necessary to enable them to decide whether they should take any action to safeguard or promote the child's welfare.

[…[8]][2]

(2) Where a local authority have obtained an emergency protection order with respect to a child, they shall make, or cause to be made, such enquiries as they consider necessary to enable them to decide what action they should take to safeguard or promote the child's welfare.

(3) The enquiries shall, in particular, be directed towards establishing –

- (a) whether the authority should make any application to the court, or exercise any of their other powers under this Act [or section 11 of the Crime and Disorder Act 1998 (child safety orders)]², with respect to the child;
- (b) whether, in the case of a child –
   - (i) with respect to whom an emergency protection order has been made; and
   - (ii) who is not in accommodation provided by or on behalf of the authority,

   it would be in the child's best interests (while an emergency protection order remains in force) for him to be in such accommodation; and
- (c) whether, in the case of a child who has been taken into police protection, it would be in the child's best interests for the authority to ask for an application to be made under section 46(7).

(4) Where enquiries are being made under subsection (1) with respect to a child, the local authority concerned shall (with a view to enabling them to determine what action, if any, to take with respect to him) take such steps as are reasonably practicable –

- (a) to obtain access to him; or
- (b) to ensure that access to him is obtained, on their behalf, by a person authorised by them for the purpose,

unless they are satisfied that they already have sufficient information with respect to him.

(5) Where, as a result of any such enquiries, it appears to the authority that there are matters connected with the child's education which should be investigated, they shall consult [the local authority (as defined in section 579(1) of the Education 1996), if different, specified in subsection (5ZA).

(5ZA) The local authority referred to in subsection (5) is –

- (a) the local authority who –
   - (i) maintain any school at which the child is a pupil, or
   - (i) make arrangements for the provision of education for the child otherwise than at school pursuant to section 19 of the Education Act 1996, or

(b)in a case where the child is a pupil at a school which is not maintained by a local authority, the local authority in whose area the school is situated.]⁷

[(5A) For the purposes of making a determination under this section as to the action to be taken with respect to a child, a local authority shall, so far as is reasonably practicable and consistent with the child's welfare –

Part I Statutes

(a) ascertain the child's wishes and feelings regarding the action to be taken with respect to him; and
(b) give due consideration (having regard to his age and understanding) to such wishes and feelings of the child as they have been able to ascertain.]⁵

(6) Where, in the course of enquiries made under this section –

(a) any officer of the local authority concerned; or
(b) any person authorised by the authority to act on their behalf in connection with those enquiries –
    (i) is refused access to the child concerned; or
    (ii) is denied information as to his whereabouts,

the authority shall apply for an emergency protection order, a child assessment order, a care order or a supervision order with respect to the child unless they are satisfied that his welfare can be satisfactorily safeguarded without their doing so.

(7) If, on the conclusion of any enquiries or review made under this section, the authority decide not to apply for an emergency protection order, a care order, a child assessment order or a supervision order they shall –

(a) consider whether it would be appropriate to review the case at a later date; and
(b) if they decide that it would be, determine the date on which that review is to begin.

(8) Where, as a result of complying with this section, a local authority conclude that they should take action to safeguard or promote the child's welfare they shall take that action (so far as it is both within their power and reasonably practicable for them to do so).

(9) Where a local authority are conducting enquiries under this section, it shall be the duty of any person mentioned in subsection (11) to assist them with those enquiries (in particular by providing relevant information and advice) if called upon by the authority to do so.

(10) Subsection (9) does not oblige any person to assist a local authority where doing so would be unreasonable in all the circumstances of the case.

(11) The persons are –

(a) any local authority;
(b) ...⁷
(c) any local housing authority;
(d) any [[Local Health Board]⁶, Special Health Authority]¹[, Primary Care Trust]³[, National Health Service trust or NHS foundation trust]⁴; and
(e) any person authorised by the Secretary of State for the purposes of this section.

(12) Where a local authority are making enquiries under this section with respect to a child who appears to them to be ordinarily resident within the area

of another authority, they shall consult that other authority, who may undertake the necessary enquiries in their place.

NOTES

Amendments.[1] Words substituted: Health Authorities Act 1995, s 2(1), Sch 1, Pt III, para 118(1), (7).[2] Words inserted: Crime and Disorder Act 1998, ss 15(4), 119, Sch 8, para 69.[3] Words inserted: Health Act 1999 (Supplementary, Consequential etc Provisions) Order 2000, SI 2000/90.[4] Words substituted: Health and Social Care (Community Health and Standards) Act 2003, s 34, Sch 4, paras 75, 79.[5] Subsection inserted: Children Act 2004, s 53(3).[6] Words substituted: SI 2007/961. [7] Words and subsection substituted and paragraph repealed: SI 2010/1158.[8] Paragraph and word repealed: Policing and Crime Act 2009, s 112(2), Sch 8, Pt 13.

Definitions. 'Care order': s 31(11); 'child': s 105(1); 'child assessment order': s 43(2); 'emergency protection order': s 44(4); 'harm': s 31(9); 'health authority': s 105(1); 'local authority': s 105(1); 'local education authority': s 105(1); 'local housing authority': s 105(1); 'ordinary residence': s 105(6); 'police protection': s 46(2); 'significant harm': s 31(10); 'supervision order': s 31(11); 'the court': s 92(7).

48 Powers to assist in discovery of children who may be in need of emergency protection

(1) Where it appears to a court making an emergency protection order that adequate information as to the child's whereabouts –

(a) is not available to the applicant for the order; but
(b) is available to another person,

it may include in the order a provision requiring that other person to disclose, if asked to do so by the applicant, any information that he may have as to the child's whereabouts.

(2) No person shall be excused from complying with such a requirement on the ground that complying might incriminate him or his spouse [or civil partner][3] of an offence; but a statement or admission made in complying shall not be admissible in evidence against either of them in proceedings for any offence other than perjury.

(3) An emergency protection order may authorise the applicant to enter premises specified by the order and search for the child with respect to whom the order is made.

(4) Where the court is satisfied that there is reasonable cause to believe that there may be another child on those premises with respect to whom an emergency protection order ought to be made, it may make an order authorising the applicant to search for that other child on those premises.

(5) Where –

(a) an order has been made under subsection (4);
(b) the child concerned has been found on the premises; and
(c) the applicant is satisfied that the grounds for making an emergency protection order exist with respect to him,

the order shall have effect as if it were an emergency protection order.

(6) Where an order has been made under subsection (4), the applicant shall notify the court of its effect.

(7) A person shall be guilty of an offence if he intentionally obstructs any person exercising the power of entry and search under subsection (3) or (4).

(8) A person guilty of an offence under subsection (7) shall be liable on summary conviction to a fine not exceeding level 3 on the standard scale.

(9) Where, on an application made by any person for a warrant under this section, it appears to the court –

(a) that a person attempting to exercise powers under an emergency protection order has been prevented from doing so by being refused entry to the premises concerned or access to the child concerned; or
(b) that any such person is likely to be so prevented from exercising any such powers,

it may issue a warrant authorising any constable to assist the person mentioned in paragraph (a) or (b) in the exercise of those powers, using reasonable force if necessary.

(10) Every warrant issued under this section shall be addressed to, and executed by, a constable who shall be accompanied by the person applying for the warrant if –

(a) that person so desires; and
(b) the court by whom the warrant is issued does not direct otherwise.

(11) A court granting an application for a warrant under this section may direct that the constable concerned may, in executing the warrant, be accompanied by a registered medical practitioner, registered nurse or [registered midwife][2] if he so chooses.

[(11A) The reference in subsection (11) to a registered midwife is to such a midwife who is also registered in the Specialist Community Public Health Nurses' Part of the register maintained under article 5 of the Nursing and Midwifery Order 2001.]][1]

(12) An application for a warrant under this section shall be made in the manner and form prescribed by rules of court.

(13) Wherever it is reasonably practicable to do so, an order under subsection (4), an application for a warrant under this section and any such warrant shall name the child; and where it does not name him it shall describe him as clearly as possible.

NOTES

Amendments.[1] Words substituted and subsection inserted: SI 2004/1771.[2] Words substituted: Nursing and Midwifery Order 2001 [*sic*], SI 2002/253, art 54(3), Sch 5, para 10(b).[3] Words inserted: Civil Partnership Act 2004, s 261(1), Sch 27, para 130.

Definitions. 'Child': s 105(1); 'emergency protection order': s 44(4); 'the applicant': s 44(1); 'the court': s 92(7).

49 Abduction of children in care etc

(1) A person shall be guilty of an offence if, knowingly and without lawful authority or reasonable excuse, he –

   (a) takes a child to whom this section applies away from the responsible person;
   (b) keeps such a child away from the responsible person; or
   (c) induces, assists or incites such a child to run away or stay away from the responsible person.

(2) This section applies in relation to a child who is –

   (a) in care;
   (b) the subject of an emergency protection order; or
   (c) in police protection,

and in this section 'the responsible person' means any person who for the time being has care of him by virtue of the care order, the emergency protection order, or section 46, as the case may be.

(3) A person guilty of an offence under this section shall be liable on summary conviction to imprisonment for a term not exceeding six months, or to a fine not exceeding level 5 on the standard scale, or to both.

NOTES

Definitions. 'Care order': ss 31(11), 105(1); 'child': s 105(1); 'emergency protection order': s 44(4); 'police protection': s 46(2); 'responsible person': s 49(2).

50 Recovery of abducted children etc

(1) Where it appears to the court that there is reason to believe that a child to whom this section applies –

   (a) has been unlawfully taken away or is being unlawfully kept away from the responsible person;
   (b) has run away or is staying away from the responsible person; or
   (c) is missing,

the court may make an order under this section ('a recovery order').

(2) This section applies to the same children to whom section 49 applies and in this section 'the responsible person' has the same meaning as in section 49.

(3) A recovery order –

   (a) operates as a direction to any person who is in a position to do so to produce the child on request to any authorised person;
   (b) authorises the removal of the child by any authorised person;
   (c) requires any person who has information as to the child's whereabouts to disclose that information, if asked to do so, to a constable or an officer of the court;
   (d) authorises a constable to enter any premises specified in the order and search for the child, using reasonable force if necessary.

(4) The court may make a recovery order only on the application of –

(a) any person who has parental responsibility for the child by virtue of a care order or emergency protection order; or
(b) where the child is in police protection, the designated officer.

(5) A recovery order shall name the child and –

(a) any person who has parental responsibility for the child by virtue of a care order or emergency protection order; or
(b) where the child is in police protection, the designated officer.

(6) Premises may only be specified under subsection (3)(d) if it appears to the court that there are reasonable grounds for believing the child to be on them.

(7) In this section –

'an authorised person' means –
(a) any person specified by the court;
(b) any constable;
(c) any person who is authorised –
(i) after the recovery order is made; and
(ii) by a person who has parental responsibility for the child by virtue of a care order or an emergency protection order,
to exercise any power under a recovery order; and

'the designated officer' means the officer designated for the purposes of section 46.

(8) Where a person is authorised as mentioned in subsection (7)(c) –

(a) the authorisation shall identify the recovery order; and
(b) any person claiming to be so authorised shall, if asked to do so, produce some duly authenticated document showing that he is so authorised.

(9) A person shall be guilty of an offence if he intentionally obstructs an authorised person exercising the power under subsection (3)(b) to remove a child.

(10) A person guilty of an offence under this section shall be liable on summary conviction to a fine not exceeding level 3 on the standard scale.

(11) No person shall be excused from complying with any request made under subsection (3)(c) on the ground that complying with it might incriminate him or his spouse [or civil partner][1] of an offence; but a statement or admission made in complying shall not be admissible in evidence against either of them in proceedings for an offence other than perjury.

(12) Where a child is made the subject of a recovery order whilst being looked after by a local authority, any reasonable expenses incurred by an authorised person in giving effect to the order shall be recoverable from the authority.

(13) A recovery order shall have effect in Scotland as if it had been made by the Court of Session and as if that court had had jurisdiction to make it.

(14) In this section 'the court', in relation to Northern Ireland, means a magistrates' court within the meaning of the Magistrates' Courts (Northern Ireland) Order 1981.

NOTES

Amendments.[1] Words inserted: Civil Partnership Act 2004, s 261(1), Sch 27, para 131.

Definitions. 'Authorised person': s 50(7); 'care order': s 31(11); 'child': s 105(1); 'child who is looked after by a local authority': s 22(1); 'emergency protection order': s 44(4); 'local authority': s 105(1); 'parental responsibility': s 3; 'police protection': s 46(2); 'recovery order': s 50(1); 'responsible person': s 49(2); 'the court': s 92(7); 'the designated officer': s 50(7).

51 Refuges for children at risk

(1) Where it is proposed to use a voluntary home or [private][2] children's home to provide a refuge for children who appear to be at risk of harm, the Secretary of State may issue a certificate under this section with respect to that home.

(2) Where a local authority or voluntary organisation arrange for a foster parent to provide such a refuge, the Secretary of State may issue a certificate under this section with respect to that foster parent.

(3) In subsection (2) 'foster parent' means a person who is, or who from time to time is, a local authority foster parent or a foster parent with whom children are placed by a voluntary organisation.

(4) The Secretary of State may by regulations –

   (a) make provision as to the manner in which certificates may be issued;
   (b) impose requirements which must be complied with while any certificate is in force; and
   (c) provide for the withdrawal of certificates in prescribed circumstances.

(5) Where a certificate is in force with respect to a home, none of the provisions mentioned in subsection (7) shall apply in relation to any person providing a refuge for any child in that home.

(6) Where a certificate is in force with respect to a foster parent, none of those provisions shall apply in relation to the provision by him of a refuge for any child in accordance with arrangements made by the local authority or voluntary organisation.

(7) The provisions are –

   (a) section 49;
   [(b) sections 82 (recovery of certain fugitive children) and 83 (harbouring) of the Children (Scotland) Act 1995, so far as they apply in relation to anything done in England and Wales;][1]
   (c) section 32(3) of the Children and Young Persons Act 1969 (compelling, persuading, inciting or assisting any person to be absent from detention, etc), so far as it applies in relation to anything done in England and Wales;
   (d) section 2 of the Child Abduction Act 1984.

Part I   Statutes

NOTES

Amendments.[1] Subsection substituted: Children (Scotland) Act 1995, s 105(4), Sch 4, para 48(1), (3).[2] Word substituted: Care Standards Act 2000, s 116, Sch 4, para 14.

Definitions. 'Child': s 105(1); 'foster parent': s 51(3); 'harm': s 31(9); 'local authority': s 105(1); 'local authority foster parent': s 23(3); 'prescribed': s 105(1); 'registered children's home': s 63(8); 'voluntary home': s 60(3); 'voluntary organisation': s 105(1).

52 Rules and regulations

(1) Without prejudice to section 93 or any other power to make such rules, rules of court may be made with respect to the procedure to be followed in connection with proceedings under this Part.

(2) The rules may in particular make provision –

(a)   as to the form in which any application is to be made or direction is to be given;

(b)   prescribing the persons who are to be notified of –
  (i)   the making, or extension, of an emergency protection order; or
  (ii) the making of an application under section 45(4) or (8) or 46(7); and

(c)   as to the content of any such notification and the manner in which, and person by whom, it is to be given.

(3) The Secretary of State may by regulations provide that, where –

(a)   an emergency protection order has been made with respect to a child;

(b)   the applicant for the order was not the local authority within whose area the child is ordinarily resident; and

(c)   that local authority are of the opinion that it would be in the child's best interests for the applicant's responsibilities under the order to be transferred to them,

that authority shall (subject to their having complied with any requirements imposed by the regulations) be treated, for the purposes of this Act, as though they and not the original applicant had applied for, and been granted, the order.

(4) Regulations made under subsection (3) may, in particular, make provision as to –

(a)   the considerations to which the local authority shall have regard in forming an opinion as mentioned in subsection (3)(c); and

(b)   the time at which responsibility under any emergency protection order is to be treated as having been transferred to a local authority.

NOTES

Definitions. 'Child': s 105(1); 'emergency protection order': s 44(4); 'local authority': s 105(1); 'ordinary residence': s 105(6).

PART VI
COMMUNITY HOMES

53 Provision of community homes by local authorities

(1) Every local authority shall make such arrangements as they consider appropriate for securing that homes ('community homes') are available –

(a) for the care and accommodation of children looked after by them; and
(b) for purposes connected with the welfare of children (whether or not looked after by them),

and may do so jointly with one or more other local authorities.

(2) In making such arrangements, a local authority shall have regard to the need for ensuring the availability of accommodation –

(a) of different descriptions; and
(b) which is suitable for different purposes and the requirements of different descriptions of children.

(3) A community home may be a home –

(a) provided, [equipped, maintained and (subject to subsection (3A)) managed]¹ by a local authority; or
(b) provided by a voluntary organisation but in respect of which a local authority and the organisation –
   (i) propose that, in accordance with an instrument of management, the [equipment, maintenance and (subject to subsection (3B)) management]¹ of the home shall be the responsibility of the local authority; or
   (ii) so propose that the management, equipment and maintenance of the home shall be the responsibility of the voluntary organisation.

[(3A) A local authority may make arrangements for the management by another person of accommodation provided by the local authority for the purpose of restricting the liberty of children.

(3B) Where a local authority are to be responsible for the management of a community home provided by a voluntary organisation, the local authority may, with the consent of the body of managers constituted by the instrument of management for the home, make arrangements for the management by another person of accommodation provided for the purpose of restricting the liberty of children.]¹

(4) Where a local authority are to be responsible for the management of a community home provided by a voluntary organisation, the authority shall designate the home as a controlled community home.

(5) Where a voluntary organisation are to be responsible for the management of a community home provided by the organisation, the local authority shall designate the home as an assisted community home.

Part I   Statutes

(6) Schedule 4 shall have effect for the purpose of supplementing the provisions of this Part.

NOTES

Amendments.[1] Words or subsections inserted: Criminal Justice and Public Order Act 1994, s 22.

Definitions. 'Assisted community home': s 53(5); 'child': s 105(1); 'child who is looked after by the local authority': s 22(1); 'community home': s 53(1); 'controlled community home': s 53(4); 'local authority': s 105(1); 'voluntary organisation': s 105(1).

54

...[1]

NOTES

Amendments.[1] Section repealed: Care Standards Act 2000, s 117, Sch 6.

55 Determination of disputes relating to controlled and assisted community homes

(1) Where any dispute relating to a controlled community home arises between the local authority specified in the home's instrument of management and –

(a) the voluntary organisation by which the home is provided; or
(b) any other local authority who have placed, or desire or are required to place, in the home a child who is looked after by them,

the dispute may be referred by either party to the Secretary of State for his determination.

(2) Where any dispute relating to an assisted community home arises between the voluntary organisation by which the home is provided and any local authority who have placed, or desire to place, in the home a child who is looked after by them, the dispute may be referred by either party to the Secretary of State for his determination.

(3) Where a dispute is referred to the Secretary of State under this section he may, in order to give effect to his determination of the dispute, give such directions as he thinks fit to the local authority or voluntary organisation concerned.

(4) This section applies even though the matter in dispute may be one which, under or by virtue of Part II of Schedule 4, is reserved for the decision, or is the responsibility, of –

(a) the local authority specified in the home's instrument of management; or
(b) (as the case may be) the voluntary organisation by which the home is provided.

(5) Where any trust deed relating to a controlled or assisted community home contains provision whereby a bishop or any other ecclesiastical or denominational authority has power to decide questions relating to religious

instruction given in the home, no dispute which is capable of being dealt with in accordance with that provision shall be referred to the Secretary of State under this section.

(6) In this Part 'trust deed', in relation to a voluntary home, means any instrument (other than an instrument of management) regulating –

(a) the maintenance, management or conduct of the home; or
(b) the constitution of a body of managers or trustees of the home.

NOTES

Definitions. 'Assisted community home': s 53(5); 'child': s 105(1); 'child who is looked after by a local authority': s 22(1); 'community home': s 53(1); 'controlled community home': s 53(4); 'local authority': s 105(1); 'trust deed': s 55(6); 'voluntary home': s 60(3); 'voluntary organisation': s 105(1).

56 Discontinuance by voluntary organisation of controlled or assisted community home

(1) The voluntary organisation by which a controlled or assisted community home is provided shall not cease to provide the home except after giving to the Secretary of State and the local authority specified in the home's instrument of management not less than two years' notice in writing of their intention to do so.

(2) A notice under subsection (1) shall specify the date from which the voluntary organisation intend to cease to provide the home as a community home.

(3) Where such a notice is given and is not withdrawn before the date specified in it, the home's instrument of management shall cease to have effect on that date and the home shall then cease to be a controlled or assisted community home.

(4) Where a notice is given under subsection (1) and the home's managers give notice in writing to the Secretary of State that they are unable or unwilling to continue as its managers until the date specified in the subsection (1) notice, the Secretary of State may by order –

(a) revoke the home's instrument of management; and
(b) require the local authority who were specified in that instrument to conduct the home until –
  (i) the date specified in the subsection (1) notice; or
  (ii) such earlier date (if any) as may be specified for the purposes of this paragraph in the order,
as if it were a community home provided by the local authority.

(5) Where the Secretary of State imposes a requirement under subsection (4)(b) –

(a) nothing in the trust deed for the home shall affect the conduct of the home by the local authority;

(b) the Secretary of State may by order direct that for the purposes of any provision specified in the direction and made by or under any enactment relating to community homes (other than this section) the home shall, until the date or earlier date specified as mentioned in subsection (4)(b), be treated as a controlled or assisted community home;

(c) except in so far as the Secretary of State so directs, the home shall until that date be treated for the purposes of any such enactment as a community home provided by the local authority; and

(d) on the date or earlier date specified as mentioned in subsection (4)(b) the home shall cease to be a community home.

NOTES

Definitions. 'Assisted community home': s 53(5); 'community home': s 53(1); 'controlled community home': s 53(4); 'local authority': s 105(1); 'trust deed': s 55(6); 'voluntary organisation': s 105(1).

57 Closure by local authority of controlled or assisted community home

(1) The local authority specified in the instrument of management for a controlled or assisted community home may give –

(a) the Secretary of State; and
(b) the voluntary organisation by which the home is provided,

not less than two years' notice in writing of their intention to withdraw their designation of the home as a controlled or assisted community home.

(2) A notice under subsection (1) shall specify the date ('the specified date') on which the designation is to be withdrawn.

(3) Where –

(a) a notice is given under subsection (1) in respect of a controlled or assisted community home;
(b) the home's managers give notice in writing to the Secretary of State that they are unable or unwilling to continue as managers until the specified date; and
(c) the managers' notice is not withdrawn,

the Secretary of State may by order revoke the home's instrument of management from such date earlier than the specified date as may be specified in the order.

(4) Before making an order under subsection (3), the Secretary of State shall consult the local authority and the voluntary organisation.

(5) Where a notice has been given under subsection (1) and is not withdrawn, the home's instrument of management shall cease to have effect on –

(a) the specified date; or
(b) where an earlier date has been specified under subsection (3), that earlier date,

and the home shall then cease to be a community home.

NOTES

Definitions. 'Assisted community home': s 53(5); 'controlled community home': s 53(4); 'community home': s 53(1); 'local authority': s 105(1); 'the specified date': s 57(2); 'voluntary organisation': s 105(1).

58 Financial provisions applicable on cessation of controlled or assisted community home or disposal etc of premises

(1) Where –

(a) the instrument of management for a controlled or assisted community home is revoked or otherwise ceases to have effect under section . . .³ 56(3) or (4)(a) or 57(3) or (5); or

(b) any premises used for the purposes of such a home are (at any time after 13th January 1987) disposed of, or put to use otherwise than for those purposes,

the proprietor shall become liable to pay compensation ('the appropriate compensation') in accordance with this section.

(2) Where the instrument of management in force at the relevant time relates –

(a) to a controlled community home; or

(b) to an assisted community home which, at any time before the instrument came into force, was a controlled community home,

the appropriate compensation is a sum equal to that part of the value of any premises which is attributable to expenditure incurred in relation to the premises, while the home was a controlled community home, by the authority who were then the responsible authority.

(3) Where the instrument of management in force at the relevant time relates –

(a) to an assisted community home; or

(b) to a controlled community home which, at any time before the instrument came into force, was an assisted community home,

the appropriate compensation is a sum equal to that part of the value of the premises which is attributable to the expenditure of money provided by way of grant under section 82, section 65 of the Children and Young Persons Act 1969 or section 82 of the Child Care Act 1980.

(4) Where the home is, at the relevant time, conducted in premises which formerly were used as an approved school or were an approved probation hostel or home, the appropriate compensation is a sum equal to that part of the value of the premises which is attributable to the expenditure –

(a) of sums paid towards the expenses of the managers of an approved school under section 104 of the Children and Young Persons Act 1933; . . .²

(b) of sums paid under section 51(3)(c) of the Powers of Criminal Courts Act 1973 [or section 20(1)(c) of the Probation Service Act 1993]¹ in relation to expenditure on approved probation hostels or homes [; or

(c) of sums paid under section 3, 5 or 9 of the Criminal Justice and Court Services Act 2000 in relation to expenditure on approved premises (within the meaning of Part I of that Act).][2]

(5) The appropriate compensation shall be paid –

(a) in the case of compensation payable under subsection (2), to the authority who were the responsible authority at the relevant time; and
(b) in any other case, to the Secretary of State.

(6) In this section –

'disposal' includes the grant of a tenancy and any other conveyance, assignment, transfer, grant, variation or extinguishment of an interest in or right over land, whether made by instrument or otherwise;
'premises' means any premises or part of premises (including land) used for the purposes of the home and belonging to the proprietor;
'the proprietor' means –
    (a) the voluntary organisation by which the home is, at the relevant time, provided; or
    (b) if the premises are not, at the relevant time, vested in that organisation, the persons in whom they are vested;
'the relevant time' means the time immediately before the liability to pay arises under subsection (1); and
'the responsible authority' means the local authority specified in the instrument of management in question.

(7) For the purposes of this section an event of a kind mentioned in subsection (1)(b) shall be taken to have occurred –

(a) in the case of a disposal, on the date on which the disposal was completed or, in the case of a disposal which is effected by a series of transactions, the date on which the last of those transactions was completed;
(b) in the case of premises which are put to different use, on the date on which they first begin to be put to their new use.

(8) The amount of any sum payable under this section shall be determined in accordance with such arrangements –

(a) as may be agreed between the voluntary organisation by which the home is, at the relevant time, provided and the responsible authority or (as the case may be) the Secretary of State; or
(b) in default of agreement, as may be determined by the Secretary of State.

(9) With the agreement of the responsible authority or (as the case may be) the Secretary of State, the liability to pay any sum under this section may be discharged, in whole or in part, by the transfer of any premises.

(10) This section has effect regardless of –

(a) anything in any trust deed for a controlled or assisted community home;
(b) the provisions of any enactment or instrument governing the disposition of the property of a voluntary organisation.

NOTES

Amendments. [1] Words inserted: Probation Service Act 1993, s 32, Sch 3, para 9(2). [2] Word omitted or words inserted: Criminal Justice and Court Services Act 2000, ss 74, 75, Sch 7, paras 87, 93, Sch 8. [3] Word repealed: Care Standards Act 2000, s 117, Sch 6.

Definitions. 'Appropriate compensation': s 58(1)–(4); 'assisted community home': s 53(5); 'community home': s 53(1); 'controlled community home': s 53(4); 'disposal': s 58(6); 'local authority': s 105(1); 'premises': s 58(6); 'the proprietor': s 58(6); 'the relevant time': s 58(6); 'the responsible authority': s 58(6); 'trust deed': s 55(6); 'voluntary organisation': s 105(1).

PART VII
VOLUNTARY HOMES AND VOLUNTARY ORGANISATIONS

59 Provision of accommodation by voluntary organisations

(1) Where a voluntary organisation provide accommodation for a child, they shall do so by –

(a) placing him (subject to subsection (2)) with –
   (i) a family;
   (ii) a relative of his; or
   (iii) any other suitable person,
   on such terms as to payment by the organisation and otherwise as the organisation may determine [(subject to section 49 of the Children Act 2004)][2];
[(aa) maintaining him in an appropriate children's home;
(b)–(e) ...][1]
(f) making such other arrangements (subject to subsection (3)) as seem appropriate to them.

[(1A) Where under subsection (1)(aa) a local authority maintains a child in a home provided, equipped and maintained by [an appropriate national authority][3] under section 82(5), it shall do so on such terms as [that national authority][3] may from time to time determine.][1]

(2) The [appropriate national authority][3] may make regulations as to the placing of children with foster parents by voluntary organisations and the regulations may, in particular, make provision which (with any necessary modifications) is similar to the provision that may be made under section 23(2)(f).

(3) The [appropriate national authority][3] may make regulations as to the arrangements which may be made under subsection (1)(f) and the regulations may in particular make provision which (with any necessary modifications) is similar to the provision that may be made under section 23(2)(f).

(4) The [appropriate national authority][3] may make regulations requiring any voluntary organisation who are providing accommodation for a child –

Part I   Statutes

(a) to review his case; and
(b) to consider any representations (including any complaint) made to them by any person falling within a prescribed class of person,

in accordance with the provisions of the regulations.

(5) Regulations under subsection (4) may in particular make provision which (with any necessary modifications) is similar to the provision that may be made under section 26.

(6) Regulations under subsections (2) to (4) may provide that any person who, without reasonable excuse, contravenes or fails to comply with a regulation shall be guilty of an offence and liable on summary conviction to a fine not exceeding level 4 on the standard scale.

[(7) In this Part 'appropriate national authority' means –

(a) in relation to England, the Secretary of State; and
(b) in relation to Wales, the Welsh Ministers.]³

NOTES

Amendments.¹ Paragraph (aa) substituted for paras (b)–(e) and subsection inserted: Care Standards Act 2000, s 116, Sch 4, para 14(8).² Words inserted: Children Act 2004, s 49(4).³ Words substituted and subsection inserted: Children and Young Persons Act 2008, s 39, Sch 3, paras 1, 23.

Definitions. 'Child': s 105(1); 'community home': s 53(1); 'registered children's home': s 63(8); 'relative': s 105(1); 'voluntary home': s 60(2); 'voluntary organisation': s 105(1).

60 [Voluntary homes]¹

(1), (2) ...²

[(3) In this Act 'voluntary home' means a children's home which is carried on by a voluntary organisation but does not include a community home.]¹

(4) Schedule 5 shall have effect for the purpose of supplementing the provisions of this Part.

NOTES

Amendments.¹ Section heading and subsection substituted: Care Standards Act 2000, s 116, Sch 4, para 14(1), (9).² Subsections repealed: Care Standards Act 2000, s 117, Sch 6.

Definitions. 'Child': s 105(1); 'community home': s 53(1); 'health service hospital': s 105(1); 'mental nursing home': s 105(1); 'nursing home': s 105(1); 'residential care home': s 105(1); 'school': s 105(1); 'voluntary home': s 60(3); 'voluntary organisation': s 105(1).

61 Duties of voluntary organisations

(1) Where a child is accommodated by or on behalf of a voluntary organisation, it shall be the duty of the organisation –

(a) to safeguard and promote his welfare;
(b) to make such use of the services and facilities available for children cared for by their own parents as appears to the organisation reasonable in his case; and

(c) to advise, assist and befriend him with a view to promoting his welfare when he ceases to be so accommodated.

(2) Before making any decision with respect to any such child the organisation shall, so far as is reasonably practicable, ascertain the wishes and feelings of –

(a) the child;
(b) his parents;
(c) any person who is not a parent of his but who has parental responsibility for him; and
(d) any other person whose wishes and feelings the organisation consider to be relevant,

regarding the matter to be decided.

(3) In making any such decision the organisation shall give due consideration –

(a) having regard to the child's age and understanding, to such wishes and feelings of his as they have been able to ascertain;
(b) to such other wishes and feelings mentioned in subsection (2) as they have been able to ascertain; and
(c) to the child's religious persuasion, racial origin and cultural and linguistic background.

NOTES

Definitions. 'Child': s 105(1); 'parental responsibility': s 3; 'voluntary organisation': s 105(1).

62 Duties of local authorities

(1) Every local authority shall satisfy themselves that any voluntary organisation providing accommodation –

(a) within the authority's area for any child; or
(b) outside that area for any child on behalf of the authority,

are satisfactorily safeguarding and promoting the welfare of the children so provided with accommodation.

(2) Every local authority shall arrange for children who are accommodated within their area by or on behalf of voluntary organisations to be visited, from time to time, in the interests of their welfare.

(3) The [appropriate national authority][3] may make regulations –

(a) requiring every child who is accommodated within a local authority's area, by or on behalf of a voluntary organisation, to be visited by an officer of the authority –
   (i) in prescribed circumstances; and
   (ii) on specified occasions or within specified periods; and
(b) imposing requirements which must be met by any local authority, or officer of a local authority, carrying out functions under this section.

(4) Subsection (2) does not apply in relation to community homes.

(5) Where a local authority are not satisfied that the welfare of any child who is accommodated by or on behalf of a voluntary organisation is being satisfactorily safeguarded or promoted they shall –
   (a) unless they consider that it would not be in the best interests of the child, take such steps as are reasonably practicable to secure that the care and accommodation of the child is undertaken by –
      (i) a parent of his;
      (ii) any person who is not a parent of his but who has parental responsibility for him; or
      (iii) a relative of his; and
   (b) consider the extent to which (if at all) they should exercise any of their functions with respect to the child.

(6) Any person authorised by a local authority may, for the purpose of enabling the authority to discharge their duties under this section –
   (a) enter, at any reasonable time, and inspect any premises in which children are being accommodated as mentioned in subsection (1) or (2);
   (b) inspect any children there;
   (c) require any person to furnish him with such records of a kind required to be kept by regulations made under [section 22 of the Care Standards Act 2000][1] [or section 20 of the Health and Social Care Act 2008] (in whatever form they are held), or allow him to inspect such records, as he may at any time direct.

(7) Any person exercising the power conferred by subsection (6) shall, if asked to do so, produce some duly authenticated document showing his authority to do so.

(8) Any person authorised to exercise the power to inspect records conferred by subsection (6) –
   (a) shall be entitled at any reasonable time to have access to, and inspect and check the operation of, any computer and any associated apparatus or material which is or has been in use in connection with the records in question; and
   (b) may require –
      (i) the person by whom or on whose behalf the computer is or has been so used; or
      (ii) any person having charge of, or otherwise concerned with the operation of, the computer, apparatus or material,
   to afford him such assistance as he may reasonably require.

(9) Any person who intentionally obstructs another in the exercise of any power conferred by subsection (6) or (8) shall be guilty of an offence and liable on summary conviction to a fine not exceeding level 3 on the standard scale.

[(10) This section does not apply in relation to any voluntary organisation which is an institution within the further education sector, as defined in section 91 of the Further and Higher Education Act 1992, or a school.][2]

NOTES

Amendments.[1] Words substituted: Care Standards Act 2000, s 116, Sch 4, para 14(10). [2] Subsection inserted: Care Standards Act 2000, s 105(5). [3] Words substituted: Children and Young Persons Act 2008, s 39, Sch 3, paras 1, 24. [4] Words in italics prospectively inserted with effect from 1 October 2010: SI 2010/813.

Definitions. 'Child': s 105(1); 'community home': s 53(1); 'functions', 'local authority': s 105(1); 'parental responsibility': s 3; 'prescribed', 'relative', 'voluntary organisation': s 105(1).

PART VIII
REGISTERED CHILDREN'S HOMES

63 [Private children's homes etc][2]

(1)–(10) ...[1]

(11) Schedule 6 shall have effect with respect to [private][2] children's homes.

(12) Schedule 7 shall have effect for the purpose of setting out the circumstances in which a person may foster more than three children without being treated [, for the purposes of this Act and the Care Standards Act 2000,][2] as carrying on a children's home.

NOTES

Amendments.[1] Subsections repealed: Care Standards Act 2000, s 117, Sch 6. [2] Section heading substituted and words inserted: Care Standards Act 2000, s 116, Sch 4, para 14(1), (11).

Definitions. 'A privately fostered child': s 66(1); 'child': s 105(1); 'children's home': s 63(3); 'community home': s 53(1); 'health service hospital': s 105(1); 'home': s 63(9); 'independent school', 'mental nursing home', 'nursing home': s 105(1); 'parental responsibility': s 3; 'registered children's home': s 63(8); 'relative', 'residential care home', 'school': s 105(1); 'voluntary home': s 60(3); 'voluntary organisation': s 105(1).

64 Welfare of children in children's homes

(1) Where a child is accommodated in a [private][1] children's home, it shall be the duty of the person carrying on the home to –

  (a) safeguard and promote the child's welfare;
  (b) make such use of the services and facilities available for children cared for by their own parents as appears to that person reasonable in the case of the child; and
  (c) advise, assist and befriend him with a view to promoting his welfare when he ceases to be so accommodated.

(2) Before making any decision with respect to any such child the person carrying on the home shall, so far as is reasonably practicable, ascertain the wishes and feelings of –

  (a) the child;
  (b) his parents;
  (c) any other person who is not a parent of his but who has parental responsibility for him; and

Part I Statutes

(d) any person whose wishes and feelings the person carrying on the home considers to be relevant,

regarding the matter to be decided.

(3) In making any such decision the person concerned shall give due consideration –

(a) having regard to the child's age and understanding, to such wishes and feelings of his as he has been able to ascertain;
(b) to such other wishes and feelings mentioned in subsection (2) as he has been able to ascertain; and
(c) to the child's religious persuasion, racial origin and cultural and linguistic background.

(4) Section 62, except subsection (4), shall apply in relation to any person who is carrying on a [private]¹ children's home as it applies in relation to any voluntary organisation.

NOTES

Amendments.¹ Word inserted: Care Standards Act 2000, s 116, Sch 4, para 14(12).

Definitions. 'Child': s 105(1); 'children's home': s 63(3); 'parental responsibility': s 3; 'voluntary organisation': s 105(1).

65 Persons disqualified from carrying on, or being employed in, children's homes

(1) A person who is disqualified (under section 68) from fostering a child privately shall not carry on, or be otherwise concerned in the management of, or have any financial interest in, a children's home unless he has –

(a) disclosed to [the appropriate authority]¹ the fact that he is so disqualified; and
(b) obtained [its]¹ written consent.

(2) No person shall employ a person who is so disqualified in a children's home unless he has –

(a) disclosed to [the appropriate authority]¹ the fact that that person is so disqualified; and
(b) obtained [its]¹ written consent.

(3) Where [the appropriate authority refuses to give its consent under this section, it]¹ shall inform the applicant by a written notice which states –

(a) the reason for the refusal;
[(b) the applicant's right to appeal under section 65A against the refusal to the [First-tier Tribunal]⁴]¹; and
(c) the time within which he may do so.

(4) Any person who contravenes subsection (1) or (2) shall be guilty of an offence and liable on summary conviction to imprisonment for a term not exceeding six months or to a fine not exceeding level 5 on the standard scale or to both.

(5) Where a person contravenes subsection (2) he shall not be guilty of an offence if he proves that he did not know, and had no reasonable grounds for believing, that the person whom he was employing was disqualified under section 68.

[(6) In this section and section 65A 'appropriate authority' means–

(a) in relation to England, [[Her Majesty's Chief Inspector of Education, Children's Services and Skills]³]²; and
(b) in relation to Wales, the National Assembly for Wales.]¹

NOTES

Amendments.¹ Words substituted and subsection inserted: Care Standards Act 2000, s 116, Sch 4, para 14(13). ² Words substituted: Health and Social Care (Community Health and Standards) Act 2003, s 147, Sch 9, para 10(1), (2).³ Words substituted: Education and Inspections Act 2006, s 157, Sch 14, paras 9, 12.⁴ Words substituted: SI 2008/2833.

Definitions. 'Child': s 105(1); 'children's home': s 63(3); 'responsible authority': Sch 6, para 3(1); 'to foster a child privately': s 66(1)(b).

[65A Appeal against refusal of authority to give consent under section 65

(1) An appeal against a decision of an appropriate authority under section 65 shall lie to the [First-tier Tribunal]².

(2) On an appeal the Tribunal may confirm the authority's decision or direct it to give the consent in question.]¹

NOTES

Amendments.¹ Section inserted: Care Standards Act 2000, s 116, Sch 4, para 14(14).² Words substituted: SI 2008/2833.

PART IX
PRIVATE ARRANGEMENTS FOR FOSTERING CHILDREN

66 Privately fostered children

(1) In this Part –

(a) 'a privately fostered child' means a child who is under the age of sixteen and who is cared for, and provided with accommodation [in their own home]¹ by, someone other than –
    (i) a parent of his;
    (ii) a person who is not a parent of his but who has parental responsibility for him; or
    (iii) a relative of his; and
(b) 'to foster a child privately' means to look after the child in circumstances in which he is a privately fostered child as defined by this section.

(2) A child is not a privately fostered child if the person caring for and accommodating him –

(a) has done so for a period of less than 28 days; and

Part I Statutes

(b) does not intend to do so for any longer period.

(3) Subsection (1) is subject to –

(a) the provisions of section 63; and
(b) the exceptions made by paragraphs 1 to 5 of Schedule 8.

(4) In the case of a child who is disabled, subsection (1)(a) shall have effect as if for 'sixteen' there were substituted 'eighteen'.

[(4A) The Secretary of State may by regulations make provision as to the circumstances in which a person who provides accommodation to a child is, or is not, to be treated as providing him with accommodation in the person's own home.]¹

(5) Schedule 8 shall have effect for the purposes of supplementing the provision made by this Part.

NOTES

Amendments.¹ Words and subsection inserted: Care Standards Act 2000, s 116, Sch 4, para 14(1), (15).

Definitions. 'Child': s 105(1); 'disabled': s 17(11); 'parental responsibility': s 3; 'privately fostered child': s 66(1); 'relative': s 105(1); 'to foster a child privately': s 66(1).

67 Welfare of privately fostered children

(1) It shall be the duty of every local authority to satisfy themselves that the welfare of children who are [or are proposed to be]¹ privately fostered within their area is being [or will be]¹ satisfactorily safeguarded and promoted and to secure that such advice is given to those [concerned with]¹ them as appears to the authority to be needed.

(2) The Secretary of State may make regulations –

(a) requiring every child who is privately fostered within a local authority's area to be visited by an officer of the authority –
    (i) in prescribed circumstances; and
    (ii) on specified occasions or within specified periods; and
(b) imposing requirements which are to be met by any local authority, or officer of a local authority, in carrying out functions under this section.

[(2A) Regulations under subsection (2)(b) may impose requirements as to the action to be taken by a local authority for the purposes of discharging their duty under subsection (1) where they have received notification of a proposal that a child be privately fostered.]¹

(3) Where any person who is authorised by a local authority [for the purpose]¹ has reasonable cause to believe that –

(a) any privately fostered child is being accommodated in premises within the authority's area; or
(b) it is proposed to accommodate any such child in any such premises,

he may at any reasonable time inspect those premises and any children there.

(4) Any person exercising the power under subsection (3) shall, if so required, produce some duly authenticated document showing his authority to do so.

(5) Where a local authority are not satisfied that the welfare of any child who is [or is proposed to be]¹ privately fostered within their area is being [or will be]¹ satisfactorily safeguarded or promoted they shall –

(a) unless they consider that it would not be in the best interests of the child, take such steps as are reasonably practicable to secure that the care and accommodation of the child is undertaken by –
(i) a parent of his;
(ii) any person who is not a parent of his but who has parental responsibility for him; or
(iii) a relative of his; and
(b) consider the extent to which (if at all) they should exercise any of their functions under this Act with respect to the child.

[(6) The Secretary of State may make regulations requiring a local authority to monitor the way in which the authority discharge their functions under this Part (and the regulations may in particular require the authority to appoint an officer for that purpose).]¹

NOTES

Amendments.¹ Words inserted or substituted and subsections inserted: Children Act 2004, s 44.

Definitions. 'Child': s 105(1); 'functions': s 105(1); 'local authority': s 105(1); 'parental responsibility': s 3; 'prescribed': s 105(1); 'privately fostered child': s 66(1); 'relative': s 105(1).

68 Persons disqualified from being private foster parents

(1) Unless he has disclosed the fact to the appropriate local authority and obtained their written consent, a person shall not foster a child privately if he is disqualified from doing so by regulations made by the Secretary of State for the purposes of this section.

(2) The regulations may, in particular, provide for a person to be so disqualified where –

(a) an order of a kind specified in the regulations has been made at any time with respect to him;
(b) an order of a kind so specified has been made at any time with respect to any child who has been in his care;
(c) a requirement of a kind so specified has been imposed at any time with respect to any such child, under or by virtue of any enactment;
(d) he has been convicted of any offence of a kind so specified, or …¹ discharged absolutely or conditionally for any such offence;
(e) a prohibition has been imposed on him at any time under section 69 or under any other specified enactment;
(f) his rights and powers with respect to a child have at any time been vested in a specified authority under a specified enactment.

[(2A) A conviction in respect of which a probation order was made before 1st October 1992 (which would not otherwise be treated as a conviction) is to be treated as a conviction for the purposes of subsection (2)(d).]¹

(3) Unless he has disclosed the fact to the appropriate local authority and obtained their written consent, a person shall not foster a child privately if –

(a) he lives in the same household as a person who is himself prevented from fostering a child by subsection (1); or
(b) he lives in a household at which any such person is employed.

[(3A) A person shall not foster a child privately if –

(a) he is barred from regulated activity relating to children (within the meaning of section 3(2) of the Safeguarding Vulnerable Groups Act 2006); or
(b) he lives in the same household as a person who is barred from such activity.]²

(4) Where an authority refuse to give their consent under this section, they shall inform the applicant by a written notice which states –

(a) the reason for the refusal;
(b) the applicant's right under paragraph 8 of Schedule 8 to appeal against the refusal; and
(c) the time within which he may do so.

(5) In this section –

'the appropriate authority' means the local authority within whose area it is proposed to foster the child in question; and
'enactment' means any enactment having effect, at any time, in any part of the United Kingdom.

NOTES

Amendments. ¹ Words repealed and subsection inserted: Criminal Justice Act 2003, ss 304, 332, Sch 32, Pt 1, paras 59, 60, Sch 37, Pt 7. ² Subsection inserted: Safeguarding Vulnerable Groups Act 2006, s 63(1), Sch 9, Pt 2, para 12.

Definitions. 'Appropriate authority': s 68(5); 'child': s 105(1); 'enactment': s 68(5); 'local authority': s 105(1); 'to foster a child privately': s 66(1).

69 Power to prohibit private fostering

(1) This section applies where a person –

(a) proposes to foster a child privately; or
(b) is fostering a child privately.

(2) Where the local authority for the area within which the child is proposed to be, or is being, fostered are of the opinion that –

(a) he is not a suitable person to foster a child;
(b) the premises in which the child will be, or is being, accommodated are not suitable; or

(c) it would be prejudicial to the welfare of the child for him to be, or continue to be, accommodated by that person in those premises,

the authority may impose a prohibition on him under subsection (3).

(3) A prohibition imposed on any person under this subsection may prohibit him from fostering privately –

- (a) any child in any premises within the area of the local authority; or
- (b) any child in premises specified in the prohibition;
- (c) a child identified in the prohibition, in premises specified in the prohibition.

(4) A local authority who have imposed a prohibition on any person under subsection (3) may, if they think fit, cancel the prohibition –

- (a) of their own motion; or
- (b) on an application made by that person,

if they are satisfied that the prohibition is no longer justified.

(5) Where a local authority impose a requirement on any person under paragraph 6 of Schedule 8, they may also impose a prohibition on him under subsection (3).

(6) Any prohibition imposed by virtue of subsection (5) shall not have effect unless –

- (a) the time specified for compliance with the requirement has expired; and
- (b) the requirement has not been complied with.

(7) A prohibition imposed under this section shall be imposed by notice in writing addressed to the person on whom it is imposed and informing him of –

- (a) the reason for imposing the prohibition;
- (b) his right under paragraph 8 of Schedule 8 to appeal against the prohibition; and
- (c) the time within which he may do so.

NOTES

Definitions. 'Child': s 105(1); 'local authority': s 105(1); 'to foster a child privately': s 66(1).

70 Offences

(1) A person shall be guilty of an offence if –

- (a) being required, under any provision made by or under this Part, to give any notice or information –
  - (i) he fails without reasonable excuse to give the notice within the time specified in that provision; or
  - (ii) he fails without reasonable excuse to give the information within a reasonable time; or

(iii) he makes, or causes or procures another person to make, any statement in the notice or information which he knows to be false or misleading in a material particular;
(b) he refuses to allow a privately fostered child to be visited by a duly authorised officer of a local authority;
(c) he intentionally obstructs another in the exercise of the power conferred by section 67(3);
(d) he contravenes section 68;
(e) he fails without reasonable excuse to comply with any requirement imposed by a local authority under this Part;
(f) he accommodates a privately fostered child in any premises in contravention of a prohibition imposed by a local authority under this Part;
(g) he knowingly causes to be published, or publishes, an advertisement which he knows contravenes paragraph 10 of Schedule 8.

(2) Where a person contravenes section 68(3), he shall not be guilty of an offence under this section if he proves that he did not know, and had no reasonable ground for believing, that any person to whom section 68(1) applied was living or employed in the premises in question.

(3) A person guilty of an offence under subsection (1)(a) shall be liable on summary conviction to a fine not exceeding level 5 on the standard scale.

(4) A person guilty of an offence under subsection (1)(b), (c) or (g) shall be liable on summary conviction to a fine not exceeding level 3 on the standard scale.

(5) A person guilty of an offence under subsection (1)(d) or (f) shall be liable on summary conviction to imprisonment for a term not exceeding six months, or to a fine not exceeding level 5 on the standard scale, or to both.

(6) A person guilty of an offence under subsection (1)(e) shall be liable on summary conviction to a fine not exceeding level 4 on the standard scale.

(7) If any person who is required, under any provision of this Part, to give a notice fails to give the notice within the time specified in that provision, proceedings for the offence may be brought at any time within six months from the date when evidence of the offence came to the knowledge of the local authority.

(8) Subsection (7) is not affected by anything in section 127(1) of the Magistrates' Courts Act 1980 (time limit for proceedings).

NOTES
Definitions. 'Child': s 105(1); 'local authority': s 105(1); 'privately fostered child': s 66(1).

PART X
CHILD MINDING AND DAY CARE FOR YOUNG CHILDREN

…[1]

NOTES

Amendments.[1] Part X repealed in relation to England and Wales: Care Standards Act 2000, s 79(5).

[PART XA
CHILD MINDING AND DAY CARE FOR CHILDREN IN ...[1] WALES

NOTES

Amendment.[1] Words omitted: Childcare Act 2006, s 103, Sch 2, para 5, Sch 3, Pt 2.

Introductory

79A Child minders and day care providers

(1) This section and section 79B apply for the purposes of this Part.

(2) 'Act as a child minder' means (subject to the following subsections) look after one or more children under the age of eight on domestic premises for reward; and 'child minding' shall be interpreted accordingly.

(3) A person who –

 (a) is the parent, or a relative, of a child;
 (b) has parental responsibility for a child;
 (c) is a local authority foster parent in relation to a child;
 (d) is a foster parent with whom a child has been placed by a voluntary organisation; or
 (e) fosters a child privately,

does not act as a child minder when looking after that child.

(4) Where a person –

 (a) looks after a child for the parents ('P1'), or
 (b) in addition to that work, looks after another child for different parents ('P2'),

and the work consists (in a case within paragraph (a)) of looking after the child wholly or mainly in P1's home or (in a case within paragraph (b)) of looking after the children wholly or mainly in P1's home or P2's home or both, the work is not to be treated as child minding.

(5) In subsection (4), 'parent', in relation to a child, includes –

 (a) a person who is not a parent of the child but who has parental responsibility for the child;
 (b) a person who is a relative of the child.

(6) 'Day care' means care provided at any time for children under the age of eight on premises other than domestic premises.

(7) This Part does not apply in relation to a person who acts as a child minder, or provides day care on any premises, unless the period, or the total of the

periods, in any day which he spends looking after children or (as the case may be) during which the children are looked after on the premises exceeds two hours.

(8) In determining whether a person is required to register under this Part for child minding, any day on which he does not act as a child minder at any time between 2 am and 6 pm is to be disregarded.

79B Other definitions, etc

(1) ...[5]

[(2) In this Act 'the Assembly' means the National Assembly for Wales.][5]

(3) A person is qualified for registration for child minding if –

(a) he, and every other person looking after children on any premises on which he is or is likely to be child minding, is suitable to look after children under the age of eight;

(b) every person living or employed on the premises in question is suitable to be in regular contact with children under the age of eight;

(c) the premises in question are suitable to be used for looking after children under the age of eight, having regard to their condition and the condition and appropriateness of any equipment on the premises and to any other factor connected with the situation, construction or size of the premises; and

(d) he is complying with regulations under section 79C and with any conditions imposed [under this Part][2].

(4) A person is qualified for registration for providing day care on particular premises if –

[(a) he has made adequate arrangements to ensure that –
   (i) every person (other than himself and the responsible individual) looking after children on the premises is suitable to look after children under the age of eight; and
   (ii) every person (other than himself and the responsible individual) living or working on the premises is suitable to be in regular contact with children under the age of eight;

(b) the responsible individual –
   (i) is suitable to look after children under the age of eight, or
   (ii) if he is not looking after such children, is suitable to be in regular contact with them;][3]

(c) the premises are suitable to be used for looking after children under the age of eight, having regard to their condition and the condition and appropriateness of any equipment on the premises and to any other factor connected with the situation, construction or size of the premises; and

(d) he is complying with regulations under section 79C and with any conditions imposed [under this Part][2].

(5) For the purposes of subsection [(4)(a)]³ a person is not treated as working on the premises in question if –

(a) none of his work is done in the part of the premises in which children are looked after; or
(b) he does not work on the premises at times when children are looked after there.

[(5ZA) For the purposes of subsection (4), 'the responsible individual' means –

(a) in a case of one individual working on the premises in the provision of day care, that person;
(b) in a case of two or more individuals so working, the individual so working who is in charge.]³

[(5A) Where, for the purposes of determining a person's qualification for registration under this Part –

(a) [the Assembly]⁵ requests any person ('A') to consent to the disclosure to the authority by another person ('B') of any information relating to A which is held by B and is of a prescribed description, and
(b) A does not give his consent (or withdraws it after having given it),

[the Assembly]⁵ may, if regulations so provide and it thinks it appropriate to do so, regard A as not suitable to look after children under the age of eight, or not suitable to be in regular contact with such children.]¹

(6) 'Domestic premises' means any premises which are wholly or mainly used as a private dwelling and 'premises' includes any area and any vehicle.

[(7) 'Regulations' means regulations made by the Assembly.]⁵

(8) ...⁶

(9) Schedule 9A (which supplements the provisions of this Part) shall have effect.

NOTES

Amendments.¹ Subsection inserted: Education Act 2002, s 152, Sch 13, para 1.² Words substituted: Children Act 2004, s 48, Sch 4, paras 1, 2.³ Subsection inserted and paragraphs and words substituted: Children Act 2004, s 48, Sch 4, paras 1, 6.⁴ Words substituted: Education and Inspections Act 2006, s 157, Sch 14, paras 9, 13.⁵ Subsections repealed and substituted and words substituted: Childcare Act 2006, s 103, Sch 2, paras 6, 7, Sch 3, Pt 2.⁶ Subsection repealed: SI 2008/2833.

Regulations

79C Regulations etc governing child minders and day care providers

(1) ...¹

(2) The Assembly may make regulations governing the activities of registered persons who act as child minders, or provide day care, on premises in Wales.

(3) The regulations under this section may deal with the following matters (among others) –

(a) the welfare and development of the children concerned;
(b) suitability to look after, or be in regular contact with, children under the age of eight;
(c) qualifications and training;
(d) the maximum number of children who may be looked after and the number of persons required to assist in looking after them;
(e) the maintenance, safety and suitability of premises and equipment;
(f) the keeping of records;
(g) the provision of information.

(4), (5) ...[1]

(6) If the regulations require any person (other than [the Assembly][1]) to have regard to or meet factors, standards and other matters prescribed by or referred to in the regulations, they may also provide for any allegation that the person has failed to do so to be taken into account –

(a) by [the Assembly][1] in the exercise of its functions under this Part, or
(b) in any proceedings under this Part.

(7) Regulations may provide –

(a) that a registered person who without reasonable excuse contravenes, or otherwise fails to comply with, any requirement of the regulations shall be guilty of an offence; and
(b) that a person guilty of the offence shall be liable on summary conviction to a fine not exceeding level 5 on the standard scale.

NOTES

Amendments.[1] Subsections repealed and words substituted: Childcare Act 2006, s 103, Sch 2, paras 6, 8, Sch 3, Pt 2.

Registration

79D Requirement to register

[(1) No person shall act as a child minder in Wales unless he is registered under this Part for child minding by the Assembly.][1]

(2) Where it appears to [the Assembly][1] that a person has contravened subsection (1), the authority may serve a notice ('an enforcement notice') on him.

(3) An enforcement notice shall have effect for a period of one year beginning with the date on which it is served.

(4) If a person in respect of whom an enforcement notice has effect contravenes subsection (1) without reasonable excuse ...[1], he shall be guilty of an offence.

(5) No person shall provide day care on any premises [in Wales][1] unless he is registered under this Part for providing day care on those premises by [the Assembly][1].

(6) If any person contravenes subsection (5) without reasonable excuse, he shall be guilty of an offence.

(7) A person guilty of an offence under this section shall be liable on summary conviction to a fine not exceeding level 5 on the standard scale.

NOTES

Amendments.[1] Subsection substituted, and words substituted and inserted: Childcare Act 2006, s 103(1), Sch 2, paras 6, 9, Sch 3, Pt 2.

79E Applications for registration

(1) A person who wishes to be registered under this Part shall make an application to [the Assembly][2].

(2) The application shall –

 (a) give prescribed information about prescribed matters;
 (b) give any other information which [the Assembly][2] reasonably requires the applicant to give
 [(c) be accompanied by the prescribed fee][1].

(3) Where a person provides, or proposes to provide, day care on different premises, he shall make a separate application in respect of each of them.

(4) Where [the Assembly][2] has sent the applicant notice under section 79L(1) of its intention to refuse an application under this section, the application may not be withdrawn without the consent of the authority.

(5) A person who, in an application under this section, knowingly makes a statement which is false or misleading in a material particular shall be guilty of an offence and liable, on summary conviction, to a fine not exceeding level 5 on the standard scale.

NOTES

Amendments.[1] Paragraph inserted: Children Act 2004, s 48, Sch 4, paras 1, 3(1).[2] Words substituted: Childcare Act 2006, s 103(1), Sch 2, para 6.

79F Grant or refusal of registration

(1) If, on an application [under section 79E][1] by a person for registration for child minding –

 (a) [the Assembly][3] is of the opinion that the applicant is, and will continue to be, qualified for registration for child minding (so far as the conditions of section 79B(3) are applicable); …[2]
 (b) …[2]

[the Assembly][3] shall grant the application; otherwise, it shall refuse it.

(2) If, on an application [under section 79E][1] by any person for registration for providing day care on any premises –

Part I   Statutes

(a) [the Assembly]³ is of the opinion that the applicant is, and will continue to be, qualified for registration for providing day care on those premises (so far as the conditions of section 79B(4) are applicable); ...²
(b) ...²

[the Assembly]³ shall grant the application; otherwise, it shall refuse it.

(3) An application may, as well as being granted subject to any conditions [the Assembly]³ thinks necessary or expedient for the purpose of giving effect to regulations under section 79C, be granted subject to any other conditions [the Assembly]³ thinks fit to impose.

(4) [The Assembly]³ may as it thinks fit vary or remove any condition to which the registration is subject or impose a new condition.

(5) Any register kept by [the Assembly]³ of persons who act as child minders or provide day care shall be open to inspection by any person at all reasonable times.

(6) A registered person who without reasonable excuse contravenes, or otherwise fails to comply with, any condition imposed on his registration shall be guilty of an offence.

(7) A person guilty of an offence under subsection (6) shall be liable on summary conviction to a fine not exceeding level 5 on the standard scale.

NOTES

Amendments.¹ Words inserted: Children Act 2004, s 48, Sch 4, paras 1, 3(2)(a).² Words or paragraphs repealed: Children Act 2004, ss 48, 64, Sch 4, paras 1, 3(2)(b), Sch 5, Pt 2.³ Words substituted: Childcare Act 2006, s 103(1), Sch 2, para 6.

79G Cancellation of registration

(1) [The Assembly]³ may cancel the registration of any person if –

(a) in the case of a person registered for child minding, [the Assembly]³ is of the opinion that the person has ceased or will cease to be qualified for registration for child minding;
(b) in the case of a person registered for providing day care on any premises, [the Assembly]³ is of the opinion that the person has ceased or will cease to be qualified for registration for providing day care on those premises,

or if [a fee]² which is due from the person has not been paid.

(2) Where a requirement to make any changes or additions to any services, equipment or premises has been imposed on a registered person ...¹, his registration shall not be cancelled on the ground of any defect or insufficiency in the services, equipment or premises if –

(a) the time set for complying with the requirements has not expired; and
(b) it is shown that the defect or insufficiency is due to the changes or additions not having been made.

(3) Any cancellation under this section must be in writing.

NOTES

Amendments.[1] Words repealed: Children Act 2004, ss 48, 64, Sch 4, paras 1, 2(2), Sch 5, Pt 2.[2] Words substituted: Children Act 2004, s 48, Sch 4, paras 1, 4(1).[3] Words substituted: Childcare Act 2006, s 103(1), Sch 2, para 6.

79H Suspension of registration

(1) Regulations may provide for the registration of any person for acting as a child minder or providing day care to be suspended for a prescribed period by [the Assembly][2] in prescribed circumstances.

(2) Any regulations made under this section shall include provision conferring on the person concerned a right of appeal to the [First-tier][3] Tribunal against suspension.

[(3) ...[2]

(4) A person registered under this Part for child minding by the Assembly shall not act as a child minder in Wales at a time when that registration is so suspended.

(5) A person registered under this Part for providing day care on any premises shall not provide day care on those premises at any time when that registration is so suspended.

(6) If any person contravenes subsection (3), (4) or (5) without reasonable excuse, he shall be guilty of an offence and liable on summary conviction to a fine not exceeding level 5 on the standard scale.][1]

NOTES

Amendments.[1] Subsections inserted: Education Act 2002, s 152, Sch 13, para 2.[2] Words substituted and subsection repealed: Childcare Act 2006, s 103, Sch 2, paras 6, 10, Sch 3, Pt 2.[3] Words inserted: SI 2008/2833.

79J Resignation of registration

(1) A person who is registered for acting as a child minder or providing day care may by notice in writing to [the Assembly][1] resign his registration.

(2) But a person may not give a notice under subsection (1) –

 (a) if [the Assembly][1] has sent him a notice under section 79L(1) of its intention to cancel the registration, unless the authority has decided not to take that step; or
 (b) if [the Assembly][1] has sent him a notice under section 79L(5) of its decision to cancel the registration and the time within which an appeal may be brought has not expired or, if an appeal has been brought, it has not been determined.

NOTES

Amendments.[1] Words substituted: Childcare Act 2006, s 103(1), Sch 2, para 6.

79K Protection of children in an emergency

(1) If, in the case of any person registered [under this Part]¹ for acting as a child minder or providing day care –

- (a) [the Assembly]¹ applies to a justice of the peace for an order –
    - (i) cancelling the registration;
    - (ii) varying or removing any condition to which the registration is subject; or
    - (iii) imposing a new condition; and
- (b) it appears to the justice that a child who is being, or may be, looked after by that person, or (as the case may be) in accordance with the provision for day care made by that person, is suffering, or is likely to suffer, significant harm,

the justice may make the order.

(2) The cancellation, variation, removal or imposition shall have effect from the time when the order is made.

(3) An application under subsection (1) may be made without notice.

(4) An order under subsection (1) shall be made in writing.

(5) Where an order is made under this section, [the Assembly]¹ shall serve on the registered person, as soon as is reasonably practicable after the making of the order –

- (a) a copy of the order;
- (b) a copy of any written statement of [the Assembly's]¹ reasons for making the application for the order which supported that application; and
- (c) notice of any right of appeal conferred by section 79M.

(6) Where an order has been so made, [the Assembly]¹ shall, as soon as is reasonably practicable after the making of the order, notify the local authority in whose area the person concerned acts or acted as a child minder, or provides or provided day care, of the making of the order.

NOTES

Amendments.¹ Words inserted and substituted: Childcare Act 2006, s 103(1), Sch 2, paras 6, 11.

79L Notice of intention to take steps

(1) Not less than 14 days before –

- (a) refusing an application for registration;
- (b) cancelling a registration;
- (c) removing or varying any condition to which a registration is subject or imposing a new condition; or
- (d) refusing to grant an application for the removal or variation of any condition to which a registration is subject,

[the Assembly]¹ shall send to the applicant, or (as the case may be) registered person, notice in writing of its intention to take the step in question.

(2) Every such notice shall –

(a) give [the Assembly's]¹ reasons for proposing to take the step; and
(b) inform the person concerned of his rights under this section.

(3) Where the recipient of such a notice informs [the Assembly]¹ in writing of his desire to object to the step being taken, [the Assembly]¹ shall afford him an opportunity to do so.

(4) Any objection made under subsection (3) may be made orally or in writing, by the recipient of the notice or a representative.

(5) If [the Assembly]¹, after giving the person concerned an opportunity to object to the step being taken, decides nevertheless to take it, it shall send him written notice of its decision.

(6) A step of a kind mentioned in subsection (1)(b) or (c) shall not take effect until the expiry of the time within which an appeal may be brought under section 79M or, where such an appeal is brought, before its determination.

(7) Subsection (6) does not prevent a step from taking effect before the expiry of the time within which an appeal may be brought under section 79M if the person concerned notifies [the Assembly]¹ in writing that he does not intend to appeal.

NOTES

Amendments.¹ Words substituted: Childcare Act 2006, s 103(1), Sch 2, para 6.

79M Appeals

(1) An appeal against –

(a) the taking of any step mentioned in section 79L(1); ...¹
(b) an order under section 79K, [or
(c) a determination made by [the Assembly]² under this Part (other than one falling within paragraph (a) or (b)) which is of a prescribed description,]¹

shall lie to the [First-tier]³ Tribunal.

(2) On an appeal, the [First-tier]³ Tribunal may –

(a) confirm the taking of the step or the making of the order [or determination]¹ or direct that it shall not have, or shall cease to have, effect; and
(b) impose, vary or cancel any condition.

NOTES

Amendments.¹ Words repealed and inserted: Education Act 2002, ss 149(2), 152, 215(2), Sch 13, para 3, Sch 22, Pt 3.² Words substituted: Childcare Act 2006, s 103(1), Sch 2, para 6.³ Words inserted: SI 2008/2833.

Part I Statutes

Inspection: England

79N General functions of the Chief Inspector

…[1]

NOTES

Amendments.[1] Section repealed: Childcare Act 2006, s 103, Sch 2, para 12, Sch 3, Pt 2.

79P

…[1]

NOTES

Amendments.[1] Section repealed: Education Act 2005, ss 53, 123, Sch 7, Pt 1, para 2, Sch 19, Pt 1.

79Q Inspection of provision of child minding and day care in England

…[1]

NOTES

Amendments.[1] Section repealed: Childcare Act 2006, s 103, Sch 2, para 12, Sch 3, Pt 2.

79R Reports of inspections

…[1]

NOTES

Amendments.[1] Section repealed: Childcare Act 2006, s 103, Sch 2, para 12, Sch 3, Pt 2.

Inspection: Wales

79S General functions of the Assembly

(1) The Assembly may secure the provision of training for persons who provide or assist in providing child minding or day care, or intend to do so.

(2) In relation to child minding and day care provided in Wales, the Assembly shall have any additional function specified in regulations made by the Assembly; …[1]

NOTES

Amendments.[1] Words repealed: Childcare Act 2006, s 103, Sch 2, para 13, Sch 3, Pt 2.

79T Inspection: Wales

(1) The Assembly may at any time require any registered person to provide it with any information connected with the person's activities as a child minder or provision of day care which the Assembly considers it necessary to have for the purposes of its functions under this Part.

(2) The Assembly may by regulations make provision –

(a) for the inspection of the quality and standards of child minding provided in Wales by registered persons and of day care provided by registered persons on premises in Wales;
(b) for the publication of reports of the inspections in such manner as the Assembly considers appropriate.

(3) The regulations may provide for the inspections to be organised by –

(a) the Assembly; or
(b) Her Majesty's Chief Inspector of Education and Training in Wales, or any other person, under arrangements made with the Assembly.

(4) The regulations may provide for subsections (2) to (4) of section 42A of the School Inspections Act 1996 to apply with modifications in relation to the publication of reports under the regulations.

Supplementary

79U Rights of entry etc

(1) [Any person authorised for the purposes of this subsection by [the Assembly]³]¹ may at any reasonable time enter any premises in …³ Wales on which child minding or day care is at any time provided.

(2) Where [a person authorised for the purposes of this subsection by [the Assembly]³]¹ has reasonable cause to believe that a child is being looked after on any premises in contravention of this Part, he may enter those premises at any reasonable time.

[(2A) Authorisation under subsection (1) or (2) –

(a) may be given for a particular occasion or period;
(b) may be given subject to conditions.]¹

(3) [A person entering premises under this section may (subject to any conditions imposed under subsection (2A)(b)]¹ –

(a) inspect the premises;
(b) inspect, and take copies of –
    (i) any records kept by the person providing the child minding or day care; and
    (ii) any other documents containing information relating to its provision;
(c) seize and remove any document or other material or thing found there which he has reasonable grounds to believe may be evidence of a failure to comply with any condition or requirement imposed by or under this Part;
(d) require any person to afford him such facilities and assistance with respect to matters within the person's control as are necessary to enable him to exercise his powers under this section;
(e) take measurements and photographs or make recordings;
(f) inspect any children being looked after there, and the arrangements made for their welfare;

(g) interview in private the person providing the child minding or day care; and
(h) interview in private any person looking after children, or living or working, there who consents to be interviewed.

(4) [Section 58 of the Education Act 2005][2] (inspection of computer records for purposes of Part I of that Act) shall apply for the purposes of subsection (3) as it applies for the purposes of Part I of that Act.

(5) ...[1]

(6) A person exercising any power conferred by this section shall, if so required, produce some duly authenticated document showing his authority to do so.

(7) It shall be an offence wilfully to obstruct a person exercising any such power.

(8) Any person guilty of an offence under subsection (7) shall be liable on summary conviction to a fine not exceeding level 4 on the standard scale.

(9) In this section –

...[1]

'documents' and 'records' each include information recorded in any form.

NOTES

Amendments.[1] Words and subsection inserted, and subsection and definition repealed: Education Act 2002, s 152, Sch 13, para 5.[2] Words substituted: Education Act 2005, s 53, Sch 7, Pt 1, para 6.[3] Words repealed and substituted: Childcare Act 2006, s 103, Sch 2, paras 6, 14, Sch 3, Pt 2.

79V Function of local authorities

Each local authority [in Wales][1] shall, in accordance with regulations, secure the provision –

(a) of information and advice about child minding and day care; and
(b) of training for persons who provide or assist in providing child minding or day care.

NOTES

Amendments.[1] Words inserted: Childcare Act 2006, s 103(1), Sch 2, para 15.

Checks on suitability of persons working with children over the age of seven

79W Requirement for certificate of suitability

(1) This section applies to any person not required to register under this Part who looks after, or provides care for, children [in Wales][1] and meets the following conditions.

References in this section to children are to those under the age of 15 or (in the case of disabled children) 17.

(2) The first condition is that the period, or the total of the periods, in any week which he spends looking after children or (as the case may be) during which the children are looked after exceeds five hours.

(3) The second condition is that he would be required to register under this Part (or, as the case may be, this Part if it were subject to prescribed modifications) if the children were under the age of eight.

(4) Regulations may require a person to whom this section applies to hold a certificate issued by [the Assembly]² as to his suitability, and the suitability of each prescribed person, to look after children.

(5) The regulations may make provision about –

 (a) applications for certificates;
 (b) the matters to be taken into account by [the Assembly]² in determining whether to issue certificates;
 (c) the information to be contained in certificates;
 (d) the period of their validity.

(6) The regulations may provide that a person to whom this section applies shall be guilty of an offence –

 (a) if he does not hold a certificate as required by the regulations; or
 (b) if, being a person who holds such a certificate, he fails to produce it when reasonably required to do so by a prescribed person.

(7) The regulations may provide that a person who, for the purpose of obtaining such a certificate, knowingly makes a statement which is false or misleading in a material particular shall be guilty of an offence.

(8) The regulations may provide that a person guilty of an offence under the regulations shall be liable on summary conviction to a fine not exceeding level 5 on the standard scale.

NOTES

Amendments.[1] Words inserted: Childcare Act 2006, s 103(1), Sch 2, para 16.[2] Words substituted: Childcare Act 2006, s 103(1), Sch 2, para 6.

Time limit for proceedings

79X Time limit for proceedings

Proceedings for an offence under this Part or regulations made under it may be brought within a period of six months from the date on which evidence sufficient in the opinion of the prosecutor to warrant the proceedings came to his knowledge; but no such proceedings shall be brought by virtue of this section more than three years after the commission of the offence.][1]

NOTES

Amendments.[1] Part inserted: Care Standards Act 2000, s 79(1).

PART XI
SECRETARY OF STATE'S SUPERVISORY FUNCTIONS AND RESPONSIBILITIES

80 Inspection of children's homes etc by persons authorised by Secretary of State

(1) The Secretary of State may cause to be inspected from time to time any –

(a) [private][4] children's home;
(b) premises in which a child who is being looked after by a local authority is living;
(c) premises in which a child who is being accommodated by or on behalf of a [local authority in the exercise of education functions or a][9] voluntary organisation is living;
(d) premises in which a child who is being accommodated by or on behalf of a [[Local Health Board][8], Special Health Authority][2][, Primary Care Trust][3][, National Health Service trust or NHS foundation trust][6] is living;
(e) ...[7]
(f) ...[7]
(g) premises in which a privately fostered child, or child who is treated as a foster child by virtue of paragraph 9 of Schedule 8, is living or in which it is proposed that he will live;
(h) premises on which any person is acting as a child minder;
(i) premises with respect to which a person is registered under section 71(1)(b) [or with respect to which a person is registered for providing day care under Part XA][4];
(j) [care home or independent hospital used to accommodate children;][4]
(k) premises which are provided by a local authority and in which any service is provided by that authority under Part III;
(l) [school or college][5] providing accommodation for any child.

(2) An inspection under this section shall be conducted by a person authorised to do so by the Secretary of State.

(3) An officer of a local authority shall not be authorised except with the consent of that authority.

(4) The Secretary of State may require any person of a kind mentioned in subsection (5) to furnish him with such information, or allow him to inspect such records (in whatever form they are held), relating to –

(a) any premises to which subsection (1) or, in relation to Scotland, subsection (1)(h) or (i) applies;
(b) any child who is living in any such premises;
(c) the discharge by the Secretary of State of any of his functions under this Act;
(d) the discharge by any local authority of any of their functions under this Act,

as the Secretary of State may at any time direct.

(5) The persons are any –

(a) local authority;
(b) voluntary organisation;
(c) person carrying on a [private][4] children's home;
(d) proprietor of an independent school [or governing body of any other school][5];
[(da) governing body of an institution designated under section 28 of the Further and Higher Education Act 1992;
(db) further education corporation;][5]
[(dc) sixth form college corporation;][10]
(e) person fostering any privately fostered child or providing accommodation for a child on behalf of a local authority, ...[9] [[Local Health Board][8], Special Health Authority][2] [, Primary Health Care Trust][3][, National Health Service trust][1] [, NHS foundation trust][6] or voluntary organisation;
(f) ...[9]
(g) person employed in a teaching or administrative capacity at any educational establishment (whether or not maintained by [a local authority][9]) at which a child is accommodated on behalf of a local authority ...[9];
(h) person who is the occupier of any premises in which any person acts as a child minder (within the meaning of Part X) or provides day care for young children (within the meaning of that Part);
[(hh) person who is the occupier of any premises –
  (i) in which any person required to be registered for child minding under Part XA acts as a child minder (within the meaning of that Part); or
  (ii) with respect to which a person is required to be registered under that Part for providing day care;][4]
(i) person carrying on any home of a kind mentioned in subsection (1)(j);
[(j) person carrying on a fostering agency.][5]

(6) Any person inspecting any home or other premises under this section may –

(a) inspect the children there; and
(b) make such examination into the state and management of the home or premises and the treatment of the children there as he thinks fit.

(7) Any person authorised by the Secretary of State to exercise the power to inspect records conferred by subsection (4) –

(a) shall be entitled at any reasonable time to have access to, and inspect and check the operation of, any computer and any associated apparatus or material which is or has been in use in connection with the records in question; and
(b) may require –
  (i) the person by whom or on whose behalf the computer is or has been so used; or
  (ii) any person having charge of, or otherwise concerned with the operation of, the computer, apparatus or material,

to afford him such reasonable assistance as he may require.

(8) A person authorised to inspect any premises under this section shall have a right to enter the premises for that purpose, and for any purpose specified in subsection (4), at any reasonable time.

(9) Any person exercising that power shall, if so required, produce some duly authenticated document showing his authority to do so.

(10) Any person who intentionally obstructs another in the exercise of that power shall be guilty of an offence and liable on summary conviction to a fine not exceeding level 3 on the standard scale.

(11) The Secretary of State may by order provide for subsections (1), (4) and (6) not to apply in relation to such homes, or other premises, as may be specified in the order.

(12) Without prejudice to section 104, any such order may make different provision with respect to each of those subsections.

[(13) In this section –

'college' means an institution within the further education sector as defined in section 91 of the Further and Higher Education Act 1992;
'fostering agency' has the same meaning as in the Care Standards Act 2000;
'further education corporation' has the same meaning as in the Further and Higher Education Act 1992.
['sixth form college corporation' has the same meaning as in that Act.][10]][5]

NOTES

Amendments.[1] Words inserted: National Health Service and Community Care Act 1990, s 66(1), Sch 9, para 36(4)(b).[2] Words substituted: Health Authorities Act 1995, s 2(1), Sch 1, Pt III, para 118(1), (9).[3] Words inserted: Health Act 1999 (Supplementary, Consequential etc Provisions) Order 2000, SI 2000/90.[4] Paragraph and words inserted or substituted: Care Standards Act 2000, ss 116, 117(2), Sch 4, paras 14(1), (16).[5] Subsection, paragraphs and words inserted or substituted: Care Standards Act 2000, s 109 (applies to England only).[6] Words substituted or inserted: Health and Social Care (Community Health and Standards) Act 2003, s 34, Sch 4, paras 75, 80.[7] Paragraphs repealed: Adoption and Children Act 2002, s 139(1), (3), Sch 3, paras 54, 65, Sch 5.[8] Words substituted: SI 2007/961. [9] Words substituted and repealed, and words and paragraph repealed: SI 2010/1158. [10] Paragraph and definition inserted: SI 2010/1080.

Definitions. 'Adoption agency': s 105(1); 'child': s 105(1); 'child minder': s 71(2)(a); 'child who is looked after by a local authority': s 22(1); 'children's home': s 63(3); 'day care': ss 18, 71(2)(b); 'functions': s 105(1); 'health authority': s 105(1); 'independent school': s 105(1); 'local authority': s 105(1); 'local education authority': s 105(1); 'mental nursing home': s 105(1); 'nursing home': s 105(1); 'privately fostered child': s 105(1); 'residential care home': s 105(1); 'voluntary home': s 60(3); 'voluntary organisation': s 105(1).

81

…[1]

NOTES

Amendments.[1] Section repealed: Inquiries Act 2005, ss 48(1), 49(2), Sch 2, Pt 1, para 12, Sch 3.

82 Financial support by Secretary of State

(1) The Secretary of State may (with the consent of the Treasury) defray or contribute towards –

  (a) any fees or expenses incurred by any person undergoing approved child care training;
  (b) any fees charged, or expenses incurred, by any person providing approved child care training or preparing material for use in connection with such training; or
  (c) the cost of maintaining any person undergoing such training.

(2) The Secretary of State may make grants to local authorities in respect of expenditure incurred by them in providing secure accommodation in community homes other than assisted community homes.

(3) Where –

  (a) a grant has been made under subsection (2) with respect to any secure accommodation; but
  (b) the grant is not used for the purpose for which it was made or the accommodation is not used as, or ceases to be used as, secure accommodation,

the Secretary of State may (with the consent of the Treasury) require the authority concerned to repay the grant, in whole or in part.

(4) The Secretary of State may make grants to voluntary organisations towards –

  (a) expenditure incurred by them in connection with the establishment, maintenance or improvement of voluntary homes which, at the time when the expenditure was incurred –
     (i) were assisted community homes; or
     (ii) were designated as such; or
  (b) expenses incurred in respect of the borrowing of money to defray any such expenditure.

(5) The Secretary of State may arrange for the provision, equipment and maintenance of homes for the accommodation of children who are in need of particular facilities and services which –

  (a) are or will be provided in those homes; and
  (b) in the opinion of the Secretary of State, are unlikely to be readily available in community homes.

(6) In this Part –

  'child care training' means training undergone by any person with a view to, or in the course of –
     (a) his employment for the purposes of any of the functions mentioned in section 83(9) or in connection with the adoption of children or with the accommodation of children in a [care home or independent hospital][1]; or

Part I   Statutes

(b) his employment by a voluntary organisation for similar purposes;

'approved child care training' means child care training which is approved by the Secretary of State; and

'secure accommodation' means accommodation provided for the purpose of restricting the liberty of children.

(7) Any grant made under this section shall be of such amount, and shall be subject to such conditions, as the Secretary of State may (with the consent of the Treasury) determine.

NOTES

Amendments.[1] Words substituted: Care Standards Act 2000, s 116, Sch 4, para 14(18).

Definitions. 'Approved child care training': s 82(6); 'assisted community home': s 53(5); 'child': s 105(1); 'child care training': s 82(6); 'community home': s 53(1); 'functions': s 105(1); 'mental nursing home': s 105(1); 'nursing home': s 105(1); 'residential care home': s 105(1); 'secure accommodation': s 82(6); 'voluntary home': s 60(3); 'voluntary organisation': s 105(1).

83 Research and returns of information

(1) The Secretary of State may conduct, or assist other persons in conducting, research into any matter connected with –

(a) his functions, or the functions of local authorities, under the enactments mentioned in subsection (9);
[(aa) the functions of Local Safeguarding Children Boards;][5]
(b) the adoption of children; or
(c) the accommodation of children in a [care home or independent hospital][2].

(2) Any local authority may conduct, or assist other persons in conducting, research into any matter connected with –

(a) their functions under the enactments mentioned in subsection (9);
[(aa) the functions of Local Safeguarding Children Boards;][5]
(b) the adoption of children; or
(c) the accommodation of children in a [care home or independent hospital][2].

(3) Every local authority shall, at such times and in such form as the Secretary of State may direct, transmit to him such particulars as he may require with respect to –

(a) the performance by the local authority of all or any of their functions –
  (i) under the enactments mentioned in subsection (9); or
  (ii) in connection with the accommodation of children in a [care home or independent hospital][2]; and
(b) the children in relation to whom the authority have exercised those functions[; and

(c) the performance by the Local Safeguarding Children Board established by them under the Children Act 2004 of all or any of its functions][5].

(4) Every voluntary organisation shall, at such times and in such form as the Secretary of State may direct, transmit to him such particulars as he may require with respect to children accommodated by them or on their behalf.

[(4A) Particulars required to be transmitted under subsection (3) or (4) may include particulars relating to and identifying individual children.][3]

(5) The Secretary of State may direct the [designated officer for][1] each magistrates' court to which the direction is expressed to relate to transmit –

(a) to such person as may be specified in the direction; and
(b) at such times and in such form as he may direct,

such particulars as he may require with respect to proceedings of the court which relate to children.

(6) The Secretary of State shall in each year lay before Parliament a consolidated and classified abstract of the information transmitted to him under subsections (3) to (5).

(7) The Secretary of State may institute research designed to provide information on which requests for information under this section may be based.

(8) The Secretary of State shall keep under review the adequacy of the provision of child care training and for that purpose shall receive and consider any information from or representations made by –

(a) the Central Council for Education and Training in Social Work;
(b) such representatives of local authorities as appear to him to be appropriate; or
(c) such other persons or organisations as appear to him to be appropriate,

concerning the provision of such training.

(9) The enactments are –

(a) this Act;
(b) the Children and Young Persons Acts 1933 to 1969;
(c) section 116 of the Mental Health Act 1983 (so far as it relates to children looked after by local authorities);
[(ca) Part 1 of the Adoption and Children Act 2002;
(cb) the Children Act 2004;
(cc) the Children and Young Persons Act 2008;][5]
(d) …[4]

NOTES

Amendments. [1] Words substituted: Courts Act 2003, s 109(1), Sch 8, para 336. [2] Words substituted: Care Standards Act 2000, s 116, Sch 4, para 14(19). [3] Subsection inserted: Children Act 2004, s 54. [4] Paragraph repealed: SI 2005/2078, art 16(1), Sch 3. [5] Paragraphs inserted: Children and Young Persons Act 2008, s 33(1)–(5).

Definitions. 'Child': s 105(1); 'child care training': s 82(6); 'functions': s 105(1); 'local authority': s 105(1); 'mental nursing home': s 105(1); 'nursing home': s 105(1); 'residential care home': s 105(1); 'voluntary organisation': s 105(1).

84 Local authority failure to comply with statutory duty: default power of Secretary of State

(1) If the Secretary of State is satisfied that any local authority has failed, without reasonable excuse, to comply with any of the duties imposed on them by or under this Act he may make an order declaring that authority to be in default with respect to that duty.

(2) An order under subsection (1) shall give the Secretary of State's reasons for making it.

(3) An order under subsection (1) may contain such directions for the purpose of ensuring that the duty is complied with, within such period as may be specified in the order, as appear to the Secretary of State to be necessary.

(4) Any such direction shall, on the application of the Secretary of State, be enforceable by mandamus.

PART XII
MISCELLANEOUS AND GENERAL

Notification of children accommodated in certain establishments

85 Children accommodated by health authorities and local education authorities

(1) Where a child is provided with accommodation by any [[Local Health Board][4], Special Health Authority][2], [Primary Care Trust,][3] [National Health Service trust][1] [or NHS foundation trust or by a local authority in the exercise of education functions][5] ('the accommodating authority') –

    (a) for a consecutive period of at least three months; or
    (b) with the intention, on the part of that authority, of accommodating him for such a period,

the accommodating authority shall notify the responsible authority.

(2) Where subsection (1) applies with respect to a child, the accommodating authority shall also notify the responsible authority when they cease to accommodate the child.

[(2A) In a case where the child is provided with accommodation by a local authority in the exercise of education functions, subsections (1) and (2) apply only if the local authority providing the accommodation is different from the responsible authority.][5]

(3) In this section 'the responsible authority' means –

    (a) the local authority appearing to the accommodating authority to be the authority within whose area the child was ordinarily resident immediately before being accommodated; or

(b) where it appears to the accommodating authority that a child was not ordinarily resident within the area of any local authority, the local authority within whose area the accommodation is situated.

(4) Where a local authority have been notified under this section, they shall –

(a) take such steps as are reasonably practicable to enable them to determine whether the child's welfare is adequately safeguarded and promoted while he is accommodated by the accommodating authority; and

(b) consider the extent to which (if at all) they should exercise any of their functions under this Act with respect to the child.

NOTES

Amendments.[1] Words inserted: National Health Service and Community Care Act 1990, s 66(1), Sch 9, para 36(5).[2] Words inserted: Health Authorities Act 1995, s 2(1), Sch 1, Pt III, para 118(1), (9).[3] Words inserted: Health Act 1999 (Supplementary, Consequential etc Provisions) Order 2000, SI 2000/90.[4] Words substituted: SI 2007/961.[5] Words substituted and subsection inserted: SI 2010/1158.

Definitions. 'Child': s 105(1); 'functions': s 105(1); 'health authority': s 105(1); 'local authority': s 105(1); 'local education authority': s 105(1); 'the accommodating authority': s 85(1); 'the responsible authority': s 85(3).

86 [Children accommodated in care homes or independent hospitals][1]

(1) Where a child is provided with accommodation in any [care home or independent hospital][1] –

(a) for a consecutive period of at least three months; or

(b) with the intention, on the part of the person taking the decision to accommodate him, of accommodating him for such period,

the person carrying on the home shall notify the local authority within whose area the home is carried on.

(2) Where subsection (1) applies with respect to a child, the person carrying on the home shall also notify that authority when he ceases to accommodate the child in the home.

(3) Where a local authority have been notified under this section, they shall –

(a) take such steps as are reasonably practicable to enable them to determine whether the child's welfare is adequately safeguarded and promoted while he is accommodated in the home; and

(b) consider the extent to which (if at all) they should exercise any of their functions under this Act with respect to the child.

(4) If the person carrying on any home fails, without reasonable excuse, to comply with this section he shall be guilty of an offence.

(5) A person authorised by a local authority may enter any [care home or independent hospital][1] within the authority's area for the purpose of establishing whether the requirements of this section have been complied with.

(6) Any person who intentionally obstructs another in the exercise of the power of entry shall be guilty of an offence.

(7) Any person exercising the power of entry shall, if so required, produce some duly authenticated document showing his authority to do so.

(8) Any person committing an offence under this section shall be liable on summary conviction to a fine not exceeding level 3 on the standard scale.

NOTES

Amendments.[1] Words substituted: Care Standards Act 2000, s 116, Sch 4, para 14(20).

Definitions. 'Child': s 105(1); 'functions': s 105(1); 'local authority': s 105(1); 'mental nursing home': s 105(1); 'nursing home': s 105(1); 'residential care home': s 105(1).

[86A Visitors for children notified to local authority under section 85 or 86

(1) This section applies if the appropriate officer of a local authority –

- (a) has been notified with respect to a child under section 85(1) or 86(1); and
- (b) has not been notified with respect to that child under section 85(2) or, as the case may be, 86(2).

(2) The local authority must, in accordance with regulations made under this section, make arrangements for the child to be visited by a representative of the authority ("a representative").

(3) It is the function of a representative to provide advice and assistance to the local authority on the performance of their duties under section 85(4) or, as the case may be, 86(3).

(4) Regulations under this section may make provision about –

- (a) the frequency of visits under visiting arrangements;
- (b) circumstances in which visiting arrangements must require a child to be visited; and
- (c) additional functions of a representative.

(5) Regulations under this section are to be made by the Secretary of State and the Welsh Ministers acting jointly.

(6) In choosing a representative a local authority must satisfy themselves that the person chosen has the necessary skills and experience to perform the functions of a representative.

(7) In this section 'visiting arrangements' means arrangements made under subsection (2).][1]

NOTES

Amendment.[1] Section inserted for certain purposes: Children and Young Persons Act 2008, s 18.

87 [Welfare of children in boarding schools and colleges]¹

[(1) Where a school or college provides accommodation for any child, it shall be the duty of the relevant person to safeguard and promote the child's welfare.

(2) Subsection (1) does not apply in relation to a school or college which is a children's home or care home.

(3) Where accommodation is provided for a child by any school or college the appropriate authority shall take such steps as are reasonably practicable to enable them to determine whether the child's welfare is adequately safeguarded and promoted while he is accommodated by the school or college.

(4) Where the [the Chief Inspector for England is][4] of the opinion that there has been a failure to comply with subsection (1) in relation to a child provided with accommodation by a school or [college in England, he shall][4] –

(a) in the case of a school other than an independent school or a special school, notify the [local authority][5] for the area in which the school is situated;

(b) in the case of a special school which is maintained by a [local authority][5], notify that authority;

(c) in any other case, notify the Secretary of State.

(4A) Where the National Assembly for Wales are of the opinion that there has been a failure to comply with subsection (1) in relation to a child provided with accommodation by a school or college [in Wales][4], they shall –

(a) in the case of a school other than an independent school or a special school, notify the [local authority][5] for the area in which the school is situated;

(b) in the case of a special school which is maintained by a [local authority][5], notify that authority;

(5) Where accommodation is, or is to be, provided for a child by any school or college, a person authorised by the appropriate authority may, for the purpose of enabling that authority to discharge its duty under this section, enter at any time premises which are, or are to be, premises of the school or college.]¹

(6) Any person [exercising]¹ the power conferred by subsection (5) may carry out such inspection of premises, children and records as is prescribed by regulations made by the Secretary of State for the purposes of this section.

(7) Any person exercising that power shall, if asked to do so, produce some duly authenticated document showing his authority to do so.

(8) Any person authorised by the regulations to inspect records –

(a) shall be entitled at any reasonable time to have access to, and inspect and check the operation of, any computer and any associated apparatus or material which is or has been in use in connection with the records in question; and

(b) may require –

(i) the person by whom or on whose behalf the computer is or has been so used; or
(ii) any person having charge of, or otherwise concerned with the operation of, the computer, apparatus or material,

to afford him such assistance as he may reasonably require.

(9) Any person who intentionally obstructs another in the exercise of any power conferred by this section or the regulations shall be guilty of an offence and liable on summary conviction to a fine not exceeding level 3 on the standard scale.

[(9A) Where [the Chief Inspector for England][4] or the National Assembly for Wales exercises the power conferred by subsection (5) in relation to a child, [that authority must][4] publish a report on whether the child's welfare is adequately safeguarded and promoted while he is accommodated by the school or college.

(9B) Where [the Chief Inspector for England][4] or the National Assembly for Wales publishes a report under this section, [that authority must][4] –

(a) send a copy of the report to the school or college concerned; and
(b) make copies of the report available for inspection at its offices by any person at any reasonable time.

(9C) Any person who requests a copy of a report published under this section is entitled to have one on payment of such reasonable fee (if any) as [the Chief Inspector for England][4] or the National Assembly for Wales (as the case may be) considers appropriate.][2]

[(10) In this section and sections 87A to 87D –

'the 1992 Act' means the Further and Higher Education Act 1992;
'appropriate authority' means –
(a) in relation to England, [[the Chief Inspector for England][4]][3];
(b) in relation to Wales, the National Assembly for Wales;

['the Chief Inspector for England' means Her Majesty's Chief Inspector of Education, Children's Services and Skills;][4]
'college' means an institution within the further education sector as defined in section 91 of the 1992 Act;
...[4];
'further education corporation' has the same meaning as in the 1992 Act;
'[local authority][5]' and 'proprietor' have the same meanings as in the Education Act 1996.
['sixth form college corporation' has the same meaning as in the 1992 Act.][6]

(11) In this section and sections 87A and 87D 'relevant person' means –

(a) in relation to an independent school, the proprietor of the school;
(b) in relation to any other school, or an institution designated under section 28 of the 1992 Act, the governing body of the school or institution;

(c) in relation to an institution conducted by a further education corporation [or sixth form college corporation][6], the corporation.

(12) Where a person other than the proprietor of an independent school is responsible for conducting the school, references in this section to the relevant person include references to the person so responsible.][1]

NOTES

Amendments.[1] Subsections and words substituted: Care Standards Act 2000, ss 105, 116, Sch 4, para 14(1), (21).[2] Subsections inserted: Health and Social Care (Community Health and Standards) Act 2003, s 111.[3] Words substituted: Health and Social Care (Community Health and Standards) Act 2003, s 147, Sch 9, para 10(1), (3).[4] Words inserted, substituted and repealed: Education and Inspections Act 2006, s 157, Sch 14, paras 9, 16(1)–(5), Sch 18, Pt 5. [5] Words substituted: SI 2010/1158. [6] Definition and words inserted: SI 2010/1080.

Definitions. 'Child': s 105(1); 'children's home': s 63(3); 'independent school': s 105(1); 'local authority': s 105(1); 'proprietor': s 87(10); 'residential care home': s 105(1).

[87A Suspension of duty under section 87(3)

(1) The Secretary of State may appoint a person to be an inspector for the purposes of this section if –

(a) that person already acts as an inspector for other purposes in relation to schools or colleges to which section 87(1) applies, and
(b) the Secretary of State is satisfied that the person is an appropriate person to determine whether the welfare of children provided with accommodation by such schools or colleges is adequately safeguarded and promoted while they are accommodated by them.

(2) Where –

(a) the relevant person enters into an agreement in writing with a person appointed under subsection (1),
(b) the agreement provides for the person so appointed to have in relation to the school or college the function of determining whether section 87(1) is being complied with, and
(c) the appropriate authority receive from the person mentioned in paragraph (b) ('the inspector') notice in writing that the agreement has come into effect,

the authority's duty under section 87(3) in relation to the school or college shall be suspended.

(3) Where the appropriate authority's duty under section 87(3) in relation to any school or college is suspended under this section, it shall cease to be so suspended if the appropriate authority receive –

(a) a notice under subsection (4) relating to the inspector, or
(b) a notice under subsection (5) relating to the relevant agreement.

(4) The Secretary of State shall terminate a person's appointment under subsection (1) if –

(a) that person so requests, or

(b) the Secretary of State ceases, in relation to that person, to be satisfied that he is such a person as is mentioned in paragraph (b) of that subsection,

and shall give notice of the termination of that person's appointment to the appropriate authority.

(5) Where –

(a) the appropriate authority's duty under section 87(3) in relation to any school or college is suspended under this section, and
(b) the relevant agreement ceases to have effect,

the inspector shall give to the appropriate authority notice in writing of the fact that it has ceased to have effect.

(6) In this section references to the relevant agreement, in relation to the suspension of the appropriate authority's duty under section 87(3) as regards any school or college, are to the agreement by virtue of which the appropriate authority's duty under that provision as regards that school or college is suspended.][1]

NOTES

Amendments.[1] Section substituted: Care Standards Act 2000, s 106(1).

[87B Duties of inspectors under section 87A

(1) The Secretary of State may impose on a person appointed under section 87A(1) ('an authorised inspector') such requirements relating to, or in connection with, the carrying out under substitution agreements of the function mentioned in section 87A(2)(b) as the Secretary of State thinks fit.

(2) Where, in the course of carrying out under a substitution agreement the function mentioned in section 87A(2)(b), it appears to an authorised inspector that there has been a failure to comply with section 87(1) in the case of a child provided with accommodation by the school [or college][2] to which the agreement relates, the inspector shall give notice of that fact –

[(a) in the case of a school other than an independent school or a special school, to the [local authority][3] for the area in which the school is situated;
(b) in the case of a special school which is maintained by a [local authority][3], to that authority;
(c) in any other case, to the Secretary of State.][2]

(3) Where, in the course of carrying out under a substitution agreement the function mentioned in section 87A(2)(b), it appears to an authorised inspector that a child provided with accommodation by the school [or college][2] to which the agreement relates is suffering, or is likely to suffer, significant harm, the inspector shall –

(a) give notice of that fact to the local authority in whose area the school is situated, and

(b) where the inspector is required to make inspection reports to the Secretary of State, supply that local authority with a copy of the latest inspection report to have been made by the inspector to the Secretary of State in relation to the school.

[(4) In this section 'substitution agreement' means an agreement by virtue of which the duty of the appropriate authority under section 87(3) in relation to a school or college is suspended.]²]¹

NOTES

Amendments.¹ Section inserted: Deregulation and Contracting Out Act 1994, s 38.² Subsection substituted and words inserted: Care Standards Act 2000, s 106. ³ Words substituted: SI 2010/1158.

[87C Boarding schools: national minimum standards

(1) The Secretary of State may prepare and publish statements of national minimum standards for safeguarding and promoting the welfare of children for whom accommodation is provided in a school or college.

(2) The Secretary of State shall keep the standards set out in the statements under review and may publish amended statements whenever he considers it appropriate to do so.

(3) Before issuing a statement, or an amended statement which in the opinion of the Secretary of State effects a substantial change in the standards, the Secretary of State shall consult any persons he considers appropriate.

(4) The standards shall be taken into account –

(a) in the making by the appropriate authority of any determination under section 87(4) or (4A);
(b) in the making by a person appointed under section 87A(1) of any determination under section 87B(2); and
(c) in any proceedings under any other enactment in which it is alleged that the person has failed to comply with section 87(1).]¹

NOTES

Amendments.¹ Section inserted: Care Standards Act 2000, s 107.

[87D Annual fee for boarding school inspections

(1) Regulations under subsection (2) may be made in relation to any school or college in respect of which the appropriate authority is required to take steps under section 87(3).

(2) The Secretary of State may by regulations require the relevant person to pay the appropriate authority an annual fee of such amount, and within such time, as the regulations may specify.

(3) A fee payable by virtue of this section may, without prejudice to any other method of recovery, be recovered summarily as a civil debt.]¹

NOTES

Amendments.¹ Section inserted: Care Standards Act 2000, s 108.

Adoption

88 Amendments of adoption legislation

(1) ...[1]

(2) ...[2]

NOTES

Amendments.[1] Subsection repealed: Adoption and Children Act 2002, s 139(1), (3), Sch 3, paras 54, 67, Sch 5. [2] Subsection repealed: Adoption and Children (Scotland) Act 2007, s 120(2), Sch 3.

89

...[1]

NOTES

Amendments.[1] Section repealed: Child Support, Pensions and Social Security Act 2000, s 85, Sch 9, Part IX.

Criminal care and supervision orders

90 Care and supervision orders in criminal proceedings

(1) The power of a court to make an order under subsection (2) of section 1 of the Children and Young Persons Act 1969 (care proceedings in [youth courts][1]) where it is of the opinion that the condition mentioned in paragraph (f) of that subsection ('the offence condition') is satisfied is hereby abolished.

(2) The powers of the court to make care orders –

(a) under section 7(7)(a) of the Children and Young Persons Act 1969 (alteration in treatment of young offenders etc.); and

(b) under section 15(1) of that Act, on discharging a supervision order made under section 7(7)(b) of that Act,

are hereby abolished.

(3) The powers given by that Act to include requirements in supervision orders shall have effect subject to amendments made by Schedule 12.

NOTES

Amendments.[1] Words substituted: Criminal Justice Act 1991, s 100, Sch 11, para 40(1), (2)(r).

Effect and duration of orders etc

91 Effect and duration of orders etc

(1) The making of a residence order with respect to a child who is the subject of a care order discharges the care order.

(2) The making of a care order with respect to a child who is the subject of any section 8 order discharges that order.

[(2A) Where a contact activity direction has been made as regards contact with a child, the making of a care order with respect to the child discharges the direction.]⁵

(3) The making of a care order with respect to a child who is the subject of a supervision order discharges that other order.

(4) The making of a care order with respect to a child who is a ward of court brings that wardship to an end.

(5) The making of a care order with respect to a child who is the subject of a school attendance order made under [section 437 of the Education Act 1996]¹ discharges the school attendance order.

[(5A) The making of a special guardianship order with respect to a child who is the subject of –

(a) a care order; or
(b) an order under section 34,

discharges that order.]²

(6) Where an emergency protection order is made with respect to a child who is in care, the care order shall have effect subject to the emergency protection order.

(7) Any order made under section 4(1) [4ZA(1),]⁶ [4A(1)]³ or 5(1) shall continue in force until the child reaches the age of eighteen, unless it is brought to an end earlier.

(8) Any –

(a) agreement under section 4[, 4ZA]⁶ [or 4A]³; or
(b) appointment under section 5(3) or (4),

shall continue in force until the child reaches the age of eighteen, unless it is brought to an end earlier.

(9) An order under Schedule 1 has effect as specified in that Schedule.

(10) A section 8 order [other than a residence order]⁷ shall, if it would otherwise still be in force, cease to have effect when the child reaches the age of sixteen, unless it is to have effect beyond that age by virtue of section 9(6) [...⁷]⁴.

(11) Where a section 8 order has effect with respect to a child who has reached the age of sixteen, it shall, if it would otherwise still be in force, cease to have effect when he reaches the age of eighteen.

(12) Any care order, other than an interim care order, shall continue in force until the child reaches the age of eighteen, unless it is brought to an end earlier.

(13) Any order made under any other provision of this Act in relation to a child shall, if it would otherwise still be in force, cease to have effect when he reaches the age of eighteen.

(14) On disposing of any application for an order under this Act, the court may (whether or not it makes any other order in response to the application)

order that no application for an order under this Act of any specified kind may be made with respect to the child concerned by any person named in the order without leave of the court.

(15) Where an application ('the previous application') has been made for –

(a) the discharge of a care order;
(b) the discharge of a supervision order;
(c) the discharge of an education supervision order;
(d) the substitution of a supervision order for a care order; or
(e) a child assessment order,

no further application of a kind mentioned in paragraphs (a) to (e) may be made with respect to the child concerned, without leave of the court, unless the period between the disposal of the previous application and the making of the further application exceeds six months.

(16) Subsection (15) does not apply to applications made in relation to interim orders.

(17) Where –

(a) a person has made an application for an order under section 34;
(b) the application has been refused; and
(c) a period of less than six months has elapsed since the refusal,

that person may not make a further application for such an order with respect to the same child, unless he has obtained the leave of the court.

NOTES

Amendments.[1] Words substituted: Education Act 1996, s 582(1), Sch 37, Pt I, para 90.[2] Subsection inserted: Adoption and Children Act 2002, s 139(a), (3), Sch 3, paras 54, 68(a).[3] Words inserted: Adoption and Children Act 2002, s 139(a), (3), Sch 3, paras 54, 68(b), (c).[4] Words inserted: Adoption and Children Act 2002, s 114(3).[5] Subsection inserted: Children and Adoption Act 2006, s 15(1), Sch 2, paras 7, 9.[6] References inserted: Human Fertilisation and Embryology Act 2008, s 56, Sch 6, Pt 1, para 29. [7] Words inserted or repealed: Children and Young Persons Act 2008, s 37(3)(a).

Definitions. 'A section 8 order': s 8(2); 'care order': ss 31(11), 105(1); 'child': s 105(1); 'child assessment order': s 43(2); 'education supervision order': s 36(2); 'emergency protection order': s 44(4); 'residence order': s 8(1); 'supervision order': s 31(11); 'the court': s 92(7).

Jurisdiction and procedure etc

92 Jurisdiction of courts

(1) The name 'domestic proceedings', given to certain proceedings in magistrates' courts, is hereby changed to 'family proceedings' and the names 'domestic court' and 'domestic court panel' are hereby changed to 'family proceedings court' and 'family panel', respectively.

(2) Proceedings under this Act shall be treated as family proceedings in relation to magistrates' courts.

(3) Subsection (2) is subject to the provisions of section 65(1) and (2) of the Magistrates' Courts Act 1980 (proceedings which may be treated as not being family proceedings), as amended by this Act.

(4) A magistrates' court shall not be competent to entertain any application, or make any order, involving the administration or application of –

(a) any property belonging to or held in trust for a child; or
(b) the income of any such property.

(5) The powers of a magistrates' court under section 63(2) of the Act of 1980 to suspend or rescind orders shall not apply in relation to any order made under this Act.

(6) Part I of Schedule 11 makes provision, including provision for the Lord Chancellor to make orders, with respect to the jurisdiction of courts and justices of the peace in relation to –

(a) proceedings under this Act; and
(b) proceedings under certain other enactments.

(7) For the purposes of this Act 'the court' means the High Court, a county court or a magistrates' court.

(8) Subsection (7) is subject to the provision made by or under Part I of Schedule 11 and to any express provision as to the jurisdiction of any court made by any other provision of this Act.

(9) The Lord Chancellor may[, after consulting the Lord Chief Justice,]¹ by order make provision for the principal registry of the Family Division of the High Court to be treated as if it were a county court for such purposes of this Act, or of any provision made under this Act, as may be specified in the order.

(10) Any order under subsection (9) may make such provision as the Lord Chancellor thinks expedient[, after consulting the Lord Chief Justice,]¹ for the purpose of applying (with or without modifications) provisions which apply in relation to the procedure in county courts to the principal registry when it acts as if it were a county court.

[(10A) The Lord Chief Justice may nominate a judicial office holder (as defined in section 109(4) of the Constitutional Reform Act 2005) to exercise his functions under subsection (9) or (10).]¹

(11) Part II of Schedule 11 makes amendments consequential on this section.

NOTES

Amendments.¹ Words and subsection inserted: Constitutional Reform Act 2005, s 15(1), Sch 4, Pt 1, paras 203, 205(1)–(4).

Definitions. 'Family panel': s 92(1); 'family proceedings': s 92(2); 'family proceedings court': s 92(1); 'the court': s 92(7).

93 Rules of Court

(1) An authority having power to make rules of court may make such provision for giving effect to –

- (a) this Act;
- (b) the provisions of any statutory instrument made under this Act; or
- (c) any amendment made by this Act in any other enactment,

as appears to that authority to be necessary or expedient.

(2) The rules may, in particular, make provision –

- (a) with respect to the procedure to be followed in any relevant proceedings (including the manner in which any application is to be made or other proceedings commenced);
- (b) as to the persons entitled to participate in any relevant proceedings, whether as parties to the proceedings or by being given the opportunity to make representations to the court;
- [(bb) for children to be separately represented in relevant proceedings,][2]
- (c) with respect to the documents and information to be furnished, and notices to be given, in connection with any relevant proceedings;
- (d) applying (with or without modification) enactments which govern the procedure to be followed with respect to proceedings brought on a complaint made to a magistrates' court to relevant proceedings in such a court brought otherwise than on a complaint;
- (e) with respect to preliminary hearings;
- (f) for the service outside [England and Wales][1], in such circumstances and in such manner as may be prescribed, of any notice of proceedings in a magistrates' court;
- (g) for the exercise by magistrates' courts, in such circumstances as may be prescribed, of such powers as may be prescribed (even though a party to the proceedings in question is [or resides][1] outside England and Wales);
- (h) enabling the court, in such circumstances as may be prescribed, to proceed on any application even though the respondent has not been given notice of the proceedings;
- (i) authorising a single justice to discharge the functions of a magistrates' court with respect to such relevant proceedings as may be prescribed;
- (j) authorising a magistrates' court to order any of the parties to such relevant proceedings as may be prescribed, in such circumstances as may be prescribed, to pay the whole or part of the costs of all or any of the other parties.

(3) In subsection (2) –

'notice of proceedings' means a summons or such other notice of proceedings as is required; and 'given', in relation to a summons, means 'served';

'prescribed' means prescribed by the rules; and

'relevant proceedings' means any application made, or proceedings brought, under any of the provisions mentioned in paragraphs (a) to (c) of subsection (1) and any part of such proceedings.

(4) This section and any other power in this Act to make rules of court are not to be taken as in any way limiting any other power of the authority in question to make rules of court.

(5) When making any rules under this section an authority shall be subject to the same requirements as to consultation (if any) as apply when the authority makes rules under its general rule making power.

NOTES

Amendments.[1] Words substituted and inserted: Courts and Legal Services Act 1990, s 116, Sch 16, para 22.[2] Paragraph inserted: Adoption and Children Act 2002, s 122(2).

Definitions. 'Notice of proceedings': s 93(3); 'prescribed': s 93(3); 'relevant proceedings': s 93(3); 'the court': s 92(7).

94 Appeals

(1) [Subject to any express provision to the contrary made by or under this Act, an][1] appeal shall lie to [a county court][4] against –

(a) the making by a magistrates' court of any order under this Act [or the Adoption and Children Act 2002][2]; or

(b) any refusal by a magistrates' court to make such an order.

(2) Where a magistrates' court has power, in relation to any proceedings under this Act [or the Adoption and Children Act 2002][2], to decline jurisdiction because it considers that the case can more conveniently be dealt with by another court, no appeal shall lie against any exercise by that magistrates' court of that power.

(3) Subsection (1) does not apply in relation to an interim order for periodical payments made under Schedule 1.

(4) On an appeal under this section, [a county court][4] may make such orders as may be necessary to give effect to its determination of the appeal.

(5) Where an order is made under subsection (4) [a county court][4] may also make such incidental or consequential orders as appear to it to be just.

(6) Where an appeal from a magistrates' court relates to an order for the making of periodical payments, [a county court][4] may order that its determination of the appeal shall have effect from such date as it thinks fit to specify in the order.

(7) The date so specified must not be earlier than the earliest date allowed in accordance with rules of court made for the purposes of this section.

(8) Where, on an appeal under this section in respect of an order requiring a person to make periodical payments, [a county court][4] reduces the amount of those payments or discharges the order –

(a) it may order the person entitled to the payments to pay to the person making them such sum in respect of payments already made as [the county court]⁴ thinks fit; and
(b) if any arrears are due under the order for periodical payments, it may remit payment of the whole, or part, of those arrears.

(9) Any order of [a county court]⁴ made on an appeal under this section (other than one directing that an application be re-heard by a magistrates' court) shall, for the purposes –

(a) of the enforcement of the order; and
(b) of any power to vary, revive or discharge orders,

be treated as if it were an order of the magistrates' court from which the appeal was brought and not an order of [a county court]⁴.

(10) The Lord Chancellor may[, after consulting the Lord Chief Justice,]³ by order make provision as to the circumstances in which appeals may be made against decisions taken by courts on questions arising in connection with the transfer, or proposed transfer, of proceedings by virtue of any order under paragraph 2 of Schedule 11.

(11) Except to the extent provided for in any order made under subsection (10), no appeal may be made against any decision of a kind mentioned in that subsection.

[(12) The Lord Chief Justice may nominate a judicial office holder (as defined in section 109(4) of the Constitutional Reform Act 2005) to exercise his functions under subsection (10).]³

NOTES

Amendments.[1] Words inserted: Courts and Legal Services Act 1990, s 116, Sch 16, para 23.[2] Words inserted: Adoption and Children Act 2002, s 100.[3] Words and subsection inserted: Constitutional Reform Act 2005, s 15(1), Sch 4, Pt 1, paras 203, 206(1)–(3).[4] Words substituted: SI 2009/871.

95 Attendance of child at hearing under Part IV or V

(1) In any proceedings in which a court is hearing an application for an order under Part IV or V, or is considering whether to make any such order, the court may order the child concerned to attend such stage or stages of the proceedings as may be specified in the order.

(2) The power conferred by subsection (1) shall be exercised in accordance with rules of court.

(3) Subsections (4) to (6) apply where –

(a) an order under subsection (1) has not been complied with; or
(b) the court has reasonable cause to believe that it will not be complied with.

(4) The court may make an order authorising a constable, or such person as may be specified in the order –

(a) to take charge of the child and to bring him to the court; and

(b) to enter and search any premises specified in the order if he has reasonable cause to believe that the child may be found on the premises.

(5) The court may order any person who is in a position to do so to bring the child to the court.

(6) Where the court has reason to believe that a person has information about the whereabouts of the child it may order him to disclose it to the court.

NOTES

Definitions. 'Child': s 105(1); 'the court': s 92(7).

96 Evidence given by, or with respect to, children

(1) Subsection (2) applies in any civil proceedings where a child who is called as a witness in any civil proceedings does not, in the opinion of the court, understand the nature of an oath.

(2) The child's evidence may be heard by the court if, in its opinion –

(a) he understands that it is his duty to speak the truth; and
(b) he has sufficient understanding to justify his evidence being heard.

(3) The Lord Chancellor may[, with the concurrence of the Lord Chief Justice,][2] by order make provision for the admissibility of evidence which would otherwise be inadmissible under any rule of law relating to hearsay.

(4) An order under subsection (3) may only be made with respect to –

(a) civil proceedings in general or such civil proceedings, or class of civil proceedings, as may be prescribed; and
(b) evidence in connection with the upbringing, maintenance or welfare of a child.

(5) An order under subsection (3) –

(a) may, in particular, provide for the admissibility of statements which are made orally or in a prescribed form or which are recorded by any prescribed method of recording;
(b) may make different provision for different purposes and in relation to different descriptions of court; and
(c) may make such amendments and repeals in any enactment relating to evidence (other than in this Act) as the Lord Chancellor considers necessary or expedient in consequence of the provision made by the order.

(6) Subsection (5)(b) is without prejudice to section 104(4).

(7) In this section –

['civil proceedings' means civil proceedings, before any tribunal, in relation to which the strict rules of evidence apply, whether as a matter of law or by agreement of the parties, and references to 'the court' shall be construed accordingly;][1] and

Part I Statutes

'prescribed' means prescribed by an order under subsection (3).

NOTES

Amendments.[1] Definition substituted: Civil Evidence Act 1995, s 15(1), Sch 1, para 16. [2] Words inserted: Constitutional Reform Act 2005, s 15(1), Sch 4, Pt 1, paras 203, 207.

Definitions. 'Child': s 105(1); 'civil proceedings': s 96(7); 'court': s 92(7); 'prescribed': s 96(7); 'upbringing': s 105(1).

97 Privacy for children involved in certain proceedings

(1) Rules made under section 144 of the Magistrates' Courts Act 1980 may make provision for a magistrates' court to sit in private in proceedings in which any powers under this Act [or the Adoption and Children Act 2002][6] may be exercised by the court with respect to any child.

(2) No person shall publish [to the public at large or any section of the public][5] any material which is intended, or likely, to identify –

   (a) any child as being involved in any proceedings before [the High Court, a county court or][4] a magistrates' court in which any power under this Act [or the Adoption and Children Act 2002][6] may be exercised by the court with respect to that or any other child; or
   (b) an address or school as being that of a child involved in any such proceedings.

(3) In any proceedings for an offence under this section it shall be a defence for the accused to prove that he did not know, and had no reason to suspect, that the published material was intended, or likely, to identify the child.

(4) The court or the [Lord Chancellor][3] may, if satisfied that the welfare of the child requires it [and, in the case of the Lord Chancellor, if the Lord Chief Justice agrees][7], by order dispense with the requirements of subsection (2) to such extent as may be specified in the order.

(5) For the purposes of this section –

   'publish' includes –
      (a) include in a programme service (within the meaning of the Broadcasting Act 1990);][1] or
      (b) cause to be published; and

   'material' includes any picture or representation.

(6) Any person who contravenes this section shall be guilty of an offence and liable, on summary conviction, to a fine not exceeding level 4 on the standard scale.

(7) Subsection (1) is without prejudice to –

   (a) the generality of the rule making power in section 144 of the Act of 1980; or
   (b) any other power of a magistrates' court to sit in private.

(8) [Sections 69 (sittings of magistrates' courts for family proceedings) and 71 (newspaper reports of certain proceedings) of the Act of 1980]² shall apply in relation to any proceedings [(before a magistrates' court)]⁴ to which this section applies subject to the provisions of this section.

[(9) The Lord Chief Justice may nominate a judicial office holder (as defined in section 109(4) of the Constitutional Reform Act 2005) to exercise his functions under subsection (4).]⁷

NOTES

Amendments.¹ Words substituted: Broadcasting Act 1990, s 203(1), Sch 20, para 53.² Words substituted: Courts and Legal Services Act 1990, s 116, Sch 16, para 24.³ Words substituted: Transfer of Functions (Magistrates' Courts and Family Law) Order 1992, SI 1992/709.⁴ Words inserted: Access to Justice Act 1999, s 72.⁵ Words inserted: Children Act 2004, s 62(1).⁶ Words inserted: Adoption and Children Act 2002, s 101(3).⁷ Words and subsection inserted: Constitutional Reform Act 2005, s 15(1), Sch 4, Pt 1, paras 203, 208(1)–(3).

Definitions. 'Child': s 105(1); 'material': s 97(5); 'publish': s 97(5); 'school': s 105(1); 'the court': s 92(7).

98 Self-incrimination

(1) In any proceedings in which a court is hearing an application for an order under Part IV or V, no person shall be excused from –

(a) giving evidence on any matter; or
(b) answering any question put to him in the course of his giving evidence,

on the ground that doing so might incriminate him or his spouse [or civil partner]¹ of an offence.

(2) A statement or admission made in such proceedings shall not be admissible in evidence against the person making it or his spouse [or civil partner]¹ in proceedings for an offence other than perjury.

NOTES

Amendments.¹ Words inserted: Civil Partnership Act 2004, s 261(1), Sch 27, para 132.

99

…¹

NOTES

Amendments.¹ Section repealed: Access to Justice Act 1999, s 106, Sch 15, Pt I.

100 Restrictions on use of wardship jurisdiction

(1) Section 7 of the Family Law Reform Act 1969 (which gives the High Court power to place a ward of court in the care, or under the supervision, of a local authority) shall cease to have effect.

(2) No court shall exercise the High Court's inherent jurisdiction with respect to children –

(a) so as to require a child to be placed in the care, or put under the supervision, of a local authority;
(b) so as to require a child to be accommodated by or on behalf of a local authority;
(c) so as to make a child who is the subject of a care order a ward of court; or
(d) for the purpose of conferring on any local authority power to determine any question which has arisen, or which may arise, in connection with any aspect of parental responsibility for a child.

(3) No application for any exercise of the court's inherent jurisdiction with respect to children may be made by a local authority unless the authority have obtained the leave of the court.

(4) The court may only grant leave if it is satisfied that –

(a) the result which the authority wish to achieve could not be achieved through the making of any order of a kind to which subsection (5) applies; and
(b) there is reasonable cause to believe that if the court's inherent jurisdiction is not exercised with respect to the child he is likely to suffer significant harm.

(5) This subsection applies to any order –

(a) made otherwise than in the exercise of the court's inherent jurisdiction; and
(b) which the local authority is entitled to apply for (assuming, in the case of any application which may only be made with leave, that leave is granted).

NOTES

Definitions. 'Care order': ss 31(11), 105(1); 'child': s 105(1); 'harm': s 31(9); 'local authority': s 105(1); 'parental responsibility': s 3; 'significant harm': s 31(10); 'the court': s 92(7).

101 Effect of orders as between England and Wales and Northern Ireland, the Channel Islands or the Isle of Man

(1) The Secretary of State may make regulations providing –

(a) for prescribed orders which –
   (i) are made by a court in Northern Ireland; and
   (ii) appear to the Secretary of State to correspond in their effect to orders which may be made under any provision of this Act,
   to have effect in prescribed circumstances, for prescribed purposes of this Act, as if they were orders of a prescribed kind made under this Act;
(b) for prescribed orders which –
   (i) are made by a court in England and Wales; and
   (ii) appear to the Secretary of State to correspond in their effect to orders which may be made under any provision in force in Northern Ireland,

to have effect in prescribed circumstances, for prescribed purposes of the law of Northern Ireland, as if they were orders of a prescribed kind made in Northern Ireland.

(2) Regulations under subsection (1) may provide for the order concerned to cease to have effect for the purposes of the law of Northern Ireland, or (as the case may be) the law of England and Wales, if prescribed conditions are satisfied.

(3) The Secretary of State may make regulations providing for prescribed orders which –

(a) are made by a court in the Isle of Man or in any of the Channel Islands; and
(b) appear to the Secretary of State to correspond in their effect to orders which may be made under this Act,

to have effect in prescribed circumstances for prescribed purposes of this Act, as if they were orders of a prescribed kind made under this Act.

(4) Where a child who is in the care of a local authority is lawfully taken to live in Northern Ireland, the Isle of Man or in any of the Channel Islands, the care order in question shall cease to have effect if the conditions prescribed in regulations by the Secretary of State are satisfied.

(5) Any regulations made under this section may –

(a) make such consequential amendments (including repeals) in –
   (i) section 25 of the Children and Young Persons Act 1969 (transfers between England and Wales and Northern Ireland); or
   (ii) section 26 (transfers between England and Wales and Channel Islands or Isle of Man) of that Act,
   as the Secretary of State considers necessary or expedient; and
(b) modify any provision of this Act, in its application (by virtue of the regulations) in relation to an order made otherwise than in England and Wales.

NOTES

Definitions. 'Care order': ss 31(11), 105(1); 'child': s 105(1); 'local authority': s 105(1); 'prescribed': s 105(1); 'the court': s 92(7).

Search warrants

102 Power of constable to assist in exercise of certain powers to search for children or inspect premises

(1) Where, on an application made by any person for a warrant under this section, it appears to the court –

(a) that a person attempting to exercise powers under any enactment mentioned in subsection (6) has been prevented from doing so by being refused entry to the premises concerned or refused access to the child concerned; or

(b) that any such person is likely to be so prevented from exercising any such powers,

it may issue a warrant authorising any constable to assist that person in the exercise of those powers, using reasonable force if necessary.

(2) Every warrant issued under this section shall be addressed to, and executed by, a constable who shall be accompanied by the person applying for the warrant if –

(a) that person so desires; and
(b) the court by whom the warrant is issued does not direct otherwise.

(3) A court granting an application for a warrant under this section may direct that the constable concerned may, in executing the warrant, be accompanied by a registered medical practitioner, registered nurse or [registered midwife]^1 if he so chooses.

[(3A) The reference in subsection (3) to a registered midwife is to such a midwife who is also registered in the Specialist Community Public Health Nurses' Part of the register maintained under article 5 of the Nursing and Midwifery Order 2001.]^2

(4) An application for a warrant under this section shall be made in the manner and form prescribed by rules of court.

(5) Where –

(a) an application for a warrant under this section relates to a particular child; and
(b) it is reasonably practicable to do so,

the application and any warrant granted on the application shall name the child; and where it does not name him it shall describe him as clearly as possible.

(6) The enactments are –

(a) sections 62, 64, 67, 76, 80, 86 and 87;
(b) paragraph 8(1)(b) and (2)(b) of Schedule 3;
(c) …^{3}

NOTES

Amendments.^{1} Words substituted: SI 2002/253.^{2} Subsection inserted: SI 2004/1771.^{3} Paragraph repealed: Adoption and Children Act 2002, s 139(1), (3), Sch 3, paras 54, 69, Sch 5.

Definitions. 'Child': s 105(1); 'the court': s 92(7).

General

103 Offences by bodies corporate

(1) This section applies where any offence under this Act is committed by a body corporate.

(2) If the offence is proved to have been committed with the consent or connivance of or to be attributable to any neglect on the part of any director, manager, secretary or other similar officer of the body corporate, or any person who was purporting to act in any such capacity, he (as well as the body corporate) shall be guilty of the offence and shall be liable to be proceeded against and punished accordingly.

104 Regulations and orders

(1) Any power of the Lord Chancellor[, the Treasury][2][, the Secretary of State or the National Assembly for Wales][4] under this Act to make an order, regulations, or rules, except an order under section ...[1] 56(4)(a), 57(3), 84 or 97(4) or paragraph 1(1) of Schedule 4, shall be exercisable by statutory instrument.

(2) Any such statutory instrument, except one made under section [4(1)(b),][3] [4ZA(3),][6] 17(4), 107 or 108(2) [or one containing regulations which fall within subsection (3B) or (3C)][7], shall be subject to annulment in pursuance of a resolution of either House of Parliament.

[(2A) ...[8]][5]

[(3A) An order under section 4(1B)[, 4ZA(3)][11] or 17(4) or regulations which fall within subsection (3B) or (3C) shall not be made by the Secretary of State unless a draft of the statutory instrument containing the order or regulations has been laid before, and approved by a resolution of, each House of Parliament.

(3B) Regulations fall within this subsection if they are the first regulations to be made by the Secretary of State in the exercise of the power conferred by section 23C(5B)(b).

(3C) Regulations fall within this subsection if they are the first regulations to be made by the Secretary of State in the exercise of the power conferred by paragraph 6(2) of Schedule 2.][9]

(4) Any statutory instrument made under this Act may –

    (a)   make different provision for different cases;
    (b)   provide for exemptions from any of its provisions; and
    (c)   contain ...[10] incidental, supplemental and transitional provisions ...[10].

NOTES

Amendments.[1] Word repealed: Care Standards Act 2000, s 117, Sch 6.[2] Words inserted: Tax Credits Act 2002, s 47, Sch 3.[3] Words inserted: Adoption and Children Act 2002, s 111(6).[4] Words substituted: Children and Adoption Act 2006, s 15(1), Sch 2, paras 7, 10(a).[5] Subsection inserted: Children and Adoption Act 2006, s 15(1), Sch 2, paras 7, 10(b).[6] Reference inserted: Human Fertilisation and Embryology Act 2008, s 56, Sch 6, Pt 1, para 30(a).[7] Words inserted: Children and Young Persons Act 2008, s 39, Sch 3, paras 1, 25(1), (2).[8] Subsection repealed: Children and Young Persons Act 2008, ss 39, 42, Sch 3, paras 1, 25(1), (3), Sch 4.[9] Subsections substituted: Children and Young Persons Act 2008, s 39, Sch 3, paras 1, 25(1), (4).[10] Words repealed: Children and Young Persons Act 2008, ss 39, 42, Sch 3, paras 1, 25(1), (5), Sch 4.[11] Reference inserted: SI 2009/1892.

[104A Regulations and orders made by the Welsh Ministers under Part 3 etc

(1) Any power of the Welsh Ministers under Part 3, Part 7 or section 86A to make an order or regulations shall be exercisable by statutory instrument.

(2) Any such statutory instrument, except one made under section 17(4) or one containing regulations which fall within subsection (4) or (5), shall be subject to annulment in pursuance of a resolution of the National Assembly for Wales.

(3) An order under section 17(4) or regulations which fall within subsection (4) or (5) shall not be made by the Welsh Ministers unless a draft of the statutory instrument containing the order or regulations has been laid before and approved by a resolution of the National Assembly for Wales.

(4) Regulations fall within this subsection if they are the first regulations to be made by the Welsh Ministers in the exercise of the power conferred by section 23C(5B)(b).

(5) Regulations fall within this subsection if they are the first regulations to be made by the Welsh Ministers in the exercise of the power conferred by paragraph 6(2) of Schedule 2.][1]

NOTES

Amendments.[1] Section inserted: Children and Young Persons Act 2008, s 39, Sch 3, paras 1, 26.

105 Interpretation

(1) In this Act –

'adoption agency' means a body which may be referred to as an adoption agency by virtue of [section 2 of the Adoption and Children Act 2002][16];
['appropriate children's home' has the meaning given by section 23;][12]
'bank holiday' means a day which is a bank holiday under the Banking and Financial Dealings Act 1971;
['care home' has the same meaning as in the Care Standards Act 2000;][12]
'care order' has the meaning given by section 31(11) and also includes any order which by or under any enactment has the effect of, or is deemed to be, a care order for the purposes of this Act; and any reference to a child who is in the care of an authority is a reference to a child who is in their care by virtue of a care order;
'child' means, subject to paragraph 16 of Schedule 1, a person under the age of eighteen;
'child assessment order' has the meaning given by section 43(2);
'child minder' has the meaning given by section 71;
['child of the family', in relation to parties to a marriage, or to two people who are civil partners of each other, means –
   (a)   a child of both of them, and
   (b)   any other child, other than a child placed with them as foster parents by a local authority or voluntary organisation, who has been treated by both of them as a child of their family;][19]

['children's home', has the meaning given by section 23;][12]

'community home' has the meaning given by section 53;
['contact activity condition' has the meaning given by section 11C;
'contact activity direction' has the meaning given by section 11A;][22]
'contact order' has the meaning given by section 8(1);
'day care' [(except in Part XA)][11] has the same meaning as in section 18;
'disabled', in relation to a child, has the same meaning as in section 17(11); ...[3]
'domestic premises' has the meaning given by section 71(12);
['dwelling-house' includes –
    (a) any building or part of a building which is occupied as a dwelling;
    (b) any caravan, house-boat or structure which is occupied as a dwelling; and any yard, garage or outhouse belonging to it and occupied with it;][6]

['education functions' has the meaning given by section 579(1) of the Education Act 1996;][27]
'education supervision order' has the meaning given in section 36;
'emergency protection order' means an order under section 44;
['enforcement order' has the meaning given by section 11J;][22]
'family assistance order' has the meaning given in section 16(2);
'family proceedings' has the meaning given by section 8(3);
'functions' includes powers and duties;
'guardian of a child' means a guardian (other than a guardian of the estate of a child) appointed in accordance with the provisions of section 5;
'harm' has the same meaning as in section 31(9) and the question of whether harm is significant shall be determined in accordance with section 31(10);
[...[20]][3]
'health service hospital' [means a health service hospital within the meaning given by the National Health Service Act 2006 or the National Health Service (Wales) Act 2006][20];
'hospital' [(except in Schedule 9A)][12] has the same meaning as in the Mental Health Act 1983, except that it does not include a [hospital at which high security psychiatric services within the meaning of that Act are provided][7];
'ill-treatment' has the same meaning as in section 31(9);
['income-based jobseeker's allowance' has the same meaning as in the Jobseekers Act 1995;][4]
['income-related employment and support allowance' means an income-related allowance under Part 1 of the Welfare Reform Act 2007 (employment and support allowance);][23]
['independent hospital' has the same meaning as in the Care Standards Act 2000;][12]
['*independent hospital*' –
    (a) *in relation to England, means a hospital as defined by section 275 of the National Health Service Act 2006 that is not a health service hospital as defined by that section; and*
    (b) *in relation to Wales, has the same meaning as in the Care Standards Act 2000;*][28]

'independent school' has the same meaning as in [the Education Act 1996]⁵;
'local authority' means, in relation to England ...², the council of a county, a metropolitan district, a London Borough or the Common Council of the City of London [, in relation to Wales, the council of a county or a county borough]² and, in relation to Scotland, a local authority within the meaning of section 1(2) of the Social Work (Scotland) Act 1968;
'local authority foster parent' has the same meaning as in section 23(3);
['Local Health Board' means a Local Health Board established under section 11 of the National Health Service (Wales) Act 2006;]²¹
...²⁷
'local housing authority' has the same meaning as in the Housing Act 1985;
...¹²
['officer of the Service' has the same meaning as in the Criminal Justice and Court Services Act 2000;]⁹
'parental responsibility' has the meaning given in section 3;
'parental responsibility agreement' has the meaning given in [sections 4(1)[, 4ZA(4)]²⁴ and 4A(2)]¹⁶;
'prescribed' means prescribed by regulations made under this Act;
['private children's home' means a children's home in respect of which a person is registered under Part II of the Care Standards Act 2000 which is not a community home or a voluntary home;]¹²
['Primary Care Trust' means a Primary Care Trust established under [section 18 of the National Health Service Act 2006]²⁰;]⁷
'privately fostered child' and 'to foster a child privately' have the same meaning as in section 66;
'prohibited steps order' has the meaning given by section 8(1);
...¹⁸
...¹²
'registered pupil' has the same meaning as in [the Education Act 1996]⁵;
'relative', in relation to a child, means a grandparent, brother, sister, uncle or aunt (whether of the full blood or half blood or [by marriage or civil partnership)]¹⁹ or step-parent;
'residence order' has the meaning given by section 8(1);
...¹²
'responsible person', in relation to a child who is the subject of a supervision order, has the meaning given in paragraph 1 of Schedule 3;
'school' has the same meaning as in [the Education Act 1996]⁵ or, in relation to Scotland, in the Education (Scotland) Act 1980;
['section 31A plan' has the meaning given by section 31A(6);]¹⁷
'service', in relation to any provision made under Part III, includes any facility;
'signed', in relation to any person, includes the making by that person of his mark;
'special educational needs' has the same meaning as in [the Education Act 1993]⁵;
['special guardian' and 'special guardianship order' have the meaning given by section 14A;]¹⁷

['Special Health Authority' means a Special Health Authority established under [section 28 of the National Health Service Act 2006 or section 22 of the National Health Service (Wales) Act 2006,][20];][3]

'specific issue order' has the meaning given by section 8(1);

['Strategic Health Authority' means a Strategic Health Authority established under [section 13 of the National Health Service Act 2006][20];][13]

'supervision order' has the meaning given by section 31(11);

'supervised child' and 'supervisor', in relation to a supervision order or an education supervision order, mean respectively the child who is (or is to be) under supervision and the person under whose supervision he is (or is to be) by virtue of the order;

'upbringing', in relation to any child, includes the care of the child but not his maintenance;

'voluntary home' has the meaning given by section 60;

'voluntary organisation' means a body (other than a public or local authority) whose activities are not carried on for profit.

['Welsh family proceedings officer' has the meaning given by section 35 of the Children Act 2004][15].

(2) References in this Act to a child whose father and mother were, or (as the case may be) were not, married to each other at the time of his birth must be read with section 1 of the Family Law Reform Act 1987 (which extends the meaning of such references).

(3) References in this Act to –

(a) a person with whom a child lives, or is to live, as the result of a residence order; or

(b) a person in whose favour a residence order is in force,

shall be construed as references to the person named in the order as the person with whom the child is to live.

(4) References in this Act to a child who is looked after by a local authority have the same meaning as they have (by virtue of section 22) in Part III.

(5) References in this Act to accommodation provided by or on behalf of a local authority are references to accommodation so provided in the exercise of functions [of that or any other local authority which are social services functions within the meaning of][10] the Local Authority Social Services Act 1970.

[(5A) References in this Act to a child minder shall be construed –

(a) ...[14]

(b) in relation to ...[25] Wales, in accordance with section 79A.][11]

[(5B) *(Applies to Scotland only)*][14]

(6) In determining the 'ordinary residence' of a child for any purpose of this Act, there shall be disregarded any period in which he lives in any place –

(a) which is a school or other institution;

(b) in accordance with the requirements of a supervision order under this Act ...[26]

[(ba) in accordance with the requirements of a youth rehabilitation order under Part 1 of the Criminal Justice and Immigration Act 2008; or][26]

(c) while he is being provided with accommodation by or on behalf of a local authority.

(7) References in this Act to children who are in need shall be construed in accordance with section 17.

(8) Any notice or other document required under this Act to be served on any person may be served on him by being delivered personally to him, or being sent by post to him in a registered letter or by the recorded delivery service at his proper address.

(9) Any such notice or other document required to be served on a body corporate or a firm shall be duly served if it is served on the secretary or clerk of that body or a partner of that firm.

(10) For the purposes of this section, and of section 7 of the Interpretation Act 1978 in its application to this section, the proper address of a person –

(a) in the case of a secretary or clerk of a body corporate, shall be that of the registered or principal office of that body;
(b) in the case of a partner of a firm, shall be that of the principal office of the firm; and
(c) in any other case, shall be the last known address of the person to be served.

NOTES

Amendments.[1] Words inserted: Registered Homes (Amendment) Act 1991, s 2(6).[2] Words repealed or inserted: Local Government (Wales) Act 1994, Sch 10, para 13, Sch 18.[3] Definitions repealed or substituted: Health Authorities Act 1995, ss 2(1), 5(1), Sch 1, Pt III, para 118(1), (10).[4] Definition inserted: Jobseekers Act 1995, s 41(4), Sch 2, para 19.[5] Words substituted: Education Act 1996, s 582(1), Sch 37, Pt I, para 91.[6] Definition inserted: Family Law Act 1996, s 52, Sch 6, para 5.[7] Definitions inserted or amended: Health Act 1999 (Supplementary, Consequential etc Provisions) Order 2000, SI 2000/90.[8] Words substituted: Powers of Criminal Courts (Sentencing) Act 2000, s 165(1), Sch 9, para 128.[9] Definition inserted: Criminal Justice and Court Services Act 2000, s 74, Sch 7, paras 87, 95.[10] Words substituted: Local Government Act 2000, s 107, Sch 5, para 22.[11] Definition amended and subsection inserted: Care Standards Act 2000, s 116, Sch 4, para 14(1), 23.[12] Definitions and words repealed, inserted and substituted: Care Standards Act 2000, s 116, Sch 4, para 14(23).[13] Definition inserted: National Health Service Reform and Health Care Professions Act 2002 (Supplementary, Consequential etc Provisions) Regulations 2002, SI 2002/2469.[14] Paragraph repealed and subsection inserted: Regulation of Care (Scotland) Act 2001, s 79, Sch 3, para 15.[15] Definition inserted: Children Act 2004, s 40, Sch 3, paras 5, 11.[16] Words substituted: Adoption and Children Act 2002, s 139(1), Sch 3, paras 54, 70(a),(c).[17] Definition inserted: Adoption and Children Act 2002, s 139(1), Sch 3, paras 54, 70(b), (e).[18] Definition repealed: Adoption and Children Act 2002, s 139(1), Sch 3, paras 54, 70(d).[19] Definition and words substituted: Civil Partnership Act 2004, s 75(1), (3), (4).[20] Words repealed and substituted: National Health Service (Consequential Provisions) Act 2006, s 2, Sch 1, paras 124, 125.[21] Definition inserted: SI 2007/961.[22] Definitions inserted: Children and Adoption Act 2006, s 15(1), Sch 2, paras 7, 11.[23] Definition inserted: Welfare Reform Act 2007, s 28(1), Sch 3, para 6(1), (5).[24] Reference inserted: Human Fertilisation and Embryology Act 2008, s 56, Sch 6, Pt 1, para 31.[25] Words repealed: Childcare Act 2006, s 103, Sch 2, para 17, Sch 3, Pt 2. [26] Words repealed and paragraph inserted: Criminal Justice and Immigration Act 2008, ss 6(2), 149, Sch 4,

Pt 1, paras 33, 36, Sch 28, Pt 1. [27] Definitions inserted and repealed: SI 2010/1158. [28] Definition 'independent hospital' in italics prospectively substituted for preceding definition with effect from 1 October 2010: SI 2010/813.

106 Financial provisions

(1) Any –

(a) grants made by the Secretary of State under this Act; and
(b) any other expenses incurred by the Secretary of State under this Act,

shall be payable out of money provided by Parliament.

(2) Any sums received by the Secretary of State under section 58, or by way of the repayment of any grant made under section 82(2) or (4) shall be paid into the Consolidated Fund.

107 Application to the Channel Islands

Her Majesty may by Order in Council direct that any of the provisions of this Act shall extend to any of the Channel Islands with such exceptions and modifications as may be specified in the Order.

108 Short title, commencement, extent, etc

(1) This Act may be cited as the Children Act 1989.

(2) Sections 89 and 96(3) to (7), and paragraph 35 of Schedule 12, shall come into force on the passing of this Act and paragraph 36 of Schedule 12 shall come into force at the end of the period of two months beginning with the day on which this Act is passed but otherwise this Act shall come into force on such date as may be appointed by order made by the Lord Chancellor or the Secretary of State, or by both acting jointly.

(3) Different dates may be appointed for different provisions of this Act in relation to different cases.

(4) The minor amendments set out in Schedule 12 shall have effect.

(5) The consequential amendments set out in Schedule 13 shall have effect.

(6) The transitional provisions and savings set out in Schedule 14 shall have effect.

(7) The repeals set out in Schedule 15 shall have effect.

(8) An order under subsection (2) may make such transitional provisions or savings as appear to the person making the order to be necessary or expedient in connection with the provisions brought into force by the order, including –

(a) provisions adding to or modifying the provisions of Schedule 14; and
(b) such adaptations –
  (i) of the provisions brought into force by the order; and
  (ii) of any provisions of this Act then in force,
  as appear to him necessary or expedient in consequence of the partial operation of this Act.

(9) The Lord Chancellor may by order make such amendments or repeals, in such enactments as may be specified in the order, as appear to him to be necessary or expedient in consequence of any provision of this Act.

(10) This Act shall, in its application to the Isles of Scilly, have effect subject to such exceptions, adaptations and modifications as the Secretary of State may by order prescribe.

(11) The following provisions of this Act extend to Scotland –

...²
section 25(8);
...²
section 88;
section 104 (so far as necessary);
section 105 (so far as necessary);
subsections (1) to (3), (8) and (9) and this subsection;
in Schedule 2, paragraph 24;
in Schedule 12, paragraphs 1, 7 to 10, 18, 27, 30(a) and 41 to 44;
in Schedule 13, paragraphs 18 to 23, 32, 46, 47, 50, 57, 62, 63, 68(a) and (b) and 71;
in Schedule 14, paragraphs 1, 33 and 34;
in Schedule 15, the entries relating to –
- (a) the Custody of Children Act 1891;
- (b) the Nurseries and Child Minders Regulation Act 1948;
- (c) section 53(3) of the Children and Young Persons Act 1963;
- (d) section 60 of the Health Services and Public Health Act 1968;
- (e) the Social Work (Scotland) Act 1968;
- (f) the Adoption (Scotland) Act 1978;
- (g) the Child Care Act 1980;
- (h) the Foster Children (Scotland) Act 1984;
- (i) the Child Abduction and Custody Act 1985; and
- (j) the Family Law Act 1986.

(12) The following provisions of this Act extend to Northern Ireland –

section 101(1)(b), (2) and (5)(a)(i);
subsections (1) to (3), (8) and (9) and this subsection;
in Schedule 2, paragraph 24;
in Schedule 12, paragraphs 7 to 10, 18 and 27;
in Schedule 13, paragraphs 21, 22, 46, 47, 57, 62, 63, 68(c) to (e) and 69 to 71;
in Schedule 14, paragraphs ...¹ 28 to 30 and 38(a); and
in Schedule 15, the entries relating to the Guardianship of Minors Act 1971, the Children Act 1975, the Child Care Act 1980, and the Family Law Act 1986.

NOTES

Amendments.[1] Word repealed: Courts and Legal Services Act 1990, ss 116, 125(7), Sch 16, para 25, Sch 20.[2] Words repealed: Regulation of Care (Scotland) Act 2001, s 80(1), Sch 4.

[SCHEDULE A1
ENFORCEMENT ORDERS

PART 1
UNPAID WORK REQUIREMENT

General

1. Subject to the modifications in paragraphs 2 and 3, Chapter 4 of Part 12 of the Criminal Justice Act 2003 has effect in relation to an enforcement order as it has effect in relation to a community order (within the meaning of Part 12 of that Act).

References to an offender

2. Subject to paragraph 3, references in Chapter 4 of Part 12 of the Criminal Justice Act 2003 to an offender are to be treated as including references to a person subject to an enforcement order.

Specific modifications

3. (1) The power of the Secretary of State by order under section 197(3) to amend the definition of 'responsible officer' and to make consequential amendments includes power to make any amendments of this Part (including further modifications of Chapter 4 of Part 12 of the Criminal Justice Act 2003) that appear to the Secretary of State to be necessary or expedient in consequence of any amendment made by virtue of section 197(3)(a) or (b).

(2) In section 198 (duties of responsible officer) –

   (a)   in subsection (1) –
       (i)   at the end of paragraph (a) insert 'and', and
       (ii) omit paragraph (c) and the word 'and' immediately preceding it, and
   (b)   after subsection (1) insert –

'(1A) Subsection (1B) applies where –

   (a)   an enforcement order is in force, and
   (b)   an officer of the Children and Family Court Advisory and Support Service or a Welsh family proceedings officer (as defined in section 35 of the Children Act 2004) is required under section 11M of the Children Act 1989 to report on matters relating to the order.

(1B) The officer of the Service or the Welsh family proceedings officer may request the responsible officer to report to him on such matters relating to the order as he may require for the purpose of making a report under section 11M(1)(c) or (d); and it shall be the duty of the responsible officer to comply with such a request.'

(3) In section 199 (unpaid work requirement) –

(a) in subsection (2) (minimum and maximum hours of unpaid work) for paragraph (b) substitute –

'(b) not more than 200.',

(b) omit subsections (3) and (4), and
(c) in subsection (5) for the words from the beginning to 'of them' substitute 'Where on the same occasion and in relation to the same person the court makes more than one enforcement order imposing an unpaid work requirement'.

(4) In section 200 (obligations of person subject to unpaid work requirement), for subsection (2) substitute –

'(2) Subject to paragraphs 7 and 9 of Schedule A1 to the Children Act 1989, the work required to be performed under an unpaid work requirement imposed by an enforcement order must be performed during a period of twelve months.

(2A) But the period of twelve months is not to run while the enforcement order is suspended under section 11J(9) of the Children Act 1989.'

(5) Section 217 (requirement to avoid conflict with religious beliefs, etc) is omitted.

(6) In section 218 (availability of arrangements in local area), subsection (1) (condition for imposition of unpaid work requirement) is omitted.

(7) Section 219 (provision of copies of relevant order) is omitted.

(8) The power of the Secretary of State to make rules under section 222 in relation to persons subject to relevant orders may also be exercised in relation to persons subject to enforcement orders.

(9) The power of the Secretary of State by order under section 223(1) to amend the provision mentioned in section 223(1)(a) includes power to amend this Part so as to make such modifications of Chapter 4 of Part 12 of the Criminal Justice Act 2003 as appear to the Secretary of State to be necessary or expedient in consequence of any amendment of the provision mentioned in section 223(1)(a).

PART 2
REVOCATION, AMENDMENT OR BREACH OF ENFORCEMENT ORDER

Power to revoke

4. (1) This paragraph applies where a court has made an enforcement order in respect of a person's failure to comply with a contact order and the enforcement order is in force.

(2) The court may revoke the enforcement order if it appears to the court that –

(a) in all the circumstances no enforcement order should have been made,

(b) having regard to circumstances which have arisen since the enforcement order was made, it would be appropriate for the enforcement order to be revoked, or

(c) having regard to the person's satisfactory compliance with the contact order or any contact order that has effect in its place, it would be appropriate for the enforcement order to be revoked.

(3) The enforcement order may be revoked by the court under sub-paragraph (2) of its own motion or on an application by the person subject to the enforcement order.

(4) In deciding whether to revoke the enforcement order under sub-paragraph (2)(b), the court is to take into account –

(a) the extent to which the person subject to the enforcement order has complied with it, and

(b) the likelihood that the person will comply with the contact order or any contact order that has effect in its place in the absence of an enforcement order.

(5) In deciding whether to revoke the enforcement order under sub-paragraph (2)(c), the court is to take into account the likelihood that the person will comply with the contact order or any contact order that has effect in its place in the absence of an enforcement order.

Amendment by reason of change of residence

5. (1) This paragraph applies where a court has made an enforcement order in respect of a person's failure to comply with a contact order and the enforcement order is in force.

(2) If the court is satisfied that the person has changed, or proposes to change, his residence from the local justice area specified in the order to another local justice area, the court may amend the order by substituting the other area for the area specified.

(3) The enforcement order may be amended by the court under sub-paragraph (2) of its own motion or on an application by the person subject to the enforcement order.

Amendment of hours specified under unpaid work requirement

6. (1) This paragraph applies where a court has made an enforcement order in respect of a person's failure to comply with a contact order and the enforcement order is in force.

(2) If it appears to the court that, having regard to circumstances that have arisen since the enforcement order was made, it would be appropriate to do so, the court may reduce the number of hours specified in the order (but not below the minimum specified in section 199(2)(a) of the Criminal Justice Act 2003).

(3) In amending the enforcement order under sub-paragraph (2), the court must be satisfied that the effect on the person of the enforcement order as

proposed to be amended is no more than is required to secure his compliance with the contact order or any contact order that has effect in its place.

(4) The enforcement order may be amended by the court under sub-paragraph (2) of its own motion or on an application by the person subject to the enforcement order.

Amendment to extend unpaid work requirement

7. (1) This paragraph applies where a court has made an enforcement order in respect of a person's failure to comply with a contact order and the enforcement order is in force.

(2) If it appears to the court that, having regard to circumstances that have arisen since the enforcement order was made, it would be appropriate to do so, the court may, in relation to the order, extend the period of twelve months specified in section 200(2) of the Criminal Justice Act 2003 (as substituted by paragraph 3).

(3) The period may be extended by the court under sub-paragraph (2) of its own motion or on an application by the person subject to the enforcement order.

Warning and report following breach

8. (1) This paragraph applies where a court has made an enforcement order in respect of a person's failure to comply with a contact order.

(2) If the responsible officer is of the opinion that the person has failed without reasonable excuse to comply with the unpaid work requirement imposed by the enforcement order, the officer must give the person a warning under this paragraph unless –

    (a)   the person has within the previous twelve months been given a warning under this paragraph in relation to a failure to comply with the unpaid work requirement, or

    (b)   the responsible officer reports the failure to the appropriate person.

(3) A warning under this paragraph must –

    (a)   describe the circumstances of the failure,

    (b)   state that the failure is unacceptable, and

    (c)   inform the person that, if within the next twelve months he again fails to comply with the unpaid work requirement, the warning and the subsequent failure will be reported to the appropriate person.

(4) The responsible officer must, as soon as practicable after the warning has been given, record that fact.

(5) If –

    (a)   the responsible officer has given a warning under this paragraph to a person subject to an enforcement order, and

(b) at any time within the twelve months beginning with the date on which the warning was given, the responsible officer is of the opinion that the person has since that date failed without reasonable excuse to comply with the unpaid work requirement imposed by the enforcement order,

the officer must report the failure to the appropriate person.

(6) A report under sub-paragraph (5) must include a report of the warning given to the person subject to the enforcement order.

(7) The appropriate person, in relation to an enforcement order, is the officer of the Service or the Welsh family proceedings officer who is required under section 11M to report on matters relating to the enforcement order.

(8) 'Responsible officer', in relation to a person subject to an enforcement order, has the same meaning as in section 197 of the Criminal Justice Act 2003 (as modified by paragraph 2).

Breach of an enforcement order

9. (1) This paragraph applies where a court has made an enforcement order ('the first order') in respect of a person's failure to comply with a contact order.

(2) If the court is satisfied beyond reasonable doubt that the person has failed to comply with the unpaid work requirement imposed by the first order, the court may –

(a) amend the first order so as to make the requirement more onerous, or
(b) make an enforcement order ('the second order') in relation to the person and (if the first order is still in force) provide for the second order to have effect either in addition to or in substitution for the first order.

(3) But the court may not exercise its powers under sub-paragraph (2) if it is satisfied that the person had a reasonable excuse for failing to comply with the unpaid work requirement imposed by the first order.

(4) The burden of proof as to the matter mentioned in sub-paragraph (3) lies on the person claiming to have had a reasonable excuse, and the standard of proof is the balance of probabilities.

(5) The court may exercise its powers under sub-paragraph (2) in relation to the first order only on the application of a person who would be able to apply under section 11J for an enforcement order if the failure to comply with the first order were a failure to comply with the contact order to which the first order relates.

(6) Where the person proposing to apply to the court is the child with respect to whom the contact order was made, subsections (6) and (7) of section 11J have effect in relation to the application as they have effect in relation to an application for an enforcement order.

(7) An application to the court to exercise its powers under sub-paragraph (2) may only be made while the first order is in force.

(8) The court may not exercise its powers under sub-paragraph (2) in respect of a failure by the person to comply with the unpaid work requirement imposed by the first order unless it is satisfied that before the failure occurred the person had been given (in accordance with rules of court) a copy of, or otherwise informed of the terms of, a notice under section 11N relating to the first order.

(9) In dealing with the person under sub-paragraph (2)(a), the court may –

(a) increase the number of hours specified in the first order (but not above the maximum specified in section 199(2)(b) of the Criminal Justice Act 2003, as substituted by paragraph 3);

(b) in relation to the order, extend the period of twelve months specified in section 200(2) of the Criminal Justice Act 2003 (as substituted by paragraph 3).

(10) In exercising its powers under sub-paragraph (2), the court must be satisfied that, taking into account the extent to which the person has complied with the unpaid work requirement imposed by the first order, the effect on the person of the proposed exercise of those powers –

(a) is no more than is required to secure his compliance with the contact order or any contact order that has effect in its place, and

(b) is no more than is proportionate to the seriousness of his failures to comply with the contact order and the first order.

(11) Where the court exercises its powers under sub-paragraph (2) by making an enforcement order in relation to a person who has failed to comply with another enforcement order –

(a) sections 11K(4), 11L(2) to (7), 11M and 11N have effect as regards the making of the order in relation to the person as they have effect as regards the making of an enforcement order in relation to a person who has failed to comply with a contact order;

(b) this Part of this Schedule has effect in relation to the order so made as if it were an enforcement order made in respect of the failure for which the other order was made.

(12) Sub-paragraph (2) is without prejudice to section 63(3) of the Magistrates' Courts Act 1980 as it applies in relation to enforcement orders.

Provision relating to amendment of enforcement orders

10. Sections 11L(2) to (7) and 11M have effect in relation to the making of an order under paragraph 6(2), 7(2) or 9(2)(a) amending an enforcement order as they have effect in relation to the making of an enforcement order; and references in sections 11L(2) to (7) and 11M to an enforcement order are to be read accordingly.][1]

NOTES

Amendments.[1] Schedule inserted: Children and Adoption Act 2006, s 4(2), Sch 1.

SCHEDULE 1
FINANCIAL PROVISION FOR CHILDREN

Section 15(1)

Orders for financial relief against parents

1. (1) On an application made by a parent[, guardian or special guardian]² of a child, or by any person in whose favour a residence order is in force with respect to a child, the court may –

(a) in the case of an application to the High Court or a county court, make one or more of the orders mentioned in sub-paragraph (2);

(b) in the case of an application to a magistrates' court, make one or both of the orders mentioned in paragraphs (a) and (c) of that sub-paragraph.

(2) The orders referred to in sub-paragraph (1) are –

(a) an order requiring either or both parents of a child –
   (i) to make to the applicant for the benefit of the child; or
   (ii) to make to the child himself,
   such periodical payments, for such term, as may be specified in the order;

(b) an order requiring either or both parents of a child –
   (i) to secure to the applicant for the benefit of the child; or
   (ii) to secure to the child himself,
   such periodical payments, for such term, as may be so specified;

(c) an order requiring either or both parents of a child –
   (i) to pay to the applicant for the benefit of the child; or
   (ii) to pay to the child himself,
   such lump sum as may be so specified;

(d) an order requiring a settlement to be made for the benefit of the child, and to the satisfaction of the court, of property –
   (i) to which either parent is entitled (either in possession or in reversion); and
   (ii) which is specified in the order;

(e) an order requiring either or both parents of a child –
   (i) to transfer to the applicant, for the benefit of the child; or
   (ii) to transfer to the child himself,
   such property to which the parent is, or the parents are, entitled (either in possession or in reversion) as may be specified in the order.

(3) The powers conferred by this paragraph may be exercised at any time.

(4) An order under sub-paragraph (2)(a) or (b) may be varied or discharged by a subsequent order made on the application of any person by or to whom payments were required to be made under the previous order.

(5) Where a court makes an order under this paragraph –

(a) it may at any time make a further such order under sub-paragraph (2)(a), (b) or (c) with respect to the child concerned if he has not reached the age of eighteen;
(b) it may not make more than one order under sub-paragraph (2)(d) or (e) against the same person in respect of the same child.

(6) On making, varying or discharging a residence order [or a special guardianship order][3] the court may exercise any of its powers under this Schedule even though no application has been made to it under this Schedule.

[(7) Where a child is a ward of court, the court may exercise any of its powers under this Schedule even though no application has been made to it.][1]

NOTES

Amendments.[1] Sub-paragraph added: Courts and Legal Services Act 1990, s 116, Sch 16, para 10(2).[2] Words substituted: Adoption and Children Act 2002, s 139(1), Sch 3, paras 54, 71(a)(i).[3] Words inserted: Adoption and Children Act 2002, s 139(1), Sch 3, paras 54, 71(a)(ii).

Definitions. 'Child': s 105(1); 'parent': Sch 1, para 16(2); 'residence order': s 8(1); 'the court': s 92(7).

Orders for financial relief for persons over eighteen

2. (1) If, on an application by a person who has reached the age of eighteen, it appears to the court –

(a) that the applicant is, will be or (if an order were made under this paragraph) would be receiving instruction at an educational establishment or undergoing training for a trade, profession or vocation, whether or not while in gainful employment; or
(b) that there are special circumstances which justify the making of an order under this paragraph,

the court may make one or both of the orders mentioned in sub-paragraph (2).

(2) The orders are –

(a) an order requiring either or both of the applicant's parents to pay to the applicant such periodical payments, for such term, as may be specified in the order;
(b) an order requiring either or both of the applicant's parents to pay to the applicant such lump sum as may be so specified.

(3) An applicant may not be made under this paragraph by any person if, immediately before he reached the age of sixteen, a periodical payments order was in force with respect to him.

(4) No order shall be made under this paragraph at a time when the parents of the applicant are living with each other in the same household.

(5) An order under sub-paragraph (2)(a) may be varied or discharged by a subsequent order made on the application of any person by or to whom payments were required to be made under the previous order.

(6) In sub-paragraph (3) 'periodical payments order' means an order made under –

- (a) this Schedule;
- (b) ...¹
- (c) section 23 or 27 of the Matrimonial Causes Act 1973;
- (d) Part I of the Domestic Proceedings and Magistrates' Courts Act 1978,
- [(e) Part 1 or 9 of Schedule 5 to the Civil Partnership Act 2004 (financial relief in the High Court or a county court etc);
- (f) Schedule 6 to the 2004 Act (financial relief in the magistrates' courts etc),]²

for the making or securing of periodical payments.

(7) The powers conferred by this paragraph shall be exercisable at any time.

(8) Where the court makes an order under this paragraph it may from time to time while that order remains in force make a further such order.

NOTES

Amendments.¹ Words repealed: Child Support Act 1991, s 58(14).² Subparagraphs inserted: Civil Partnership Act 2004, s 78(1), (2).

Definitions. 'Periodical payments order': Sch 1, para 2(6); 'the court': s 92(7).

Duration of orders for financial relief

3. (1) The term to be specified in an order for periodical payments made under paragraph 1(2)(a) or (b) in favour of a child may begin with the date of the making of an application for the order in question or any later date [or a date ascertained in accordance with sub-paragraph (5) or (6)]¹ but –

- (a) shall not in the first instance extend beyond the child's seventeenth birthday unless the court thinks it right in the circumstances of the case to specify a later date; and
- (b) shall not in any event extend beyond the child's eighteenth birthday.

(2) Paragraph (b) of sub-paragraph (1) shall not apply in the case of a child if it appears to the court that –

- (a) the child is, or will be (if an order were made without complying with that paragraph) would be receiving instruction at an educational establishment or undergoing training for a trade, profession or vocation, whether or not while in gainful employment; or
- (b) there are special circumstances which justify the making of an order without complying with that paragraph.

(3) An order for periodical payments made under paragraph 1(2)(a) or 2(2)(a) shall, notwithstanding anything in the order, cease to have effect on the death of the person liable to make payments under the order.

(4) Where an order is made under paragraph 1(2)(a) or (b) requiring periodical payments to be made or secured to the parent of a child, the order shall cease to have effect if –

Part I Statutes

(a) any parent making or securing the payments; and
(b) any parent to whom the payments are made or secured,

live together for a period of more than six months.

[(5) Where –

(a) a maintenance assessment ('the current assessment') is in force with respect to a child; and
(b) an application is made for an order under paragraph 1(2)(a) or (b) of this Schedule for periodical payments in favour of that child –
   (i) in accordance with section 8 of the Child Support Act 1991; and
   (ii) before the end of the period of 6 months beginning with the making of the current assessment,

the term to be specified in any such order made on that application may be expressed to begin on, or at any time after, the earliest permitted date.

(6) For the purposes of subsection (5) above, 'the earliest permitted date' is whichever is the later of –

(a) the date 6 months before the application is made; or
(b) the date on which the current assessment took effect or, where successive maintenance assessments have been continuously in force with respect to a child, on which the first of those assessments took effect.

(7) Where –

(a) a maintenance assessment ceases to have effect or is cancelled by or under any provision of the Child Support Act 1991, and
(b) an application is made, before the end of the period of 6 months beginning with the relevant date, for an order for periodical payments under paragraph 1(2)(a) or (b) in favour of a child with respect to whom that maintenance assessment was in force immediately before it ceased to have effect or was cancelled,

the term to be specified in any such order, or in any interim order under paragraph 9, made on that application may begin with the date on which that maintenance assessment ceased to have effect or, as the case may be, the date with effect from which it was cancelled, or any later date.

(8) In sub-paragraph (7)(b) –

(a) where the maintenance assessment ceased to have effect, the relevant date is the date on which it so ceased; and
(b) where the maintenance assessment was cancelled, the relevant date is the later of –
   (i) the date on which the person who cancelled it did so, and
   (ii) the date from which the cancellation first had effect.][1]

NOTES

Amendments.[1] Words and subparagraphs inserted: Maintenance Orders (Backdating) Order 1993, SI 1993/623.

Matters to which court is to have regard in making orders for financial relief

4. (1) In deciding whether to exercise its powers under paragraph 1 or 2, and if so in what manner, the court shall have regard to all the circumstances including –

- (a) the income, earning capacity, property and other financial resources which each person mentioned in sub-paragraph (4) has or is likely to have in the foreseeable future;
- (b) the financial needs, obligations and responsibilities which each person mentioned in sub-paragraph (4) has or is likely to have in the foreseeable future;
- (c) the financial needs of the child;
- (d) the income, earning capacity (if any), property and other financial resources of the child;
- (e) any physical or mental disability of the child;
- (f) the manner in which the child was being, or was expected to be, educated or trained.

(2) In deciding whether to exercise its powers under paragraph 1 against a person who is not the mother or father of the child, and if so in what manner, the court shall in addition have regard to –

- (a) whether that person had assumed responsibility for the maintenance of the child, and, if so, the extent to which and basis on which he assumed that responsibility and the length of the period during which he met that responsibility;
- (b) whether he did so knowing that the child was not his child;
- (c) the liability of any other person to maintain the child.

(3) Where the court makes an order under paragraph 1 against a person who is not the father of the child, it shall record in the order that the order is made on the basis that the person against whom the order is made is not the child's father.

(4) The persons mentioned in sub-paragraph (1) are –

- (a) in relation to a decision whether to exercise its powers under paragraph 1, any parent of the child;
- (b) in relation to a decision whether to exercise its powers under paragraph 2, the mother and father of the child;
- (c) the applicant for the order;
- (d) any other person in whose favour the court proposes to make the order.

[(5) In the case of a child who has a parent by virtue of section 42 or 43 of the Human Fertilisation and Embryology Act 2008, any reference in sub-paragraph (2), (3) or (4) to the child's father is a reference to the woman who is a parent of the child by virtue of that section.][1]

NOTES

Amendments.[1] Subparagraph inserted: Human Fertilisation and Embryology Act 2008, s 56, Sch 6, Pt 1, para 32(1), (2).

Provisions relating to lump sums

5. (1) Without prejudice to the generality of paragraph 1, an order under that paragraph for the payment of a lump sum may be made for the purpose of enabling any liabilities or expenses –

(a) incurred in connection with the birth of the child or in maintaining the child; and
(b) reasonably incurred before the making of the order,

to be met.

(2) The amount of any lump sum required to be paid by an order made by a magistrates' court under paragraph 1 or 2 shall not exceed £1000 or such larger amount as the [Lord Chancellor][1] may[, after consulting the Lord Chief Justice,][2] from time to time by order fix for the purposes of this sub-paragraph.

(3) The power of the court under paragraph 1 or 2 to vary or discharge an order for the making or securing of periodical payments by a parent shall include power to make an order under that provision for the payment of a lump sum by that parent.

(4) The amount of any lump sum which a parent may be required to pay by virtue of sub-paragraph (3) shall not, in the case of an order made by a magistrates' court, exceed the maximum amount that may at the time of the making of the order be required to be paid under sub-paragraph (2), but a magistrates' court may make an order for the payment of a lump sum not exceeding that amount even though the parent was required to pay a lump sum by a previous order under this Act.

(5) An order made under paragraph 1 or 2 for the payment of a lump sum may provide for the payment of that sum by instalments.

(6) Where the court provides for the payment of a lump sum by instalments the court, on an application made either by the person liable to pay or the person entitled to receive that sum, shall have power to vary that order by varying –

(a) the number of instalments payable;
(b) the amount of any instalment payable;
(c) the date on which any instalment becomes payable.

[(7) The Lord Chief Justice may nominate a judicial office holder (as defined in section 109(4) of the Constitutional Reform Act 2005) to exercise his functions under this paragraph.][2]

NOTES

Amendments.[1] Words substituted: Transfer of Functions (Magistrates' Courts and Family Law) Order 1992, SI 1992/709. [2] Words and subparagraph inserted: Constitutional Reform Act 2005, s 15(1), Sch 4, Pt 1, paras 203, 209(1)–(3).

Definitions. 'Child': s 105(1), Sch 1, para 16(1); 'parent': Sch 1, para 16(2); 'the court': s 92(7).

Variation etc of orders for periodical payments

6. (1) In exercising its powers under paragraph 1 or 2 to vary or discharge an order for the making or securing of periodical payments the court shall have regard to all the circumstances of the case, including any change in any of the matters to which the court was required to have regard when making the order.

(2) The power of the court under paragraph 1 or 2 to vary an order for the making or securing of periodical payments shall include power to suspend any provision of the order temporarily and to revive any provision so suspended.

(3) Where on an application under paragraph 1 or 2 for the variation or discharge of an order for the making or securing of periodical payments the court varies the payments required to be made under that order, the court may provide that the payments as so varied shall be made from such date as the court may specify [except that, subject to sub-paragraph (9), the date shall not be][1] earlier than the date of the making of the application.

(4) An application for the variation of an order made under paragraph 1 for the making or securing of periodical payments to or for the benefit of a child may, if the child has reached the age of sixteen, be made by the child himself.

(5) Where an order for the making or securing of periodical payments made under paragraph 1 ceases to have effect on the date on which the child reaches the age of sixteen, or at any time after that date but before or on the date on which he reaches the age of eighteen, the child may apply to the court which made the order for an order for its revival.

(6) If on such an application it appears to the court that –

(a) the child is, will be or (if an order were made under this sub-paragraph) would be receiving instruction at an educational establishment or undergoing training for a trade, profession or vocation, whether or not while in gainful employment; or

(b) there are special circumstances which justify the making of an order under this paragraph,

the court shall have power by order to revive the order from such date as the court may specify, not being earlier than the date of the making of the application.

(7) Any order which is revived by an order under sub-paragraph (5) may be varied or discharged under that provision, on the application of any person by whom or to whom payments are required to be made under the revived order.

(8) An order for the making or securing of periodical payments made under paragraph 1 may be varied or discharged, after the death of either parent, on the application of a guardian [or special guardian][2] of the child concerned.

[(9) Where –

(a) an order under paragraph 1(2)(a) or (b) for the making or securing of periodical payments in favour of more than one child ('the order') is in force;

(b) the order requires payments specified in it to be made to or for the benefit of more than one child without apportioning those payments between them;
(c) a maintenance assessment ('the assessment') is made with respect to one or more, but not all, of the children with respect to whom those payments are to be made; and
(d) an application is made, before the end of the period of 6 months beginning with the date on which the assessment was made, for the variation or discharge of the order,

the court may, in exercise of its powers under paragraph 1 to vary or discharge the order, direct that the variation or discharge shall take effect from the date on which the assessment took effect or any later date.]¹

NOTES

Amendments.¹ Words substituted or subparagraph inserted: Maintenance Orders (Backdating) Order 1993, SI 1993/623.² Words inserted: Adoption and Children Act 2002, s 139(1), Sch 3, paras 54, 71(b).

[Variation of orders for periodical payments etc made by magistrates' courts

6A. (1) Subject to sub-paragraphs (7) and (8), the power of a magistrates' court –

(a) under paragraph 1 or 2 to vary an order for the making of periodical payments, or
(b) under paragraph 5(6) to vary an order for the payment of a lump sum by instalments,

shall include power, if the court is satisfied that payment has not been made in accordance with the order, to exercise one of its powers under paragraphs (a) to (d) of section 59(3) of the Magistrates' Courts Act 1980.

(2) In any case where –

(a) a magistrates' court has made an order under this Schedule for the making of periodical payments or for the payment of a lump sum by instalments, and
(b) payments under the order are required to be made by any method of payment falling within section 59(6) of the Magistrates' Courts Act 1980 (standing order, etc),

any person entitled to make an application under this Schedule for the variation of the order (in this paragraph referred to as 'the applicant') may apply to [a magistrates' court acting in the same local justice area as the court which made the order]³ for the order to be varied as mentioned in sub-paragraph (3).

(3) Subject to sub-paragraph (5), where an application is made under sub-paragraph (2), [a justices' clerk]³, after giving written notice (by post or otherwise) of the application to any interested party and allowing that party, within the period of 14 days beginning with the date of the giving of that

notice, an opportunity to make written representations, may vary the order to provide that payments under the order shall be made [to the designated officer for the court]³.

(4) The clerk may proceed with an application under sub-paragraph (2) notwithstanding that any such interested party as is referred to in sub-paragraph (3) has not received written notice of the application.

(5) Where an application has been made under sub-paragraph (2), the clerk may, if he considers it inappropriate to exercise his power under sub-paragraph (3), refer the matter to the court which, subject to sub-paragraphs (7) and (8), may vary the order by exercising one of its powers under paragraphs (a) to (d) of section 59(3) of the Magistrates' Courts Act 1980.

(6) Subsection (4) of section 59 of the Magistrates' Courts Act 1980 (power of court to order that account be opened) shall apply for the purposes of sub-paragraphs (1) and (5) as it applies for the purposes of that section.

(7) Before varying the order by exercising one of its powers under paragraphs (a) to (d) of section 59(3) of the Magistrates' Courts Act 1980, the court shall have regard to any representations made by the parties to the application.

(8) If the court does not propose to exercise its power [under paragraph (c), (cc) or (d)]² of subsection (3) of section 59 of the Magistrates' Courts Act 1980, the court shall, unless upon representations expressly made in that behalf by the applicant for the order it is satisfied that it is undesirable to do so, exercise its power under paragraph (b) of that subsection.

(9) None of the powers of the court, or of [a justices' clerk]³, conferred by this paragraph shall be exercisable in relation to an order under this Schedule for the making of periodical payments, or for the payment of a lump sum by instalments, which is not a qualifying maintenance order (within the meaning of section 59 of the Magistrates' Courts Act 1980).

(10) In sub-paragraphs (3) and (4) 'interested party', in relation to an application made by the applicant under sub-paragraph (2), means a person who would be entitled to be a party to an application for the variation of the order made by the applicant under any other provision of this Schedule if such an application were made.]¹

NOTES

Amendments.¹ Paragraph inserted: Maintenance Enforcement Act 1991, s 6.² Words substituted: Child Support Act 1991 (Consequential Amendments) Order 1994, SI 1994/731.³ Words substituted: Courts Act 2003, s 109(1), Sch 8, para 338(1)–(3).

Variation of orders for secured periodical payments after death of parent

7. (1) Where the parent liable to make payments under a secured periodical payments order has died, the persons who may apply for the variation or discharge of the order shall include the personal representatives of the deceased parent.

(2) No application for the variation of the order shall, except with the permission of the court, be made after the end of the period of six months from the date on which representation in regard to the estate of that parent is first taken out.

(3) The personal representatives of a deceased person against whom a secured periodical payments order was made shall not be liable for having distributed any part of the estate of the deceased after the end of the period of six months referred to in sub-paragraph (2) on the ground that they ought to have taken into account the possibility that the court might permit an application for variation to be made after that period by the person entitled to payments under the order.

(4) Sub-paragraph (3) shall not prejudice any power to recover any part of the estate so distributed arising by virtue of the variation of an order in accordance with this paragraph.

(5) Where an application to vary a secured periodical payments order is made after the death of the parent liable to make payments under the order, the circumstances to which the court is required to have regard under paragraph 6(1) shall include the changed circumstances resulting from the death of the parent.

(6) In considering for the purposes of sub-paragraph (2) the question when representation was first taken out, a grant limited to settled land or to trust property shall be left out of account and a grant limited to real estate or to personal estate shall be left out of account unless a grant limited to the remainder of the estate has previously been made or is made at the same time.

(7) In this paragraph 'secured periodical payments order' means an order for secured periodical payments under paragraph 1(2)(b).

NOTES

Definitions. 'Child': s 105(1), Sch 1, para 16(1); 'parent': Sch 1, para 16(2); 'secured periodical payments order': Sch 1, para 7(7); 'the court': s 92(7).

Financial relief under other enactments

8. (1) This paragraph applies where a residence order [or a special guardianship order][1] is made with respect to a child at a time when there is in force an order ('the financial relief order') made under any enactment other than this Act and requiring a person to contribute to the child's maintenance.

(2) Where this paragraph applies, the court may, on the application of –

(a) any person required by the financial relief order to contribute to the child's maintenance; or
(b) any person in whose favour a residence order [or a special guardianship order][1] with respect to the child is in force,

make an order revoking the financial relief order, or varying it by altering the amount of any sum payable under that order or by substituting the applicant for the person to whom any such sum is otherwise payable under that order.

NOTES

Amendments.[1] Words inserted: Adoption and Children Act 2002, s 139(1), Sch 3, paras 54, 71(c).

Interim orders

9. (1) Where an application is made under paragraph 1 or 2 the court may, at any time before it disposes of the application, make an interim order –

(a) requiring either or both parents to make such periodical payments, at such times and for such term as the court thinks fit; and
(b) giving any direction which the court thinks fit.

(2) An interim order made under this paragraph may provide for payments to be made from such date as the court may specify [except that, subject to paragraph 3(5) and (6), the date shall not be][1] earlier than the date of the making of the application under paragraph 1 or 2.

(3) An interim order made under this paragraph shall cease to have effect when the application is disposed of or, if earlier, on the date specified for the purposes of this paragraph in the interim order.

(4) An interim order in which a date has been specified for the purposes of sub-paragraph (3) may be varied by substituting a later date.

NOTES

Amendments.[1] Words substituted: Maintenance Orders (Backdating) Order 1993, SI 1993/623.

Definitions. 'Child': s 105(1); 'parent': Sch 1, para 16(2); 'residence order': s 8(1); 'the court': s 92(7); 'the financial relief order': Sch 1, para 8(1).

Alteration of maintenance agreements

10. (1) In this paragraph and in paragraph 11 'maintenance agreement' means any agreement in writing made with respect to a child, whether before or after the commencement of this paragraph, which –

(a) is or was made between the father and mother of the child; and
(b) contains provision with respect to the making or securing of payments, or the disposition or use of any property, for the maintenance or education of the child,

and any such provisions are in this paragraph, and paragraph 11, referred to as 'financial arrangements'.

(2) Where a maintenance agreement is for the time being subsisting and each of the parties to the agreement is for the time being either domiciled or resident in England and Wales, then, either party may apply for an order under this paragraph.

(3) If the court to which the application is made is satisfied either –

(a) that, by reason of a change in the circumstances in the light of which any financial arrangements contained in the agreement were made

(including a change foreseen by the parties when making the agreement), the agreement should be altered so as to make different financial arrangements; or
(b) that the agreement does not contain proper financial arrangements with respect to the child,

then that court may by order make such alterations in the agreement by varying or revoking any financial arrangements contained in it as may appear to it to be just having regard to all the circumstances.

(4) If the maintenance agreement is altered by an order under this paragraph, the agreement shall have effect thereafter as if the alteration had been made by agreement between the parties and for valuable consideration.

(5) Where a court decides to make an order under this paragraph altering the maintenance agreement –

(a) by inserting provision for the making or securing by one of the parties to the agreement of periodical payments for the maintenance of the child; or
(b) by increasing the rate of periodical payments required to be made or secured by one of the parties for the maintenance of the child,

then, in deciding the term for which under the agreement as altered by the order the payments or (as the case may be) the additional payments attributable to the increase are to be made or secured for the benefit of the child, the court shall apply the provisions of sub-paragraphs (1) and (2) of paragraph 3 as if the order were an order under paragraph 1(2)(a) or (b).

(6) A magistrates' court shall not entertain an application under sub-paragraph (2) unless both the parties to the agreement are resident in England and Wales and .[the court acts in, or is authorised by the Lord Chancellor to act for, a local justice area in which at least one of the parties is resident][1], and shall not have power to make any order on such an application except –

(a) in a case where the agreement contains no provision for periodical payments by either of the parties, an order inserting provision for the making by one of the parties of periodical payments for the maintenance of the child;
(b) in a case where the agreement includes provision for the making by one of the parties of periodical payments, an order increasing or reducing the rate of, or terminating, any of those payments.

(7) For the avoidance of doubt it is hereby declared that nothing in this paragraph affects any power of a court before which any proceedings between the parties to a maintenance agreement are brought under any other enactment to make an order containing financial arrangements or any right of either party to apply for such an order in such proceedings.

[(8) In the case of a child who has a parent by virtue of section 42 or 43 of the Human Fertilisation and Embryology Act 2008, the reference in sub-paragraph (1)(a) to the child's father is a reference to the woman who is a parent of the child by virtue of that section.][2]

NOTES

Amendments.[1] Words substituted: Courts Act 2003, s 109(1), Sch 8, para 339. [2] Subparagraph inserted: Human Fertilisation and Embryology Act 2008, s 56, Sch 6, Pt 1, para 32(1), (3).

11. (1) Where a maintenance agreement provides for the continuation, after the death of one of the parties, of payments for the maintenance of a child and that party dies domiciled in England and Wales, the surviving party or the personal representatives of the deceased party may apply to the High Court or a county court for an order under paragraph 10.

(2) If a maintenance agreement is altered by a court on an application under this paragraph, the agreement shall have effect thereafter as if the alteration had been made, immediately before the death, by agreement between the parties and for valuable consideration.

(3) An application under this paragraph shall not, except with leave of the High Court or a county court, be made after the end of the period of six months beginning with the day on which representation in regard to the estate of the deceased is first taken out.

(4) In considering for the purposes of sub-paragraph (3) the question when representation was first taken out, a grant limited to settled land or to trust property shall be left out of account and a grant limited to real estate or to personal estate shall be left out of account unless a grant limited to the remainder of the estate has previously been made or is made at the same time.

(5) A county court shall not entertain an application under this paragraph, or an application for leave to make an application under this paragraph, unless it would have jurisdiction to hear and determine proceedings for an order under section 2 of the Inheritance (Provision for Family and Dependants) Act 1975 in relation to the deceased's estate by virtue of section 25 of the County Courts Act 1984 (jurisdiction under the Act of 1975).

(6) The provisions of this paragraph shall not render the personal representatives of the deceased liable for having distributed any part of the estate of the deceased after the expiry of the period of six months referred to in sub-paragraph (3) on the ground that they ought to have taken into account the possibility that a court might grant leave for an application by virtue of this paragraph to be made by the surviving party after that period.

(7) Sub-paragraph (6) shall not prejudice any power to recover any part of the estate so distributed arising by virtue of the making of an order in pursuance of this paragraph.

NOTES

Definitions. 'Child': s 105(1); 'financial arrangements': Sch 1, para 10(1); 'maintenance agreement': Sch 1, para 10(1); 'the court': s 92(7).

Enforcement of orders for maintenance

12. (1) Any person for the time being under an obligation to make payments in pursuance of any order for the payment of money made by a magistrates' court under this Act shall give notice of any change of address to such person (if any) as may be specified in the order.

(2) Any person failing without reasonable excuse to give such a notice shall be guilty of an offence and liable on summary conviction to a fine not exceeding level 2 on the standard scale.

(3) An order for the payment of money made by a magistrates' court under this Act shall be enforceable as a magistrates' court maintenance order within the meaning of section 150(1) of the Magistrates' Courts Act 1980.

Direction for settlement of instrument by conveyancing counsel

13. Where the High Court or a county court decides to make an order under this Act for the securing of periodical payments or for the transfer or settlement of property, it may direct that the matter be referred to one of the conveyancing counsel of the court to settle a proper instrument to be executed by all necessary parties.

Financial provision for child resident in country outside England and Wales

14. (1) Where one parent of a child lives in England and Wales and the child lives outside England and Wales with –

(a) another parent of his;
(b) a guardian [or special guardian][1] of his; or
(c) a person in whose favour a residence order is in force with respect to the child,

the court shall have power, on an application made by any of the persons mentioned in paragraphs (a) to (c), to make one or both of the orders mentioned in paragraph 1(2)(a) and (b) against the parent living in England and Wales.

(2) Any reference in this Act to the powers of the court under paragraph 1(2) or to an order made under paragraph 1(2) shall include a reference to the powers which the court has by virtue of sub-paragraph (1) or (as the case may be) to an order made by virtue of sub-paragraph (1).

NOTES

Amendments.[1] Words inserted: Adoption and Children Act 2002, s 139(1), Sch 3, paras 54, 71(d).

Local authority contribution to child's maintenance

15. (1) Where a child lives, or is to live, with a person as the result of a residence order, a local authority may make contributions to that person towards the cost of the accommodation and maintenance of the child.

(2) Sub-paragraph (1) does not apply where the person with whom the child lives, or is to live, is a parent of the child or the husband or wife [or civil partner][1] of a parent of the child.

NOTES

Amendments.[1] Words inserted: Civil Partnership Act 2004, s 78(1), (3).

Interpretation

16. (1) In this Schedule 'child' includes, in any case where an application is made under paragraph 2 or 6 in relation to a person who has reached the age of eighteen, that person.

[(2) In this Schedule, except paragraphs 2 and 15, 'parent' includes –

(a) any party to a marriage (whether or not subsisting) in relation to whom the child concerned is a child of the family, and

(b) any civil partner in a civil partnership (whether or not subsisting) in relation to whom the child concerned is a child of the family;

and for this purpose any reference to either parent or both parents shall be read as a reference to any parent of his and to all of his parents.][2]

[(3) In this Schedule, 'maintenance assessment' has the same meaning as it has in the Child Support Act 1991 by virtue of section 54 of that Act as read with any regulations in force under that section.][1]

NOTES

Amendments.[1] Words added: Maintenance Orders (Backdating) Order 1993, SI 1993/623.
[2] Subparagraph substituted: Civil Partnership Act 2004, s 78(1), (4).

Definitions. 'Child': s 105(1), Sch 1, para 16(1); 'child of the family': s 105(1); 'local authority': s 105(1); 'parent': Sch 1, para 16(2); 'residence order': s 8(1).

SCHEDULE 2
LOCAL AUTHORITY SUPPORT FOR CHILDREN AND FAMILIES

Sections 17, 23 and 29

PART I
PROVISION OF SERVICES FOR FAMILIES

Identification of children in need and provision of information

1. (1) Every local authority shall take reasonable steps to identify the extent to which there are children in need within their area.

(2) Every local authority shall –

(a) publish information
  (i) about services provided by them under sections 17, 18, [20, 23B to 23D, 24A and 24B][1]; and
  (ii) where they consider it appropriate, about the provision by others (including, in particular, voluntary organisations) of services which the authority have power to provide under those sections; and

(b) take such steps as are reasonably practicable to ensure that those who might benefit from the services receive the information relevant to them.

NOTES

Amendments.[1] Words substituted: Children (Leaving Care) Act 2000, s 7(1), (4).

1A. ...[1]

NOTES

Amendments.[1] Paragraph repealed: Children Act 2004, s 64, Sch 5, Pt 1.

Maintenance of a register of disabled children

2. (1) Every local authority shall open and maintain a register of disabled children within their area.

(2) The register may be kept by means of a computer.

Assessment of children's needs

3. Where it appears to a local authority that a child within their area is in need, the authority may assess his needs for the purposes of this Act at the same time as any assessment of his needs is made under –

(a) the Chronically Sick and Disabled Persons Act 1970;
(b) [Part IV of the Education Act 1996][1];
(c) the Disabled Persons (Services, Consultation and Representation) Act 1986; or
(d) any other enactment.

Prevention of neglect and abuse

4. (1) Every local authority shall take reasonable steps, through the provision of services under Part III of this Act, to prevent children within their area suffering ill-treatment or neglect.

(2) Where a local authority believe that a child who is at any time within their area –

(a) is likely to suffer harm; but
(b) lives or proposes to live in the area of another local authority they shall inform that other local authority.

(3) When informing that other local authority they shall specify –

(a) the harm that they believe he is likely to suffer; and
(b) (if they can) where the child lives or proposes to live.

Provision of accommodation in order to protect child

5. (1) Where –

(a) it appears to a local authority that a child who is living on particular premises is suffering, or is likely to suffer, ill treatment at the hands of another person who is living on those premises; and

(b) that other person proposes to move from the premises,

the authority may assist that other person to obtain alternative accommodation.

(2) Assistance given under this paragraph may be in cash.

(3) Subsections (7) to (9) of section 17 shall apply in relation to assistance given under this paragraph as they apply in relation to assistance given under that section.

Provision for disabled children

6. Every local authority shall provide services designed –

(a) to minimise the effect on disabled children within their area of their disabilities; and

(b) to give such children the opportunity to lead lives which are as normal as possible.

[(2) The duty imposed by sub-paragraph (1)(c) shall be performed in accordance with regulations made by the appropriate national authority.][1]

NOTES

Amendments.[1] Subparagraph inserted for the purpose of making regulations: Children and Young Persons Act 2008, s 25(1), (4).

Provision to reduce need for care proceedings etc.

7. Every local authority shall take reasonable steps designed –

(a) to reduce the need to bring –
 (i) proceedings for care or supervision orders with respect to children within their area;
 (ii) criminal proceedings against such children;
 (iii) any family or other proceedings with respect to such children which might lead to them being placed in the authority's care; or
 (iv) proceedings under the inherent jurisdiction of the High Court with respect to children;

(b) to encourage children within their area not to commit criminal offences; and

(c) to avoid the need for children within their area to be placed in secure accommodation.

Provision for children living with their families

8. Every local authority shall make such provision as they consider appropriate for the following services to be available with respect to children in need within their area while they are living with their families –

(a) advice, guidance and counselling;

(b) occupational, social, cultural or recreational activities;
(c) home help (which may include laundry facilities);
(d) facilities for, or assistance with, travelling to and from home for the purpose of taking advantage of any other service provided under this Act or of any similar service;
(e) assistance to enable the child concerned and his family to have a holiday.

Family centres

9. (1) Every local authority shall provide such family centres as they consider appropriate in relation to children within their area.

(2) 'Family centre' means a centre at which any of the persons mentioned in sub-paragraph (3) may –

(a) attend for occupational, social, cultural or recreational activities;
(b) attend for advice, guidance or counselling; or
(c) be provided with accommodation while he is receiving advice, guidance or counselling.

(3) The persons are –

(a) a child;
(b) his parents;
(c) any person who is not a parent of his but who has parental responsibility for him;
(d) any other person who is looking after him.

Maintenance of the family home

10. Every local authority shall take such steps as are reasonably practicable, where any child within their area who is in need and whom they are not looking after is living apart from his family –

(a) to enable him to live with his family; or
(b) to promote contact between him and his family,

if, in their opinion, it is necessary to do so in order to safeguard or promote his welfare.

Duty to consider racial groups to which children in need belong

11. Every local authority shall, in making any arrangements –

(a) for the provision of day care within their area; or
(b) designed to encourage persons to act as local authority foster parents,

have regard to the different racial groups to which children within their area who are in need belong.

NOTES

Amendments.[1] Words substituted: Education Act 1996, s 582(1), Sch 37, Pt I, para 92.

Definitions. 'Care order': ss 31(11), 105(1); 'child': s 105(1); 'child in need': s 17(10); 'day care': ss 18(4), 105(1); 'disabled': ss 17(11), 105(1); 'family': s 17(10); 'family centre': Sch 2, para 9(2); 'family proceedings': s 8(3); 'harm': ss 31(9), 105(1); 'ill-treatment': ss 31(9), 105(1); 'local authority': s 105(1); 'local authority foster parent': s 23(3); 'parental responsibility': s 3; 'secure accommodation': s 25(1); 'significant harm': ss 31(10), 105(1); 'supervision order': s 31(11); voluntary organisation': s 105(1).

PART II
CHILDREN LOOKED AFTER BY LOCAL AUTHORITIES

[Regulations as to conditions under which child in care is allowed to live with parent, etc

12A. Regulations under section 22C may, in particular, impose requirements on a local authority as to –

(a) the making of any decision by a local authority to allow a child in their care to live with any person falling within section 22C(3) (including requirements as to those who must be consulted before the decision is made and those who must be notified when it has been made);
(b) the supervision or medical examination of the child concerned;
(c) the removal of the child, in such circumstances as may be prescribed, from the care of the person with whom the child has been allowed to live;
(d) the records to be kept by local authorities.

Regulations as to placements of a kind specified in section 22C(6)(d)

12B. Regulations under section 22C as to placements of the kind specified in section 22C(6)(d) may, in particular, make provision as to –

(a) the persons to be notified of any proposed arrangements;
(b) the opportunities such persons are to have to make representations in relation to the arrangements proposed;
(c) the persons to be notified of any proposed changes in arrangements;
(d) the records to be kept by local authorities;
(e) the supervision by local authorities of any arrangements made.

Placements out of area

12C. Regulations under section 22C may, in particular, impose requirements which a local authority must comply with –

(a) before a child looked after by them is provided with accommodation at a place outside the area of the authority; or
(b) if the child's welfare requires the immediate provision of such accommodation, within such period of the accommodation being provided as may be prescribed.

Avoidance of disruption in education

12D. (1) Regulations under section 22C may, in particular, impose requirements which a local authority must comply with before making any decision concerning a child's placement if he is in the fourth key stage.

(2) A child is 'in the fourth key stage' if he is a pupil in the fourth key stage for the purposes of Part 6 or 7 of the Education 2002 (see section 82 and 103 of that Act).

Regulations as to placing of children with local authority foster parents

12E. Regulations under section 22C may, in particular, make provision –

(a) with regard to the welfare of children placed with local authority foster parents;

(b) as to the arrangements to be made by local authorities in connection with the health and education of such children;

(c) as to the records to be kept by local authorities;

(d) for securing that where possible the local authority foster parent with whom a child is to be placed is –
  (i) of the same religious persuasion as the child; or
  (ii) gives an undertaking that the child will be brought up in that religious persuasion;

(e) for securing the children placed with local authority foster parents, and the premises in which they are accommodated, will be supervised and inspected by a local authority and that the children will be removed from those premises if their welfare appears to require it.

12F. (1) Regulations under section 22C may, in particular, also make provision –

(a) for securing that a child is not placed with a local authority foster parent unless that person is for the time being approved as a local authority foster parent by such local authority as may be prescribed;

(b) establishing a procedure under which any person in respect of whom a qualifying determination has been made may apply to the appropriate national authority for a review of that determination by a panel constituted by that national authority.

(2) A determination is a qualifying determination if –

(a) it relates to the issue of whether a person should be approved, or should continue to be approved, as a local authority foster parent; and

(b) it is of a prescribed description.

(3) Regulations made by virtue of sub-paragraph (1)(b) may include provision as to –

(a) the duties and powers of a panel;

(b) the administration and procedures of a panel;

(c) the appointment of members of a panel (including the number, or any limit on the number, of members who may be appointed and any conditions for appointment);
(d) the payment of fees to members of a panel;
(e) the duties of any person in connection with a review conducted under the regulations;
(f) the monitoring of any such reviews.

(4) Regulations made by virtue of sub-paragraph (3)(e) may impose a duty to pay to the appropriate national authority such sum as that national authority may determine; but such a duty may not be imposed upon a person who has applied for a review of a qualifying determination.

(5) The appropriate national authority must secure that, taking one financial year with another, the aggregate of the sums which become payable to it under regulations made by virtue of sub-paragraph (4) does not exceed the cost to it of performing its independent review functions.

(6) The appropriate national authority may make an arrangement with an organisation under which independent review functions are performed by the organisation on the national authority's behalf.

(7) If the appropriate national authority makes such an arrangement with an organisation, the organisation is to perform its functions under the arrangement in accordance with any general or special directions given by that national authority.

(8) The arrangement may include provision for payments to be made to the organisation by the appropriate national authority.

(9) Payments made by the appropriate national authority in accordance with such provision shall be taken into account in determining (for the purpose of sub-paragraph (5)) the cost to that national authority of performing its independent review functions.

(10) Where the Welsh Ministers are the appropriate national authority, sub-paragraphs (6) and (8) also apply as if references to an organisation included references to the Secretary of State.

(11) In this paragraph –

'financial year' means a period of twelve months ending with 31st March;
'independent review function' means a function conferred or imposed on a national authority by regulations made by virtue of sub-paragraph (1)(b);
'organisation' includes a public body and a private or voluntary organisation.

12G. Regulations under section 22C may, in particular, also make provision as to the circumstances in which local authorities may make arrangements for duties imposed on them by the regulations to be discharged on their behalf.]⁹

Promotion and maintenance of contact between child and family

15. (1) Where a child is being looked after by a local authority, the authority shall, unless it is not reasonably practicable or consistent with his welfare, endeavour to promote contact between the child and –

(a) his parents;
(b) any person who is not a parent of his but who has parental responsibility for him; and
(c) any relative, friend or other person connected with him.

(2) Where a child is being looked after by a local authority –

(a) the authority shall take such steps as are reasonably practicable to secure that
   (i) his parents; and
   (ii) any person who is not a parent of his but who has parental responsibility for him,
   are kept informed of where he is being accommodated; and
(b) every such person shall secure that the authority are kept informed of his or her address.

(3) Where a local authority ('the receiving authority') take over the provision of accommodation for a child from another local authority ('the transferring authority') under section 20(2) –

(a) the receiving authority shall (where reasonably practicable) inform
   (i) the child's parents; and
   (ii) any person who is not a parent of his but who has parental responsibility for him;
(b) sub-paragraph (2)(a) shall apply to the transferring authority, as well as the receiving authority, until at least one such person has been informed of the change; and
(c) sub-paragraph (2)(b) shall not require any person to inform the receiving authority of his address until he has been so informed.

(4) Nothing in this paragraph requires a local authority to inform any person of the whereabouts of a child if –

(a) the child is in the care of the authority; and
(b) the authority has reasonable cause to believe that informing the person would prejudice the child's welfare.

(5) Any person who fails (without reasonable excuse) to comply with sub-paragraph (2)(b) shall be guilty of an offence and liable on summary conviction to a fine not exceeding level 2 on the standard scale.

(6) It shall be a defence in any proceedings under sub-paragraph (5) to prove that the defendant was residing at the same address as another person who was the child's parent or had parental responsibility for the child and had reasonable cause to believe that the other person had informed the appropriate authority that both of them were residing at that address.

Visits to or by children: expenses

16. (1) This paragraph applies where –

(a) a child is being looked after by a local authority; and
(b) the conditions mentioned in sub-paragraph (3) are satisfied.

(2) The authority may –

(a) make payments to –
  (i) a parent of the child;
  (ii) any person who is not a parent of his but who has parental responsibility for him; or
  (iii) any relative, friend or other person connected with him,
  in respect of travelling, subsistence or other expenses incurred by that person in visiting the child; or
(b) make payments to the child, or to any person on his behalf, in respect of travelling, subsistence or other expenses incurred by or on behalf of the child in his visiting –
  (i) a parent of his;
  (ii) any person who has parental responsibility for him; or
  (iii) any relative, friend or other person connected with him.

(3) The conditions are that –

(a) it appears to the authority that the visit in question could not otherwise be made without undue financial hardship; and
(b) the circumstances warrant the making of the payments.

Appointment of visitor for child who is not being visited

17. (1) Where it appears to a local authority in relation to any child that they are looking after that –

(a) communication between the child and –
  (i) a parent of his, or
  (ii) any person who is not a parent of his but who has parental responsibility for him,
  has been infrequent; or
(b) he has not visited or been visited by (or lived with) any such person during the preceding twelve months,

and that it would be in the child's best interests for an independent person to be appointed to be his visitor for the purposes of this paragraph, they shall appoint such a visitor.

(2) A person so appointed shall –

(a) have the duty of visiting, advising and befriending the child; and
(b) be entitled to recover from the authority who appointed him any reasonable expenses incurred by him for the purposes of his functions under this paragraph.

(3) A person's appointment as a visitor in pursuance of this paragraph shall be determined if –

(a) he gives notice in writing to the authority who appointed him that he resigns the appointment; or
(b) the authority give him notice in writing that they have terminated it.

(4) The determination of such an appointment shall not prejudice any duty under this paragraph to make a further appointment.

(5) Where a local authority propose to appoint a visitor for a child under this paragraph, the appointment shall not be made if –

(a) the child objects to it; and
(b) the authority are satisfied that he has sufficient understanding to make an informed decision.

(6) Where a visitor has been appointed for a child under this paragraph, the local authority shall determine the appointment if –

(a) the child objects to its continuing; and
(b) the authority are satisfied that he has sufficient understanding to make an informed decision.

(7) The [appropriate national authority][8] may make regulations as to the circumstances in which a person appointed as a visitor under this paragraph is to be regarded as independent of the local authority appointing him.

Power to guarantee apprenticeship deeds etc

18. (1) While a child is being looked after by a local authority, or is a person qualifying for advice and assistance, the authority may undertake any obligation by way of guarantee under any deed of apprenticeship or articles of clerkship which he enters into.

(2) Where a local authority have undertaken any such obligation under any deed or articles they may at any time (whether or not they are still looking after the person concerned) undertake the like obligation under any supplemental deed or articles.

Arrangements to assist children to live abroad

19. (1) A local authority may only arrange for, or assist in arranging for, any child in their care to live outside England and Wales with the approval of the court.

(2) A local authority may, with the approval of every person who has parental responsibility for the child arrange for, or assist in arranging for, any other child looked after by them to live outside England and Wales.

(3) The court shall not give its approval under sub-paragraph (1) unless it is satisfied that –

(a) living outside England and Wales would be in the child's best interests;

(b) suitable arrangements have been, or will be, made for his reception and welfare in the country in which he will live;
(c) the child has consented to living in that country; and
(d) every person who has parental responsibility for the child has consented to his living in that country.

(4) Where the court is satisfied that the child does not have sufficient understanding to give or withhold his consent, it may disregard sub-paragraph (3)(c) and give its approval if the child is to live in the country concerned with a parent, guardian, [special guardian,][4] or other suitable person.

(5) Where a person whose consent is required by sub-paragraph (3)(d) fails to give his consent, the court may disregard that provision and give its approval if it is satisfied that that person –

(a) cannot be found;
(b) is incapable of consenting; or
(c) is withholding his consent unreasonably.

(6) [Section 85 of the Adoption and Children Act 2002 (which imposes restrictions on taking children out of the United Kingdom)][5] shall not apply in the case of any child who is to live outside England and Wales with the approval of the court given under this paragraph.

(7) Where a court decides to give its approval under this paragraph it may order that its decision is not to have effect during the appeal period.

(8) In sub-paragraph (7) 'the appeal period' means –

(a) where an appeal is made against the decision, the period between the making of the decision and the determination of the appeal; and
(b) otherwise, the period during which an appeal may be made against the decision.

[(9) This paragraph does not apply to a local authority placing a child for adoption with prospective adopters.][6]

[Preparation for ceasing to be looked after

19A. It is the duty of the local authority looking after a child to advise, assist and befriend him with a view to promoting his welfare when they have ceased to look after him.

19B. (1) A local authority shall have the following additional functions in relation to an eligible child whom they are looking after.

(2) In sub-paragraph (1) 'eligible child' means, subject to sub-paragraph (3), a child who –

(a) is aged sixteen or seventeen; and
(b) has been looked after by a local authority for a prescribed period, or periods amounting in all to a prescribed period, which began after he reached a prescribed age and ended after he reached the age of sixteen.

(3) The [appropriate national authority][8] may prescribe –

(a) additional categories of eligible children; and
(b) categories of children who are not to be eligible children despite falling within sub-paragraph (2).

(4) For each eligible child, the local authority shall carry out an assessment of his needs with a view to determining what advice, assistance and support it would be appropriate for them to provide him under this Act –

(a) while they are still looking after him; and
(b) after they cease to look after him,

and shall then prepare a pathway plan for him.

(5) The local authority shall keep the pathway plan under regular review.

(6) Any such review may be carried out at the same time as a review of the child's case carried out by virtue of section 26.

(7) The [appropriate national authority][8] may by regulations make provision as to assessments for the purposes of sub-paragraph (4).

(8) The regulations may in particular provide for the matters set out in section 23B(6).

Personal advisers

19C. A local authority shall arrange for each child whom they are looking after who is an eligible child for the purposes of paragraph 19B to have a personal adviser.][2]

Death of children being looked after by local authorities

20. (1) If a child who is being looked after by a local authority dies, the authority –

(a) shall notify the [appropriate national authority][8] [[and (in the case of a local authority in England) Her Majesty's Chief Inspector of Education, Children's Services and Skills][7]][3];
(b) shall, so far as is reasonably practicable, notify the child's parents and every person who is not a parent of his but who has parental responsibility for him;
(c) may, with the consent (so far as it is reasonably practicable to obtain it) of every person who has parental responsibility for the child, arrange for the child's body to be buried or cremated; and
(d) may, if the conditions mentioned in sub-paragraph (2) are satisfied, make payments to any person who has parental responsibility for the child, or any relative, friend or other person connected with the child, in respect of travelling, subsistence or other expenses incurred by that person in attending the child's funeral.

(2) The conditions are that –

(a) it appears to the authority that the person concerned could not otherwise attend the child's funeral without undue financial hardship; and

(b) that the circumstances warrant the making of the payments.

(3) Sub-paragraph (1) does not authorise cremation where it does not accord with the practice of the child's religious persuasion.

(4) Where a local authority have exercised their power under sub-paragraph (1)(c) with respect to a child who was under sixteen when he died, they may recover from any parent of the child any expenses incurred by them.

(5) Any sums so recoverable shall, without prejudice to any other method of recovery, be recoverable summarily as a civil debt.

(6) Nothing in this paragraph affects any enactment regulating or authorising the burial, cremation or anatomical examination of the body of a deceased person.

NOTES

Amendments.[1] Sub-paragraph added: Courts and Legal Services Act 1990, s 116, Sch 16, para 27.[2] Paragraphs inserted: Children (Leaving Care) Act 2000, s 1.[3] Words inserted: Health and Social Care (Community Health and Standards) Act 2003, s 147, Sch 9, para 10(1), (4).[4] Words inserted: Adoption and Children Act 2002, s 139(1), Sch 3, paras 54, 72(a).[5] Words substituted: Adoption and Children Act 2002, s 139(1), Sch 3, paras 54, 72(b).[6] Subparagraph inserted: Adoption and Children Act 2002, s 139(1), Sch 3, paras 54, 72(c).[7] Words substituted: Education and Inspections Act 2006, s 157, Sch 14, paras 9, 17.[8] Words substituted: Children and Young Persons Act 2008, s 39, Sch 3, paras 1, 27(1), (2). [9] Paras 12A–12G substituted for paras 12–14 as originally enacted: Children and Young Persons Act 2008, s 8(2), Sch 1, para 4.

Definitions. 'Child': s 105(1); 'child who is looked after by a local authority': s 22(1); 'functions': s 105(1); 'local authority': s 105(1); 'local authority foster parent': s 23(3); 'parental responsibility': s 3; 'person qualifying for advice and assistance': s 24(2); 'prescribed': s 105(1); 'relative': s 105(1); 'receiving authority': Sch 2, para 15(3); 'the appeal period': Sch 2, para 19(8); 'the court': s 92(7); 'the transferring authority': Sch 2, para 15(3).

PART III
CONTRIBUTIONS TOWARDS MAINTENANCE OF CHILDREN

Liability to contribute

21. (1) Where a local authority are looking after a child (other than in the cases mentioned in sub-paragraph (7)) they shall consider whether they should recover contributions towards the child's maintenance from any person liable to contribute ('a contributor').

(2) An authority may only recover contributions from a contributor if they consider it reasonable to do so.

(3) The persons liable to contribute are –

(a) where the child is under sixteen, each of his parents;
(b) where he has reached the age of sixteen, the child himself.

(4) A parent is not liable to contribute during any period when he is in receipt of income support [under][3] [Part VII of the Social Security Contributions and

Benefits Act 1992]¹[, of any element of child tax credit other than the family element, of working tax credit]³[, of an income-based jobseeker's allowance or of an income-related employment and support allowance]⁵.

(5) A person is not liable to contribute towards the maintenance of a child in the care of a local authority in respect of any period during which the child is allowed by the authority (under section 23(5)) to live with a parent of his.

(6) A contributor is not obliged to make any contribution towards a child's maintenance except as agreed or determined in accordance with this Part of this Schedule.

(7) The cases are where the child is looked after by a local authority under –

- (a) section 21;
- (b) an interim care order;
- (c) [section 92 of the Powers of Criminal Courts (Sentencing) Act 2000]⁴.

NOTES

Amendments.¹ Words substituted: Social Security (Consequential Provisions) Act 1992, s 4, Sch 2, para 108.² Words inserted: Jobseekers Act 1995, s 41(4), Sch 2, para 19.³ Words substituted or inserted: Tax Credits Act 2002, s 47, Sch 3, paras 15, 20.⁴ Words substituted: Powers of Criminal Courts (Sentencing) Act 2000, s 165(1), Sch 9, para 131.⁵ Words substituted: Welfare Reform Act 2007, s 28(1), Sch 3, para 6(1), (6).

Agreed contributions

22. (1) Contributions towards a child's maintenance may only be recovered if the local authority have served a notice ('a contribution notice') on the contributor specifying –

- (a) the weekly sum which they consider that he should contribute; and
- (b) arrangements for payment.

(2) The contribution notice must be in writing and dated.

(3) Arrangements for payment shall, in particular, include –

- (a) the date on which liability to contribute begins (which must not be earlier than the date of the notice);
- (b) the date on which liability under the notice will end (if the child has not before that date ceased to be looked after by the authority); and
- (c) the date on which the first payment is to be made.

(4) The authority may specify in a contribution notice a weekly sum which is a standard contribution determined by them for all children looked after by them.

(5) The authority may not specify in a contribution notice a weekly sum greater than that which they consider –

- (a) they would normally be prepared to pay if they had placed a similar child with local authority foster parents; and
- (b) it is reasonably practicable for the contributor to pay (having regard to his means).

(6) An authority may at any time withdraw a contribution notice (without prejudice to their power to serve another).

(7) Where the authority and the contributor agree –

(a) the sum which the contributor is to contribute; and
(b) arrangements for payment,

(whether as specified in the contribution notice or otherwise) and the contributor notifies the authority in writing that he so agrees, the authority may recover summarily as a civil debt any contribution which is overdue and unpaid.

(8) A contributor may, by serving a notice in writing on the authority, withdraw his agreement in relation to any period of liability falling after the date of service of the notice.

(9) Sub-paragraph (7) is without prejudice to any other method of recovery.

Contribution orders

23. (1) Where a contributor has been served with a contribution notice and has –

(a) failed to reach any agreement with the local authority as mentioned in paragraph 22(7) within the period of one month beginning with the day on which the contribution notice was served; or
(b) served a notice under paragraph 22(8) withdrawing his agreement,

the authority may apply to the court for an order under this paragraph.

(2) On such an application the court may make an order ('a contribution order') requiring the contributor to contribute a weekly sum towards the child's maintenance in accordance with arrangements for payment specified by the court.

(3) A contribution order –

(a) shall not specify a weekly sum greater than that specified in the contribution notice; and
(b) shall be made with due regard to the contributor's means.

(4) A contribution order shall not –

(a) take effect before the date specified in the contribution notice; or
(b) have effect while the contributor is not liable to contribute (by virtue of paragraph 21); or
(c) remain in force after the child has ceased to be looked after by the authority who obtained the order.

(5) An authority may not apply to the court under sub-paragraph (1) in relation to a contribution notice which they have withdrawn.

(6) Where –

(a) a contribution order is in force;

(b) the authority serve another contribution notice; and
(c) the contributor and the authority reach an agreement under paragraph 22(7) in respect of that other contribution notice,

the effect of the agreement shall be to discharge the order from the date on which it is agreed that the agreement shall take effect.

(7) Where an agreement is reached under sub-paragraph (6) the authority shall notify the court –

(a) of the agreement; and
(b) of the date on which it took effect.

(8) A contribution order may be varied or revoked on the application of the contributor or the authority.

(9) In proceedings for the variation of a contribution order, the authority shall specify –

(a) the weekly sum which, having regard to paragraph 22, they propose that the contributor should contribute under the order as varied; and
(b) the proposed arrangements for payment.

(10) Where a contribution order is varied, the order –

(a) shall not specify a weekly sum greater than that specified by the authority in the proceedings for variation; and
(b) shall be made with due regard to the contributor's means.

(11) An appeal shall lie in accordance with rules of court from any order made under this paragraph.

Enforcement of contribution orders etc

24. (1) A contribution order made by a magistrates' court shall be enforceable as a magistrates' court maintenance order (within the meaning of section 150(1) of the Magistrates' Courts Act 1980).

(2) Where a contributor has agreed, or has been ordered, to make contributions to a local authority, any other local authority within whose area the contributor is for the time being living may –

(a) at the request of the local authority who served the contribution notice; and
(b) subject to agreement as to any sum to be deducted in respect of services rendered,

collect from the contributor any contributions due on behalf of the authority who served the notice.

(3) In sub-paragraph (2) the reference to any other local authority includes a reference to –

(a) a local authority within the meaning of section 1(2) of the Social Work (Scotland) Act 1968; and

(b) a Health and Social Services Board established under Article 16 of the Health and Personal Social Services (Northern Ireland) Order 1972.

(4) The power to collect sums under sub-paragraph (2) includes the power to –

(a) receive and give a discharge for any contributions due; and
(b) (if necessary) enforce payment of any contributions,

even though those contributions may have fallen due at a time when the contributor was living elsewhere.

(5) Any contributions collected under sub-paragraph (2) shall be paid (subject to any agreed deduction) to the local authority who served the contribution notice.

(6) In any proceedings under this paragraph, a document which purports to be –

(a) a copy of an order made by a court under or by virtue of paragraph 23; and
(b) certified as a true copy by the [designated officer for][1] the court,

shall be evidence of the order.

(7) In any proceedings under this paragraph, a certificate which –

(a) purports to be signed by the clerk or some other duly authorised officer of the local authority who obtained the contribution order; and
(b) states that any sum due to the authority under the order is overdue and unpaid,

shall be evidence that the sum is overdue and unpaid.

Regulations

25. The [appropriate national authority][2] may make regulations –

(a) as to the considerations which a local authority must take into account in deciding –
    (i) whether it is reasonable to recover contributions; and
    (ii) what the arrangements for payment should be;
(b) as to the procedures [a local authority][2] must follow in reaching agreements with –
    (i) contributors (under paragraph 22 and 23); and
    (ii) any other local authority (under paragraph 23).

NOTES

Amendments.[1] Words substituted: Courts Act 2003, s 109(1), Sch 8, para 340. [2] Words substituted: Children and Young Persons Act 2008, s 39, Sch 3, paras 1, 27(1), (5).

Definitions. 'Child': s 105(1); 'child who is looked after by a local authority': s 22(1); 'contribution notice': Sch 2, para 22(1); 'contribution order': Sch 2, para 23(2); 'contributor': Sch 2, para 21(1); 'local authority': s 105(1); 'local authority foster parent': s 23(3); 'signed': s 105(1); 'the court': s 92(7).

SCHEDULE 3
SUPERVISION ORDERS

Sections 35 and 36

PART I
GENERAL

Meaning of 'responsible person'

1. In this Schedule, 'the responsible person', in relation to a supervised child, means –

- (a) any person who has parental responsibility for the child; and
- (b) any other person with whom the child is living.

Power of supervisor to give directions to supervised child

2. (1) A supervision order may require the supervised child to comply with any directions given from time to time by the supervisor which require him to do all or any of the following things –

- (a) to live at a place or places specified in the directions for a period or periods so specified;
- (b) to present himself to a person or persons specified in the directions at a place or places and on a day or days so specified;
- (c) to participate in activities specified in the directions on a day or days so specified.

(2) It shall be for the supervisor to decide whether, and to what extent, he exercises his power to give directions and to decide the form of any directions which he gives.

(3) Sub-paragraph (1) does not confer on a supervisor power to give directions in respect of any medical or psychiatric examination or treatment (which are matters dealt with in paragraphs 4 and 5).

Imposition of obligations on responsible person

3. (1) With the consent of any responsible person, a supervision order may include a requirement –

- (a) that he take all reasonable steps to ensure that the supervised child complies with any direction given by the supervisor under paragraph 2;
- (b) that he take all reasonable steps to ensure that the supervised child complies with any requirement included in the order under paragraph 4 or 5;
- (c) that he comply with any directions given by the supervisor requiring him to attend at a place specified in the directions for the purpose of taking part in activities so specified.

(2) A direction given under sub-paragraph (1)(c) may specify the time at which the responsible person is to attend and whether or not the supervised child is required to attend with him.

(3) A supervision order may require any person who is a responsible person in relation to the supervised child to keep the supervisor informed of his address, if it differs from the child's.

Psychiatric and medical examinations

4. (1) A supervision order may require the supervised child –

(a) to submit to a medical or psychiatric examination; or
(b) to submit to any such examination from time to time as directed by the supervisor.

(2) Any such examination shall be required to be conducted –

(a) by, or under the direction of, such registered medical practitioner as may be specified in the order;
(b) at a place specified in the order and at which the supervised child is to attend as a non-resident patient; or
(c) at –
  (i) a health service hospital; or
  (ii) in the case of a psychiatric examination, a hospital [, independent hospital or care home]¹,
at which the supervised child is, or is to attend as, a resident patient.

(3) A requirement of a kind mentioned in sub-paragraph (2)(c) shall not be included unless the court is satisfied, on the evidence of a registered medical practitioner, that –

(a) the child may be suffering from a physical or mental condition that requires, and may be susceptible to, treatment; and
(b) a period as a resident patient is necessary if the examination is to be carried out properly.

(4) No court shall include a requirement under this paragraph in a supervision order unless it is satisfied that –

(a) where the child has sufficient understanding to make an informed decision, he consents to its inclusion; and
(b) satisfactory arrangements have been, or can be, made for the examination.

Psychiatric and medical treatment

5. (1) Where a court which proposes to make or vary a supervision order is satisfied, on the evidence of a registered medical practitioner approved for the purposes of section 12 of the Mental Health Act 1983, that the mental condition of the supervised child –

(a) is such as requires, and may be susceptible to, treatment; but
(b) is not such as to warrant his detention in pursuance of a hospital order under Part III of that Act,

the court may include in the order a requirement that the supervised child shall, for a period specified in the order, submit to such treatment as is so specified.

(2) The treatment specified in accordance with sub-paragraph (1) must be –

(a) by, or under the direction of, such registered medical practitioner as may be specified in the order;
(b) as a non-resident patient at such a place as may be so specified; or
(c) as a resident patient in a hospital [, independent hospital or care home]¹.

(3) Where a court which proposes to make or vary a supervision order is satisfied, on the evidence of a registered medical practitioner, that the physical condition of the supervised child is such as requires, and may be susceptible to, treatment, the court may include in the order a requirement that the supervised child shall, for a period specified in the order, submit to such treatment as is so specified.

(4) The treatment specified in accordance with sub-paragraph (3) must be –

(a) by, or under the direction of, such registered medical practitioner as may be specified in the order;
(b) as a non-resident patient at such place as may be so specified; or
(c) as a resident patient in a health service hospital.

(5) No court shall include a requirement under this paragraph in a supervision order unless it is satisfied –

(a) where the child has sufficient understanding to make an informed decision, that he consents to its inclusion; and
(b) that satisfactory arrangements have been, or can be, made for the treatment.

(6) If a medical practitioner by whom or under whose direction a supervised person is being treated in pursuance of a requirement included in a supervision order by virtue of this paragraph is unwilling to continue to treat or direct the treatment of the supervised child or is of the opinion that –

(a) the treatment should be continued beyond the period specified in the order;
(b) the supervised child needs different treatment;
(c) he is not susceptible to treatment; or
(d) he does not require further treatment,

the practitioner shall make a report in writing to that effect to the supervisor.

(7) On receiving a report under this paragraph the supervisor shall refer it to the court, and on such a reference the court may make an order cancelling or varying the requirement.

NOTES

Amendments.¹ Words substituted: Care Standards Act 2000, s 116, Sch 4, para 14(24).

Definitions. 'Child': s 105(1); 'health service hospital': s 105(1); 'hospital': s 105(1); 'mental nursing home': s 105(1); 'parental responsibility': s 3; 'supervised child': s 105(1); 'supervision order': s 31(11); 'supervisor': s 105(1); 'the court': s 92(7); 'the responsible person': Sch 3, para 1.

PART II
MISCELLANEOUS

Life of supervision order

6. (1) Subject to sub-paragraph (2) and section 91, a supervision order shall cease to have effect at the end of the period of one year beginning with the date on which it was made.

(2) A supervision order shall also cease to have effect if an event mentioned in section 25(1)(a) or (b) of the Child Abduction and Custody Act 1985 (termination of existing orders) occurs with respect to the child.

(3) Where the supervisor applies to the court to extend, or further extend, a supervision order the court may extend the order for such period as it may specify.

(4) A supervision order may not be extended so as to run beyond the end of the period of three years beginning with the date on which it was made.

7. ...[1]

Information to be given to supervisor etc.

8. (1) A supervision order may require the supervised child –

(a) to keep the supervisor informed of any change in his address; and
(b) to allow the supervisor to visit him at the place where he is living.

(2) The responsible person in relation to any child with respect to whom a supervision order is made shall –

(a) if asked by the supervisor, inform him of the child's address (if it is known to him); and
(b) if he is living with the child, allow the supervisor reasonable contact with the child.

Selection of supervisor

9. (1) A supervision order shall not designate a local authority as the supervisor unless –

(a) the authority agree; or
(b) the supervised child lives or will live within their area.

(2)–(5) ...[2]

Effect of supervision order on earlier orders

10. The making of a supervision order with respect to any child brings to an end any earlier care or supervision order which –

(a) was made with respect to that child; and
(b) would otherwise continue in force.

Part I Statutes

Local authority functions and expenditure

11. (1) The Secretary of State may make regulations with respect to the exercise by a local authority of their functions where a child has been placed under their supervision by a supervision order.

(2) Where a supervision order requires compliance with directions given by virtue of this section, any expenditure incurred by the supervisor for the purposes of the directions shall be defrayed by the local authority designated in the order.

NOTES

Amendments.[1] Paragraph repealed: Courts and Legal Services Act 1990, ss 116, 125(7), Sch 16, para 27, Sch 20.[2] Subparagraphs omitted: Criminal Justice and Court Services Act 2000, ss 74, 75, Sch 7, paras 87, 96, Sch 8.

Definitions. 'Care order': ss 31(11), 105(1); 'child': s 105(1); 'local authority': s 105(1); 'supervised child': s 105(1); 'supervision order': s 31(11); 'supervisor': s 105(1); 'the appropriate authority': Sch 3, para 9(3); 'the responsible person': Sch 3, para 1.

PART III
EDUCATION SUPERVISION ORDERS

Effect of orders

12. (1) Where an education supervision order is in force with respect to a child, it shall be the duty of the supervisor –

(a) to advise, assist and befriend, and give directions to –
   (i) the supervised child; and
   (ii) his parents;
   in such a way as will, in the opinion of the supervisor, secure that he is properly educated;
(b) where any such directions given to
   (i) the supervised child; or
   (ii) a parent of his,
   have not been complied with, to consider what further steps to take in the exercise of the supervisor's powers under this Act.

(2) Before giving any directions under sub-paragraph (1) the supervisor shall, so far as is reasonably practicable, ascertain the wishes and feelings of –

(a) the child; and
(b) his parents;

including, in particular, their wishes as to the place at which the child should be educated.

(3) When settling the terms of any such directions, the supervisor shall give due consideration –

(a) having regard to the child's age and understanding, to such wishes and feelings of his as the supervisor has been able to ascertain; and
(b) to such wishes and feelings of the child's parents as he has been able to ascertain.

(4) Directions may be given under this paragraph at any time while the education supervision order is in force.

13. (1) Where an education supervision order is in force with respect to a child, the duties of the child's parents under [sections 7 and 444 of the Education Act 1996 (duties to secure education of children and]¹ to secure regular attendance of registered pupils) shall be superseded by their duty to comply with any directions in force under the education supervision order.

(2) Where an education supervision order is made with respect to a child –

- (a) any school attendance order –
    - (i) made under [section 437 of the Education Act 1996]¹ with respect to the child; and
    - (ii) in force immediately before the making of the education supervision order,

    shall cease to have effect; and
- (b) while the education supervision order remains in force, the following provisions shall not apply with respect to the child –
    - (i) [section 437]¹ of that Act (school attendance orders);
    - (ii) [section 9 of that Act]¹ (pupils to be educated in accordance with wishes of their parents);
    - (iii) [sections 411 and 423 of that Act]¹ (parental preference and appeals against admission decisions);
- [(c) a youth rehabilitation order made under Part 1 of the Criminal Justice and Immigration Act 2008 with respect to the child, while the education supervision order is in force, may not include an education requirement (within the meaning of that Part);]³
- (d) any education requirement of a kind mentioned in paragraph (c), which was in force with respect to the child immediately before the making of the education supervision order, shall cease to have effect.

Effect where child also subject to supervision order

14. (1) This paragraph applies where an education supervision order and a supervision order, or [youth rehabilitation order (within the meaning of Part 1 of the Criminal Justice and Immigration Act 2008)]³, are in force at the same time with respect to the same child.

(2) Any failure to comply with a direction given by the supervisor under the education supervision order shall be disregarded if it would not have been reasonably practicable to comply with it without failing to comply with a direction [or instruction]³ given under the other order.

Duration of orders

15. (1) An education supervision order shall have effect for a period of one year, beginning with the date on which it is made.

(2) An education supervision order shall not expire if, before it would otherwise have expired, the court has (on the application of the authority in whose favour the order was made) extended the period during which it is in force.

(3) Such an application may not be made earlier than three months before the date on which the order would otherwise expire.

(4) The period during which an education supervision order is in force may be extended under sub-paragraph (2) on more than one occasion.

(5) No one extension may be for a period of more than three years.

(6) An education supervision order shall cease to have effect on –

- (a) the child's ceasing to be of compulsory school age; or
- (b) the making of a care order with respect to the child;

and sub-paragraphs (1) to (4) are subject to this sub-paragraph.

Information to be given to supervisor etc.

16. (1) An education supervision order may require the child –

- (a) to keep the supervisor informed of any change in his address; and
- (b) to allow the supervisor to visit him at the place where he is living.

(2) A person who is the parent of a child with respect to whom an education supervision order has been made shall –

- (a) if asked by the supervisor, inform him of the child's address (if it is known to him); and
- (b) if he is living with the child, allow the supervisor reasonable contact with the child.

Discharge of orders

17. (1) The court may discharge any education supervision order on the application of –

- (a) the child concerned;
- (b) a parent of his; or
- (c) [the local authority designated in the order][4].

(2) On discharging an education supervision order, the court may direct the local authority within whose area the child lives, or will live, to investigate the circumstances of the child.

Offences

18. (1) If a parent of a child with respect to whom an education supervision order is in force persistently fails to comply with a direction given under the order he shall be guilty of an offence.

(2) It shall be a defence for any person charged with such an offence to prove that –

(a) he took all reasonable steps to ensure that the direction was complied with;
(b) the direction was unreasonable; or
(c) he had complied with –
  (i) a requirement included in a supervision order made with respect to the child; or
  (ii) directions given under such a requirement,
and that it was not reasonably practicable to comply both with the direction and with the requirement or directions mentioned in this paragraph.

(3) A person guilty of an offence under this paragraph shall be liable on summary conviction to a fine not exceeding level 3 on the standard scale.

Persistent failure of child to comply with directions

19. (1) Where a child with respect to whom an education supervision order is in force persistently fails to comply with any direction given under the order, [the local authority designated in the order shall notify the appropriate local authority, if different][4].

(2) Where a local authority have been notified under sub-paragraph (1) they shall investigate the circumstances of the child.

(3) In this paragraph 'the appropriate local authority' has the same meaning as in section 36.

Miscellaneous

20. The Secretary of State may by regulations make provision modifying, or displacing, the provisions of any enactment about education in relation to any child with respect to whom an education supervision order is in force to such extent as appears to the Secretary of State to be necessary or expedient in consequence of the provision made by this Act with respect to such orders.

Interpretation

21. In this part of this Schedule 'parent' has the same meaning as in [the Education Act 1996][1].

NOTES

Amendments.[1] Words substituted: Education Act 1996, s 582(1), Sch 37, Pt I, para 93.[2] Words substituted: Powers of Criminal Courts (Sentencing) Act 2000, s 165(1), Sch 9, para 131. 3 [3] Subparagraph and words substituted, and words inserted: Criminal Justice and Immigration Act 2008, s 6(2), Sch 4, Pt 1, paras 33, 37(1)–(3). [4] Words substituted: SI 2010/1158.

Definitions. 'Care order': ss 31(11), 105(1); 'child': s 105(1); 'education supervision order': s 36(2); 'local education authority': s 105(1); 'parent': Sch 3, para 21; 'supervised child': s 105(1); 'supervision order': s 31(11); 'supervisor': s 105(1); 'the appropriate local authority': Sch 3, para 19(3); 'the court': s 92(7).

SCHEDULE 4
MANAGEMENT AND CONDUCT OF COMMUNITY HOMES

Section 53(6)

PART I
INSTRUMENTS OF MANAGEMENT

Instruments of management for controlled and assisted community homes

1. (1) The Secretary of State may by order make an instrument of management providing for the constitution of a body of managers for any ...[1] home which is designated as a controlled or assisted community home.

(2) Sub-paragraph (3) applies where two or more ...[1] homes are designated as controlled community homes or as assisted community homes.

(3) If –

(a) those homes are, or are to be, provided by the same voluntary organisation; and

(b) the same local authority is to be represented on the body of managers for those homes,

a single instrument of management may be made by the Secretary of State under this paragraph constituting one body of managers for those homes or for any two or more of them.

(4) The number of persons who, in accordance with an instrument of management, constitute the body of managers for a ...[1] home shall be such number (which must be a multiple of three) as may be specified in the instrument.

(5) The instrument shall provide that the local authority specified in the instrument shall appoint –

(a) in the case of a ...[1] home which is designated as a controlled community home, two-thirds of the managers; and

(b) in the case of a ...[1] home which is designated as an assisted community home, one-third of them.

(6) An instrument of management shall provide that the foundation managers shall be appointed, in such manner and by such persons as may be specified in the instrument –

(a) so as to represent the interests of the voluntary organisation by which the home is, or is to be, provided; and

(b) for the purpose of securing that
 (i) so far as is practicable, the character of the home ...[1] will be preserved; and
 (ii) subject to paragraph 2(3), the terms of any trust deed relating to the home are observed.

(7) An instrument of management shall come into force on such date as it may specify.

(8) If an instrument of management is in force in relation to a ...¹ home the home shall be (and be known as) a controlled community home or an assisted community home, according to its designation.

(9) In this paragraph –

'foundation managers', in relation to a ...¹ home, means those of the managers of the home who are not appointed by a local authority in accordance with sub-paragraph (5); and

'designated' means designated in accordance with section 53.

2. (1) An instrument of management shall contain such provisions as the Secretary of State considers appropriate.

(2) Nothing in the instrument of management shall affect the purposes for which the premises comprising the home are held.

(3) Without prejudice to the generality of sub-paragraph (1), an instrument of management may contain provisions –

- (a) specifying the nature and purpose of the home (or each of the homes) to which it relates;
- (b) requiring a specified number or proportion of the places in that home (or those homes) to be made available to local authorities and to any other body specified in the instrument; and
- (c) relating to the management of that home (or those homes) and the charging of fees with respect to –
    - (i) children placed there; or
    - (ii) places made available to any local authority or other body.

(4) Subject to sub-paragraphs (1) and (2), in the event of any inconsistency between the provisions of any trust deed and an instrument of management, the instrument of management shall prevail over the provisions of the trust deed in so far as they relate to the home concerned.

(5) After consultation with the voluntary organisation concerned and with the local authority specified in its instrument of management, the Secretary of State may by order vary or revoke any provisions of the instrument.

NOTES

Amendments.[1] Words repealed: Courts and Legal Services Act 1990, ss 116, 125(7), Sch 16, para 28, Sch 20.

Definitions. 'Assisted community home': s 53(5); 'child': s 105(1); 'community home': s 53(1); 'controlled community home': s 53(4); 'designated': Sch 4, para 1(9); 'foundation managers': Sch 4, para 1(9); 'local authority': s 105(1); 'trust deed': s 55(6); 'voluntary home': s 60(3); 'voluntary organisation': s 105(1).

PART II
MANAGEMENT OF CONTROLLED AND ASSISTED COMMUNITY HOMES

3. (1) The management, equipment and maintenance of a controlled community home shall be the responsibility of the local authority specified in its instrument of management.

(2) The management, equipment and maintenance of an assisted community home shall be the responsibility of the voluntary organisation by which the home is provided.

(3) In this paragraph –

'home' means a controlled community home or (as the case may be) assisted community home; and
'the managers', in relation to a home, means the managers constituted by its instrument of management; and
'the responsible body', in relation to a home, means the local authority or (as the case may be) voluntary organisation responsible for its management, equipment and maintenance.

(4) The functions of a home's responsible body shall be exercised through the managers [, except in so far as, under section 53(3B), any of the accommodation is to be managed by another person][1].

(5) Anything done, liability incurred or property acquired by a home's managers shall be done, incurred or acquired by them as agents of the responsible body [; and similarly, to the extent that a contract so provides, as respects anything done, liability incurred or property acquired by a person by whom, under section 53(3B), any of the accommodation is to be managed][1].

(6) In so far as any matter is reserved for the decision of a home's responsible body by –

(a) sub-paragraph (8);
(b) the instrument of management;
(c) the service by the body on the managers, or any of them, of a notice reserving any matter,

that matter shall be dealt with by the body and not by the managers.

(7) In dealing with any matter so reserved, the responsible body shall have regard to any representations made to the body by the managers.

(8) The employment of persons at a home shall be a matter reserved for the decision of the responsible body.

(9) Where the instrument of management of a controlled community home so provides, the responsible body may enter into arrangements with the voluntary organisation by which that home is provided whereby, in accordance with such terms as may be agreed

between them and the voluntary organisation, persons who are not in the employment of the responsible body shall undertake duties at that home.

(10) Subject to sub-paragraph (11) –

(a) where the responsible body for an assisted community home proposes to engage any person to work at that home or to terminate without notice the employment of any person at that home, it shall consult the local authority specified in the instrument of management and, if that authority so direct, the responsible body shall not carry out its proposal without their consent; and

(b) that local authority may, after consultation with the responsible body, require that body to terminate the employment of any person at that home.

(11) Paragraphs (a) and (b) of sub-paragraph (10) shall not apply –

(a) in such cases or circumstances as may be specified by notice in writing given by the local authority to the responsible body; and

(b) in relation to the employment of any persons or class of persons specified in the home's instrument of management.

(12) The accounting year of the managers of a home shall be such as may be specified by the responsible body.

(13) Before such date in each accounting year as may be so specified, the managers of a home shall submit to the responsible body estimates, in such form as the body may require, of expenditure and receipts in respect of the next accounting year.

(14) Any expenses incurred by the managers of a home with the approval of the responsible body shall be defrayed by that body.

(15) The managers of a home shall keep –

(a) proper accounts with respect to the home; and
(b) proper records in relation to the accounts.

(16) Where an instrument of management relates to more than one home, one set of accounts and records may be kept in respect of all the homes to which it relates.

NOTES

Amendments.[1] Words inserted: Criminal Justice and Public Order Act 1994, s 22.

Definitions. 'Assisted community home': s 53(5); 'community home': s 53(1); 'controlled community home': s 53(4); 'functions': s 105(1); 'home': Sch 4, para 3(3); 'local authority': s 105(1); 'the managers': Sch 4, para 3(3); 'the responsible body': Sch 4, para 3(3).

PART III
REGULATIONS

4. (1) The Secretary of State may make regulations –

(a) as to the placing of children in community homes;

(b)–(c) …[1]

(2), (3) …[1]

NOTES

Amendments.[1] Paragraphs repealed: Care Standards Act 2000, s 117, Sch 6.

SCHEDULE 5
VOLUNTARY HOMES AND VOLUNTARY ORGANISATIONS

Section 60(4)

PART I
REGISTRATION OF VOLUNTARY HOMES

1.–6. ...[1]

NOTES

Amendments.[1] Part repealed: Care Standards Act 2000, s 117, Sch 6

PART II
REGULATIONS AS TO VOLUNTARY HOMES

Regulations as to conduct of voluntary homes

7. (1) The [appropriate national authority][2] may make regulations –

(a) as to the placing of children in voluntary homes;

(b)–(c) ...[1]

(2)–(4) ...[1]

8. ...[1]

NOTES

Amendments.[1] Paragraph and sub-paragraphs repealed: Care Standards Act 2000, s 117, Sch 6. [2] Words substituted: Children and Young Persons Act 2008, s 39, Sch 3, paras 1, 28.

SCHEDULE 6
[PRIVATE CHILDREN'S HOMES][1]

Section 63(11)

PART I
REGISTRATION

1.–9. ...[2]

NOTES

Amendments.[1] Heading substituted: Care Standards Act 2000, s 116, Sch 4, para 14(1), (25)(a). [2] Part repealed: Care Standards Act 2000, s 117, Sch 6.

PART II
REGULATIONS

10. (1) The Secretary of State may make regulations –

(a) as to the placing of children in [private][1] children's homes;

(b)–(c) ...²

(2) The regulations may in particular –

(a)–(k) ...²

(l) make provision similar to that made by regulations under section 26.

(3), (4) ...²

NOTES

Amendments.¹ Word substituted: Care Standards Act 2000, s 116, Sch 4, para 14(25).² Paragraphs and sub-paragraphs repealed: Care Standards Act 2000, s 117, Sch 6.

SCHEDULE 7
FOSTER PARENTS: LIMITS ON NUMBER OF FOSTER CHILDREN

Section 63(12)

Interpretation

1. For the purposes of this Schedule, a person fosters a child if –

(a) he is a local authority foster parent in relation to the child;
(b) he is a foster parent with whom the child has been placed by a voluntary organisation; or
(c) he fosters the child privately.

The usual fostering limit

2. Subject to what follows, a person may not foster more than three children ('the usual fostering limit').

Siblings

3. A person may exceed the usual fostering limit if the children concerned are all siblings with respect to each other.

Exemption by local authority

4. (1) A person may exceed the usual fostering limit if he is exempted from it by the local authority within whose area he lives.

(2) In considering whether to exempt a person, a local authority shall have regard, in particular, to –

(a) the number of children whom the person proposes to foster;
(b) the arrangements which the person proposes for the care and accommodation of the fostered children;
(c) the intended and likely relationship between the person and the fostered children;
(d) the period of time for which he proposes to foster the children; and
(e) whether the welfare of the fostered children (and of any other children who are or will be living in the accommodation) will be safeguarded and promoted.

(3) Where a local authority exempt a person, they shall inform him by notice in writing –

(a) that he is so exempted;
(b) of the children, described by name, whom he may foster; and
(c) of any condition to which the exemption is subject.

(4) A local authority may at any time by notice in writing –

(a) vary or cancel an exemption; or
(b) impose, vary or cancel a condition to which the exemption is subject,

and, in considering whether to do so, they shall have regard in particular to the considerations mentioned in sub-paragraph (2).

(5) The Secretary of State may make regulations amplifying or modifying the provisions of this paragraph in order to provide for cases where children need to be placed with foster parents as a matter of urgency.

Effect of exceeding fostering limit

5. (1) A person shall cease to be treated [, for the purposes of this Act and the Care Standards Act 2000]¹ as fostering and shall be treated as carrying on a children's home if –

(a) he exceeds the usual fostering limit; or
(b) where he is exempted under paragraph 4 –
  (i) he fosters any child not named in the exemption; and
  (ii) in so doing, he exceeds the usual fostering limit.

(2) Sub-paragraph (1) does not apply if the children concerned are all siblings in respect of each other.

NOTES

Amendments.¹ Words inserted: Care Standards Act 2000, s 116, Sch 4, para 14(26).

Complaints etc

6. (1) Every local authority shall establish a procedure for considering any representations (including any complaint) made to them about the discharge of their functions under paragraph 4 by a person exempted or seeking to be exempted under that paragraph.

(2) In carrying out any consideration of representations under subparagraph (1), a local authority shall comply with any regulations made by the Secretary of State for the purposes of this paragraph.

NOTES

Definitions. 'Child': s 105(1); 'children's home': s 63(3); 'foster': Sch 7, para 1; 'local authority': s 105(1); 'local authority foster parent': s 23(3); 'the usual fostering limit': Sch 7, para 2; 'voluntary organisation': s 105(1).

SCHEDULE 8
PRIVATELY FOSTERED CHILDREN

Section 66(5)

Exemptions

1. A child is not a privately fostered child while he is being looked after by a local authority.

2. (1) A child is not a privately fostered child while he is in the care of any person –

- (a) in premises in which any –
    - (i) parent of his;
    - (ii) person who is not a parent of his but who has parental responsibility for him; or
    - (iii) person who is a relative of his and who has assumed responsibility for his care,

    is for the time being living;
- (b) ...[1]
- (c) in accommodation provided by or on behalf of any voluntary organisation;
- (d) in any school in which he is receiving full-time education;
- (e) in any health service hospital;
- (f) [in any care home or independent hospital;][2]
- (g) in any home or institution not specified in this paragraph but provided, equipped and maintained by the Secretary of State.

(2) Sub-paragraph [(1)(c)][1] to (g) does not apply where the person caring for the child is doing so in his personal capacity and not in the course of carrying out his duties in relation to the establishment mentioned in the paragraph in question.

NOTES

Amendments.[1] Sub-paragraph repealed and word substituted: Care Standards Act 2000, s 116, Sch 4, para 14(27). [2] Sub-paragraph substituted: Care Standards Act 2000, s 116, Sch 4, para 14(28).

3. A child is not a privately fostered child while he is in the care of any person in compliance with –

- [(a) a youth rehabilitation order made under section 1 of the Criminal Justice and Immigration Act 2008;][2]; or
- (b) a supervision requirement within the meaning of [Part II of the Children (Scotland) Act 1995][1].

NOTES

Amendments.[1] Words substituted: Children (Scotland) Act 1995, s 105(4), Sch 4, para 48(1), (5). [2] Subparagraph substituted: Criminal Justice and Immigration Act 2008, s 6(2), Sch 4, Pt 1, paras 33, 38.

4. A child is not a privately fostered child while he is liable to be detained, or subject to guardianship, under the Mental Health Act 1983.

5. A child is not a privately fostered child while [he is placed in the care of a person who proposes to adopt him under arrangements made by an adoption agency within the meaning of –

(a) section 2 of the Adoption and Children Act 2002;
(b) section 1 of the Adoption (Scotland) Act 1978; or
(c) Article 3 of the Adoption (Northern Ireland) Order 1987][1]

[or while he is a child in respect of whom a local authority have functions by virtue of regulations under section 83(6)(b) of the Adoption and Children Act 2002 (which relates to children brought into the United Kingdom for adoption), or corresponding functions by virtue of regulations under section 1 of the Adoption (Intercountry Aspects) Act 1999 (regulations to give effect to Hague Convention on Protection of Children and Co-operation in respect of Intercountry Adoption)][2]

NOTES

Amendments.[1] Words substituted: Adoption and Children Act 2002, s 139(1), Sch 3, paras 54, 73. [2] Words inserted: Children and Adoption Act 2006, s 14(3).

Power of local authority to impose requirements

6. (1) Where a person is fostering any child privately, or proposes to foster any child privately, the appropriate local authority may impose on him requirements as to –

(a) the number, age and sex of the children who may be privately fostered by him;
(b) the standard of the accommodation and equipment to be provided for them;
(c) the arrangements to be made with respect to their health and safety; and
(d) particular arrangements which must be made with respect to the provision of care for them,

and it shall be his duty to comply with any such requirement before the end of such period as the authority may specify unless, in the case of a proposal, the proposal is not carried out.

(2) A requirement may be limited to a particular child, or class of child.

(3) A requirement (other than one imposed under sub-paragraph (1)(a)) may be limited by the authority so as to apply only when the number of children fostered by the person exceeds a specified number.

(4) A requirement shall be imposed by notice in writing addressed to the person on whom it is imposed and informing him of –

(a) the reason for imposing the requirement;
(b) his right under paragraph 8 to appeal against it; and
(c) the time within which he may do so.

(5) A local authority may at any time vary any requirement, impose any additional requirement or remove any requirement.

(6) In this Schedule –
   (a) 'the appropriate local authority' means –
      (i) the local authority within whose area the child is being fostered; or
      (ii) in the case of a proposal to foster a child, the local authority within whose area it is proposed that he will be fostered; and
   (b) 'requirement', in relation to any person, means a requirement imposed on him under this paragraph.

Regulations requiring notification of fostering etc

7. (1) The Secretary of State may by regulations make provision as to –
   (a) the circumstances in which notification is required to be given in connection with children who are, have been or are proposed to be fostered privately; and
   (b) the manner and form in which such notification is to be given.

(2) The regulations may, in particular –
   (a) require any person who is, or proposes to be, involved (whether or not directly) in arranging for a child to be fostered privately to notify the appropriate authority;
   (b) require any person who is –
      (i) a parent of a child; or
      (ii) a person who is not a parent of his but who has parental responsibility for a child,
      and who knows that it is proposed that the child should be fostered privately, to notify the appropriate authority;
   (c) require any parent of a privately fostered child, or person who is not a parent of such a child but who has parental responsibility for him, to notify the appropriate authority of any change in his address;
   (d) require any person who proposes to foster a child privately, to notify the appropriate authority of his proposal;
   (e) require any person who is fostering a child privately, or proposes to do so, to notify the appropriate authority of –
      (i) any offence of which he has been convicted;
      (ii) any disqualification imposed on him under section 68; or
      (iii) any prohibition imposed on him under section 69;
   (f) require any person who is fostering a child privately, to notify the appropriate authority of any change in his address;
   (g) require any person who is fostering a child privately to notify the appropriate authority in writing of any person who begins, or ceases, to be part of his household;
   (h) require any person who has been fostering a child privately, but has ceased to do so, to notify the appropriate authority (indicating, where the child has died, that that is the reason).

Part I Statutes

[**7A.** Every local authority must promote public awareness in their area of requirements as to notification for which provision is made under paragraph 7.]¹

NOTES

Amendments.¹ Paragraph inserted in relation to England: Children Act 2004, s 44(7).

Appeals

8. (1) A person aggrieved by –

(a) a requirement imposed under paragraph 6;
(b) a refusal of consent under section 68;
(c) a prohibition imposed under section 69;
(d) a refusal to cancel such a prohibition;
(e) a refusal to make an exemption under paragraph 4 of Schedule 7;
(f) a condition imposed in such an exemption; or
(g) a variation or cancellation of such an exemption,

may appeal to the court.

(2) The appeal must be made within fourteen days from the date on which the person appealing is notified of the requirement, refusal, prohibition, condition, variation or cancellation.

(3) Where the appeal is against –

(a) a requirement imposed under paragraph 6;
(b) a condition of an exemption imposed under paragraph 4 of Schedule 7; or
(c) a variation or cancellation of such an exemption,

the requirement, condition, variation or cancellation shall not have effect while the appeal is pending.

(4) Where it allows an appeal against a requirement or prohibition, the court may, instead of cancelling the requirement or prohibition –

(a) vary the requirement, or allow more time for compliance with it; or
(b) if an absolute prohibition has been imposed, substitute for it a prohibition on using the premises after such time as the court may specify unless such specified requirements as the local authority had power to impose under paragraph 6 are complied with.

(5) Any requirement or prohibition specified or substituted by a court under this paragraph shall be deemed for the purposes of Part IX (other than this paragraph) to have been imposed by the local authority under paragraph 6 or (as the case may be) section 69.

(6) Where it allows an appeal against a refusal to make an exemption, a condition imposed in such an exemption or a variation or cancellation of such an exemption, the court may –

(a) make an exemption;

(b) impose a condition; or
(c) vary the exemption.

(7) Any exemption made or varied under sub-paragraph (6), or any condition imposed under that sub-paragraph, shall be deemed for the purposes of Schedule 7 (but not for the purposes of this paragraph) to have been made, varied or imposed under that Schedule.

(8) Nothing in sub-paragraph (1)(e) to (g) confers any right of appeal on –

(a) a person who is, or would be if exempted under Schedule 7, a local authority foster parent; or
(b) a person who is, or would be if so exempted, a person with whom a child is placed by a voluntary organisation.

Extension of Part IX to certain school children during holidays

9. (1) Where a child under sixteen who is a pupil at a school . . .[1] lives at the school during school holidays for a period of more than two weeks, Part IX shall apply in relation to the child as if –

(a) while living at the school, he were a privately fostered child; and
(b) paragraphs [2(1)(c) and (d)][2] and 6 were omitted.

[But this sub-paragraph does not apply to a school which is an appropriate children's home.][2]

(2) Sub-paragraph (3) applies to any person who proposes to care for and accommodate one or more children at a school in circumstances in which some or all of them will be treated as private foster children by virtue of this paragraph.

(3) That person shall, not less than two weeks before the first of those children is treated as a private foster child by virtue of this paragraph during the holiday in question, give written notice of his proposal to the local authority within whose area the child is ordinarily resident ('the appropriate authority'), stating the estimated number of the children.

(4) A local authority may exempt any person from the duty of giving notice under sub-paragraph (3).

(5) Any such exemption may be granted for a special period or indefinitely and may be revoked at any time by notice in writing given to the person exempted.

(6) Where a child who is treated as a private foster child by virtue of this paragraph dies, the person caring for him at the school shall, not later than 48 hours after the death, give written notice of it –

(a) to the appropriate local authority; and
(b) where reasonably practicable, to each parent of the child and to every person who is not a parent of his but who has parental responsibility for him.

(7) Where a child who is treated as a foster child by virtue of this paragraph ceases for any other reason to be such a child, the person caring for him at the school shall give written notice of the fact to the appropriate local authority.

NOTES

Amendments.[1] Words repealed: Care Standards Act 2000, s 110.[2] Words inserted and substituted: Care Standards Act 2000, s 116, Sch 4, para 14(27).

Prohibition of advertisements relating to fostering

10. No advertisement indicating that a person will undertake, or will arrange for, a child to be privately fostered shall be published, unless it states that person's name and address.

Avoidance of insurances on lives of privately fostered children

11. A person who fosters a child privately and for reward shall be deemed for the purposes of the Life Assurance Act 1774 to have no interest in the life of the child.

NOTES

Definitions. 'Child': s 105(1); 'child who is looked after by a local authority': s 22(1); 'children's home': s 63(3); 'health service hospital': s 105(1); 'local authority': s 105(1); 'local authority foster parent': s 23(3); 'local education authority': s 105(1); 'mental nursing home': s 105(1); 'nursing home': s 105(1); 'parental responsibility': s 3; 'privately fostered child': s 66; 'relative': s 105(1); 'requirement': Sch 8, para 6(6); 'residential care home': s 105(1); 'school': s 105(1); 'the appropriate local authority': Sch 8, para 6(6); 'the court': s 92(7); 'to foster a child privately': s 66; 'voluntary organisation': s 105(1).

[Schedule 9 ceases to extend to England and Wales.]

[SCHEDULE 9A
CHILD MINDING AND DAY CARE FOR YOUNG CHILDREN [IN WALES][1]

NOTES

Amendments.[1] Words inserted: Childcare Act 2006, s 103(1), Sch 2, para 18(1), (2).

Exemption of certain schools

1. (1) Except in prescribed circumstances, Part XA does not apply to provision of day care within sub-paragraph (2) for any child looked after in –

    (a)   a maintained school;
    (b)   a school assisted by a [local authority][2];
    (c)   a school in respect of which payments are made by ...[1] the Assembly under section 485 of the Education Act 1996;
    (d)   an independent school.

(2) The provision mentioned in sub-paragraph (1) is provision of day care made by –

    (a)   the person carrying on the establishment in question as part of the establishment's activities; or

(b) a person employed to work at that establishment and authorised to make that provision as part of the establishment's activities.

(3) In sub-paragraph (1) –

'assisted' has the same meaning as in the Education Act 1996;
'maintained school' has the meaning given by section 20(7) of the School Standards and Framework Act 1998.

NOTES

Amendments.[1] Words repealed: Childcare Act 2006, s 103, Sch 2, para 18(1), (3), Sch 3, Pt 2.
[2] Words substituted: SI 2010/1158.

Exemption for other establishments

2. (1) Part XA does not apply to provision of day care within sub-paragraph (2) for any child looked after –

(a) in an appropriate children's home;
(b) in a care home;
(c) as a patient in a hospital (within the meaning of the Care Standards Act 2000);
(d) in a residential family centre.

(2) The provision mentioned in sub-paragraph (1) is provision of day care made by –

(a) the department, authority or other person carrying on the establishment in question as part of the establishment's activities; or
(b) a person employed to work at that establishment and authorised to make that provision as part of the establishment's activities.

[**2A.** (1) Part XA does not apply to provision of day care in a hotel, guest house or other similar establishment for children staying in that establishment where –

(a) the provision takes place only between 6pm and 2 am; and
(b) the person providing the care is doing so for no more than two different clients at the same time.

(2) For the purposes of sub-paragraph (1)(b), a 'client' is a person at whose request (or persons at whose joint request) day care is provided for a child.][1]

NOTES

Amendments. [1] Paragraph inserted: Children Act 2004, s 48, Sch 4, paras 1, 7.

Exemption for occasional facilities

3. (1) Where day care is provided on particular premises on less than six days in any year, that provision shall be disregarded for the purposes of Part XA if the person making it has notified [the Assembly][1] in writing before the first occasion on which the premises concerned are so used in that year.

(2) In sub-paragraph (1) 'year' means the year beginning with the day (after the commencement of paragraph 5 of Schedule 9) on which the day care in question was or is first provided on the premises concerned and any subsequent year.

NOTES

Amendments.[1] Words substituted: Childcare Act 2006, s 103(1), Sch 2, para 6.

Disqualification for registration

4. (1) Regulations may provide for a person to be disqualified for registration for child minding or providing day care [in Wales][6].

(2) The regulations may, in particular, provide for a person to be disqualified where –

- (a) he is included in the list kept under section 1 of the Protection of Children Act 1999;
- [(b) he is subject to a direction under section 142 of the Education Act 2002, given on the grounds that he is unsuitable to work with children [or on grounds relating to his health][5]][2];
- [(ba) he is barred from regulated activity relating to children (within the meaning of section 3(2) of the Safeguarding Vulnerable Groups Act 2006);][24]
- (c) an order of a prescribed kind has been made at any time with respect to him;
- (d) an order of a prescribed kind has been made at any time with respect to any child who has been in his care;
- (e) a requirement of a prescribed kind has been imposed at any time with respect to such a child, under or by virtue of any enactment;
- (f) he has at any time been refused registration under Part X or Part XA[, or Part 3 of the Childcare Act 2006,][6] or any prescribed enactment or had any such registration cancelled;
- (g) he has been convicted of any offence of a prescribed kind, or has been ...[4] discharged absolutely or conditionally for any such offence;
- [(ga) he has been given a caution in respect of any offence of a prescribed kind;][5]
- (h) he has at any time been disqualified from fostering a child privately;
- (j) a prohibition has been imposed on him at any time under section 69, section 10 of the Foster Children (Scotland) Act 1984 or any prescribed enactment;
- (k) his rights and powers with respect to a child have at any time been vested in a prescribed authority under a prescribed enactment.

(3) Regulations may provide for a person who lives –

- (a) in the same household as a person who is himself disqualified for registration for child minding or providing day care [in Wales]; or
- (b) in a household at which any such person is employed,

to be disqualified for registration for child minding or providing day care [in Wales].

[(3A) Regulations under this paragraph may provide for a person not to be disqualified for registration [(and may in particular provide for a person not to be disqualified for registration for the purposes of sub-paragraphs (4) and (5))][3] by reason of any fact which would otherwise cause him to be disqualified if –

(a) he has disclosed the fact to [the Assembly][6], and
(b) [the Assembly][6] has consented in writing ...[3] and has not withdrawn that consent.][1]

(4) A person who is disqualified for registration for providing day care [in Wales][6] shall not provide day care, or be [directly][3] concerned in the management of ...[3] any provision of day care [in Wales][6].

(5) No person shall employ, in connection with the provision of day care [in Wales][6], a person who is disqualified for registration for providing day care [in Wales][6].

[(6) In this paragraph –

'caution' includes a reprimand or warning within the meaning of section 65 of the Crime and Disorder Act 1998;
'enactment' means any enactment having effect, at any time, in any part of the United Kingdom.][5]

[(7) A conviction in respect of which a probation order was made before 1st October 1992 (which would not otherwise be treated as a conviction) is to be treated as a conviction for the purposes of this paragraph.][4]

NOTES

Amendments.[1] Sub-paragraph inserted: Education Act 2002, s 152, Sch 13, para 6.[2] Subparagraph substituted: Education Act 2002, s 215(1), Sch 21, para 9.[3] Words inserted or repealed in relation to England: Children Act 2004, ss 48, 64, Sch 4, paras 1, 5, 8, Sch 5, Pt 2.[4] Words repealed and subparagraph inserted: Criminal Justice Act 2003, ss 304, 332, Sch 32, Pt 1, paras 59, 61(1)–(3), Sch 37, Pt 7.[5] Words and subparagraph inserted, and subparagraph substituted: Childcare Act 2006, s 102(1), (2)(a).[6] Words inserted and substituted: Childcare Act 2006, s 103(1), Sch 2, paras 6, 18(1), (4).[7] Subparagraph inserted: Safeguarding Vulnerable Groups Act 2006, s 63(1), Sch 9, Pt 1, para 1. [25] Words substituted: SI 2010/1158.

5. (1) If any person –

(a) acts as a child minder [in Wales][1] at any time when he is disqualified for registration for child minding [in Wales][1]; or
(b) contravenes [sub-paragraph (4) or (5)][2] of paragraph 4,

he shall be guilty of an offence.

[(2) A person who contravenes sub-paragraph (4) of paragraph 4 shall not be guilty of an offence under this paragraph if –

(a) he is disqualified for registration by virtue only of regulations made under sub-paragraph (3) of paragraph 4, and

Part I Statutes

(b) he proves that he did not know, and had no reasonable grounds for believing, that he was living in the same household as a person who was disqualified for registration or in a household in which such a person was employed.]²

(3) Where a person contravenes sub-paragraph (5) of paragraph 4, he shall not be guilty of an offence under this paragraph if he proves that he did not know, and had no reasonable grounds for believing, that the person whom he was employing was disqualified.

(4) A person guilty of an offence under this paragraph shall be liable on summary conviction to imprisonment for a term not exceeding six months, or to a fine not exceeding level 5 on the standard scale, or to both.

NOTES

Amendments.¹ Words inserted: Childcare Act 2006, s 103(1), Sch 2, para 18(1), (5).² Words and subparagraph substituted in relation to England: Childcare Act 2006, s 103(1), Sch 2, para 18(1), (5).

[Provision of day care: unincorporated associations

5A. (1) References in Part XA to a person, so far as relating to the provision of day care, include an unincorporated association.

(2) Proceedings for an offence under Part XA which is alleged to have been committed by an unincorporated association must be brought in the name of the association (and not in that of any of its members).

(3) For the purpose of any such proceedings, rules of court relating to the service of documents are to have effect as if the association were a body corporate.

(4) In proceedings for an offence under Part XA brought against an unincorporated association, section 33 of the Criminal Justice Act 1925 and Schedule 3 to the Magistrates' Courts Act 1980 (procedure) apply as they do in relation to a body corporate.

(5) A fine imposed on an unincorporated association on its conviction of an offence under Part XA is to be paid out of the funds of the association.

(6) If an offence under Part XA committed by an unincorporated association is shown –

(a) to have been committed with the consent or connivance of an officer of the association or a member of its governing body, or
(b) to be attributable to any neglect on the part of such an officer or member,

the officer or member as well as the association is guilty of the offence and liable to proceeded against and punished accordingly.]¹

NOTES

Amendments.¹ Paragraph inserted: Children Act 2004, s 48, Sch 4, paras 1, 9.

Certificates of registration

6. (1) If an application for registration is granted, [the Assembly]¹ shall give the applicant a certificate of registration.

(2) A certificate of registration shall give prescribed information about prescribed matters.

(3) Where, due to a change of circumstances, any part of the certificate requires to be amended, [the Assembly]¹ shall issue an amended certificate.

(4) Where [the Assembly]¹ is satisfied that the certificate has been lost or destroyed, the authority shall issue a copy, on payment by the registered person of any prescribed fee.

(5) For the purposes of Part XA, a person is –

- (a) registered for providing child minding [in Wales]¹; or
- (b) registered for providing day care on any premises [in Wales]¹,

if a certificate of registration to that effect is in force in respect of him.

NOTES

Amendments.¹ Words substituted and inserted: Childcare Act 2006, s 103(1), Sch 2, paras 6, 18(1), (6).

...¹ Fees

7. Regulations may require registered persons to pay to [the Assembly]²[, at or by the prescribed times, fees of the prescribed amounts in respect of the discharge by [the Assembly]² of its functions under Part XA]¹.

NOTES

Amendments.¹ Word repealed and words substituted: Children Act 2004, ss 48, 64, Sch 4, paras 1, 4(2), Sch 5, Pt 2.² Words substituted: Childcare Act 2006, s 103(1), Sch 2, para 6.

Co-operation between authorities

8. (1) ...¹

(2) Where it appears to the Assembly that any local authority in Wales could, by taking any specified action, help in the exercise of any of its functions under Part XA, the Assembly may request the help of that authority specifying the action in question.

(3) An authority whose help is so requested shall comply with the request if it is compatible with their own statutory or other duties and obligations and does not unduly prejudice the discharge of any of their functions.]²

NOTES

Amendments.¹ Subparagraph repealed: Childcare Act 2006, s 103, Sch 2, para 18(1), (7), Sch 3, Pt 2.² Schedule inserted: Care Standards Act 2000, s 79(2), Sch 3.

SCHEDULE 10
AMENDMENTS OF ADOPTION LEGISLATION

[not reproduced]

SCHEDULE 11
JURISDICTION

Section 92

PART I
GENERAL

Commencement of proceedings

1. (1) The Lord Chancellor may[, after consulting the Lord Chief Justice,]⁴ by order specify proceedings under this Act or [the Adoption and Children Act 2002]³ which may only be commenced in –

(a) a specified level of court;
(b) a court which falls within a specified class of court; or
(c) a particular court determined in accordance with, or specified in, the order.

(2) The Lord Chancellor may[, after consulting the Lord Chief Justice,]⁴ by order specify circumstances in which specified proceedings under this Act or [the Adoption and Children Act 2002]³ (which might otherwise be commenced elsewhere) may only be commenced in –

(a) a specified level of court;
(b) a court which falls within a specified class of court; or
(c) a particular court determined in accordance with, or specified in, the order.

[(2A) Sub-paragraphs (1) and (2) shall also apply in relation to proceedings –

[(a) under section 55A of the Family Law Act 1986 (declarations of parentage); or]²
(b) which are to be dealt with in accordance with an order made under section 45 [of the Child Support Act 1991]² (jurisdiction of courts in certain proceedings under that Act).]¹

(3) The Lord Chancellor may[, after consulting the Lord Chief Justice,]⁴ by order make provision by virtue of which, where specified proceedings with respect to a child under –

(a) this Act;
(b) [the Adoption and Children Act 2002]³;
[(bb) section 20 (appeals) ...² of the Child Support Act 1991;]¹ or
(c) the High Court's inherent jurisdiction with respect to children,

have been commenced in or transferred to any court (whether or not by virtue of an order under this Schedule), any other specified family proceedings which may affect, or are otherwise connected with, the child may, in specified circumstances, only be commenced in that court.

(4) A class of court specified in an order under this Schedule may be described by reference to a description of proceedings and may include different levels of court.

Transfer of proceedings

2. (1) The Lord Chancellor may[, after consulting the Lord Chief Justice,][4] by order provide that in specified circumstances the whole, or any specified part of, specified proceedings to which this paragraph applies shall be transferred to –

(a) a specified level of court;
(b) a court which falls within a specified class of court; or
(c) a particular court determined in accordance with, or specified in, the order.

(2) Any order under this paragraph may provide for the transfer to be made at any stage, or specified stage, of the proceedings and whether or not the proceedings, or any part of them, have already been transferred.

(3) The proceedings to which this paragraph applies are –

(a) any proceedings under this Act;
(b) any proceedings under [the Adoption and Children Act 2002][3];
[(ba) any proceedings under section 55A of the Family Law Act 1986][2]
[(bb) [any proceedings under][2] section 20 (appeals) …[2] of the Child Support Act 1991;][1]
(c) any other proceedings which –
   (i) are family proceedings for the purposes of this Act, other than proceedings under the inherent jurisdiction of the High Court; and
   (ii) may affect, or are otherwise connected with, the child concerned.

(4) Proceedings to which this paragraph applies by virtue of sub-paragraph (3)(c) may only be transferred in accordance with the provisions of an order made under this paragraph for the purpose of consolidating them with proceedings under –

(a) this Act;
(b) [the Adoption and Children Act 2002][3]; or
(c) the High Court's inherent jurisdiction with respect to children.

(5) An order under this paragraph may make such provision as the Lord Chancellor thinks appropriate[, after consulting the Lord Chief Justice,][4] for excluding proceedings to which this paragraph applies from the operation of any enactment which would otherwise govern the transfer of those proceedings, or any part of them.

Part I Statutes

Hearings by single justice

3. (1) In such circumstances as the Lord Chancellor may[, after consulting the Lord Chief Justice,]⁴ by order specify –

(a) the jurisdiction of a magistrates' court to make an emergency protection order;

(b) any specified question with respect to the transfer of specified proceedings to or from a magistrates' court in accordance with the provisions of an order under paragraph 2,

may be exercised by a single justice.

(2) Any provision made under this paragraph shall be without prejudice to any other enactment or rule of law relating to the functions which may be performed by a single justice of the peace.

General

4. (1) For the purposes of this Schedule –

(a) the commencement of proceedings under this Act includes the making of any application under this Act in the course of proceedings (whether or not those proceedings are proceedings under this Act); and

(b) there are three levels of court, that is to say the High Court, any county court and any magistrates' court.

(2) In this Schedule 'specified' means specified by an order made under this Schedule.

(3) Any order under paragraph 1 may make provision as to the effect of commencing proceedings in contravention of any of the provisions of the order.

(4) An order under paragraph 2 may make provision as to the effect of a failure to comply with any of the provisions of the order.

(5) An order under this Schedule may –

(a) make such consequential, incidental or transitional provision as the Lord Chancellor considers expedient, [after consulting the Lord Chief Justice,]⁴ including provision amending any other enactment so far as it concerns the jurisdiction of any court or justice of the peace;

(b) make provision for treating proceedings which are –
  (i) in part proceedings of a kind mentioned in paragraph (a) or (b) of paragraph 2(3); and
  (ii) in part proceedings of a kind mentioned in paragraph (c) of paragraph 2(3),
as consisting entirely of proceedings of one or other of those kinds, for the purposes of the application of any order made under paragraph 2.

[(6) The Lord Chief Justice may nominate a judicial office holder (as defined in section 109(4) of the Constitutional Reform Act 2005) to exercise his functions under this Part of this Schedule.]

NOTES

Amendments.[1] Words inserted: Child Support Act 1991, s 45(3)–(5).[2] Words inserted, substituted or repealed: Child Support, Pensions and Social Security Act 2000, ss 83, 85, Sch 8, para 10(1)–(3), Sch 9, Part IX.[3] Words substituted: Adoption and Children Act 2002, s 139(1), Sch 3, paras 54, 75.[4] Words and subparagraph inserted: Constitutional Reform Act 2005, s 15(1), Sch 4, Pt 1, paras 203, 210(1)–(2).

Definitions. 'Child': s 105(1); 'class of court': Sch 11, para 1(4); 'emergency protection order': s 44(4); 'family proceedings': s 8(3); 'functions': s 105(1); 'levels of court': Sch 11, para 4(1); 'specified': Sch 11, para 4(2); 'the commencement of proceedings under this Act': Sch 11, para 4(1).

PART II
CONSEQUENTIAL AMENDMENTS

[not reproduced]

SCHEDULE 12
MINOR AMENDMENTS

[not reproduced]

SCHEDULE 13
CONSEQUENTIAL AMENDMENTS

[not reproduced]

SCHEDULE 14
TRANSITIONALS AND SAVINGS

Section 108(6)

Pending Proceedings, etc

1. (1) [Subject to sub-paragraphs (1A) and (4)][1], nothing in any provision of this Act (other than the repeals mentioned in sub-paragraph (2)) shall affect any proceedings which are pending immediately before the commencement of that provision.

[(1A) Proceedings pursuant to section 7(2) of the Family Law Reform Act 1969 (committal or wards of court to care of local authority) or in the exercise of the High Court's inherent jurisdiction with respect to children which are pending in relation to a child who has been placed or allowed to remain in the care of a local authority shall not be treated as pending proceedings after 13th October 1992 for the purposes of this Schedule if no final order has been made by that date pursuant to section 7(2) of the 1969 Act or in the exercise of the High Court's inherent jurisdiction in respect of the child's care.][1]

(2) The repeals are those of –

    (a) section 42(3) of the Matrimonial Causes Act 1973 (declaration by court that party to marriage unfit to have custody of children of family); and

    (b) section 38 of the Sexual Offences Act 1956 (power of court to divest person of authority over girl or boy in cases of incest).

(3) For the purposes of the following provisions of this Schedule, any reference to an order in force immediately before the commencement of a provision of this Act shall be construed as including a reference to an order made after that commencement in proceedings pending before that commencement.

(4) Sub-paragraph (3) is not to be read as making the order in question have effect from a date earlier than that on which it was made.

(5) An order under section 96(3) may make such provision with respect to the application of the order in relation to proceedings which are pending when the order comes into force as the Lord Chancellor considers appropriate.

2. Where, immediately before the day on which Part IV comes into force, there was in force an order under section 3(1) of the Children and Young Persons Act 1963 (order directing a local authority to bring a child or young person before a [youth court][6] under section 1 of the Children and Young Persons Act 1969), the order shall cease to have effect on that day.

CUSTODY ORDERS, ETC

Cessation of declarations of unfitness, etc.

3. Where, immediately before the day on which Parts I and II come into force, there was in force –

(a) a declaration under section 42(3) of the Matrimonial Causes Act 1973 (declaration by court that party to marriage unfit to have custody of children of family); or

(b) an order under section 38(1) of the Sexual Offences Act 1956 divesting a person of authority over a girl or boy in a case of incest;

the declaration or, as the case may be, the order shall cease to have effect on that day.

The Family Law Reform Act 1987 (c. 42)

Conversion of orders under section 4

4. Where, immediately before the day on which Parts I and II come into force, there was in force an order under section 4(1) of the Family Law Reform Act 1987 (order giving father parental rights and duties in relation to a child), then, on and after that day, the order shall be deemed to be an order under section 4 of this Act giving the father parental responsibility for the child.

Orders to which paragraphs 6 to 11 apply

5. (1) In paragraphs 6 to 11 'an existing order' means any order which –

(a) is in force immediately before the commencement of Parts I and II;
(b) was made under any enactment mentioned in sub-paragraph (2);
(c) determines all or any of the following –
  (i) who is to have custody of a child;

(ii) who is to have care and control of a child;
(iii) who is to have access to a child;
(iv) any matter with respect to a child's education or upbringing; and
(d) is not an order of a kind mentioned in paragraph 15(1).

(2) The enactments are –

(a) the Domestic Proceedings and Magistrates' Courts Act 1978;
(b) the Children Act 1975;
(c) the Matrimonial Causes Act 1973;
(d) the Guardianship of Minors Acts 1971 and 1973;
(e) the Matrimonial Causes Act 1965;
(f) the Matrimonial Proceedings (Magistrates' Courts) Act 1960.

(3) For the purposes of this paragraph and paragraphs 6 to 11 'custody' includes legal custody and joint as well as sole custody but does not include access.

Parental responsibility of parents

6. (1) Where –

(a) a child's father and mother were married to each other at the time of his birth; and
(b) there is an existing order with respect to the child,

each parent shall have parental responsibility for the child in accordance with section 2 as modified by sub-paragraph (3).

(2) Where –

(a) a child's father and mother were not married to each other at the time of his birth; and
(b) there is an existing order with respect to the child,

section 2 shall apply as modified by sub-paragraphs (3) and (4).

(3) The modification is that for section 2(8) there shall be substituted –

'(8) The fact that a person has parental responsibility for a child does not entitle him to act in a way which would be incompatible with any existing order or any order made under this Act with respect to the child'.

(4) The modifications are that –

(a) for the purposes of section 2(2), where the father has custody or care and control of the child by virtue of any existing order, the court shall be deemed to have made (at the commencement of that section) an order under section 4(1) giving him parental responsibility for the child; and
(b) where by virtue of paragraph (a) a court is deemed to have made an order under section 4(1) in favour of a father who has care and control of a child by virtue of an existing order, the court shall not bring the order under section 4(1) to an end at any time while he has care and control of the child by virtue of the order.

Part I Statutes

Persons who are not parents but who have custody or care and control

7. (1) Where a person who is not the parent or guardian of a child has custody or care and control of him by virtue of an existing order, that person shall have parental responsibility for him so long as he continues to have that custody or care and control by virtue of the order.

(2) Where sub-paragraph (1) applies, [Parts I and II and paragraph 15 of Schedule 1][1] shall have effect as modified by this paragraph.

(3) The modifications are that –

    (a)   for section 2(8) there shall be substituted –

'(8) The fact that a person has parental responsibility for a child does not entitle him to act in a way which would be incompatible with any existing order or with any order made under this Act with respect to the child';

    (b)   at the end of section 9(4) there shall be inserted –

'(c) any person who has custody or care and control of a child by virtue of any existing order'; and

    (c)   at the end of section 34(1)(c) there shall be inserted –

'(cc) where immediately before the care order was made there was an existing order by virtue of which a person had custody or care and control of the child, that person.'

    [(d)   for paragraph 15 of Schedule I there shall be substituted –

'**15.** Where a child lives with a person as the result of a custodianship order within the meaning of section 33 of the Children Act 1975, a local authority may make contributions to that person towards the cost of the accommodation and maintenance of the child so long as that person continues to have legal custody of that child by virtue of the order.'][1]

Persons who have care and control

8. (1) Sub-paragraphs (2) to (6) apply where a person has care and control of a child by virtue of an existing order, but they shall cease to apply when that order ceases to have effect.

(2) Section 5 shall have effect as if –

    (a)   for any reference to a residence order in favour of a parent or guardian there were substituted a reference to any existing order by virtue of which the parent or guardian has care and control of the child; and
    (b)   for subsection (9) there were substituted –

'(9) Subsections (1) and (7) do not apply if the existing order referred to in paragraph (b) of those subsections was one by virtue of which a surviving parent of the child also had care and control of him.'

(3) Section 10 shall have effect as if for subsection (5)(c)(i) there were substituted –

'(i) in any case where by virtue of an existing order any person or persons has or have care and control of the child, has the consent of that person or each of those persons'.

(4) Section 20 shall have effect as if for subsection (9)(a) there were substituted 'who has care and control of the child by virtue of an existing order.'

(5) Section 23 shall have effect as if for subsection (4)(c) there were substituted –

'(c) where the child is in care and immediately before the care order was made there was an existing order by virtue of which a person had care and control of the child, that person.'

(6) In Schedule 1, paragraphs 1(1) and 14(1) shall have effect as if for the words 'in whose favour a residence order is in force with respect to the child' there were substituted 'who has been given care and control of the child by virtue of an existing order'.

Persons who have access

9. (1) Sub-paragraphs (2) to (4) apply where a person has access by virtue of an existing order.

(2) Section 10 shall have effect as if after subsection (5) there were inserted –

'(5A) Any person who has access to a child by virtue of an existing order is entitled to apply for a contact order.'

(3) Section 16(2) shall have effect as if after paragraph (b) there were inserted –

'(bb) any person who has access to the child by virtue of an existing order.'

(4) Sections 43(11), 44(13) and 46(10), shall have effect as if in each case after paragraph (d) there were inserted –

'(dd) any person who has been given access to him by virtue of an existing order.'

Enforcement of certain existing orders

10. (1) Sub-paragraph (2) applies in relation to any existing order which, but for the repeal by this Act of –

(a) section 13(1) of the Guardianship of Minors Act 1971;
(b) section 43(1) of the Children Act 1975; or
(c) section 33 of the Domestic Proceedings and Magistrates' Courts Act 1978,

(provisions concerning the enforcement of custody orders) might have been enforced as if it were an order requiring a person to give up a child to another person.

(2) Where this sub-paragraph applies, the existing order may, after the repeal of the enactments mentioned in sub-paragraph (1)(a) to (c), be enforced under section 14 as if –

(a) any reference to a residence order were a reference to the existing order; and
(b) any reference to a person in whose favour the residence order is in force were a reference to a person to whom actual custody of the child is given by an existing order which is in force.

(3) In sub-paragraph (2) 'actual custody', in relation to a child, means the actual possession of his person.

Discharge of existing orders

11. (1) The making of a residence order or a care order with respect to a child who is the subject of an existing order discharges the existing order.

(2) Where the court makes any section 8 order (other than a residence order) with respect to a child with respect to whom any existing order is in force, the existing order shall have effect subject to the section 8 order.

(3) The court may discharge an existing order which is in force with respect to a child –

(a) in any family proceedings relating to the child or in which any question arises with respect to the child's welfare; or
(b) on the application of –
   (i) any parent or guardian of the child;
   (ii) the child himself; or
   (iii) any person named in the order.

(4) A child may not apply for the discharge of an existing order except with the leave of the court.

(5) The power in sub-paragraph (3) to discharge an existing order includes the power to discharge any part of the order.

(6) In considering whether to discharge an order under the power conferred by sub-paragraph (3) the court shall, if the discharge of the order is opposed by any party to the proceedings, have regard in particular to the matters mentioned in section 1(3).

GUARDIANS

Existing guardians to be guardians under this Act

12. (1) Any appointment of a person as guardian of a child which –

(a) was made –
   (i) under sections 3 to 5 of the Guardianship of Minors Act 1971;
   (ii) under section 38(3) of the Sexual Offences Act 1956; or

(iii) under the High Court's inherent jurisdiction with respect to children; and
(b) has taken effect before the commencement of section 5(4),

shall (subject to sub-paragraph (2)) be deemed, on and after the commencement of section 5(4), to be an appointment made and having effect under that section.

(2) Where an appointment of a person as guardian of a child has effect under section 5 by virtue of sub-paragraph (1)(a)(ii), the appointment shall not have effect for a period which is longer than any period specified in the order.

Appointment of guardian not yet in effect

13. Any appointment of a person to be a guardian of a child –
(a) which was made as mentioned in paragraph 12(1)(a)(i); but
(b) which, immediately before the commencement of section 5(4), had not taken effect,

shall take effect in accordance with section 5 (as modified, where it applies, by paragraph 8(2)).

Persons deemed to be appointed as guardians under existing wills

14. For the purposes of the Wills Act 1837 and of this Act any disposition by will and testament or devise of the custody and tuition of any child, made before the commencement of section 5(4) and paragraph 1 of Schedule 13, shall be deemed to be an appointment by will of a guardian of the child.

CHILDREN IN CARE

Children in compulsory care

15. (1) Sub-paragraph (2) applies where, immediately before the day on which Part IV comes into force, a person was –
(a) in care by virtue of –
   (i) a care order under section 1 of the Children and Young Persons Act 1969;
   (ii) a care order under section 15 of that Act, on discharging a supervision order made under section 1 of that Act; or
   (iii) an order or authorisation under section 25 or 26 of that Act;
(b) ...[5]

to be the subject of a care order under the Children and Young Persons Act 1969;
(c) in care –
   (i) under section 2 of the Child Care Act 1980; or
   (ii) by virtue of paragraph 1 of Schedule 4 to that Act (which extends the meaning of a child in care under section 2 to include children in care under section 1 of the Children Act 1948),

and a child in respect of whom a resolution under section 3 of the Act of 1980 or section 2 of the Act of 1948 was in force;
(d) a child in respect of whom a resolution had been passed under section 65 of the Child Care Act 1980;
(e) in care by virtue of an order under –
  (i) section 2(1)(e) of the Matrimonial Proceedings (Magistrates' Courts) Act 1960;
  (ii) section 7(2) of the Family Law Reform Act 1969;
  (iii) section 43(1) of the Matrimonial Causes Act 1973; or
  (iv) section 2(2)(b) of the Guardianship Act 1973;
  (v) section 10 of the Domestic Proceedings and Magistrates' Courts Act 1978,
(orders having effect for certain purposes as if the child had been received into care under section 2 of the Child Care Act 1980);
(f) in care by virtue of an order made, on the revocation of a custodianship order, under section 36 of the Children Act 1975; ...[2]
(g) in care by virtue of an order made, on the refusal of an adoption order, under section 26 of the Adoption Act 1976 or any order having effect (by virtue of paragraph 1 of Schedule 2 to that Act) as if made under that section [; or
(h) in care by virtue of an order of the court made in the exercise of the High Court's inherent jurisdiction with respect to children.][2]

(2) Where this sub-paragraph applies, then, on and after the day on which Part IV commences –
(a) the order or resolution in question shall be deemed to be a care order;
(b) the authority in whose care the person was immediately before that commencement shall be deemed to be the authority designated in that deemed care order; and
(c) any reference to a child in the care of a local authority shall include a reference to a person who is the subject of such a deemed care order,

and the provisions of this Act shall apply accordingly, subject to paragraph 16.

Modifications

16. (1) Sub-paragraph (2) only applies where a person who is the subject of a care order by virtue of paragraph 15(2) is a person falling within sub-paragraph (1)(a) ...[5] of that paragraph.

(2) Where the person would otherwise have remained in care until reaching the age of nineteen, by virtue of –

(a) section 20(3)(a) or 21(1) of the Children and Young Persons Act 1969; ...[5]
(b) ...[5]

this Act applies as if in section 91(12) for the word 'eighteen' there were substituted 'nineteen'.

(3) ...[5]

[(3A) Where in respect of a child who has been placed or allowed to remain in the care of a local authority pursuant to section 7(2) of the Family Law Reform Act 1969 or in the exercise of the High Court's inherent jurisdiction and the child is still in the care of a local authority, proceedings have ceased by virtue of paragraph 1(1A) to be treated as pending, paragraph 15(2) shall apply on 14th October 1992 as if the child was in care pursuant to an order as specified in paragraph 15(1)(e)(ii) or (h) as the case may be.]¹

(4) [Sub-paragraphs (5) and (6) only apply]³ where a child who is the subject of a care order by virtue of paragraph 15(2) is a person falling within sub-paragraph (1)(e) to [(h)]² of that paragraph.

(5) [Subject to sub-paragraph (6),]³ where a court, on making the order, or at any time thereafter, gave directions under –

[(a) section 4(4)(a) of the Guardianship Act 1973;
(b) section 43(5)(a) of the Matrimonial Causes Act 1973; or
(c) in the exercise of the High Court's inherent jurisdiction with respect to children,]²

as to the exercise by the authority of any powers, those directions shall[, subject to the provisions of section 25 of this Act and of any regulations made under that section,]³ continue to have effect (regardless of any conflicting provision in this Act [other than section 25]³) until varied or discharged by a court under this sub-paragraph.

[(6) Where directions referred to in sub-paragraph (5) are to the effect that a child be placed in accommodation provided for the purpose of restricting liberty then the directions shall cease to have effect upon the expiry of the maximum period specified by regulations under section 25(2)(a) in relation to children of his description, calculated from 14th October 1991.]³

Cessation of wardship where ward in care

[**16A.** (1) Where a child who is a ward of court is in care by virtue of –

(a) an order under section 7(2) of the Family Law Reform Act 1969; or
(b) an order made in the exercise of the High Court's inherent jurisdiction with respect to children,

he shall, on the day on which Part IV commences, cease to be a ward of court.]²

[(2) Where immediately before the day on which Part IV commences a child was in the care of a local authority and as the result of an order –

(a) pursuant to section 7(2) of the Family Law Reform Act 1969; or
(b) made in the exercise of the High Court's inherent jurisdiction with respect to children,

continued to be in the care of a local authority and was made a ward of court, he shall on the day on which Part IV commences, cease to be a ward of court.

(3) Sub-paragraphs (1) and (2) do not apply in proceedings which are pending.]¹

Children placed with parent etc. while in compulsory care

17. (1) This paragraph applies where a child is deemed by paragraph 15 to be in the care of a local authority under an order or resolution which is deemed by that paragraph to be a care order.

(2) If, immediately before the day on which Part III comes into force, the child was allowed to be under the charge and control of –

    (a)   a parent or guardian under section 21(2) of the Child Care Act 1980; or

    (b)   a person who, before the child was in the authority's care, had care and control of the child by virtue of an order falling within paragraph 5,

on and after that day the provision made by and under section 23(5) shall apply as if the child had been placed with the person in question in accordance with that provision.

Orders for access to children in compulsory care

18. (1) This paragraph applies to any access order –

    (a)   made under section 12C of the Child Care Act 1980 (access orders with respect to children in care of local authorities); and

    (b)   in force immediately before the commencement of Part IV

(2) On and after the commencement of Part IV, the access order shall have effect as an order made under section 34 in favour of the person named in the order.

[**18A.** (1) This paragraph applies to any decision of a local authority to terminate arrangements for access or to refuse to make such arrangements –

    (a)   of which notice has been given under, and in accordance with, section 12B of the Child Care Act 1980 (termination of access); and

    (b)   which is in force immediately before the commencement of Part IV.

(2) On and after the commencement of Part IV, a decision to which this paragraph applies shall have effect as a court order made under section 34(4) authorising the local authority to refuse to allow contact between the child and the person to whom notice was given under section 12B of the Child Care Act 1980.][3]

19. (1) This paragraph applies where, immediately before the commencement of Part IV, an access order made under section 12C of the Act of 1980 was suspended by virtue of an order made under section 12E of that Act (suspension of access orders in emergencies).

(2) The suspending order shall continue to have effect as if this Act had not been passed.

(3) If –

    (a)   before the commencement of Part IV; and

(b) during the period for which the operation of the access order is suspended,

the local authority concerned made an application for its variation or discharge to an appropriate juvenile court, its operation shall be suspended until the date on which the application to vary or discharge it is determined or abandoned.

Children in voluntary care

20. (1) This paragraph applies where, immediately before the day on which Part III comes into force –

   (a) a child was in the care of a local authority –
      (i) under section 2(1) of the Child Care Act 1980; or
      (ii) by virtue of paragraph 1 of Schedule 4 to that Act (which extends the meaning of references to children in care under section 2 to include references to children in care under section 1 of the Children Act 1948); and
   (b) he was not a person in respect of whom a resolution under section 3 of the Act of 1980 or section 2 of the Act of 1948 was in force.

(2) Where this paragraph applies, the child shall, on and after the day mentioned in sub-paragraph (1), be treated for the purposes of this Act as a child who is provided with accommodation by the local authority under Part III, but he shall cease to be so treated once he ceases to be so accommodated in accordance with the provisions of Part III.

(3) Where –

   (a) this paragraph applies; and
   (b) the child, immediately before the day mentioned in sub-paragraph (1), was (by virtue of section 21(2) of the Act of 1980) under the charge and control of a person falling within paragraph 17(2)(a) or (b),

the child shall not be treated for the purposes of this Act as if he were being looked after by the authority concerned.

Boarded out children

21. (1) Where, immediately before the day on which Part III comes into force, a child in the care of a local authority –

   (a) was –
      (i) boarded out with a person under section 21(1)(a) of the Child Care Act 1980; or
      (ii) placed under the charge and control of a person, under section 21(2) of that Act; and
   (b) the person with whom he was boarded out, or (as the case may be) placed, was not a person falling within paragraph 17(2)(a) or (b),

on and after that day, he shall be treated (subject to sub-paragraph (2)) as having been placed with a local authority foster parent and shall cease to be so treated when he ceases to be placed with that person in accordance with the provisions of this Act.

(2) Regulations made under section 23(2)(a) shall not apply in relation to a person who is a local authority foster parent by virtue of sub-paragraph (1) before the end of the period of twelve months beginning with the day on which Part III comes into force and accordingly that person shall for that period be subject –

(a) in a case falling within sub-paragraph (1)(a)(i), to terms and regulations mentioned in section 21(1)(a) of the Act of 1980; and
(b) in a case falling within sub-paragraph (1)(a)(ii), to terms fixed under section 21(2) of that Act and regulations made under section 22A of that Act,

as if that Act had not been repealed by this Act.

Children in care to qualify for advice and assistance

22. Any reference in Part III to a person qualifying for advice and assistance shall be construed as including a reference to a person within the area of the local authority in question who is under twenty-one and who was, at any time after reaching the age of sixteen but while still a child –

(a) a person falling within –
   (i) any of paragraphs (a) to [(h)]^2 of paragraph 15(1); or
   (ii) paragraph 20(1); or
(b) the subject of a criminal care order (within the meaning of paragraph 34).

Emigration of children in care

23. Where –

(a) the Secretary of State has received a request in writing from a local authority that he give his consent under section 24 of the Child Care Act 1980 to the emigration of a child in their care; but
(b) immediately before the repeal of the Act of 1980 by this Act, he has not determined whether or not to give his consent,

section 24 of the Act of 1980 shall continue to apply (regardless of that repeal) until the Secretary of State has determined whether or not to give his consent to the request.

Contributions for maintenance of children in care

24. (1) Where, immediately before the day on which Part III of Schedule 2 comes into force, there was in force an order made (or having effect as if made) under any of the enactments mentioned in sub-paragraph (2), then, on and after that day –

(a) the order shall have effect as if made under paragraph 23(2) of Schedule 2 against a person liable to contribute; and
(b) Part III of Schedule 2 shall apply to the order, subject to the modifications in sub-paragraph (3).

(2) The enactments are –

(a) section 11(4) of the Domestic Proceedings and Magistrates' Courts Act 1978;
(b) section 26(2) of the Adoption Act 1976;
(c) section 36(5) of the Children Act 1975;
(d) section 2(3) of the Guardianship Act 1973;
(e) section 2(1)(h) of the Matrimonial Proceedings (Magistrates' Courts) Act 1960,

(provisions empowering the court to make an order requiring a person to make periodical payments to a local authority in respect of a child in care).

(3) The modifications are that, in paragraph 23 of Schedule 2 –

(a) in sub-paragraph (4), paragraph (a) shall be omitted;
(b) for sub-paragraph (6) there shall be substituted –

'(6) Where –

(a) a contribution order is in force;
(b) the authority serve a contribution notice under paragraph 22; and
(c) the contributor and the authority reach an agreement under paragraph 22(7) in respect of the contribution notice,

the effect of the agreement shall be to discharge the order from the date on which it is agreed that the agreement shall take effect'; and

(c) at the end of sub-paragraph (10) there shall be inserted –

'and
(c) where the order is against a person who is not a parent of the child, shall be made with due regard to –
(i) whether that person had assumed responsibility for the maintenance of the child, and, if so, the extent to which and basis on which he assumed that responsibility and the length of the period during which he met that responsibility;
(ii) whether he did so knowing that the child was not his child;
(iii) the liability of any other person to maintain the child.'

SUPERVISION ORDERS

Orders under section 1(3)(b) or 21(2) of the 1969 Act

25. (1) This paragraph applies to any supervision order –

(a) made –

(i) under section 1(3)(b) of the Children and Young Persons Act 1969; or
(ii) under section 21(2) of that Act on the discharge of a care order made under section 1(3)(c) of that Act; and
(b) in force immediately before the commencement of Part IV.

(2) On and after the commencement of Part IV, the order shall be deemed to be a supervision order made under section 31 and –

(a) any requirement of the order that the child reside with a named individual shall continue to have effect while the order remains in force, unless the court otherwise directs
(b) any other requirement imposed by the court, or directions given by the supervisor, shall be deemed to have been imposed or given under the appropriate provisions of Schedule 3.

(3) Where, immediately before the commencement of Part IV, the order had been in force for a period of [six months or more]³, it shall cease to have effect at the end of the period of six months beginning with the day on which Part IV comes into force unless –

(a) the court directs that it shall cease to have effect at the end of a different period (which shall not exceed three years);
(b) it ceased to have effect earlier in accordance with section 91; or
(c) it would have ceased to have had effect earlier had this Act not been passed.

(4) Where sub-paragraph (3) applies, paragraph 6 of Schedule 3 shall not apply.

(5) Where, immediately before the commencement of Part IV, the order had been in force for less than six months it shall cease to have effect in accordance with section 91 and paragraph 6 of Schedule 3 unless –

(a) the court directs that it shall cease to have effect at the end of a different period (which shall not exceed three years); or
(b) it would have ceased to have had effect earlier had this Act not been passed.

Other supervision orders

26. (1) This paragraph applies to any order for the supervision of a child which was in force immediately before the commencement of Part IV and was made under –

(a) section 2(1)(f) of the Matrimonial Proceedings (Magistrates' Courts) Act 1960;
(b) section 7(4) of the Family Law Reform Act 1969;
(c) section 44 of the Matrimonial Causes Act 1973;
(d) section 2(2)(a) of the Guardianship Act 1973;
(e) section 34(5) or 36(3)(b) of the Children Act 1975;
(f) section 26(1)(a) of the Adoption Act 1976; or

(g) section 9 of the Domestic Proceedings and Magistrates' Courts Act 1978.

(2) The order shall not be deemed to be a supervision order made under any provision of this Act but shall nevertheless continue in force for a period of one year beginning with the day on which Part IV comes into force unless –

(a) the court directs that it shall cease to have effect at the end of a lesser period; or
(b) it would have ceased to have had effect earlier had this Act not been passed.

PLACE OF SAFETY ORDERS

27. (1) This paragraph applies to –

(a) any order or warrant authorising the removal of a child to a place of safety which –
   (i) was made, or issued, under any of the enactments mentioned in sub-paragraph (2); and
   (ii) was in force immediately before the commencement of Part IV; and
(b) any interim order made under section 23(5) of the Children and Young Persons Act 1963 or section 28(6) of the Children and Young Persons Act 1969.

(2) The enactments are –

(a) section 40 of the Children and Young Persons Act 1933 (warrant to search for or remove child);
(b) section 28(1) of the Children and Young Persons Act 1969 (detention of child in place of safety);
(c) section 34(1) of the Adoption Act 1976 (removal of protected children from unsuitable surroundings);
(d) section 12(1) of the Foster Children Act 1980 (removal of foster children kept in unsuitable surroundings).

(3) The order or warrant shall continue to have effect as if this Act had not been passed.

(4) Any enactment repealed by this Act shall continue to have effect in relation to the order or warrant so far as is necessary for the purposes of securing that the effect of the order is what it would have been had this Act not been passed.

(5) Sub-paragraph (4) does not apply to the power to make an interim order or further interim order given by section 23(5) of the Children and Young Persons Act 1963 or section 28(6) of the Children and Young Persons Act 1969.

(6) Where, immediately before section 28 of the Children and Young Persons Act 1969 is repealed by this Act, a child is being detained under the powers granted by that section, he may continue to be detained in accordance with that section but subsection (6) shall not apply.

RECOVERY OF CHILDREN

28. The repeal by this Act of subsection (1) of section 16 of the Child Care Act 1980 (arrest of child absent from compulsory care) shall not affect the operation of that section in relation to any child arrested before the coming into force of the repeal.

29. (1) This paragraph applies where –

(a) a summons has been issued under section 15 or 16 of the Child Care Act 1980 (recovery of children in voluntary or compulsory care); and

(b) the child concerned is not produced in accordance with the summons before the repeal of that section by this Act comes into force.

(2) The summons, any warrant issued in connection with it and section 15 or (as the case may be) section 16, shall continue to have effect as if this Act had not been passed.

30. The amendment by paragraph 27 of Schedule 12 of section 32 of the Children and Young Persons Act 1969 (detention of absentees) shall not affect the operation of that section in relation to –

(a) any child arrested; or

(b) any summons or warrant issued,

under that section before the coming into force of that paragraph.

VOLUNTARY ORGANISATIONS: PARENTAL RIGHTS RESOLUTIONS

31. (1) This paragraph applies to a resolution –

(a) made under section 64 of the Child Care Act 1980 (transfer of parental rights and duties to voluntary organisations); and

(b) in force immediately before the commencement of Part IV.

(2) The resolution shall continue to have effect until the end of the period of six months beginning with the day on which Part IV comes into force unless it is brought to an end earlier in accordance with the provisions of the Act of 1980 preserved by this paragraph.

(3) While the resolution remains in force, any relevant provisions of, or made under, the Act of 1980 shall continue to have effect with respect to it.

(4) Sub-paragraph (3) does not apply to –

(a) section 62 of the Act of 1980 and any regulations made under that section (arrangements by voluntary organisations for emigration of children); or

(b) section 65 of the Act of 1980 (duty of local authority to assume parental rights and duties).

(5) Section 5(2) of the Act of 1980 (which is applied to resolutions under Part VI of that Act by section 64(7) of that Act) shall have effect with respect to the resolution as if the reference in paragraph (c) to an appointment of a

guardian under section 5 of the Guardianship of Minors Act 1971 were a reference to an appointment of a guardian under section 5 of this Act.

FOSTER CHILDREN

32. (1) This paragraph applies where –

(a) immediately before the commencement of Part VIII, a child was a foster child within the meaning of the Foster Children Act 1980; and

(b) the circumstances of the case are such that, had Parts VIII and IX then been in force, he would have been treated for the purposes of this Act as a child who was being provided with accommodation in a children's home and not as a child who was being privately fostered.

(2) If the child continues to be cared for and provided with accommodation as before, section 63(1) and (10) shall not apply in relation to him if –

(a) an application for registration of the home in question is made under section 63 before the end of the period of three months beginning with the day on which Part VIII comes into force; and

(b) the application has not been refused or, if it has been refused –
   (i) the period for an appeal against the decision has not expired; or
   (ii) an appeal against the refusal has been made but has not been determined or abandoned.

(3) While section 63(1) and (10) does not apply, the child shall be treated as a privately fostered child for the purposes of Part IX.

NURSERIES AND CHILD MINDING

33. (1) Sub-paragraph (2) applies where, immediately before the commencement of Part X, any premises are registered under section 1(1)(a) of the Nurseries and Child-Minders Regulation Act 1948 (registration of premises, other than premises wholly or mainly used as private dwellings, where children are received to be looked after).

(2) During the transitional period, the provisions of the Act of 1948 shall continue to have effect with respect to those premises to the exclusion of Part X.

(3) Nothing in sub-paragraph (2) shall prevent the local authority concerned from registering any person under section 71(1)(b) with respect to the premises.

(4) In this paragraph 'the transitional period' means the period ending with –

(a) the first anniversary of the commencement of Part X; or

(b) if earlier, the date on which the local authority concerned registers any person under section 71(1)(b) with respect to the premises.

34. (1) Sub-paragraph (2) applies where, immediately before the commencement of Part X –

(a) a person is registered under section 1(1)(b) of the Act of 1948 (registration of persons who for reward receive into their homes children under the age of five to be looked after); and

(b) all the children looked after by him as mentioned in section 1(1)(b) of that Act are under the age of five.

(2) During the transitional period, the provisions of the Act of 1948 shall continue to have effect with respect to that person to the exclusion of Part X.

(3) Nothing in sub-paragraph (2) shall prevent the local authority concerned from registering that person under section 71(1)(a).

(4) In this paragraph 'the transitional period' means the period ending with –

(a) the first anniversary of the commencement of Part X; or
(b) if earlier, the date on which the local authority concerned registers that person under section 71(1)(a).

CHILDREN ACCOMMODATED IN CERTAIN ESTABLISHMENTS

35. In calculating, for the purposes of section 85(1)(a) or 86(1)(a), the period of time for which a child has been accommodated any part of that period which fell before the day on which that section came into force shall be disregarded.

CRIMINAL CARE ORDERS

36. (1) This paragraph applies where, immediately before the commencement of section 90(2) there was in force an order ('a criminal care order') made –

(a) under section 7(7)(a) of the Children and Young Persons Act 1969 (alteration in treatment of young offenders etc.); or
(b) under section 15(1) of that Act, on discharging a supervision order made under section 7(7)(b) of that Act.

(2) The criminal care order shall continue to have effect until the end of the period of six months beginning with the day on which section 90(2) comes into force unless it is brought to an end earlier in accordance with –

(a) the provisions of the Act of 1969 preserved by sub-paragraph (3)(a); or
(b) this paragraph.

(3) While the criminal care order remains in force, any relevant provisions –

(a) of the Act of 1969; and
(b) of the Child Care Act 1980,

shall continue to have effect with respect to it.

(4) While the criminal care order remains in force, a court may, on the application of the appropriate person, make –

(a) a residence order;

(b) a care order or a supervision order under section 31;
(c) an education supervision order under section 36 (regardless of subsection (6) of that section); or
(d) an order falling within sub-paragraph (5),

and shall, on making any of those orders, discharge the criminal care order.

(5) The order mentioned in sub-paragraph (4)(d) is an order having effect as if it were a supervision order of a kind mentioned in section 12AA of the Act of 1969 (as inserted by paragraph 23 of Schedule 12), that is to say, a supervision order –

(a) imposing a requirement that the child shall live for a specified period in local authority accommodation; but
(b) in relation to which the conditions mentioned in [subsection (6)]² of section 12AA are not required to be satisfied.

(6) The maximum period which may be specified in an order made under sub-paragraph (4)(d) is six months and such an order may stipulate that the child shall not live with a named person.

(7) Where this paragraph applies, section 5 of the Rehabilitation of Offenders Act 1974 (rehabilitation periods for particular sentences) shall have effect regardless of the repeals in it made by this Act.

(8) In sub-paragraph (4) 'appropriate person' means –

(a) in the case of an application for a residence order, any person (other than a local authority) who has the leave of the court;
(b) in the case of an application for an education supervision order, a local education authority; and
(c) in any other case, the local authority to whose care the child was committed by the order.

MISCELLANEOUS

Consents under the Marriage Act 1949 (c. 76)

37. (1) In the circumstances mentioned in sub-paragraph (2), section 3 of and Schedule 2 to the Marriage Act 1949 (consents to marry) shall continue to have effect regardless of the amendment of that Act by paragraph 5 of Schedule 12.

(2) The circumstances are that –

(a) immediately before the day on which paragraph 5 of Schedule 12 comes into force, there is in force –
  (i) an existing order, as defined in paragraph 5(1); or
  (ii) an order of a kind mentioned in paragraph 16(1); and
(b) section 3 of and Schedule 2 to the Act of 1949 would, but for this Act, have applied to the marriage of the child who is the subject of the order.

Part I   Statutes

The Children Act 1975 (c. 72)

38. The amendments of other enactments made by the following provisions of the Children Act 1975 shall continue to have effect regardless of the repeal of the Act of 1975 by this Act –

(a) section 68(4), (5) and (7) (amendments of section 32 of the Children and Young Persons Act 1969); and
(b) in Schedule 3 –
 (i) paragraph 13 (amendments of Births and Deaths Registration Act 1953);
 (ii) paragraph 43 (amendment of Perpetuities and Accumulations Act 1964);
 (iii) paragraphs 46 and 47 (amendments of Health Services and Public Health Act 1968); and
 (iv) paragraph 77 (amendment of Parliamentary and Other Pensions Act 1972).

The Child Care Act 1980 (c. 5)

39. The amendment made to section 106(2)(a) of the Children and Young Persons Act 1933) by paragraph 26 of Schedule 5 to the Child Care Act 1980 shall continue to have effect regardless of the repeal of the Act of 1980 by this Act.

Legal aid

40. ...[7]

NOTES

Amendments.[1] Words inserted or substituted: SI 1991/1990, amending SI 1991/828.[2] Words repealed, inserted or substituted: Courts and Legal Services Act 1990, ss 116, 125(7), Sch 16, para 33, Sch 20.[3] Words inserted or substituted: Children Act 1989 (Commencement and Transitional Provisions) Order 1991, SI 1991/828, art 4, Sch.[4] References in paras 12, 13 and 14 to 'the commencement of section 5' shall be construed as references to the commencement of sub-ss (1)–(10) and (13) of that section (14 Oct 1991) except in relation to the appointment of a guardian of the estate of any child in which case they shall be construed as a reference to the commencement of sub-ss (11) and (12) of that section (1 Feb 1992): SI 1991/1990, amending SI 1991/828.[5] Words repealed: Armed Forces Act 1991, s 26(2), Sch 3.[6] Words substituted: Criminal Justice Act 1991, s 100, Sch 11, para 40(2)(r).[7] Paragraph repealed: Access to Justice Act 1999, s 106, Sch 15, Pt I.

Definitions. 'A section 8 order': s 8(2); 'actual custody': Sch 14, para 10(3); 'appropriate person': Sch 14, para 36(8); 'care order': ss 31(11), 105(1); 'child': s 105(1); 'children's home': s 63(3); 'contact order': s 8(1); 'contribution notice': Sch 2, para 22(1); 'contribution order': Sch 2, para 23(2); 'contributor': Sch 2, para 21(1); 'criminal care order': Sch 14, para 36(1); 'custody': Sch 14, para 5(3); 'education supervision order': s 36(2); 'existing order': Sch 14, para 5(1), (2); 'family proceedings': s 8(3); 'local authority': s 105(1); 'local authority foster parent': s 23(3); 'local education authority': s 105(1); 'order in force immediately before the commencement of ... this Act': Sch 14, para (1), (3), (4); 'parental responsibility': s 3; 'privately fostered child': s 66(1); 'residence order': s 8(1); 'supervision order': s 31(11); 'supervisor': s 105(1); 'the transitional period': Sch 14, para 33(4); 'upbringing': s 105(1).

Part II
STATUTORY INSTRUMENTS

ALLOCATION AND TRANSFER OF PROCEEDINGS ORDER 2008

SI 2008/2836

ARRANGEMENT OF ARTICLES

PART 1
PRELIMINARY

Article		Page
1	Citation, commencement, interpretation and application	282
2	Classes of county court	283
3	Principal Registry of the Family Division	283
4	Contravention of a provision of this Order	284

PART 2
STARTING PROCEEDINGS

Section 1
Starting Proceedings in Specified Level of Court

5	Proceedings which must be started in a magistrates' court	284
6	Proceedings which must be started in a county court	285
7	Proceedings which may be started in the High Court	285
8	Proceedings which must be started in the court where proceedings under the 2002 Act are pending	286

Section 2
Starting Proceedings in Specified Class of County Court

9	Starting proceedings under the 1989 Act	286
10	Starting proceedings under Part 4A of the 1996 Act	286
11	Starting proceedings under the 2002 Act	287

PART 3
TRANSFER OF PROCEEDINGS

Section 1
General

12	Disapplication of enactments about transfer	287
13	General rules about transfer of proceedings	287

Section 2
Transfer of Proceedings to Specified Level of Court

14	Transfer of proceedings from one magistrates' court to another	287
15	Transfer of proceedings from magistrates' court to county court	288
16	Transfer of proceedings from county court to magistrates' court	288
17	Transfer of proceedings from one county court to another	288
18	Transfer of proceedings from county court to High Court	289
19	Transfer of proceedings from High Court	289

Section 3
Transfer of Proceedings to a Specified Class of County Court

20	Transfer of proceedings under the 1989 Act	289
21	Transfer of proceedings under the 2002 Act	289

22	Transfer of proceedings under Part 4A of the 1996 Act	290

Section 4
Transfer of Proceedings to Particular Court

23	Transfer of proceedings when arrested for breach of order under Part 4 of the 1996 Act	290
24	Transfer of proceedings when arrested for breach of order under Part 4A of the 1996 Act	290

PART 4
APPLICATION FOLLOWING REFUSAL TO TRANSFER FROM MAGISTRATES' COURT TO COUNTY COURT AND APPEAL AGAINST TRANSFER TO MAGISTRATES' COURT BY COUNTY COURT

25	Application following refusal to order transfer of proceedings from magistrates' court to county court	291
26	Appeal against transfer of proceedings to magistrates' court by county court	291

PART 5
REVOCATIONS, CONSEQUENTIAL AMENDMENTS AND TRANSITIONAL PROVISIONS

27	Revocations	291
28	Consequential amendments	291
29	Transitional provisions	292
	Schedule 1 – Classes of County Court	293

PART 1
PRELIMINARY

1 Citation, commencement, interpretation and application

(1) This Order may be cited as the Allocation and Transfer of Proceedings Order 2008 and, subject to paragraph (2), shall come into force on 25 November 2008.

(2) Articles 6(a)(i), 9(1) and 20(1), in so far as they apply to section 11J(6) or 11O(7) of, and paragraphs 4 to 7 and 9 of Schedule A1 to, the 1989 Act, shall come into force on the same day as sections 4 and 5 of the Children and Adoption Act 2006 come into force.

(3) In this Order –

'the 1989 Act' means the Children Act 1989;
'the 1996 Act' means the Family Law Act 1996;
'the 2002 Act' means the Adoption and Children Act 2002;
'Convention adoption order' means an adoption order under the 2002 Act which, by virtue of regulations under section 1 of the Adoption (Intercountry Aspects) Act 1999 (regulations giving effect to the Convention), is made as a Convention adoption order;
'proceedings' means, unless the context otherwise requires, proceedings under –

(a) section 55A of the Family Law Act 1986 (declarations of parentage);
(b) the 1989 Act;
(c) section 20 of the Child Support Act 1991 (appeals);
(d) [section 54 of the Human Fertilisation and Embryology Act 2008][1] (parental orders);
(e) Part 4 of the 1996 Act; and
(f) the 2002 Act.

(4) The provisions in this Order apply unless any enactment or rule provides otherwise.

NOTES

Amendments.[1] Words substituted: SI 2010/986.

2 Classes of county court

For the purposes of this Order there are the following classes of county court –

(a) family hearing centres, being those courts against which the word yes appears in column 2 of the table in Schedule 1;
(b) care centres, being those courts against which the word yes appears in column 3 of that table;
(c) adoption centres, being those courts against which the word yes appears in column 4 of that table;
(d) intercountry adoption centres, being those courts against which the word yes appears in column 5 of that table; and
(e) forced marriage county courts, being those courts against which the word yes appears in column 6 of that table.

3 Principal Registry of the Family Division

[(1)][1] The principal registry of the Family Division of the High Court is treated, for the purposes of this Order, as if it were –

(a) a family hearing centre;
(b) a care centre;
(c) an adoption centre;
(d) an intercountry adoption centre; and
(e) a forced marriage county court.

[(2) The principal registry of the Family Division of the High Court is treated as if it were a county court for the purposes of appeals from decisions of a magistrates' court under –

(a) section 94 of the 1989 Act; and
(b) section 61 of the 1996 Act.][1]

NOTES

Amendments.[1] Paragraph renumbered and paragraph inserted: SI 2009/871.

4 Contravention of a provision of this Order

Where proceedings are started or transferred in contravention of a provision of this Order, the contravention does not have the effect of making the proceedings invalid.

PART 2
STARTING PROCEEDINGS

Section 1
Starting Proceedings in Specified Level of Court

5 Proceedings which must be started in a magistrates' court

(1) Proceedings under the following provisions must be started in a magistrates' court –

- (a) section 79K of the 1989 Act (protection of children in an emergency);
- (b) paragraph 23 of Schedule 2 to the 1989 Act (contribution order);
- (c) paragraph 8 of Schedule 8 to the 1989 Act (certain appeals);
- (d) section 23 of the 2002 Act (varying placement order);
- (e) section 50 or 51 of the 2002 Act (adoption order), unless any local authority will be a party to the proceedings or article 6(c) or (d) applies;
- (f) section 20 of the Child Support Act 1991 (appeals) where the proceedings are to be dealt with in accordance with the Child Support Appeals (Jurisdiction of Courts) Order 2002; and
- (g) [section 54 of the Human Fertilisation and Embryology Act 2008][1] (parental orders).

(2) Subject to paragraphs (3) and (4), proceedings under the following provisions must be started in a magistrates' court –

- (a) section 4 of the 1989 Act (acquisition of parental responsibility by father);
- (b) section 4A of the 1989 Act (acquisition of parental responsibility by step-parent);
- (c) section 25 of the 1989 Act (use of accommodation for restricting liberty);
- (d) section 31 of the 1989 Act (care and supervision orders);
- (e) section 33(7) of the 1989 Act (leave to change surname of, or remove from United Kingdom, child in care);
- (f) section 34 of the 1989 Act (parental contact etc. with children in care);
- (g) section 36 of the 1989 Act (education supervision orders);
- (h) section 43 of the 1989 Act (child assessment orders);
- (i) section 44 of the 1989 Act (emergency protection orders);
- (j) section 45 of the 1989 Act (extension, variation or discharge of emergency protection order);
- (k) section 46(7) of the 1989 Act (emergency protection order by police officer);

(l) section 48 of the 1989 Act (powers to assist in discovery of children etc.);
(m) section 50 of the 1989 Act (recovery orders);
(n) section 102 of the 1989 Act (warrant authorising a constable to assist in exercise of certain powers to search for children etc.); and
(o) paragraph 19 of Schedule 2 to the 1989 Act (approval of arrangements to assist child to live abroad).

(3) Proceedings to which paragraph (2) applies which –
   (a) concern a child who is the subject of proceedings which are pending in a county court or the High Court; and
   (b) arise out of the same circumstances as gave rise to those proceedings

may be started in the court in which those proceedings are pending.

(4) Proceedings under section 4 or 4A of the 1989 Act which are started at the same time as proceedings in a county court or the High Court for an order under section 8 of the 1989 Act (residence, contact and other applications in relation to children) in relation to the same child must be started in the court in which proceedings under section 8 are started.

NOTES
Amendments.[1] Words substituted: SI 2010/986.

6 Proceedings which must be started in a county court

Subject to article 7, proceedings –

(a) brought by an applicant who is under the age of eighteen under –
   (i) section 10(2)(b), 11J(6) or 11O(7) of, or paragraph 9(6) of Schedule A1 to, the 1989 Act (leave of the court to make an application); or
   (ii) Part 4 of the 1996 Act;
(b) under section 43 of the 1996 Act (leave of the court for applications by children under sixteen);
(c) for a Convention adoption order; or
(d) for an adoption order under the 2002 Act where section 83 of that Act (restriction on bringing children in) applies,

must be started in a county court.

7 Proceedings which may be started in the High Court

Subject to articles 5(3) and (4) and 8, proceedings may be started in the High Court only if –

(a) the proceedings are exceptionally complex;
(b) the outcome of the proceedings is important to the public in general; or
(c) there is another substantial reason for the proceedings to be started in the High Court.

8 Proceedings which must be started in the court where proceedings under the 2002 Act are pending

(1) Where proceedings under section 50 or 51 of the 2002 Act (adoption order) are pending, proceedings concerning the same child under –

(a) section 29(4)(b) of the 2002 Act (leave to apply for a residence order);
(b) section 29(5)(b) of the 2002 Act (leave to apply for a special guardianship order);
(c) section 8 of the 1989 Act where section 28(1)(a) or 29(4)(b) of the 2002 Act applies (leave obtained to make application for a residence order);
(d) section 14A of the 1989 Act where section 28(1)(b) or 29(5)(b) of the 2002 Act applies (leave obtained to make application for a special guardianship order);
(e) section 37(a) of the 2002 Act (leave to remove the child); or
(f) section 47(3) or (5) of the 2002 Act (leave to oppose the making of an adoption order),

must be started in the court in which the proceedings under section 50 or 51 are pending.

(2) Where proceedings under section 22 of the 2002 Act (placement order) are pending, proceedings under section 30(2)(b) of that Act (leave to remove a child from accommodation provided by the local authority) must be started in the court in which the proceedings under section 22 are pending.

(3) Where proceedings under section 42(6) of the 2002 Act (leave to apply for an adoption order) are pending, proceedings under section 38(3)(a) or 40(2)(a) of that Act (leave to remove a child) must be started in the court in which the proceedings under section 42(6) are pending.

Section 2
Starting Proceedings in Specified Class of County Court

9 Starting proceedings under the 1989 Act

(1) Subject to article 8(1)(c) and (d), proceedings under Part 1 or 2 of, or Schedule 1 or paragraphs 4 to 7 or 9 of Schedule A1 to, the 1989 Act which are to be started in a county court must be started in a family hearing centre.

(2) Proceedings under Part 3, 4 or 5 of the 1989 Act which are to be started in a county court must be started in a care centre.

10 Starting proceedings under Part 4A of the 1996 Act

(1) Proceedings under Part 4A of the 1996 Act which are to be started in a county court must be started in a forced marriage county court.

(2) Article 7 applies to proceedings under Part 4A of the 1996 Act as it applies to other proceedings.

11 Starting proceedings under the 2002 Act

(1) Subject to paragraph (2), proceedings under the 2002 Act which are to be started in a county court must be started in an adoption centre.

(2) Proceedings for –

(a) a Convention adoption order; or
(b) an adoption order under the 2002 Act where section 83 of that Act applies

which are to be started in a county court must be started in an intercountry adoption centre.

PART 3
TRANSFER OF PROCEEDINGS

Section 1
General

12 Disapplication of enactments about transfer

The proceedings to which this Order applies are excluded from the operation of sections 38 and 39 of the Matrimonial and Family Proceedings Act 1984 (transfer of family proceedings).

13 General rules about transfer of proceedings

(1) When making any decision about the transfer of proceedings under articles 14, 15, 17 and 18 the court must have regard to the need to avoid delay in the proceedings.

(2) Articles 16 and 19 do not apply if the transfer of proceedings would cause the determination of the proceedings to be delayed.

(3) The transfer of proceedings under this Part may be made at any stage of the proceedings and whether or not the proceedings have already been transferred.

Section 2
Transfer of Proceedings to Specified Level of Court

14 Transfer of proceedings from one magistrates' court to another

A magistrates' court (the 'transferring court') may transfer proceedings to another magistrates' court (the 'receiving court') only if the transferring court considers that –

(a) the transfer will significantly accelerate the determination of the proceedings;
(b) it is more convenient for the parties or for the child who is the subject of the proceedings for the proceedings to be dealt with by the receiving court; or

Part II Statutory Instruments

(c) there is another good reason for the proceedings to be transferred.

15 Transfer of proceedings from magistrates' court to county court

(1) Subject to paragraphs (2) and (3), a magistrates' court may transfer the whole or any part of proceedings to a county court only if the magistrates' court considers that –

- (a) the transfer will significantly accelerate the determination of the proceedings;
- (b) there is a real possibility of difficulty in resolving conflicts in the evidence of witnesses;
- (c) there is a real possibility of a conflict in the evidence of two or more experts;
- (d) there is a novel or difficult point of law;
- (e) there are proceedings concerning the child in another jurisdiction or there are international law issues;
- (f) there is a real possibility that enforcement proceedings may be necessary and the method of enforcement or the likely penalty is beyond the powers of a magistrates' court;
- (g) there is a real possibility that a guardian ad litem will be appointed under rule 9.5 of the Family Proceedings Rules 1991;
- (h) there is a real possibility that a party to proceedings is a person lacking capacity within the meaning of the Mental Capacity Act 2005 to conduct the proceedings; or
- (i) there is another good reason for the proceedings to be transferred.

(2) Proceedings under any of the provisions mentioned in articles 5(1)(a) to (c) or 5(2)(i) to (*l*) may not be transferred from a magistrates' court.

(3) Proceedings under section 25 of the 1989 Act (use of accommodation for restricting liberty) may not be transferred from a magistrates' court which is not a family proceedings court within the meaning of section 67 of the Magistrates' Courts Act 1980.

16 Transfer of proceedings from county court to magistrates' court

(1) A county court must transfer to a magistrates' court proceedings which were transferred under article 15(1) if the county court considers that none of the criteria in article 15(1) applies.

(2) Subject to articles 5(3) and (4), 6 and 8, a county court must transfer to a magistrates' court proceedings which were started in the county court if the county court considers that none of the criteria in article 15(1)(b) to (*i*) applies.

17 Transfer of proceedings from one county court to another

Subject to articles 16, 20, 21 and 22 a county court (the 'transferring court') may transfer proceedings to another county court (the 'receiving court') only if the transferring court considers that –

(a) the transfer will significantly accelerate the determination of the proceedings;
(b) it is more convenient for the parties or for the child who is the subject of the proceedings for the proceedings to be dealt with by the receiving court;
(c) the proceedings involve the determination of a question of a kind mentioned in section 59(1) of the 1996 Act and the property in question is situated in the district of the receiving court; or
(d) there is another good reason for the proceedings to be transferred.

18 Transfer of proceedings from county court to High Court

A county court may transfer proceedings to the High Court only if the county court considers that –

(a) the proceedings are exceptionally complex;
(b) the outcome of the proceedings is important to the public in general; or
(c) there is another substantial reason for the proceedings to be transferred.

19 Transfer of proceedings from High Court

The High Court must transfer to a county court or a magistrates' court proceedings which were started in, or transferred to, the High Court if the High Court considers that none of the criteria in article 18 applies.

Section 3
Transfer of Proceedings to a Specified Class of County Court

20 Transfer of proceedings under the 1989 Act

(1) Where proceedings under Part 1 or 2 of, or Schedule 1 or paragraphs 4 to 7 or 9 of Schedule A1 to, the 1989 Act are to be transferred to a county court, they must be transferred to a family hearing centre.

(2) Where proceedings under Part 3, 4 or 5 of the 1989 Act are to be transferred to a county court, they must be transferred to a care centre.

21 Transfer of proceedings under the 2002 Act

(1) Subject to paragraph (2), where proceedings under the 2002 Act are to be transferred to a county court, they must be transferred to an adoption centre.

(2) Where proceedings for –

(a) a Convention Adoption Order; or
(b) an adoption order under the 2002 Act where section 83 of that Act applies,

are to be transferred to a county court, they must be transferred to an intercountry adoption centre.

22 Transfer of proceedings under Part 4A of the 1996 Act

(1) Where proceedings under Part 4A of the 1996 Act are to be transferred to a county court, they must be transferred to a forced marriage county court.

(2) Articles 17 to 19 apply to the transfer of proceedings under Part 4A of the 1996 Act as they apply to the transfer of other proceedings but as if the modification in paragraph (3) were made.

(3) Article 19 is to be read as if 'or a magistrates' court' were omitted.

Section 4
Transfer of Proceedings to Particular Court

23 Transfer of proceedings when arrested for breach of order under Part 4 of the 1996 Act

Where a person is brought before –

(a) the relevant judicial authority in accordance with section 47(7)(a) of the 1996 Act (arrest for breach of order); or
(b) a court by virtue of a warrant issued under section 47(9) of the 1996 Act,

and the matter is not then disposed of immediately, the relevant judicial authority or the court may transfer the matter to the relevant judicial authority or court which attached the power of arrest under section 47(2) or (3) of the 1996 Act or which issued the warrant.

24 Transfer of proceedings when arrested for breach of order under Part 4A of the 1996 Act

Where a person is brought before –

(a) the relevant judge in accordance with section 63I(3) of the 1996 Act (arrest for breach of order); or
(b) a court by virtue of a warrant issued under section 63J(3) of the 1996 Act,

and the matter is not then disposed of immediately, the relevant judge or the court may transfer the matter to the relevant judge or court which attached the power of arrest under section 63H(2) or (4) of the 1996 Act or which issued the warrant.

PART 4
APPLICATION FOLLOWING REFUSAL TO TRANSFER FROM MAGISTRATES' COURT TO COUNTY COURT AND APPEAL AGAINST TRANSFER TO MAGISTRATES' COURT BY COUNTY COURT

25 Application following refusal to order transfer of proceedings from magistrates' court to county court

(1) Where a magistrates' court refuses to order the transfer of proceedings to a county court under article 15(1), an application may be made for an order transferring proceedings to a county court.

(2) An application under paragraph (1) must be made –

(a) in relation to proceedings under the 2002 Act, to an adoption centre;
(b) in relation to proceedings under Parts 3, 4 and 5, to a care centre; and
(c) in any other case, to a family hearing centre.

(3) In this article, 'proceedings' means the proceedings under the 1989 Act or the 2002 Act and proceedings under section 55A of the Family Law Act 1986 (declarations of parentage).

26 Appeal against transfer of proceedings to magistrates' court by county court

Where a county court orders the transfer of proceedings to a magistrates' court under article 16, an appeal may be made against that decision –

(a) where the decision was made by a district judge or deputy district judge of a county court, to a circuit judge; or
(b) where the decision was made by a district judge or deputy district judge of the principal registry of the Family Division, to a judge of the Family Division of the High Court.

PART 5
REVOCATIONS, CONSEQUENTIAL AMENDMENTS AND TRANSITIONAL PROVISIONS

27 Revocations

Subject to article 29(2) and (3), the instruments listed in column 1 of the table in Schedule 2 (which have the references listed in column 2) are revoked to the extent indicated in column 3.

28 Consequential amendments

(1) Subject to article 29(4), the Family Proceedings Rules 1991 are amended as follows –

(a) in rule 2.39(1) for 'where no such application as is referred to in rule 2.40(1) is pending the', substitute 'The';
(b) omit rule 2.40;

(c) in rule 3.8(2) omit 'but shall be treated, in the first instance, as an application to the High Court for leave';

(d) for rule 4.22(2A) substitute –

'(2A) In relation to an appeal to the High Court under section 94, the documents required to be filed by paragraph (2) shall be filed in the district registry, being in the same place as a care centre within the meaning of article 2(b) of the Allocation and Transfer of Proceedings Order 2008, which is nearest to the court below.'; and

(e) in rule 4.26 after paragraph (5) add –

'(6) Where a local authority makes an application to a magistrates' court for a care or supervision order with respect to the child in relation to whom the direction was given, the local authority must inform the court that gave the direction of the application in writing.'.

(2) Subject to article 29(4), for rule 3A(8) of the Family Proceedings Courts (Matrimonial Proceedings etc) Rules 1991 substitute –

'(8) Subject to any enactment, where an application for an occupation order or a non-molestation order is pending, the court may transfer the proceedings to another court of its own motion or on the application of either party; and any order for transfer shall be made in Form FL417.'.

29 Transitional provisions

(1) This Order applies, so far as practicable, to proceedings started before but not concluded by 25 November 2008.

(2) Where, by reason of paragraph (1), this Order does not apply to particular proceedings which have been started but not concluded before the 25 November 2008, the Children (Allocation of Proceedings) Order 1991 or the Family Law Act 1996 (Part IV) (Allocation of Proceedings) Order 1997, as the case may be, continue to apply to those proceedings.

(3) The Children (Allocation of Proceedings) (Appeals) Order 1991 continues to apply to –

(a) an appeal started before 25 November 2008; and
(b) an appeal in proceedings to which the Children (Allocation of Proceedings) Order 1991 still applies by virtue of paragraph (2).

(4) The amendments in article 28 do not apply in relation to proceedings to which the Children (Allocation of Proceedings) Order 1991 or the Family Law Act 1996 (Part IV) (Allocation of Proceedings) Order 1997 still apply by virtue of paragraph (2).

(5) In relation to an appeal in respect of a type of case before the commencement of section 10 of the Child Support, Pensions and Social Security Act 2000 for the purposes of that type of case, the reference to the Child Support Appeals (Jurisdiction of Courts) Order 2002 in article 5(1)(f) is to be read as a reference to the Child Support Appeals (Jurisdiction of Courts) Order 1993.

Allocation and Transfer of Proceedings Order 2008, Sch 1

SCHEDULE 1

Article 2

CLASSES OF COUNTY COURT

Column 1	Column 2	Column 3	Column 4	Column 5	Column 6
County court	Family Hearing Centre	Care Centre	Adoption Centre	Inter-country Adoption Centre	Forced Marriage county court
Aberystwyth County Court	Yes		Yes		
Accrington County Court	Yes				
Aldershot County Court	Yes				
Altrincham County Court	Yes				
Barnet County Court	Yes				
Barnsley County Court	Yes				
Barnstaple County Court	Yes				
Barrow in Furness County Court	Yes				
Basingstoke County Court	Yes				
Bath County Court	Yes				
Bedford County Court	Yes				
Birkenhead County Court	Yes				
Birmingham County Court	Yes	Yes	Yes	Yes	Yes
Bishop Auckland County Court	Yes				
Blackburn County Court	Yes	Yes	Yes		Yes
Blackpool County Court	Yes				

Part II Statutory Instruments

Column 1	Column 2	Column 3	Column 4	Column 5	Column 6
County court	Family Hearing Centre	Care Centre	Adoption Centre	Intercountry Adoption Centre	Forced Marriage county court
Blackwood County Court	Yes				
Bodmin County Court	Yes				
Bolton County Court	Yes		Yes		
Boston County Court	Yes				
Bournemouth County Court	Yes	Yes	Yes	Yes	
Bow County Court	Yes		Yes		
Bradford County Court	Yes		Yes		Yes
Brecon County Court	Yes				
Brentford County Court	Yes		Yes		
Bridgend County Court	Yes				
Brighton County Court	Yes	Yes	Yes		
Bristol County Court	Yes	Yes	Yes	Yes	Yes
Bromley County Court	Yes		Yes		
Burnley County Court	Yes				
Burton-on-Trent County Court	Yes				
Bury County Court	Yes				
Bury St. Edmunds County Court	Yes				
Caernarfon County Court	Yes	Yes			
Cambridge County Court	Yes	Yes	Yes		

Allocation and Transfer of Proceedings Order 2008, Sch 1

Column 1	Column 2	Column 3	Column 4	Column 5	Column 6
County court	Family Hearing Centre	Care Centre	Adoption Centre	Inter-country Adoption Centre	Forced Marriage county court
Canterbury County Court	Yes	Yes	Yes		
Cardiff County Court	Yes	Yes	Yes	Yes	Yes
Carlisle County Court	Yes	Yes	Yes		
Carmarthen County Court	Yes				
Chelmsford County Court	Yes	Yes	Yes		
Chester County Court	Yes	Yes	Yes	Yes	
Chesterfield County Court	Yes				
Chichester County Court	Yes				
Chorley County Court	Yes				
Clerkenwell & Shoreditch County Court	Yes				
Colchester and Clacton County Court	Yes				
Consett County Court	Yes				
Coventry County Court	Yes	Yes	Yes		
Crewe County Court	Yes				
Croydon County Court	Yes		Yes		
Darlington County Court	Yes				
Dartford County Court	Yes				

Part II Statutory Instruments

Column 1 County court	Column 2 Family Hearing Centre	Column 3 Care Centre	Column 4 Adoption Centre	Column 5 Intercountry Adoption Centre	Column 6 Forced Marriage county court
Derby County Court	Yes	Yes	Yes		Yes
Dewsbury County Court	Yes				
Doncaster County Court	Yes				
Dudley County Court	Yes				
Durham County Court	Yes				
Eastbourne County Court	Yes				
Edmonton County Court	Yes				
Epsom County Court	Yes				
Exeter County Court	Yes	Yes	Yes	Yes	
Gateshead County Court	Yes				
Gloucester County Court	Yes				
Grimsby County Court	Yes				
Guildford County Court	Yes	Yes	Yes		
Halifax County Court	Yes				
Harlow County Court	Yes				
Harrogate County Court	Yes				
Hartlepool County Court	Yes				
Hastings County Court	Yes				

Column 1	Column 2	Column 3	Column 4	Column 5	Column 6
County court	Family Hearing Centre	Care Centre	Adoption Centre	Inter-country Adoption Centre	Forced Marriage county court
Haverfordwest County Court	Yes				
Hereford County Court	Yes				
Hertford County Court	Yes				
Hitchin County Court	Yes				
Horsham County Court	Yes				
Huddersfield County Court	Yes				
Ilford County Court	Yes				
Ipswich County Court	Yes	Yes	Yes		
Keighley County Court	Yes				
Kendal County Court	Yes				
King's Lynn County Court	Yes				
Kingston-upon-Hull County Court	Yes	Yes	Yes		
Kingston-upon-Thames County Court	Yes				
Lambeth County Court	Yes				
Lancaster County Court	Yes	Yes	Yes		
Leeds County Court	Yes	Yes	Yes	Yes	Yes
Leicester County Court	Yes	Yes	Yes		Yes
Leigh County Court	Yes				
Lincoln County Court	Yes	Yes	Yes		

Part II   Statutory Instruments

Column 1 County court	Column 2 Family Hearing Centre	Column 3 Care Centre	Column 4 Adoption Centre	Column 5 Intercountry Adoption Centre	Column 6 Forced Marriage county court
Liverpool County Court	Yes	Yes	Yes	Yes	
Llanelli County Court	Yes				
Llangefni County Court	Yes		Yes		
Lowestoft County Court	Yes				
Luton County Court	Yes	Yes	Yes		Yes
Macclesfield County Court	Yes		Yes		
Maidstone County Court	Yes				
Manchester County Court	Yes	Yes	Yes	Yes	Yes
Mansfield County Court	Yes				
Medway County Court	Yes	Yes	Yes		
Merthyr Tydfil County Court	Yes				
Middlesbrough County Court at Teesside Combined Court	Yes	Yes	Yes		Yes
Milton Keynes County Court	Yes	Yes	Yes		
Morpeth County Court	Yes				
Neath County Court	Yes				
…					
Newcastle-upon-Tyne County Court	Yes	Yes	Yes	Yes	Yes

Column 1	Column 2	Column 3	Column 4	Column 5	Column 6
County court	Family Hearing Centre	Care Centre	Adoption Centre	Inter-country Adoption Centre	Forced Marriage county court
Newport (Gwent) County Court	Yes	Yes	Yes		
Newport (Isle of Wight) County Court	Yes				
Northampton County Court	Yes	Yes	Yes		
North Shields County Court	Yes				
Norwich County Court	Yes	Yes	Yes		
Nottingham County Court	Yes	Yes	Yes	Yes	
Oldham County Court	Yes				
Oxford County Court	Yes	Yes	Yes		
Penrith County Court	Yes				
Penzance County Court	Yes				
Peterborough County Court	Yes	Yes	Yes		
Plymouth County Court	Yes	Yes	Yes		
Pontefract County Court	Yes				
Pontypridd County Court	Yes	Yes	Yes		
Portsmouth County Court	Yes	Yes	Yes	Yes	
Preston County Court	Yes				
Rawtenstall County Court	Yes				

Part II Statutory Instruments

Column 1	Column 2	Column 3	Column 4	Column 5	Column 6
County court	Family Hearing Centre	Care Centre	Adoption Centre	Inter-country Adoption Centre	Forced Marriage county court
Reading County Court	Yes	Yes	Yes		
Reigate County Court	Yes				
Rhyl County Court	Yes	Yes	Yes		
Romford County Court	Yes		Yes		Yes
Rotherham County Court	Yes				
Runcorn County Court	Yes				
St. Helens County Court	Yes				
Salford County Court	Yes				
Salisbury County Court	Yes				
Scarborough County Court	Yes				
Scunthorpe County Court	Yes				
Sheffield County Court	Yes	Yes	Yes		
Shrewsbury County Court	Yes				
Skipton County Court	Yes				
Slough County Court	Yes				
Southampton County Court	Yes		Yes		
Southend County Court	Yes				
Southport County Court	Yes				

Allocation and Transfer of Proceedings Order 2008, Sch 1

Column 1	Column 2	Column 3	Column 4	Column 5	Column 6
County court	Family Hearing Centre	Care Centre	Adoption Centre	Intercountry Adoption Centre	Forced Marriage county court
South Shields County Court	Yes				
Stafford County Court	Yes				
Staines County Court	Yes				
Stockport County Court	Yes		Yes		
Stoke-on-Trent County Court	Yes	Yes	Yes		
Sunderland County Court	Yes	Yes	Yes		
Swansea County Court	Yes	Yes	Yes		
Swindon County Court	Yes	Yes	Yes		
Tameside County Court	Yes				
Taunton County Court	Yes	Yes	Yes		
Telford County Court	Yes	Yes	Yes		
Thanet County Court	Yes				
Torquay County Court	Yes				
Trowbridge County Court	Yes				
Truro County Court	Yes	Yes	Yes		
Tunbridge Wells County Court	Yes				
Uxbridge County Court	Yes				
Wakefield County Court	Yes				

Part II Statutory Instruments

Column 1	Column 2	Column 3	Column 4	Column 5	Column 6
County court	Family Hearing Centre	Care Centre	Adoption Centre	Intercountry Adoption Centre	Forced Marriage county court
Walsall County Court	Yes				
Wandsworth County Court	Yes				
Warrington County Court	Yes	Yes	Yes		
Watford County Court	Yes	Yes	Yes		
Welshpool and Newtown County Court	Yes				
Weston Super Mare County Court	Yes				
Weymouth County Court	Yes				
Whitehaven County Court	Yes				
Wigan County Court	Yes				
Willesden County Court	Yes				Yes
Winchester County Court	Yes				
Wolverhampton County Court	Yes	Yes	Yes		
Woolwich County Court	Yes				
Worcester County Court	Yes	Yes	Yes		
Worthing County Court	Yes				
Wrexham County Court	Yes	Yes	Yes	Yes	
Yeovil County Court	Yes				
York County Court	Yes	Yes	Yes		

Allocation and Transfer of Proceedings Order 2008, Sch 1

NOTES

Amendments.[1] Entry 'Nelson County Court' revoked: SI 2009/3319.

****

Part II Statutory Instruments

FAMILY PROCEEDINGS RULES 1991

SI 1991/1247

ARRANGEMENT OF RULES

PART I
PRELIMINARY

Rule		Page
1.1	Citation and commencement	310
1.2	Interpretation	310
1.3	Application of other rules	315
1.4	County court proceedings in principal registry	315
1.5	Computation of time	316

PART II
MATRIMONIAL AND CIVIL PARTNERSHIP CAUSES

2.38	Respondent's statement as to arrangements for children	316
2.39	Procedure for complying with section 41 of Act of 1973 or section 63 of Act of 2004	317
2.40	Applications relating to children of the family	318
2.57	Children to be separately represented on certain applications	318

PART III
OTHER MATRIMONIAL ETC PROCEEDINGS

3.1	Application in case of failure to provide reasonable maintenance	319
3.2	Application for alteration of maintenance agreement during lifetime of parties	320
3.3	Application for alteration of maintenance agreement after death of one party	321
3.4	Further proceedings on application under rule 3.3	322
3.5	Application of other rules to proceedings under section 35 or 36 of Act of 1973 or under paragraph 69 or 73 of Schedule 5 to Act of 2004	323
3.6	Married Women's Property Act 1882 or section 66 of Act of 2004	323
3.7	Exercise in principal registry of county court jurisdiction under section 17 of Married Women's Property Act 1882 or under section 66 of Act of 2004	325
3.8	Applications under Part IV of the Family Law Act 1996 (Family Homes and Domestic Violence)	326
3.9	Hearing of applications under Part IV of the Family Law Act 1996	327
3.9A	Enforcement of orders made on applications under Part IV of the Family Law Act 1996	328
3.10	Applications under Part IV of the Family Law Act 1996: bail	330
3.11	Proceedings in respect of polygamous marriage	331
3.12	Application under section 55 of Act of 1986 for declaration as to marital status	332
3.12A	Application under section 58 of Act of 2004 for declaration as to civil partnership status	334
3.13	Application under section 55A of Act of 1986 for declaration of parentage	335
3.14	Application under section 56(1)(b) and (2) of Act of 1986 for a declaration of legitimacy or legitimation	337

3.15	Application under section 57 of Act of 1986 for declaration as to adoption effected overseas	337
3.16	General provisions as to proceedings under rules 3.12, 3.13, 3.14 and 3.15	338
3.17	Application for leave under section 13 of Act of 1984 or under paragraph 4 of Schedule 7 to Act of 2004	339
3.18	Application for order for financial relief or avoidance of transaction order under Part III of Act of 1984 or under Schedule 7 to Act of 2004	340
3.19	Application for order under section 24 of Act of 1984 or under paragraph 17 of Schedule 7 to Act of 2004 preventing transaction	342
3.20	Consent to marriage of minor	342
3.20A	Consent to registration of civil partnership of child	343
3.21	Application under section 27 of the Act of 1991 for declaration of parentage	343
3.22	Appeal under section 20 of the Act of 1991 …	344
3.23	Appeal from Upper Tribunal	344
3.24	Reference under section 8(5) of the Gender Recognition Act 2004	344
3.25	Proceedings under Part 4A of the Family Law Act 1996: interpretation of rules and forms	345
3.26	Applications under Part 4A of the Family Law Act 1996 for forced marriage protection orders	346
3.27	Leave stage for forced marriage protection orders	346
3.28	Service of the application for a forced marriage protection order	347
3.29	Transfer of proceedings	347
3.30	Parties to proceedings for a forced marriage protection order	347
3.31	Orders for disclosure against a person not a party	348
3.32	Claim to withhold inspection or disclosure of a document	349
3.33	Hearing of applications for forced marriage protection orders	349
3.34	Forced marriage protection orders made by the court of its own motion	350
3.35	Enforcement of forced marriage protection orders	351
3.36	Applications under Part 4A of the Family Law Act 1996: bail	352

PART IIIA
APPLICATIONS FOR ORDERS PREVENTING AVOIDANCE UNDER SECTION 32L OF THE CHILD SUPPORT ACT 1991

3A.1	Scope of this Part	353
3A.2	Interpretation	353
3A.3	Application of CPR	353
3A.4	Where and how to start proceedings	353
3A.5	Who the parties are	354
3A.6	Service of the application	355
3A.7	Applications without notice	355

PART IV
PROCEEDINGS UNDER THE CHILDREN ACT 1989, ETC

4.1	Interpretation and application	356
4.2	Matters prescribed for the purposes of the Act of 1989	357
4.3	Application for leave to commence proceedings	358
4.4	Application	359
4.4A	Application for a warning notice or application to amend enforcement order by reason of change of residence	361
4.5	Withdrawal of application	361
4.6	Transfer	362
4.7	Parties	363

4.8	Service	364
4.9	Answer to application	366
4.10	Appointment of children's guardian	366
4.11	Powers and duties of officers of the service and Welsh family proceedings officers	368
4.11A	Additional powers and duties of children's guardian	368
4.11AA	Additional powers and duties of officers of the service and Welsh family proceedings officers: family assistance order reports and risk assessments	370
4.11B	Additional powers and duties of a children and family reporter	372
4.12	Solicitor for child	373
4.13	Welfare officer	374
4.13A	Local authority officers preparing family assistance order reports	374
4.13B	Section 11J or 11O: duties of person notified	375
4.14	Directions	375
4.14A	Timetable for the Child in proceedings for a care order or supervision order	377
4.15	Timing of proceedings	377
4.16	Attendance at directions appointment and hearing	378
4.17	Documentary evidence	379
4.17A	Disclosure of report under section 14A(8) or (9)	380
4.17AA	Service of risk assessments	380
4.18	Expert evidence – examination of child	381
4.19	Amendment	381
4.20	Oral evidence	382
4.21	Hearing	382
4.21AA	Service of enforcement order or order amending or revoking enforcement order	383
4.21A	Attachment of penal notice	383
4.21B	Order with notice attached: committal	384
4.22		384
4.23		384
4.24	Notification of consent	384
4.24A	Exclusion requirements: interim care orders and emergency protection orders	385
4.25	Secure accommodation – evidence	386
4.26	Investigation under section 37	386
4.27	Direction to local authority to apply for education supervision order	387
4.27A	Stay under the Council Regulation	387
4.28	Transitional provision	388

PART IVA
PROCEEDINGS UNDER SECTION 54 OF THE HUMAN FERTILISATION AND EMBRYOLOGY ACT 2008

4A.1	Interpretation	388
4A.2	Application of this Part	388
4A.3	Application of Part IV	388
4A.4	Application for a parental order	388
4A.5	How to start parental order proceedings	389
4A.6	Personal details	389
4A.7	Who the parties are	389
4A.8	What the court shall do when the application has been issued	390
4A.9	What a proper officer shall do	390
4A.10	Service of the application and other documents	390
4A.11	Acknowledgement	390
4A.12	Date for first directions hearing	390
4A.13	The first directions hearing	390

4A.14	Where the agreement of the other parent or the woman who carried the child is not required	392
4A.15	Agreement	393
4A.16	Parental order reporter	393
4A.17	Reports of the parental order reporter and disclosure to the parties	393
4A.18	Notice of final hearing	394
4A.19	The final hearing	394
4A.20	Proof of identity of the child	394
4A.21	Disclosing information to an adult who was subject to a parental order	395
4A.22	Application for recovery orders	395
4A.23	Custody, inspection and disclosure of documents and information	395
4A.24	Documents held by the court not to be inspected or copied without the court's leave	396
4A.25	Orders	396
4A.26	Copies of orders	396
4A.27	Amendment and revocation of orders	397

PART V
WARDSHIP

5.1	Application to make a minor a ward of court	398
5.2	Enforcement of order by tipstaff	399
5.3	Where minor ceases to be a ward of court	399
5.4	Adoption of minor who is a ward of court	399
5.5	Orders for use of secure accommodation	400
5.6	Notice to provider of refuge	400

PART VI
CHILD ABDUCTION AND CUSTODY

6.1	Interpretation	400
6.2	Mode of application	400
6.3	Contents of originating summons: general provisions	401
6.4	Contents of originating summons: particular provisions	401
6.5	Defendants	402
6.6	Acknowledgement of service	402
6.7	Evidence	402
6.8	Hearing	402
6.9	Dispensing with service	403
6.10	Adjournment of summons	403
6.11	Stay of proceedings	403
6.11A	Stay under the Council Regulation	404
6.12	Transfer of proceedings	404
6.13	Interim directions	405
6.14		405
6.15	Revocation and variation of registered decisions	405
6.16	Orders for disclosure of information	405
6.17	Applications and orders under sections 33 and 34 of the Family Law Act 1986	405
6.18	Registration of registered decisions	406

PART VII
ENFORCEMENT OF ORDERS

Chapter 1
General

7.1	Enforcement of order for payment of money etc	406
7.2	Committal and injunction	407

Part II   Statutory Instruments

| 7.3 | Transfer of county court order to High Court | 408 |

Chapter 3
Registration and Enforcement of Custody Orders

7.7	Registration under Family Law Act 1986	408
7.8	Application to register English Part I order	409
7.9	Registration of orders made in Scotland, Northern Ireland or a specified dependent territory	410
7.10	Revocation and variation of English order	411
7.11	Registration of revoked, recalled or varied orders made in Scotland, Northern Ireland or a specified dependent territory	411
7.12	Interim directions	412
7.13	Staying and dismissal of enforcement proceedings	412
7.14	Particulars of other proceedings	412
7.15	Inspection of register	412

PART VIII
APPEALS

8.A1	Interpretation	413
8.1	Appeals from district judges	413
8.1A		414
8.1B		414
8.2	Appeals to a county court and appeals from district judges under the Act of 1989 or Parts 4 and 4A of the Family Law Act 1996 or relating to deduction order appeals	414
8.2A	Notice of appeal	415
8.2B	Respondents	416
8.2C	Stay	417
8.2D	Amendment of appeal notice	417
8.2E	Powers of a district judge	418
8.2F	Appeal court's powers	418
8.2FF	Appeal court's powers: deduction order appeals	418
8.2G	Hearing of appeals	419
8.2H	Appeals from orders made under Parts 4 and 4A of the Family Law Act 1996	419
8.3	Appeals under section 13 of the Administration of Justice Act 1960	420
8.4	Appeal under section 8(1) of the Gender Recognition Act 2004	420

PART IX
DISABILITY

9.1	Interpretation and application of Part IX	421
9.2	Child or protected party must sue by next friend etc	421
9.2A	Certain children may sue without next friend etc	423
9.3	Service on child or protected party	425
9.4	Petition for nullity on ground of mental disorder	426
9.5	Separate representation of children	426

PART X
PROCEDURE (GENERAL)

10.1	Application	427
10.2	Service on solicitors	427
10.3	Service on person acting in person	427
10.4	Service by bailiff in proceedings in principal registry	428
10.5	Proof of service by officer of court etc	428
10.6	Service out of England and Wales	428
10.7	Mode of giving notice	429

10.8	Notice of intention to defend	429
10.9	Mode of making applications	430
10.10	Orders for transfer of family proceedings	430
10.11	Procedure on transfer of cause or application	431
10.12	Evidence by affidavit	432
10.13	Taking of affidavit in county court proceedings	432
10.14	Evidence of marriage or overseas relationship outside England and Wales	432
10.14A	Power of court to limit cross-examination	433
10.15	Official shorthand note etc of proceedings	433
10.16	Copies of decrees and orders	434
10.17	Service of order	434
10.18	No notice of intention to proceed after year's delay	434
10.19	Filing of documents at place of hearing etc	435
10.20	Inspection etc of documents retained in court	435
10.20A		435
10.21	Disclosure of addresses	435
10.21A	Disclosure of information under the Act of 1991	436
10.21B	Documents in family proceedings concerning gender recognition	436
10.22	Practice to be observed in district registries and designated county courts	437
10.23	Transitional provisions	437
10.24	Applications for relief which is precluded by the Act of 1991	437
10.25	Modification of rule 10.24 in relation to non-free-standing applications	439
10.26	Human Rights Act 1998	439
10.27	Costs	442
10.28	Attendance at private hearings	442

PART XI
COMMUNICATION OF INFORMATION: PROCEEDINGS RELATING TO CHILDREN

11.1	Application	444
11.2	Communication of information: general	444
11.3	Instruction of experts	444
11.4	Communication of information for purposes connected with the proceedings	445
11.5	Communication of information by a party etc for other purposes	445
11.6	Communication for the effective functioning of Cafcass and CAFCASS CYMRU	448
11.7	Communication to and by Ministers of the Crown and Welsh Ministers	449
11.8	Communication by persons lawfully in receipt of information	451
11.9	Interpretation	451

	Appendix 1 – Forms	453
	Appendix 3 – Notices and Respondents	459
	Appendix 4	473

NOTES

Commencement. 14 Oct 1991.

Enabling power. Matrimonial and Family Proceedings Act 1984, s 40(1).

PART I
PRELIMINARY

1.1 Citation and commencement

These rules may be cited as the Family Proceedings Rules 1991 and shall come into force on 14th October 1991.

1.2 Interpretation

(1) In these rules, unless the context otherwise requires –

'the Act of 1973' means the Matrimonial Causes Act 1973;
'the Act of 1984' means the Matrimonial and Family Proceedings Act 1984;
'the Act of 1986' means the Family Law Act 1986;
'the Act of 1989' means the Children Act 1989;
['the Act of 1991' means the Child Support Act 1991;][2]
['the Act of 2004' means the Civil Partnership Act 2004;][11]
['the Act of 2006' means the Children and Adoption Act 2006;][12]
['the Allocation Order' means any order made by the Lord Chancellor under Part 1 of Schedule 11 to the Act of 1989;][14]
'ancillary relief ' means –
    (a)   an avoidance of disposition order,
    (b)   a financial provision order,
    (c)   an order for maintenance pending suit,
    [(ca) an order for maintenance pending outcome of proceedings,][11]
    (d)   a property adjustment order, ...[5]
    (e)   a variation order; [or
    (f)   a pension sharing order;][6]
['avoidance of disposition order' means –
    (a)   in matrimonial proceedings, an order under section 37(2)(b) or (c) of the Act of 1973, and
    (b)   in civil partnership proceedings, an order under paragraph 74(3) or (4) of Schedule 5 to the Act of 2004;][11]
'business day' has the meaning assigned to it by rule 1.5(6);
['cause' means –
    (a)   a matrimonial cause or a civil partnership cause, or
    (b)   proceedings under section 19 of the Act of 1973 (presumption of death and dissolution of marriage), or
    (c)   proceedings under section 55 of the Act of 2004 (presumption of death);
'child', except in Part IV, in relation to one or both of the parties to a marriage or civil partnership, includes an illegitimate child of that party or, as the case may be, of both parties;
'child of the family' has, except in Part IV, the meaning assigned to it by section 105(1) of the Act of 1989;
'civil partnership cause' has the meaning assigned to it by section 32 of the Act of 1984;

'civil partnership order' means one of the orders mentioned in section 37 of the Act of 2004;
'civil partnership proceedings county court' means a county court so designated by the Lord Chancellor under section 36A of the Act of 1984;
['Commission' means the Child Maintenance and Enforcement Commission;][15]
'consent order' means –
- (a) in matrimonial proceedings, an order under section 33A of the Act of 1973, and
- (b) in civil partnership proceedings, an order under paragraph 66 of Schedule 5 to the Act of 2004;][11]

['Contracting State' means –
- [(a) one of the parties to the Council Regulation, that is to say, Belgium, Cyprus, Czech Republic, Germany, Greece, Spain, Estonia, France, Hungary, Ireland, Italy, Latvia, Lithuania, Luxembourg, Malta, Netherlands, Austria, Poland, Portugal, Slovakia, Slovenia, Finland, Sweden and the United Kingdom,][8] and
- (b) a party which has subsequently adopted the Council Regulation;][7]

['the Council Regulation' means Council Regulation (EC) No [2201/2003 of 27th November 2003 concerning][8] jurisdiction and the recognition and enforcement of judgments in matrimonial matters and [the][8] matters of parental responsibility …[8];][7]
'court' means a judge or the district judge;
['court of trial' means –
- (a) in matrimonial proceedings, a divorce county court designated by the Lord Chancellor as a court of trial pursuant to section 33(1) of the Act of 1984, and
- (b) in civil partnership proceedings, a civil partnership proceedings county court designated by the Lord Chancellor as a court of trial pursuant to section 36A(1)(b) of the Act of 1984, and

in matrimonial proceedings pending in a divorce county court or in civil partnership proceedings pending in a civil partnership proceedings county court, the principal registry shall be treated as a court of trial having its place of sitting at the Royal Courts of Justice;][11]

'defended cause' means a cause not being an undefended cause;
['designated county court' means a court designated as –
- (a) a divorce county court, or
- (b) a civil partnership proceedings county court, or
- (c) both a divorce county court and a civil partnership proceedings county court;

'dissolution town', in relation to any civil partnership proceedings, means a place at which sittings of the High Court are authorised to be held outside the Royal Courts of Justice for the hearing of such proceedings or proceedings of the class to which they belong;][11]

'district judge', in relation to proceedings in the principal registry, a district registry or a county court, means the district judge or one of the district judges of that registry or county court, as the case may be;

['district registry' ...[13] means –
- (a) in matrimonial proceedings, any district registry having a divorce county court within its district;
- (b) in civil partnership proceedings, any district registry having a civil partnership proceedings county court within its district; and
- (c) in any other case, any district registry having a designated county court within its district;][11]

'divorce county court' means a county court so designated by the Lord Chancellor pursuant to section 33(1) of the Act of 1984;

'divorce town', in relation to any matrimonial proceedings, means a place at which sittings of the High Court are authorised to be held outside the Royal Courts of Justice for the hearing of such proceedings or proceedings of the class to which they belong;

'document exchange' means any document exchange for the time being approved by the Lord Chancellor;

'family proceedings' has the meaning assigned to it by section 32 of the Act of 1984;

['financial provision order' means –
- (a) in matrimonial proceedings, any of the orders mentioned in section 21(1) of the Act of 1973, except an order under section 27(6) of that Act, and
- (b) in civil partnership proceedings, any of the orders mentioned in paragraph 2(1) of Schedule 5 to the Act of 2004, made under Part 1 of Schedule 5 to that Act;

'financial relief' has –
- (a) in matrimonial proceedings, the meaning assigned to it by section 37 of the Act of 1973, and
- (b) in civil partnership proceedings, the meaning assigned to it by paragraph 74 of Schedule 5 to the Act of 2004;][11]

'judge' does not include a district judge;

['matrimonial cause' has the meaning assigned to it by section 32 of the Act of 1984;][11]

'notice of intention to defend' has the meaning assigned to it by rule 10.8;

['officer of the service' has the same meaning as in the Criminal Justice and Court Services Act 2000;][7]

['order for maintenance pending outcome of proceedings' means an order under paragraph 38 of Schedule 5 to the Act of 2004;][11]

'order for maintenance pending suit' means an order under section 22 of the Act of 1973;

'person named' includes a person described as 'passing under the name of A.B.';

'the President' means the President of the Family Division or, in the case of his absence or incapacity through illness or otherwise or of a vacancy in the office of President, the senior puisne judge of that Division;

['the President of Gender Recognition Panels' means the office in paragraph 2(1) of Schedule 1 to the Gender Recognition Act 2004;][9]

'principal registry' means the Principal Registry of the Family Division;

'proper officer' means –
   (a) in relation to the principal registry, the [family proceedings department manager][3], and
   (b) in relation to any other court or registry, the [court manager][3], or other officer of the court or registry acting on his behalf in accordance with directions given by the Lord Chancellor;

['property adjustment order' means –
   (a) in matrimonial proceedings, any of the orders mentioned in section 21(2) of the Act of 1973, and
   (b) in civil partnership proceedings, any of the orders mentioned in paragraph 7(1) of Schedule 5 to the Act of 2004;][11]

['registry for the divorce town or dissolution town'][11] shall be construed in accordance with rule 2.32(6);

'Royal Courts of Justice', in relation to matrimonial proceedings pending in a divorce county court [or civil partnership proceedings pending in a civil partnership proceedings county court][11], means such place, being the Royal Courts of Justice or elsewhere, as may be specified in directions given by the Lord Chancellor pursuant to section 42(2)(a) of the Act of 1984;

'senior district judge' means the senior district judge of the Family Division or, in his absence from the principal registry, the senior of the district judges in attendance at the registry;

'special procedure list' has the meaning assigned to it by rule 2.24(3);

'undefended cause' means –
   (i) a cause in which no answer has been filed or any answer filed has been struck out, or
   (ii) a cause which is proceeding only on the respondent's answer and in which no reply or answer to the respondent's answer has been filed or any such reply or answer has been struck out, or
   (iii) a cause to which rule 2.12(4) applies and in which no notice has been given under that rule or any notice so given has been withdrawn, or
   (iv) a cause in which an answer has been filed claiming relief but in which no pleading has been filed opposing the grant of a decree [or civil partnership order, as the case may be,][11] on the petition or answer or any pleading or part of a pleading opposing the grant of such relief has been struck out, or
   (v) any cause not within (i) to (iv) above in which a decree [or civil partnership order, as the case may be,][11] has been pronounced;

['variation order' means –
(a) in matrimonial proceedings, an order under section 31 of the Act of 1973, and
(b) in civil partnership proceedings, an order under Part 11 of Schedule 5 to the Act of 2004][11];

['Welsh family proceedings officer' has the same meaning as in the Children Act 2004][10].

(2) Unless the context otherwise requires, a cause begun by petition shall be treated as pending for the purposes of these rules notwithstanding that a final decree [or civil partnership order has been made on the petition, or it has been otherwise finally disposed of][11].

(3) Unless the context otherwise requires, a rule or Part referred to by number means the rule or Part so numbered in these rules.

(4) In these rules a form referred to by number means the form so numbered in Appendix 1 [or 1A][4] to these rules with such variation as the circumstances of the particular case may require.

(5) In these rules any reference to an Order and rule is –

(a) if prefixed by the letters 'CCR', a reference to that Order and rule in the County Court Rules 1981, and
(b) if prefixed by the letters 'RSC', a reference to that Order and rule in the Rules of the Supreme Court 1965.

[(5A) In these rules a reference to a Part or rule, if prefixed by the letters 'CPR' is a reference to that Part or rule in the Civil Procedure Rules 1998.][4]

[(6) References in these rules to a county court shall –

(a) in matrimonial proceedings, be construed as references to a divorce county court, and
(b) in civil partnership proceedings, be construed as references to a civil partnership proceedings county court.][11]

(7) In this rule and in rule 1.4, 'matrimonial proceedings' means proceedings of a kind with respect to which divorce county courts have jurisdiction by or under section 33, 34 or 35 of the Act of 1984.

[(8) In this rule and in rule 1.4, 'civil partnership proceedings' means proceedings of a kind with respect to which civil partnership proceedings county courts have jurisdiction by or under section 36A, 36B or 36C of the Act of 1984.

(9) In these Rules –

(a) a reference to a conditional order is a reference to an order made under Chapter 2 of Part 2 of the Act of 2004 of a kind mentioned in section 37(1)(a), (b) or (c) of that Act which has not been made final; and
(b) except in rule 8.1 ...[13], a reference to a final order is a reference to such an order which has been made final.][11]

NOTES

Amendments.[1] Words inserted: SI 1992/2067.[2] Definition inserted: SI 1993/295.[3] Definition amended: SI 1997/1056.[4] Words and paragraph inserted: SI 1999/3491.[5] Word omitted: SI 2000/2267.[6] Definition inserted: SI 2000/2267.[7] Definition inserted: SI 2001/821.[8] Words and paragraph substituted and words repealed: SI 2005/264.[9] Definition inserted: SI 2005/559.[10] Definition inserted: SI 2005/559.[11] Definitions, words and paragraphs substituted and inserted: SI 2005/2922.[12] Definition inserted: SI 2008/2861.[13] Words revoked: SI 2009/636. [14] Definition inserted: SI 2010/1064.[15] Definition inserted: SI 2010/786.

References. References in para (5) to the County Court Rules 1981 and the Rules of the Supreme Court 1965 are references to the County Court Rules and the Rules of the Supreme Court in force immediately before 26 April 1999 and references to provisions of those Rules in the Family Proceedings Rules 1991 shall be read accordingly.

1.3 Application of other rules

(1) Subject to the provisions of these rules and of any enactment the County Court Rules 1981 and the Rules of the Supreme Court 1965 shall [continue to][1] apply, with the necessary modifications, to family proceedings in a county court and the High Court respectively.

(2) For the purposes of paragraph (1) any provision of these rules authorising or requiring anything to be done in family proceedings shall be treated as if it were, in the case of proceedings pending in a county court, a provision of the County Court Rules 1981 and, in the case of proceedings pending in the High Court, a provision of the Rules of the Supreme Court 1965.

NOTES

Amendments.[1] Words inserted: SI 1999/1012.

References. References in this rule to the County Court Rules 1981 and the Rules of the Supreme Court 1965 are references to the County Court Rules and the Rules of the Supreme Court in force immediately before 26 April 1999 and references to provisions of those Rules in the Family Proceedings Rules 1991 shall be read accordingly.

1.4 County court proceedings in principal registry

[(1) Subject to the provisions of these rules –

(a) matrimonial proceedings pending at any time in the principal registry which, if they had been begun in a divorce county court, would be pending at that time in such a court, shall be treated, for the purposes of these rules and of any provision of the County Court Rules 1981 and the County Courts Act 1984, as pending in a divorce county court and not in the High Court, and

(b) civil partnership proceedings pending at any time in the principal registry which, if they had been begun in a civil partnership proceedings county court, would be pending at that time in such a court, shall be treated, for the purposes of these rules and of any provision of the County Court Rules 1981 and the County Courts Act 1984, as pending in a civil partnership proceedings county court and not in the High Court.][1]

(2) Unless the context otherwise requires, any reference to a divorce county court [or a civil partnership proceedings county court or a designated county court]¹ in any provision of these rules which relates to the commencement or prosecution of proceedings in ...¹, or the transfer of proceedings to or from[,]¹ such a court, includes a reference to the principal registry.

NOTES

Amendments.¹ Paragraph substituted and words inserted and revoked: SI 2005/2922.

References. Reference in this rule to the County Court Rules 1981 is a reference to the County Court Rules in force immediately before 26 April 1999 and references to provisions of those Rules in the Family Proceedings Rules 1991 shall be read accordingly.

1.5 Computation of time

(1) Any period of time fixed by these rules, or by any rules applied by these rules, or by any decree, judgment, order or direction for doing any act shall be reckoned in accordance with the following provisions of this rule.

(2) Where the act is required to be done not less than a specified period before a specified date, the period starts immediately after the date on which the act is done and ends immediately before the specified date.

(3) Where the act is required to be done within a specified period after or from a specified date, the period starts immediately after that date.

(4) Where, apart from this paragraph, the period in question, being a period of seven days or less, would include a day which is not a business day, that day shall be excluded.

(5) Where the time so fixed for doing an act in the court office expires on a day on which the office is closed, and for that reason the act cannot be done on that day, the act shall be in time if done on the next day on which the office is open.

(6) In these rules 'business day' means any day other than –

    (a)   a Saturday, Sunday, Christmas Day or Good Friday; or
    (b)   a bank holiday under the Banking and Financial Dealings Act 1971, in England and Wales.

[PART II
MATRIMONIAL AND CIVIL PARTNERSHIP CAUSES]¹

NOTES

Amendments.¹ Part heading substituted: SI 2005/2922.

****

2.38 Respondent's statement as to arrangements for children

(1) A respondent on whom there is served a statement in accordance with rule 2.2(2) may, whether or not he agreed that statement, file in the court office a written statement of his views on the present and proposed arrangements for

the children, and on receipt of such a statement from the respondent the proper officer shall send a copy to the petitioner.

(2) Any such statement of the respondent's views shall, if practicable, be filed within the time limited for giving notice of intention to defend and in any event before the district judge considers the arrangements or proposed arrangements for the upbringing and welfare of the children of the family under section 41(1) of the Act of 1973 [or under section 63(1) of the Act of 2004, as the case may be][1].

NOTES

Amendments.[1] Words inserted: SI 2005/2922.

2.39 Procedure for complying with section 41 of Act of 1973 [or section 63 of Act of 2004][1]

(1) [The][2] district judge shall, after making his certificate under rule 2.36(1)(a) or after the provision of evidence pursuant to a direction under rule 2.24(4), as the case may be, proceed to consider the matters specified in section 41(1) of the Act of 1973 [or in section 63(1) of the Act of 2004, as the case may be,][1] in accordance with the following provisions of this rule.

(2) Where, on consideration of the relevant evidence, including any further evidence or report provided pursuant to this rule and any statement filed by the respondent under rule 2.38, the district judge is satisfied that –

- [(a) there are no children of the family to whom –
    - (i) in a matrimonial cause, section 41 of the Act of 1973 applies; or
    - (ii) in a civil partnership cause, section 63 of the Act of 2004 applies, or][1]
- (b) there are such children but the court need not exercise its powers under the Act of 1989 with respect to any of them or give [a relevant direction][1],

the district judge shall certify accordingly and, in a case to which sub-paragraph (b) applies, the petitioner and the respondent shall each be sent a copy of the certificate by the proper officer.

(3) Where the district judge is not satisfied as mentioned in paragraph (2) above he may, without prejudice to his powers under the Act of 1989 or [his power to give a relevant direction][1], give one or more of the following directions –

- (a) that the parties, or any of them, shall file further evidence relating to the arrangements for the children (and the direction shall specify the matters to be dealt with in further evidence);
- (b) that a welfare report on the children, or any of them, be prepared;
- (c) that the parties, or any of them, shall attend before him at the date, time and place specified in the direction;

and the parties shall be notified accordingly.

(4) Where the court gives a [relevant direction]¹, notice of the direction shall be given to the parties.

[(5) In this rule –

(a) 'parties' means the petitioner, the respondent and any person who appears to the court to have the care of the child; and
(b) 'relevant direction' means a direction –
  (i) in a matrimonial cause, under section 41(2) of the Act of 1973, and
  (ii) in a civil partnership cause, under section 63(2) of the Act of 2004.]¹

NOTES

Amendments.¹ Words substituted and inserted and paragraph substituted: SI 2005/2922.² Word substituted: SI 2008/2836.

2.40 Applications relating to children of the family

...¹

NOTES

Amendments.¹ Rule revoked: SI 2008/2836.

****

2.57 Children to be separately represented on certain applications

(1) Where an application is made to the High Court or a [designated county court]¹ for an order for a variation of settlement, the court shall, unless it is satisfied that the proposed variation does not adversely affect the rights or interests of any children concerned, direct that the children be separately represented on the application, either by a solicitor or by a solicitor and counsel, and may appoint the Official Solicitor or other fit person to be guardian ad litem of the children for the purpose of the application.

(2) On any other application for ancillary relief the court may give such a direction or make such appointment as it is empowered to give or make by paragraph (1).

(3) Before a person other than the Official Solicitor is appointed guardian ad litem under this rule there shall be filed a certificate by the solicitor acting for the children that the person proposed as guardian has no interest in the matter adverse to that of the children and that he is a proper person to be such guardian.

NOTES

Amendments.¹ Words substituted: SI 2005/2922.

****

PART III
OTHER MATRIMONIAL ETC PROCEEDINGS

3.1 Application in case of failure to provide reasonable maintenance

(1) Every application under section 27 of the Act of 1973 [or under Part 9 of Schedule 5 to the Act of 2004][3] shall be made by originating application in Form M19.

[(2) The application may be made

(a) in the case of an application under the Act of 1973, to any divorce county court, and
(b) in the case of an application under the Act of 2004, to any civil partnership proceedings county court,

and there shall be filed with the application an affidavit by the applicant and also a copy of the application and of the affidavit for service on the respondent.][3]

(3) The affidavit shall state –

(a) the same particulars regarding the marriage [or the civil partnership, as the case may be][3], the court's jurisdiction, the children and the previous proceedings as are required in the case of a petition by sub-paragraphs (a), (c), (d), (f) and (i) of paragraph 1 of Appendix 2;
(b) particulars of the respondent's failure to provide reasonable maintenance for the applicant, or, as the case may be, of the respondent's failure to provide, or to make a proper contribution towards, reasonable maintenance for the children of the family; and
(c) full particulars of the applicant's property and income and of the respondent's property and income, so far as may be known to the applicant.

(4) A copy of the application and of the affidavit referred to in paragraph (2) shall be served on the respondent, together with a notice in Form M20 with [Form M23A][2].

(5) Subject to paragraph (6), the respondent shall, within 14 days after the time allowed for sending the acknowledgement of service, file an affidavit stating –

(a) whether the alleged failure to provide, or to make proper contribution towards, reasonable maintenance is admitted or denied, and, if denied, the grounds on which he relies;
(b) any allegation which he wishes to make against the applicant; and
(c) full particulars of his property and income, unless otherwise directed.

(6) Where the respondent challenges the jurisdiction of the court to hear the application he shall, within 14 days after the time allowed for sending the acknowledgement of service, file an affidavit setting out the grounds of the challenge; and the obligation to file an affidavit under paragraph (5) shall not arise until 14 days after the question of jurisdiction has been determined and the court has decided that the necessary jurisdiction exists.

(7) Where the respondent's affidavit contains an allegation of adultery or of an improper association with a person named, the provisions of [sub-paragraphs (4) to (7) of paragraph 4 of Appendix 4][3] (which deal with service on, and [filing of a statement in answer by][1], a named person) shall apply.

(8) If the respondent does not file an affidavit in accordance with paragraph (5), the court may order him to file an affidavit containing full particulars of his property and income, and in that case the respondent shall serve a copy of any such affidavit on the applicant.

(9) Within 14 days after being served with a copy of any affidavit filed by the respondent, the applicant may file a further affidavit as to means and as to any fact in the respondent's affidavit which is disputed, and in that case the applicant shall serve a copy on the respondent.

No further affidavit shall be filed without leave.

[(10) The following provisions shall apply to applications under section 27 of the Act of 1973 and Part 9 of Schedule 5 to the Act of 2004 –

(a) rule 10.10 with such modifications as may be appropriate and as if the application were an application for ancillary relief; and
(b) paragraphs 5 to 9 of Appendix 4.][3]

NOTES

Amendments.[1] Words inserted: SI 1999/3491. [2] Words inserted: SI 2005/559. [3] Words inserted and substituted and paragraph substituted: SI 2005/2922.

References. References to rules 2.52 to 2.70 shall be read as references to those rules before SI 1999/3491 introducing the new ancillary relief rules came into force.

3.2 Application for alteration of maintenance agreement during lifetime of parties

(1) An application under section 35 of the Act of 1973 [or under paragraph 69 of Schedule 5 to the Act of 2004][2] for the alteration of a maintenance agreement shall be made by originating application containing, unless otherwise directed, the information required by Form M21.

[(2) The application may be made –

(a) in the case of an application under the Act of 1973, to any divorce county court, and
(b) in the case of an application under the Act of 2004, to any civil partnership proceedings county court,

and may be heard and determined by the district judge.][2]

(3) There shall be filed with the application an affidavit by the applicant exhibiting a copy of the agreement and verifying the statements in the application and also a copy of the application and of the affidavit for service on the respondent.

(4) A copy of the application and of the affidavit referred to in paragraph (3) shall be served on the respondent, together with a notice in Form M20 with [Form M23A]¹ attached.

(5) The respondent shall, within 14 days after the time limited for giving notice of intention to defend [in Form M23A]¹, file an affidavit in answer to the application containing full particulars of his property and income and, if he does not do so, the court may order him to file an affidavit containing such particulars.

(6) A respondent who files an affidavit under paragraph (5) shall at the same time file a copy which the proper officer shall serve on the applicant.

NOTES

Amendments.¹ Words inserted: SI 2005/559. ² Words inserted and paragraph substituted: SI 2005/2922.

3.3 Application for alteration of maintenance agreement after death of one party

(1) An application under section 36 of the Act of 1973 [or under paragraph 73 of Schedule 5 to the Act of 2004]¹ for the alteration of a maintenance agreement after the death of one of the parties shall be made –

(a) in the High Court, by originating summons out of the principal registry or any district registry, or
(b) in a county court, by originating application,

in Form M22.

(2) There shall be filed in support of the application an affidavit by the applicant exhibiting a copy of the agreement and an official copy of the grant of representation to the deceased's estate and of every testamentary document admitted to proof and stating –

(a) whether the deceased died domiciled in England and Wales;
[(b) the place and date of the marriage between the parties to the agreement, or the place at and date on which they formed their civil partnership, as the case may be;]¹
(c) the name of every child of the family and of any other child for whom the agreement makes financial arrangements, and –
  (i) the date of birth of each such child who is still living (or, if it be the case, that he has attained 18) and the place where and the person with whom any such minor child is residing,
  (ii) the date of death of any such child who has died since the agreement was made;
(d) whether there have been in any court any, and if so what, previous proceedings with reference to the agreement or to the marriage [or civil partnership, as the case may be,]¹ or to the children of the family or any other children for whom the agreement makes financial arrangements, and the date and effect of any order or decree made in such proceedings;

(e) whether there have been in any court any proceedings by the applicant against the deceased's estate under the Inheritance (Provision for Family and Dependants) Act 1975 or any Act repealed by that Act and the date and effect of any order made in such proceedings;

(f) in the case of an application by the surviving party, the applicant's means;

(g) in the case of an application by the personal representatives of the deceased, the surviving party's means, so far as they are known to the applicants, and the information mentioned in sub-paragraphs (a), (b) and (c) of rule 3.4(4);

(h) the facts alleged by the applicant as justifying an alteration in the agreement and the nature of the alteration sought;

(i) if the application is made after the end of the period of six months from the date on which representation in regard to the deceased's estate was first taken out, the grounds on which the court's permission to entertain the application is sought.

(3) CCR Order 48, rules 3(1), 7 and 9 shall apply to an originating application under the said section 36 as they apply to an application under section 1 of the Inheritance (Provision for Family and Dependants) Act 1975.

(4) In this rule and the next following rule 'the deceased' means the deceased party to the agreement to which the application relates.

NOTES

Amendments.[1] Words inserted and paragraph substituted: SI 2005/2922.

3.4 Further proceedings on application under rule 3.3

(1) Without prejudice to his powers under RSC Order 15 (which deals with parties and other matters), the district judge may at any stage of the proceedings direct that any person be added as a respondent to an application under rule 3.3.

(2) RSC Order 15, rule 13 (which enables the court to make representation orders in certain cases), shall apply to the proceedings as if they were mentioned in paragraph (1) of the said rule 13.

(3) Where the application is in a county court, the references in paragraphs (1) and (2) to RSC Order 15 and Order 15, rule 13 shall be construed as references to CCR Order 5 and Order 5, rule 6 respectively.

(4) A respondent who is a personal representative of the deceased shall, within 14 days after the time limited for giving notice of intention to defend, file an affidavit in answer to the application stating –

(a) full particulars of the value of the deceased's estate for probate, after providing for the discharge of the funeral, testamentary and administration expenses, debts and liabilities payable thereout, including the amount of the [inheritance tax or any other tax replaced by that tax][1] and interest thereon;

(b) the persons or classes of persons beneficially interested in the estate (giving the names and addresses of all living beneficiaries) and the value of their interests so far as ascertained, and

(c) if such be the case, that any living beneficiary (naming him) is a [child][2] or a [protected party][2] within the meaning of rule 9.1.

(5) If a respondent who is a personal representative of the deceased does not file an affidavit stating the matters mentioned in paragraph (4) the district judge may order him to do so.

(6) A respondent who is not a personal representative of the deceased may, within 14 days after the time limited for giving notice of intention to defend, file an affidavit in answer to the application.

(7) Every respondent who files an affidavit in answer to the application shall at the same time lodge a copy, which the proper officer shall serve on the applicant.

NOTES

Amendments.[1] Words substituted: SI 1991/2113. [2] Words substituted: SI 2007/2187.

3.5 Application of other rules to proceedings under section 35 or 36 of Act of 1973 [or under paragraph 69 or 73 of Schedule 5 to Act of 2004][1]

[(1) The following provisions shall apply to an application under section 35 or 36 of the Act of 1973 or under paragraph 69 or 73 of Schedule 5 to the Act of 2004 –

(a) in the case of an application under either section or paragraph –
  (i) rule 10.10 with such modifications as may be appropriate and as if the application were an application for ancillary relief; and
  (ii) paragraphs 4, 7 and 8 of Appendix 4, and
(b) in the case of an application under section 35 or paragraph 69, paragraph 9 of Appendix 4; and
(c) in the case of an application under section 36 or paragraph 73, paragraph 9(5) to (7) of Appendix 4.][1]

(2) Subject to paragraph (1) and to the provisions of rules 3.2 to 3.4, these rules shall, so far as applicable, apply with the necessary modifications to an application under [section 35 or section 36 of the Act of 1973 or paragraph 69 or paragraph 73 of Schedule 5 to the Act of 2004, as the case may be][1], as if the application were a cause, the originating application or summons a petition, and the applicant the petitioner.

NOTES

Amendments.[1] Words inserted and substituted: SI 2005/2922.

3.6 Married Women's Property Act 1882 [or section 66 of Act of 2004][2]

(1) Subject to paragraph (2) below, an application under section 17 of the Married Women's Property Act 1882 ...[2] [or under section 66 of the Act of 2004][2] shall be made –

Part II   Statutory Instruments

   (a)   in the High Court, by originating summons, which may be issued out of the principal registry or any district registry, or
   (b)   in a county court, by originating application,

in Form M23 and shall be supported by affidavit.

[(2) An order –

   (a)   in a matrimonial cause, under section 17, and
   (b)   in a civil partnership cause, under section 66,

may be made in any ancillary relief proceedings upon the application of any party thereto by notice of application or summons.]²

(3) An application under section 17 [or section 66]² to a county court shall be filed –

   (a)   subject to sub-paragraph (b) [and (c)]², in the court for the district in which the applicant or respondent resides, or
   [(b) in the case of an application under section 17, in the divorce county court in which any pending matrimonial cause has been commenced by or on behalf of either the applicant or the respondent or in which any matrimonial cause is intended to be commenced by the applicant, and
   (c)   in the case of an application under section 66, in the civil partnership proceedings county court in which any pending civil partnership cause has been commenced by or on behalf of either the applicant or the respondent or in which any civil partnership cause is intended to be commenced by the applicant]².

(4) Where the application concerns the title to or possession of land, the originating summons or application shall –

   (a)   state whether the title to the land is registered or unregistered and, if registered, the Land Registry title number; and
   (b)   give particulars, so far as known to the applicant, of any mortgage of the land or any interest therein.

(5) The application shall be served on the respondent, together with a copy of the affidavit in support and an acknowledgement of service in [Form M23A]¹.

(6) Where particulars of a mortgage are given pursuant to paragraph (4), the applicant shall file a copy of the originating summons or application, which shall be served on the mortgagee; and any person so served may apply to the court in writing, within 14 days after service, for a copy of the affidavit in support; and within 14 days of receiving such affidavit may file an affidavit in answer and shall be entitled to be heard on the application.

(7) If the respondent intends to contest the application, he shall, within 14 days after the time allowed for sending the acknowledgement of service, file an affidavit in answer to the application setting out the grounds on which he relies, and lodge in the court office a copy of the affidavit for service on the applicant.

(8) If the respondent fails to comply with paragraph (7), the applicant may apply for directions; and the district judge may give such directions as he thinks fit, including a direction that the respondent shall be debarred from defending the application unless an affidavit is filed within such time as the district judge may specify.

(9) A district judge may grant an injunction in proceedings under section 17 [or under section 66][2] if, but only so far as, the injunction is ancillary or incidental to any relief sought in those proceedings.

(10) Paragraphs (7) and (9) of Appendix 4 shall apply to an application under section 17 or under section 66.][2]

(11) Subject to the provisions of this rule, these rules shall apply, with the necessary modifications, to an application under section 17 [or under section 66][2] as if the application were a cause, the originating summons or application a petition, and the applicant a petitioner.

[(12) In this rule and in rule 3.7 –

(a) a reference to section 17 is to section 17 of the Married Women's Property Act 1882; and
(b) a reference to section 66 is to section 66 of the Act of 2004.][2]

NOTES

Amendments.[1] Words revoked or substituted: SI 2005/559. [2] Words inserted and substituted: SI 2005/2922.

3.7 Exercise in principal registry of county court jurisdiction under section 17 of Married Women's Property Act 1882 [or under section 66 of Act of 2004][1]

(1) Where any proceedings for divorce, nullity [of marriage][1] or judicial separation which are either pending in the principal registry, or are intended to be commenced there by the applicant, are or will be treated as pending in a divorce county court, an application under section 17 by one of the parties to the marriage may be made to the principal registry as if it were a county court.

[(1A) Where any proceedings for dissolution, nullity of civil partnership or separation which are either pending in the principal registry, or are intended to be commenced there by the applicant are or will be treated as pending in a civil partnership proceedings county court, an application under section 66 by one of the parties to the civil partnership may be made to the principal registry as if it were a county court.][1]

(2) In relation to proceedings commenced or intended to be commenced in the principal registry under paragraph (1) [or (1A)][1] of this rule or transferred from the High Court to the principal registry by an order made under section 38 of the Act of 1984 –

(a) section 42 of the Act of 1984 and the rules made thereunder shall have effect, with the necessary modifications, as they have effect in relation to proceedings commenced in or transferred to the principal registry under that section; and

(b) CCR Order 4, rule 8 and rule 3.6(3) (which relate to venue) shall not apply.

(3) Rule 1.4(1)[(a)]¹ shall apply, with the necessary modifications, to proceedings in, or intended to be commenced in, the principal registry under paragraph (1) of this rule as it applies to matrimonial proceedings.

[(4) Rule 1.4(1)(b) shall apply, with necessary modifications, to proceedings in, or intended to be commenced in, the principal registry under paragraph (1A) of this rule as it applies to civil partnership proceedings.]¹

NOTES

Amendments.¹ Words revoked or substituted: SI 2005/559.² Words inserted or substituted: SI 2005/2922.

[3.8 Applications under Part IV of the Family Law Act 1996 (Family Homes and Domestic Violence)

(1) An application for an occupation order or a non-molestation order under Part IV of the Family Law Act 1996 shall be made in Form FL401.

(2) An application for an occupation order or a non-molestation order made by a child under the age of sixteen shall be made in Form FLA401 ...².

(3) An application for an occupation order or a non-molestation order which is made in other proceedings which are pending shall be made in Form FL401.

(4) An application in Form FL401 shall be supported by a statement which is signed by the applicant and is sworn to be true.

(5) Where an application is made without giving notice, the sworn statement shall state the reasons why notice was not given.

(6) An application made on notice (together with the sworn statement and a notice in Form FL402) shall be served by the applicant on the respondent personally not less than 2 days before the date on which the application will be heard.

(7) The court may abridge the period specified in paragraph (6).

(8) Where the applicant is acting in person, service of the application shall be effected by the court if the applicant so requests.

This does not affect the court's power to order substituted service.

[(9) Subject to any enactment, where an application for an occupation order or a non-molestation order is pending, the court may transfer the proceedings to another court of its own motion or on the application of either party; and any order for transfer shall be made in Form FL417.]³

(10) Rule 9.2A shall not apply to an application for an occupation order or a non-molestation order under Part IV of the Family Law Act 1996.

(11) A copy of an application for an occupation order under section 33, 35 or 36 of the Family Law Act 1996 shall be served by the applicant by first-class post on the mortgagee or, as the case may be, the landlord of the

dwelling-house in question, with a notice in Form FL416 informing him of his right to make representations in writing or at any hearing.

(12) Where the application is for the transfer of a tenancy, notice of the application shall be served by the applicant on the other cohabitant[, spouse or civil partner][1] and on the landlord (as those terms are defined by paragraph 1 of Schedule 7 to the Family Law Act 1996) and any person so served shall be entitled to be heard on the application.

(13) [Paragraph 7 of Appendix 4 shall apply] to –
   (a) an application for an occupation order under section 33, 35 or 36 of the Family Law Act 1996, and
   (b) an application for the transfer of a tenancy ...[1]

(14) Rule 3.6(7) to (9) ...[1] shall apply, with the necessary modifications, to an application for the transfer of a tenancy, as they apply to an application under rule 3.6.

(15) The applicant shall file a statement in Form FL415 after he has served the application.

NOTES

Amendments.[1] Words inserted, substituted or revoked: SI 2005/2922.[2] Words revoked: SI 2008/2836.[3] Paragraph substituted: SI 2008/2446.

3.9 Hearing of applications under Part IV of the Family Law Act 1996

(1) An application for an occupation order or a non-molestation order under Part IV of the Family Law Act 1996 shall be dealt with in chambers unless the court otherwise directs.

(2) Where an order is made on an application made ex parte, a copy of the order together with a copy of the application and of the sworn statement in support shall be served by the applicant on the respondent personally.

(3) Where the application is for an occupation order under section 33, 35 or 36 of the Family Law Act 1996, a copy of any order made on the application shall be served by the applicant by first-class post on the mortgagee or, as the case may be, the landlord of the dwelling-house in question.

(4) A copy of an order made on an application heard inter partes shall be served by the applicant on the respondent personally.

(5) Where the applicant is acting in person, service of a copy of any order made on the hearing of the application shall be effected by the court if the applicant so requests.

(6) The following forms shall be used in connection with hearings of applications under Part IV of the Family Law Act 1996 –
   (a) a record of the hearing shall be made on Form FL405, ...[1]
   (b) any [occupation][1] order made on the hearing shall be issued in Form FL404[, and

(c) any non-molestation order made on the hearing shall be issued in Form FL404a]¹.

(7) The court may direct that a further hearing be held in order to consider any representations made by a mortgagee or a landlord.

(8) An application to vary, extend or discharge an order made under Part IV of the Family Law Act 1996 shall be made in Form FL403 and this rule shall apply to the hearing of such an application.

NOTES

Amendments.¹ Words revoked and inserted and subpara inserted: SI 2007/1622.

3.9A Enforcement of orders made on applications under Part IV of the Family Law Act 1996

[(1) Where a power of arrest is attached to one or more of the provisions ('the relevant provisions') of an occupation order under the Family Law Act 1996, the relevant provisions shall be set out in Form FL406 and the form shall not include any provisions of the order to which the power of arrest was not attached.

(1A) Where the court makes a non-molestation order under that Act or paragraph (1) applies, the following documents shall be delivered to the officer for the time being in charge of any police station for the applicant's address or of such other police station as the court may specify –

- (a) a copy of Form FL404a or FL406, as the case may be; and
- (b) a statement showing that the respondent has been served with the order or informed of its terms (whether by being present when the order was made or by telephone or otherwise).

(1B) The documents referred to in paragraphs (1A)(a) and (b) shall be delivered by –

- (a) the applicant, if the applicant is responsible for serving the order on the respondent in accordance with rule 3.9(2) or (4); or
- (b) the court, if the court is responsible for serving the order on the respondent in accordance with rule 3.9(5).]²

(2) Where an order is made varying or discharging the relevant provisions [of an occupation order or, as the case may be, any provisions of a non-molestation order]², the proper officer shall –

- (a) immediately inform the officer who received a copy of the [any form under paragraph (1A)]² and, if the applicant's address has changed, the officer for the time being in charge of the police station for the new address; and
- (b) deliver a copy of the order to any officer so informed.

(3) An application for the issue of a warrant for the arrest of the respondent [under section 47(8) of the Family Law Act 1996]² shall be made in Form FL407 and the warrant shall be issued in Form FL408.

Family Proceedings Rules 1991, r 3.9A

(4) The court before whom a person is brought following his arrest may –

    (a) determine whether the facts, and the circumstances which led to the arrest, amounted to disobedience of the order, or

    (b) adjourn the proceedings and, where such an order is made, the arrested person may be released and –

        (i) [Unless the court directs otherwise,]² be dealt with within 14 days of the day on which he was arrested; and

        (ii) be given not less than 2 days' notice of the adjourned hearing.

Nothing in this paragraph shall prevent the issue of a notice under CCR Order 29, rule 1(4) if the arrested person is not dealt with within the period mentioned in sub-paragraph (b)(i) above.

(5) The following provisions shall apply, with the necessary modifications, to the enforcement of orders made …¹ under Part IV of the Family Law Act 1996 –

    (a) RSC Order 52, rule 7 (powers to suspend execution of committal order);

    (b) (in a case where an application for an order of committal is made to the High Court) RSC Order 52, rule 2 (application for leave);

    (c) CCR Order 29, rule 1 (committal for breach of order);

    (d) CCR Order 29, rule 1A (undertakings);

    (e) CCR Order 29, rule 3 (discharge of person in custody); and CCR Order 29, rule 1 shall have effect, as if for paragraph (3), there were substituted the following –

'(3) At the time when the order is drawn up, the proper officer shall –

    (a) where the order made is (or includes) a non-molestation order and

    (b) where the order made is an occupation order and the court so directs,

issue a copy of the order, indorsed with or incorporating a notice as to the consequences of disobedience, for service in accordance with paragraph (2).'.

(6) The court may adjourn consideration of the penalty to be imposed for contempts found provided and such consideration may be restored if the respondent does not comply with any conditions specified by the court.

(7) Where the court makes a hospital order in Form FL413 or a guardianship order in Form FL414 under the Mental Health Act 1983, the proper officer shall –

    (a) send to the hospital any information which will be of assistance in dealing with the patient;

    (b) inform the applicant when the respondent is being transferred to hospital.

(8) Where a transfer direction given by the Secretary of State under section 48 of the Mental Health Act 1983 is in force in respect of a person remanded in custody by the court under Schedule 5 to the Family Law Act 1996, the proper officer shall notify –

(a) the governor of the prison to which that person was remanded; and
(b) the hospital where he is detained,

of any committal hearing which that person is required to attend and the proper officer shall give notice in writing to the hospital where that person is detained of any further remand under paragraph 3 of Schedule 5 to the Family Law Act 1996.

(9) An order for the remand of the respondent shall be in form FL409.

(10) In paragraph (4) 'arrest' means arrest under a power of arrest attached to [an occupation order under section 47(2) or (3) of the Family Law Act 1996]² or under a warrant of arrest [issued on an application under section 47(8) of that Act]².

NOTES

Amendments.[1] Words revoked: SI 2005/559.[2] Paras (1), (1A), (1B) substituted for para (1), and words inserted and substituted: SI 2007/1622.

3.10 Applications under Part IV of the Family Law Act 1996: bail

(1) An application for bail made by a person arrested under a power of arrest [attached to an occupation order under section 47(2) or (3) of the Family Law Act 1996]² or a warrant of arrest [issued on an application under section 47(8) of that Act]² may be made either orally or in writing.

(2) Where an application is made in writing, it shall contain the following particulars –

(a) the full name of the person making the application;
(b) the address of the place where the person making the application is detained at the time when the application is made;
(c) the address where the person making the application would reside if he were to be granted bail;
(d) the amount of the recognizance in which he would agree to be bound; and
(e) the grounds on which the application is made and, where a previous application has been refused, full particulars of any change in circumstances which has occurred since that refusal.

(3) An application made in writing shall be signed by the person making the application or by a person duly authorised by him in that behalf or, where the person making the application is a minor or is for any reason incapable of acting, by a guardian ad litem acting on his behalf and a copy shall be served by the person making the application on the applicant for the Part IV order.

(4) The persons prescribed for the purposes of paragraph 4 of Schedule 5 to the Family Law Act 1996 (postponement of taking of recognizance) are –

(a) a district judge,
(b) a justice of the peace,
(c) a justices' clerk,
(d) a police officer of the rank of inspector or above or in charge of a police station, and
(e) (where the person making the application is in his custody) the governor or keeper of a prison.

(5) The person having custody of the person making the application shall –

(a) on receipt of a certificate signed by or on behalf of the district judge stating that the recognizance of any sureties required have been taken, or on being otherwise satisfied that all such recognizances have been taken; and
(b) on being satisfied that the person making the application has entered into his recognizance,

release the person making the application.

(6) The following forms shall be used –

(a) the recognizance of the person making the application shall be in Form FL410 and that of a surety in Form FL411;
(b) a bail notice in Form FL412 shall be given to the respondent where he is remanded on bail.][1]

NOTES

Amendments.[1] Rules substituted: SI 1997/1893.[2] Words inserted: SI 2007/1622.

3.11 Proceedings in respect of polygamous marriage

(1) The provisions of this rule shall have effect where a petition, originating application or originating summons asks for matrimonial relief within the meaning of section 47(2) of the Act of 1973 in respect of a marriage [where either party to the marriage is, or has during the subsistence of the marriage been, married to more than one person][1] (in this rule referred to as a polygamous marriage).

(2) The petition, originating application or originating summons –

(a) shall state that the marriage in question is polygamous;
(b) shall state whether or not there is, to the knowledge of the petitioner or applicant, any living spouse of his or hers additional to the respondent or, as the case may be, any living spouse of the respondent additional to the petitioner or applicant (in this rule referred to as an additional spouse); and
(c) if there is any additional spouse, shall give his or her full name and address and the date and place of his or her marriage to the petitioner or applicant or, as the case may be, to the respondent, or state, so far as may be applicable, that such information is unknown to the petitioner or applicant.

(3) Without prejudice to its powers under RSC Order 15 (which deals with parties) or CCR Order 15 (which deals with amendment) the court may order that any additional spouse –

(a) be added as a party to the proceedings; or
(b) be given notice of –
   (i) the proceedings; or
   (ii) of any application in the proceedings for any such order as is mentioned in section 47(2)(d) of the Act of 1973.

(4) Any order under paragraph (3) may be made at any stage of the proceedings and either on the application of any party or by the court of its own motion and, where an additional spouse is mentioned in a petition or an acknowledgement of service of a petition, the petitioner shall, on making any application in the proceedings or, if no previous application has been made in the proceedings, on making a request for directions for trial, ask for directions as to whether an order should be made under paragraph (3).

(5) Any person to whom notice is given pursuant to an order under paragraph (3) shall be entitled, without filing an answer or affidavit, to be heard in the proceedings or on the application to which the notice relates.

NOTES
Amendments.[1] Words substituted: SI 1996/816.

3.12 Application under section 55 of Act of 1986 for declaration as to marital status

(1) Unless otherwise directed, a petition by which proceedings are begun under section 55 of the Act of 1986 for a declaration as to marital status shall state –

(a) the names of the parties to the marriage to which the application relates and the residential address of each of them at the date of the presentation of the petition;
(b) the place and date of any ceremony of marriage to which the application relates;
(c) the grounds on which the application is made and all other material facts alleged by the petitioner to justify the making of the declaration;
(d) whether there have been or are continuing any proceedings in any court, tribunal or authority in England and Wales or elsewhere between the parties which relate to, or are capable of affecting, the validity or subsistence of the marriage, divorce, annulment or legal separation to which the application relates, or which relate to the matrimonial [or civil partnership][1] status of either of the parties, and, if so –
   (i) the nature, and either the outcome or present state of those proceedings,
   (ii) the court, tribunal or authority before which they were begun,
   (iii) the date when they were begun,
   (iv) the names of the parties to them,
   (v) the date or expected date of the trial,

(vi) any other facts relevant to the question whether the petition should be stayed under Schedule 1 to the Domicile and Matrimonial Proceedings Act of 1973;

and any such proceedings shall include any which are instituted otherwise than in a court of law in any country outside England and Wales, if they are instituted before a tribunal or other authority having power under the law having effect there to determine questions of status, and shall be treated as continuing if they have begun and have not been finally disposed of;

(e) where it is alleged that the court has jurisdiction based on domicile, which of the parties to the marriage to which the application relates is domiciled in England and Wales on the date of the presentation of the petition, or died before that date and was at death domiciled in England and Wales.

(f) where it is alleged that the court has jurisdiction based on habitual residence, which of the parties to the marriage to which the application relates has been habitually resident in England and Wales, or died before that date and had been habitually resident in England and Wales throughout the period of one year ending with the date of death;

(g) where the petitioner was not a party to the marriage to which the application relates, particulars of his interest in the determination of the application.

(2) Where the proceedings are for a declaration that the validity of a divorce, annulment or legal separation obtained in any country outside England or Wales in respect of the marriage either is or is not entitled to recognition in England and Wales, the petition shall in addition state the date and place of the divorce, annulment or legal separation.

(3) There shall be annexed to the petition a copy of the certificate of any marriage to which the application relates, or, as the case may be, a certified copy of any decree of divorce, annulment or order for legal separation to which the application relates.

(4) Where a document produced by virtue of paragraph (3) is not in English it shall, unless otherwise directed, be accompanied by a translation certified by a notary public or authenticated by affidavit.

(5) The parties to the marriage in respect of which a declaration is sought shall be petitioner and respondent respectively to the application, unless a third party is applying for a declaration, in which case he shall be the petitioner and the parties to the marriage shall be respondents to the application.

NOTES
Amendments.[1] Words inserted: SI 2005/2922.

[3.12A Application under section 58 of Act of 2004 for declaration as to civil partnership status

(1) Unless the court otherwise directs, a petition by which proceedings are begun under section 58 of the Act of 2004 for a declaration as to civil partnership status must state –

- (a) the names of each party to the civil partnership to which the application relates and the residential address of each of them at the date of the presentation of the petition;
- (b) the place at, and the date on which, the civil partnership was formed;
- (c) the grounds on which the application is made and all other material facts alleged by the petitioner to justify the making of the declaration;
- (d) whether there have been or are continuing any proceedings in any court, tribunal or authority in England and Wales or elsewhere between the parties which relate to, or are capable of affecting, the validity or subsistence of the civil partnership, dissolution, annulment or legal separation to which the application relates, or which relate to the civil partnership or matrimonial status of either of the parties;
- (e) in relation to any proceedings to which paragraph (d) applies –
  - (i) the nature, and either the outcome or present state of those proceedings,
  - (ii) the court, tribunal or authority before which they were begun,
  - (iii) the date when they were begun,
  - (iv) the names of the parties to them,
  - (v) the date or expected date of the trial,
  - (vi) any other facts relevant to the question whether the petition should be stayed under the Family Proceedings (Civil Partnership: Staying of Proceedings) Rules 2005;
- (f) where it is alleged that the court has jurisdiction based on domicile, which of the parties to the civil partnership to which the application relates –
  - (i) is domiciled in England and Wales on the date of the presentation of the petition, or
  - (ii) died before that date and was at death domiciled in England and Wales;
- (g) where it is alleged that the court has jurisdiction based on habitual residence, which of the parties to the civil partnership to which the application relates –
  - (i) has been habitually resident in England and Wales, or
  - (ii) died before that date and had been habitually resident in England and Wales throughout the period of one year ending with the date of death;
- (h) where the petitioner was not a party to the civil partnership to which the application relates, particulars of his interest in the determination of the application.

(2) Proceedings to which paragraph (1)(d) applies –

(a) include any proceedings instituted otherwise than in a court of law in any country outside England and Wales, if they are instituted before a tribunal or other authority having power under the law having effect there to determine questions of status, and

(b) are treated as continuing if they have begun and have not been finally disposed of.

(3) Where the proceedings are for a declaration that the validity of a dissolution, annulment or legal separation obtained in any country outside England or Wales in respect of the civil partnership either is or is not entitled to recognition in England and Wales, the petition must in addition state the date and place of the dissolution, annulment or legal separation.

(4) There must be annexed to the petition a copy of the certificate of any civil partnership, or, as the case may be, a certified copy of any order for dissolution, annulment or legal separation, to which the application relates.

(5) Where a document produced by virtue of paragraph (4) is not in English it must, unless otherwise directed, be accompanied by a translation certified by a notary public or authenticated by affidavit.

(6) The parties to the civil partnership in respect of which a declaration is sought shall be the petitioner and respondent respectively to the application, unless a third party is applying for a declaration, in which case he shall be the petitioner and the parties to the civil partnership shall be the respondents.][1]

NOTES
Amendments.[1] Rule inserted: SI 2005/2922.

[3.13 Application under section 55A of Act of 1986 for declaration of parentage

(1) Unless otherwise directed, a petition by which proceedings are begun under section 55A of the Act of 1986 for a declaration of parentage shall state –

(a) the full name and the sex, date and place of birth and residential address of the petitioner (except where the petitioner is the Secretary of State);

(b) where the case is not an excepted case within section 55A(4) of the Act of 1986, either the petitioner's interest in the determination of the application, or that section 27(2) of the Act of 1991 applies;

(c) if they are known, the full name and the sex, date and place of birth and residential address of each of the following persons (unless that person is the petitioner) –
  (i) the person whose parentage is in issue;
  (ii) the person whose parenthood is in issue; and
  (iii) any person who is acknowledged to be the [parent][3] of the person whose parentage is in issue;

(d) if the petitioner, the person whose parentage is in issue or the person whose parenthood is in issue, is known by a name other than that which appears in the certificate of his birth, that other name shall also be stated in the petition and in any decree made thereon;

[(e) where the mother, or alleged mother, of the person whose parentage is in issue has previously been known by different names, if known –
  (i) each full name by which she has previously been known; and
  (ii) the dates between which she was known by each name;]⁴
(f) the grounds on which the petitioner relies and all other material facts alleged by him to justify the making of the declaration;
(g) whether there are or have been any other proceedings in any court, tribunal or authority in England or Wales or elsewhere relating to the parentage of the person whose parentage is in issue or to the parenthood of the person whose parenthood is in issue, and, if so –
  (i) particulars of the proceedings, including the court, tribunal or authority before which they were begun, and their nature, outcome or present state;
  (ii) the date they were begun;
  (iii) the names of the parties; and
  (iv) the date or expected date of any trial in the proceedings;
(h) that either the person whose parentage is in issue or the person whose parenthood is in issue –
  (i) is domiciled in England and Wales on the date of the presentation of the petition;
  (ii) has been habitually resident in England and Wales throughout the period of one year ending with that date; or
  (iii) died before that date and either was at death domiciled in England and Wales or had been habitually resident in England and Wales throughout the period of one year ending with the date of death; and
(i) the nationality, citizenship or immigration status of the person whose parentage is in issue and of the person whose parenthood is in issue, and the effect which the granting of a declaration of parentage would have upon the status of each of them as regards his nationality, citizenship or right to be in the United Kingdom.

(2) Unless otherwise directed, there shall be annexed to the petition a copy of the birth certificate of the person whose parentage is in issue.

(3) The respondents to the application shall be –
  (i) the person whose parentage is in issue; and
  (ii) any person who is, or who is alleged to be, the [parent]³ of the person whose parentage is in issue;

excluding the petitioner.

[(4) The prescribed officer for the purposes of section 55A(7) of the Act of 1986 shall be the proper officer within the meaning of rule 1.2(1).]²

(5) Within 21 days after a declaration of parentage has been made, the prescribed officer shall send to the Registrar General a copy of the declaration in Form M30 and the petition.]¹

NOTES

Amendments.[1] Rule substituted: SI 2001/821.[2] Paragraph substituted: SI 2003/184.[3] Words substituted: SI 2005/2922.[4] Subparagraph substituted: SI 2009/636.

3.14 Application under section 56(1)(b) and (2) of Act of 1986 for a declaration of legitimacy or legitimation

(1) Unless otherwise directed, a petition by which proceedings are begun under section 56(1)(b) and (2) of the Act of 1986 for a declaration of legitimacy or legitimation shall state –

(a) the name of the petitioner, and if the petitioner is known by a name other than that which appears in the certificate of his birth, that other name shall be stated in the petition and in any decree made thereon;
(b) the date and place of birth of the petitioner;
[(c) if it is known, the name of the petitioner's father and his residential address at the time of the presentation of the petition;
(cc) if it is known, the name of the petitioner's mother at her birth and, if it is different, her current name and her residential address at the time of presentation of the petition;][1]
(d) the grounds on which the petitioner relies and all other material facts alleged by him to justify the making of the declaration; and
(e) either that the petitioner is domiciled in England and Wales on the date of the presentation of the petition or that he has been habitually resident in England and Wales throughout the period of one year ending with that date.

(2) Unless otherwise directed, there shall be annexed to the petition a copy of the petitioner's birth certificate.

(3) The petitioner's father and mother, or the survivor of them, shall be respondents to the application.

NOTES

Amendments.[1] Subparagraphs substituted: SI 2009/2027.

3.15 Application under section 57 of Act of 1986 for declaration as to adoption effected overseas

(1) Unless otherwise directed, a petition by which proceedings are begun under section 57 of the Act of 1986 for a declaration as to an adoption effected overseas shall state –

(a) the names of those persons who are to be respondents pursuant to paragraph (4) and the residential address of each of them at the date of the presentation of the petition;
(b) the date and place of the petitioner's birth;
(c) the date and place of the adoption order and the court or other tribunal or authority which made it;
(d) all other material facts alleged by the petitioner to justify the making of the declaration and the grounds on which the application is made;

(e) either that the petitioner is domiciled in England and Wales on the date of the presentation of the petition or that he has been habitually resident in England and Wales throughout the period of one year ending with that date.

(2) There shall be annexed to the petition a copy of the petitioner's birth certificate (if it is available this certificate should be the one made after the adoption referred to in the petition) and, unless otherwise directed, a certified copy of the adoption order effected under the law of any country outside the British Islands.

(3) Where a document produced by virtue of paragraph (2) is not in English, it shall, unless otherwise directed, be accompanied by a translation certified by a notary public or authenticated by affidavit.

(4) The following shall, if alive, be respondents to the application, either –

(a) those whom the petitioner claims are his adoptive parents for the purposes of section 39 of the Adoption Act 1976 [or section 67 of the Adoption and Children Act 2002][1]; or
(b) those whom the petitioner claims are not his adoptive parents for the purposes of that section.

NOTES
Amendments.[1] Words inserted: SI 2005/2922.

3.16 General provisions as to proceedings under rules 3.12, 3.13, 3.14 and 3.15

(1) A petition under rule 3.12, [3.12A,][2] 3.13, 3.14 or 3.15 shall be supported by an affidavit by the petitioner verifying the petition and giving particulars of every person whose interest may be affected by the proceedings and his relationship to the petitioner.

Provided that if the petitioner is under the age of 18, the affidavit shall, unless otherwise directed, be made by his next friend.

(2) Where the jurisdiction of the court to entertain a petition is based on habitual residence the petition shall include a statement of the addresses of the places of residence of the person so resident and the length of residence at each place either during the period of one year ending with the date of the presentation of the petition or, if that person is dead, throughout the period of one year ending with the date of death.

(3) An affidavit for the purposes of paragraph (1) may contain statements of information or belief with the sources and grounds thereof.

(4) [Except in the case of a petition under rule 3.13, a copy of the petition][1] and every document accompanying it shall be sent by the petitioner to the Attorney General at least one month before the petition is filed and it shall not be necessary thereafter to serve these documents upon him.

[(5) If the Attorney General has notified the court that he wishes to intervene in the proceedings, the proper officer shall send to him a copy of any answer and, in the case of a petition under rule 3.13, of the petition and every document accompanying it.][1]

(6) When all answers to the petition have been filed the petitioner shall issue and serve on all respondents to the application a request for directions as to any other persons who should be made respondents to the petition or given notice of the proceedings.

(7) When giving directions in accordance with paragraph (6) the court shall consider whether it is [desirable][1] that the Attorney General should argue before it any question relating to the proceedings, and if it does so consider [and the Attorney General agrees to argue that question][1], the Attorney General need not file an answer and the court shall give directions requiring him to serve on all parties to the proceedings a summary of his argument.

(8) Persons given notice of proceedings pursuant to directions given in accordance with paragraph (6) shall within 21 days after service of the notice upon them be entitled to apply to the court to be joined as parties.

(9) The Attorney General may file an answer to the petition within 21 days after directions have been given under paragraph (7) and no directions for trial shall be given until that period and the period referred to in paragraph (8) have expired.

(10) The Attorney General, in deciding whether it is necessary or expedient to intervene in the proceedings, may have a search made for, and may inspect and bespeak a copy of, any document filed or lodged in the court offices which relates to any other family proceedings referred to in proceedings.

[(11) Declarations made in accordance with –
(a) section 55, section 55A and section 56(1)(b) and (2) of the Act of 1986 shall be in the forms prescribed respectively in Forms M29, M30 and M31; and
(b) section 58 of the Act of 2004 shall be the form prescribed in Form M29A.][2]

(12) Subject to rules 3.12, [3.12A,] 3.13, 3.14 and 3.15 and this rule, these rules shall, so far as applicable and with the exception of rule 2.6(1), apply with the necessary modifications to the proceedings as if they were a cause.

NOTES
Amendments.[1] Text substituted or inserted: SI 2001/821.[2] Text substituted or inserted: SI 2005/2922.

3.17 Application for leave under section 13 of Act of 1984 [or under paragraph 4 of Schedule 7 to Act of 2004][1]

(1) An application for leave to apply for an order for financial relief [to which this rule applies][1] shall be made ex parte by originating summons issued in Form M25 out of the principal registry and shall be supported by an affidavit by the applicant...[1].

[(1A) The affidavit in support shall state the facts relied on in support of the application with particular reference –

(a) in the case of an application under the Act of 1984, to the matters set out in section 16(2) of that Act, and
(b) in the case of an application under the Act of 2004, to the matters set out in paragraph 8(3) of Schedule 7 to that Act.]¹

(2) The affidavit in support shall give particulars of the judicial or other proceedings by means of which the marriage [or civil partnership, as the case may be,]¹ to which the application relates was dissolved or annulled or by which the parties to the marriage [or civil partnership]¹ were legally separated and shall state, so far as is known to the applicant –

[(a) in the case of an application under the Act of 1984, the names of the parties to the marriage and the date and place of the marriage;
(ab) in the case of an application under the Act of 2004, the names of the parties to the civil partnership and the date on, and place at which it was formed;]¹
(b) the occupation and residence of each of the parties to the marriage [or civil partnership, as the case may be]¹;
(c) whether there are any living children of the family and, if so, the number of such children and the full names (including surname) of each and his date of birth or, if it be the case, that he is over 18;
[(d) whether either party to the marriage or civil partnership has subsequently married or formed a civil partnership;]¹
(e) an estimate in summary form of the appropriate amount or value of the capital resources and net income of each party and of any minor child of the family;
(f) the grounds on which it is alleged that the court has jurisdiction to entertain an application for an order for financial relief under Part III of the Act of 1984[;]
[(g) this rule and rule 3.18 apply to an application for financial relief under –
  (i) Part III of the Act of 1984; and
  (ii) Schedule 7 to the Act of 2004].

(3) The proper officer shall fix a date, time and place for the hearing of the application by a judge in chambers and give notice thereof to the applicant.

NOTES

Amendments.¹ Text inserted or substituted: SI 2005/2922.

3.18 Application for order for financial relief or avoidance of transaction order under Part III of Act of 1984 [or under Schedule 7 to Act of 2004]²

(1) An application for an order for financial relief [to which this rule applies]² shall be made by originating summons issued in Form M26 out of the principal registry and at the same time the applicant, unless otherwise directed, shall file an affidavit in support of the summons giving full particulars of his property and income.

(2) The applicant shall serve a sealed copy of the originating summons on the respondent and shall annex thereto a copy of the affidavit in support, if one has been filed, and a notice of proceedings and acknowledgement of service in Form M28, and rule 10.8 shall apply to such an acknowledgement of service as if the references in paragraph (1) of that rule to Form M6 [and M6A]² and in paragraph (2) of that rule to seven days were, respectively, references to Form M28 and 31 days.

[(3) Rule 2.70 and paragraphs 2, 3, 5, 7 (4) to (6) and 9(6) and (7) of Appendix 4 shall apply to an application for an order for financial relief under this rule and the court may order the attendance of any person for the purpose of being examined or cross-examined and the discovery and production of any document.]²

(4) An application for an interim order for maintenance ...² or an avoidance of transaction order ...² may be made, unless the court otherwise directs, in the originating summons under paragraph (1) or by summons in accordance with rule 10.9(1) and an application for [an avoidance of transaction order]² shall be supported by an affidavit, which may be the affidavit filed under paragraph (1), stating the facts relied on.

(5) If the respondent intends to contest the application he shall, within 28 days after the time limited for giving notice to defend, file an affidavit in answer to the application setting out the grounds on which he relies and shall serve a copy on the applicant.

(6) In respect of any application for an avoidance of transaction order the court may give such a direction or make such appointment as it is empowered to give or make by paragraph (3) and [paragraph 3 of Appendix 4 shall apply to such an application]².

(7) Where the originating summons contains an application for an order under section 22 of the Act of 1984 the applicant shall serve a copy on the landlord of the dwelling house and he shall be entitled to be heard on the application.

(8) An application for an order for financial relief ...² or for an avoidance of transaction order shall be determined by a judge.

[(9) In this rule –
- (a) 'avoidance of transaction order' means –
  - (i) in relation to an application under the Act of 1984, an application under section 23 of that Act, and
  - (ii) in relation to an application under the Act of 2004, an application under paragraph 15 of Schedule 7 to that Act; and
- (b) 'interim order for maintenance' means –
  - (i) in relation to an application under the Act of 1984, an order under section 14 of that Act, and
  - (ii) in relation to an application under the Act of 2004, an order under paragraph 5 of Schedule 7 to that Act.]²

Part II   Statutory Instruments

NOTES

Amendments.¹ Words revoked: SI 2005/559.² Text inserted, substituted or revoked: SI 2005/2922.

3.19 Application for order under section 24 of Act of 1984 [or under paragraph 17 of Schedule 7 to Act of 2004]¹ preventing transaction

(1) An application under section 24 of the Act of 1984 [or under paragraph 17 of Schedule 7 to Act of 2004]¹ for an order preventing a transaction shall be made by originating summons issued in Form M27 out of the principal registry and shall be supported by an affidavit by the applicant stating the facts relied on in support of the application.

(2) The applicant shall serve a sealed copy of the originating summons on the respondent and shall annex thereto a copy of the affidavit in support and a notice of proceedings and acknowledgement of service in Form M28 and rule 10.8 shall apply to such an acknowledgement of service as if the references in paragraph (1) of that rule to Form M6 [and M6A]¹ and in paragraph (2) of that rule to seven days were, respectively, references to Form M28 and 31 days.

(3) If the respondent intends to contest the application he shall, within 28 days after the time limited for giving notice of intention to defend, file an affidavit in answer to the application setting out the grounds on which he relies and shall serve a copy on the applicant.

(4) The application shall be determined by a judge.

[(5) Paragraph 9 of Appendix 4 (except sub-paragraphs (5), (8), (9) and (10)) shall apply to an application to which this rule applies.]¹

NOTES

Amendments.¹ Text inserted or substituted: SI 2005/2922.

3.20 Consent to marriage of minor

(1) An application under section 3 of the Marriage Act 1949 (in this rule referred to as 'section 3') for the consent of the court to the marriage of a minor shall be dealt with in chambers unless the court otherwise directs.

(2) The application may be heard and determined by a district judge.

(3) An application under section 3 may be brought without the intervention of the applicant's next friend, unless the court otherwise directs.

(4) Where an application under section 3 follows a refusal to give consent to the marriage every person who has refused consent shall be made a defendant to the summons or a respondent to the application, as appropriate.

(5) The application shall, unless the court orders otherwise, be served not less than seven days before the date upon which the application is to be heard.

[3.20A Consent to registration of civil partnership of child

(1) An application under paragraph 3, 4 or 10 of Schedule 2 to the Act of 2004 for the consent of the court to a child registering as the civil partner of another shall be dealt with in chambers unless the court otherwise directs.

(2) The application may be heard and determined by a district judge.

(3) The application may be brought without the intervention of the applicant's next friend, unless the court otherwise directs.

(4) Where an application to which this rule relates follows a refusal to give consent to the child registering as the civil partner of another person, every person who has refused consent shall be made a defendant to the summons or a respondent to the application, as the case may be.

(5) The application shall, unless the court orders otherwise, be served not less than seven days before the date upon which the application is to be heard.]¹

NOTES

Amendments.¹ Text inserted or substituted: SI 2005/2922.

[3.21 Application under section 27 of the Act of 1991 for declaration of parentage

(1) Rule 4.6 shall apply to an application under [section 55A of the Act of 1986 (declarations of parentage)]² as it applies to an application under the Act of 1989.

(2) Where an application under [section 55A of the Act of 1986]² has been transferred to the High Court or a county court the court shall, as soon as practicable after a transfer has occurred, consider what directions to give for the conduct of the proceedings.

(3) Without prejudice to the generality of paragraph (2), the court may, in particular, direct that –

   (a) the proceedings shall proceed as if they had been commenced by originating summons or originating application;

   (b) any document served or other thing done while the proceedings were pending in another court, including a magistrates' court, shall be treated for such purposes as may be specified in the direction as if it had been such document or other thing, being a document or other thing provided for by the rules of court applicable in the court to which the proceedings have been transferred, as may be specified in the direction and had been served or done pursuant to any such rule;

   (c) a pre-trial hearing shall be held to determine what further directions, if any, should be given.

(4) The application may be heard and determined by a district judge.]¹

NOTES

Amendments.¹ Rule inserted: SI 1993/295. ² Words substituted: SI 2001/821.

Part II Statutory Instruments

[3.22 Appeal under section 20 of the Act of 1991 ...²

(1) Rule 4.6 shall apply to an appeal under section 20 of the Act of 1991 ([appeals to [First-tier Tribunal]³]²) as it applies to an application under the Act of 1989.

(2) Where an appeal under section 20 of the Act of 1991 is transferred to the High Court or a county court, Rule 3.21(2) and (3) shall apply to the appeal as it applies to an application under [section 55A of the Act of 1986]².]¹

NOTES

Amendments.¹ Rule inserted: SI 1993/295. ² Words deleted or substituted: SI 2001/821. ³ Words substituted: SI 2008/2446.

[3.23 Appeal from [Upper Tribunal]²

(1) This rule shall apply to any appeal to the Court of Appeal under section [13 of the Tribunals, Courts and Enforcement Act 2007 (right to appeal to Court of Appeal etc)]²).

(2) Where leave to appeal is granted by the [Upper Tribunal]², the notice of appeal must be served within 6 weeks from the date on which notice of the grant was given in writing to the appellant.

(3) Where leave to appeal is granted by the Court of Appeal upon an application made within 6 weeks of the date on which notice of the [Upper Tribunal's]² refusal of leave to appeal was given in writing to the appellant, the notice of appeal must be served –

    (a)   before the end of the said period of 6 weeks; or
    (b)   within 7 days after the date on which leave is granted,

whichever is the later, or within such other period as the Court of Appeal may direct.]¹

NOTES

Amendments.¹ Rule inserted: SI 1993/295. ² Words substituted: SI 2008/2446.

[3.24 Reference under section 8(5) of the Gender Recognition Act 2004

(1) A reference to the High Court under section 8(5) of the Gender Recognition Act 2004 must be made by an originating summons issued out of the principal registry.

(2) The Secretary of State is to be referred to as the applicant and the respondent is the person whose application under section 1(1), 5(2) or 6(1) of the Gender Recognition Act 2004 was granted.

(3) The originating summons must be served on the President of Gender Recognition Panels and such other persons as the court may direct.

(4) Where the applicant knows that –

    (a)   the respondent is a party to a cause in which the petition or answer prays for a decree of nullity [of marriage]² under section 12(g) of, or

paragraph 11(1)(e) of Schedule 1 to, the Act of 1973 [or for an order for nullity of civil partnership under section 50(1)(d) of the Act of 2004]², he must –
  (i) give particulars of those proceedings in the originating summons, and
  (ii) serve the originating summons on the court in which that petition is pending (where he has sufficient information to do so);
(b) a full gender recognition certificate has been issued to the respondent under section 5(1) of the Gender Recognition Act 2004, he must give particulars of this in the originating summons.

(5) A copy of any order of the court made on the reference must be served on –
  (a) the parties,
  (b) the President of Gender Recognition Panels,
  (c) where sufficient particulars have been provided under paragraph (4)(a)(i), on the court in which any such cause is pending,
and may be served on such other persons as the court thinks fit.]¹

NOTES

Amendments.¹ Rule inserted: SI 2005/559. ² Words inserted: SI 2005/2922.

[3.25 Proceedings under Part 4A of the Family Law Act 1996: interpretation of rules and forms

[(1) In rules 3.26 to 3.36 –

'a forced marriage protection order' means an order under section 63A of the Family Law Act 1996;
'the person who is the subject of the proceedings' means the person who will be protected by the forced marriage protection order applied for or being considered by the court of its own motion, if that order is made, or who is being protected by such an order.

(2) In connection with proceedings under Part 4A of the Family Law Act 1996, references in the forms mentioned below to 'respondent' are to be read –

(a) in Forms FL408, FL413 and FL414, as references to the respondent or other person who has failed to comply with the forced marriage protection order or is otherwise in contempt of court in relation to the order;
(b) in Forms FL409, FL410, FL411 and FL412, as references to the respondent or other person arrested under section 63I or 63J of the Family Law Act 1996.]¹

NOTES

Amendments.¹ Rule inserted: SI 2008/2446.

[3.26 Applications under Part 4A of the Family Law Act 1996 for forced marriage protection orders

(1) An application for a forced marriage protection order, including an application for a forced marriage protection order which is made in other proceedings which are pending, shall be made in Form FL401A.

(2) An application for a forced marriage protection order made by an organisation shall state –

    (a) the name and address of the person submitting the application; and
    (b) the position which that person holds in the organisation.

(3) Where an application is made without notice, it shall be supported by a sworn statement explaining why notice has not been given.][1]

NOTES

Amendments.[1] Rule inserted: SI 2008/2446.

[3.27 Leave stage for forced marriage protection orders

(1) Where the leave of the court is required to apply for a forced marriage protection order, the person seeking leave shall file –

    (a) a written request for leave in Form FL430 setting out –
        (i) the reasons for the application;
        (ii) the applicant's connection with the person to be protected;
        (iii) the applicant's knowledge of the circumstances of the person to be protected; and
        (iv) the applicant's knowledge of the wishes and feelings of the person to be protected; and
    (b) a draft of the application for the making of which leave is sought, together with sufficient copies for one to be served on each respondent and the person to be protected.

(2) As soon as practicable after receiving a request under paragraph (1), the court shall –

    (a) grant the request, or
    (b) direct that a date be fixed for the hearing of the request and fix the date,

and the proper officer shall inform the following persons of the court's action under this paragraph –

        (i) the person making the request,
        (ii) the respondent,
        (iii) (if different) the person to be protected, and
        (iv) any other person directed by the court.

(3) Where leave is granted to bring proceedings, the application shall proceed in accordance with rule 3.26.][1]

NOTES

Amendments.[1] Rule inserted: SI 2008/2446.

[3.28 Service of the application for a forced marriage protection order

(1) Subject to paragraph (3), in every application made on notice the applicant shall serve a copy of the application, together with the notice of proceedings in Form FL402A, on –

(a) the respondent,
(b) the person who is the subject of the proceedings (if not the applicant), and
(c) any other person directed by the court,

personally not less than 2 days before the date on which the application will be heard.

(2) The court may abridge the period specified in paragraph (1).

(3) Service of the application shall be effected by the court if the applicant so requests.

This does not affect the court's power to order substituted service.

(4) The applicant shall file a statement in Form FL415 after the application has been served.][1]

NOTES

Amendments.[1] Rule inserted: SI 2008/2446.

[3.29 Transfer of proceedings

(1) Subject to any enactment, where proceedings under Part 4A of the Family Law Act 1996 are pending, the court may transfer the proceedings to another court of its own motion or on the application of a party or (if not a party) the person who is the subject of the proceedings.

(2) The order for transfer shall be in Form FL417.][1]

NOTES

Amendments.[1] Rule inserted: SI 2008/2446.

[3.30 Parties to proceedings for a forced marriage protection order

(1) In proceedings under Part 4A of the Family Law Act 1996, a person may file a request in Form FL431 for that person or another person to –

(a) be joined as a party, or
(b) cease to be a party.

(2) As soon as practicable after receiving a request under paragraph (1), the court shall do one of the following –

(a) in the case only of a request under paragraph (1)(a), grant the request;
(b) order that the request be considered at a hearing, and fix a date for the hearing; or

(c) invite written representations as to whether the request should be granted, to be filed within a specified period, and upon expiry of that period act under sub-paragraph (a) or (b) as it sees fit;

and the proper officer shall inform the following persons of the court's action under this paragraph –
- (i) the person making the request,
- (ii) the applicant and the respondent,
- (iii) (if different) the person who is the subject of the proceedings, and
- (iv) any other person directed by the court.

(3) The court may direct –

(a) that a person who would not otherwise be a respondent under these rules be joined as a party to the proceedings; or

(b) that a party to the proceedings cease to be a party;

and such a direction may be made by the court of its own motion as well as upon a request under paragraph (1).]¹

NOTES

Amendments.¹ Rule inserted: SI 2008/2446.

[3.31 Orders for disclosure against a person not a party

(1) This rule applies where an application is made to the court under any Act for disclosure by a person who is not a party to the proceedings.

(2) The application must be supported by evidence.

(3) The court may make an order under this rule only where –

(a) the documents of which disclosure is sought are likely to support the case of the applicant or adversely affect the case of one of the other parties to the proceedings; and

(b) disclosure is necessary in order to dispose fairly of the proceedings or to save costs.

(4) An order under this rule shall –

(a) specify the documents or the classes of documents which the non-party must disclose; and

(b) require the non-party, when making disclosure, to specify any of those documents –
- (i) which are no longer in his control; or
- (ii) in respect of which he claims a right or duty to withhold inspection.

(5) Such an order may –

(a) require the non-party to indicate what has happened to any documents which are no longer in his control; and

(b) specify the time and place for disclosure and inspection.]¹

NOTES

Amendments.[1] Rule inserted: SI 2008/2446.

[3.32 Claim to withhold inspection or disclosure of a document

(1) A person may apply, without notice, for an order permitting him to withhold disclosure of a document on the ground that disclosure would damage the public interest.

(2) Unless the court orders otherwise, an order of the court under paragraph (1) –

(a) must not be served on any other person; and
(b) must not be open to inspection by any person.

(3) A person who wishes to claim that he has a right or duty to withhold inspection of a document, or part of a document, must state in writing –

(a) that he has such a right or duty; and
(b) the grounds on which he claims that right or duty.

(4) The statement referred to in paragraph (3) must be made to the person wishing to inspect the document.

(5) A party or (if different) the person who is the subject of the proceedings may apply to the court to decide whether a claim made under paragraph (3) should be upheld.

(6) For the purpose of deciding an application under paragraph (1) (application to withhold disclosure) or paragraph (3) (claim to withhold inspection), the court may –

(a) require the person seeking to withhold disclosure or inspection of a document to produce that document to the court; and
(b) invite any person, whether or not a party, to make representations.

(7) An application under paragraph (1) or paragraph (3) shall be supported by evidence.

(8) This rule does not affect any rule of law which permits or requires a document to be withheld from disclosure or inspection on the ground that its disclosure or inspection would damage the public interest.][1]

NOTES

Amendments.[1] Rule inserted: SI 2008/2446.

[3.33 Hearing of applications for forced marriage protection orders

(1) The hearing of an application for a forced marriage protection order shall be in chambers unless the court otherwise directs.

(2) A record of the hearing shall be made in Form FL405.

(3) The order made on the hearing shall be issued in Form FL404B.

(4) The court may direct the withholding of any submissions made, or any evidence adduced, for or at the hearing –

(a) in order to protect the person who is the subject of the proceedings or any other person, or
(b) for any other good reason.

(5) The applicant shall serve –

(a) a copy of the order;
(b) a copy of the record of the hearing; and
(c) where the order is made without notice, a copy of the application together with any statement supporting it;

on the respondent, the person being protected by the order (if neither the applicant nor a respondent) and any other person named in the order, personally as soon as reasonably practical.

(6) Service of the documents mentioned in paragraph (5) shall be effected by the court if the applicant so requests or where the court made the order of its own motion.

(7) The court may direct that a further hearing be held to consider any representations made by the respondent, the person being protected by the order (if neither the applicant nor a respondent) and any other person named in the order.

(8) An application to vary, extend or discharge a forced marriage protection order shall be made in Form FL403A and this rule shall apply to the hearing of such an application.]¹

NOTES

Amendments.¹ Rule inserted: SI 2008/2446.

[3.34 Forced marriage protection orders made by the court of its own motion

(1) Where the court makes a forced marriage protection order of its own motion under section 63C of the Family Law Act 1996, it shall set out in the order –

(a) a summary of its reasons for making the order; and
(b) the names of the persons who are to be served with the order.

(2) The court may order service of the order on –

(a) any of the parties to the current proceedings;
(b) (if different) the person being protected by the order; and
(c) any other persons whom the court considers should be served.

(3) The court will give directions as to how the order is to be served.

(4) The court may direct that a further hearing be held to consider any representations made by any of the persons named in the order.

(5) Rule 3.33(8) applies to an order made under this rule as it applies to an order made under rule 3.33.]¹

NOTES

Amendments.¹ Rule inserted: SI 2008/2446.

[3.35 Enforcement of forced marriage protection orders

(1) Subject to the following modifications, rule 3.9A shall apply to a forced marriage protection order as it applies to an order made under Part IV of the Family Law Act 1996.

(2) In paragraph (1) –

   (a) for 'an occupation order', substitute 'a forced marriage protection order'; and
   (b) for 'FL406', substitute 'FL406A'.

(3) For paragraph (1A), substitute –

   '(1A) Where paragraph (1) applies, the following documents shall be delivered to the officer for the time being in charge of any police station for the address of the person being protected by the order or of such other police station as the court may specify –

   (a) Form FL406A, and
   (b) a statement showing that the respondents and any other persons directed by the court to be served with the order have been so served or informed of its terms (whether by being present when the order was made or by telephone or otherwise).'

(4) In paragraph (1B) –

   (a) delete the words 'on the respondent' in both places where they occur;
   (b) in sub-paragraph (a), for '3.9(2) or (4)', substitute '3.33(5)'; and
   (c) in sub-paragraph (b), for '3.9(5)', substitute '3.33(6) or 3.34(3)'.

(5) In paragraph (2) –

   (a) for 'an occupation order or, as the case may be, any provisions of a non-molestation order', substitute 'a forced marriage protection order'; and
   (b) for 'the applicant's address', substitute 'the address of the person being protected by the order'.

(6) For paragraph (3), substitute –

   '(3) An application for the issue of a warrant for the arrest of a person under section 63J(2) of the Family Law Act 1996 shall be –

   (a) made in Form FL407A; and
   (b) accompanied by a sworn statement.

   (3A) An application for the issue of a warrant of arrest made by a person who is neither the person being protected by the order nor (if different) the person who applied for the order shall be treated, in the first instance, as an application for leave and the court shall either –

(a) grant the application; or
(b) direct that a date be fixed for the hearing of the application and fix a date,

and shall in either case inform the following persons of the court's action –

(i) the person applying for the issue of the warrant;
(ii) the person being protected by the order;
(iii) any other person directed by the court.

(3B) The warrant shall be issued in Form FL408.'

(7) In paragraph (5) –

(a) for 'IV', substitute '4A'; and
(b) for the words from 'and CCR Order 29' to the end, substitute 'and CCR Order 29, rule 1 shall have effect, as if for paragraph (3) there was substituted the following –

'(3) At the time when the order is drawn up, the proper officer shall, where the order made is (or includes) a forced marriage protection order, issue a copy of the order, indorsed with or incorporating a notice as to the consequences of disobedience, for service in accordance with paragraph (2).'

(8) In paragraph (6), for 'respondent', substitute 'arrested person'.

(9) In paragraph (7)(b) –

(a) after 'applicant', insert 'and (if different) the person being protected by the order'; and
(b) for 'respondent', substitute 'person who has failed to comply with the order or is otherwise in contempt of court in relation to the order'.

(10) In paragraph (9), for 'respondent', substitute 'arrested person'.

(11) In paragraph (10) –

(a) for 'an occupation order', substitute 'a forced marriage protection order';
(b) for '47(2) or (3)', substitute '63H(2) or (4)'; and
(c) for '47(8)', substitute '63J(2)'.][1]

NOTES

Amendments.[1] Rule inserted: SI 2008/2446.

[3.36 Applications under Part 4A of the Family Law Act 1996: bail

(1) Subject to the following modifications, rule 3.10 shall apply to a forced marriage protection order as it applies to an order made under Part IV of the Family Law Act 1996.

(2) In paragraph (1) –

(a) for 'an occupation order', substitute 'a forced marriage protection order';
(b) for '47(2) or (3)', substitute '63H(2) or (4)';
(c) for '47(8)', substitute '63J(2)'.

(3) In paragraph (3), for 'the applicant for the Part IV order', substitute –

'–

(a) the applicant for the forced marriage protection order;
(b) the (or any other) respondent to the application for the order;
(c) (if different) the person being protected by the order; and
(d) any other person named in the order.'

(4) In paragraph (4), omit sub-paragraphs (b) and (c).][1]

NOTES

Amendments.[1] Rule inserted: SI 2008/2446.

[PART IIIA
APPLICATIONS FOR ORDERS PREVENTING AVOIDANCE UNDER SECTION 32L OF THE CHILD SUPPORT ACT 1991

3A.1 Scope of this Part

Subject to rule 3A.7, the rules in this Part apply to applications made under section 32L(1) and (2) of the Act of 1991.

3A.2 Interpretation

In this Part –

'child support maintenance' has the meaning assigned to it in section 3(6) of the Act of 1991;

'reviewable disposition' has the meaning assigned to it in section 32L(5) of the Act of 1991.

3A.3 Application of CPR

Subject to the provisions of this Part, CPR Part 8 (alternative procedure for claims) and CPR rules 31.17 to 31.19 apply as appropriate with any necessary modifications to proceedings in this Part.

3A.4 Where and how to start proceedings

(1) The application shall be made to the High Court by originating summons out of –

(a) the principal registry; or
(b) any district registry.

(2) The application may be heard by –

(a) a judge;
(b) a district judge of the principal registry; or
(c) if directed by a judge, a district judge in a district registry.

(3) Unless the court directs otherwise, the application shall –

(a) include the following information –
   (i) the name and address of the person who owes child support maintenance;
   (ii) the amount of outstanding child support maintenance and the period during which that amount has been outstanding;
   (iii) details of the calculation of the amount of outstanding child support maintenance;
   (iv) any steps taken to date to enforce payment of the amount of outstanding child support maintenance; and
   (v) in the case of applications made without notice, the reasons why notice has not been given;
(b) where the application relates to land –
   (i) state whether the title to the land is registered or unregistered and, if registered, the Land Registry title number; and
   (ii) give particulars, as far as known to the applicant, of any mortgagee of the land or any other interest in the land;
(c) in the case of an application under section 32L(2) of the Act of 1991, the name and address of the person in whose favour the reviewable disposition is alleged to have been made; and
(d) state the facts relied on in support of the application including –
   (i) in the case of an application under section 32L(1) of the Act of 1991, the identity of the proposed disposition or other dealing with property which would have the consequence of making ineffective a step that has been or may be taken to recover the amount of outstanding child support maintenance;
   (ii) in the case of an application under section 32L(2) of the Act of 1991, the identity of the disposition which is alleged to be reviewable and has had the consequence of making ineffective a step taken, or which may have been taken, to recover the amount of outstanding child support maintenance.

(4) Where the Commission is not relying on evidence to give rise to the presumption under section 32L(7) of the Act of 1991 (that the person who disposed of or is about to dispose of or deal with property did so or, as the case may be is about to do so, with the intention of avoiding payment of child support maintenance) then the Commission shall give other evidence supporting the person's intention of avoiding such payment.

3A.5 Who the parties are

(1) The applicant in the proceedings is the Commission and the respondent is the person who has failed to pay child support maintenance.

(2) The court may at any time direct that –

(a) any person be made a party to proceedings; or
(b) a party be removed from the proceedings.

3A.6 Service of the application

(1) The applicant shall serve the application, a copy of any sworn statement in support and the acknowledgement of service on –

(a) any respondent;
(b) the person in whose favour the reviewable disposition is alleged to have been made; and
(c) such other persons as the court directs.

(2) Where an application includes an application relating to land, the applicant shall serve a copy of the application on any –

(a) mortgagee;
(b) trustee of a trust of land or settlement; and
(c) other person who has an interest in the land,

of whom particulars are given in the application.

(3) Any person served under paragraph (2) may make a request to the court in writing, within 14 days beginning with the date of service of the application, for a copy of the applicant's sworn statement in support of the application.

(4) Any person who –

(a) is served with copies of the application and the applicant's sworn statement in support of the application under paragraph (1); or
(b) receives a copy of the applicant's sworn statement in support of the application following a request under paragraph (3),

may within 14 days beginning with the date of service or receipt file a statement in answer.

(5) A statement in answer filed under paragraph (4) shall be sworn to be true.

3A.7 Applications without notice

(1) This rule applies to an application under section 32L(1) of the Act of 1991.

(2) The court may grant an application made without notice if it appears to the court that there are good reasons for not giving notice.

(3) If the applicant makes an application without giving notice, the sworn statement in support of the application shall state the reasons why notice has not been given.

(4) If the court grants an application under paragraph (2) –

(a) the order shall include a provision allowing any respondent to apply to the court for the order to be reconsidered as soon as just and convenient at a full hearing; and

(b) the applicant shall, as soon as reasonably practicable, serve upon each respondent a copy of the order and copies of the application and sworn statement in support of the application.]¹

NOTES

Amendments.¹ Part inserted: SI 2010/786.

PART IV
PROCEEDINGS UNDER THE CHILDREN ACT 1989[, ETC]¹

NOTES

Amendments.¹ Word inserted: SI 2009/636.

4.1 Interpretation and application

(1) In this Part of these rules, unless a contrary intention appears –

a section or schedule referred to means the section or schedule so numbered in the Act of 1989;
'a section 8 order' has the meaning assigned to it by section 8(2);
'application' means an application made under or by virtue of the Act of 1989 or under these rules, and 'applicant' shall be construed accordingly;
'child', in relation to proceedings to which this Part applies –
  (a) means, subject to sub-paragraph (b), a person under the age of 18 with respect to whom the proceedings are brought, and
  (b) where the proceedings are under Schedule 1, also includes a person who has reached the age of 18;
['children and family reporter' means an officer of the service [or a Welsh family proceedings officer]⁴ who has been asked to prepare a welfare report under section 7(1)(a);]²
['children's guardian' –
  (a) means an officer of the service [or a Welsh family proceedings officer]⁴ appointed under section 41 for the child with respect to whom the proceedings are brought; but
  (b) does not include such an officer appointed in relation to proceedings specified by Part IVA;]²
['contact activity condition' has the meaning assigned to it by section 11C(2);
'contact activity direction' has the meaning assigned to it by section 11A(3);
'contact order' has the meaning assigned to it by section 8(1);]⁷
'directions appointment' means a hearing for directions under rule 4.14(2);
'emergency protection order' means an order under section 44;
['enforcement order' has the meaning assigned to it by section 11J(2);]⁷
['family assistance order report' means a report to the court pursuant to a direction in a family assistance order under section 16(6);]⁶
['financial compensation order' means an order made under section 11O(2);]⁷
…²
'leave' includes permission and approval;
'note' includes a record made by mechanical means;

'parental responsibility' has the meaning assigned to it by section 3;
'recovery order' means an order under section 50;
['risk assessment' has the meaning assigned to it by section 16A(3);][6]
['special guardianship order' has the meaning assigned to it by section 14A;][5]
'specified proceedings' has the meaning assigned to it by section 41(6) and rule 4.2(2);
['warning notice' means a notice attached to a contact order pursuant to section 8(2) of the Act of 2006;][7] and
'welfare officer' means a person who has been asked to prepare a welfare report under [section 7(1)(b)][2].

(2) Except where the contrary intention appears, the provisions of this Part apply to proceedings in the High Court and the county courts –

(a) on an application for a section 8 order;
(b) on an application for a care order or a supervision order;
(c) on an application under section [4(1)(c)][3], 4(3), [4A(1)(b), 4A(3),][5] [4ZA(1)(c), 4ZA(6),][9] 5(1), 6(7), [11J(5), 11O(5),][7] 13(1), [14A, 14C(3), 14D,][5] ...[6], 33(7), 34(2), 34(3), 34(4), 34(9), 36(1), 38(8)(b), 39(1), 39(2), 39(3), 39(4), 43(1), 43(12), 44, 45, 46(7), 48(9) [, 50(1) or 102(1)];[1]
(d) under Schedule 1, except where financial relief is also sought by or on behalf of an adult;
[(da) on an application under paragraph 4(3), 5(3), 6(4), 7(3) or 9(5) of Schedule A1;][7]
(e) on an application under paragraph 19(1) of Schedule 2;
(f) on an application under paragraph 6(3), 15(2) or 17(1) of Schedule 3;
(g) on an application under paragraph 11(3) or 16(5) of Schedule 14; ...[7]
(h) under section 25[...[8]][7]
(i) on an application for a warning notice.][7][or]
[(j) on an application for a warrant under section 79 of the Childcare Act 2006.][8]

NOTES

Amendments.[1] Words substituted: SI 1991/2113.[2] Definition inserted or deleted, or words substituted: SI 2001/821.[3] Reference substituted: SI 2003/2839.[4] Words inserted: SI 2005/559.[5] Definition and references inserted: SI 2005/2922.[6] Definitions inserted and reference revoked: SI 2007/2187.[7] Definitions, references and subparagraph inserted, and word revoked: SI 2008/2861.[8] Word revoked and subparagraph inserted: SI 2009/636. [9] References inserted: SI 2009/2027.

4.2 Matters prescribed for the purposes of the Act of 1989

(1) The parties to proceedings in which directions are given under section 38(6), and any person named in such a direction, form the prescribed class for the purposes of section 38(8) (application to vary directions made with interim care or interim supervision order).

(2) The following proceedings are specified for the purposes of section 41 in accordance with subsection (6)(i) thereof –

(a) proceedings under section 25;
(b) applications under section 33(7);

(c) proceedings under paragraph 19(1) of Schedule 2;
(d) applications under paragraph 6(3) of Schedule 3.
[(e) appeals against the determination of proceedings of a kind set out in sub-paragraphs (a) to (d).]¹

(3) The applicant for an order that has been made under section 43(1) and the persons referred to in section 43(11) may, in any circumstances, apply under section 43(12) for a child assessment order to be varied or discharged.

(4) The following persons form the prescribed class for the purposes of section 44(9) (application to vary directions) –

(a) the parties to the application for the order in respect of which it is sought to vary the directions;
(b) the [children's guardian]²;
(c) the local authority in whose area the child concerned is ordinarily resident;
(d) any person who is named in the directions.

NOTES
Amendments.¹ Words inserted: SI 1991/2113. ² Words substituted: SI 2001/821.

4.3 Application for leave to commence proceedings

(1) Where the leave of the court is required to bring any proceedings to which this Part applies, the person seeking leave shall file –

(a) a written request for leave [in Form C2]¹ setting out the reasons for the application; and
[(b) a draft of the application (being the documents referred to in rule 4.4 (1A)) for the making of which leave is sought together with sufficient copies for one to be served on each respondent.]¹

(2) On considering a request for leave filed under paragraph (1), the court shall –

(a) grant the request, whereupon the proper officer shall inform the person making the request [and any local authority that is preparing, or has prepared, a report under section 14A(8) or (9)]² of the decision, or
(b) direct that a date be fixed for the hearing of the request, whereupon the proper officer shall fix such a date and give such notice as the court directs to the person making the request [and any local authority that is preparing, or has prepared, a report under section 14A(8) or (9)]² and such other persons as the court requires to be notified, of the date so fixed.

(3) Where leave is granted to bring proceedings to which this Part applies the application shall proceed in accordance with rule 4.4; but paragraph (1)(a) of that rule shall not apply.

(4) In the case of a request for leave to bring proceedings under Schedule 1, the draft application under paragraph (1) shall be accompanied by a statement

setting out the financial details which the person seeking leave believes to be relevant to the request and containing a declaration that it is true to the maker's best knowledge and belief, together with sufficient copies for one to be served on each respondent.

NOTES

Amendments.[1] Words inserted or substituted: SI 1994/3155.[2] Words inserted: SI 2005/2922.

4.4 Application

(1) Subject to paragraph (4) [and rule 4.4A][5], an applicant shall –

- [(a) file the documents referred to in paragraph (1A) below (which documents shall together be called the 'application') together with sufficient copies for one to be served on each respondent, and][3]
- (b) serve a copy of the application, [together with Form C6 and such (if any) of Forms [C1A,][4] C7 and C10A as are given to him by the proper officer under paragraph (2)(b)][3] on each respondent such number of days prior to the date fixed under paragraph (2)(a) as is specified for that application in column (ii) of Appendix 3 to these rules.

[(1A) the documents to be filed under paragraph (1)(a) above are –

- (a)
  - (i) whichever is appropriate of Forms [C1, [C100,][5] [C110,][9] C2, C3, C4][4][,][5] ...[8] [or C79][5], and
  - [(ii) supplemental Forms C10, C11, C12 and C13A to C20 as appropriate,][9]
  - (iiA) in the case of an application for a care order or supervision order, such of the documents specified in the Annex to Form C110 as are available, and[9] [and
  - (iii) in the case of an application for a section 8 order or an order under section 4(1)(c)[, 4ZA(1)(c) or 4A(1)(b)][7] where question 7 on Form C1, [or (as the case may be) question 5 on Form C100,][5] or question 4 on Form C2, is answered in the affirmative, supplemental Form C1A][4], or
- (b) where there is no appropriate form a statement in writing of the order sought, and where the application is made in respect of more than one child, all the children shall be included in one application.][3]

(2) On receipt of the documents filed under paragraph (1)(a) the proper officer shall –

- (a) fix the date for a hearing or a directions appointment, allowing sufficient time for the applicant to comply with paragraph (1)(b),
- (b) endorse the date so fixed upon [Form C6 and, where appropriate, Form C6A][3], and
- [(c) return forthwith to the applicant the copies of the application and Form C10A if filed with it, together with Form C6 and such of Forms

C6A and C7 as are appropriate[, and, in the case of an application for a section 8 order or an order under section 4(1)(c)[, 4ZA(1)(c) or 4A(1)(b)][7], Form C1A][4].][3]

[(3) The applicant shall, at the same time as complying with paragraph (1)(b), serve Form C6A on the persons set out for the relevant class of proceedings in column (iv) of Appendix 3 to these rules.][3]

[(3A) In the case of an application under –

(a) section 11J; or
(b) section 11O,

in addition to complying with paragraph (3), the applicant shall serve a copy of the application on the person who was the children's guardian, guardian ad litem, next friend or legal representative as referred to in the relevant entry in column (iv) of Appendix 3 to these rules.][5]

(4) An application for –

(a) a [section 8 order][2],
(b) an emergency protection order,
(c) a warrant under section 48(9), ...[1]
(d) a recovery order, [...][6]
(e) a warrant under section 102(1)][1] [or][6]
[(f) a warrant under section 79 of the Childcare Act 2006,][6]

may be made ex parte in which case the applicant shall –

(i) file the application ...[1] in the appropriate form in Appendix 1 to these rules –
  (a) where the application is made by telephone, within 24 hours after the making of the application, or
  (b) in any other case, at the time when the application is made, and
(ii) in the case of an application for a [section 8 order][2] or an emergency protection order, serve a copy of the application on each respondent within 48 hours after the making of the order.

(5) Where the court refuses to make an order on an ex parte application it may direct that the application be made inter partes.

(6) In the case of proceedings under Schedule 1, the application under paragraph (1) shall be accompanied by a statement [in Form C10A][3] setting out the financial details which the applicant believes to be relevant to the application ...[3], together with sufficient copies for one to be served on each respondent.

NOTES

Amendments.[1] Words revoked or inserted: SI 1991/2113. [2] Words substituted: SI 1992/2067. [3] Words inserted, repealed or substituted: SI 1994/3155. [4] Words and sub-paragraph inserted: SI 2004/3375. [5] Words, references and paragraph inserted and word substituted by comma: SI 2008/2861. [6] Word revoked, and word and subparagraph inserted: SI 2009/636. [7] References inserted: SI 2009/2027. [8] Reference revoked: SI 2010/1064. [9] Reference inserted and subparagraphs substituted and inserted: SI 2010/786.

[4.4A Application for a warning notice or application to amend enforcement order by reason of change of residence

(1) This rule applies in relation to an application for a warning notice or for an order under paragraph 5 of Schedule A1 (to amend an enforcement order by reason of change of residence).

(2) The application shall be made –

- (a) in the case of an application for a warning notice, ex parte on Form C78; or
- (b) in the case of an application for an order under paragraph 5 of Schedule A1, ex parte on Form C79.

(3) The court may deal with the application without a hearing.

(4) Where the court determines that the application shall be dealt with at a hearing –

- (a) rule 4.4(1)(b) and (3) shall apply; and
- (b) rule 4.4(2) shall apply as if for the words before 'the proper officer' there were substituted 'On the court determining that the application shall be dealt with at a hearing'.][1]

NOTES

Amendments.[1] Rule inserted: SI 2008/2861.

4.5 Withdrawal of application

(1) An application may be withdrawn only with leave of the court.

(2) Subject to paragraph (3), a person seeking leave to withdraw an application shall file and serve on the parties a written request for leave setting out the reasons for the request.

(3) The request under paragraph (2) may be made orally to the court if the parties and ...[4] the [children's guardian][1][,][3] [welfare officer[,][3] children and family reporter][1][, or the officer of the service or the Welsh family proceedings officer who is [acting or has acted under a duty referred to in rule 4.11AA(1)(a) to (g)][4]][3] are present.

(4) Upon receipt of a written request under paragraph (2) the court shall –

- (a) if –
    - (i) the parties consent in writing,
    - (ii) the [children's guardian][1] has had an opportunity to make representations, and
    - (iii) the court thinks fit,

    grant the request, in which case the proper officer shall notify the parties, [any local authority that is preparing, or has prepared, a report under section 14A(8) or (9),][2] the [children's guardian][1] and the [welfare officer or children and family reporter][1] [or the officer of the

service or the Welsh family proceedings officer who is [acting or has acted under a duty referred to in rule 4.11AA(1)(a) to (g)]⁴]³ of the granting of the request, or

(b) direct that a date be fixed for the hearing of the request in which case the proper officer shall give at least 7 days' notice to the parties, [any local authority that is preparing, or has prepared, a report under section 14A(8) or (9),]² the [children's guardian]¹[,]³ [welfare officer[,]³ children and family reporter]¹ [and the officer of the service or the Welsh family proceedings officer who is [acting or has acted under a duty referred to in rule 4.11AA(1)(a) to (g)]⁴]³, of the date fixed.

NOTES

Amendments.¹ Words substituted: SI 2001/821.² Words inserted: SI 2005/2922.³ Commas substituted and words inserted: SI 2007/2187.⁴ Word revoked and words substituted: SI 2008/2861.

4.6 Transfer

(1) Where an application is made, in accordance with the provisions of [the Allocation Order]¹, to a county court for an order transferring proceedings from a magistrates' court following the refusal of the magistrates' court to order such a transfer, the applicant shall –

(a) file the application in Form [C2]², together with a copy of the certificate issued by the magistrates' court, and
(b) serve a copy of the documents mentioned in sub-paragraph (a) personally on all parties to the proceedings which it is sought to have transferred,

within 2 days after receipt by the applicant of the certificate.

(2) Within 2 days after receipt of the documents served under paragraph (1)(b), any party other than the applicant may file written representations.

(3) The court shall, not before the fourth day after the filing of the application under paragraph (1), unless the parties consent to earlier consideration, consider the application and either –

(a) grant the application, whereupon the proper officer shall inform the parties [and any local authority that is preparing, or has prepared, a report under section 14A(8) or (9)]³ of that decision, or
(b) direct that a date be fixed for the hearing of the application, whereupon the proper officer shall fix such a date and give not less than 1 day's notice to the parties [and any local authority that is preparing, or has prepared, a report under section 14A(8) or (9)]³ of the date so fixed.

(4) Where proceedings are transferred from a magistrates' court to a county court in accordance with the provisions of [the Allocation Order]¹, the county court shall consider whether to transfer those proceedings to the High Court in accordance with that Order and either –

(a) determine that such an order need not be made,
(b) make such an order,

(c) order that a date be fixed for the hearing of the question whether such an order should be made, whereupon the proper officer shall give such notice to the parties [and any local authority that is preparing, or has prepared, a report under section 14A(8) or (9)]³ as the court directs of the date so fixed, or

(d) invite the parties to make written representations, within a specified period, as to whether such an order should be made; and upon receipt of the representations the court shall act in accordance with sub-paragraph (a), (b) or (c).

(5) The proper officer shall notify the parties [and any local authority that is preparing, or has prepared, a report under section 14A(8) or (9)]³ of an order transferring the proceedings from a county court or from the High Court made in accordance with the provisions of [the Allocation Order]¹.

[(6) Before ordering the transfer of proceedings from a county court to a magistrates' court in accordance with the Allocation Order, the county court shall notify the magistrates' court of its intention to make such an order and invite the views of the clerk to the justices on whether such an order should be made.

(7) An order transferring proceedings from a county court to a magistrates' court in accordance with the Allocation Order shall –

(a) be in form [C49]², and
(b) be served by the court on the parties.

(8) ...³]¹

NOTES

Amendments.¹ Words or subsections substituted or inserted: SI 1991/2113. ² Words substituted: SI 1994/3155. ³ Words inserted: SI 2005/2922. ³ Paragraph revoked: SI 2010/1064.

4.7 Parties

(1) The respondents to proceedings to which this Part applies shall be those persons set out in the relevant entry in [column (iii)]¹ of Appendix 3 to these rules.

(2) In proceedings to which this Part applies, a person may file a request [in Form C2]² that he or another person –

(a) be joined as a party, or
(b) cease to be a party.

(3) On considering a request under paragraph (2) the court shall, subject to paragraph (4) –

(a) grant it without a hearing or representations, save that this shall be done only in the case of a request under paragraph (2)(a), whereupon the proper officer shall inform the parties [and any local authority that is preparing, or has prepared, a report under section 14A(8) or (9)]³ and the person making the request of that decision, or

(b) order that a date be fixed for the consideration of the request, whereupon the proper officer shall give notice of the date so fixed, together with a copy of the request –
   (i) in the case of a request under paragraph (2)(a), to the applicant [and any local authority that is preparing, or has prepared, a report under section 14A(8) or (9)][3], and
   (ii) in the case of a request under paragraph (2)(b), to the parties, or
(c) invite the parties or any of them to make written representations, within a specified period, as to whether the request should be granted; and upon the expiry of the period the court shall act in accordance with sub-paragraph (a) or (b).

(4) Where a person with parental responsibility requests that he be joined under paragraph (2)(a), the court shall grant his request.

(5) In proceedings to which this Part applies the court may direct –
   (a) that a person who would not otherwise be a respondent under these rules be joined as a party to the proceedings, or
   (b) that a party to the proceedings cease to be a party.

NOTES

Amendments. [1] Words substituted: SI 1992/2067. [2] Words substituted: SI 1994/3155. [3] Words inserted: SI 2922.

4.8 Service

(1) Subject to the requirement in rule 4.6(1)(b) of personal service, where service of a document is required under this Part (and not by a provision to which section 105(8) (Service of notice or other document under the Act) applies) it may be effected –

(a) if the person to be served is not known by the person serving to be acting by solicitor –
   (i) by delivering it to him personally, or
   (ii) by delivering it at, or by sending it by first-class post to, his residence or his last known residence, or
(b) if the person to be served is known by the person serving to be acting by solicitor –
   (i) by delivering the document at, or sending it by first-class post to, the solicitor's address for service,
   (ii) where the solicitor's address for service includes a numbered box at a document exchange, by leaving the document at that document exchange or at a document exchange which transmits documents on every business day to that document exchange, or
   (iii) by sending a legible copy of the document by facsimile transmission to the solicitor's office.

(2) In this rule 'first-class post' means first-class post which has been pre-paid or in respect of which pre-payment is not required.

(3) Where a child who is a party to proceedings to which this Part applies [is not prosecuting or defending them without a next friend or guardian ad litem under rule 9.2A and]¹ is required by these rules or other rules of court to serve a document, service shall be effected by –

(a) the solicitor acting for the child, or
(b) where there is no such solicitor, [the children's guardian or]⁴ the guardian ad litem, or
(c) where there is neither such a solicitor [nor a children's guardian]⁴ nor a guardian ad litem, the court.

(4) Service of any document on a child [who is not prosecuting or defending the proceedings concerned without a next friend or guardian ad litem under rule 9.2A]¹ shall, subject to any direction of the court, be effected by service on –

(a) the solicitor acting for the child, or
(b) where there is no such solicitor, [the children's guardian or]⁴ the guardian ad litem, or
(c) where there is neither such a solicitor [nor a children's guardian]⁴ nor a guardian ad litem, with leave of the court, the child.

(5) Where the court refuses leave under paragraph (4)(c) it shall give a direction under paragraph (8).

(6) A document shall, unless the contrary is proved, be deemed to have been served –

(a) in the case of service by first-class post, on the second business day after posting, and
(b) in the case of service in accordance with paragraph (1)(b)(ii), on the second business day after the day on which it is left at the document exchange.

(7) At or before the first directions appointment in, or hearing of, proceedings to which this Part applies the applicant shall file a statement [in Form C9]³ that service of –

(a) a copy of the application [and other documents referred to in rule 4.4(1)(b)]³ has been effected on each respondent, ...⁴
(b) notice of the proceedings has been effected under rule 4.4(3); [and
(c) a copy of the application has been effected under rule 4.4(3A);]⁴

and the statement shall indicate –
  (i) the manner, date, time and place of service, or
  (ii) where service was effected by post, the date, time and place of posting.

[(8) In proceedings to which this Part applies, where these rules or other rules of court require a document to be served, the court may, without prejudice to any power under rule 4.14, direct that –

(a) the requirement shall not apply;

(b) the time specified by the rules for complying with the requirement shall be abridged to such extent as may be specified in the direction;
(c) service shall be effected in such manner as may be specified in the direction.]²

NOTES

Amendments.¹ Words inserted: SI 1992/456. ² Words substituted: SI 1992/2067. ³ Words inserted: SI 1994/3155. ³ Words inserted: SI 2001/821. ⁴ Word revoked and subparagraph and preceding word inserted: SI 2008/2861.

4.9 Answer to application

[(1) Within 14 days of service of an application for –
- (a) an order under section 4(1)(c)[, 4ZA(1)(c) or 4A(1)(b)]⁵;
- (b) a section 8 order;
- (c) an enforcement order;
- (d) a financial compensation order;
- (e) a special guardianship order;
- (f) an order under Schedule 1;
- (g) an order under Part 2 of Schedule A1; or
- (h) an order for a warning notice to which rule 4.4A(4) applies,

each respondent shall file, and serve on the parties, an acknowledgement of the application in Form C7 and, if both parts of question 6 or question 7 (or both) on Form C7 are answered in the affirmative, Form C1A.]⁴

(2) ...¹

[(3) Following service of an application to which this Part applies, other than –
- (a) an application under rule 4.3; and
- (b) an application referred to in paragraph (1)(a), (b), (e) or (h),

a respondent may, subject to paragraph (4), file a written answer, which shall be served on the other parties.]⁴

(4) An answer under paragraph (3) shall, except in the case of an application under section 25, 31, 34, 38, 43, 44, 45, 46, 48 or 50, be filed, and served, not less than 2 days before the date fixed for the hearing of the application.

NOTES

Amendments.¹ Words inserted, repealed or substituted: SI 1994/3155. ² Words inserted: SI 2004/3375. ³ Words inserted: SI 2005/2922. ⁴ Paragraphs substituted: SI 2008/2861. ⁵ References inserted: SI 2009/2027.

4.10 Appointment of [children's guardian]²

(1) As soon as practicable after the commencement of specified proceedings, or the transfer of such proceedings to the court, the court shall appoint a [children's guardian]², unless –
- (a) such an appointment has already been made by the court which made the transfer and is subsisting, or

(b) the court considers that such an appointment is not necessary to safeguard the interests of the child.

(2) At any stage in specified proceedings a party may apply, without notice to the other parties unless the court directs otherwise, for the appointment of a [children's guardian][2].

(3) The court shall grant an application under paragraph (2) unless it considers such an appointment not to be necessary to safeguard the interests of the child, in which case it shall give its reasons; and a note of such reasons shall be taken by the proper officer.

(4) At any stage in specified proceedings the court may, of its own motion, appoint a [children's guardian][2].

[(4A) The court may, in specified proceedings, appoint more than one children's guardian in respect of the same child.][2]

(5) The proper officer shall, as soon as practicable, notify the parties and any [welfare officer or children and family reporter][2] of an appointment under this rule or, as the case may be, of a decision not to make such an appointment.

(6) Upon the appointment of a [children's guardian][2] the proper officer shall, as soon as practicable, notify him of the appointment and serve on him copies of the application and of documents filed under rule 4.17(1).

[(7) A children's guardian appointed by the court under this rule shall not –

(a) be a member, officer or servant of a local authority which, or an authorised person (within the meaning of section 31(9)) who, is a party to the proceedings;

(b) be, or have been, a member, officer or servant of a local authority or voluntary organisation (within the meaning of section 105(1)) who has been directly concerned in that capacity in arrangements relating to the care, accommodation or welfare of the child during the five years prior to the commencement of the proceedings; or

(c) be a serving probation officer who has, in that capacity, been previously concerned with the child or his family.][2]

(8) When appointing a [children's guardian][2] the court shall consider the appointment of anyone who has previously acted as [children's guardian][2] of the same child.

(9) The appointment of a [children's guardian][2] under this rule shall continue for such time as is specified in the appointment or until terminated by the court.

(10) When terminating an appointment in accordance with paragraph (9), the court shall give its reasons in writing for so doing.

(11) Where the court appoints a [children's guardian][2] in accordance with this rule or refuses to make such an appointment, the court or the proper officer shall record the appointment or refusal in Form [C47][1].

NOTES

Amendments.[1] Word substituted: SI 1994/3155. [2] Words inserted or substituted: SI 2001/821.

[4.11 Powers and duties of officers of the service [and Welsh family proceedings officers][2]

(1) In carrying out his duty under section 7(1)(a) [or][4] section 41(2) [or in acting under a duty referred to in rule 4.11AA(1)][4], the officer of the service shall have regard to the principle set out in section 1(2) and the matters set out in section 1(3)(a) to (f) as if for the word 'court' in that section there were substituted the words ['officer of the Service or Welsh family proceedings officer'][2].

(2) The officer of the service [or the Welsh family proceedings officer][2] shall make such investigations as may be necessary for him to carry out his duties and shall, in particular–

   (a) contact or seek to interview such persons as he thinks appropriate or as the court directs;
   (b) obtain such professional assistance as is available to him which he thinks appropriate or which the court directs him to obtain.

(3) In addition to his duties, under other paragraphs of this rule, or rules 4.11A[, 4.11AA][3] and 4.11B, the officer of the service [or the Welsh family proceedings officer][2] shall provide to the court such other assistance as it may require.

(4) A party may question the officer of the service [or the Welsh family proceedings officer][2] about oral or written advice tendered by him to the court.][1]

NOTES

Amendments.[1] Rule substituted: SI 2001/821. [2] Words inserted or substituted: SI 2005/559. [3] Words substituted and reference inserted: SI 2007/2187. [4] Word substituted and inserted: SI 2008/2861.

[4.11A Additional powers and duties of children's guardian

(1) The children's guardian shall–

   (a) appoint a solicitor to represent the child unless such a solicitor has already been appointed; and
   (b) give such advice to the child as is appropriate having regard to his understanding and, subject to rule 4.12(1)(a), instruct the solicitor representing the child on all matters relevant to the interests of the child including possibilities for appeal, arising in the course of proceedings.

(2) Where the children's guardian is an officer of the service authorised by the Service in the terms mentioned by and in accordance with section 15(1) of the Criminal Justice and Court Services Act 2000, paragraph (1)(a) shall not require him to appoint a solicitor for the child if he intends to have conduct of the proceedings on behalf of the child unless–

(a) the child wishes to instruct a solicitor direct; and
(b) the children's guardian or the court considers that he is of sufficient understanding to do so.

[(2A) Where the children's guardian is a Welsh family proceedings officer authorised by the National Assembly for Wales in the terms mentioned by and in accordance with section 37(1) of the Children Act 2004, paragraph (1)(a) shall not require him to appoint a solicitor for the child if he intends to have conduct of the proceedings on behalf of the child unless –

(a) the child wishes to instruct a solicitor direct; and
(b) the children's guardian or the court considers that he is of sufficient understanding to do so.][2]

(3) Where it appears to the children's guardian that the child–

(a) is instructing his solicitor direct; or
(b) intends to conduct and is capable of conducting the proceedings on his own behalf,

he shall inform the court and from then he–

(i) shall perform all of his duties set out in rule 4.11 and this rule, other than those duties under paragraph (1)(a) of this rule, and such other duties as the court may direct;
(ii) shall take such part in the proceedings as the court may direct; and
(iii) may, with the leave of the court, have legal representation in the conduct of those duties.

(4) Unless excused by the court, the children's guardian shall attend all directions appointments in and hearings of the proceedings and shall advise the court on the following matters–

(a) whether the child is of sufficient understanding for any purpose including the child's refusal to submit to a medical or psychiatric examination or other assessment that the court has the power to require, direct or order.
(b) the wishes of the child in respect of any matter relevant to the proceedings including his attendance at court;
(c) the appropriate forum for the proceedings;
(d) the appropriate timing of the proceedings or any part of them;
(e) the options available to it in respect of the child and the suitability of each such option including what order should be made in determining the application; and
(f) any other matter concerning which the court seeks his advice or concerning which he considers that the court should be informed.

(5) The advice given under paragraph (4) may, subject to any order of the court, by given orally or in writing; and if the advice be given orally, a note of it shall be taken by the court or the proper officer.

(6) The children's guardian shall, where practicable, notify any person whose joinder as a party to those proceedings would be likely, in the opinion of the

children's guardian, to safeguard the interests of the child of that person's right to apply to be joined under rule 4.7(2) and shall inform the court–
   (a)   of any such notification given;
   (b)   of anyone whom he attempted to notify under this paragraph but was unable to contact; and
   (c)   of anyone whom he believes may wish to be joined to the proceedings.

(7) The children's guardian shall, unless the court otherwise directs, not less than 14 days before the date fixed for the final hearing of the proceedings–
   (a)   file a written report advising on the interests of the child; and
   (b)   serve a copy of the filed report on the other parties [and any local authority that is preparing, or has prepared, a report under section 14A(8) or (9)]³.

(8) The children's guardian shall serve and accept service of documents on behalf of the child in accordance with rule 4.8(3)(b) and (4)(b) and, where the child has not himself been served, and has sufficient understanding, advise the child of the contents of any document so served.

(9) If the children's guardian inspects records of the kinds referred to in section 42, he shall bring to the attention of–
   (a)   the court; and
   (b)   unless the court otherwise directs, the other parties to the proceedings,

all records and documents which may, in his opinion, assist in the proper determination of the proceedings.

(10) The children's guardian shall ensure that, in relation to a decision made by the court in the proceedings–
   (a)   if he considers it appropriate to the age and understanding of the child, the child is notified of that decision; and
   (b)   if the child is notified of the decision, it is explained to the child in a manner appropriate to his age and understanding.]¹

NOTES
Amendments.¹ Rule inserted: SI 2001/821.² Paragraph inserted: SI 2005/559.³ Words inserted: SI 2005/2922.

[4.11AA Additional powers and duties of officers of the service and Welsh family proceedings officers: family assistance order reports and risk assessments

[(1) This rule applies where an officer of the service or a Welsh family proceedings officer is acting under a duty in accordance with –
   (a)   section 11E(7) (providing the court with information as to the making of a contact activity direction or a contact activity condition);
   (b)   section 11G(2) (monitoring compliance with a contact activity direction or a contact activity condition);
   (c)   section 11H(2) (monitoring compliance with a contact order);

(d) section 11L(5) (providing the court with information as to the making of an enforcement order);
(e) section 11M(1) (monitoring compliance with an enforcement order);
(f) section 16(6) (providing a family assistance order report to the court); and
(g) section 16A (making a risk assessment).][2]

(2) When an officer of the service or a Welsh family proceedings officer is [acting under a duty referred to in paragraph (1)(a) to (g)][2] he must consider whether –

(a) to notify the child of such of the contents of [any report or risk assessment he makes][2] as he considers appropriate to the age and understanding of the child;
(b) to recommend in [any report or risk assessment he makes][2] that the court lists a hearing for the purposes of considering the report or assessment;
(c) it is in the best interests of the child for the child to be made a party to the proceedings.

(3) If the officer of the service or the Welsh family proceedings officer decides to notify the child of any of the contents of [any report or risk assessment he makes][2], he must explain those contents to the child in a manner appropriate to the child's age and understanding.

(4) If the officer of the service or the Welsh family proceedings officer considers that the child should be made a party to the proceedings he must notify the court of his opinion together with the reasons for that opinion.

(5) If the officer of the service or the Welsh family proceedings officer considers that the court should exercise its discretion under rule 4.17AA(2) in relation to service of a risk assessment, he must state in the risk assessment –

(a) the way in which he considers the court should exercise its discretion (including his view on the length of any suggested delay in service); and
(b) his reasons for reaching his view.

(6) The officer of the service or the Welsh family proceedings officer must file [any report or risk assessment he makes][2] with the court –

(a) at or by the time directed by the court;
(b) in the absence of any such direction, at least 14 days before a relevant hearing; or
(c) where there has been no direction from the court and no relevant hearing is listed, as soon as possible following completion of [any report or risk assessment he makes][2].

(7) In paragraph (6), a hearing is a relevant hearing if the proper officer has given the officer of the service or the Welsh family proceedings officer notice that the report or assessment is to be considered at it.

(8) When an officer of the service or a Welsh family proceedings officer prepares [a report as a result of acting under a duty referred to in paragraph (1)(a) to (f)]², he shall, as soon as practicable, serve copies of that report on –

(a) each party; and
(b) any local authority that is preparing or has prepared a report under section 14A(8) or (9).

(9) At any hearing where [a report prepared as a result of acting under a duty referred to in paragraph (1)(a) to (f)]² or a risk assessment is considered, any party may question the officer of the service or the Welsh family proceedings officer about the report or assessment.]¹

NOTES

Amendments.¹ Rule inserted: SI 2007/2187. ² Paragraph and words substituted: SI 2008/2861.

[4.11B Additional powers and duties of a children and family reporter

(1) The children and family reporter shall–

(a) notify the child of such contents of his report (if any) as he considers appropriate to the age and understanding of the child, including any reference to the child's own views on the application and the recommendation of the children and family reporter; and
(b) if he does notify the child of any contents of his report, explain them to the child in a manner appropriate to his age and understanding.

(2) Where the court has–

(a) directed that a written report be made by a children and family reporter; and
(b) notified the children and family reporter that his report is to be considered at a hearing,

the children and family reporter shall–

(i) file the report; and
(ii) serve a copy on the other parties[, any local authority that is preparing, or has prepared, a report under section 14A(8) or (9)]² and on the children's guardian (if any),

by such time as the court may direct, and if no direction is given, not less than 14 days before that hearing.

(3) The court may direct that the children and family reporter attend any hearing at which his report is to be considered.

(4) The children and family reporter shall advise the court if he considers that the joinder of a person as a party to the proceedings would be likely to safeguard the interests of the child.

(5) The children and family reporter shall consider whether it is in the best interests of the child for the child to be made a party to the proceedings.

(6) If the children and family reporter considers the child should be made a party to the proceedings he shall notify the court of his opinion together with the reasons for that opinion.][1]

NOTES

Amendments.[1] Rule inserted: SI 2001/821. [2] Words inserted: SI 2005/2922.

4.12 Solicitor for child

(1) A solicitor appointed under section 41(3) or in accordance with [rule 4.11A(1)(a)][2] shall represent the child –

    (a) in accordance with instructions received from the [children's guardian][2] (unless the solicitor considers, having taken into account the views of the [children's guardian][2] and any direction of the court under [rule 4.11A(3)][2], that the child wishes to give instructions which conflict with those of the [children's guardian][2] and that he is able, having regard to his understanding, to give such instructions on his own behalf in which case he shall conduct the proceedings in accordance with instructions received from the child), or

    (b) where no [children's guardian][2] has been appointed for the child and the condition in section 41(4)(b) is satisfied, in accordance with instructions received from the child, or

    (c) in default of instructions under (a) or (b), in furtherance of the best interests of the child.

(2) A solicitor appointed under section 41(3) or in accordance with [rule 4.11A(1)(a)][2] shall serve and accept service of documents on behalf of the child in accordance with rule 4.8(3)(a) and (4)(a) and, where the child has not himself been served and has sufficient understanding, advise the child of the contents of any document so served.

(3) Where the child wishes an appointment of a solicitor under section 41(3) or in accordance with [rule 4.11A(1)(a)][2] to be terminated, he may apply to the court for an order terminating the appointment; and the solicitor and the [children's guardian][2] shall be given an opportunity to make representations.

(4) Where the [children's guardian][2] wishes an appointment of a solicitor under section 41(3) to be terminated, he may apply to the court for an order terminating the appointment; and the solicitor and, if he is of sufficient understanding, the child, shall be given an opportunity to make representations.

(5) When terminating an appointment in accordance with paragraph (3) or (4), the court shall give its reasons for so doing, a note of which shall be taken by the court or the proper officer.

(6) Where the court appoints a solicitor under section 41(3) or refuses to make such an appointment, the court or the proper officer shall record the appointment or refusal in Form [C48][1].

NOTES

Amendments.¹ Word substituted: SI 1994/3155. ² Words substituted: SI 2001/821.

[4.13 Welfare officer

(1) Where the court has directed that a written report be made by a welfare officer [in accordance with section 7(1)(b)]², the report shall be filed at or by such time as the court directs or, in the absence of such a direction, at least 14 days before a relevant hearing; and the proper officer shall, as soon as practicable, serve a copy of the report on the parties[, any local authority that is preparing, or has prepared, a report under section 14A(8) or (9)]³ and any [children's guardian]².

(2) In paragraph (1), a hearing is relevant if the proper officer has given the welfare officer notice that his report is to be considered at it.

(3) After the filing of a report by a welfare officer, the court may direct that the welfare officer attend any hearing at which the report is to be considered; and

(a) except where such a direction is given at a hearing attended by the welfare officer, the proper officer shall inform the welfare officer of the direction; and
(b) at the hearing at which the report is considered any party may question the welfare officer about his report.

[(3A) The welfare officer shall consider whether it is in the best interests of the child for the child to be made a party to the proceedings.

(3B) If the welfare officer considers the child should be made a party to the proceedings he shall notify the court of his opinion together with the reasons for that opinion.]²

(4) This rule is without prejudice to any power to give directions under rule 4.14.]¹

NOTES

Amendments.¹ Rule substituted: SI 1992/2067, except in relation to a written report the making of which was directed before 5 October 1992. ² Words inserted or substituted: SI 2001/821. ³ Words inserted: SI 2005/2922.

[4.13A Local authority officers preparing family assistance order reports

Where a family assistance order directs a local authority officer to prepare a family assistance order report, rules 4.5, 4.13, 4.14(1)(a)(i) and (2), 4.15(2) and 4.17(1) shall apply to, or in respect of, the local authority officer preparing a family assistance order report as they would apply to, or in respect of, a welfare officer preparing a report in accordance with section 7(1)(b).]¹

NOTES

Amendments.¹ Rule inserted: SI 2007/2187.

[4.13B Section 11J or 11O: duties of person notified

Where there has been a notification of an application in accordance with rule 4.4(3A), the person notified shall –

(a) consider whether it is in the best interests of the child for the child to be a party to the proceedings to which that application relates; and
(b) before the date fixed for the first hearing or directions appointment, notify the court, orally or in writing, of his opinion on this question, together with the reasons for this opinion.][1]

NOTES

Amendments.[1] Rule inserted: SI 2008/2861.

4.14 Directions

[(1) In this rule, 'party' includes the children's guardian and, where a request or direction is or are concerned with –

(a) a report under –
   (i) section 7, the welfare officer or children and family reporter;
   (ii) section 14A(8) or (9), the local authority preparing that report;
(b) [a duty referred to in rule 4.11AA(1)(a) to (f)][5], the officer of the service or the Welsh family proceedings officer who is [acting under the duty in question][5];
(c) a risk assessment, the officer of the service or the Welsh family proceedings officer who is preparing the assessment.]][4][3]

(2) In proceedings to which this Part applies the court may, subject to paragraph (3) [and rule 4.14A][6], give, vary or revoke directions for the conduct of the proceedings, including –

(a) the timetable for the proceedings;
(b) varying the time within which or by which an act is required, by these rules or by other rules of court, to be done;
(c) the attendance of the child;
[(d) the appointment of a children's guardian, a guardian ad litem, or a solicitor under section 41(3);][2]
(e) the service of documents;
(f) the submission of evidence including experts' reports;
(g) the preparation of welfare reports under section 7;
(h) the transfer of the proceedings to another court;
[(i) consolidation with other proceedings;
(j) the preparation of reports under section 14A(8) or (9);
(k) the attendance of the person who prepared the report under section 14A(8) or (9) at any hearing at which the report is to be considered][3][;
(l) the preparation of family assistance order reports;
(m) listing a hearing for the purposes of considering the contents of a risk assessment][4][;

Part II   Statutory Instruments

(n) the exercise by an officer of the service or a Welsh family proceedings officer of any duty referred to in rule 4.11AA(1)(a) to (e).][5]

(3) Directions under paragraph (2) may be given, varied or revoked either –

(a) of the court's own motion having given the parties notice of its intention to do so, and an opportunity to attend and be heard or to make written representations,

(b) on the written request [in Form C2][1] of a party specifying the direction which is sought, filed and served on the other parties, or

(c) on the written request [in Form C2][1] of a party specifying the direction which is sought, to which the other parties consent and which they or their representatives have signed.

(4) In an urgent case the request under paragraph (3)(b) may, with the leave of the court, be made –

(a) orally, or
(b) without notice to the parties, or
(c) both as in sub-paragraph (a) and as in sub-paragraph (b).

(5) On receipt of a written request under paragraph (3)(b) the proper officer shall fix a date for the hearing of the request and give not less than 2 days' notice [in Form C6][1] to the parties of the date so fixed.

(6) On considering a request under paragraph (3)(c) the court shall either –

(a) grant the request, whereupon the proper officer shall inform the parties of the decision, or

(b) direct that a date be fixed for the hearing of the request, whereupon the proper officer shall fix such a date and give not less than 2 days' notice to the parties of the date so fixed.

(7) A party may apply for an order to be made under section 11(3) or, if he is entitled to apply for such an order, under section 38(1) in accordance with paragraph (3)(b) or (c).

(8) Where a court is considering making, of its own motion, a section 8 order, or an order under section [14A, 14D,][3] 31, 34 or 38 [or under paragraph 4, 5, 6 or 7 of Schedule A1][5], the power to give directions under paragraph (2) shall apply.

(9) Directions of a court which are still in force immediately prior to the transfer of proceedings to which this Part applies to another court shall continue to apply following the transfer, subject to any changes of terminology which are required to apply those directions to the court to which the proceedings are transferred, unless varied or discharged by directions under paragraph (2).

[(9A) After the filing of [a report prepared as a result of acting under a duty referred to in rule 4.11AA(1)(a) to (f)][5] or a risk assessment, the court may direct that the officer of the service or the Welsh family proceedings officer attend any hearing at which the report or assessment is to be considered.][4]

(10) The court or the proper officer shall take a note of the giving, variation or revocation of a direction under this rule and serve, as soon as practicable, a copy of the note on any party who was not present at the giving, variation or revocation.

NOTES

Amendments.[1] Words inserted: SI 1994/3155.[2] Words substituted: SI 2001/821.[3] Text inserted: SI 2005/2922.[4] Paragraphs substituted and inserted, and subparas inserted: SI 2007/2187.[5] Words substituted and inserted and subparagraph inserted: SI 2008/2861.[6] Words inserted: SI 2010/786.

[4.14A Timetable for the Child in proceedings for a care order or supervision order

(1) In proceedings for a care order or a supervision order, the court shall set the timetable of the proceedings in accordance with the Timetable for the Child.

(2) The 'Timetable for the Child' means the timetable set by the court in accordance with its duties under sections 1 and 32 of the Act of 1989 and shall –

(a) take into account dates of the significant steps in the life of the child who is the subject of the proceedings; and
(b) be appropriate for that child.][1]

NOTES

Amendments.[1] Rule inserted: SI 2010/786.

4.15 Timing of proceedings

(1) Where these rules or other rules of court provide a period of time within which or by which a certain act is to be performed in the course of proceedings to which this Part applies, that period may not be extended otherwise than by direction of the court under rule 4.14.

(2) At the –

(a) transfer to a court of proceedings to which this Part applies,
(b) postponement or adjournment of any hearing or directions appointment in the course of proceedings to which this Part applies, or
(c) conclusion of any such hearing or directions appointment other than one at which the proceedings are determined, or so soon thereafter as is practicable, the court or the proper officer shall –
   (i) fix a date upon which the proceedings shall come before the court again for such purposes as the court directs, which date shall, where paragraph (a) applies, be as soon as possible after the transfer, and
   (ii) give notice to the parties, [any local authority that is preparing, or has prepared, a report under section 14A(8) or (9),][2] the [children's guardian][1][,][3] the [welfare officer[, the][3] children and family reporter][1] [or the officer of the service or the Welsh family

proceedings officer who is [acting or has acted under a duty referred to in rule 4.11AA(1)(a) to (g)]⁴]³ of the date so fixed.

NOTES

Amendments.¹ Words substituted: SI 2001/821.² Words inserted: SI 2005/2922.³ Comma substituted, and words substituted and inserted: SI 2007/2187.⁴ Words substituted: SI 2008/2861.

4.16 Attendance at directions appointment and hearing

(1) Subject to paragraph (2), a party shall attend a directions appointment of which he has been given notice in accordance with rule 4.14(5) unless the court otherwise directs.

[(1A) Paragraphs (2) to (4) do not apply where –
  (a) the hearing relates to –
     (i) a decision about whether to make a contact activity direction or to attach a contact activity condition to a contact order; or
     (ii) an application for a fi2861cial compensation order, an enforcement order or an order under paragraph 9(2) of Schedule A1; and
  (b) the court has yet to obtain sufficient evidence from, or in relation to, the person who may be the subject of the direction, condition or order to enable it to determine the matter.]²

(2) Proceedings or any part of them shall take place in the absence of any party, including the child, if –
  (a) the court considers it in the interests of the child, having regard to the matters to be discussed or the evidence likely to be given, and
  (b) the party is represented by a [children's guardian]¹ or solicitor;

and when considering the interests of the child under sub-paragraph (a) the court shall give the [children's guardian]¹, the solicitor for the child and, if he is of sufficient understanding, the child an opportunity to make representations.

(3) Subject to paragraph (4), where at the time and place appointed for a hearing or directions appointment the applicant appears but one or more of the respondents do not, the court may proceed with the hearing or appointment.

(4) The court shall not begin to hear an application in the absence of a respondent unless –
  (a) it is proved to the satisfaction of the court that he received reasonable notice of the date of the hearing; or
  (b) the court is satisfied that the circumstances of the case justify proceeding with the hearing.

(5) Where, at the time and place appointed for a hearing or directions appointment one or more of the respondents appear but the applicant does not, the court may refuse the application or, if sufficient evidence has previously been received, proceed in the absence of the applicant.

(6) Where at the time and place appointed for a hearing or directions appointment neither the applicant nor any respondent appears, the court may refuse the application.

(7) Unless the court otherwise directs, a hearing of, or directions appointment in, proceedings to which this Part applies shall be in chambers.

NOTES

Amendments.[1] Words substituted: SI 2001/821.[2] Paragraph inserted: SI 2008/2861.

4.17 Documentary evidence

(1) Subject to paragraphs (4) and (5), in proceedings to which this Part applies a party shall file and serve on the parties, [any local authority that is preparing, or has prepared, a report under section 14A(8) or (9),][3] any [welfare officer[, any][4] children and family reporter][2][, any officer of the service or any Welsh family proceedings officer who is [acting or has acted under a duty referred to in rule 4.11AA(1)(a) to (g)][5]][4] and any [children's guardian][2] of whose appointment he has been given notice under rule 4.10(5) –

(a) written statements of the substance of the oral evidence which the party intends to adduce at a hearing of, or a directions appointment in, those proceedings, which shall –
   (i) be dated,
   (ii) be signed by the person making the statement, ...[1]
   (iii) contain a declaration that the maker of the statement believes it to be true and understands that it may be placed before the court; and
   [(iv) show in the top right hand corner of the first page –
      (a) the initials and surname of the person making the statement,
      (b) the number of the statement in relation to the maker,
      (c) the date on which the statement was made, and
      (d) the party on whose behalf it is filed; and][1]

(b) copies of any documents, including experts' reports, upon which the party intends to rely at a hearing of, or a directions appointment in, those proceedings,

at or by such time as the court directs or, in the absence of a direction, before the hearing or appointment.

(2) A party may, subject to any direction of the court about the timing of statements under this rule, file and serve on the parties a statement which is supplementary to a statement served under paragraph (1).

(3) At a hearing or a directions appointment a party may not, without the leave of the court –

(a) adduce evidence, or
(b) seek to rely on a document,

in respect of which he has failed to comply with the requirements of paragraph (1).

(4) In proceedings for a section 8 order [or a special guardianship order]³ a party shall –

(a) neither file nor serve any document other than as required or authorised by these rules, and
(b) in completing a form prescribed by these rules, neither give information, nor make a statement, which is not required or authorised by that form,

without the leave of the court.

(5) In proceedings for a section 8 order [or a special guardianship order]³ no statement or copy may be filed under paragraph (1) until such time as the court directs.

NOTES

Amendments.¹ Words inserted or revoked: SI 1992/2067.² Words substituted: SI 2001/821.³ Words inserted: SI 2005/2922.⁴ Words substituted: SI 2007/2187.⁵ Words substituted: SI 2008/2861.

[4.17A Disclosure of report under section 14A(8) or (9)

(1) In proceedings for a special guardianship order, the local authority shall file the report under section 14A(8) or (9) within the timetable fixed by the court.

(2) The court shall consider whether to give a direction that the report under section 14A(8) or (9) be disclosed to each party to the proceedings.

(3) Before giving such a direction the court shall consider whether any information should be deleted including information which reveals the party's address in a case where he has declined to reveal it in accordance with rule 10.21 (disclosure of addresses).

(4) The court may direct that the report will not be disclosed to a party.

(5) The proper officer shall serve a copy of the report filed under paragraph (1) –

(i) in accordance with any direction given under paragraph (2); and
(ii) on any children's guardian, welfare officer or children and family reporter.]¹

NOTES

Amendments.¹ Rule inserted: SI 2005/2922.

[4.17AA Service of risk assessments

(1) Where an officer of the service or a Welsh family proceedings officer has filed a risk assessment with the court, subject to paragraph (2), the proper officer shall as soon as practicable serve copies of the risk assessment on –

(a) each party; and

(b) any local authority that is preparing or has prepared a report under section 14A(8) or (9).

(2) Before serving the risk assessment, the court must consider whether, in order to prevent a risk of harm to the child, it is necessary for –

(a) information to be deleted from a copy of the risk assessment before that copy is served on a party; or
(b) service of a copy of the risk assessment (whether with information deleted from it or not) on a party to be delayed for a specified period,

and may direct accordingly.][1]

NOTES

Amendments.[1] Rule inserted: SI 2007/2187.

4.18 Expert evidence – examination of child

(1) No person may, without the leave of the court, cause the child to be medically or psychiatrically examined, or otherwise assessed, for the purpose of the preparation of expert evidence for use in the proceedings.

(2) An application for leave under paragraph (1) shall, unless the court otherwise directs, be served on all parties to the proceedings and on the [children's guardian][1].

(3) Where the leave of the court has not been given under paragraph (1), no evidence arising out of an examination or assessment to which that paragraph applies may be adduced without the leave of the court.

NOTES

Amendments.[1] Words substituted: SI 2001/821.

4.19 Amendment

(1) Subject to rule 4.17(2), a document which has been filed or served in proceedings to which this Part applies, may not be amended without the leave of the court which shall, unless the court otherwise directs, be requested in writing.

(2) On considering a request for leave to amend a document the court shall either –

(a) grant the request, whereupon the proper officer shall inform the person making the request of that decision, or
(b) invite the parties or any of them to make representations, within a specified period, as to whether such an order should be made.

(3) A person amending a document shall file it and serve it on those persons on whom it was served prior to amendment; and the amendments shall be identified.

4.20 Oral evidence

The court or the proper officer shall keep a note of the substance of the oral evidence given at a hearing of, or directions appointment in, proceedings to which this Part applies.

4.21 Hearing

(1) The court may give directions as to the order of speeches and evidence at a hearing, or directions appointment, in the course of proceedings to which this Part applies.

(2) Subject to directions under paragraph (1), at a hearing of, or directions appointment in, proceedings to which this Part applies, the parties and the [children's guardian][4] shall adduce their evidence in the following order –

- (a) the applicant,
- (b) any party with parental responsibility for the child,
- (c) other respondents,
- (d) the [children's guardian][4],
- (e) the child, if he is a party to the proceedings and there is no [children's guardian][4].

[(2A) At the hearing at which the report under section 14A(8) or (9) is considered a party to whom the report, or part of it, has been disclosed may question the person who prepared the report about it.][5]

(3) After the final hearing of proceedings to which this Part applies, the court shall deliver its judgment as soon as is practicable.

[(4) When making an order or when refusing an application, the court shall –

- (a) where it makes a finding of fact state such finding and complete Form C22; and
- (b) state the reasons for the court's decision.][3]

(5) An order made in proceedings to which this Part applies shall be recorded, by the court or the proper officer, either in the appropriate form in Appendix 1 to these rules or, where there is no such form, in writing.

(6) Subject to paragraph (7) [and rule 4.21AA][6], a copy of an order made in accordance with paragraph (5) shall, as soon as practicable after it has been made, be served by the proper officer on the parties to the proceedings in which it was made [and][1] on any person with whom the child is living[, and where applicable, on the local authority that prepared the report under section 14A(8) or (9)][5].

(7) Within 48 hours after the making ex parte of –

- (a) a [section 8 order][2], or
- (b) an order under section 44, 48(4), 48(9) or 50,

the applicant shall serve a copy of the order in the appropriate form in Appendix 1 to these Rules on –

- (i) each party,

(ii) any person who has actual care of the child or who had such care immediately prior to the making of the order, and

(iii) in the case of an order referred to in sub-paragraph (b), the local authority in whose area the child lives or is found.

(8) At a hearing of, or directions appointment in, an application which takes place outside the hours during which the court office is normally open, the court or the proper officer shall take a note of the substance of the proceedings.

NOTES

Amendments.[1] Word inserted: SI 1992/456.[2] Words substituted: SI 1992/2067.[3] Words inserted: SI 1994/3155.[4] Words substituted: SI 2001/821.[5] Words and paragraph inserted: SI 2005/2922. [6] Words inserted: SI 2008/2861.

[4.21AA Service of enforcement order or order amending or revoking enforcement order

(1) Paragraphs (2) and (3) apply where an enforcement order or an order under paragraph 9(2) of Schedule A1 is made by the court.

(2) As soon as practicable after an order has been made, a copy of it shall be served by the proper officer on –

(a) the parties, except the person against whom the order is made;
(b) the officer of the service or the Welsh family proceedings officer who is obliged to comply with a request under section 11M;
(c) the responsible officer.

(3) Unless the court directs otherwise, the applicant shall serve a copy of the order personally on the person against whom the order is made.

(4) As soon as practicable after an order had been made under paragraph 4, 5, 6 or 7 of Schedule A1, a copy of the order shall be served by the proper officer on –

(a) the parties;
(b) the officer of the service or the Welsh family proceedings officer who is obliged to comply with a request under section 11M;
(c) the responsible officer; and
(d) in the case of an order made under paragraph 5 of Schedule A1, the responsible officer in the former local justice area.

(5) In this rule, 'responsible officer' has the meaning given in paragraph 8(8) of Schedule A1.][1]

NOTES

Amendments.[1] Rule inserted: SI 2008/2861.

[4.21A Attachment of penal notice

CCR Order 29, rule 1 (committal for breach of order or undertaking) shall apply to section 8 orders [(except those referred to in rule 4.21B(a))][3] and orders under section 14A, 14B(2)(b), 14C(3)(b), or 14D as if for paragraph (3) of that rule there were substituted the following –

'(3) In the case of a section 8 order (within the meaning of section 8(2) of the Children Act 1989) or an order under section 14A, 14B(2)(b), 14C(3)(b), or 14D of the Children Act 1989 enforceable by committal order under paragraph (1), the judge or the district judge may, on the application of the person entitled to enforce the order, direct that the proper officer issue a copy of the order, endorsed with or incorporating a notice as to the consequences of disobedience, for service in accordance with paragraph (2); and no copy of the order shall be issued with any such notice endorsed or incorporated save in accordance with such a direction.][1,2]

NOTES

Amendments.[1] Rule inserted: SI 1992/2067.[2] Rule substituted: SI 2005/2922.[3] Words inserted: SI 2008/2861.

[4.21B Order with notice attached: committal

CCR Order 29, rule 1 (committal for breach of order or undertaking) shall apply to –

(a) contact orders within the meaning of section 8(1) of the Children Act 1989 to which a notice has been attached under section 11I of that Act or under section 8(2) of the Children and Adoption Act 2006;
(b) enforcement orders made under section 11J of the Children Act 1989;
(c) enforcement orders amended or made pursuant to paragraph 9 of Schedule A1 to the Children Act 1989

as if paragraph (3) were omitted.][1]

NOTES

Amendments.[1] Rule inserted: SI 2008/2861.

4.22

...[1]

NOTES

Amendments.[1] Rule revoked: SI 2009/636.

4.23

...[1]

NOTES

Amendments.[1] Rule revoked: SI 2005/1976.

4.24 Notification of consent

[(1)][2] Consent for the purposes of –

(a) section 16(3), [or][1]
(b) [section 38A(2)(b)(ii) or 44A(2)(b)(ii), or][2]
(c) paragraph 19(3)(c) or (d) of Schedule 2,

shall be given either –

(i) orally in court, or
(ii) in writing to the court signed by the person giving his consent.

[(2) Any written consent given for the purposes of subsection (2) of section 38A or section 44A, shall include a statement that the person giving consent –

(a) is able and willing to give to the child the care which it would be reasonable to expect a parent to give him; and
(b) understands that the giving of consent could lead to the exclusion of the relevant person from the dwelling-house in which the child lives.]²

NOTES

Amendments.[1] Words inserted and repealed: SI 1992/456.[2] Paragraph numbering, words and paragraph inserted: SI 1997/1893.

[4.24A Exclusion requirements: interim care orders and emergency protection orders

(1) This rule applies where the court includes an exclusion requirement in an interim care order or an emergency protection order.

(2) The applicant for an interim care order or emergency protection order shall –

(a) prepare a separate statement of the evidence in support of the application for an exclusion requirement;
(b) serve the statement personally on the relevant person with a copy of the order containing the exclusion requirement (and of any power of arrest which is attached to it);
(c) inform the relevant person of his right to apply to vary or discharge the exclusion requirement.

(3) Where a power of arrest is attached to an exclusion requirement in an interim care order or an emergency protection order, a copy of the order shall be delivered to the officer for the time being in charge of the police station for the area in which the dwelling-house in which the child lives is situated (or of such other station as the court may specify) together with a statement showing that the relevant person has been served with the order or informed of its terms (whether by being present when the order was made or by telephone or otherwise).

(4) Rules 3.9(5), 3.9A (except paragraphs (1) and (3)) and 3.10 shall apply, with the necessary modifications, for the service, variation, discharge and enforcement of any exclusion requirement to which a power of arrest is attached as they apply to an order made on an application under Part IV of the Family Law Act 1996.

(5) The relevant person shall serve the parties to the proceedings with any application which he makes for the variation or discharge of the exclusion requirement.

(6) Where an exclusion requirement ceases to have effect whether –

(a) as a result of the removal of a child under section 38A(10) or 44A(10),
(b) because of the discharge of the interim care order or emergency protection order, or
(c) otherwise,

the applicant shall inform –

(i) the relevant person,
(ii) the parties to the proceedings,
(iii) any officer to whom a copy of the order was delivered under paragraph (3), and
(iv) (where necessary) the court.

(7) Where the court includes an exclusion requirement in an interim care order or an emergency protection order of its own motion, paragraph (2) shall apply with the omission of any reference to the statement of the evidence.][1]

NOTES

Amendments.[1] Rule inserted: SI 1997/1893.

4.25 Secure accommodation – evidence

In proceedings under section 25, the court shall, if practicable, arrange for copies of all written reports before it to be made available before the hearing to –

(a) the applicant;
(b) the parent or guardian of the child;
(c) any legal representative of the child;
(d) the [children's guardian][1]; and
(e) the child, unless the court otherwise directs;

and copies of such reports may, if the court considers it desirable, be shown to any person who is entitled to notice of the proceedings in accordance with these rules.

NOTES

Amendments.[1] Words substituted: SI 2001/821.

4.26 Investigation under section 37

(1) This rule applies where a direction is given to an appropriate authority by the High Court or a county court under section 37(1).

(2) On giving a direction the court shall adjourn the proceedings and the court or the proper officer shall record the direction [in Form C40][1].

(3) A copy of the direction recorded under paragraph (2) shall, as soon as practicable after the direction is given, be served by the proper officer on the parties to the proceedings in which the direction is given and, where the appropriate authority is not a party, on that authority.

(4) When serving the copy of the direction on the appropriate authority the proper officer shall also serve copies of such of the documentary evidence which has been, or is to be, adduced in the proceedings as the court may direct.

(5) Where a local authority informs the court of any of the matters set out in section 37(3)(a) to (c) it shall do so in writing.

[(6) Where a local authority makes an application to a magistrates' court for a care or supervision order with respect to the child in relation to whom the direction was given, the local authority must inform the court that gave the direction of the application in writing.][2]

NOTES

Amendments.[1] Words substituted: SI 1994/3155.[2] Paragraph inserted: SI 2008/2836.

4.27 [Direction to local authority to apply for education supervision order][2]

(1) For the purposes of section 40(3) and (4) of the Education Act 1944 a direction by the High Court or a county court to a [local authority][2] to apply for an education supervision order shall be given [in writing][1].

(2) Where, following such a direction, a [local authority][2] informs the court that they have decided not to apply for an education supervision order, they shall do so in writing.

NOTES

Amendments.[1] Words substituted: SI 1997/1893. [2] Words substituted: SI 2010/1172.

[4.27A Stay under the Council Regulation

(1) An application for an order under Article 19 of the Council Regulation shall be made to a district judge, who may determine the application or refer the application, or any question arising thereon, to a judge for his decision.

(2) Where at any time after an application under rule 4.4 is made, it appears to the court that, under Articles 16 to 19 of the Council Regulation, the court does not have jurisdiction to hear the application and is required or may be required to stay the proceedings, the court will stay the proceedings and fix a date for a hearing to determine the questions of jurisdiction and whether there should be a stay or other order and shall serve notice of the hearing on the parties to the proceedings.

(3) The court must give reasons for its decision under Articles 16 to 19 of the Council Regulation and, where it makes a finding of fact state such a finding of fact.

(4) A declaration under Article 17 of the Council Regulation that the court has no jurisdiction over the proceedings shall be recorded by the court or proper officer in writing.

(5) The court may, if all parties agree, deal with any question about the jurisdiction of the court without a hearing.][1]

NOTES

Amendments.[1] Rule inserted: SI 2005/264.

4.28 Transitional provision

Nothing in any provision of this Part of these rules shall affect any proceedings which are pending (within the meaning of paragraph 1 of Schedule 14 to the Act of 1989) immediately before these rules come into force.

[[PART IVA
PROCEEDINGS UNDER SECTION 54 OF THE HUMAN FERTILISATION AND EMBRYOLOGY ACT 2008

4A.1 Interpretation

In this Part of these Rules –

> 'the Act of 2002' means the Adoption and Children Act 2002 as applied with modifications by the Human Fertilisation and Embryology (Parental Orders) Regulations 2010;
> 'the Act of 2008' means the Human Fertilisation and Embryology Act 2008;
> 'the other parent' means any person who is a parent of the child but is not one of the applicants or the woman who carried the child (including any man who is the father by virtue of section 35 or 36 of the Act of 2008 or any woman who is a parent by virtue of section 42 or 43 of that Act);
> 'parental order' means an order under section 54 of the Act of 2008;
> 'parental order proceedings' means proceedings for the making of a parental order under the Act of 2008 or an order under any provision of the Act of 2002;
> 'parental order reporter' means an officer of the service or a Welsh family proceedings officer appointed to act on behalf of a child who is the subject of parental order proceedings;
> 'provision for contact' means a contact order under section 8 or 34 of the Act of 1989.

4A.2 Application of this Part

Except where the contrary intention appears, the Rules in this Part apply to parental order proceedings.

4A.3 Application of Part IV

Subject to the other provisions of this Part, rules 4.1(1), 4.5, 4.6, 4.8, 4.10(2) to (10), 4.11, 4.11A(4) to (10), 4.11B, 4.14(3)(b) and (c), (4) and (6), 4.16(7), 4.17, 4.19, 4.20, and 4.21 apply as appropriate with any necessary modifications to parental order proceedings.

4A.4 Application for a parental order

(1) The application for a parental order shall be made in Form C51.

(2) The applicants shall file Form C51 and any documents referred to in it with the court together with sufficient copies for one to be served on each respondent.

4A.5 How to start parental order proceedings

(1) Parental order proceedings are started when a proper officer issues an application in Form C51 at the request of the applicant.

(2) An application is issued on the date entered in Form C51 by the proper officer.

4A.6 Personal details

(1) The court may direct that a party is not required to reveal –
- (a) the address or telephone number of their private residence;
- (b) the address of the child; or
- (c) the name of a person with whom the child is living, if that person is not the applicant.

(2) Where the court directs that a party is not required to reveal any of the particulars in paragraph (1), that party shall give notice of those particulars to the court in Form C8 and the particulars shall not be revealed to any person unless the court directs otherwise.

(3) Where a party changes his home address during the course of proceedings, that party shall give notice of the change to the court.

4A.7 Who the parties are

(1) In parental order proceedings –
- (a) the applicants may be such of the following who satisfy the conditions in section 54(1) of the Act of 2008 –
  - (i) a husband and wife;
  - (ii) civil partners of each other; or
  - (iii) two persons who are living as partners in an enduring family relationship who are not within the prohibited degrees of relationship in relation to each other; and
- (b) the respondents shall be –
  - (i) the woman who carried the child;
  - (ii) the other parent (if any);
  - (iii) any person in whose favour there is provision for contact; and
  - (iv) any other person or body with parental responsibility for the child at the date of the application.

(2) The court shall direct that a person with parental responsibility for the child be made a party to proceedings where that person requests to be one.

(3) The court may at any time direct that –
- (a) any other person or body be made a respondent to the proceedings; or
- (b) a respondent be removed from the proceedings.

(4) If the court makes a direction for the addition or removal of a party, it may give consequential directions about –

- (a) serving a copy of the application form on any new respondent;
- (b) serving relevant documents on the new party; and
- (c) the management of the proceedings.

4A.8 What the court shall do when the application has been issued

(1) As soon as practicable after the application has been issued the court shall –

- (a) if section 48(1) of the Act of 2002 applies (restrictions on making adoption orders), consider whether it is proper to hear the application;
- (b) subject to paragraph (2), set a date for the first directions hearing;
- (c) appoint a parental order reporter; and
- (d) set a date for the hearing of the application.

(2) Where it considers it appropriate the court may, instead of setting a date for a first directions appointment, give the directions provided for in rule 4A.13.

4A.9 What a proper officer shall do

As soon as practicable after the issue of proceedings a proper officer shall –

- (a) return to the applicants the copies of Form C51 together with Forms C6, C6A and C52 as are appropriate; and
- (b) send a copy of the certified copy of the entry in the register of live births to the parental order reporter.

4A.10 Service of the application and other documents

The applicants shall serve –

- (a) Form C51 and any documents referred to in it, Form C6 and Form C52 on the respondents within 14 days before the hearing or first directions hearing; and
- (b) Form C6A on any local authority or voluntary organisation that has at any time provided accommodation for the child.

4A.11 Acknowledgement

Within 7 days of the service of an application for a parental order, each respondent shall file and serve on all other parties an acknowledgement in Form C52.

4A.12 Date for first directions hearing

Unless the court directs otherwise, the first directions hearing shall be within 4 weeks beginning with the date on which the application is issued.

4A.13 The first directions hearing

(1) At the first directions hearing in the proceedings the court shall –

(a) fix a timetable for the filing of –
  (i) any report from a parental order reporter;
  (ii) if a statement of facts has been filed, any amended statement of facts; and
  (iii) any other evidence;
(b) give directions relating to the report of the parental order reporter and other evidence;
(c) consider whether any other person should be a party to the proceedings and, if so, give directions in accordance with rule 4A.7(2) or (3) joining that person as a party;
(d) give directions relating to the appointment of a guardian ad litem or next friend for any protected person unless a guardian ad litem or next friend has already been appointed;
(e) consider whether the case needs to be transferred to another court and, if so, give directions to transfer the proceedings to another court in accordance with the Allocation Order;
(f) give directions about –
  (i) tracing the other parent or the woman who carried the child;
  (ii) service of documents;
  (iii) subject to paragraph (2), disclosure, as soon as possible, of information and evidence to the parties; and
  (iv) the final hearing.

(2) Rule 4A.17 (reports of the parental order reporter and disclosure to parties) applies to any direction given under paragraph (1)(f)(iii) as it applies to a direction given under rule 4A.17(1).

(3) The parties or their legal representatives shall attend the first directions hearing unless the court directs otherwise.

(4) Directions may also be given at any stage in the proceedings –

(a) of the court's own motion; or
(b) on the application in Form C2 of a party or the parental order reporter.

(5) Where the court proposes to exercise the powers in paragraph (1) of its own motion, the court shall first give the parties –

(a) notice of its intention to do so; and
(b) an opportunity to attend and be heard or to make written representations.

(6) Where there is an application for directions to be made under paragraph (1), rule 4.14(3)(b) and (c),(4) and (6) as applied by rule 4A.3 shall apply.

(7) For the purposes of giving directions or for such purposes as the court directs –

(a) the court may set a date for a further directions hearing or other hearing; and
(b) the proper officer shall give notice of any date so fixed to the parties and to the parental order reporter.

(8) Directions of a court which are still in force immediately prior to the transfer of proceedings to another court shall continue to apply following the transfer subject to –

   (a)   any changes of terminology which are required to apply those directions to the court to which the proceedings are transferred; and
   (b)   any variation or revocation of the direction.

(9) The court or proper officer shall –

   (a)   take a note of the giving, variation or revocation of a direction under this rule; and
   (b)   as soon as practicable serve a copy of the note on every party.

(10) After the first directions hearing the court shall monitor compliance by the parties with the court's timetable and directions.

4A.14 Where the agreement of the other parent or the woman who carried the child is not required

(1) The following paragraphs apply where the agreement of the other parent or the woman who carried the child to the making of the parental order is not required as the person in question cannot be found or is incapable of giving agreement.

(2) The applicants shall –

   (a)   state that the agreement is not required in Form C51 or at a later stage in a written note to be filed with the court;
   (b)   file a statement of facts setting out a summary of the history of the case and any other facts to satisfy the court that the other parent or the woman who carried the child cannot be found or is incapable of giving agreement.

(3) On receipt of Form C51 or written note –

   (a)   a proper officer shall –
      (i)   unless the other parent or woman who carried the child cannot be found, inform the other parent or woman who carried the child that their agreement is not required;
      (ii)   send a copy of the statement of facts filed in accordance with paragraph (2)(b) to –
         (aa)   the other parent unless the other parent cannot be found;
         (bb)   the woman who carried the child unless the woman cannot be found; and
         (cc)   the parental order reporter; and
   (b)   if the applicants consider that the other parent or the woman who carried the child is incapable of giving agreement, the court shall consider whether to –
      (i)   appoint a guardian ad litem for the other parent or the woman who carried the child; or
      (ii)   give directions for an application to be made under rule 9.2(5),

unless a guardian ad litem has already been appointed for the other parent or the woman who carried the child.

4A.15 Agreement

(1) Unless the court directs otherwise, agreement of the other parent or the woman who carried the child to the making of the parental order may be given in Form A101A or a form to like effect.

(2) Any form of agreement executed in Scotland shall be witnessed by a Justice of the Peace or a Sheriff.

(3) Any form of agreement executed in Northern Ireland shall be witnessed by a Justice of the Peace.

(4) Any form of agreement executed outside the United Kingdom shall be witnessed by –

(a) any person for the time being authorised by law in the place where the document is executed to administer an oath for any judicial or other legal purpose;
(b) a British Consular officer;
(c) a notary public; or
(d) if the person executing the document is serving in any of the regular armed forces of the Crown, an officer holding a commission in any of those forces.

4A.16 Parental order reporter

(1) A parental order reporter is appointed to act on behalf of a child who is the subject of parental order proceedings and has a duty to safeguard the interests of that child.

(2) In addition to such of the matters set out in rules 4.11 and 4.11A as applied by rule 4A.3 as are appropriate to parental order proceedings, the parental order reporter shall –

(a) investigate the matters set out in section 54(1) to (8) of the Act of 2008;
(b) so far as the parental order reporter considers necessary, investigate any matter contained in the application form or other matter which appears relevant to the making of the parental order;
(c) advise the court on whether there is any reason under section 1 of the Act of 2002 to refuse the parental order.

4A.17 Reports of the parental order reporter and disclosure to the parties

(1) The court shall consider whether to give a direction that a confidential report of the parental order reporter be disclosed to each party to the proceedings.

(2) Before giving such a direction the court shall consider whether any information should be deleted including information which discloses the

particulars referred to in rule 4A.6(1) where a party has given notice under rule 4A.6(2) (disclosure of personal details).

(3) The court may direct that the report shall not be disclosed to a party.

4A.18 Notice of final hearing

A proper officer shall give notice in Form C6 to the parties and the parental order reporter –

(a) of the date and place where the application shall be heard; and
(b) of the fact that, unless the person wishes or the court requires, the person need not attend.

4A.19 The final hearing

(1) Any person who has been given notice in accordance with rule 4A.18 may attend the final hearing and be heard on the question of whether an order should be made.

(2) The court may direct that any person shall attend a final hearing.

4A.20 Proof of identity of the child

(1) Unless the contrary is shown, the child referred to in the application shall be deemed to be the child referred to in the form of agreement to the making of the parental order where the conditions in paragraph (2) apply.

(2) The conditions are –

(a) the application identifies the child by reference to a full certified copy of an entry in the registers of live-births;
(b) the form of agreement identifies the child by reference to a full certified copy of an entry in the registers of live-births attached to the form; and
(c) the copy of the entry in the registers of live-births referred to in sub-paragraph (a) is the same or relates to the same entry in the registers of live-births as the copy of the entry in the registers of live-births attached to the form of agreement.(3) Where the precise date of the child's birth is not proved to the satisfaction of the court, the court shall determine the probable date of birth.

(4) The probable date of the child's birth may be specified in the parental order as the date of the child's birth.

(5) Where the child's place of birth cannot be proved to the satisfaction of the court –

(a) the child may be treated as having been born in the registration district of the court where it is probable that the child may have been born in –
   (i) the United Kingdom;
   (ii) the Channel Islands; or
   (iii) the Isle of Man; or

(b) in any other case, the particulars of the country of birth may be omitted from the parental order.

4A.21 Disclosing information to an adult who was subject to a parental order

(1) Subject to paragraph (2) the person who was subject to the parental order has the right, on request in Form A64A, to receive from the court which made the parental order a copy of the following –

(a) the application form for a parental order (but not the documents attached to that form);
(b) the parental order and any other orders relating to the parental order proceedings;
(c) any transcript of the court's decision; and
(d) a report made to the court by the parental order reporter.

(2) The court shall not provide a copy of a document or order referred to in paragraph (1) unless the person making the request has completed the certificate relating to counselling in Form A64A.

(3) This rule does not apply to a person under the age of 18 years.

4A.22 Application for recovery orders

(1) An application for any of the orders referred to in section 41(2) of the Act of 2002 (recovery orders) may be made without notice in which case the applicant shall file the application –

(a) where the application is made by telephone, the next business day after the making of the application; or
(b) in any other case, at the time when the application is made.

(2) Where the court refuses to make an order on an application without notice it may direct that the application is made on notice in which case the application shall proceed in accordance with rules 4A.1 to 4A.19.

(3) An application for any of the orders referred to in section 41(2) of the Act of 2002 shall be made in Form C2.

(4) The respondents to an application under this rule are –

(a) in a case where parental order proceedings are pending, all parties to those proceedings;
(b) any person having parental responsibility for the child;
(c) any person in whose favour there is provision for contact;
(d) any person who was caring for the child immediately prior to the making of the application; and
(e) any person whom the applicant alleges to have effected, or to have been or to be responsible for, the taking or keeping of the child.

4A.23 Custody, inspection and disclosure of documents and information

(1) All documents relating to parental order proceedings shall, while they are in the custody of the court, be kept in a place of special security.

(2) Any person who obtains any information in the course of, or relating to, parental order proceedings shall treat that information as confidential and shall only disclose it if –

(a) the disclosure is necessary for the proper exercise of that person's duties; or
(b) the information is requested by –
   (i) a court or public authority (whether in Great Britain or not) having power to determine parental order proceedings and related matters, for the purpose of that court or authority discharging its duties relating to those proceedings and matters; or
   (ii) a person who is authorised in writing by the Secretary of State to obtain the information for the purposes of research.

4A.24 Documents held by the court not to be inspected or copied without the court's leave

Subject to the provisions of these Rules or any direction given by the court –

(a) no document or order held by the court in parental order proceedings and related proceedings under the Act of 2002 shall be open to inspection by any person; and
(b) no copy of any such document or order, or of an extract from any such document or order, shall be taken by or given to any person.

4A.25 Orders

(1) A parental order takes effect from the date when it is made, or such later date as the court may specify.

(2) In proceedings in Wales a party may request that an order be drawn up in Welsh as well as in English.

4A.26 Copies of orders

(1) Within 7 days beginning with the date on which the final order was made in proceedings, or such shorter time as the court may direct, a proper officer shall send –

(a) a copy of the order in Form C53 to the applicant;
(b) a copy which is sealed, authenticated with the stamp of the court or certified as a true copy of a parental order, to the Registrar General;
(c) a notice of the making or refusal of –
   (i) the final order; or
   (ii) an order quashing or revoking a parental order or allowing an appeal against an order in proceedings,

to every respondent and, with the leave of the court, any other person.

(2) A notice of refusal of a parental order shall be in Form C54.

(3) The proper officer shall also send notice of the making of a parental order to –

(a) any court in Great Britain which appears to the proper officer to have made any such order as is referred to in section 46(2) of the Act of 2002 (order relating to parental responsibility for, and maintenance of, the child); and

(b) the principal registry, if it appears to the proper officer that a parental responsibility agreement has been recorded at the principal registry.

(4) A copy of any final order may be sent to any other person with the leave of the court.

(5) The proper officer shall send a copy of any order made during the course of the proceedings to all the parties to those proceedings unless the court directs otherwise.

(6) If an order has been drawn up in Welsh as well as in English in accordance with rule 4A.25(2), any reference in this rule to sending an order is to be taken as a reference to sending both the Welsh and English orders.

4A.27 Amendment and revocation of orders

(1) This rule applies to an application under paragraph 4 of Schedule 1 to the Act of 2002 (amendment of a parental order and revocation of direction).

(2) The application shall be made in Form C2.

(3) Subject to paragraph (4), an application may be made without serving a copy of the application.

(4) The court may direct that an application be served on such persons as it thinks fit.

(5) Where the court makes an order granting the application, a proper officer shall send the Registrar General a notice –

(a) specifying the amendments; or
(b) informing the Registrar General of the revocation,

giving sufficient particulars of the order to enable the Registrar General to identify the case.]²]¹

NOTES

Amendments.¹ Part inserted: SI 1994/2165. ² Part substituted: SI 2010/1064.

PART V
WARDSHIP

5.1 Application to make a minor a ward of court

(1) An application to make a minor a ward of court shall be made by originating summons and, unless the court otherwise directs, the plaintiff shall file an affidavit in support of the application when the originating summons is issued.

(2) Rule 4.3 shall, so far as applicable, apply to an application by a local authority for the leave of the court under section 100(3) of the Act of 1989.

(3) Where there is no person other than the minor who is a suitable defendant, an application may be made ex parte to a district judge for leave to issue either an ex parte originating summons or an originating summons with the minor as defendant thereto; and, except where such leave is granted, the minor shall not be made a defendant to an originating summons under this rule in the first instance.

(4) Particulars of any summons issued under this rule in a district registry shall be sent by the proper officer to the principal registry for recording in the register of wards.

(5) The date of the minor's birth shall, unless otherwise directed, be stated in the summons, and the plaintiff shall –

  (a) on issuing the summons or before or at the first hearing thereof lodge in the registry out of which the summons issued a certified copy of the entry in the Register of Births or, as the case may be, in the Adopted Children Register relating to the minor, or
  (b) at the first hearing of the summons apply for directions as to proof of birth of the minor in some other manner.

(6) The name of each party to the proceedings shall be qualified by a brief description, in the body of the summons, of his interest in, or relation to, the minor.

(7) Unless the court otherwise directs, the summons shall state the whereabouts of the minor or, as the case may be, that the plaintiff is unaware of his whereabouts.

(8) Upon being served with the summons, every defendant other than the minor shall forthwith lodge in the registry out of which the summons issued a notice stating the address of the defendant and the whereabouts of the minor or, as the case may be, that the defendant is unaware of his whereabouts and, unless the court otherwise directs, serve a copy of the same upon the plaintiff.

(9) Where any party other than the minor changes his address or becomes aware of any change in the whereabouts of the minor after the issue or, as the case may be, service of the summons, he shall, unless the court otherwise directs, forthwith lodge notice of the change in the registry out of which the summons issued and serve a copy of the notice on every other party.

(10) The summons shall contain a notice to the defendant informing him of the requirements of paragraphs (8) and (9).

(11) In this rule any reference to the whereabouts of a minor is a reference to the address at which and the person with whom he is living and any other information relevant to the question where he may be found.

5.2 Enforcement of order by tipstaff

The power of the High Court to secure, through an officer attending upon the court, compliance with any direction relating to a ward of court may be exercised by an order addressed to the tipstaff.

5.3 Where minor ceases to be a ward of court

(1) A minor who, by virtue of section 41(2) of the [Senior Courts Act 1981][1],, becomes a ward of court on the issue of a summons under rule 5.1 shall cease to be a ward of court –

   (a) if an application for an appointment for the hearing of the summons is not made within the period of 21 days after the issue of the summons, at the expiration of that period;
   (b) if an application for such an appointment is made within that period, on the determination of the application made by the summons unless the court hearing it orders that the minor be made a ward of court.

(2) Nothing in paragraph (1) shall be taken as affecting the power of the court under section 41(3) of the said Act to order that any minor who is for the time being a ward of court shall cease to be a ward of court.

(3) If no application for an appointment for the hearing of a summons under rule 5.1 is made within the period of 21 days after the issue of the summons, a notice stating whether the applicant intends to proceed with the application made by the summons must be left at the registry in which the matter is proceeding immediately after the expiration of that period.

NOTES
Amendments.[1] Words inserted: Constitutional Reform Act 2005, s 59(5), Sch 11, Pt 1, para 1(2).

5.4 Adoption of minor who is a ward of court

(1) An application for leave –

   (a) to commence proceedings to adopt a minor who is a ward or
   (b) to commence proceedings to [place or][1] free such a minor for adoption,

may be ex parte to a district judge.

(2) Where a local authority has been granted leave to place a minor who is a ward with foster parents with a view to adoption it shall not be necessary for an application to be made for leave under paragraph (1)(a) or (b) unless the court otherwise directs.

Part II Statutory Instruments

(3) If the applicant for leave under paragraph (1)(a) or (b), or a local authority which has applied for leave as referred to in paragraph (2), or a foster parent so requests, the district judge may direct that any subsequent proceedings shall be conducted with a view to securing that the proposed adopter is not seen by or made known to any respondent or prospective respondent who is not already aware of his identity except with his consent.

(4) In paragraphs (1) and (3) 'proceedings' means proceedings in the High Court or in a county court.

NOTES

Amendments.[1] Words inserted: 2005/2922.

[5.5 Orders for use of secure accommodation

No order shall be made with the effect of placing or keeping a minor in secure accommodation, within the meaning of section 25(1) of the Act of 1989 [unless the minor has been made a party to the summons.][2].][1]

NOTES

Amendments.[1] Rule inserted: SI 1991/2113. [2] Words substituted: SI 1992/456.

[5.6 Notice to provider of refuge

Where a child is staying in a refuge which is certified under section 51(1) or 51(2) of the Act of 1989, the person who is providing that refuge shall be given notice of any application under this Part of these rules in respect of that child.][1]

NOTES

Amendments.[1] Rule inserted: SI 1991/2113.

PART VI
CHILD ABDUCTION AND CUSTODY ...[1]

NOTES

Amendments.[1] Words repealed: SI 1994/3155.

6.1 Interpretation

In this Part, unless the context otherwise requires –

(a) 'the Act' means the Child Abduction and Custody Act 1985 and words or expressions bear the same meaning as in that Act;
(b) 'the Hague Convention' means the convention defined in section 1[1] of the Act and 'the European Convention' means the convention defined in section 12[1] of the Act 1965.

6.2 Mode of application

(1) Except as otherwise provided by this Part, every application under the Hague Convention and the European Convention shall be made by originating

summons, which shall be in Form No. 10 in Appendix A to the Rules of the Supreme Court [and issued out of the principal registry][1].

(2) An application in custody proceedings for a declaration under section 23(2) of the Act shall be made by summons in those proceedings.

NOTES

Amendments.[1] Words inserted: SI 1997/1893.

6.3 Contents of originating summons: general provisions

(1) The originating summons under which any application is made under the Hague Convention or the European Convention shall state –

(a) the name and date of birth of the child in respect of whom the application is made;
(b) the names of the child's parents or guardians;
(c) the whereabouts or suspected whereabouts of the child;
(d) the interest of the plaintiff in the matter and the grounds of the application; and
(e) particulars of any proceedings (including proceedings out of the jurisdiction and concluded proceedings) relating to the child,

and shall be accompanied by all relevant documents including but not limited to the documents specified in Article 8 of the Hague Convention or, as the case may be, Article 13 of the European Convention.

6.4 Contents of originating summons: particular provisions

(1) In applications under the Hague Convention, in addition to the matters specified in rule 6.3 –

(a) the originating summons under which an application is made for the purposes of Article 8 for the return of a child shall state the identity of the person alleged to have removed or retained the child and, if different, the identity of the person with whom the child is presumed to be;
(b) the originating summons under which an application is made for the purposes of Article 15 for a declaration shall identify the proceedings in which the request that such a declaration be obtained was made.

(2) In applications under the European Convention, in addition to the matters specified in rule 6.3, the originating summons shall identify the decision relating to custody or rights of access which is sought to be registered or enforced or in relation to which a declaration that it is not to be recognised is sought.

[(3) Where the application is one to which the Council Regulation also applies, in addition to the matters specified in rule 6.3, the originating summons shall also identify –

(a) any details of measures taken by courts or authorities to ensure the protection of the child after its return to the Member State of habitual residence of which the applicant is aware; and

(b) details of any person with parental responsibility who is not already listed in accordance with rule 6.3.][1]

NOTES

Amendments.[1] Paragraph inserted: SI 2005/264.

6.5 Defendants

The defendants to an application under the Act shall be –

(a) the person alleged to have brought into the United Kingdom the child in respect of whom an application under the Hague Convention is made;

(b) the person with whom the child is alleged to be;

(c) any parent or guardian of the child who is within the United Kingdom and is not otherwise a party;

(d) the person in whose favour a decision relating to custody has been made if he is not otherwise a party; and

(e) any other person who appears to the court to have a sufficient interest in the welfare of the child.

6.6 Acknowledgement of service

The time limited for acknowledging service of an originating summons by which an application is made under the Hague Convention or the European Convention shall be seven days after service of the originating summons (including the day of service) or, in the case of a defendant referred to in rule 6.5(d) or (e), such further time as the Court may direct.

6.7 Evidence

(1) The plaintiff, on issuing an originating summons under the Hague Convention or the European Convention, may lodge affidavit evidence in the principal registry in support of his application and serve a copy of the same on the defendant with the originating summons.

(2) A defendant to an application under the Hague Convention or the European Convention may lodge affidavit evidence in the principal registry and serve a copy of the same on the plaintiff within seven days after service of the originating summons on him.

(3) The plaintiff in an application under the Hague Convention or the European Convention may within seven days thereafter lodge in the principal registry a statement in reply and serve a copy thereof on the defendant.

6.8 Hearing

Any application under the Act (other than an application (a) to join a defendant, (b) to dispense with service or extend the time for acknowledging service, or (c) for the transfer of proceedings) shall be heard and determined by a judge and shall be dealt with in chambers unless the court otherwise directs.

6.9 Dispensing with service

The court may dispense with service of any summons (whether originating or ordinary) in any proceedings under the Act.

6.10 Adjournment of summons

The hearing of the originating summons under which an application under the Hague Convention or the European Convention is made may be adjourned for a period not exceeding 21 days at any one time.

6.11 Stay of proceedings

(1) A party to proceedings under the Hague Convention shall, where he knows that an application relating to the merits of rights of custody is pending in or before a relevant authority, file in the principal registry a concise statement of the nature of the application which is pending, including the authority before which it is pending.

(2) A party –
  (a) to pending proceedings under section 16 of the Act, or
  (b) to proceedings as a result of which a decision relating to custody has been registered under section 16 of the Act,

shall, where he knows that such an application as is specified in section 20(2) of the Act [or section 42(2) of the Child Custody Act 1987 (an Act of Tynwald)][1] is pending in or before a relevant authority, file a concise statement of the nature of the application which is pending.

(3) The proper officer shall on receipt of such a statement as is mentioned in paragraph (1) or (2) notify the relevant authority in which or before whom the application is pending and shall subsequently notify it or him of the result of the proceedings.

(4) On the court receiving notification under paragraph (3) above or equivalent notification from the Court of Session [, the High Court in Northern Ireland or the High Court of Justice of the Isle of Man][1] –

  (a) where the application relates to the merits of rights of custody, all further proceedings in the action shall be stayed unless and until the proceedings under the Hague Convention in the High Court, Court of Session [, High Court in Northern Ireland or the High Court of Justice of the Isle of Man,][1], as the case may be, are dismissed, and the parties to the action shall be notified by the proper officer of the stay and of any such dismissal accordingly, and
  (b) where the application is such a one as is specified in section 20(2) of the Act, the proper officer shall notify the parties to the action.

(5) In this rule 'relevant authority' includes the High Court, a county court, a magistrates' court, the Court of Session, a sheriff court, a children's hearing within the meaning of Part III of the Social Work (Scotland) Act 1968, [the High Court in Northern Ireland or the High Court of Justice of the Isle of Man][1], a county court in Northern Ireland, a court of summary jurisdiction in Northern Ireland [, the High Court of Justice of the Isle of Man, a court of summary jurisdiction in the Isle of Man][1] or the Secretary of State.

NOTES

Amendments.[1] Words inserted or substituted: SI 1994/2890.

[6.11A Stay under the Council Regulation

Rule 4.27A applies to proceedings under this Part as it applies to proceedings under Part 4 but as if –

(a) for 'application under rule 4.4 is made' there is read 'presentation of an originating summons'; and
(b) for 'application' in sub-paragraph (2) there is read 'originating summons'.][1]

NOTES

Amendments.[1] Rule inserted: SI 2005/264.

6.12 Transfer of proceedings

(1) At any stage in the proceedings under the Act the court may, of its own motion or on the application by summons of any party to the proceedings issued on two days' notice, order that the proceedings be transferred to the Court of Session [, the High Court in Northern Ireland or the High Court of Justice of the Isle of Man][1].

(2) Where an order is made under paragraph (1) the proper officer shall send a copy of the order, which shall state the grounds therefor, together with the originating summons, the documents accompanying it and any evidence, to the Court of Session [, the High Court in Northern Ireland or the High Court of Justice of the Isle of Man][1], as the case may be.

(3) Where proceedings are transferred to the Court of Session [, the High Court in Northern Ireland or the High Court of Justice of the Isle of Man][1] the costs of the whole proceedings both before and after the transfer shall be at the discretion of the Court to which the proceedings are transferred.

(4) Where proceedings are transferred to the High Court from the Court of Session [, the High Court in Northern Ireland or the High Court of Justice of the Isle of Man][1] the proper officer shall notify the parties of the transfer and the proceedings shall continue as if they had begun by originating summons under rule 6.2.

NOTES

Amendments.[1] Words substituted: SI 1994/2890.

6.13 Interim directions

An application for interim directions under section 5 or section 19 of the Act may where the case is one of urgency be made ex parte on affidavit but shall otherwise be made by summons.

6.14

...[1]

NOTES

Amendments.[1] Rule revoked: SI 1992/2067.

6.15 Revocation and variation of registered decisions

(1) This rule applies to decisions which have been registered under section 16 of the Act and are subsequently varied or revoked by an authority in the Contracting State in which they were made.

(2) The court shall, on cancelling the registration of a decision which has been revoked, notify –

   (a) the person appearing to the court to have care of the child,
   (b) the person on whose behalf the application for registration of the decision was made, and
   (c) any other party to that application,

of the cancellation.

(3) The court shall, on being notified of the variation of a decision, notify –

   (a) the person appearing to the court to have care of the child, and
   (b) any party to the application for registration of the decision

of the variation and any such person may apply by summons in the proceedings for the registration of the decision, for the purpose of making representations to the court before the registration is varied.

(4) Any person appearing to the court to have an interest in the matter may apply by summons in the proceedings for the registration of a decision for the cancellation or variation of the registration.

6.16 Orders for disclosure of information

At any stage in proceedings under the European Convention the court may, if it has reason to believe that any person may have relevant information about the child who is the subject of those proceedings, order that person to disclose such information and may for that purpose order that the person attend before it or file affidavit evidence.

[6.17 Applications and orders under sections 33 and 34 of the Family Law Act 1986

(1) In this rule 'the 1986 Act' means the Family Law Act 1986.

(2) An application under section 33 of the 1986 Act shall be in Form C4 and an order made under that section shall be in Form C30.

(3) An application under section 34 of the 1986 Act shall be in Form C3 and an order made under that section shall be in Form C31.

(4) An application under section 33 or section 34 of the 1986 Act may be made ex parte in which case the applicant shall file the application –

    (a) where the application is made by telephone, within 24 hours after the making of the application, or

    (b) in any other case at the time when the application is made,

and shall serve a copy of the application on each respondent 48 hours after the making of the order.

(5) Where the court refuses to make an order on an ex parte application it may direct that the application be made inter partes.][1]

NOTES

Amendments.[1] Rule inserted: SI 1994/3155.

[6.18 Registration of registered decisions

There shall be kept in the principal registry by the proper officer a register of decisions registered under section 16 of the Act together with any variation of those decisions as made under section 17 of the Act][1]

NOTES

Amendments.[1] Rule inserted: SI 2005/264.

PART VII
ENFORCEMENT OF ORDERS

Chapter 1
General

7.1 Enforcement of order for payment of money etc

(1) Before any process is issued for the enforcement of an order made in family proceedings for the payment of money to any person, an affidavit shall be filed verifying the amount due under the order and showing how that amount is arrived at.

In a case to which CCR Order 25 rule 11 (which deals with the enforcement of a High Court judgment in the county court) applies, the information required to be given in an affidavit under this paragraph may be given in the affidavit filed pursuant to that rule.

(2) Except with the leave of the district judge, no writ of fieri facias or warrant of execution shall be issued to enforce payment of any sum due under an order for ancillary relief or an order made under the provisions of section 27 of the

Act of 1973 [or an order under Part 9 of Schedule 5 to the Act of 2004][1] where an application for a variation order is pending.

(3) Where a warrant of execution has been issued to enforce an order made in family proceedings pending in the principal registry which are treated as pending in a [designated county court][1], the goods and chattels against which the warrant has been issued shall, wherever they are situate, be treated for the purposes of section 103 of the County Courts Act 1984 as being out of the jurisdiction of the principal registry.

(4) The Attachment of Earnings Act 1971 and CCR Order 27 (which deals with attachment of earnings) shall apply to the enforcement of an order made in family proceedings in the principal registry which are treated as pending in a [designated county court][1] as if the order were an order made by such a court.

[(5) Where –

(a) an application under CCR Order 25, rule 3 (which deals with the oral examination of a judgment debtor) relates to an order made by a divorce county court, the application shall be made to such divorce county court as in the opinion of the applicant is nearest to the place where the debtor resides, or carries on business,

(b) an application under CCR Order 25, rule 3 (which deals with the oral examination of a judgment debtor) relates to an order made by a civil partnership proceedings county court, the application shall be made to such civil partnership proceedings county court as in the opinion of the applicant is nearest to the place where the debtor resides, or carries on business, and

(c) in either case, paragraph (2) of rule 3 shall not apply.

(6) In a case to which paragraph (5) relates there shall be filed the affidavit required by paragraph (1) of this rule and, except where the application is made to the court in which the order sought to be enforced was made, a copy of the order shall be exhibited to the affidavit.][1]

NOTES

Amendments.[1] Words and paragraphs inserted or substituted: SI 2005/2922.

7.2 Committal and injunction

(1) Subject to RSC Order 52, rule 6 (which, except in certain cases, requires an application for an order of committal to be heard in open court) an application for an order of committal in family proceedings pending in the High Court shall be made by summons.

(2) Where no judge is conveniently available to hear the application, then, without prejudice to CCR Order 29, rule 3(2) (which in certain circumstances gives jurisdiction to a district judge) an application for –

(a) the discharge of any person committed, or
(b) the discharge by consent of an injunction granted by a judge,

may be made to the district judge who may, if satisfied of the urgency of the matter and that it is expedient to do so, make any order on the application which a judge could have made.

(3) Where an order or warrant for the committal of any person to prison has been made or issued in family proceedings pending in the principal registry which are treated as pending in a [designated county court][2] [or a county court][1], that person shall, wherever he may be, be treated for the purposes of section 122 of the County Courts Act 1984 as being out of the jurisdiction of the principal registry; but if the committal is for failure to comply with the terms of an injunction, the order or warrant may, if [the court][1] so directs, be executed by the tipstaff within any county court district.

[(3A) Where an order or warrant for the arrest or committal of any person has been made or issued in proceedings under Part IV of the Family Law Act 1996 pending in the principal registry which are treated as pending in a county court, the order or warrant may, if the court so directs, be executed by the tipstaff within any county court district.][1]

(4) For the purposes of section 118 of the County Courts Act 1984 in its application to the hearing of family proceedings at the Royal Courts of Justice [or the principal registry][1], the tipstaff shall be deemed to be an officer of the court.

NOTES

Amendments.[1] Words inserted or substituted and paragraph inserted: SI 1997/1893.[2] Words substituted: SI 2005/2922.

7.3 Transfer of county court order to High Court

(1) Any person who desires the transfer to the High Court of any order made by a [designated county court][1] in family proceedings except an order for periodical payments or for the recovery of arrears of periodical payments shall apply to the court ex parte by affidavit stating the amount which remains due under the order, and on the filing of the application the transfer shall have effect.

(2) Where an order is so transferred, it shall have the same force and effect and the same proceedings may be taken on it as if it were an order of the High Court.

NOTES

Amendments.[1] Words substituted: SI 2005/2922.

****

Chapter 3
Registration and Enforcement of Custody Orders

7.7 Registration under Family Law Act 1986

(1) In this Chapter, unless the context otherwise requires –

'the appropriate court', means in relation to Scotland, the Court of Session and, in relation to Northern Ireland, the High Court [and, in relation to a specified dependent territory, the corresponding court in that territory][1];

['the appropriate officer' means, in relation to the Court of Session, the Deputy Principal Clerk of Session, in relation to the High Court in Northern Ireland, the Master (Care and Protection) of that court and, in relation to the appropriate court in a specified dependent territory, the corresponding officer of that court;][1]

...[1]

'Part I order' means an order under Part I of the Act of 1986;

...[1]

'registration' means registration under Part I of the Act of 1986, and 'register' and 'registered' shall be construed accordingly;

['specified dependent territory' means a dependent territory specified in column 1 of Schedule 1 to the Family Law Act 1986 (Dependent Territories) Order 1991.][1]

(2) The prescribed officer for the purposes of sections 27(4) and 28(1) of the Act shall be the [family proceedings department manager][2] of the principal registry and the functions of the court under sections 27(3) and 28(1) of the Act of 1986 shall be performed by the proper officer.

NOTES

Amendments.[1] Words inserted or repealed: SI 1994/2890. [2] Words substituted: SI 1997/1056.

7.8 Application to register English Part I order

(1) An application under section 27 of the Act of 1986 for the registration of a Part I order made by the High Court shall be made by lodging in the principal registry or the district registry, as the case may be, a certified copy of the order, together with a copy of any order which has varied any of the terms of the original order and an affidavit by the applicant in support of his application, with a copy thereof.

(2) An application under section 27 of the Act of 1986 for the registration of a Part I order made by a county court shall be made by filing in that court a certified copy of the order, together with a certified copy of any order which has varied any of the terms of the original order and an affidavit in support of the application, with a copy thereof.

(3) The affidavit in support under paragraphs (1) and (2) above shall state –

(a) the name and address of the applicant and his interest under the order;
(b) the name and date of birth of the child in respect of whom the order was made, his whereabouts or suspected whereabouts and the name of any person with whom he is alleged to be;
(c) the name and address of any other person who has an interest under the order and whether it has been served on him;
[(d) in which of the jurisdictions of Scotland, Northern Ireland or a specified dependent territory the order is to be registered;][1]

(e) that, to the best of the applicant's information and belief, the order is in force;
(f) whether, and if so where, the order is already registered; and
(g) details of any order known to the applicant which affects the child and is in force in the jurisdiction in which the Part I order is to be registered;

and there shall be exhibited to the affidavit any document relevant to the application.

(4) Where the documents referred to in paragraphs (1) and (3), or (2) and (3), as the case may be are to be sent to the appropriate court, the proper officer shall –

(a) retain the original affidavit and send the other documents to [the appropriate officer]¹;
(b) record the fact of transmission in the records of the court; and
(c) file a copy of the documents.

(5) On receipt of notice of the registration of a Part I order in the appropriate court the proper officer shall record the fact of registration in the records of the court.

(6) If it appears to the proper officer that the Part I is no longer in force or that the child has attained the age of 16, he shall refuse to send the documents to the appropriate court and shall within 14 days of such refusal give notice of it, and the reason for it, to the applicant.

(7) If the proper officer refuses to send the documents to the appropriate court, the applicant may apply to the judge in chambers for an order that the documents (or any of them) be sent to the appropriate court.

NOTES
Amendments.¹ Words substituted: SI 1994/2890.

7.9 [Registration of orders made in Scotland, Northern Ireland or a specified dependent territory]¹

On receipt of a certified copy of an order made in [Scotland, Northern Ireland or a specified dependent territory]¹ for registration, the prescribed officer shall –

(a) record the order in the register by entering particulars of –
  (i) the name and address of the applicant and his interest under the order;
  (ii) the name and whereabouts or suspected whereabouts of the child, his date of birth, and the date on which he will attain the age of 16; and
  (iii) the terms of the order, its date and the court which made it;
(b) file the certified copy and accompanying documents; and
(c) give notice to the court which sent the certified copy and to the applicant for registration that the order has been registered.

NOTES

Amendments.[1] Words substituted: SI 1994/2890.

7.10 Revocation and variation of English order

(1) Where a Part I order which is registered in the appropriate court is revoked or varied, the proper officer of the court making the subsequent order shall –

   (a) send a certified copy of that order to [the appropriate officer][1], as the case may be, and to the court which made the Part I order, if that court is different from the court making the subsequent order, for filing by that court;
   (b) record the fact of transmission in the records of the court; and
   (c) file a copy of the order.

(2) On receipt of notice from the appropriate court of the amendment of its register, the proper officer in the court which made the Part I order and in the court which made the subsequent order shall each record the fact of amendment.

NOTES

Amendments.[1] Words substituted: SI 1994/2890.

7.11 [Registration of revoked, recalled or varied orders made in Scotland, Northern Ireland or a specified dependent territory][1]

(1) On receipt of a certified copy of an order made in [Scotland, Northern Ireland or a specified dependent territory][1] which revokes, recalls or varies a registered Part I order, the proper officer shall enter particulars of the revocation, recall or variation, as the case may be, in the register, and give notice of the entry to –

   (a) the court which sent the certified copy,
   (b) if different, the court which made the Part I order,
   (c) the applicant for registration, and
   (d) if different, the applicant for the revocation, recall or variation of the order.

(2) An application under section 28(2) of the Act of 1986 shall be made by summons and may be heard and determined by a district judge.

(3) If the applicant for the Part I order is not the applicant under section 28(2) of the Act of 1986 he shall be made a defendant to the application.

(4) Where the court cancels a registration of its own motion or on an application under paragraph (2), the proper officer shall amend the register accordingly and shall give notice of the amendment to the court which made the Part I order.

NOTES

Amendments.[1] Words substituted: SI 1994/2890.

7.12 Interim directions

(1) An application for interim directions under section 29 of the Act of 1986 may be heard and determined by a district judge.

(2) The parties to the proceedings for enforcement and, if he is not a party thereto, the applicant for the Part I order, shall be made parties to the application.

7.13 Staying and dismissal of enforcement proceedings

(1) An application under section 30(1) or 31(1) of the Act of 1986 may be heard and determined by a district judge.

(2) The parties to the proceedings for enforcement which are sought to be stayed and, if he is not a party thereto, the applicant for the Part I order shall be made parties to an application under either of the said sections.

(3) Where the court makes an order under section 30(2) or (3) or section 31(3) of the Act of 1986, the proper officer shall amend the register accordingly and shall give notice of the amendment to the court which made the Part I order and to the applicants for registration, for enforcement and for the stay or dismissal of the proceedings for enforcement.

7.14 Particulars of other proceedings

A party to proceedings for or relating to a Part I order who knows of other proceedings (including proceedings out of the jurisdiction and concluded proceedings) which relate to the child concerned shall file an affidavit stating –

(a) in which jurisdiction and court the other proceedings were instituted;
(b) the nature and current state of such proceedings and the relief claimed or granted;
(c) the names of the parties to such proceedings and their relationship to the child; and
(d) if applicable, and if known, the reasons why the relief claimed in the proceedings for or relating to the Part I order was not claimed in the other proceedings.

7.15 Inspection of register

The following persons, namely –

(a) the applicant for registration of a registered Part I order,
(b) any person who satisfies a district judge that he has an interest under the Part I order, and
(c) any person who obtains the leave of a district judge,

may inspect any entry in the register relating to the order and may bespeak copies of the order and of any document relating thereto.

****

PART VIII
APPEALS

[[8.A1 Interpretation

(1) In this Part –

(a) 'the court below' means the court from which, or the person from whom, the appeal lies;
(b) 'the appeal court' means the court to which the appeal is made;
(c) ...³
(d) 'deduction order appeal' means an appeal under regulation 25AB(1)(a) to (d) of the Child Support (Collection and Enforcement) Regulations 1992.

(2) For the purposes of a deduction order appeal –

(a) 'the appellant' means the person who brings or seeks to bring an appeal; and
(b) 'the respondent' means –
   (i) the Commission and any person other than the appellant who was served with an order under section 32A(1), 32E(1) or 32F(1) of the Act of 1991; and
   (ii) a person who is permitted by the appeal court to be a party to the appeal.]¹]²

NOTES

Amendments.¹ Rule inserted: SI 2009/636. ² Rule substituted: SI 2009/2027. ³ Paragraph revoked: SI 2010/786.

8.1 Appeals from district judges

(1) Except where paragraph (2) applies, any party may appeal from an order or decision made or given by the district judge in family proceedings in a county court to a judge on notice; and in such a case –

(a) CCR Order 13 rule 1(10) (which enables the judge to vary or rescind an order made by the district judge in the course of proceedings), and
(b) CCR Order 37 rule 6 (which gives a right of appeal to the judge from a judgment or final decision of the district judge),

shall not apply to the order or decision.

(2) Any order or decision granting or varying an order (or refusing to do so) –

(a) on an application for ancillary relief, or
(b) in proceedings to which rules 3.1, 3.2, 3.3, [or 3.6]¹ apply,

shall be treated as a final order for the purposes of CCR Order 37, rule 6.

[(3) On any appeal to which paragraph (2) applies –

(a) the appeal shall be limited to a review of the decision or order of the district judge unless the judge considers that in the circumstances of the case it would be in the interests of justice to hold a rehearing;

(b) oral evidence or evidence which was not before the district judge may be admitted if in all circumstances of the case it would be in the interests of justice to do so, irrespective of whether the appeal be by way of review or rehearing.]²

(4) Unless the court otherwise orders, any notice under this rule must be issued within 14 days of the order or decision appealed against and served not less than 14 days before the day fixed for the hearing of the appeal.

(5) Appeals under this rule shall be heard in chambers unless the judge otherwise directs.

(6) Unless the court otherwise orders, an appeal under this rule shall not operate as a stay of proceedings on the order or decision appealed against.

[[(7) This rule does not apply to –
- (a) the proceedings referred to in rule 8.2; and
- (b) any appeal by a party to proceedings for the assessment of costs against a decision in those proceedings.]³]²

NOTES

Amendments.¹ Words substituted: SI 1997/1893.² Paragraphs substituted and inserted: SI 2003/184.³ Paragraph substituted: SI 2009/636.

[8.1A

...²]¹

NOTES

Amendments.¹ Rule inserted: SI 1997/1893.² Rule revoked: SI 2009/636.

[8.1B

...²]¹

NOTES

Amendments.¹ Rule inserted: SI 2008/2446.² Rule revoked: SI 2009/636.

[8.2 [Appeals to a county court and appeals from district judges under the Act of 1989 or Parts 4 and 4A of the Family Law Act 1996 or relating to deduction order appeals]²

(1) Rules 8.2A to 8.2H apply where –
- (a) there is an appeal under –
  - (i) section 4(7) of the Maintenance Orders Act 1958;
  - (ii) section 29 of the Domestic Proceedings and Magistrates' Courts Act 1978;
  - (iii) section 60(5) of the Act of 1986;
  - (iv) section 94(1) to (9) of the Act of 1989;
  - (v) section 61 of the Family Law Act 1996; ...²
  - [(vi) any other enactment giving a person a right of appeal against a decision of a magistrates' court; or

(vii) regulation 25AB(1)(a) to (d) of the Child Support (Collection and Enforcement) Regulations 1992; or]²
(b) an appeal lies from any decision of a district judge to the judge of the court in which the decision was made in proceedings –
  (i) listed in rule 4.1(2); …²
  (ii) to which Parts 4 and 4A of the Family Law Act 1996 apply[; or
  (iii) relating to a deduction order appeal]².

(2) In proceedings referred to in paragraph (1)(b)…², any party may appeal from an order or decision made or given by the district judge in a county court to a judge on notice and CCR Order 13, rule 1(10) and Order 37, rule 6 shall not apply.

(3) Appeals under paragraph (1)(b) shall be heard in chambers unless the judge directs otherwise.

(4) Rules 8.2A to 8.2H are subject to any enactment.]¹.

NOTES

Amendments.¹ Rule substituted: SI 2009/636. ² Heading substituted, words revoked and inserted, and subparas substituted and inserted: SI 2009/2027.

[8.2A Notice of appeal

(1) The appellant shall file and serve on –

(a) the parties to the proceedings in the court below [and in the case of a deduction order appeal, the Commission and any other respondent]²;
(b) any children's guardian; and
(c) where applicable, the local authority that prepared a report under section 14A(8) or (9) of the Act of 1989,

the documents set out in paragraph (2).

(2) The documents referred to in paragraph (1) are –

(a) notice in writing of the appeal, setting out the grounds of the appeal;
(b) a certified copy of the summons or application and of the order appealed against, and of any order staying its execution;
(c) a copy of any notes of the evidence; and
(d) a copy of any reasons given for the decision.

(3) The appellant shall file and serve the notice of appeal in accordance with paragraph (1) –

(a) within 14 days after the determination against which the appeal is brought;
(b) in the case of an appeal against an order under section 38(1) of the Act of 1989, within 7 days after the making of the order;
(c) in the case of an appeal against an order under section 29 of the Domestic Proceedings and Magistrates' Courts Act 1978, within 21 days after the making of the order; …²
[(cc) in the case of a deduction order appeal, within 21 days of –
  (i) where the appellant is a deposit-taker, service of the order;

(ii) where the appellant is a liable person, receipt of the order; or
(iii) where the appellant is either a deposit-taker or a liable person, the date of receipt of notification of the decision; or][2]
(d) with the leave of the court to which, or judge to whom, the appeal is brought, within such other time as that court or judge may direct.

(4) Subject to any direction of the court to which, or judge to whom, the appeal is brought, the appellant shall file and serve the documents mentioned in paragraph (2)(b) to (d) as soon as practicable after filing and service of the notice of appeal ...[2].

(5) Where the magistrates' court is the court below, the appellant shall serve the documents mentioned in paragraph (2)(a) and (b) on the designated officer for that court.][1]

[(6) In the case of a deduction order appeal, the Commission shall provide to the court and serve on all other parties to the appeal any information and evidence relevant to the making of the decision or order being appealed, within 14 days of receipt of the notice of appeal.

(7) For the purposes of paragraph (3)(cc) –

(a) references to 'liable person' and 'deposit-taker' are to be interpreted in accordance with section 32E of the Act of 1991 and regulation 25A(2) of the Child Support (Collection and Enforcement) Regulations 1992 and section 54 of that Act, respectively; and
(b) the liable person is to be treated as having received the order or notification of the decision 2 days after it was posted by the Commission.][2]

NOTES

Amendments.[1] Rule substituted for r 8.2 as originally enacted: SI 2009/636. [2] Words inserted and deleted, and paragraphs and subparagraph inserted: SI 2009/2027.

[8.2B Respondents

(1) Subject to [paragraphs (2) and (3)][2], a respondent who wishes to contend –

(a) on the appeal that the decision of the court below [or, in a deduction order appeal, the order or decision of the Commission][2] should be varied, either in any event or in the event of the appeal being allowed in whole or in part;
(b) that the decision of the court below [or, in a deduction order appeal, the order or decision of the Commission][2] should be affirmed on grounds other than those relied upon by that court; or
(c) by way of cross-appeal that the decision of the court below [or, in a deduction order appeal, the order or decision of the Commission][2] was wrong in whole or in part,

shall, within 14 days of receipt of notice of the appeal, file and serve on all other parties to the appeal a notice in writing, setting out the grounds upon which the respondent relies.

(2) No notice under paragraph (1) may be filed or served in an appeal against an order under section 38 of the Act of 1989.

[(3) Where the Commission as a respondent, wishes to contend that its order or decision should be –

(a) varied, either in any event or in the event of the appeal being allowed in whole or in part; or
(b) affirmed on different grounds from those on which it relied when making the order or decision,

it shall, within 14 days of receipt of notice of the appeal, file and serve on all other parties to the appeal a notice in writing, setting out the grounds upon which it relies.]²]¹

NOTES

Amendments.¹ Rule substituted for r 8.2 as originally enacted: SI 2009/636. ² Words substituted and inserted, and paragraph inserted: SI 2009/2027.

[[8.2C Stay

(1) Subject to paragraph (2), unless the court orders otherwise, an appeal under rule 8.2(1) shall not operate as a stay of proceedings on the order or decision appealed against.

(2) Paragraph (1) shall not apply to an appeal made against an order under section 32F(1) of the Act of 1991.]²]¹

NOTES

Amendments.¹ Rule substituted for r 8.2 as originally enacted: SI 2009/636. ² Rule further substituted: SI 2009/2027.

[8.2D Amendment of appeal notice

(1) The appellant may amend the appeal notice, without leave, by serving a supplementary notice not less than 7 days before the date of the hearing of the appeal, on each of the persons on whom the notice to be amended was served.

(2) Within 2 days after service of a supplementary notice under paragraph (1) the appellant must file two copies of the notice in the court in which the appeal notice was filed.

(3) Except with the leave of the court hearing the appeal, the appellant may not rely on grounds other than those stated in the notice of appeal or any supplementary notice under paragraph (1).

(4) The court may amend the grounds of appeal or make any other order, on such terms as it thinks just, to ensure the determination on the merits of the real question in controversy between the parties.]¹

NOTES

Amendments.¹ Rule substituted for r 8.2 as originally enacted: SI 2009/636.

[8.2E Powers of a district judge

(1) A district judge may –

    (a)   dismiss an appeal to which this rule applies –
          (i)   for want of prosecution; or
          (ii)   with the consent of the parties; or
    (b)   give leave for the appeal to be withdrawn,

and may deal with any question of costs arising out of the dismissal or withdrawal.

(2) Unless the court directs otherwise, any interlocutory application in an appeal under rule 8.2 (1)(a) may be made to a district judge.

[(3) A district judge may hear any deduction order appeal.][2]][1]

NOTES

Amendments.[1] Rule substituted for r 8.2 as originally enacted: SI 2009/636. [2] Paragraph inserted: SI 2009/2027.

[8.2F Appeal court's powers

(1) In relation to an appeal the appeal court has all the powers of the court below.

(2) The appeal court has power to –

    (a)   affirm, set aside or vary any order or judgment made or given by the court below;
    (b)   refer any application or issue for determination by the court below;
    (c)   order a new hearing;
    (d)   make orders for the payment of interest;
    (e)   make a costs order.

(3) The appeal court may exercise its powers in relation to the whole or part of an order of the lower court.

[(4) Paragraph (2)(d) of this rule does not apply in the case of an appeal against the decision of a district judge in proceedings relating to a deduction order appeal.

(5) This rule does not apply to a deduction order appeal.[2]][1]

NOTES

Amendments.[1] Rule substituted for r 8.2 as originally enacted: SI 2009/636. [2] Paragraphs inserted: SI 2009/2027.

[8.2FF Appeal court's powers: deduction order appeals

In the case of a deduction order appeal –

    (a)   the appeal court has power to –
          (i)   affirm or set aside the order or decision;
          (ii)   remit the matter to the Commission for the order or decision to be reconsidered, with appropriate directions;

(iii) refer any application or issue for determination by the Commission;
(iv) make a costs order; and
(b) the appeal court may exercise its powers in relation to the whole or part of an order or decision of the Commission.][1]

NOTES

Amendments.[1] Rule inserted: SI 2009/2027.

[8.2G Hearing of appeals

(1) [Subject to paragraph (2A), every][2] appeal will be limited to a review of the decision of the court below unless –

(a) an enactment makes different provision for a particular category of appeal; or
(b) the court considers that in the circumstances of an individual appeal it would be in the interests of justice to hold a re-hearing.

(2) [Subject to paragraph (2A), unless][2] it orders otherwise, the appeal court will not receive –

(a) oral evidence; or
(b) evidence which was not before the court below.

[(2A) In the case of a deduction order appeal, the appeal will be a re-hearing, unless the appeal court orders otherwise.][2]

(3) The appeal court will allow an appeal where the decision of the court below [or, in a deduction order appeal, the order or decision of the Commission][2] was –

(a) wrong; or
[(b) unjust because of a serious procedural or other irregularity in –
  (i) the proceedings in the court below; or
  (ii) the making of an order or decision by the Commission][2]

(4) The appeal court may draw any inference of fact which it considers justified on the evidence.][1]

NOTES

Amendments.[1] Rule substituted for r 8.2 as originally enacted: SI 2009/636. [2] Words substituted, paragraph inserted and subparagraph substituted: SI 2009/2027.

[8.2H Appeals from orders made under Parts 4 and 4A of the Family Law Act 1996

Where an appeal is brought against the making of a hospital order or a guardianship order under the Mental Health Act 1983 a copy of any written evidence considered by the magistrates' court under section 37(1) of the 1983 Act shall be sent by the designated officer to the county court in which the documents relating to the appeal are filed.][1]

Part II Statutory Instruments

NOTES

Amendments.¹ Rule substituted for r 8.2 as originally enacted: SI 2009/636.

[8.3 Appeals under section 13 of the Administration of Justice Act 1960

[(1)]² Proceedings within paragraph 3(d) of Schedule 1 to the [Senior Courts Act 1981]³ shall be heard and determined by a Divisional Court of the Family Division ...².

[(2) On entering the appeal, or as soon as practicable thereafter, the appellant shall, unless otherwise directed, lodge in the principal registry –

(a) three certified copies of the summons and of the order appealed against, and of any order staying its execution;
(b) three copies of the clerk's notes of the evidence;
(c) three copies of the justices' reasons for their decision;
(d) a certificate that notice of motion has been duly served on the clerk and on every party affected by the appeal; and
(e) where the notice of motion includes an application to extend the time for bringing the appeal, a certificate (and a copy) by the appellant's solicitor, or the appellant if he is acting in person, setting out the reasons for the delay and the relevant dates.]²]¹

NOTES

Amendments.¹ Rule inserted: SI 1991/2113.² Paragraph numbered as such, words revoked and paragraph inserted: SI 2009/636. ³ Words substituted: Constitutional Reform Act 2005, s 59(5), Sch 11, Pt 1, para 1(2).

[8.4 Appeal under section 8(1) of the Gender Recognition Act 2004

(1) RSC Order 55 applies to an appeal to the High Court under section 8(1) of the Gender Recognition Act 2004 subject to the modifications made by this rule.

(2) The notice of the originating motion must be –

(a) issued out of the principal registry;
(b) served on the Secretary of State in addition to the person to be served under RSC Order 55, rule 4(1).

(3) The Secretary of State may appear and be heard in the proceedings on the appeal.

(4) Where the High Court issues a gender recognition certificate under section 8(3)(a) of the Gender Recognition Act 2004, the proper officer must send a copy of that certificate to the Secretary of State.]¹

NOTES

Amendments.¹ Rule inserted: SI 2005/559.

PART IX
DISABILITY

9.1 Interpretation and application of Part IX

(1) In this Part –

['the 2005 Act' means the Mental Capacity Act 2005;
'child' means a person under 18;
'deputy' has the meaning given in section 16(2)(b) of the 2005 Act;
'enduring power of attorney' has the meaning given in Schedule 4 to the 2005 Act;
'lasting power of attorney' has the meaning given in section 9 of the 2005 Act;][3]
...[3]
...[3]
...[3]
['protected party' means a party, or an intended party, who lacks capacity (within the meaning of the 2005 Act) to conduct the proceedings;][3]

(2) So far as they relate to [children][3] [who are the subject of applications],[1] the provisions of this Part of these rules shall not apply to proceedings which are specified proceedings within the meaning of section 41(6) of the Children Act 1989 and, with respect to proceedings which are dealt with together with specified proceedings, this Part shall have effect subject to the said section 41 and Part IV of these rules.

[(3) Rule 9.2A shall apply only to proceedings under the Act of 1989[, Part 4A of the Family Law Act 1996][4] or the inherent jurisdiction of the High Court with respect to [children][3].][2]

NOTES

Amendments.[1] Words inserted: SI 1991/2113. [2] Words inserted: SI 1992/456. [3] Definitions inserted and revoked, and words substituted: SI 2007/2187. [4] Words inserted: SI 2008/2446.

9.2 [Child or protected party][3] must sue by next friend etc

(1) [Except where rule 9.2A or any other rule otherwise provides, a [child or protected party][3] may begin and prosecute any family proceedings only by his next friend and may defend any such proceedings only][2] by his guardian ad litem and, except as otherwise provided by this rule, it shall not be necessary for a guardian ad litem to be appointed by the court.

(2) No person's name shall be used in any proceedings as next friend of a [child or protected party][3] unless he is the Official Solicitor or the documents mentioned in paragraph (7) have been filed.

(3) Where a person [has authority as a deputy][3] under Part VII to conduct legal proceedings in the name of a [protected party][3] or on his behalf, that person shall, subject to [paragraph (2)][1] be entitled to be next friend or guardian ad litem of the [protected party][3] in any family proceedings to which his [power][3] extends.

(4) Where a person entitled to defend any family proceedings is a [protected party]³ and there is no person [with authority as a deputy]³ under Part VII to defend the proceedings in his name or on his behalf, then –

(a) the Official Solicitor shall, if he consents, be the [protected party's]³ guardian ad litem, but at any stage of the proceedings an application may be made on not less than four days' notice to the Official Solicitor, for the appointment of some other person as guardian;

(b) in any other case, an application may be made on behalf of the [protected party]³ for the appointment of a guardian ad litem;

and there shall be filed in support of any application under this paragraph the documents mentioned in paragraph (7).

(5) Where a petition, answer, originating application or originating summons has been served on a person whom there is reasonable ground for believing to be a [child or protected party]³ and no notice of intention to defend has been given, or answer or affidavit in answer filed, on his behalf, the party at whose instance the document was served shall, before taking any further steps in the proceedings, apply to a district judge for directions as to whether a guardian ad litem should be appointed to act for that person in the cause, and on any such application the district judge may, if he considers it necessary in order to protect the interests of the person served, order that some proper person be appointed his guardian ad litem.

(6) [Except where a [child]³ is prosecuting or defending proceedings under rule 9.2A, no]² notice of intention to defend shall be given, or answer or affidavit in answer filed, by or on behalf of a person under disability unless the person giving the notice or filing the answer or affidavit –

(a) is the Official Solicitor or, in a case to which paragraph (4) applies, is the Official Solicitor or has been appointed by the court to be guardian ad litem; or

(b) in any other case, has filed the documents mentioned in paragraph (7).

(7) The documents referred to in paragraphs (2), (4) and (6) are –

(a) a written consent to act by the proposed next friend or guardian ad litem;

(b) where the person ...³ is a [protected party]³ and the proposed next friend or guardian ad litem [has authority as a deputy]³ to conduct the proceedings in his name or on his behalf, an office copy, sealed with the seal of the Court of Protection, of [the document conferring his authority to act]³; and

(c) except where the proposed next friend or guardian ad litem is authorised as mentioned in sub-paragraph (b), a certificate by the solicitor acting for the person under disability –

(i) that he knows or believes that the person to whom the certificate relates is a [child]³ or [protected party]³, stating (in the case of a [protected party]³) the grounds of his knowledge or belief and, where the person ...³ is a [protected party]³, that there is no person [with authority as a deputy to conduct the proceedings in the name of a protected party or on his behalf]³, and

(ii) that the person named in the certificate as next friend or guardian ad litem has no interest in the cause or matter in question adverse to that of the [child or protected party]³ and that he is a proper person to be next friend or guardian.

NOTES

Amendments.¹ Words substituted: SI 1991/2113.² Words substituted: SI 1992/456.³ Words substituted and revoked: SI 2007/2187.

[9.2A Certain [children]³ may sue without next friend etc

(1) Where a person entitled to begin, prosecute or defend any proceedings to which this rule applies, is a [child]³ to whom this Part applies, he may subject to paragraph (4), begin, prosecute or defend, as the case may be, such proceedings without a next friend or guardian ad litem –

(a) where he has obtained the leave of the court for that purpose; or
(b) where a solicitor –
  (i) considers that the [child]³ is able, having regard to his understanding, to give instructions in relation to the proceedings; and
  (ii) has accepted instructions from the [child]³ to act for him in the proceedings and, where the proceedings have begun, is so acting.

(2) A [child]³ shall be entitled to apply for the leave of the court under paragraph (1)(a) without a next friend or guardian ad litem either –

(a) by filing a written request for leave setting out the reasons for the application, or
(b) by making an oral request for leave at any hearing in the proceedings.

(3) On considering a request for leave filed under paragraph (2)(a), the court shall either –

(a) grant the request, whereupon the proper officer shall communicate the decision to the [child]³ and, where the leave relates to the prosecution or defence of existing proceedings, to the other parties to those proceedings, or
(b) direct that the request be heard ex parte, whereupon the proper officer shall fix a date for such a hearing and give to the [child]³ making the request such notice of the date so fixed as the court may direct.

(4) Where a [child]³ has a next friend or guardian ad litem in proceedings and the [child]³ wishes to prosecute or defend the remaining stages of the proceedings without a next friend or guardian ad litem, the [child]³ may apply to the court for leave for that purpose and for the removal of the next friend or guardian ad litem; and paragraph (2) shall apply to the application as if it were an application under paragraph (1)(a).

(5) On considering a request filed under paragraph (2) by virtue of paragraph (4), the court shall either –

(a) grant the request, whereupon the proper officer shall communicate the decision to the [child]³ and next friend or guardian ad litem concerned and to all other parties to the proceedings, or

(b) direct that the request be heard, whereupon the proper officer shall fix a date for such a hearing and give to the [child]³ and next friend or guardian ad litem concerned such notice of the date so fixed as the court may direct;

provided that the court may act under sub-paragraph (a) only if it is satisfied that the next friend or guardian ad litem does not oppose the request.

(6) Where the court is considering whether to –

(a) grant leave under paragraph (1)(a), or
(b) grant leave under paragraph (4) and remove a next friend or guardian ad litem,

it shall grant the leave sought and, as the case may be, remove the next friend or guardian ad litem if it considers that the [child]³ concerned has sufficient understanding to participate as a party in the proceedings concerned or proposed without a next friend or guardian ad litem.

[(6A) In exercising its powers under paragraph (6) the court may order the next friend or guardian ad litem to take such part in the proceedings as the court may direct.]²

(7) Where a request for leave is granted at a hearing fixed under paragraph (3)(b) (in relation to the prosecution or defence of proceedings already begun) or (5)(b), the proper officer shall forthwith communicate the decision to the other parties to the proceedings.

(8) The court may revoke any leave granted under paragraph (1)(a) where it considers that the child does not have sufficient understanding to participate as a party in the proceedings concerned without a next friend or guardian ad litem.

(9) Without prejudice to any requirement of CCR Order 50, rule 5 or RSC Order 67, where a solicitor is acting for a [child]³ in proceedings which the [child]³ is prosecuting or defending without a next friend or guardian ad litem by virtue of paragraph (1)(b) and either of the conditions specified in the paragraph (1)(b)(i) and (ii) cease to be fulfilled, he shall forthwith so inform the court.

(10) Where –

(a) the court revokes any leave under paragraph (8), or
(b) either of the conditions specified in paragraph (1)(b)(i) and (ii) is no longer fulfilled,

the court may, if it considers it necessary in order to protect the interests of the [child]³ concerned, order that some proper person be appointed his next friend or guardian ad litem.

(11) Where a [child]³ is of sufficient understanding to begin, prosecute or defend proceedings without a next friend or guardian ad litem –
- (a) he may nevertheless begin, prosecute or defend them by his next friend or guardian ad litem; and
- (b) where he is prosecuting or defending proceedings by his next friend or guardian ad litem, the respective powers and duties of the [child]³ and next friend or guardian ad litem, except those conferred or imposed by this rule, shall not be affected by the [child]³'s ability to dispense with a next friend or guardian ad litem under the provisions of this rule.]¹

NOTES

Amendments.¹ Rule inserted: SI 1992/456.² Paragraph inserted: SI 1997/1893.³ Words substituted: SI 2007/2187.

9.3 Service on [child or protected party]²

(1) Where a document to which rule 2.9 applies is required to be served on a [child or protected party]² ...¹, it shall be served –
- (a) in the case of a [child]² who is not also a [protected party]², on his [parent]³ or, if he has no [parent]³, on the person with whom he resides or in whose care he is;
- (b) in the case of a [protected party]² –
  - [(i) on the person (if any) who is the attorney of a registered enduring power of attorney, donee of a lasting power of attorney or deputy of the protected party, or]²
  - (ii) if there is no [attorney of a registered enduring power of attorney, donee of a lasting power of attorney or deputy of the protected party]², on the Official Solicitor if he has consented under rule 9.2(4) to be the guardian ad litem of the [protected party]², or
  - (iii) in any other case, on the person with whom the [protected party]² resides or in whose care he is –

  Provided that the court may order that a document which has been, or is to be, served on the [child or protected party]² or on a person other than one mentioned in sub-paragraph (a) or (b) shall be deemed to be duly served on the [child or protected party]².

(2) Where a document is served in accordance with paragraph (1) it shall be indorsed with a notice in Form M24; and after service has been effected the person at whose instance the document was served shall, unless the Official Solicitor is the guardian ad litem of the [child or protected party]² or the court otherwise directs, file an affidavit by the person on whom the document was served stating whether the contents of the document were, or its purport was, communicated to the [child or protected party]² and, if not, the reasons for not doing so.

NOTES

Amendments.¹ Words revoked: SI 1992/2067.² Words substituted: SI 2007/2197.³ Word substituted: SI 2009/636.

9.4 Petition for nullity on ground of mental disorder

(1) Where a petition for nullity [of marriage]¹ has been presented on the ground that at the time of the marriage the respondent was suffering from mental disorder within the meaning of the Mental Health Act 1983 of such a kind or to such an extent as to be unfitted for marriage, then, whether or not the respondent gives notice of intention to defend, the petitioner shall not proceed with the cause without the leave of the district judge.

[(1A) Where a petition for nullity of civil partnership has been presented on the ground that at the time of the formation of the civil partnership the respondent was suffering from mental disorder within the meaning of the Mental Health Act 1983 of such a kind or to such an extent as to be unfitted for civil partnership, then, whether or not the respondent gives notice of intention to defend, the petitioner shall not proceed with the cause without the leave of the district judge.]¹

(2) The district judge by whom an application for leave is heard may make it a condition of granting leave that some proper person be appointed to act as guardian ad litem of the respondent.

NOTES

Amendments.¹ Words and paragraph inserted: SI 2005/2922.

9.5 Separate representation of children

[(1) Without prejudice to rules 2.57 and 9.2A [and to paragraph 2 of Appendix 4]³, if in any family proceedings it appears to the court that it is in the best interest of any child to be made a party to the proceedings, the court may appoint –

- (a) an officer of the service [or a Welsh family proceedings officer]²;
- (b) (if he consents) the Official Solicitor; or
- (c) (if he consents) some other proper person,

to be the guardian ad litem of the child with authority to take part in the proceedings on the child's behalf.]¹

(2) An order under paragraph (1) may be made by the court of its own motion or on the application of a party to the proceedings or of the proposed guardian ad litem.

(3) The court may at any time direct that an application be made by a party for an order under paragraph (1) and may stay the proceedings until the application has been made.

(4) …¹

(5) Unless otherwise directed, a person appointed under this rule or rule 2.57 [or under paragraph 2 of Appendix 4]³ to be the guardian ad litem of a child in any family proceedings shall be treated as a party for the purpose of any provision of these rules requiring a document to be served on or notice to be given to a party to the proceedings.

[(6) Where the guardian ad litem appointed under this rule is an officer of the service [or a Welsh family proceedings officer][2], rules 4.11 and 4.11A shall apply to him as they apply to a children's guardian appointed under section 41 of the Children Act 1989.][1]

NOTES

Amendments.[1] Paragraph substituted, omitted or inserted: SI 2001/821.[2] Words inserted: SI 2005/559.[3] Words inserted: SI 2005/2922.

PART X
PROCEDURE (GENERAL)

10.1 Application

The provisions of this Part apply to all family proceedings, but have effect subject to the provisions of any other Part of these rules.

10.2 Service on solicitors

(1) Where a document is required by these rules to be sent to any person who is acting by a solicitor, service shall, subject to any other direction or order, be effected –

(a) by sending the document by first class post to the solicitor's address for service; or

(b) where that address includes a numbered box at a document exchange, at that document exchange or at a document exchange which transmits documents every business day to that document exchange; or

(c) by FAX (as defined by RSC Order 1, rule 4(1)) in accordance with the provisions of RSC Order 65, rule 5(2B).

(2) Any document which is left at a document exchange in accordance with paragraph (1)(b) shall, unless the contrary is proved, be deemed to have been served on the second day after the day on which it is left.

(3) Where no other mode of service is prescribed, directed or ordered, service may additionally be effected by leaving the document at the solicitor's address.

10.3 Service on person acting in person

(1) Subject to paragraph (3) and to any other direction or order, where a document is required by these rules to be sent to any person who is acting in person, service shall be effected by sending the document by first class post to the address given by him or, if he has not given an address for service, to his last known address.

(2) Subject to paragraph (3), where no other mode of service is prescribed, directed or ordered, service may additionally be effected by delivering the document to him or by leaving it at the address specified in paragraph (1).

(3) Where it appears to the district judge that it is impracticable to deliver the document to the person to be served and that, if the document were left at, or

sent by post to, the address specified in paragraph (1), it would be unlikely to reach him, the district judge may dispense with service of the document.

10.4 Service by bailiff in proceedings in principal registry

Where, in any proceedings pending in the principal registry which are treated as pending in a [designated county court][1], a document is to be served by bailiff, it shall be sent for service to the proper officer of the county court within the district of which the document is to be served.

NOTES

Amendments.[1] Words substituted: SI 2005/2922.

10.5 Proof of service by officer of court etc

(1) Where a petition is sent to any person by an officer of the court, he shall note the date of posting in the records of the court.

(2) Without prejudice to section 133 of the County Court Act 1984 (proof of service of summonses etc) a record made pursuant to paragraph (1) shall be evidence of the facts stated therein.

(3) Where the court has authorised notice by advertisement to be substituted for service and the advertisement has been inserted by some person other than the proper officer, that person shall file copies of the newspapers containing the advertisement.

10.6 Service out of England and Wales

(1) Any document in family proceedings may be served out of England and Wales without leave either in the manner prescribed by these rules or –

- (a) where the proceedings are pending in the High Court, in accordance with RSC Order 11, rules 5 and 6 (which relates to the service of a writ abroad); or
- (b) where the proceedings are pending in a [designated county court][1], in accordance with CCR Order 8, rules 8 to 10 (which relate to the service of process abroad).

(2) Where the document is served in accordance with RSC Order 11, rules 5 and 6, those rules and rule 8 of the said Order 11 (which deals with the expenses incurred by the Secretary of State) shall have effect in relation to service of the document as they have effect in relation to service of notice of a writ, except that the official certificate of service referred to in paragraph (5) of the said rule 5 shall, if the document was served personally, show the server's means of knowledge of the identity of the person served.

(3) Where the document is served in accordance with CCR Order 8, rules 8 to 10, those rules shall have effect subject to the following modifications –

- (a) the document need not be served personally on the person required to be served so long as it is served in accordance with the law of the country in which service is effected;

(b) the official certificate or declaration with regard to service referred to in paragraph (6) of the said rule 10 shall, if the document was served personally, show the server's means of knowledge of the identity of the person served; and

(c) in paragraph (7) of the said rule 10 the words 'or in the manner in which default summonses are required to be served' shall be omitted.

(4) Where a petition is to be served on a person out of England and Wales, then –

(a) the time within which that person must give notice of intention to defend shall be determined having regard to the practice adopted under RSC Order 11, rule 4(4) (which requires an order for leave to serve a writ out of the jurisdiction to limit the time for appearance) and the notice in Form M5 [or Form M5A, as the case may be,][1] shall be amended accordingly;

(b) if the petition is to be served otherwise than in accordance with RSC Order 11, rules 5 and 6, or CCR Order 8, rules 8 to 10, and there is reasonable ground for believing that the person to be served does not understand English, the petition shall be accompanied by a translation, approved by the district judge, of the notice in Form M5, [or Form M5A, as the case may be,][1] in the official language of the country in which service is to be effected or, if there is more than one official language of that country, in any one of those languages which is appropriate to the place where service is to be effected; but this sub-paragraph shall not apply in relation to a document which is to be served in a country in which the official language, or one of the official languages, is English.

(5) Where a document specifying the date of hearing of any proceedings is to be served out of England and Wales, the date shall be fixed having regard to the time which would be limited under paragraph (4)(a) for giving notice of intention to defend if the document were a petition.

NOTES

Amendments.[1] Words substituted or inserted: SI 2005/2922.

10.7 Mode of giving notice

Unless otherwise directed, any notice which is required by these rules to be given to any person shall be in writing, and may be given in any manner in which service may be effected under RSC Order 65, rule 5.

10.8 Notice of intention to defend

(1) In these rules (other than rule 3.2(5)) any reference to a notice of intention to defend is a reference to an acknowledgement of service –

(a) in proceedings other than under the Act of 2004, in Form M6, and
(b) in proceedings under the Act of 2004, in Form M6A,

containing a statement to the effect that the person by whom or on whose behalf it is signed intends to defend the proceedings to which the acknowledgement relates, and any reference to giving notice of intention to defend is a reference to returning such a notice to the court office.][1]

(2) In relation to any person on whom there is served a document requiring or authorising an acknowledgment of service to be returned to the court office, references in these rules to the time limited for giving notice of intention to defend are references –

(a) to seven days after service of the document, in the case of notice of intention to defend a petition under Part II of these rules, and
(b) in any other case, to 14 days or such other time as may be fixed.

(3) Subject to paragraph (2) a person may give notice of intention to defend notwithstanding that he has already returned to the court office an acknowledgment of service not constituting such a notice.

NOTES

Amendments.[1] Paragraph substituted: SI 2005/2922.

10.9 Mode of making applications

Except where these rules, or any rules applied by these rules, otherwise provide, every application in family proceedings –

(a) shall be made to a district judge;
(b) shall, if the proceedings are pending in the High Court, be made by summons or, if the proceedings are pending in a [designated county court][1], be made in accordance with CCR Order 13, rule 1 (which deals with applications in the course of proceedings).

NOTES

Amendments.[1] Words substituted: SI 2005/2922.

10.10 Orders for transfer of family proceedings

(1) Where a [matrimonial][1] cause is pending in the High Court, the district judge of the registry in which the cause is pending or a judge may order that the cause be transferred to another registry.

[(1A) Where a civil partnership cause is pending in the High Court, the district judge of the registry in which the cause is pending or a judge may order that the cause be transferred to another district registry.][1]

(2) Where a cause is pending in a divorce county court, the court may order that the cause be transferred to another divorce county court.

[(2A) Where a cause is pending in a civil partnership proceedings county court, the court may order that the cause be transferred to another civil partnership proceedings county court.][1]

(3) Paragraphs [(1) to (2A)][1] shall apply to applications in causes as they apply to causes; but before making an order for transfer of an application the court

shall consider whether it would be more convenient to transfer the cause under paragraph [(1), (1A), (2) or (2A)]¹, as the case may be.

(4) The court shall not, either of its own motion or on the application of any party, make an order under [any of paragraphs (1) to (3)]¹ unless the parties have either –

    (a)   had an opportunity of being heard on the question, or
    (b)   consented to such an order.

(5) Where the parties, or any of them, desire to be heard on the question of a transfer, the court shall give the parties notice of a date, time and place at which the question will be considered.

(6) Paragraphs (4) and (5) shall apply with the necessary modifications to an order for the transfer of family proceedings under section 38 or 39 of the Act of 1984 as they apply to an order under paragraph [(1), (1A), (2) or (2A)]¹ of this rule.

(7) Paragraphs (4) and (5) shall not apply where the court makes an order for transfer under [any of paragraphs (1) to (3)]¹ in compliance with the provisions of any Order made under Part I of Schedule 11 to the Children Act 1989.

NOTES

Amendments.¹ Words inserted and substituted and paragraphs inserted: SI 2005/2922.

10.11 Procedure on transfer of cause or application

(1) Where any cause or application is ordered to be transferred from one court or registry to another, the proper officer of the first-mentioned court or registry shall, unless otherwise directed, give notice of the transfer to the parties.

(2) Any provision in these rules, or in any order made or notice given pursuant to these rules, for the transfer of proceedings between a [designated county court]¹ and the High Court shall, in relation to proceedings which, after the transfer, are to continue in the principal registry, be construed –

    (a)   in the case of a transfer from the High Court to a [designated county court]¹, as a provision for the proceedings to be treated as pending in a [designated county court]¹, and
    (b)   in the case of a transfer from a [designated county court]¹ to the High Court, as a provision for the proceedings no longer to be treated as pending in a [designated county court]¹.

(3) Proceedings transferred from a [designated county court]¹ to the High Court pursuant to any provision in these rules shall, unless the order of transfer otherwise directs, proceed in the registry nearest to the [designated county court]¹ from which they are transferred, but nothing in this paragraph shall prejudice any power under these rules to order the transfer of the proceedings to a different registry.

NOTES

Amendments.¹ Words substituted: SI 2005/2922.

10.12 Evidence by affidavit

On any application made –

(a) in a county court, by originating application or in accordance with CCR Order 13, rule 1 (which deals with applications in the course of proceedings) or

(b) in the High Court, by originating summons, notice or motion,

evidence may be given by affidavit unless these rules otherwise provide or the court otherwise directs, but the court may, on the application of any party, order the attendance for cross-examination of the person making any such affidavit; and where, after such an order has been made, that person does not attend, his affidavit shall not be used as evidence without the leave of the court.

10.13 Taking of affidavit in county court proceedings

In relation to family proceedings pending or treated as pending in a [designated county court]¹, section 58(1) of the County Courts Act 1984 shall have effect as if after paragraph (c) there were inserted the following words –

'or

(d) a district judge of the principal registry; or
(e) any officer of the principal registry authorised by the President under section 2 of the Commissioners for Oaths Act 1889; or
(f) any clerk in the Central Office of the Royal Courts of Justice authorised to take affidavits for the purposes of proceedings in the Supreme Court.'.

NOTES
Amendments.¹ Words substituted: SI 2005/2922.

10.14 Evidence of marriage [or overseas relationship]¹ outside England and Wales

(1) The celebration of a marriage outside England and Wales and its validity under the law of the country where it was celebrated may, in any family proceedings in which the existence and validity of the marriage is not disputed, be proved by the evidence of one of the parties to the marriage and the production of a document purporting to be –

(a) a marriage certificate or similar document issued under the law in force in that country; or
(b) a certified copy of an entry in a register of marriages kept under the law in force in that country.

[(1A) The formation of an overseas relationship other than a marriage, outside England and Wales and its validity under the law of the country where it was formed may, in any family proceedings in which the existence and validity of that relationship is not disputed, be proved by the evidence of one of the parties to it and the production of a document purporting to be –

(a) a certificate or similar document issued under the law in force in that country evidencing its formation; or
(b) a certified copy of an entry in a register of such relationships kept under the law in force in that country.]¹

(2) Where a document produced by virtue of paragraph (1) [or 1A]¹ is not in English it shall, unless otherwise directed, be accompanied by a translation certified by a notary public or authenticated by affidavit.

(3) This rule shall not be construed as precluding the proof of a marriage [or the existence of an overseas relationship which is not a marriage]¹ in accordance with the Evidence (Foreign, Dominion and Colonial Documents) Act 1933 or in any other manner authorised apart from this rule.

NOTES

Amendments.¹ Text inserted: SI 2005/2922.

[10.14A Power of court to limit cross-examination

The court may limit the issues on which an officer of the service [or a Welsh family proceedings officer]² may be cross-examined.]¹

NOTES

Amendments.¹ Rule inserted: SI 2001/821. ² Words inserted: SI 2005/559.

10.15 Official shorthand note etc of proceedings

(1) Unless the judge otherwise directs, an official shorthand note shall be taken of the proceedings at the trial in open court of every cause pending in the High Court.

(2) An official shorthand note may be taken of any other proceedings before a judge or district judge if directions for the taking of such a note are given by the Lord Chancellor.

(3) The shorthand writer shall sign the note and certify it to be a correct shorthand note of the proceedings and shall retain the note unless he is directed by the district judge to forward it to the court.

(4) On being so directed the shorthand writer shall furnish the court with a transcript of the whole or such part as may be directed of the shorthand note.

(5) Any party, any person who has intervened in a cause, the Queen's Proctor or, where a declaration of parentage has been made under [section 55A]¹ of the Act of 1986, the Registrar General shall be entitled to require from the shorthand writer a transcript of the shorthand note, and the shorthand writer shall, at the request of any person so entitled, supply that person with a transcript of the whole or any part of the note on payment of the shorthand writer's charges authorised by any scheme in force providing for the taking of official shorthand notes of legal proceedings.

(6) Except as aforesaid, the shorthand writer shall not, without the permission of the court, furnish the shorthand note or a transcript of the whole or any part thereof to anyone.

(7) In these Rules references to a shorthand note include references to a record of the proceedings made by mechanical means and in relation to such a record references to the shorthand writer shall have effect as if they were references to the person responsible for transcribing the record.

NOTES

Amendments.[1] Text substituted: SI 2001/821.

10.16 Copies of decrees and orders

(1) A copy of every decree [or civil partnership order, as the case may be,][1] shall be sent by the proper officer to every party to the cause.

(2) A sealed or other copy of a decree[, civil partnership order or other order][1] or order made in open court shall be issued to any person requiring it on payment of the prescribed fee.

NOTES

Amendments.[1] Text inserted: SI 2005/2922.

10.17 Service of order

(1) Where an order made in family proceedings has been drawn up, the proper officer of the court where the order is made shall, unless otherwise directed, send a copy of the order to every party affected by it.

(2) Where a party against whom the order is made is acting by a solicitor, a copy may, if the district judge thinks fit, be sent to that party as if he were acting in person, as well as to his solicitor.

(3) It shall not be necessary for the person in whose favour the order was made to prove that a copy of the order has reached any other party to whom it is required to be sent.

(4) This rule is without prejudice to RSC Order 45, rule 7 (which deals with the service of an order to do or abstain from doing an act), CCR Order 29 rule 1 (which deals with orders enforceable by committal) and any other rule or enactment for the purposes of which an order is required to be served in a particular way.

10.18 No notice of intention to proceed after year's delay

RSC Order 3, rule 6 (which requires a party to give notice of intention to proceed after a year's delay) shall not apply to any proceedings pending in the High Court.

10.19 Filing of documents at place of hearing etc

Where the file of any family proceedings has been sent from one [designated county court]¹ or registry to another for the purpose of a hearing or for some other purpose, any document needed for that purpose and required to be filed shall be filed in the other court or registry.

NOTES

Amendments.¹ Words substituted: SI 2005/2922.

10.20 Inspection etc of documents retained in court

(1) Subject to rule 10.21, a party to any family proceedings or his solicitor or the Queen's Proctor or a person appointed under rule 2.57 or 9.5 [or under paragraph 2 of Appendix 4]³ to be the guardian ad litem of a child in any family proceedings may have a search made for, and may inspect and bespeak a copy of, any document filed or lodged in the court office in those proceedings.

(2) Any person not entitled to a copy of a document under paragraph (1) above who intends to make an application under the Hague Convention (as defined in section 1(1) of the Child Abduction and Custody Act 1985) in a Contracting State (as defined in section 2 of that Act) other than the United Kingdom shall, if he satisfies the [court]¹ that he intends to make such an application, be entitled to obtain a copy bearing the seal of the court of any order relating to the custody of the child in respect of whom the application is to be made.

(3) Except as provided by rules 2.36(4) [and (5)]³[, 3.16(10) and [Part XI]⁴]² and 3.16(10) and paragraphs (1) and (2) of this rule, no document filed or lodged in the court office other than a decree[, civil partnership order or other]³ order made in open court shall be open to inspection by any person without the leave of the district judge, and no copy of any such document, or of an extract from any such document, shall be taken by, or issued to, any person without such leave.

NOTES

Amendments.¹ Word substituted: SI 1992/2067. ² Words inserted: SI 2005/1976. ³ Words inserted or substituted: SI 2005/2922. ⁴ Words substituted: SI 2009/857.

[10.20A

…²]¹

NOTES

Amendments.¹ Rule inserted: SI 2005/1976. ² Rule revoked: SI 2009/857.

10.21 Disclosure of addresses

(1) [Subject to rule 2.3]¹ nothing in these rules shall be construed as requiring any party to reveal the address of their private residence (or that of any child) save by order of the court.

[(1A) In proceedings under Part 4A of the Family Law Act 1996, a party is also not required to reveal the address of –

(a) the person who is the subject of the proceedings; or
(b) any witness;

unless the court directs otherwise.]³

(2) Where a party declines to reveal an address in reliance upon [this rule]³, he shall give notice of that address to the court in Form [C8]² and that address shall not be revealed to any person save by order of the court.

NOTES

Amendments.¹ Words inserted: SI 1991/2113. ² Words substituted: SI 1994/3155. ³ Paragraph inserted and words substituted: SI 2008/2446.

[10.21A Disclosure of information under the Act of 1991

[(1)]² Where the Secretary of State requires a person mentioned in regulation 2(2) or (3)(a) of the Child Support (Information, Evidence and Disclosure) Regulations 1992 to furnish information or evidence for a purpose mentioned in regulation 3(1) of those Regulations, [nothing in rules 10.20 (inspection etc of documents in court), [Part XI (communication of information: proceedings relating to children)]⁴]² or 10.21 (disclosure of addresses) shall prevent that person from furnishing the information or evidence sought or require him to seek leave of the court before doing so.

(2) For the purposes of the law relating to contempt of court, information relating to ancillary relief proceedings held in private may be communicated, subject to any direction of the court, by a party to the proceedings to –

(a) the Secretary of State;
(b) a McKenzie Friend or a lay adviser; or
(c) [the First-tier Tribunal]³ dealing with an appeal made under section 20 of the Child Support Act 1991

for the purposes of making or responding to an appeal under section 20 of the Act of 1991 or the determination of such an appeal.

(3) For the purposes of this rule the definitions of 'McKenzie Friend' and 'lay adviser' in rule 10.20A apply.]²]¹

NOTES

Amendments.¹ Rule inserted: SI 1993/295. ² Para (1) numbered as such, and paras (2), (3) inserted: SI 2007/2187. ³ Words substituted: SI 2008/2446. ⁴ Words substituted: SI 2009/857.

[10.21B Documents in family proceedings concerning gender recognition

(1) This rule applies to all documents in family proceedings brought under –

(a) section 12(g) or (h) of, or paragraph 11(1)(e) of Schedule 1 to, the Act of 1973;
[(b) section 50(1)(d) or (e) of the Act of 2004;]²
[(c)]² the Gender Recognition Act 2004.

(2) Documents to which this rule applies must, while they are in the custody of the court, be kept in a place of special security.]

NOTES

Amendments.[1] Rule inserted: SI 2005/559.[2] Subparagraphs inserted and renumbered: SI 2005/2922.

10.22 Practice to be observed in district registries and [designated county courts][1]

(1) The President and the senior district judge may, with the concurrence of the Lord Chancellor, issue directions for the purpose of securing in the district registries and the [designated county courts][1] due observance of statutory requirements and uniformity of practice in family proceedings.

(2) RSC Order 63, rule 11 (which requires the practice of the Central Office to be followed in the district registries) shall not apply to family proceedings.

NOTES

Amendments.[1] Words substituted: SI 2005/2922.

10.23 Transitional provisions

(1) Subject to paragraph (2) below, these rules shall apply, so far as practicable, to any proceedings pending on the day on which they come into force.

(2) Rule 8.1 shall not apply to an appeal from an order or decision made or given by a district judge in matrimonial proceedings in a divorce county court where notice of appeal has been filed before the day on which these rules come into force.

(3) Where, by reason of paragraph (1) above, these rules do not apply to particular proceedings pending on the day on which they come into force, the rules in force immediately before that day shall continue to apply to those proceedings.

(4) Nothing in this rule shall be taken as prejudicing the operation of the provisions of the Interpretation Act 1978 as regards the effect of repeals.

(5) Without prejudice to the generality of paragraph (1) above (and for the avoidance of doubt) rule 2.39 shall not apply to any proceedings which are pending within the meaning of paragraph 1(1) of Schedule 14 to the Children Act 1989.

[10.24 Applications for relief which is precluded by the Act of 1991

(1) Where an application is made for an order which, in the opinion of the district judge, the court would be prevented from making by section 8 or 9 of the Act of 1991, the proper officer may send a notice in Form M34 to the applicant.

(2) In the first instance, the district judge shall consider the matter under paragraph (1) himself, without holding a hearing.

(3) Where a notice is sent under paragraph (1), no requirement of these rules, except for those of this rule, as to the service of the application by the proper officer or as to any other procedural step to follow the making of an application of the type in question, shall apply unless and until the court directs that they shall apply or that they shall apply to such extent and subject to such modifications as may be specified in the direction.

(4) Where an applicant who has been sent a notice under paragraph (1) informs the proper officer in writing, within 14 days of the date of the notice, that he wishes to persist with his application, the proper officer shall refer the matter to the district judge for action in accordance with paragraph (5).

(5) Where the district judge acts in accordance with this paragraph, he shall give such directions as he considers appropriate for the matter to be heard and determined by the court and, without prejudice to the generality of the foregoing, such directions may provide for the hearing to be ex parte.

(6) Where directions are given under paragraph (5), the proper officer shall inform the applicant of the directions and, in relation to the other parties, –

- (a) send them a copy of the application;
- (b) where the hearing is to be ex parte, inform them briefly –
  - (i) of the nature and effect of the notice under this rule,
  - (ii) that the matter is being resolved ex parte, and
  - (iii) that they will be informed of the result in due course; and
- (c) where the hearing is to be inter partes, inform them of –
  - (i) the circumstances which led to the directions being given, and
  - (ii) the directions.

(7) Where a notice has been sent under paragraph (1) and the proper officer is not informed under paragraph (4), the application shall be treated as having been withdrawn.

(8) Where the matter is heard pursuant to directions under paragraph (5) and the court determines that it would be prevented by section 8 or 9 of the Act of 1991 from making the order sought by the application, it shall dismiss the application.

(9) Where the court dismisses an application under this rule it shall give its reasons in writing, copies of which shall be sent to the parties by the proper officer.

(10) In this rule, 'the matter' means the question whether the making of an order in the terms sought by the application would be prevented by section 8 or 9 of the Act of 1991.][1]

NOTES

Amendments.[1] Rule inserted: SI 1993/295.

[10.25 Modification of rule 10.24 in relation to non-free-standing applications

Where a notice is sent under rule 10.24(1) in respect of an application which is contained in a petition or other document ('the document') which contains material extrinsic to the application –

(a) the document shall, until the contrary is directed under sub-paragraph (c) of this rule, be treated as if it did not contain the application in respect of which the notice was served;
(b) the proper officer shall, when he sends copies of the document to the respondents under any provision of these rules, attach a copy of the notice under rule 10.24(1) and a notice informing the respondents of the effect of sub-paragraph (a) of this paragraph; and
(c) if it is determined, under rule 10.24, that the court would not be prevented, by section 8 or 9 of the Act of 1991, from making the order sought by the application, the court shall direct that the document shall be treated as if it contained the application, and it may give such directions as it considers appropriate for the conduct of the proceedings in consequence of that direction.][1]

NOTES

Amendments.[1] Rule inserted: SI 1993/295.

[10.26 Human Rights Act 1998

(1) In this rule –

'originating document' means a petition, application, originating application, originating summons or other originating process;
'answer' means an answer or other document filed or served by a party in reply to an originating document (but not an acknowledgement of service);
'Convention right' has the same meaning as in the Human Rights Act 1998;
'declaration of incompatibility' means a declaration of incompatibility under section 4 of the Human Rights Act 1998.

(2) A party who seeks to rely on any provision of or right arising under the Human Rights Act 1998 or seeks a remedy available under that Act –

(a) shall state that fact in his originating document or (as the case may be) answer; and
(b) shall in his originating document or (as the case may be) answer –
   (i) give precise details of the Convention right which it is alleged has been infringed and details of the alleged infringement;
   (ii) specify the relief sought;
   (iii) state if the relief sought includes a declaration of incompatibility.

(3) A party who seeks to amend his originating document (as the case may be) answer to include the matters referred to in paragraph (2) shall, unless the court orders otherwise, do so as soon as possible and in any event not less than 28 days before the hearing.

(4) The court shall not make a declaration of incompatibility unless 21 days' notice, or such other period of notice as the court directs, has been given to the Crown.

(5) Where notice has been given to the Crown a Minister, or other person permitted by the Human Rights Act 1998, shall be joined as a party on giving notice to the court.

(6) Where a party has included in his originating document or (as the case may be) answer:

(a) a claim for a declaration of incompatibility, or
(b) an issue for the court to decide which may lead to the court considering making a declaration of incompatibility,

then the court may at any time consider whether notice should be given to the Crown as required by the Human Rights Act 1998 and give directions for the content and service of the notice.

(7) In the case of an appeal for which permission to appeal is required, the court shall, unless it decides that it is appropriate to do so at another stage in the proceedings, consider the issues and give the directions referred to in paragraph (6) when deciding whether to give such permission.

(8) If paragraph (7) does not apply, and a hearing for directions would, but for this rule, be held, the court shall unless it decides that it is appropriate to do so at another stage in the proceedings, consider the issues and give the directions referred to in paragraph (6) at the hearing for directions.

(9) If neither paragraph (7) nor paragraph (8) applies, the court shall consider the issues and give the directions referred to in paragraph (6) when it considers it appropriate to do so, and may fix a hearing for this purpose.

(10) Where a party amends his originating document or (as the case may be) answer to include any matter referred to in paragraph (6)(a), then the court will consider whether notice should be given to the Crown and give directions for the content and service of the notice.

(11) In paragraphs (12) to (16), 'notice' means the notice given under paragraph (4).

(12) The notice shall be served on the person named in the list published under section 17 of the Crown Proceedings Act 1947.

(13) The notice shall be in the form directed by the court.

(14) Unless the court orders otherwise, the notice shall be accompanied by the directions given by the court and the originating document and any answers in the proceedings.

(15) Copies of the notice shall be served on all the parties.

(16) The court may require the parties to assist in the preparation of the notice.

(17) Unless the court orders otherwise, the Minister or other person permitted by the Human Rights Act 1998 to be joined as a party shall, if he wishes to be

joined, give notice of his intention to be joined as a party to the court and every other party, and where the Minister has nominated a person to be joined as a party the notice must be accompanied by the written nomination.

(18) Where a claim is made under [section 7(1)][2] of the Human Rights Act 1998 in respect of a judicial act the procedure in paragraphs (6) to (17) shall also apply, but the notice to be given to the Crown:

(a) shall be given to the Lord Chancellor and shall be served on the Treasury Solicitor on his behalf; and
(b) shall also give details of the judicial act which is the subject of the claim and of the court that made it.

(19) Where in any appeal a claim is made [under section 7(1) of that Act and section 9(3) and (4) applies][2] –

(a) that claim must be set out in the notice of appeal; and
(b) notice must be given to the Crown in accordance with paragraph (18).

(20) The appellant must in a notice of appeal to which paragraph (19)(a) applies –

(a) state that a claim is being made under [section 7(1)][2] of the Human Rights Act 1998 [in respect of a judicial act and section 9(3) applies][2]; and
(b) give details of –
  (i) the Convention right which it is alleged has been infringed;
  (ii) the infringement;
  (iii) the judicial act complained of; and
  (iv) the court which made it.

(21) Where paragraph (19) applies and the appropriate person (as defined in section 9(5) of the Human Rights Act 1998) has not applied within 21 days, or such other period as the court directs, after the notice is served to be joined as a party, the court may join the appropriate person as a party.

(22) On any application or appeal concerning –

(a) a committal order;
(b) a refusal to grant habeas corpus; or
(c) a secure accommodation order made under section 25 of the Act of 1989,

if the court ordering the release of the person concludes that his Convention rights have been infringed by the making of the order to which the application or appeal relates, the judgment or order should so state, but if the court does not do so, that failure will not prevent another court from deciding the matter.][1]

NOTES

Amendments.[1] Rule inserted: SI 2000/2267.[2] Words substituted or inserted: SI 2001/821.

[10.27 Costs

(1) Order 38 of the County Court Rules 1981 and Order 62 of the Rules of the Supreme Court 1965 shall not apply to costs in family proceedings, and CPR Parts 43, 44 (except rules 44.9 to 44.12), 47 and 48 shall apply to costs in those proceedings, with the following modifications –

- (a) in CPR rule 43.2(1)(c)(ii), 'district judge' includes a district judge of the Principal Registry of the Family Division;
- (b) CPR rule 44.3(2) (costs follow the event) shall not apply[; and
- (c) CPR rule 44.3(1) and (3) to (5) shall not apply to an application to which rule 2.71 (ancillary relief: costs) applies]².

(2) Except in the case of an appeal against a decision of an authorised court officer (to which CPR rules 47.20 to 47.23 apply), an appeal against a decision in assessment proceedings relating to costs in family proceedings shall be dealt with in accordance with the following paragraphs of this rule.

(3) An appeal within paragraph (2) above shall lie as follows –

- (a) where the decision appealed against was made by a district judge of the High Court or a costs judge (as defined by CPR rule 43.2(1)(b)), to a judge of the High Court;
- (b) where the decision appealed against was made by a district judge of a county court, to a judge of that court.

(4) CPR Part 52 applies to every appeal within paragraph (2) above, and any reference in CPR Part 52 to a judge or a district judge shall be taken to include a district judge of the Principal Registry of the Family Division.

(5) The Civil Procedure Rules 1998 shall apply to an appeal to which CPR Part 52 or CPR rules 47.20 to 47.23 apply in accordance with paragraph (2) above in the same way as they apply to any other appeal within CPR Part 52 or CPR rules 47.20 to 47.23 as the case may be; accordingly the Rules of the Supreme Court 1965 and the County Court Rules 1981 shall not apply to any such appeal.]¹

NOTES

Amendment.¹ Rule inserted: SI 2003/184. ² Subparagraph and preceding word inserted: SI 2006/352.

[10.28 Attendance at private hearings

[(1) This rule applies when proceedings are held in private except in relation to hearings –

- (a) conducted for the purpose of judicially assisted conciliation or negotiation ; or
- (b) in proceedings to which Part IVA of these Rules applies.]²

(2) For the purposes of these Rules, a reference to proceedings held 'in private' means proceedings at which the general public have no right to be present.

(3) When this rule applies no person shall be present during any hearing other than –

(a) an officer of the court;
(b) a party to the proceedings;
(c) a litigation friend for any party, or legal representative instructed to act on that party's behalf;
(d) an officer of the service or Welsh family proceedings officer;
(e) a witness;
(f) duly accredited representatives of news gathering and reporting organisations; and
(g) any other person whom the court permits to be present.

(4) At any stage of the proceedings the court may direct that persons within paragraph (3)(f) shall not attend the proceedings or any part of them, where satisfied that –

(a) this is necessary –
   (i) in the interests of any child concerned in, or connected with, the proceedings;
   (ii) for the safety or protection of a party, a witness in the proceedings, or a person connected with such a party or witness; or
   (iii) for the orderly conduct of the proceedings; or
(b) justice will otherwise be impeded or prejudiced.

(5) The court may exercise the power in paragraph (4) of its own motion or pursuant to representations made by any of the persons listed in paragraph (6), and in either case having given to any person within paragraph (3)(f) who is in attendance an opportunity to make representations.

(6) At any stage of the proceedings, the following persons may make representations to the court regarding restricting the attendance of persons within paragraph (3)(f) in accordance with paragraph (4) –

(a) a party to the proceedings;
(b) any witness in the proceedings;
(c) where appointed, any children's guardian;
(d) where appointed, an officer of the service or Welsh family proceedings officer, on behalf of the child the subject of the proceedings;
(e) the child, if of sufficient age and understanding.

(7) This rule does not affect any power of the court to direct that witnesses shall be excluded until they are called for examination.

(8) In this rule 'duly accredited' refers to accreditation in accordance with any administrative scheme for the time being approved for the purposes of this rule by the Lord Chancellor.][1]

NOTES

Amendment.[1] Rule inserted: SI 2009/857. [2] Paragraph substituted: SI 2010/1064.

[PART XI
COMMUNICATION OF INFORMATION: PROCEEDINGS RELATING TO CHILDREN

11.1 Application

The provisions of this Part apply to family proceedings which –

(a) relate to the exercise of the inherent jurisdiction of the High Court with respect to minors;
(b) are brought under the Act of 1989; or
(c) otherwise relate wholly or mainly to the maintenance or upbringing of a minor.

11.2 Communication of information: general

(1) For the purposes of the law relating to contempt of court, information relating to proceedings held in private (whether or not contained in a document filed with the court) may be communicated –

(a) where the communication is to –
   (i) a party;
   (ii) the legal representative of a party;
   (iii) a professional legal adviser;
   (iv) an officer of the service or a Welsh family proceedings officer;
   (v) the welfare officer;
   (vi) the Legal Services Commission;
   (vii) an expert whose instruction by a party has been authorised by the court for the purposes of the proceedings;
   (viii) a professional acting in furtherance of the protection of children; or
   (ix) an independent reviewing officer appointed in respect of a child who is, or has been, subject to proceedings to which this rule applies;
(b) where the court gives permission; or
(c) subject to any direction of the court, in accordance with rules 11.4 to 11.8.

(2) Nothing in this Part permits the communication to the public at large, or any section of the public, of any information relating to the proceedings.

(3) Nothing in rules 11.4 to 11.8 permits the disclosure of an unapproved draft judgment handed down by any court.

11.3 Instruction of experts

(1) No party may instruct an expert for any purpose relating to proceedings, including to give evidence in those proceedings, without the leave of the court.

(2) Where the leave of the court has not been given under paragraph (1), no evidence arising out of an unauthorised instruction may be introduced without leave of the court.

11.4 Communication of information for purposes connected with the proceedings

(1) A party or the legal representative of a party, on behalf of and upon the instructions of that party, may communicate information relating to the proceedings to any person where necessary to enable that party –

(a) by confidential discussion, to obtain support, advice or assistance in the conduct of the proceedings;
(b) to engage in mediation or other forms of alternative dispute resolution;
(c) to make and pursue a complaint against a person or body concerned in the proceedings; or
(d) to make and pursue a complaint regarding the law, policy or procedure relating to a category of proceedings to which this Part applies.

(2) Where information is communicated to any person in accordance with paragraph (1)(a) of this rule, no further communication by that person is permitted.

(3) When information relating to the proceedings is communicated to any person in accordance with paragraphs (1)(b),(c) or (d) of this rule –

(a) the recipient may communicate that information to a further recipient, provided that –
   (i) the party who initially communicated the information consents to that further communication; and
   (ii) the further communication is made only for the purpose or purposes for which the party made the initial communication; and
(b) the information may be successively communicated to and by further recipients on as many occasions as may be necessary to fulfil the purpose for which the information was initially communicated, provided that on each such occasion the conditions in sub-paragraph (a) are met.

11.5 Communication of information by a party etc for other purposes

A person specified in the first column of the following table may communicate to a person listed in the second column such information as is specified in the third column for the purpose or purposes specified in the fourth column –

| A party | A lay adviser, a McKenzie Friend, or a person arranging or providing pro bono legal services | Any information relating to the proceedings | To enable the party to obtain advice or assistance in relation to the proceedings |

A party	A health care professional or a person or body providing counselling services for children or families		To enable the party or any child of the party to obtain health care or counselling
A party	The Secretary of State, a McKenzie Friend, a lay adviser or the First-tier Tribunal dealing with an appeal made under section 20 of the Child Support Act 1991		For the purposes of making or responding to an appeal under section 20 of the Child Support Act 1991 or the determination of such an appeal
A party	An adoption panel		To enable the adoption panel to discharge its functions as appropriate
A party	The European Court of Human Rights		For the purpose of making an application to the European Court of Human Rights
A party or any person lawfully in receipt of information	The Children's Commissioner or the Children's Commissioner for Wales		To refer an issue affecting the interests of children to the Children's Commissioner or the Children's Commissioner for Wales

Family Proceedings Rules 1991, r 11.5

A party, any person lawfully in receipt of information or a proper officer	A person or body conducting an approved research project		For the purpose of an approved research project
A legal representative or a professional legal adviser	A person or body responsible for investigating or determining complaints in relation to legal representatives or professional legal advisers		For the purposes of the investigation or determination of a complaint in relation to a legal representative or a professional legal adviser
A legal representative or a professional legal adviser	A person or body assessing quality assurance systems		To enable the legal representative or professional legal adviser to obtain a quality assurance assessment
A legal representative or a professional legal adviser	An accreditation body	Any information relating to the proceedings providing that it does not, or is not likely to, identify any person involved in the proceedings	To enable the legal representative or professional legal adviser to obtain accreditation
A party	A police officer	The text or summary of the whole or part of a judgment given in the proceedings	For the purpose of a criminal investigation

PART II – Statutory Instruments

Part II Statutory Instruments

A party or any person lawfully in receipt of information	A member of the Crown Prosecution Service		To enable the Crown Prosecution Service to discharge its functions under any enactment

11.6 Communication for the effective functioning of Cafcass and CAFCASS CYMRU

An officer of the service or a Welsh family proceedings officer, as appropriate, may communicate to a person listed in the second column such information as is specified in the third column for the purpose or purposes specified in the fourth column –

A Welsh family proceedings officer	A person or body exercising statutory functions relating to inspection of CAFCASS CYMRU	Any information relating to the proceedings which is required by the person or body responsible for the inspection	For the purpose of an inspection of CAFCASS CYMRU by a body or person appointed by the Welsh Ministers
An officer of the service or a Welsh family proceedings officer	The General Social Care Council or the Care Council for Wales	Any information relating to the proceedings providing that it does not, or is not likely to, identify any person involved in the proceedings	For the purpose of initial and continuing accreditation as a social worker of a person providing services to Cafcass or CAFCASS CYMRU in accordance with s 13(2) of the Criminal Justice and Courts Services Act 2000 or s 36 of the Children Act 2004 as the case may be

An officer of the service or a Welsh family proceedings officer	A person or body providing services relating to professional development or training to Cafcass or CAFCASS CYMRU	Any information relating to the proceedings providing that it does not, or is not likely to, identify any person involved in the proceedings without that person's consent	To enable the person or body to provide the services, where the services cannot be effectively provided without such disclosure
An officer of the service or a Welsh family proceedings officer	A person employed by or contracted to Cafcass or CAFCASS CYMRU for the purposes of carrying out the functions referred to in column 4 of this row	Any information relating to the proceedings	Engagement in processes internal to Cafcass or CAFCASS CYMRU which relate to the maintenance of necessary records concerning the proceedings, or to ensuring that Cafcass or CAFCASS CYMRU functions are carried out to a satisfactory standard

11.7 Communication to and by Ministers of the Crown and Welsh Ministers

A person specified in the first column of the following table may communicate to a person listed in the second column such information as is specified in the third column for the purpose or purposes specified in the fourth column –

A party or any person lawfully in receipt of information relating to the proceedings	A Minister of the Crown with responsibility for a government department engaged, or potentially engaged, in an application before the European Court of Human Rights relating to the proceedings	Any information relating to the proceedings of which he or she is in lawful possession	To provide the department with information relevant, or potentially relevant, to the proceedings before the European Court of Human Rights
A Minister of the Crown	The European Court of Human Rights		For the purpose of engagement in an application before the European Court of Human Rights relating to the proceedings
A Minister of the Crown	Lawyers advising or representing the United Kingdom in an application before the European Court of Human Rights relating to the proceedings		For the purpose of receiving advice or for effective representation in relation to the application before the European Court of Human Rights.

A Minister of the crown or a Welsh Minister	Another Minister, or Ministers, of the Crown or a Welsh Minister		For the purpose of notification, discussion and the giving or receiving of advice regarding issues raised by the information in which the relevant departments have, or may have, an interest

11.8 Communication by persons lawfully in receipt of information

(1) This rule applies to communications made in accordance with rules 11.5, 11.6 and 11.7 and the reference in this rule to 'the table' means the table in the relevant rule.

(2) A person in the second column of the table may only communicate information relating to the proceedings received from a person in the first column for the purpose or purposes –

  (a) for which he received that information; or
  (b) of professional development or training, providing that any communication does not, or is not likely to, identify any person involved in the proceedings without that person's consent.

11.9 Interpretation

In this Part –

  'accreditation body' means –
    (a) The Law Society,
    (b) Resolution, or
    (c) The Legal Services Commission;

  'adoption panel' means a panel established in accordance with regulation 3 of the Adoption Agencies Regulations 2005 or regulation 3 of the Adoption Agencies (Wales) Regulations 2005;
  'alternative dispute resolution' means methods of resolving a dispute, including mediation, other than through the normal court process;
  'approved research project' means a project of research –
    (a) approved in writing by a Secretary of State after consultation with the President of the Family Division,
    (b) approved in writing by the President of the Family Division, or
    (c) conducted under section 83 of the Act of 1989 or section 13 of the Criminal Justice and Court Services Act 2000;

  'body assessing quality assurance systems' includes –

(a) The Law Society,
(b) The Legal Services Commission, or
(c) The General Council of the Bar;

'body or person responsible for investigating or determining complaints in relation to legal representatives or professional legal advisers' means –
(a) The Law Society,
(b) The General Council of the Bar,
(c) The Institute of Legal Executives, or
(d) The Legal Services Ombudsman;

'Cafcass' has the meaning assigned to it by section 11 of the Criminal Justice and Courts Services Act 2000;

'CAFCASS CYMRU' means the part of the Welsh Assembly Government exercising the functions of Welsh Ministers under Part 4 of the Children Act 2004;

'criminal investigation' means an investigation conducted by police officers with a view to it being ascertained –
(a) whether a person should be charged with an offence, or
(b) whether a person charged with an offence is guilty of it;

'health care professional' means –
(a) a registered medical practitioner,
(b) a registered nurse or midwife,
(c) a clinical psychologist, or
(d) a child psychotherapist;

'independent reviewing officer' means a person appointed in respect of a child in accordance with regulation 2A of the Review of Children's Cases Regulations 1991, or regulation 3 of the Review of Children's Cases (Wales) Regulations 2007;

'lay adviser' means a non-professional person who gives lay advice on behalf of an organisation in the lay advice sector;

['legal representative' means a –
(a) barrister,
(b) solicitor,
(c) solicitor's employee,
(d) manager of a body recognised under section 9 of the Administration of Justice Act 1985, or
(e) person who, for the purposes of the Legal Services Act 2007, is an authorised person in relation to an activity which constitutes the conduct of litigation (within the meaning of that Act),

who has been instructed to act for a party in relation to the proceedings;][2]

'McKenzie Friend' means any person permitted by the court to sit beside an unrepresented litigant in court to assist that litigant by prompting, taking notes and giving him advice;

'professional acting in furtherance of the protection of children' includes –
(a) an officer of a local authority exercising child protection functions,
(b) a police officer who is –

>   (i) exercising powers under section 46 of the Act of 1989, or
>   (ii) serving in a child protection unit or a paedophile unit of a police force,
>   (c) any professional person attending a child protection conference or review in relation to a child who is the subject of the proceedings to which the information relates, or
>   (d) an officer of the National Society for the Prevention of Cruelty to Children;
>
> ['professional legal adviser' means a –
>   (a) barrister,
>   (b) solicitor,
>   (c) solicitor's employee,
>   (d) manager of a body recognised under section 9 of the Administration of Justice Act 1985, or
>   (e) person who, for the purposes of the Legal Services Act 2007, is an authorised person in relation to an activity which constitutes the conduct of litigation (within the meaning of that Act),
>
> who is providing advice to a party but is not instructed to represent that party in the proceedings;][2]
>
> 'social worker' has the meaning assigned to it by section 55 of the Care Standards Act 2000;
>
> 'welfare officer' means a person who has been asked to prepare a report under section 7(1)(b) of the Act of 1989.][1]

NOTES

Amendment.[1] Part inserted: SI 2009/857. [2] Definitions substituted: SI 2009/3348.

APPENDIX 1
FORMS

M1	Statement of Information for a Consent Order
M2	General Heading of Proceedings
M3	Certificate with Regard to Reconciliation
[M4	Statement of Arrangements for Children][4]
[M5	Notice of Proceedings][4, 7, 10]
[M5A	Notice of Proceedings: Civil Partnership Act 2004][11]
[M6	Acknowledgment of Service][4, 10]
[M6A	Acknowledgement of Service: Civil Partnership Act 2004][11]
M7	Affidavit by Petitioner in Support of Petition
M8	Notice of Application for Decree Nisi to be made Absolute
M9	Certificate of Making Decree Nisi Absolute (Divorce)
[M9A	Order Making Conditional Order for Dissolution Final][11]
M10	Certificate of Making Decree Nisi Absolute (Nullity)

Part II Statutory Instruments

[M10A   Order Making Conditional Nullity Order Final]¹¹
           ...⁸

M16   Request for Issue of Judgment Summons

M17   Judgment Summons
           ...⁶

[M19   Originating Application on Ground of Failure to Provide
           Reasonable Maintenance]⁴

M20   Notice of Application Under Rule 3.1 or 3.2

[M21   Originating Application for Alteration of Maintenance Agreement
           during Parties' Lifetime]⁴

M22   Originating Application for Alteration of Maintenance Agreement
           after Death of One of the Parties

M23   Originating Summons Under Section 17 of the Married Women's
           Property Act 1882 or Section 1 of the Matrimonial Homes
           Act 1967

M24   Notice to be Indorsed on Document Served in Accordance with
           Rule 9.3

M25   Ex Parte Originating Summons Under Section 13 of the
           Matrimonial and Family Proceedings Act 1984

M26   Originating Summons Under Section 12 of the Matrimonial and
           Family Proceedings Act 1984

M27   Originating Summons Under Section 24 of the Matrimonial and
           Family Proceedings Act 1984

M28   Notice of Proceedings and Acknowledgment of Service

M29   Declaration as to Marital Status Under Section 55 of the Family
           Law Act 1986

[M29A   Declaration as to Civil Partnership Status under Section 58 of the
           Civil Partnership Act 2004]¹¹

M30   Declaration as to Parentage Under [Section 55A] of the Family
           Law Act 1986

M31   Declaration as to Legitimacy or Legitimation Under
           Section 56(1)(b) and (2) of the Family Law Act 1986

[M32   Declaration as to an Adoption Effected Overseas under Section 57
           of the Family Law Act 1986]¹

[M33   Application for registration of Maintenance Order in a
           Magistrates' Court]³

[M34   Notice under rule 10.24(1)]⁴

[[C1   Application   [[Children Act 1989 except care and supervision
                            orders, Section 8 orders and orders related to
                            enforcement of a contact order]¹⁷]¹⁴]⁹

[C100	Application	under the Children Act 1989 for a residence, contact or other section 8 order][14]
[C110	Application	under the Children Act 1989 for a care order or supervision order][17]
[C1A		Supplemental Information Form][12]
C2	Application	for an order or directions in existing family proceedings
	Application	to be joined as, or cease to be, a party in existing family proceedings
	Application	for leave to commence proceedings
C3	Application	for an order authorising search for, taking charge of, and delivery of a child
C4	Application	for an order for disclosure of a child's whereabouts
C6	Notice	of proceedings [Hearing] [Directions Appointment] (*Notice to parties*)
C6A	Notice	of proceedings [Hearing] [Directions Appointment] (Notice to non-parties)
[C7		Acknowledgement][9]
C8		Confidential Address
[C9	Statement	of Service][9]
C10	Supplement	for an application for financial provision for a child or for variation of financial provision for a child
C10A	Statement	of Means
[C11	Supplement	for an application for an Emergency Protection Order][6]
C12	Supplement	for an application for a Warrant to assist a person authorised by an Emergency Protection Order
...[17]		
[C13A	Supplement	for an application for a Special Guardianship Order][11]
C14	Supplement	for an application for authority to refuse contact with a child in care
C15	Supplement	for an application for contact with a child in care
C16	Supplement	for an application for a Child Assessment Order
C17	Supplement	for an application for an Education Supervision Order

Part II   Statutory Instruments

C17A	Supplement	for an application for an extension of an Education Supervision Order
C18	Supplement	for an application for a Recovery Order
C19	Supplement	for a Warrant of Assistance
C20	Supplement	for an application for an order to hold a child in Secure Accommodation
C21	Order or direction	Blank
C22	Record	of hearing
[C23	Order	Emergency Protection Order][6]
C24	Order	Variation of an Emergency Protection Order
		Extension of an Emergency Protection Order
		Discharge of an Emergency Protection Order
C25	Warrant	To assist a person authorised by an Emergency Protection Order
C26	Order	Authority to keep a child in Secure Accommodation
C27	Order	Authority to search for another child
C28	Warrant	To assist a person to gain access to a child or entry to premises
C29	Order	Recovery of a child
C30	Order	To disclose information about the whereabouts of a missing child
C31	Order	Authorising search for, taking charge of, and delivery of a child
C32	Order	Care Order
		Discharge of a Care Order
[C33	Order	Interim Care Order][6]
C34	Order	Contact with a child in care
		Authority to refuse contact with a child in care
C35	Order	Supervision Order
		Interim Supervision Order
C36	Order	Substitution of a Supervision Order for a Care Order
		Discharge of a Supervision Order
		Variation of a Supervision Order
		Extension of a Supervision Order
C37	Order	Education Supervision Order

C38	Order	Discharge of an Education Supervision Order
		Extension of an Education Supervision Order
C39	Order	Child Assessment Order
C40	Direction	To undertake an investigation
[C42	Order	Family Assistance Order][9]
C43	Order	Residence Order
		Contact Order
		Specific Issue Order
		Prohibited Steps Order
[C43A	Order	Special Guardianship Order][11]
C44	Order	Leave to change the surname by which a child is known
		Leave to remove a child from the United Kingdom
C45	Order	Parental Responsibility Order
		Termination of a Parental Responsibility Order
C46	Order	Appointment of a guardian
		Termination of the appointment of a guardian
[C47	Order	Making or refusing the appointment of a children's guardian
		Termination of the appointment of a children's guardian][9]
[C48	Order	Appointment of a solicitor for a child
		Refusal of the appointment of a solicitor for a child
		Termination of the appointment of a solicitor for a child][9]
C49	Order	Transfer of Proceedings to [the High Court] [a county court] [a family proceedings court]
C51		Application for a Parental Order
C52		Acknowledgement of an application for a Parental Order
C53	Order	Parental Order
C54	Notice	of Refusal of a Parental Order][5]
[C78	Application	for attachment of a warning notice to a contact order
[A64A	Application	for a recovery order
A101A	Consent	to the making of a parental order][16]

Part II   Statutory Instruments

C79	Application	related to enforcement of a contact order
C80	Order	Enforcement order
C81	Order	Revocation of enforcement order
C82	Order	Order for financial compensation][14]

[FL401   Application for a non-molestation order/an occupation order

FL402   Notice of Proceedings [Hearing] [Directions Appointment]

FL403   Application to vary, extend or discharge an order in existing proceedings

[FL404   Occupation Order][13]

[FL404a Non-Molestation Order][13]

FL405   Record of Hearing

[FL406   Record of Occupation Order][13]

FL407   Application for a Warrant of Arrest

FL408   Warrant of Arrest

FL409   Remand Order

FL410   Recognizance of respondent

FL411   Recognizance of respondent's surety

FL412   Bail Notice

FL413   Hospital Order/Interim Hospital Order

FL414   Guardianship Order

FL415   Statement of Service

FL416   Notice to Mortgagees and Landlords

FL417   Transfer of proceedings to [the High Court] [a county court] [a family proceedings court]][6]

[FL401A Application for a Forced Marriage Protection Order

FL402A Notice of proceedings

FL403A Application to vary, extend or discharge a Forced Marriage Protection Order

FL404B Forced Marriage Protection Order

FL406A Power of Arrest: Forced Marriage Protection Order

FL407A Application for Warrant of Arrest: Forced Marriage Protection Order

FL430   Application for leave to apply for a Forced Marriage Protection Order

FL431   Application to be joined as, or cease to be, a party to Forced Marriage Protection Proceedings][15]

NOTES

Amendments.[1] Forms substituted or inserted: SI 1991/2113.[2] Forms amended: SI 1992/456.[3] Forms substituted, inserted or amended: SI 1992/2067.[4] Forms substituted, inserted or amended: SI 1993/295.[5] Forms substituted: SI 1994/3155.[6] Forms deleted, substituted or inserted: SI 1997/1893.[7] Form amended: SI 1998/1901.[8] Forms omitted: SI 1999/3491.[9] Forms substituted or inserted: SI 2001/821.[10] Forms amended: SI 2005/264.[11] Entries inserted: SI 2005/2922.[12] Entry inserted: SI 2004/3375.[13] Entries substituted and inserted: SI 2007/1622.[14] Words substituted and entries inserted: SI 2008/2861.[15] Entries inserted: SI 2008/2446. [16] Entries inserted: SI 2010/1064. [17] Words substituted and entries inserted and revoked: SI 2010/786.

****

[APPENDIX 3
NOTICES AND RESPONDENTS

Rules 4.4 and 4.7

(i)	(ii)	(iii)	(iv)
Provision under which proceedings brought	*Minimum number of days prior to hearing or directions appointment for service under rule 4.4(1)(b)*	*Respondents*	*Persons to whom notice is to be given*
All applications.	See separate entries below.	Subject to separate entries below: every person whom the applicant believes to have parental responsibility for the child; where the child is the subject of a care order,	Subject to separate entries below: local authority providing accommodation for the child; persons who are caring for the child at the time when the proceedings are commenced;

(i)	(ii)	(iii)	(iv)
Provision under which proceedings brought	*Minimum number of days prior to hearing or directions appointment for service under rule 4.4(1)(b)*	*Respondents*	*Persons to whom notice is to be given*
		every person whom the applicant believes to have had parental responsibility immediately prior to the making of the care order; in the case of an application to extend, vary or discharge an order, the parties to the proceedings leading to the order which it is sought to have extended, varied or discharged; in the case of specified proceedings, the child.	in the case of proceedings brought in respect of a child who is alleged to be staying in a refuge which is certified under section 51(1) or (2), the person who is providing the refuge.

(i)	(ii)	(iii)	(iv)
Provision under which proceedings brought	*Minimum number of days prior to hearing or directions appointment for service under rule 4.4(1)(b)*	*Respondents*	*Persons to whom notice is to be given*
Section [4(1)(c)][3], 4(3), [4ZA(1)(c), 4ZA(6),][8] [4A(1)(b), 4A(3),][4] 5(1), 6(7), 8, 13(1), [14A, 14C(3), 14D,][4] ...[5], 33(7), Schedule 1, paragraph 19(1) of Schedule 2, or paragraph 11(3) or 16(5) of Schedule 14 [or, where rule 4.4A(4) applies, section 8(2)(a) of the Act of 2006][6].	14 days.	As for 'all applications' above, and: in the case of proceedings under Schedule 1, those persons whom the applicant believes to be interested in or affected by the proceedings; in the case of an application under paragraph 11(3)(b) or 16(5) of Schedule 14, any person, other than the child, named in the order or directions which it is sought to discharge or vary; [in the case of an application	As for 'all applications' above, and: in the case of an application for a section 8 order [or an application under section 14A or 14D][4], every person whom the applicant believes – (i) to be named in a court order with respect to the same child, which has not ceased to have effect, (ii) to be a party to pending proceedings in respect of the same child, or

(i)	(ii)	(iii)	(iv)
Provision under which proceedings brought	*Minimum number of days prior to hearing or directions appointment for service under rule 4.4(1)(b)*	*Respondents*	*Persons to whom notice is to be given*
		under section 14A, if a care order is in force with respect to the child, the child.]⁴	(iii) to be a person with whom the child has lived for at least 3 years prior to the application, unless, in a case to which (i) or (ii) applies, the applicant believes that the court order or pending proceedings are not relevant to the application; in the case of an application under paragraph 19(1) of Schedule 2, the parties to the proceedings leading to the care order;

(i)	(ii)	(iii)	(iv)
Provision under which proceedings brought	Minimum number of days prior to hearing or directions appointment for service under rule 4.4(1)(b)	Respondents	Persons to whom notice is to be given
			in the case of an application under section 5(1), [the father or parent (being a woman who is a parent by virtue of section 43 of the Human Fertilisation and Embryology Act 2008) of the child if that person][8] does not have parental responsibility. [in the case of an application under section 14A, if the child is not being accommodated by the local authority, the local authority in whose area the applicant is ordinarily resident; in the case of an application under section 14D – (a) as for applications under section 14A above, and

Part II Statutory Instruments

(i)	(ii)	(iii)	(iv)
Provision under which proceedings brought	*Minimum number of days prior to hearing or directions appointment for service under rule 4.4(1)(b)*	*Respondents*	*Persons to whom notice is to be given*
			(b) the local authority that prepared the report under section 14A(8) or (9) in the proceedings leading to the order which it is sought to have varied or discharged, if different from any local authority that will otherwise be notified.][4]
Section 11J or 11O	14 days	Only the person who the applicant alleges has failed to comply with the contact order	Any officer of the service or Welsh family proceedings officer exercising a duty conferred on him by section 11H(2) (monitoring compliance with a contact order)

(i)	(ii)	(iii)	(iv)
Provision under which proceedings brought	*Minimum number of days prior to hearing or directions appointment for service under rule 4.4(1)(b)*	*Respondents*	*Persons to whom notice is to be given*
			Where the child was a party to the proceedings in which the contact order was made – (a) the person who was the children's guardian, guardian ad litem or next friend of the child in those proceedings; or (b) where there was no children's guardian, guardian ad litem or next friend, the person who was the legal representative of the child in those proceedings.][6]

(i)	(ii)	(iii)	(iv)
Provision under which proceedings brought	*Minimum number of days prior to hearing or directions appointment for service under rule 4.4(1)(b)*	*Respondents*	*Persons to whom notice is to be given*
Section 36(1), 39(1), 39(2), 39(3), 39(4), 43(1), or paragraph 6(3), 15(2) or 17(1) of Schedule 3.	7 days.	As for 'all applications' above, and: in the case of an application under section 39(2) or (3), the supervisor; in the case of proceedings under paragraph 17(1) of Schedule 3, the [local authority designated in the order][10]; in the case of proceedings under section 36 or paragraph 15(2) or 17(1) of Schedule 3, the child.	As for 'all applications' above, and: in the case of an application for an order under section 43(1) – (i) every person whom the applicant believes to be a parent of the child, (ii) every person whom the applicant believes to be caring for the child, (iii) every person in whose favour a contact order is in force with respect to the child, and

Family Proceedings Rules 1991, App 3

(i)	(ii)	(iii)	(iv)
Provision under which proceedings brought	*Minimum number of days prior to hearing or directions appointment for service under rule 4.4(1)(b)*	*Respondents*	*Persons to whom notice is to be given*
Section 31, 34(2), 34(3), 34(4), 34(9) or 38(8)(b).	3 days.	As for 'all applications' above, and; in the case of an application under section 34, the person whose contact with the child is the subject of the application.	(iv) every person who is allowed to have contact with the child by virtue of an order under section 34. As for 'all applications' above, and; in the case of an application under section 31 – (i) every person whom the applicant believes to be a party to pending relevant proceedings in respect of the same child, and

PART II – Statutory Instruments

(i)	(ii)	(iii)	(iv)
Provision under which proceedings brought	*Minimum number of days prior to hearing or directions appointment for service under rule 4.4(1)(b)*	*Respondents*	*Persons to whom notice is to be given*
			(ii) every person whom the applicant believes to be a parent without parental responsibility for the child.
Section 43(12).	2 days.	As for 'all applications' above.	Those of the persons referred to in section 43(11)(a) to (e) who were not party to the application for the order which it is sought to have varied or discharged.
Section 25, 44(1), 44(9)(b), 45(4), 45(8), 46(7), 48(9), 50(1), or 102(1).	1 day.	As for 'all applications' above, and: in the case of an application under section 44(9)(b) –	Except for applications under section 102(1), as for 'all applications' above, and: in the case of an application under

(i)	(ii)	(iii)	(iv)
Provision under which proceedings brought	*Minimum number of days prior to hearing or directions appointment for service under rule 4.4(1)(b)*	*Respondents*	*Persons to whom notice is to be given*
		(i) the parties to the application for the order in respect of which it is sought to vary the directions; (ii) any person who was caring for the child prior to the making of the order, and (iii) any person whose contact with the child is affected by the direction which it is sought to have varied;	section 44(1), every person whom the applicant believes to be a parent of the child; in the case of an application under section 44(9)(b) – (i) the local authority in whose area the child is living, and (ii) any person whom the applicant believes to be affected by the direction which it is sought to have varied;

(i)	(ii)	(iii)	(iv)
Provision under which proceedings brought	*Minimum number of days prior to hearing or directions appointment for service under rule 4.4(1)(b)*	*Respondents*	*Persons to whom notice is to be given*
[Paragraph 4 of Schedule A1	14 days	in the case of an application under section 50, the person whom the applicant alleges to have effected or to have been or to be responsible for the taking or keeping of the child. Only – the person who was the applicant for the enforcement order, and where the child was a party to the proceedings in which the enforcement order was made, the child	in the case of an application under section 102(1), the person referred to in section 102(1) and any person preventing or likely to prevent such a person from exercising powers under enactments mentioned in subsection (6) of that section. Any officer of the service or Welsh family proceedings officer exercising a duty conferred on him by section 11M(1) (monitoring compliance with an enforcement order) and the responsible officer (as defined in section 197 of the Criminal Justice Act 2003 as modified by Schedule A1)

Family Proceedings Rules 1991, App 3

(i)	(ii)	(iii)	(iv)
Provision under which proceedings brought	*Minimum number of days prior to hearing or directions appointment for service under rule 4.4(1)(b)*	*Respondents*	*Persons to whom notice is to be given*
Paragraphs 5 to 7 of Schedule A1	14 days	Only the person who was the applicant for the enforcement order	Any officer of the service or Welsh family proceedings officer exercising a duty conferred on him by section 11M(1) (monitoring compliance with an enforcement order) and the responsible officer (as defined in section 197 of the Criminal Justice Act 2003 as modified by Schedule A1)

(i)	(ii)	(iii)	(iv)
Provision under which proceedings brought	*Minimum number of days prior to hearing or directions appointment for service under rule 4.4(1)(b)*	*Respondents*	*Persons to whom notice is to be given*
Paragraph 9 of Schedule A1	14 days	Only – the person who the applicant alleges has failed to comply with the unpaid work requirement imposed by an enforcement order, and where the child was a party to the proceedings in which the enforcement order was made, the child	Any officer of the service or Welsh family proceedings officer exercising a duty conferred on him by section 11M(1) (monitoring compliance with an enforcement order) and the responsible officer (as defined in section 197 of the Criminal Justice Act 2003 as modified by Schedule A1).][6]
[...[9]][2] [Section 79 of the Childcare Act 2006	1 day	Any person preventing or likely to prevent Her Majesty's Chief Inspector of Education, Children's Services and Skills from exercising a power conferred on him by section 77][7]	][1]

NOTES

Amendments.[1] Appendix substituted: SI 1992/2067.[2] Words inserted: SI 1994/2165.[3] Words substituted: SI 2003/2839.[4] Entries and words inserted: SI 2005/2922.[5] Reference revoked:

SI 2007/2187.[6] Words and entry inserted: SI 2008/2861.[7] Entry inserted: SI 2009/636. [8] References inserted and words substituted: SI 2009/2027. [9] Entry revoked: SI 2010/1064. [10] Words inserted: SI 2010/1172.

[APPENDIX 4

Rules 3.1(10), 3.5(1), 3.6(10), 3.8(13), 3.18(3) and (6), 3.19(5)

1

In this Appendix a reference to a paragraph by number alone is a reference to a paragraph of this Appendix.

2 Representation of children on applications under Act of 1984 and under Schedule 7 to the Act 2004

(1) Sub-paragraph (2) applies where, on an application for financial relief under Part III of the Act of 1984 or under Schedule 7 to the Act of 2004, an application is made for an order for a variation of settlement.

(2) The court must, unless it is satisfied that the proposed variation does not adversely affect the rights or interests of any children concerned, direct that the children be separately represented on the application, either by a solicitor or by a solicitor and counsel, and may appoint the Official Solicitor or other fit person to be guardian ad litem of the children for the purpose of the application.

(3) On any other application for financial relief under Part III of the Act of 1984 or under Schedule 7 to the Act of 2004 the court may give such a direction or make such appointment as it is empowered to give or make by sub-paragraph (2).

(4) Before a person other than the Official Solicitor is appointed guardian ad litem under this rule the solicitor acting for the children must file a certificate that the person proposed as guardian has no interest in the matter adverse to that of the children and that he is a proper person to be such guardian.

3 Evidence on application for financial relief or avoidance of transaction order under Act of 1984 or under Schedule 7 to Act of 2004

(1) Where an application is made for financial relief or an avoidance of transaction order under Part III of the Act of 1984 or under Schedule 7 to the Act of 2004, the affidavit in support must contain, so far as known to the applicant, full particulars –

    (a)   in the case of an application for a transfer or settlement of property –
           (i)   of the property in respect of which the application is made, and
           (ii) of the property to which the party against whom the application is made is entitled either in possession or reversion;
    (b)   in the case of an application for an order for a variation of settlement –
           (i)   of all relevant settlements, made on the spouses or civil partners, as the case may be, and

(ii) of the funds brought into settlement by each spouse or civil partner;
(c) in the case of an application for an avoidance of transaction order –
(i) of the property to which the disposition relates, and
(ii) of the person in whose favour the disposition is alleged to have been made,
and in the case of a disposition alleged to have been made by way of settlement, of the trustees and the beneficiaries of the settlement.

(2) Where an application for a property adjustment order or an avoidance of transaction order relates to land, the affidavit in support must identify the land and –

(a) state whether the title to the land is registered or unregistered and, if registered, the Land Registry title number; and
(b) give particulars, so far as known to the applicant, of any mortgage of the land or other interest in it.

(3) A copy of Form M26 or M27 as the case may be, together with a copy of the supporting affidavit, must, as well as being served on the respondent, be served –

(a) in the case of an application for an order for a variation of settlement, on the trustees of the settlement and the settlor if living;
(b) in the case of an application for an avoidance of transaction order, on the person in whose favour the disposition is alleged to have been made; and
(c) in the case of an application to which sub-paragraph (2) refers, on any mortgagee of whom particulars are given pursuant to that paragraph, and on such other persons, if any, as the district judge may direct.

(4) Any person who is served with an application pursuant to sub-paragraph (3) may within 14 days after service file an affidavit in answer.

(5) In this rule a relevant settlement –

(a) in relation to a marriage, is an ante-nuptial or post-nuptial settlement; and
(b) in relation to a civil partnership, is a settlement made during its subsistence or in anticipation of its formation, on the civil partners including one made by will or codicil, but not including one in the form of a pension arrangement (within the meaning of Part 4 of Schedule 5 to the Act of 2004).

4 Service of affidavit on application for alteration of maintenance agreement

(1) This paragraph applies to an affidavit filed in support of an application under section 35 or 36 of the Act of 1973 or paragraphs 69 or 73 of Schedule 5 to the Act of 2004.

(2) This paragraph, apart from sub-paragraph (3), also applies to an affidavit filed in support of an application under section 27 of the Act of 1973 or Part 9

of Schedule 5 to the Act of 2004 which contains an allegation of adultery or of an improper association with a person named.

(3) Where a person files an affidavit to which this sub-paragraph applies he must at the same time serve a copy on the opposite party.

(4) Where an affidavit to which this paragraph applies contains an allegation of adultery or of an improper association with a named person ('the named person') the court may direct that the party who filed the affidavit serve a copy of all or part of it on the named person together with Form F (the references to ancillary relief in that form being substituted by references to the provision under which the application is made).

(5) Where the court makes a direction under sub-paragraph (4) the named person may file an affidavit in answer to the allegations.

(6) The named person may intervene in the proceedings by applying for directions under paragraph 7(4) within seven days of service of the affidavit on him.

(7) Rule 2.37(3) applies to a person served with an affidavit under sub-paragraph (4) as it applies to a co-respondent.

5 Information on application for consent orders on application for failure to provide reasonable maintenance or for financial provision under Act of 1984 or Schedule 7 to Act of 2004

(1) This paragraph applies to an application for a consent order –

(a) under section 27 of the Act of 1973 or Part 9 of Schedule 5 to the Act of 2004; and

(b) under Part III of the Act of 1984 or Schedule 7 to the Act of 2004.

(2) Subject to sub-paragraphs (3) and (4), there must be lodged with every application to which this paragraph applies two copies of a draft of the order in the terms sought, one of which must be indorsed with a statement signed by the respondent to the application signifying his agreement, and a statement of information (which may be made in more than one document) which must include –

(a) the duration of the marriage or civil partnership, as the case may be, the age of each party and of any minor or dependent child of the family;

(b) an estimate in summary form of the approximate amount or value of the capital resources and net income of each party and of any minor child of the family;

(c) what arrangements are intended for the accommodation of each of the parties and any minor child of the family;

(d) whether either party has subsequently married or formed a civil partnership or has any present intention to do so or to cohabit with another person;

(e) where the order includes provision to be made –

(i) under section 17(1)(a) of the Act of 1984 of a kind which could be made by an order under section 25B or 25C of the Act of 1973;
(ii) under section 17(1)(b) of the Act of 1984; or
(iii) under paragraph 9(2) of Schedule 7 to the Act of 2004 of a kind which could be made by an order under paragraphs 15, 25 or 26 of Schedule 5 to that Act,

a statement confirming that the person responsible for the pension arrangement in question has been served with the documents required by rule 2.70(11) and that no objection to such an order has been made by that person within 21 days from such service;

(f) where the terms of the order provide for a transfer of property, a statement confirming that any mortgagee of that property has been served with notice of the application and that no objection to such a transfer has been made by the mortgagee within 14 days from such service; and

(g) any other especially significant matters.

(3) Where an application is made –

(a) for a consent order for interim periodical payments pending the determination of the application; or
(b) for an order varying an order for periodical payments,

the statement of information required by sub-paragraph (2) need include only the information in respect of net income mentioned in sub-paragraph (2)(b).

(4) Where all or any of the parties attend the hearing of an application for financial relief the court may dispense with the lodging of a statement of information in accordance with sub-paragraph (2) and give directions for the information which would otherwise be required to be given in such a statement to be given in such a manner as it sees fit.

6 Investigation by district judge of application under section 27 of Act of 1973 or under Part 9 of Schedule 5 to Act of 2004

(1) On or after the filing of a notice in Form M19 an appointment must be fixed for the hearing of the application by the district judge.

(2) An application for an avoidance of disposition order must, if practicable, be heard at the same time as any related application.

(3) Notice of the appointment must be given in Form M20 by the proper officer to every party to the application.

(4) Any party may apply to the court for an order that any person do attend an appointment (an 'inspection appointment') before the court and produce any documents to be specified or described in the order, the inspection of which appears to the court to be necessary for disposing fairly of the application to which it relates or for saving costs.

(5) No person shall be required by an order under sub-paragraph (4) to produce any document at an inspection appointment which he could not be required to produce at the final hearing of the application.

(6) The court must permit any person attending an inspection appointment pursuant to an order under sub-paragraph (4) to be represented at the appointment.

7 Further provision about certain applications

(1) This paragraph applies to –

(a) an application under section 27 of the Act of 1973 or under Part 9 of Schedule 5 to the Act of 2004;
(b) an application under section 35 and 36 of the Act of 1973 or under paragraphs 69 and 73 of Schedule 5 to the Act of 2004;
(c) an application under section 17 of the Married Women's Property Act 1882 or under section 66 of the Act of 2004;
(d) an application under section 33, 35 and 36 of the Family Law Act 1996 and applications for transfer of tenancy under that Act; and

(2) This paragraph, apart from sub-paragraph (3) also applies to an application for financial relief under Part III of the Act of 1984 or under Schedule 7 to the Act of 2004.

(3) At the hearing of an application to which this paragraph applies the district judge must, subject to paragraphs 8 and 9(5) and rule 10.10 investigate the allegations made in support of and in answer to the application, and may take evidence orally and may at any stage of the proceedings, whether before or during the hearing, order the attendance of any person for the purpose of being examined or cross-examined and order the disclosure and inspection of any document or require further affidavits.

(4) The district judge may at any stage of the proceedings give directions as to the filing and service of pleadings and as to the further conduct of the proceedings.

(5) Where any party to such an application intends on the day appointed for the hearing to apply for directions, he must file and serve on every other party a notice to that effect.

(6) Subject to any directions given by the court, any party to an application to which this sub-paragraph applies may by letter require any other party to give further information concerning any matter contained in any affidavit filed by or on behalf of that other party or any other relevant matter, or to provide a list of relevant documents or to allow inspection of any such document, and may, in default of compliance by such other party, apply to the district judge for directions.

8 Order on certain applications

(1) This paragraph applies to –

(a) an application under section 27 of the Act of 1973 or under Part 9 of Schedule 5 to the Act of 2004;
(b) an application under section 35 and 36 of the Act of 1973 or under paragraphs 69 and 73 of Schedule 5 to the Act of 2004;
(c) an application under section 17 of the Married Women's Property Act 1882 or under section 66 of the Act of 2004;

(2) Subject to paragraph 9(5) the district judge must, after completing his investigation under paragraph 7, make such order as he thinks just.

(3) Pending the final determination of the application, the district judge may make an interim order upon such terms as he thinks just.

(4) RSC Order 31, rule 1 (power to order sale of land) shall apply to applications to which this rule applies as though that application were a cause or matter in the Chancery Division.

9 Arrangements for hearing applications etc by judge

(1) This paragraph applies to

(a) an application under section 27 of the Act of 1973 or under Part 9 of Schedule 5 to the Act of 2004;
(b) an application under section 35 of the Act of 1973 or under paragraphs 69 of Schedule 5 to the Act of 2004;
(c) an application under section 17 of the Married Women's Property Act 1882 or under section 66 of the Act of 2004.

(2) This paragraph, apart from sub-paragraphs (5), (8), (9) and (10), applies to an application under section 24 of the Act of 1984 or under paragraph 17 of Schedule 7 to the Act of 2004 for an order preventing transactions.

(3) Sub-paragraphs (5) to (7) of this paragraph apply to an application under section 36 of the Act of 1973 or under paragraph 73 of Schedule 5 to the Act of 2004;

(4) Sub-paragraphs (6) and (7) of this paragraph apply to an application for financial relief under the Act of 1984 or under Schedule 7 to the Act of 2004.

(5) The district judge may at any time refer an application of a kind referred to in sub-paragraph (1), or any question arising thereon, to a judge for his decision.

(6) Where an application of a kind mentioned in sub-paragraph (1), (2) or (3) is referred or adjourned to a judge, the proper officer must fix a date, time and place for the hearing of the application or the consideration of the question and give notice of that date to all parties.

(7) The hearing or consideration must, unless the court otherwise directs, take place in chambers.

(8) In an application under the Married Women's Property Act 1882 or under section 27 or 35 of the Act of 1973, where the application is proceeding in a divorce county court which is not a court of trial or is pending in the High

Court and proceeding in a district registry which is not in a divorce town, the hearing or consideration shall take place at such court of trial or divorce town as in the opinion of the district judge is the nearest or most convenient.

(9) In an application under section 66 of the Act of 2004 or under Part 9 or paragraph 69 of Schedule 5 to the Act of 2004, where the application is proceeding in a civil partnership proceedings county court which is not a court of trial or is pending in the High Court and proceeding in a district registry which is not in a dissolution town, the hearing or consideration shall take place at such court of trial or dissolution town as in the opinion of the district judge is the nearest or most convenient.

(10) For the purposes of sub-paragraph (8) and (9) the Royal Courts of Justice shall be treated as a divorce town or a dissolution town, as the case may be.

(11) In respect of any application referred to him under this rule, a judge shall have the same powers as a district judge has under paragraph 7(4).][1]

NOTES

Amendments.[1] Appendix inserted: SI 2005/2922.

Part II Statutory Instruments

FAMILY PROCEEDINGS COURTS (CHILDREN ACT 1989) RULES 1991

SI 1991/1395

ARRANGEMENT OF RULES

PART I
INTRODUCTORY

Rule		Page
1	Citation, commencement and interpretation	482
2	Matters prescribed for the purposes of the Act of 1989 and the Childcare Act 2006	484
2A	Proceedings with respect to which a single justice may discharge the functions of a court	485

PART II
GENERAL

3	Application for leave to commence proceedings	486
4	Application	486
5	Withdrawal of application	488
6	Transfer of proceedings	489
7	Parties	489
8	Service	490
9	Acknowledgement of application	492
10	Appointment of children's guardian	492
11	Powers and duties of officers of the service and Welsh family proceedings officers	493
11A	Additional powers and duties of children's guardian	494
11AA	Additional powers and duties of officers of the service and Welsh family proceedings officers: ... reports and risk assessments	496
11B	Additional powers and duties of a children and family reporter	497
12	Solicitor for child	498
13	Welfare officer	499
13A	Local authority officer preparing a family assistance order report	500
14	Directions	500
14A	Timetable for the Child in proceedings for a care order or supervision order	502
15	Timing of proceedings	503
16	Attendance of parties at directions appointment and hearing	504
16A	Restrictions on presence of persons at directions appointment and hearing	505
17	Documentary evidence	506
17A	Disclosure of report under section 14A(8) or (9)	507
17AA	Service of risk assessment	507
18	Expert evidence – examination of child	508
19	Amendment	508
20	Oral evidence	509
21	Hearing	509

PART IIA
PROCEEDINGS UNDER SECTION 54 OF THE HUMAN FERTILISATION AND EMBRYOLOGY ACT 2008

21A	Interpretation	510
21B	Application of this Part	511
21C	Application of remaining provisions of these Rules	511
21D	Application for a parental order	511
21E	How to start parental order proceedings	511
21F	Personal details	511
21G	Who the parties are	511
21H	What the court shall do when the application has been issued	512
21I	What a designated officer for the court shall do	512
21J	Service of the application and other documents	512
21JA	Acknowledgement	513
21JB	Date for first directions appointment	513
21JC	The first directions appointment	513
21JD	Where the agreement of the other parent or the woman who carried the child is not required	514
21JE	Agreement	515
21JF	Parental order reporter	515
21JG	Reports of the parental order reporter and disclosure to the parties	516
21JH	Notice of final hearing	516
21JI	The final hearing	516
21JJ	Proof of identity of the child	516
21JK	Disclosing information to an adult who was subject to a parental order	517
21JL	Application for recovery orders	517
21JM	Keeping of registers, custody, inspection and disclosure of documents and information	518
21JN	Documents held by the court not to be inspected or copied without the court's leave	518
21JO	Orders	518
21JP	Copies of orders	519
21JQ	Amendment and revocation of orders	519
21JR	Proceedings in respect of which a single justice and a justices' clerk may discharge the functions of the court	520

PART IIB
PROCEEDINGS IN RESPECT OF THE COUNCIL REGULATION

21K	Application by a party for transfer of proceedings to a court of another Member State	520
21L	Application by a court of another Member State for transfer of proceedings	521
21M	A certified copy of a judgment for enforcement in other Member States	521
21N	Application for a certificate in accordance with Article 41	522
21P	Rectification of certificates issued under Article 41	522

PART IIC
COMMUNICATION OF INFORMATION: PROCEEDINGS RELATING TO CHILDREN

21Q	Application	523
21R	Communication of information: general	523
21S	Instruction of experts	523

21T	Communication of information for purposes connected with the proceedings	524
21U	Communication of information by a party etc for other purposes	524
21V	Communication for the effective functioning of Cafcass and CAFCASS CYMRU	527
21W	Communication to and by Ministers of the Crown and Welsh Ministers	529
21X	Communication by persons lawfully in receipt of information	530
21Y	Interpretation	531

PART III
MISCELLANEOUS

22	Costs	533
22A	Power of court to limit cross-examination	533
23	Confidentiality of documents	533
23A	Communication of information relating to proceedings	534
24	Enforcement of residence order or special guardianship order	534
25	Notification of consent	534
25A	Exclusion requirements: interim care orders and emergency protection orders	535
26	Secure accommodation	536
27	Investigation under section 37	536
28	Limits on the power of a justices' clerk or a single justice to make an order under section 11(3) or section 38(1)	537
29	Appeals to a family proceedings court under section 77(6) and paragraph 8(1) of Schedule 8	537
30	Contribution orders	537
31	Direction to local authority to apply for education supervision order	538
31A	Applications and orders under sections 33 and 34 of the Family Law Act 1986	538
32	Delegation by justices' clerk	538
33	Application of section 97 of the Magistrates' Courts Act 1980	539
33A	Disclosure of addresses	539
33B	Setting aside on failure of service	539
34	Consequential and minor amendments, savings and transitionals	539
	Schedule 1 – Forms	540
	Schedule 2 – Respondents and notice	543

NOTES

Commencement. 14 October 1991.

Enabling power. Magistrates' Courts Act 1980, s 144.

PART I
INTRODUCTORY

1 Citation, commencement and interpretation

(1) These Rules may be cited as the Family Proceedings Courts (Children Act 1989) Rules 1991 and shall come into force on 14th October 1991.

(2) Unless a contrary intention appears –

a section or schedule referred to means the section or schedule in the Act of 1989,

'application' means an application made under or by virtue of the Act of 1989 or under these Rules, and 'applicant' shall be construed accordingly,
'business day' means any day other than –
    (a)   a Saturday, Sunday, Christmas Day or Good Friday; or
    (b)   a bank holiday, that is to say, a day which is, or is to be observed as, a bank holiday, or a holiday, under the Banking and Financial Dealings Act 1971, in England and Wales,

'child'
    (a)   means, in relation to any relevant proceedings, subject to sub-paragraph (b), a person under the age of 18 with respect to whom the proceedings are brought, and
    (b)   where paragraph 16(1) of Schedule 1 applies, also includes a person who has reached the age of 18,

['children and family reporter' means an officer of the service [or a Welsh family proceedings officer][3] who has been asked to prepare a welfare report under section 7(1)(a);][1]

['children's guardian'–
    (a)   means an officer of the service [or a Welsh family proceedings officer][3] appointed under section 41 for the child with respect to whom the proceedings are brought; but
    (b)   does not include such an officer appointed in relation to proceedings specified by rule 21A;][1]

['contact activity condition' has the meaning assigned to it by section 11C(2),
'contact activity direction' has the meaning assigned to it by section 11A(3),
'contact order' has the meaning assigned to it by section 8(1),][8]
'contribution order' has the meaning assigned to it by paragraph 23(2) of Schedule 2,
['the Council Regulation' means Council Regulation (EC) 2201/2003 of 27 November 2003 concerning jurisdiction and the recognition and enforcement of judgments in matrimonial matters and the matters of parental responsibility,][4]
'court' means a family proceedings court constituted in accordance with sections 66 and 67 of the Magistrates' Courts Act 1980 or, in respect of those proceedings prescribed in rule 2(5), a single justice who is a member of a family panel,
'directions appointment' means a hearing for directions under rule 14(2) [and rule 21JC][9],
'emergency protection order' means an order under section 44,
['family assistance order report' means a report to the court pursuant to a direction in a family assistance order under section 16(6);][7]
'file' means deposit with the [designated officer for a magistrates' court][2, 5],
'form' means a form in Schedule 1 to these Rules with such variation as the circumstances of the particular case may require,
  …[1]
  …[5]][2]
'leave' includes approval,
['Member State' means –

Part II Statutory Instruments

> (a) those parties contracting to the Council Regulation, that is to say, Belgium, Cyprus, Czech Republic, Germany, Greece, Spain, Estonia, France, Hungary, Ireland, Italy, Latvia, Lithuania, Luxembourg, Malta, Netherlands, Austria, Poland, Portugal, Slovakia, Slovenia, Finland, Sweden and the United Kingdom.
> (b) a party which has subsequently adopted the Council Regulation,]⁴

'note' includes a record made by mechanical means,
['officer of the service' has the same meaning as in the Criminal Justice and Court Services Act 2000;]¹
'parental responsibility' has the meaning assigned to it by section 3,
'parties' in relation to any relevant proceedings means the respondents specified for those proceedings in the third column of Schedule 2 to these Rules, and the applicant,
'recovery order' means an order under section 50,
'relevant proceedings' has the meaning assigned to it by section 93(3),
['risk assessment' has the meaning assigned to it by section 16A(3);]⁷
'section 8 order' has the meaning assigned to it by section 8(2),
['special guardianship order' has the meaning assigned to it by section 14A,]⁶
'specified proceedings' has the meaning assigned to it by section 41(6) and rule 2(2),
'the 1981 rules' means the Magistrates' Courts Rules 1981,
'the Act of 1989' means the Children Act 1989,
'welfare officer' means a person who has been asked to prepare a welfare report under [section 7(1)(b)]¹
['Welsh family proceedings officer' has the same meaning as in the Children Act 2004]⁴.

NOTES

Amendments.¹ Words inserted or omitted: SI 2001/818. ² Words substituted: SI 2001/615. ³ Words and definition inserted: SI 2005/585. ⁴ Definitions inserted: SI 2005/229. ⁵ Words substituted and definition revoked: SI 2005/617. ⁶ Definition inserted: SI 2005/2930. ⁷ Definitions inserted: SI 2007/2188. ⁸ Definitions inserted: SI 2008/2858. ⁹ Words inserted: SI 2010/1065.

2 Matters prescribed for the purposes of the Act of 1989 [and the Childcare Act 2006]⁴

(1) The parties to proceedings in which directions are given under section 38(6), and any person named in such a direction, form the prescribed class for the purposes of section 38(8)(b) (application to vary directions made with interim care or interim supervision order).

(2) The following proceedings are specified for the purposes of section 41 in accordance with subsection (6)(i) thereof –

> (a) proceedings [(in a family proceedings court)]¹ under section 25;
> (b) applications under section 33(7);
> (c) proceedings under paragraph 19(1) of Schedule 2;
> (d) applications under paragraph 6(3) of Schedule 3.

(3) The applicant for an order that has been made under section 43(1) and the persons referred to in section 43(11) may, in any circumstances, apply under section 43(12) for a child assessment order to be varied or discharged.

(4) The following persons form the prescribed class for the purposes of section 44(9)(b) (application to vary directions) –

- (a) the parties to the application for the order in respect of which it is sought to vary the directions;
- (b) the [children's guardian][2];
- (c) the local authority in whose area the child concerned is ordinarily resident;
- (d) any person who is named in the directions.

(5) The following proceedings are prescribed for the purposes of section 93(2)(i) as being proceedings with respect to which a single justice may discharge the functions of a family proceedings court, that is to say, proceedings –

- (a) where an ex parte application is made, under sections 10, 44(1), 48(9), 50(1), ...[4] or 102(1),
- (b) subject to rule 28, under sections 11(3) or 38(1),
- (c) under sections 4(3)(b), [4ZA(6)(b),][5] [4A(3)(b),][3] 7, 14, 34(3)(b), 37, 41, 44(9)(b) and (11)(b)(iii), 48(4), 91(15) or (17), or paragraph 11(4) of Schedule 14,
- [(cc) in accordance with rule 16A(1) except that a single justice may only give permission under rule 16A(1)(g) for a person to be present at a directions appointment or a hearing which that justice is conducting,][6]
- (d) in accordance with any Order made by the Lord Chancellor under Part I of Schedule 11, and
- (e) in accordance with rules 3 to 8, [10 to 16, 17 to 19][6], 21, 22, or 27.

NOTES

Amendments.[1] Words inserted: SI 1991/1991.[2] Words substituted: SI 2001/818.[3] Reference inserted: SI 2005/2930.[4] Words inserted and reference revoked: SI 2009/637. [5] Reference inserted: SI 2009/2025. [6] Paragraph and words inserted: SI 2010/787.

[2A Proceedings with respect to which a single justice may discharge the functions of a court

Where an application is made for a warrant under section 79 of the Childcare Act 2006, a single justice may discharge the functions of a family proceedings court in relation to those proceedings.]

NOTES

Amendments.[1] Rule inserted: SI 2009/637.

PART II
GENERAL

3 Application for leave to commence proceedings

(1) Where the leave of the court is required to bring any relevant proceedings, the person seeking leave shall file –

- (a) a written request for leave [in Form C2]¹ setting out the reasons for the application, and
- [(b) a draft of the application (being the documents referred to in rule 4(1A)) for the making of which leave is sought together with sufficient copies for one to be served on each respondent.]¹

(2) On considering a request for leave filed under paragraph (1), the court shall –

- (a) grant the request, whereupon the [designated officer for the court]²,³ shall inform the person making the request of the decision, or
- (b) direct that a date be fixed for a hearing of the request, whereupon the justices' clerk shall fix such a date and [the [designated officer for the court]³ shall]² give such notice as the court directs to the person making the request [and any local authority that is preparing, or has prepared, a report under section 14A(8) or (9)]⁴ and to such other persons as the court requires to be notified, of the date so fixed.

(3) Where leave is granted to bring any relevant proceedings, the application shall proceed in accordance with rule 4; but paragraph (1)(a) of that rule shall not apply.

NOTES

Amendments.¹ Words inserted or substituted: SI 1994/3156.² Words inserted or substituted: SI 2001/615.³ Words substituted: SI 2005/617.⁴ Words inserted: SI 2005/2930.

4 Application

(1) Subject to paragraph (4), an applicant shall –

- [(a) file the documents referred to in paragraph (1A) below (which documents shall together be called the 'application') together with sufficient copies for one to be served on each respondent, and]²
- (b) serve a copy of the application [together with Form C6 and such (if any) of Forms [C1A,]⁴ C7 and C10A as are given to him by the [designated officer for the court]³,⁵ under paragraph 2(b)]² on each respondent such minimum number of days prior to the date fixed under paragraph (2)(a) as is specified in relation to that application in column (ii) of Schedule 2 to these Rules.

[(1A) the documents to be filed under paragraph (1)(a) above are –

- (a)
  - (i) whichever is appropriate of Forms [C1, [C100,]⁶ [C110,]¹⁰ C2, C3, C4, C5]⁴ or ...⁹, and

[(ii) supplemental Forms C10, C11, C12 and C13A to C20 as appropriate,]¹⁰

[(iiA) in the case of an application for a care order or supervision order, such of the documents specified in the Annex to Form C110 as are available, and]¹⁰ [and

(iii) in the case of an application for a section 8 order or an order under section 4(1)(c)[, 4ZA(1)(c) or 4A(1)(b)]⁸ where question 7 on Form C1 [or (as the case may be) question 5 on Form C100]⁶, or question 4 on Form C2, is answered in the affirmative, supplemental Form C1A,]⁴ or

(b) where there is no appropriate form a statement in writing of the order sought,

and where the application is made in respect of more than one child, all the children shall be included in one application.]²

[(2) On receipt by the [designated officer for the court]⁵ of the documents filed under paragraph (1)(a) –

(a) the justices' clerk shall fix the date, time and place for a hearing or a directions appointment, allowing sufficient time for the applicant to comply with paragraph (1)(b), and

(b) the [designated officer for the court]⁵ shall –
　(i) endorse the date, time and place so fixed upon Form C6, and where appropriate, Form C6A, and
　(ii) return forthwith to the applicant the copies of the application and Form C10A if filed with it, together with Form C6, and such of Forms C6A and C7 as are appropriate[, and, in the case of an application for a section 8 order or an order under section 4(1)(c), [4ZA(1)(c) or 4A(1)(b)]⁸ Form C1A]⁴.]³

[(3) The applicant shall, at the same time as complying with paragraph (1)(b), serve Form C6A on the persons set out in relation to the relevant class of proceedings in column (iv) of Schedule 2 to these Rules.]²

(4) An application for –

(a) a [section 8 order]¹,
(b) an emergency protection order,
(c) a warrant under section 48(9),
(d) a recovery order, ...⁷
(e) a warrant under section 102(1), [or]⁷
[(f) a warrant under section 79 of the Childcare Act 2006]⁷

may, with leave of the justices' clerk, be made ex parte in which case the applicant shall –

　(i) file with the [designated officer for the court]³,⁵ or the court the application ...² in the appropriate form in Schedule 1 to these Rules at the time when the application is made or as directed by the justices' clerk, and
　(ii) in the case of an application for a prohibited steps order, or a specific issue order, under section 8 or an emergency protection

order, ...[7] serve a copy of the application on each respondent within 48 hours after the making of the order.

(5) Where the court refuses to make an order on an ex parte application it may direct that the application be made inter partes.

(6) In the case of proceedings under Schedule 1, the application under paragraph (1) shall be accompanied by a statement [in Form C10A][2] setting out the financial details which the applicant believes to be relevant to the application ...[2], together with sufficient copies for one to be served on each respondent.

NOTES

Amendments.[1] Words substituted: SI 1992/2068.[2] Words inserted, repealed or substituted: SI 1994/3156.[3] Words or paragraphs substituted: SI 2001/615.[4] Words and sub-pararagraph inserted or substituted: SI 2004/3376.[5] Words substituted: SI 2005/617.[6] Reference and words inserted: SI 2008/2858.[7] Words revoked, and word and subparagraph inserted: SI 2009/637. [8] References inserted: SI 2009/2025. [9] Reference revoked: SI 2010/1065. [10] Reference inserted and subparagraphs substituted and inserted: SI 2010/787.

5 Withdrawal of application

(1) An application may be withdrawn only with leave of the court.

(2) Subject to paragraph (3), a person seeking leave to withdraw an application shall file and serve on the parties a written request for leave setting out the reasons for the request.

(3) The request under paragraph (2) may be made orally to the court if the parties and, if appointed, the [children's guardian][1][,][6] the [welfare officer[, the][6] children and family reporter][1] [or the officer of the service or the Welsh family proceedings officer who is acting or has acted under a duty referred to in rule 11AA(1)(a) to (e)][6] are present.

(4) Upon receipt of a written request under paragraph (2), the court shall –

    (a)   if –
        (i)   the parties consent in writing,
        (ii)   any [children's guardian][1] has had an opportunity to make representations, and
        (iii) the court thinks fit,
grant the request; in which case the [designated officer for the court][2, 3] shall notify the parties, [any local authority that is preparing, or has prepared, a report under section 14A(8) or (9),][4] the [children's guardian][1][,][5] the [welfare officer[, the][5] children and family reporter][1] [and the officer of the service or the Welsh family proceedings officer who [acting or has acted under a duty referred to in rule 11AA(1)(a) to (e)][6]][5] of the granting of the request; or
    (b)   the justices' clerk shall fix a date for the hearing of the request and [the [designated officer for the court][3] shall][2] give at least 7 days' notice to the parties, [any local authority that is preparing, or has prepared, a report under section 14A(8) or (9),][4] the [children's guardian][1][,][5] the [welfare officer[, the][5] children and family reporter][1] [and the officer of

the service or Welsh family proceedings officer who is [acting or has acted under a duty referred to in rule 11AA(1)(a) to (e)][6]][5] of the date fixed.

NOTES

Amendments. [1] Words substituted: SI 2001/818. [2] Words substituted or inserted: SI 2001/615. [3] Words substituted: SI 2005/617. [4] Words inserted: SI 2005/2930. [5] Words and punctuation substituted: SI 2007/2188. [6] Comma and words substituted: SI 2008/2858.

6 Transfer of proceedings

(1) Where, in any relevant proceedings, the [designated officer for the court][2, 4] or the court receives a request in writing from a party that the proceedings be transferred to another family proceedings court or to a county court, the [designated officer for the court][2, 4] or court shall issue [an order or certificate][1] in the appropriate form in Schedule 1 to these Rules, granting or refusing the request in accordance with any Order made by the Lord Chancellor under Part I of Schedule 11.

(2) Where a request is granted under paragraph (1), the [designated officer for the court][2, 4] shall send a copy of the [order][1] –

- (a) to the parties,
- [(aa) to any local authority that is preparing, or has prepared, a report under section 14A(8) or (9),][5]
- (b) to any [children's guardian][3], and
- (c) to the family proceedings court or to the county court to which the proceedings are to be transferred.

(3) Any consent given or refused by a justices' clerk in accordance with any Order made by the Lord Chancellor under Part I of Schedule 11 shall be recorded in writing by the justices' clerk at the time it is given or refused or as soon as practicable thereafter.

(4) Where a request to transfer proceedings to a county court is refused under paragraph (1), the person who made the request may apply in accordance with rule 4.6 of the Family Proceedings Rules 1991 for an order under any Order made by the Lord Chancellor under Part I of Schedule 11.

NOTES

Amendments. [1] Words substituted: SI 1994/3156. [2] Words substituted: SI 2001/615. [3] Words substituted: SI 2001/818. [4] Words substituted: SI 2005/617. [5] Subparagraph inserted: SI 2005/2930.

7 Parties

(1) The respondents to relevant proceedings shall be those persons set out in the relevant entry in column (iii) of Schedule 2 to these Rules.

(2) In any relevant proceedings a person may file a request [in Form C2][1] that he or another person –

- (a) be joined as a party, or
- (b) cease to be a party.

(3) On considering a request under paragraph (2) the court shall, subject to paragraph (4) –

(a) grant it without a hearing or representations, save that this shall be done only in the case of a request under paragraph (2)(a), whereupon the [designated officer for the court]$^{2,\ 3}$ shall inform the parties [and any local authority that is preparing, or has prepared, a report under section 14A(8) or (9)]^4 and the person making the request of that decision, or

(b) order that a date be fixed for the consideration of the request, whereupon the [designated officer for the court]$^{2,\ 3}$ shall give notice of the date so fixed, together with a copy of the request –
   (i) in the case of a request under paragraph (2)(a), to the applicant [and any local authority that is preparing, or has prepared, a report under section 14A(8) or (9)]^4, and
   (ii) in the case of a request under paragraph (2)(b), to the parties, or

(c) invite the parties or any of them to make written representations, within a specified period, as to whether the request should be granted; and upon the expiry of the period the court shall act in accordance with sub-paragraph (a) or (b).

(4) Where a person with parental responsibility requests that he be joined under paragraph (2)(a), the court shall grant his request.

(5) In any relevant proceedings the court may direct –

(a) that a person who would not otherwise be a respondent under these Rules be joined as a party to the proceedings, or
(b) that a party to the proceedings cease to be a party.

NOTES

Amendments.^{1} Words substituted: SI 1994/3156.^{2} Words substituted: SI 2001/615.^{3} Words substituted: SI 2005/617.^{4} Words inserted: SI 2005/2930.

8 Service

(1) Where service of a document is required by these Rules (and not by a provision to which section 105(8) (service of notice or other document under the Act) applies) it may be effected –

(a) if the person to be served is not known by the person serving to be acting by solicitor –
   (i) by delivering it to him personally, or
   (ii) by delivering it at, or by sending it by first-class post to, his residence or his last known residence, or
(b) if the person to be served is known by the person serving to be acting by solicitor –
   (i) by delivering the document at, or sending it by first-class post to, the solicitor's address for service,
   (ii) where the solicitor's address for service includes a numbered box at a document exchange, by leaving the document at that

document exchange or at a document exchange which transmits documents on every business day to that document exchange, or

(iii) by sending a legible copy of the document by facsimile transmission to the solicitor's office.

(2) In this rule, 'first-class post' means first-class post which has been pre-paid or in respect of which pre-payment is not required.

(3) Where a child who is a party to any relevant proceedings is required by these Rules to serve a document, service shall be effected by –

(a) the solicitor acting for the child,
(b) where there is no such solicitor, the [children's guardian][3], or
(c) where there is neither such a solicitor nor a [children's guardian][3], the [designated officer for the court][4, 5].

(4) Service of any document on a child shall, subject to any direction of the justices' clerk or the court, be effected by service on –

(a) the solicitor acting for the child,
(b) where there is no such solicitor, the [children's guardian][3], or
(c) where there is neither such a solicitor nor a [children's guardian][3], with leave of the justices' clerk or the court, the child.

(5) Where the justices' clerk or the court refuses leave under paragraph (4)(c), a direction shall be given under paragraph (8).

(6) A document shall, unless the contrary is proved, be deemed to have been served –

(a) in the case of service by first-class post, on the second business day after posting, and
(b) in the case of service in accordance with paragraph (1)(b)(ii), on the second business day after the day on which it is left at the document exchange.

(7) At or before the first directions appointment in, or hearing of, relevant proceedings, whichever occurs first, the applicant shall file a statement [in Form C9][2] that service of –

(a) a copy of the application [and other documents referred to in rule 4(1)(b)][2] has been effected on each respondent, and
(b) notice of the proceedings has been effected under rule 4(3);

and the statement shall indicate –

(i) the manner, date, time and place of service, or
(ii) where service was effected by post, the date, time and place of posting.

[(8) In any relevant proceedings, where these rules require a document to be served, the court or the justices' clerk may, without prejudice to any power under rule 14, direct that –

(a) the requirement shall not apply;

(b) the time specified by the rules for complying with the requirement shall be abridged to such extent as may be specified in the direction;
(c) service shall be effected in such manner as may be specified in the direction.]¹

NOTES

Amendments.¹ Words substituted: SI 1992/2068.² Words inserted: SI 1994/3156.³ Words substituted: SI 2001/818.⁴ Words substituted: SI 2001/615.⁵ Words substituted: SI 2005/617.

[9 Acknowledgement of application

Within 14 days of service of [an application for an order under section 4(1)(c)[, 4ZA(1)(c) or 4A(1)(b)]³,]² an application for a section 8 order[, a special guardianship order]³ or an application under Schedule 1, each respondent shall file and serve on the parties an acknowledgement of the application in Form C7 [and, if both parts of question 6 or question 7 (or both) on Form C7 are answered in the affirmative, Form C1A]².]¹

NOTES

Amendments.¹ Rule substituted: SI 1994/3156.² Words inserted: SI 2004/3376.³ Words inserted: SI 2005/2930. ³ References inserted: SI 2009/2025.

10 Appointment of [children's guardian]¹

(1) As soon as practicable after the commencement of specified proceedings or the transfer of such proceedings to the court, the justices' clerk or the court shall appoint a [children's guardian]¹ unless –

(a) such an appointment has already been made by the court which made the transfer and is subsisting, or
(b) the justices' clerk or the court considers that such an appointment is not necessary to safeguard the interests of the child.

(2) At any stage in specified proceedings a party may apply, without notice to the other parties unless the justices' clerk or the court otherwise directs, for the appointment of a [children's guardian]¹.

(3) The justices' clerk or the court shall grant an application under paragraph (2) unless it is considered that such an appointment is not necessary to safeguard the interests of the child, in which case reasons shall be given; and a note of such reasons shall be taken by the justices' clerk.

(4) At any stage in specified proceedings the justices' clerk or the court may appoint a [children's guardian]¹ even though no application is made for such an appointment.

[(4A) The [designated officer for the court]³ or the court may, in specified proceedings, appoint more than one children's guardian in respect of the same child.]¹

(5) The [designated officer for the court]², ³ shall, as soon as practicable, notify the parties and any [welfare officer or children and family reporter]¹ of an appointment under this rule or, as the case may be, of a decision not to make such an appointment.

(6) Upon the appointment of a [children's guardian]¹ the [designated officer for the court]², ³ shall, as soon as practicable, notify him of the appointment and serve on him copies of the application and of documents filed under rule 17(1).

[(7) A children's guardian appointed by the [designated officer for the court]³ or by the court under this rule shall not –

(a) be a member, officer or servant of a local authority which, or an authorised person (within the meaning of section 31(9)) who, is a party to the proceedings;
(b) be, or have been, a member, officer or servant of a local authority or voluntary organisation (within the meaning of section 105(1)) who has been directly concerned in that capacity in arrangements relating to the care, accommodation or welfare of the child during the five years prior to the commencement of the proceedings; or
(c) be a serving probation officer who has, in that capacity, been previously concerned with the child or his family.]¹

(8) When appointing a [children's guardian]¹, the justices' clerk or the court shall consider the appointment of anyone who has previously acted as [children's guardian]¹ of the same child.

(9) The appointment of a [children's guardian]¹ under this rule shall continue for such time as is specified in the appointment or until terminated by the court.

(10) When terminating an appointment in accordance with paragraph (9), the court shall give reasons in writing for so doing, a note of which shall be taken by the justices' clerk.

(11) Where the justices' clerk or the court appoints a [children's guardian]¹ in accordance with this rule or refuses to make such an appointment, the justices' clerk shall record the appointment or refusal in the appropriate form in Schedule 1 to these Rules.

NOTES

Amendments.¹ Words substituted or inserted: SI 2001/818. ² Words substituted: SI 2001/615. ³ Words substituted: SI 2005/617.

[11 Powers and duties of officers of the service [and Welsh family proceedings officers]²

(1) In carrying out his duty under section 7(1)(a) [...⁵]⁴ or section 41(2) [or in acting under a duty referred to in rule 11AA(1)]⁵, the officer of the service [or the Welsh family proceedings officer]² shall have regard to the principle set out in section 1(2) and the matters set out in section 1(3)(a) to (f) as if for the word 'court' in that section there were substituted the words ['officer of the service or Welsh family proceedings officer']².

(2) The officer of the service [or the Welsh family proceedings officer]² shall make such investigations as may be necessary for him to carry out his duties and shall, in particular—

(a) contact or seek to interview such persons as he thinks appropriate or as the court directs;
(b) obtain such professional assistance as is available to him which he thinks appropriate or which the justices' clerk or the court directs him to obtain.

(3) In addition to his duties, under other paragraphs of this rule, or rules [11A, 11AA or 11B]⁴, the officer of the service [or the Welsh family proceedings officer]² shall provide to the [designated officer for the court]³, the justices' clerk and the court such other assistance as he or it may require.

(4) A party may question the officer of the service [or the Welsh family proceedings officer]² about oral or written advice tendered by him to the [designated officer for the court]³, the justices' clerk or the court.]¹

NOTES

Amendments.¹ Rule substituted: SI 2001/818.² Words inserted: SI 2005/585.³ Words substituted: SI 2005/617.⁴ Words inserted and substituted: SI 2007/2188.⁵ Words revoked: SI 2008/2858.

[11A Additional powers and duties of children's guardian

(1) The children's guardian shall –

(a) appoint a solicitor to represent the child unless such a solicitor has already been appointed; and
(b) give such advice to the child as is appropriate having regard to his understanding and, subject to rule 12(1)(a), instruct the solicitor representing the child on all matters relevant to the interests of the child including possibilities for appeal, arising in the course of proceedings.

(2) Where it appears to the children's guardian that the child –

(a) is instructing his solicitor direct; or
(b) intends to conduct and is capable of conducting the proceedings on his own behalf,

he shall inform the court through the [designated officer for the court]³ and from then he –

(i) shall perform all of his duties set out in rule 11 and this rule, other than those duties under paragraph (1)(a) of this rule, and such other duties as the justices' clerk or the court may direct;
(ii) shall take such part in the proceedings as the justices' clerk or the court may direct; and
(iii) may, with the leave of the justices' clerk or the court, have legal representation in the conduct of those duties.

(3) Unless excused by the justices' clerk or the court, the children's guardian shall attend all directions appointments in and hearings of the proceedings and shall advise the court on the following matters –

(a) whether the child is of sufficient understanding for any purpose including the child's refusal to submit to a medical or psychiatric examination or other assessment that the court has the power to require, direct or order;
(b) the wishes of the child in respect of any matter relevant to the proceedings including his attendance at court;
(c) the appropriate forum for the proceedings;
(d) the appropriate timing of the proceedings or any part of them;
(e) the options available to it in respect of the child and the suitability of each such option including what order should be made in determining the application; and
(f) any other matter concerning which the [designated officer for the court][3], the justices' clerk or the court seeks his advice or concerning which he considers that the [designated officer for the court][3], the justices' clerk or the court should be informed.

(4) The advice given under paragraph (3) may, subject to any order of the court, be given orally or in writing; and if the advice be given orally, a note of it shall be taken by the justices' clerk or the court.

(5) The children's guardian shall, where practicable, notify any person whose joinder as a party to those proceedings would be likely, in the opinion of the officer of the service [or the Welsh family proceedings officer][2], to safeguard the interests of the child of that person's right to apply to be joined under rule 7(2) and shall inform the [designated officer for the court][3] or the court –

(a) of any such notification given;
(b) of anyone whom he attempted to notify under this paragraph but was unable to contact; and
(c) of anyone whom he believes may wish to be joined to the proceedings.

(6) The children's guardian shall, unless the justices' clerk or the court otherwise directs, not less than 14 days before the date fixed for the final hearing of the proceedings –

(a) file a written report advising on the interests of the child;
(b) serve a copy of the filed report on the other parties [and any local authority that is preparing, or has prepared, a report under section 14A(8) or (9)][4].

(7) The children's guardian shall serve and accept service of documents on behalf of the child in accordance with rule 8(3)(b) and (4)(b) and, where the child has not himself been served, and has sufficient understanding, advise the child of the contents of any document so served.

(8) If the children's guardian inspects records of the kinds referred to in section 42, he shall bring to the attention of –

(a) the court, through the [designated officer for the court][3]; and

Part II   Statutory Instruments

    (b)   unless the court or the justices' clerk otherwise directs, the other parties to the proceedings,

all records and documents which may, in his opinion, assist in the proper determination of the proceedings.

(9) The children's guardian shall ensure that, in relation to a decision made by the justices' clerk or the court in the proceedings –

    (a)   if he considers it appropriate to the age and understanding of the child, the child is notified of that decision; and

    (b)   if the child is notified of the decision, it is explained to the child in a manner appropriate to his age and understanding.][1]

NOTES

Amendments.[1] Rule inserted: SI 2001/818.[2] Words inserted: SI 2005/585.[3] Words substituted: SI 2005/617.[4] Words inserted: SI 2005/2930.

[11AA   Additional powers and duties of officers of the service and Welsh family proceedings officers: ...[2] reports and risk assessments

[(1) This rule applies where an officer of the service or a Welsh family proceedings officer is acting under a duty in accordance with –

    (a)   section 11E(7) (providing the court with information as to the making of a contact activity direction or a contact activity condition);

    (b)   section 11G(2) (monitoring compliance with a contact activity direction or a contact activity condition);

    (c)   section 11H(2) (monitoring compliance with a contact order);

    (d)   section 16(6) (providing a family assistance order report to the court); and

    (e)   section 16A (making a risk assessment).][2]

(2) Where an officer of the service or a Welsh family proceedings officer is [acting under a duty referred to in paragraph (1)(a) to (e)][2], he must consider whether –

    (a)   to notify the child of such of the contents of [any report or risk assessment he makes][2] as he considers appropriate to the age and understanding of the child;

    (b)   to recommend in [any report or risk assessment he makes][2] that the court lists a hearing for the purposes of considering the report or assessment;

    (c)   it is in the best interests of the child for the child to be made a party to the proceedings.

(3) If the officer of the service or the Welsh family proceedings officer decides to notify the child of any of the contents of [any report or risk assessment he makes][2], he must explain those contents to the child in a manner appropriate to the child's age and understanding.

(4) If the officer of the service or the Welsh family proceedings officer considers that the child should be made a party to the proceedings, he must notify the court of his opinion together with the reasons for that opinion.

(5) If the officer of the service or the Welsh family proceedings officer considers that the court should exercise the discretion under rule 17AA(2) in relation to service of a risk assessment, he must state in the risk assessment –

(a) the way in which he considers the discretion should be exercised (including his view on the length of any suggested delay in service); and

(b) his reasons for reaching his view.

(6) The officer of the service or the Welsh family proceedings officer must file [any report or risk assessment he makes][2] with the court –

(a) at or by the time directed by the court;

(b) in the absence of any such direction, at least 14 days before a relevant hearing; or

(c) where there has been no direction from the court and no relevant hearing is listed, as soon as possible following completion of the report or assessment.

(7) In paragraph (6), a hearing is a relevant hearing if the justices' clerk has given the officer of the service or the Welsh family proceedings officer notice that the report or assessment is to be considered at it.

(8) When an officer of the service or a Welsh family proceedings officer prepares [a report as a result of acting under a duty referred to in paragraph (1)(a) to (d)][2], he shall as soon as practicable serve copies of the report on –

(a) each party; and

(b) any local authority that is preparing or has prepared a report under section 14A(8) or (9).

(9) At any hearing where [a report or assessment prepared as a result of acting under a duty referred to in paragraph (1)(a) to (e)][2] is considered any party may question the officer of the service or the Welsh family proceedings officer about the report or the assessment.][1]

NOTES

Amendments.[1] Rule inserted: SI 2007/2188. [2] Words revoked, and paragraph and words substituted: SI 2008/2858.

[11B Additional powers and duties of a children and family reporter

(1) In addition to his duties under rule 11, the children and family reporter shall –

(a) notify the child of such contents of his report (if any) as he considers appropriate to the age and understanding of the child, including any reference to the child's own views on the application and the recommendation of the children and family reporter; and

(b) if he does notify the child of any contents of his report, explain them to the child in a manner appropriate to his age and understanding.

(2) Where the court has –
- (a) directed that a written report be made by a children and family reporter; and
- (b) notified the children and family reporter that his report is to be considered at a hearing,

the children and family reporter shall –
- (i) file his report; and
- (ii) serve a copy on the other parties[, any local authority that is preparing, or has prepared, a report under section 14A(8) or (9)][2] and on the children's guardian (if any),

by such time as the court may direct and if no direction is given, not less than 14 days before that hearing.

(3) The court may direct that the children and family reporter attend any hearing at which his report is to be considered.

(4) The children and family reporter shall advise the court if he considers that the joinder of a person as a party to the proceedings would be likely to safeguard the interests of the child.

(5) The children and family reporter shall consider whether it is in the best interests of the child for the child to be made a party to the proceedings.

(6) If the children and family reporter considers the child should be made a party to the proceedings he shall notify the court of his opinion together with the reasons for that opinion.][1]

NOTES

Amendments.[1] Rule inserted: SI 2001/818. [2] Words inserted: SI 2005/2930.

12 Solicitor for child

(1) A solicitor appointed under section 41(3) or in accordance with [rule 11A(1)(a)][1] shall represent the child –

- (a) in accordance with instructions received from the [children's guardian][1] (unless the solicitor considers, having taken into account the views of the [children's guardian][1] and any direction of the court under [rule 11A(2)][1], that the child wishes to give instructions which conflict with those of the [children's guardian][1] and that he is able, having regard to his understanding, to give such instructions on his own behalf in which case he shall conduct the proceedings in accordance with instructions received from the child), or
- (b) where no [children's guardian][1] has been appointed for the child and the condition in section 41(4)(b) is satisfied, in accordance with instructions received from the child, or

(c) in default of instructions under (a) or (b), in furtherance of the best interests of the child.

(2) A solicitor appointed under section 41(3) or in accordance with [rule 11A(1)(a)]¹ shall serve and accept service of documents on behalf of the child in accordance with rule 8(3)(a) and (4)(a) and, where the child has not himself been served and has sufficient understanding, advise the child of the contents of any document so served.

(3) Where the child wishes an appointment of a solicitor under section 41(3) or in accordance with [rule 11A(1)(a)]¹ to be terminated, he may apply to the court for an order terminating the appointment; and the solicitor and the [children's guardian]¹ shall be given an opportunity to make representations.

(4) Where the [children's guardian]¹ wishes an appointment of a solicitor under section 41(3) to be terminated, he may apply to the court for an order terminating the appointment; and the solicitor and, if he is of sufficient understanding, the child, shall be given an opportunity to make representations.

(5) When terminating an appointment in accordance with paragraph (3) or (4), the court shall give reasons for so doing, a note of which shall be taken by the justices' clerk.

(6) Where the justices' clerk or the court appoints a solicitor under section 41(3) or refuses to make such an appointment, the justices' clerk shall record the appointment or refusal in the appropriate form in Schedule 1 to these Rules and [the [designated officer for the court]³ shall]² serve a copy on the parties and, where he is appointed, on the solicitor.

NOTES

Amendments.¹ Words substituted: SI 2001/818. ² Words inserted: SI 2001/615. ³ Words substituted: SI 2005/617.

[13 Welfare officer

(1) Where the court or a justices' clerk has directed that a written report be made by a welfare officer [in accordance with section 7(1)(b)]², the report shall be filed at or by such time as the court or justices' clerk directs or, in the absence of such a direction, at least 14 days before a relevant hearing; and the [designated officer for the court]³, ⁴ shall, as soon as practicable, serve a copy of the report on the parties[, any local authority that is preparing, or has prepared, a report under section 14A(8) or (9)]⁵ and any [children's guardian]².

(2) In paragraph (1), a hearing is relevant if the [designated officer for the court]³, ⁴ has given the welfare officer notice that his report is to be considered at it.

(3) After the filing of a written report by a welfare officer, the court or the justices' clerk may direct that the welfare officer attend any hearing at which the report is to be considered; and

(a) except where such a direction is given at a hearing attended by the welfare officer, the [designated officer for the court]³, ⁴ shall inform the welfare officer of the direction; and
(b) at the hearing at which the report is considered any party may question the welfare officer about his report.

[(3A) The welfare officer shall consider whether it is in the best interests of the child for the child to be made a party to the proceedings.

(3B) If the welfare officer considers the child should be made a party to the proceedings he shall notify the court of his opinion together with the reasons for that opinion.]²

(4) This rule is without prejudice to the court's power to give directions under rule 14.]¹

NOTES

Amendments.¹ Rule substituted: SI 1992/2068, except in relation to a written report the making of which was directed before 5 October 1992.² Words substituted or inserted: SI 2001/818.³ Words substituted: SI 2001/615.⁴ Words substituted: SI 2005/617.⁵ Words inserted: SI 2005/2930.

[13A Local authority officer preparing a family assistance order report

Where a family assistance order directs a local authority officer to prepare a family assistance order report, rules 5(4)(a) and (b), 13, 14(1)(a)(i) and (2), 15(5) and 17(1) shall apply to, or in respect of, the local authority officer as they would apply to, or in respect of, a welfare officer preparing a report in accordance with section 7(1)(b).]¹

NOTES

Amendments.¹ Rule inserted: SI 2007/2188.

14 Directions

[(1) In this rule, 'party' includes the children's guardian and, where a request or directions is or are concerned with –
(a) a report under –
 (i) section 7, the welfare officer or children and family reporter;
 (ii) section 14A(8) or (9), the local authority preparing that report;
(b) [a duty referred to in rule 11AA(1)(a) to (d)]⁸, the officer of the service or the Welsh family proceedings officer who is [acting under the duty in question]⁸;
(c) a risk assessment, the officer of the service or the Welsh family proceedings officer who is preparing the assessment.]⁷

(2) In any relevant proceedings the justices' clerk or the court may, subject to paragraph (5) [and rule 14A]⁹, give, vary or revoke directions for the conduct of the proceedings, including –
(a) the timetable for the proceedings;
(b) varying the time within which or by which an act is required, by these Rules, to be done;

(c) the attendance of the child;
(d) the appointment of a [children's guardian]³ ...³, or of a solicitor under section 41(3);
(e) the service of documents;
(f) the submission of evidence including experts' reports;
(g) the preparation of welfare reports under section 7;
(h) the transfer of the proceedings to another court in accordance with any Order made by the Lord Chancellor under Part I of Schedule 11;
(i) consolidation with other proceedings;
[(j) the preparation of reports under section 14A(8) or (9);
(k) the attendance of the person who prepared the report under section 14A(8) or (9) at any hearing at which the report is to be considered;]⁵
[(l) the preparation of family assistance order reports;
(m) listing a hearing for the purposes of considering the contents of a risk assessment]⁷
[(n) the exercise by an officer of the service or a Welsh family proceedings officer of any duty referred to in rule 11AA(1)(a) to (c)]⁸

and the justices' clerk shall, on receipt of an application [by the [designated officer for the court]⁶]⁴, or where proceedings have been transferred to his court, consider whether such directions need to be given.

(3) Where the justices' clerk or a single justice who is holding a directions appointment considers, for whatever reason, that it is inappropriate to give a direction on a particular matter, he shall refer the matter to the court which may give any appropriate direction.

(4) Where a direction is given under paragraph (2)(h), [an order]² shall be issued in the appropriate form in Schedule 1 to these Rules and the [designated officer for the court]⁴, ⁶ shall follow the procedure set out in rule 6(2).

(5) Directions under paragraph (2) may be given, varied or revoked either –

(a) of the justices' clerk's or the court's own motion [the [designated officer for the court]⁶]⁴ having given the parties notice of the intention to do so and an opportunity to attend and be heard or to make written representations,
(b) on the written request [in Form C2]² of a party specifying the direction which is sought, filed and served on the other parties, or
(c) on the written request [in Form C2]² of a party specifying the direction which is sought, to which the other parties consent and which they or their representatives have signed.

(6) In an urgent case, the request under paragraph (5)(b) may, with the leave of the justices' clerk or the court, be made –

(a) orally,
(b) without notice to the parties, or
(c) both as in sub-paragraph (a) and as in sub-paragraph (b).

(7) On receipt of a request [by the [designated officer for the court]⁶]⁴ under paragraph (5)(b) the justices' clerk shall fix a date for the hearing of the request and [the [designated officer for the court]⁶ shall]⁴ give not less than 2 days' notice [in Form C6]² to the parties of the date so fixed.

(8) On considering a request under paragraph (5)(c) the justices' clerk or the court shall either –

    (a)   grant the request, whereupon the [designated officer for the court]⁴, ⁶ shall inform the parties of the decision, or

    (b)   direct that a date be fixed for the hearing of the request, whereupon the justices' clerk shall fix such a date and [the [designated officer for the court]⁶ shall]⁴ give not less than 2 days' notice to the parties of the date so fixed.

(9) Subject to rule 28, a party may request, in accordance with paragraph 5(b) or (c), that an order be made under section 11(3) or, if he is entitled to apply for such an order, under section 38(1), and paragraphs (6), (7) and (8) shall apply accordingly.

(10) Where, in any relevant proceedings, the court has power to make an order of its own motion, the power to give directions under paragraph (2) shall apply.

(11) Directions of the justices' clerk or a court which are still in force immediately prior to the transfer of relevant proceedings to another court shall continue to apply following the transfer, subject to any changes of terminology which are required to apply those directions to the court to which the proceedings are transferred, unless varied or discharged by directions under paragraph (2).

[(11A) After the filing of [a report or assessment prepared as a result of acting under a duty referred to in rule 11AA(1)(a) to (e)]⁸, the court may direct that the officer of the service or the Welsh family proceedings officer attend any hearing at which the report or assessment is to be considered.]⁷

(12) The justices' clerk or the court shall [record]¹ the giving, variation or revocation of a direction under this rule [in the appropriate form in Schedule 1 to these Rules]¹ and [the [designated officer for the court]⁶ shall]⁴ serve, as soon as practicable, a copy of [the form]¹ on any party who was not present at the giving, variation or revocation.

NOTES

Amendments.¹ Words inserted or substituted: SI 1991/1991.² Words inserted or substituted: SI 1994/3156.³ Words substituted or omitted: SI 2001/818.⁴ Words inserted or substituted: SI 2001/615.⁵ Subparagraph inserted: SI 2005/2930.⁶ Words substituted: SI 2005/617.⁷ Paragraphs inserted and substituted and subparas inserted: SI 2007/2188.⁸ Words substituted and subparagraph inserted: SI 2008/2858. ⁹ Words inserted: SI 2010/787.

[14A Timetable for the Child in proceedings for a care order or supervision order

(1) In proceedings for a care order or supervision order, the court shall set the timetable of the proceedings in accordance with the Timetable for the Child.

(2) The 'Timetable for the Child' means the timetable set by the court in accordance with its duties under sections 1 and 32 and shall –

(a) take into account dates of the significant steps in the life of the child who is the subject of the proceedings; and
(b) be appropriate for that child.][1]

NOTES

Amendments.[1] Rule inserted: SI 2010/787.

15 Timing of proceedings

(1) Any period of time fixed by these Rules, or by any order or direction, for doing any act shall be reckoned in accordance with this rule.

(2) Where the period, being a period of 7 days or less, would include a day which is not a business day, that day shall be excluded.

(3) Where the time fixed for filing a document with the [designated officer for the court][1, 3] expires on a day on which the [office of the [designated officer for the court][3]][1] is closed, and for that reason the document cannot be filed on that day, the document shall be filed in time if it is filed on the next day on which the [office of the [designated officer for the court][3]][1] is open.

(4) Where these Rules provide a period of time within which or by which a certain act is to be performed in the course of relevant proceedings, that period may not be extended otherwise than by a direction of the justices' clerk or the court under rule 14.

(5) At the –

(a) transfer to a court of relevant proceedings,
(b) postponement or adjournment of any hearing or directions appointment in the course of relevant proceedings, or
(c) conclusion of any such hearing or directions appointment other than one at which the proceedings are determined, or so soon thereafter as is practicable,
  [(i) the justices' clerk shall fix a date upon which the proceedings shall come before him or the court again for such purposes as he or the court directs, which date shall, where paragraph (a) applies, be as soon as possible after the transfer, and
  (ii) the [designated officer for the court][3] shall give notice to the parties[, any local authority that is preparing, or has prepared, a report under section 14A(8) or (9)][4] and to the [children's guardian][2][,][5] the [welfare officer[, the][5] children and family reporter][2] [or the officer of the service or the Welsh family proceedings officer who is [acting or has acted under a duty referred to in rule 11AA(1)(a) to (e)][6]][5] of the date so fixed.][1]

NOTES

Amendments.[1] Words substituted: SI 2001/615.[2] Words substituted: SI 2001/818.[3] Words substituted: SI 2005/617.[4] Words inserted: SI 2005/2930.[5] Punctuation and words inserted: SI 2007/2188.[6] Words substituted: SI 2008/2858.

16 Attendance [of parties]³ at directions appointment and hearing

(1) Subject to paragraph (2), a party shall attend a directions appointment of which he has been given notice in accordance with rule 14(5) unless the justices' clerk or the court otherwise directs.

[(1A Paragraphs (2) to (4) do not apply where –

(a) the hearing relates to a decision about whether to make a contact activity direction or to attach a contact activity condition to a contact order; and
(b) the court has yet to obtain sufficient evidence from, or in relation to, the person who may be the subject of the direction or condition to enable it to determine the matter.]²

(2) Relevant proceedings shall take place in the absence of any party including the child if –

(a) the court considers it in the interests of the child, having regard to the matters to be discussed or the evidence likely to be given, and
(b) the party is represented by a [children's guardian]¹ or solicitor;

and when considering the interests of the child under sub-paragraph (a) the court shall give the [children's guardian]¹, solicitor for the child and, if he is of sufficient understanding, the child, an opportunity to make representations.

(3) Subject to paragraph (4) below, where at the time and place appointed for a hearing or directions appointment the applicant appears but one or more of the respondents do not, the justices' clerk or the court may proceed with the hearing or appointment.

(4) The court shall not begin to hear an application in the absence of a respondent unless –

(a) it is proved to the satisfaction of the court that he received reasonable notice of the date of the hearing; or
(b) the court is satisfied that the circumstances of the case justify proceeding with the hearing.

(5) Where, at the time and place appointed for a hearing or directions appointment, one or more respondents appear but the applicant does not, the court may refuse the application or, if sufficient evidence has previously been received, proceed in the absence of the applicant.

(6) Where at the time and place appointed for a hearing or directions appointment neither the applicant nor any respondent appears, the court may refuse the application.

(7) …³

NOTES

Amendments.¹ Words substituted: SI 2001/818.² Paragraph inserted: SI 2008/2858.³ Words inserted: SI 2009/858.

[16A Restrictions on presence of persons at directions appointment and hearing

(1) No person shall be present at any directions appointment or hearing in relevant proceedings other than –

(a) an officer of the court;
(b) a party to the proceedings;
(c) a litigation friend for any party, or legal representative instructed to act on that party's behalf;
(d) an officer of the service or Welsh family proceedings officer;
(e) a witness;
(f) duly accredited representatives of news gathering and reporting organisations; and
(g) any other person whom the court permits to be present.

(2) Paragraph (1) does not entitle persons within paragraph (1)(f) to be present at any hearing conducted for the purpose of judicially assisted conciliation or negotiation.

(3) At any stage of the proceedings the court may direct that persons within paragraph (1)(f) shall not attend the proceedings or any part of them, where satisfied that –

(a) this is necessary –
  (i) in the interests of any child concerned in or connected with the proceedings;
  (ii) for the safety or protection of a party, a witness in the proceedings, or a person connected with such a party or witness; or
  (iii) for the orderly conduct of the proceedings; or
(b) justice will otherwise be impeded or prejudiced.

(4) The court may exercise the power in paragraph (3) of its own motion or pursuant to representations made by any of the persons listed in paragraph (5), and in either case having given to any person within paragraph (1)(f) who is in attendance an opportunity to make representations.

(5) At any stage of the proceedings, the following persons may make representations to the court regarding restricting the attendance of persons within paragraph (1)(f) in accordance with paragraph (3) –

(a) a party to the proceedings;
(b) any witness in the proceedings;
(c) where appointed, any children's guardian;
(d) where appointed, an officer of the service or Welsh family proceedings officer, on behalf of the child the subject of proceedings;
(e) the child, if of sufficient age and understanding.

[(5A) A justices' clerk may give permission under paragraph (1)(g) for a person to be present at a directions appointment or a hearing which that clerk is conducting.]

Part II   Statutory Instruments

(6) This rule does not affect any power of the court to direct that witnesses shall be excluded until they are called for examination.

(7) In this rule, 'duly accredited' refers to accreditation in accordance with any administrative scheme for the time being approved for the purposes of this rule by the Lord Chancellor.][1]

NOTES

Amendments.[1] Rule inserted: SI 2009/858. [2] Paragraph inserted: SI 2010/787.

17 Documentary evidence

(1) Subject to paragraphs (4) and (5), in any relevant proceedings a party shall file and serve on the parties, [any local authority that is preparing, or has prepared, a report under section 14A(8) or (9),][3] any [welfare officer[, any][4] children and family reporter][2][, any officer of the service or any Welsh family proceedings officer who is [acting or has acted under a duty referred to in rule 11AA(1)(a) to (e)][5]][4] and any [children's guardian][2] of whose appointment he has been given notice under rule 10(5) –

    (a)   written statements of the substance of the oral evidence which the party intends to adduce at a hearing of, or a directions appointment in, those proceedings, which shall –
        (i)   be dated,
        (ii)   be signed by the person making the statement, …[1]
        (iii)   contain a declaration that the maker of the statement believes it to be true and understands that it may be placed before the court, and
        [(iv)   show in the top right hand corner of the first page –
            (a)   the initials and surname of the person making the statement,
            (b)   the number of the statement in relation to the maker,
            (c)   the date on which the statement was made, and
            (d)   the party on whose behalf it is filed; and][1]
    (b)   copies of any documents, including, subject to rule 18(3), experts' reports, upon which the party intends to rely, at a hearing of, or a directions appointment in, those proceedings,

at or by such time as the justices' clerk or the court directs or, in the absence of a direction, before the hearing or appointment.

(2) A party may, subject to any direction of the justices' clerk or the court about the timing of statements under this rule, file and serve on the parties a statement which is supplementary to a statement served under paragraph (1).

(3) At a hearing or directions appointment a party may not, without the leave of the justices' clerk, in the case of a directions appointment, or the court –

    (a)   adduce evidence, or
    (b)   seek to rely on a document,

in respect of which he has failed to comply with the requirements of paragraph (1).

(4) In proceedings for a section 8 order a party shall –

(a) neither file nor serve any document other than as required or authorised by these Rules, and
(b) in completing a form prescribed by these Rules, neither give information, nor make a statement, which is not required or authorised by that form,

without the leave of the justices' clerk or the court.

(5) In proceedings for a section 8 order [or a special guardianship order][3], no statement or copy may be filed under paragraph (1) until such time as the justices' clerk or the court directs.

NOTES

Amendments.[1] Words revoked or inserted: SI 1992/2068.[2] Words substituted: SI 2001/818.[3] Words inserted: SI 2005/2930.[4] Words substituted and inserted: SI 2007/2188.[5] Words substituted: SI 2008/2858.

[17A Disclosure of report under section 14A(8) or (9)

(1) In proceedings for a special guardianship order, the local authority shall file the report under section 14A(8) or (9) within the timetable fixed by the court.

(2) The justices' clerk or the court shall consider whether to give a direction that the report under section 14A(8) or (9) be disclosed to each party to the proceedings.

(3) Before giving such a direction the justices' clerk or the court shall consider whether any information should be deleted including information which reveals the party's address in a case where he has declined to reveal it in accordance with rule 33A (disclosure of addresses).

(4) The justices' clerk or the court may direct that the report will not be disclosed to a party.

(5) The designated officer shall serve a copy of the report filed under paragraph (1) –

(a) in accordance with any direction given under paragraph (2); and
(b) on any children's guardian, welfare officer or children and family reporter.][1]

NOTES

Amendments.[1] Rule inserted: SI 2005/2930.

[17AA Service of risk assessment

(1) Where an officer of the service or Welsh family proceedings officer has filed a risk assessment with the court, subject to paragraph (2), the justices' clerk shall as soon as practicable serve copies of the risk assessment on –

Part II   Statutory Instruments

(a) each party; and
(b) any local authority that is preparing or has prepared a report under section 14A(8) or (9).

(2) Before serving the risk assessment, the court must consider whether, in order to prevent a risk of harm to the child, it is necessary for –

(a) information to be deleted from a copy of the risk assessment before that copy is served on a party; or
(b) service of a copy of the risk assessment (whether with information deleted from it or not) on a party to be delayed for a specified period,

and may direct accordingly.][1]

NOTES

Amendments.[1] Rule inserted: SI 2007/2188.

18 Expert evidence – examination of child

(1) No person may, without the leave of the justices' clerk or the court, cause the child to be medically or psychiatrically examined, or otherwise assessed, for the purpose of the preparation of expert evidence for use in the proceedings.

(2) An application for leave under paragraph (1) shall, unless the justices' clerk or the court otherwise directs, be served on all the parties to the proceedings and on the [children's guardian][1].

(3) Where the leave of the justices' clerk or the court has not been given under paragraph (1), no evidence arising out of an examination or assessment to which that paragraph applies may be adduced without the leave of the court.

NOTES

Amendments.[1] Words substituted: SI 2001/818.

19 Amendment

(1) Subject to rule 17(2), a document which has been filed or served in any relevant proceedings may not be amended without the leave of the justices' clerk or the court which shall, unless the justices' clerk or the court otherwise directs, be requested in writing.

(2) On considering a request for leave to amend a document the justices' clerk or the court shall either –

(a) grant the request, whereupon the [designated officer for the court][1,2] shall inform the person making the request of that decision, or
(b) invite the parties or any of them to make representations, within a specified period, as to whether such an order should be made.

(3) A person amending a document shall file it with the [designated officer for the court][1,2] and serve it on those persons on whom it was served prior to amendment; and the amendments shall be identified.

NOTES

Amendments.¹ Words substituted: SI 2001/615. ² Words substituted: SI 2005/617.

20 Oral evidence

The justices' clerk or the court shall keep a note of the substance of the oral evidence given at a hearing of, or directions appointment in, relevant proceedings.

21 Hearing

(1) Before the hearing, the justice or justices who will be dealing with the case shall read any documents which have been filed under rule 17 in respect of the hearing.

(2) The justices' clerk at a directions appointment, or the court at a hearing or directions appointment, may give directions as to the order of speeches and evidence.

(3) Subject to directions under paragraph (2), at a hearing of, or directions appointment in, relevant proceedings, the parties and the [children's guardian][3] shall adduce their evidence in the following order –

  (a) the applicant,
  (b) any party with parental responsibility for the child,
  (c) other respondents,
  (d) the [children's guardian][3],
  (e) the child if he is a party to the proceedings and there is no [children's guardian][3].

[(3A) At the hearing at which the report under section 14A(8) or (9) is considered a party to whom the report, or part of it, has been disclosed may question the person who prepared the report about it.][5]

(4) After the final hearing of relevant proceedings, the court shall make its decision as soon as is practicable.

(5) Before the court makes an order or refuses an application or request, the justices' clerk shall record in writing –

  (a) the names of the justice or justices constituting the court by which the decision is made, and
  (b) in consultation with the justice or justices, the reasons for the court's decision and any findings of fact.

[(6) When making an order or when refusing an application, the court, or one of the justices constituting the court by which the decision is made shall

  (a) where it makes a finding of fact state such finding and complete Form C22; and
  (b) state the reasons for the court's decision.][2]

[(7) As soon as practicable after the court announces its decision –

Part II Statutory Instruments

>   (a) the justices' clerk shall make a record of any order made in the appropriate form in Schedule 1 to these Rules or, where there is no such form, in writing; and
>   (b) subject to paragraph (8), the [designated officer for the court][6] shall serve a copy of any order made on the parties to the proceedings and on any person with whom the child is living[, and where applicable, on the local authority that prepared the report under section 14A(8) or (9)][5].][4]

(8) Within 48 hours after the making of an order under section 48(4) or the making, ex parte, of –

>   (a) a [section 8 order][1], or
>   (b) an order under section 44, 48(9), 50 [or][1] 75(1) ...[1],

the applicant shall serve a copy of the order in the appropriate form in Schedule 1 to these Rules on –

>   (i) each party,
>   (ii) any person who has actual care of the child, or who had such care immediately prior to the making of the order, and
>   (iii) in the case of an order referred to in sub-paragraph (b), the local authority in whose area the child lives or is found.

NOTES

Amendments.[1] Words inserted, substituted or revoked: SI 1992/2068.[2] Words substituted: SI 1994/3156.[3] Words substituted: SI 2001/818.[4] Words substituted: SI 2001/615.[5] Paragraph and words inserted: SI 2005/2930.[6] Words substituted: SI 2005/617.

[[PART IIA
PROCEEDINGS UNDER SECTION 54 OF THE HUMAN FERTILISATION AND EMBRYOLOGY ACT 2008

21A Interpretation

In this Part of these Rules –

> 'the Act of 2002' means the Adoption and Children Act 2002 as applied with modifications by the Human Fertilisation and Embryology (Parental Orders) Regulations 2010;
> 'the Act of 2008' means the Human Fertilisation and Embryology Act 2008;
> 'the other parent' means any person who is a parent of the child but is not one of the applicants or the woman who carried the child (including any man who is the father by virtue of section 35 or 36 of the Act of 2008 or any woman who is a parent by virtue of section 42 or 43 of that Act);
> 'parental order' means an order under section 54 of the Act of 2008;
> 'parental order proceedings' means proceedings for the making of a parental order under the Act of 2008 or an order under any provision of the Act of 2002;
> 'parental order reporter' means an officer of the service or a Welsh family proceedings officer appointed to act on behalf of a child who is the subject of parental order proceedings;

'provision for contact' means a contact order under section 8 or 34.

21B Application of this Part

Except where the contrary intention appears, the Rules in this Part apply to parental order proceedings.

21C Application of remaining provisions of these Rules

Subject to the other provisions of this Part, rules 1(2), 2(5), 5, 6, 8, 10(2) to (10), 11, 11A(3) to (9), 11B, 14(3) to (8), 17, 19 to 21, 22, 22A, 32, 33 and 33B shall apply as appropriate with any necessary modifications to parental order proceedings.

21D Application for a parental order

(1) The application for a parental order shall be made in Form C51.

(2) The applicants shall file Form C51 and any documents referred to in it with the court together with sufficient copies for one to be served on each respondent.

21E How to start parental order proceedings

(1) Parental order proceedings are started when a designated officer for the court issues an application in Form C51 at the request of the applicant.

(2) An application is issued on the date entered in Form C51 by the designated officer for the court.

21F Personal details

(1) The court may direct that a party is not required to reveal –

   (a)   the address or telephone number of their private residence;
   (b)   the address of the child; or
   (c)   the name of a person with whom the child is living, if that person is not the applicant.

(2) Where the court directs that a party is not required to reveal any of the particulars in paragraph (1), that party shall give notice of those particulars to the court in Form C8 and the particulars shall not be revealed to any person unless the court directs otherwise.

(3) Where a party changes his home address during the course of proceedings, that party shall give notice of the change to the court.

21G Who the parties are

(1) In parental order proceedings –

   (a)   the applicants may be such of the following who satisfy the conditions in section 54(1) of the Act of 2008 –
         (i)   a husband and wife;

(ii) civil partners of each other; or
(iii) two persons who are living as partners in an enduring family relationship who are not within the prohibited degrees of relationship in relation to each other; and

(b) the respondents shall be –
(i) the woman who carried the child;
(ii) the other parent (if any);
(iii) any person in whose favour there is provision for contact; and
(iv) any other person or body with parental responsibility for the child at the date of the application.

(2) The court shall direct that a person with parental responsibility for the child be made a party to proceedings where that person requests to be one.

(3) The court may at any time direct that –

(a) any other person or body be made a respondent to the proceedings; or
(b) a respondent be removed from the proceedings.

(4) If the court makes a direction for the addition or removal of a party, it may give consequential directions about –

(a) serving a copy of the application form on any new respondent;
(b) serving relevant documents on the new party; and
(c) the management of the proceedings.

21H What the court shall do when the application has been issued

(1) As soon as practicable after the application has been issued the court shall –

(a) if section 48(1) of the Act of 2002 applies (restrictions on making adoption orders), consider whether it is proper to hear the application;
(b) subject to paragraph (2), set a date for the first directions appointment;
(c) appoint a parental order reporter; and
(d) set a date for the hearing of the application.

(2) Where it considers it appropriate the court may, instead of setting a date for a first directions appointment, give the directions provided for in rule 21JC.

21I What a designated officer for the court shall do

As soon as practicable after the issue of proceedings a designated officer for the court shall –

(a) return to the applicants the copies of Form C51 together with Forms C6, C6A and C52 as appropriate; and
(b) send a copy of the certified copy of the entry in the register of live births to the parental order reporter.

21J Service of the application and other documents

The applicants shall serve –

(a) Form C51 and any documents referred to in it, Form C6 and Form C52 on the respondents within 14 days before the hearing or first directions appointment; and
(b) Form C6A on any local authority or voluntary organisation that has at any time provided accommodation for the child.

21JA Acknowledgement

Within 7 days of the service of an application for a parental order, each respondent shall file and serve on all other parties an acknowledgement in Form C52.

21JB Date for first directions appointment

Unless the court directs otherwise, the first directions appointment shall be within 4 weeks beginning with the date on which the application is issued.

21JC The first directions appointment

(1) At the first directions appointment in the proceedings the court shall –

- (a) fix a timetable for the filing of –
  - (i) any report from a parental order reporter;
  - (ii) if a statement of facts has been filed, any amended statement of facts; and
  - (iii) any other evidence;
- (b) give directions relating to the report and other evidence;
- (c) consider whether any other person should be a party to the proceedings and, if so, give directions in accordance with rule 21G(2) or (3) joining that person as a party;
- (d) consider whether the case needs to be transferred to another court and, if so, give directions to transfer the proceedings to another court in accordance with any order made by the Lord Chancellor under Part 1 of Schedule 11;
- (e) give directions about –
  - (i) tracing the other parent or the woman who carried the child;
  - (ii) service of documents;
  - (iii) subject to paragraph (2), disclosure, as soon as possible, of information and evidence to the parties; and
  - (iv) the final hearing.

(2) Rule 21JG (reports of the parental order reporter and disclosure to parties) applies to any direction given under paragraph (1)(e)(iii) as it applies to a direction given under rule 21JG(1).

(3) The parties or their legal representatives shall attend the first directions appointment unless the court directs otherwise.

(4) Directions may also be given at any stage in the proceedings –

- (a) of the court's own motion; or

(b) on the application in Form C2 of a party or the parental order reporter.

(5) Where the court proposes to exercise the powers in paragraph (1) of its own motion, the court shall first give the parties –

(a) notice of its intention to do so; and
(b) an opportunity to attend and be heard or to make written representations.

(6) Where there is an application for directions to be made under paragraph (1), rule 14(5) (b) and (c), (7) and (8) as applied by rule 21C shall apply.

(7) For the purposes of giving directions or for such purposes as the court directs –

(a) the court may set a date for a further directions appointment or other hearing; and
(b) the designated officer for the court shall give notice of any date so fixed to the parties and to the parental order reporter.

(8) Directions of a court which are still in force immediately prior to the transfer of proceedings to another court shall continue to apply following the transfer subject to –

(a) any changes of terminology which are required to apply those directions to the court to which the proceedings are transferred; and
(b) any variation or revocation of the direction.

(9) The court or designated officer for the court shall –

(a) take a note of the giving, variation or revocation of a direction under this rule; and
(b) as soon as practicable serve a copy of the note on every party.

(10 After the first directions appointment the court shall monitor compliance by the parties with the court's timetable and directions.

21JD Where the agreement of the other parent or the woman who carried the child is not required

(1) The following paragraphs apply where the agreement of the other parent or the woman who carried the child to the making of the parental order is not required as the person in question cannot be found or is incapable of giving agreement.

(2) The applicants shall –

(a) state that the agreement is not required in Form C51 or at a later stage in a written note to be filed with the court;
(b) file a statement of facts setting out a summary of the history of the case and any other facts to satisfy the court that the other parent or the woman who carried the child cannot be found or is incapable of giving agreement.

(3) On receipt of Form C51 or written note a designated officer for the court shall –

(a) unless the other parent or the woman who carried the child cannot be found, inform the other parent or the woman who carried the child that their agreement is not required;
(b) send a copy of the statement of facts filed in accordance with paragraph (2)(b) to –
   (i) the other parent unless the other parent cannot be found;
   (ii) the woman who carried the child unless the woman cannot be found; and
   (iii) the parental order reporter.

21JE Agreement

(1) Unless the court directs otherwise, agreement of the other parent or the woman who carried the child to the making of the parental order may be given in Form A101A or a form to like effect.

(2) Any form of agreement executed in Scotland shall be witnessed by a Justice of the Peace or a Sheriff.

(3) Any form of agreement executed in Northern Ireland shall be witnessed by a Justice of the Peace.

(4) Any form of agreement executed outside the United Kingdom shall be witnessed by –

(a) any person for the time being authorised by law in the place where the document is executed to administer an oath for any judicial or other legal purpose;
(b) a British Consular officer;
(c) a notary public; or
(d) if the person executing the document is serving in any of the regular armed forces of the Crown, an officer holding a commission in any of those forces.

21JF Parental order reporter

(1) A parental order reporter is appointed to act on behalf of a child who is the subject of parental order proceedings and has a duty to safeguard the interests of that child.

(2) In addition to such of the matters set out in rules 11 and 11A, as applied by rule 21C, as are appropriate to parental order proceedings, the parental order reporter shall –

(a) investigate the matters set out in section 54(1) to (8) of the Act of 2008;
(b) so far as the parental order reporter considers necessary, investigate any matter contained in the application form or other matter which appears relevant to the making of the parental order;

(c) advise the court on whether there is any reason under section 1 of the Act of 2002 to refuse the parental order.

21JG Reports of the parental order reporter and disclosure to the parties

(1) The court shall consider whether to give a direction that a confidential report of the parental order reporter be disclosed to each party to the proceedings.

(2) Before giving such a direction the court shall consider whether any information should be deleted including information which discloses the particulars referred to in rule 21F(1) where a party has given notice under rule 21F(2) (disclosure of personal details).

(3) The court may direct that the report shall not be disclosed to a party.

21JH Notice of final hearing

A designated officer for the court shall give notice in Form C6 to the parties and the parental order reporter –

(a) of the date and place where the application shall be heard; and
(b) of the fact that, unless the person wishes or the court requires, the person need not attend.

21JI The final hearing

(1) Any person who has been given notice in accordance with rule 21JH may attend the final hearing and be heard on the question of whether an order should be made.

(2) The court may direct that any person shall attend a final hearing.

21JJ Proof of identity of the child

(1) Unless the contrary is shown, the child referred to in the application shall be deemed to be the child referred to in the form of agreement to the making of the parental order where the conditions in paragraph (2) apply.

(2) The conditions are –

(a) the application identifies the child by reference to a full certified copy of an entry in the registers of live-births;
(b) the form of agreement identifies the child by reference to a full certified copy of an entry in the registers of live-births attached to the form; and
(c) the copy of the entry in the registers of live-births referred to in sub-paragraph (a) is the same or relates to the same entry in the registers of live-births as the copy of the entry in the registers of live-births attached to the form of agreement.

(3) Where the precise date of the child's birth is not proved to the satisfaction of the court, the court shall determine the probable date of birth.

(4) The probable date of the child's birth may be specified in the parental order as the date of the child's birth.

(5) Where the child's place of birth cannot be proved to the satisfaction of the court –

- (a) the child may be treated as having been born in the registration district of the court where it is probable that the child may have been born in –
  - (i) the United Kingdom;
  - (ii) the Channel Islands; or
  - (iii) the Isle of Man; or
- (b) in any other case, the particulars of the country of birth may be omitted from the parental order.

21JK Disclosing information to an adult who was subject to a parental order

(1) Subject to paragraph (2), the person who was subject to the parental order has the right, on request in Form A64A, to receive from the court which made the parental order a copy of the following –

- (a) the application form for a parental order (but not the documents attached to that form);
- (b) the parental order and any other orders relating to the parental order proceedings;
- (c) any transcript of the court's decision; and
- (d) a report made to the court by the parental order reporter.

(2) The court shall not provide a copy of a document or order referred to in paragraph (1) unless the person making the request has completed the certificate relating to counselling in Form A64A.

(3) This rule does not apply to a person under the age of 18 years.

21JL Application for recovery orders

(1) An application for any of the orders referred to in section 41(2) of the Act of 2002 (recovery orders) may be made, with the permission of the court, without notice in which case the applicant shall file the application at the time when the application is made or as directed by the court.

(2) Where the court refuses to make an order on an application without notice it may direct that the application is made on notice in which case the application shall proceed in accordance with rules 21A to 21JI.

(3) An application for any of the orders referred to in section 41(2) of the Act of 2002 shall be made in Form C2.

(4) The respondents to an application under this rule are –

- (a) in a case where parental order proceedings are pending, all parties to those proceedings;
- (b) any person having parental responsibility for the child;
- (c) any person in whose favour there is provision for contact;

(d) any person who was caring for the child immediately prior to the making of the application; and
(e) any person whom the applicant alleges to have effected, or to have been or to be responsible for, the taking or keeping of the child.

21JM Keeping of registers, custody, inspection and disclosure of documents and information

(1) Such part of the register kept in pursuance of rules made under the Magistrates' Courts Act 1980 as relates to parental order proceedings, shall be kept in a separate book and the book shall not contain particulars of any other proceedings.

(2) The book kept in pursuance of paragraph (1) and all other documents relating to parental order proceedings shall, while they are in the custody of the court, be kept in a place of special security.

(3) Any person who obtains any information in the course of, or relating to, parental order proceedings shall treat that information as confidential and shall only disclose it if –

(a) the disclosure is necessary for the proper exercise of that person's duties; or
(b) the information is requested by –
  (i) a court or public authority (whether in Great Britain or not) having power to determine parental order proceedings and related matters, for the purpose of that court or authority discharging its duties relating to those proceedings and matters; or
  (ii) a person who is authorised in writing by the Secretary of State to obtain the information for the purposes of research.

21JN Documents held by the court not to be inspected or copied without the court's leave

Subject to the provisions of these Rules or any direction given by the court –

(a) no document or order held by the court in parental order proceedings shall be open to inspection by any person; and
(b) no copy of any such document or order, or of an extract from any such document or order, shall be taken by or given to any person.

21JO Orders

(1) A parental order takes effect from the date when it is made, or such later date as the court may specify.

(2) In proceedings in Wales a party may request that an order be drawn up in Welsh as well as in English.

21JP Copies of orders

(1) Within 7 days beginning with the date on which the final order was made in proceedings, or such shorter time as the court may direct, a designated officer for the court shall send –

    (a)   a copy of the order in Form C53 to the applicant;
    (b)   a copy which is sealed, authenticated with the stamp of the court or certified as a true copy of a parental order, to the Registrar General;
    (c)   a notice of the making or refusal of –
        (i)   the final order; or
        (ii)   an order quashing or revoking a parental order or allowing an appeal against an order in proceedings,

to every respondent and, with the leave of the court, any other person.

(2) A notice of refusal of a parental order shall be in Form C54.

(3) The designated officer for the court shall also send notice of the making of a parental order to –

    (a)   any court in Great Britain which appears to the designated officer for the court to have made any such order as is referred to in section 46(2) of the Act of 2002 (order relating to parental responsibility for, and maintenance of, the child); and
    (b)   the principal registry, if it appears to the designated officer for the court that a parental responsibility agreement has been recorded at the principal registry.

(4) A copy of any final order may be sent to any other person with the leave of the court.

(5) The designated officer for the court shall send a copy of any order made during the course of the proceedings to all the parties to those proceedings unless the court directs otherwise.

(6) If an order has been drawn up in Welsh as well as in English in accordance with rule 21JO(2), any reference in this rule to sending an order is to be taken as a reference to sending both the Welsh and English orders.

21JQ Amendment and revocation of orders

(1) This rule applies to an application under paragraph 4 of Schedule 1 to the Act of 2002 (amendment of a parental order and revocation of direction).

(2) The application shall be made to a family proceedings court for the same local justice area as the family proceedings court which made the parental order, by delivering it or sending it by post to the designated officer for the court.

(3) The application shall be made in Form C2.

(4) Subject to paragraph (5), an application may be made without serving a copy of the application.

(5) The court may direct that an application notice be served on such persons as it thinks fit.

(6) Where the court makes an order granting the application, a designated officer for the court shall send the Registrar General a notice –

(a) specifying the amendments; or
(b) informing the Registrar General of the revocation,

giving sufficient particulars of the order to enable the Registrar General to identify the case.

21JR Proceedings in respect of which a single justice and a justices' clerk may discharge the functions of the court

(1) A single justice may discharge the functions of a family proceedings court in rules 21F(1) and (2), 21G(2) to (4), 21H, 21JB, 21JC(1), (3) to (5), (7), (9) and (10), 21JE(1), 21JG, 21JI(2), 21JK, 21JL(1) and (2), 21JN, 21JP(1), (4) and 21JQ(5).

(2) A justices' clerk may discharge the functions of a family proceedings court in the rules referred to in paragraph (1) except that the functions in –

(a) rule 21JP(4) may not be exercised; and
(b) rule 21G(2) and (3) may only be exercised with the consent of the parties.

(3) Where the justices' clerk or single justice who is holding a directions appointment considers, for whatever reason, that it is inappropriate to give a direction on a particular matter, the matter shall be referred to the court which may give any appropriate direction.]²]¹

NOTES

Amendments.¹ Part inserted: SI 1994/2166.² Part substituted: SI 2010/1065.

[PART IIB
PROCEEDINGS IN RESPECT OF THE COUNCIL REGULATION

21K Application by a party for transfer of proceedings to a court of another Member State

(1) A party may make an application that proceedings, or a specific part of those proceedings, be heard in another Member State pursuant to Article 15 of the Council Regulation.

(2) An application under paragraph (1) shall be made –

(a) to the court in which the relevant parental responsibility proceedings (within the meaning of the Council Regulation) are pending; and
(b) on notice in form C1; and
(c) such notice shall be filed and served on the respondents not less than 5 business days before the hearing of the application.

(3) An application made under paragraph (1) must be supported by an affidavit, which should contain evidence of the child's particular connection to the other Member State in accordance with Article 15(3) of the Council Regulation. In this paragraph the child referred to is the child subject of the parental responsibility proceedings.

(4) The respondents referred to in paragraph (2)(c) mean any other parties, the child and the Central Authority of the relevant Member State.

21L Application by a court of another Member State for transfer of proceedings

(1) A court of another Member State may make an application that proceedings, or a specific part of those proceedings, be heard in that Member State pursuant to Article 15 of the Council Regulation.

(2) An application under paragraph (1) should be made in the first instance to the Central Authority of England and Wales.

(3) The Central Authority will forward an application made under paragraph (1) to the court in which the parental responsibility proceedings are pending, or where there are no pending proceedings to the principal registry.

(4) When a court receives the application the court shall serve all other parties in England and Wales not less than 5 business days before the hearing of the application.

(5) A decision to accept or refuse jurisdiction under Article 15 of the Council Regulation is to be served on all parties, the Central Authority of the relevant Member State and the Central Authority of England and Wales. Service on a Central Authority or court of another Member State shall be made by the Central Authority of England and Wales.

21M A certified copy of a judgment for enforcement in other Member States

(1) An application for a certified copy of a judgment or certificate referred to in Article 37(1), 39 or 45(1) of the Council Regulation must be made to the court which made the order by witness statement or affidavit without notice being served on any other party.

(2) A witness statement or affidavit by which an application for a certified copy of a judgment is made must –
   (a) give particulars of the proceedings in which the judgment was obtained;
   (b) have annexed to it –
      (i) a copy of the petition or application by which the proceedings were begun;
      (ii) evidence of service on the respondent;
      (iii) copies of the pleadings and particulars, if any; and
      (iv) a statement of the grounds on which the judgment was based together, where appropriate, with any document showing that the

applicant is entitled to legal aid or assistance by way of representation for the purposes of the proceedings;
(c) state whether the respondent did or did not object to the jurisdiction, and if so, on what grounds;
(d) show that the judgment has been served in accordance with rule 8 and is not subject to any order for the stay of proceedings;
(e) state that the time for appealing has expired, or, as the case may be, the date on which it will expire and in either case whether notice of appeal against the judgment has been given; and
(f) state –
  (i) whether the judgment provides for the payment of a sum of money;
  (ii) whether interest is recoverable on the judgment or part thereof and if so, the rate of interest, the date from which interest is recoverable, and the date on which interest ceases to accrue.

(3) A witness statement or affidavit by which an application for a certificate is made must give –
(a) particulars of the proceedings in which the judgment was obtained;
(b) the full name, country and place of birth and date of birth of the parties;
(c) details of the type of certificate applied for and the reasons for making the application; and
(d) where the application is for a certificate under Annex II to the Council Regulation –
  (i) the full name and, if known, the address and the date and place of birth of any other persons with parental responsibility;
  (ii) information as to whether or not the judgment entails the return of a child wrongfully removed or retained in another Member State and, if so, the full name and address of the person to whom the child should be returned.

(4) The certified copy of the judgment shall be an office copy sealed with the seal of the court and signed by the justices' clerk and there shall be issued with the copy of the judgment a certified copy of any order which has varied any of the terms of the original order.

21N Application for a certificate in accordance with Article 41

(1) An application for a certificate in accordance with Article 41 can be made, after judgment, by any party.

(2) An application under paragraph (1) should be made to the court in which the relevant judgment was made and must be supported by an affidavit, which should contain evidence of the cross-border character of the case.

21P Rectification of certificates issued under Article 41

(1) The court may rectify an error in a certificate issued under Article 41.

(2) The court may rectify the certificate of its own motion or pursuant to an application made by any party to the proceedings, or the court or Central Authority of another Member State.]¹

NOTES

Amendments.¹ Part inserted: SI 2005/229.

[PART IIC

COMMUNICATION OF INFORMATION: PROCEEDINGS RELATING TO CHILDREN

21Q Application

The provisions of this Part apply to relevant proceedings.

21R Communication of information: general

(1) For the purposes of the law relating to contempt of court, information relating to relevant proceedings (whether or not contained in a document filed with the court) may be communicated –

(a) where the communication is to –
  (i) a party;
  (ii) the legal representative of a party;
  (iii) a professional legal adviser;
  (iv) an officer of the service or a Welsh family proceedings officer;
  (v) the welfare officer;
  (vi) the Legal Services Commission;
  (vii) an expert whose instruction by a party has been authorised by the court for the purposes of the proceedings;
  (viii) a professional acting in furtherance of the protection of children; or
  (ix) an independent reviewing officer appointed in respect of a child who is, or has been, subject to proceedings to which this rule applies;
(b) where the court gives permission; or
(c) subject to any direction of the court, in accordance with rules 21T to 21X.

(2) Nothing in this Part permits the communication to the public at large, or any section of the public, of any information relating to the proceedings.

21S Instruction of experts

(1) No party may instruct an expert for any purpose relating to relevant proceedings, including to give evidence in those proceedings, without the leave of the court.

(2) Where the leave of the court has not been given under paragraph (1), no evidence arising out of an unauthorised instruction may be introduced without leave of the court.

21T Communication of information for purposes connected with the proceedings

(1) A party or the legal representative of a party, on behalf of and upon the instructions of that party, may communicate information relating to the proceedings to any person where necessary to enable that party –

- (a) by confidential discussion, to obtain support, advice or assistance in the conduct of the proceedings;
- (b) to engage in mediation or other forms of alternative dispute resolution;
- (c) to make and pursue a complaint against a person or body concerned in the proceedings; or
- (d) to make and pursue a complaint regarding the law, policy or procedure relating to a category of proceedings to which this part applies.

(2) Where information is communicated to any person in accordance with paragraph (1)(a) of this rule, no further communication by that person is permitted.

(3) When information relating to the proceedings is communicated to any person in accordance with paragraphs (1)(b),(c) or (d) of this rule –

- (a) the recipient may communicate that information to a further recipient, provided that –
  - (i) the party who initially communicated the information consents to that further communication; and
  - (ii) the further communication is made only for the purpose or purposes for which the party made the initial communication; and
- (b) the information may be successively communicated to and by further recipients on as many occasions as may be necessary to fulfil the purpose for which the information was initially communicated, provided that on each such occasion the conditions in sub-paragraph (a) are met.

21U Communication of information by a party etc for other purposes

A person specified in the first column of the following table may communicate to a person listed in the second column such information as is specified in the third column for the purpose or purposes specified in the fourth column –

A party	A lay adviser, a McKenzie Friend, or a person arranging or providing pro bono legal services	Any information relating to the proceedings	To enable the party to obtain advice or assistance in relation to the proceedings
A party	A health care professional or a person or body providing counselling services for children or families		To enable the party or any child of the party to obtain health care or counselling
A party	The Secretary of State, a McKenzie Friend, a lay adviser or the First-tier Tribunal dealing with an appeal made under section 20 of the Child Support Act 1991		For the purposes of making or responding to an appeal under section 20 of the Child Support Act 1991 or the determination of such an appeal
A party	An adoption panel		To enable the adoption panel to discharge its functions as appropriate
A party	The European Court of Human Rights		For the purpose of making an application to the European Court of Human Rights

Part II   Statutory Instruments

A party or any person lawfully in receipt of information	The Children's Commissioner or the Children's Commissioner for Wales		To refer an issue affecting the interests of children to the Children's Commissioner or the Children's Commissioner for Wales
A party, any person lawfully in receipt of information or a proper officer	A person or body conducting an approved research project		For the purpose of an approved research project
A legal representative or a professional legal adviser	A person or body responsible for investigating or determining complaints in relation to legal representatives or professional legal advisers		For the purposes of the investigation or determination of a complaint in relation to a legal representative or a professional legal adviser
A legal representative or a professional legal adviser	A person or body assessing quality assurance systems		To enable the legal representative or professional legal adviser to obtain a quality assurance assessment
A legal representative or a professional legal adviser	An accreditation body	Any information relating to the proceedings providing that it does not, or is not likely to, identify any person involved in the proceedings	To enable the legal representative or professional legal adviser to obtain accreditation

A party	A police officer	The text or summary of the whole or part of a judgment given in the proceedings	For the purpose of a criminal investigation
A party or any person lawfully in receipt of information	A member of the Crown Prosecution Service	To enable the Crown Prosecution Service to discharge its functions under any enactment	

21V Communication for the effective functioning of Cafcass and CAFCASS CYMRU

An officer of the service or a Welsh family proceedings officer, as appropriate, may communicate to a person listed in the second column such information as is specified in the third column for the purpose or purposes specified in the fourth column –

A Welsh family proceedings officer	A person or body exercising statutory functions relating to inspection of CAFCASS CYMRU	Any information relating to the proceedings which is required by the person or body responsible for the inspection	For the purpose of an inspection of CAFCASS CYMRU by a body or person appointed by the Welsh Ministers

Part II Statutory Instruments

An officer of the service or a Welsh family proceedings officer	The General Social Care Council or the Care Council for Wales	Any information relating to the proceedings providing that it does not, or is not likely to, identify any person involved in the proceedings	For the purpose of initial and continuing accreditation as a social worker of a person providing services to Cafcass or CAFCASS CYMRU in accordance with s.13(2) of the Criminal Justice and Courts Services Act 2000 or s.36 of the Children Act 2004 as the case may be
An officer of the service or a Welsh family proceedings officer	A person or body providing services relating to professional development or training to Cafcass or CAFCASS CYMRU	Any information relating to the proceedings providing that it does not, or is not likely to, identify any person involved in the proceedings without that person's consent	To enable the person or body to provide the services, where the services cannot be effectively provided without such disclosure

An officer of the service or a Welsh family proceedings officer	A person employed by or contracted to Cafcass or CAFCASS CYMRU for the purposes of carrying out the functions referred to in column 4 of this row	Any information relating to the proceedings	Engagement in processes internal to Cafcass or CAFCASS CYMRU which relate to the maintenance of necessary records concerning the proceedings, or to ensuring that Cafcass or CAFCASS CYMRU functions are carried out to a satisfactory standard

21W Communication to and by Ministers of the Crown and Welsh Ministers

A person specified in the first column of the following table may communicate to a person listed in the second column such information as is specified in the third column for the purpose or purposes specified in the fourth column –

A party or any person lawfully in receipt of information relating to the proceedings	A Minister of the Crown with responsibility for a government department engaged, or potentially engaged, in an application before the European Court of Human Rights relating to the proceedings	Any information relating to the proceedings of which he or she is in lawful possession	To provide the department with information relevant, or potentially relevant, to the proceedings before the European Court of Human Rights

A Minister of the Crown	The European Court of Human Rights	For the purpose of engagement in an application before the European Court of Human Rights relating to the proceedings	
A Minister of the Crown	Lawyers advising or representing the United Kingdom in an application before the European Court of Human Rights relating to the proceedings	For the purpose of receiving advice or for effective representation in relation to the application before the European Court of Human Rights	
A Minister of the Crown or a Welsh Minister	Another Minister, or Ministers, of the Crown or a Welsh Minister	For the purpose of notification, discussion and the giving or receiving of advice regarding issues raised by the information in which the relevant departments have, or may have, an interest	

21X Communication by persons lawfully in receipt of information

(1) This rule applies to communications made in accordance with rules 21U, 21V and 21W and the reference in this rule to 'the table' means the table in the relevant rule.

(2) A person in the second column of the table may only communicate information relating to the proceedings received from a person in the first column for the purpose or purposes –

    (a) for which he received that information; or

(b) of professional development or training, providing that any communication does not, or is not likely to, identify any person involved in the proceedings without that person's consent.

21Y Interpretation

In this Part –

'accreditation body' means –
- (a) The Law Society,
- (b) Resolution, or
- (c) The Legal Services Commission;

'adoption panel' means a panel established in accordance with regulation 3 of the Adoption Agencies Regulations 2005 or regulation 3 of the Adoption Agencies (Wales) Regulations 2005;

'alternative dispute resolution' means methods of resolving a dispute, including mediation, other than through the normal court process;

'approved research project' means a project of research –
- (a) approved in writing by a Secretary of State after consultation with the President of the Family Division,
- (b) approved in writing by the President of the Family Division, or
- (c) conducted under section 83 of the Act of 1989 or section 13 of the Criminal Justice and Court Services Act 2000;

'body assessing quality assurance systems' includes –
- (a) The Law Society,
- (b) The Legal Services Commission, or
- (c) The General Council of the Bar;

'body or person responsible for investigating or determining complaints in relation to legal representatives or professional legal advisers' means –
- (a) The Law Society,
- (b) The General Council of the Bar,
- (c) The Institute of Legal Executives, or
- (d) The Legal Services Ombudsman;

'Cafcass' has the meaning assigned to it by section 11 of the Criminal Justice and Courts Services Act 2000;

'CAFCASS CYMRU' means the part of the Welsh Assembly Government exercising the functions of Welsh Ministers under Part 4 of the Children Act 2004;

'criminal investigation' means an investigation conducted by police officers with a view to it being ascertained –
- (a) whether a person should be charged with an offence, or
- (b) whether a person charged with an offence is guilty of it;

'health care professional' means –
- (a) a registered medical practitioner,
- (b) a registered nurse or midwife,
- (c) a clinical psychologist, or
- (d) a child psychotherapist;

'independent reviewing officer' means a person appointed in respect of a child in accordance with regulation 2A of the Review of Children's Cases Regulations 1991, or regulation 3 of the Review of Children's Cases (Wales) Regulations 2007;

'lay adviser' means a non-professional person who gives lay advice on behalf of an organisation in the lay advice sector;

['legal representative' means a –
- (a) barrister,
- (b) solicitor,
- (c) solicitor's employee,
- (d) manager of a body recognised under section 9 of the Administration of Justice Act 1985, or
- (e) person who, for the purposes of the Legal Services Act 2007, is an authorised person in relation to an activity which constitutes the conduct of litigation (within the meaning of that Act),

who has been instructed to act for a party in relation to the proceedings;][2]

'McKenzie Friend' means any person permitted by the court to sit beside an unrepresented litigant in court to assist that litigant by prompting, taking notes and giving him advice;

'professional acting in furtherance of the protection of children' includes –
- (a) an officer of a local authority exercising child protection functions,
- (b) a police officer who is –
  - (i) exercising powers under section 46 of the Act of 1989, or
  - (ii) serving in a child protection unit or a paedophile unit of a police force;
- (c) any professional person attending a child protection conference or review in relation to a child who is the subject of the proceedings to which the information relates, or
- (d) an officer of the National Society for the Prevention of Cruelty to Children;

['professional legal adviser' means a –
- (a) barrister,
- (b) solicitor,
- (c) solicitor's employee,
- (d) manager of a body recognised under section 9 of the Administration of Justice Act 1985, or
- (e) person who, for the purposes of the Legal Services Act 2007, is an authorised person in relation to an activity which constitutes the conduct of litigation (within the meaning of that Act),

who is providing advice to a party but is not instructed to represent that party in the proceedings;][2]

'social worker' has the meaning assigned to it by section 55 of the Care Standards Act 2000;

'welfare officer' means a person who has been asked to prepare a report under section 7(1)(b) of the Act of 1989.][1]

NOTES

Amendments.¹ Part inserted: SI 2009/858. ² Definitions substituted: SI 2009/3348.

PART III
MISCELLANEOUS

22 Costs

(1) In any relevant proceedings, the court may, at any time during the proceedings in that court, make an order that a party pay the whole or any part of the costs of any other party.

(2) A party against whom the court is considering making a costs order shall have an opportunity to make representations as to why the order should not be made.

[22A Power of court to limit cross-examination

The court may limit the issues on which an officer of the service [or a Welsh family proceedings officer]² may be cross-examined.]¹

NOTES

Amendments.¹ Rule inserted: SI 2001/818. ² Words inserted: SI 2005/585.

23 Confidentiality of documents

(1) [[Subject to Part IIC]⁶]⁴ no document, other than a record of an order, held by the court and relating to relevant proceedings shall be disclosed, other than to –

(a) a party,
(b) the legal representative of a party,
(c) the [children's guardian]¹,
(d) the Legal Aid Board, or
(e) a [welfare officer or children and family reporter]¹, [or
(f) an expert whose instruction by a party has been authorised by the court [for the purposes of proceedings]⁶,]¹

without leave of the justices' clerk or the court.

(2) Nothing in this rule shall prevent the notification by the court or the [designated officer for the court]², ⁵ of a direction under section 37(1) to the authority concerned.

[(3) Nothing in this rule shall prevent the disclosure of a document prepared by an officer of the service or a Welsh family proceedings officer for the purpose of –

(a) enabling a person to perform functions required under section 62(3A) of the Justices of the Peace Act 1997;
(b) enabling a person to perform functions required under section 38(1) of the Children Act 2004; or

(c) assisting an officer of the service or a Welsh family proceedings officer who is appointed by the court under any enactment to perform his functions.]³

[(4) Nothing in this rule shall prevent the disclosure of any document relating to proceedings by [an officer of the service or a Welsh family proceedings officer to any other officer of the service or Welsh family proceedings officer]³ unless that other officer is involved in the same proceedings but on behalf of a different party.]¹

NOTES

Amendments.¹ Words substituted or inserted: SI 2001/818.² Words substituted: SI 2001/615. ³ Paragraph and words substituted: SI 2005/585.⁴ Words inserted: SI 2005/1977.⁵ Words substituted: SI 2005/617.⁶ Words substituted: SI 2009/858.

[23A Communication of information relating to proceedings

...²]¹

NOTES

Amendments.¹ Rule inserted: SI 2005/1977.² Rule revoked: SI 2009/858.

24 Enforcement of residence order [or special guardianship order]²

Where a person in whose favour a residence order [or special guardianship order]² is in force wishes to enforce it he shall file a written statement describing the alleged breach of the arrangements settled by the order, whereupon the justices' clerk shall fix a date, time and place for a hearing of the proceedings and [the [designated officer for the court]³ shall]¹ give notice, as soon as practicable, to the person wishing to enforce the residence order [or special guardianship order]² and to any person whom it is alleged is in breach of the arrangements settled by that order, of the date fixed.

NOTES

Amendments.¹ Words inserted: SI 2001/615.² Words inserted: SI 2005/2930.³ Words substituted: SI 2005/617.

25 Notification of consent

[(1)]² Consent for the purposes of –

    (a) section 16(3), [or]¹
    (b) [section 38A(2)(b)(ii) or 44A(2)(b)(ii), or]²
    (c) paragraph 19(1) of Schedule 2,

shall be given either –
        (i) orally in court, or
        (ii) in writing to the [designated officer for the court]³, ⁴ or the court and signed by the person giving his consent.

[(2) Any written consent given for the purposes of subsection (2) of section 38A or section 44A, shall include a statement that the person giving consent –

(a) is able and willing to give to the child the care which it would be reasonable to expect a parent to give him; and
(b) understands that the giving of consent could lead to the exclusion of the relevant person from the dwelling-house in which the child lives.][2]

NOTES
Amendments.[1] Words inserted or revoked: SI 1992/2068.[2] Paragraph numbering and paragraph inserted and words substituted: SI 1997/1895.[3] Words substituted: SI 2001/615.[4] Words substituted: SI 2005/617.

[25A Exclusion requirements: interim care orders and emergency protection orders

(1) This rule applies where the court includes an exclusion requirement in an interim care order or an emergency protection order.

(2) The applicant for an interim care order or emergency protection order shall –

(a) prepare a separate statement of the evidence in support of the application for an exclusion requirement;
(b) serve the statement personally on the relevant person with a copy of the order containing the exclusion requirement (and of any power of arrest which is attached to it);
(c) inform the relevant person of his right to apply to vary or discharge the exclusion requirement.

(3) Where a power of arrest is attached to an exclusion requirement in an interim care order or an emergency protection order, a copy of the order shall be delivered to the officer for the time being in charge of the police station for the area in which the dwelling-house in which the child lives is situated (or of such other station as the court may specify) together with a statement that the relevant person has been served with the order or informed of its terms (whether by being present when the order was made or by telephone or otherwise).

(4) Rules 12A(3), 20 (except paragraphs (1) and (3)) and 21 of the Family Proceedings Courts (Matrimonial Proceedings etc) Rules 1991 shall apply, with the necessary modifications, for the service, variation, discharge and enforcement of any exclusion requirement to which a power of arrest is attached as they apply to an order made on an application under Part IV of the Family Law Act 1996.

(5) The relevant person shall serve the parties to the proceedings with any application which he makes for the variation or discharge of the exclusion requirement.

(6) Where an exclusion requirement ceases to have effect whether –

(a) as a result of the removal of a child under section 38A(10) or 44A(10),
(b) because of the discharge of the interim care order or emergency protection order, or
(c) otherwise,

the applicant shall inform –
- (i) the relevant person,
- (ii) the parties to the proceedings,
- (iii) any officer to whom a copy of the order was delivered under paragraph (3), and
- (iv) (where necessary) the court.

(7) Where the court includes an exclusion requirement in an interim care order or an emergency protection order of its own motion, paragraph (2) shall apply with the omission of any reference to the statement of the evidence.][1]

NOTES

Amendments.[1] Rule inserted: SI 1997/1895.

26 Secure accommodation

In proceedings under section 25, the [designated officer for the court][1, 3] shall, if practicable, arrange for copies of all written reports before the court to be made available before the hearing to –

- (a) the applicant,
- (b) the parent or guardian of the child,
- (c) any legal representative of the child,
- (d) the [children's guardian][2], and
- (e) the child, unless the justices' clerk or the court otherwise directs;

and copies of such reports may, if the court considers it desirable, be shown to any person who is entitled to notice of the proceedings in accordance with these Rules.

NOTES

Amendments.[1] Words substituted: SI 2001/615.[2] Words substituted: SI 2001/818.[3] Words substituted: SI 2005/617.

27 Investigation under section 37

(1) This rule applies where a direction is given to an appropriate authority by a family proceedings court under section 37(1).

(2) On giving a direction the court shall adjourn the proceedings and the justices' clerk or the court shall record the direction [in Form C40][1].

(3) A copy of the direction recorded under paragraph (2) shall, as soon as practicable after the direction is given, be served by the [designated officer for the court][2, 3] on the parties to the proceedings in which the direction is given and, where the appropriate authority is not a party, on that authority.

(4) When serving the copy of the direction on the appropriate authority the [designated officer for the court][2, 3] shall also serve copies of such of the documentary evidence which has been, or is to be, adduced in the proceedings as the court may direct.

(5) Where a local authority informs the court of any of the matters set out in section 37(3)(a) to (c) it shall do so in writing.

NOTES

Amendments.[1] Words substituted: SI 1994/3156.[2] Words substituted: SI 2001/615.[3] Words substituted: SI 2005/617.

28 Limits on the power of a justices' clerk or a single justice to make an order under section 11(3) or section 38(1)

A justices' clerk or single justice shall not make an order under section 11(3) or section 38(1) unless –

(a) a written request for such an order has been made to which the other parties and any [children's guardian][1] consent and which they or their representatives have signed,
(b) a previous such order has been made in the same proceedings, and
(c) the terms of the order sought are the same as those of the last such order made.

NOTES

Amendments.[1] Words substituted: SI 2001/818.

29 Appeals to a family proceedings court under section 77(6) and paragraph 8(1) of Schedule 8

(1) An appeal under section 77(6) or paragraph 8(1) of Schedule 8 shall be by application in accordance with rule 4.

(2) An appeal under section 77(6) shall be brought within 21 days from the date of the step to which the appeal relates.

30 Contribution orders

(1) An application for a contribution order under paragraph 23(1) of Schedule 2 shall be accompanied by a copy of the contribution notice served in accordance with paragraph 22(1) of that Schedule and a copy of any notice served by the contributor under paragraph 22(8) of that Schedule.

(2) Where a local authority notifies the court of an agreement reached under paragraph 23(6) of Schedule 2, it shall do so in writing through the [designated officer for the court][1, 2].

(3) An application for the variation or revocation of a contribution order under paragraph 23(8) of Schedule 2 shall be accompanied by a copy of the contribution order which it is sought to vary or revoke.

NOTES

Amendments.[1] Words substituted: SI 2001/615.[2] Words substituted: SI 2005/617.

31 [Direction to local authority to apply for education supervision order][2]

(1) For the purposes of section 40(3) and (4) of the Education Act 1944, a direction by a magistrates' court to a [local authority][2] to apply for an education supervision order shall be given [in writing][1].

(2) Where, following such a direction, a [local authority][2] informs the court that they have decided not to apply for an education supervision order, they shall do so in writing.

NOTES

Amendments.[1] Words substituted: SI 1997/1895. [2] Words substituted: SI 2010/1172.

[31A Applications and orders under sections 33 and 34 of the Family Law Act 1986

(1) In this rule 'the 1986 Act' means the Family Law Act 1986.

(2) An application under section 33 of the 1986 Act shall be in Form C4 and an order made under that section shall be in Form C30.

(3) An application under section 34 of the 1986 Act shall be in Form C3 and an order made under that section shall be in Form C31.

(4) An application under section 33 or section 34 of the 1986 Act may be made ex parte in which case the applicant shall file the application –

(a) where the application is made by telephone, within 24 hours after the making of the application, or

(b) in any other case at the time when the application is made,

and shall serve a copy of the application on each respondent 48 hours after the making of the order.

(5) Where the court refuses to make an order on an ex parte application it may direct that the application be make inter partes.][1]

NOTES

Amendments.[1] Rule inserted: SI 1994/3156.

32 Delegation by justices' clerk

(1) In this rule, 'employed as a clerk in court' has the same meaning as in rule 2(1) of the Justices' Clerks (Qualifications of Assistants) Rules 1979.

(2) Anything authorised to be done by, to or before a justices' clerk under these Rules, or under paragraphs 13 to 15C of the Justices' Clerks Rules 1970 as amended by Schedule 3 to these Rules, may be done instead by, to or before a person employed as a clerk in court where that person is appointed by the [Lord Chancellor][1] to assist him and where that person has been specifically authorised by the justices' clerk for that purpose.

(3) Any authorisation by the justices' clerk under paragraph (2) shall be recorded in writing at the time the authority is given or as soon as practicable thereafter.

NOTES

Amendments.[1] Words substituted: SI 2005/617.

33 Application of section 97 of the Magistrates' Courts Act 1980

Section 97 of the Magistrates' Courts Act 1980 shall apply to relevant proceedings in a family proceedings court as it applies to a hearing of a complaint under that section.

[33A Disclosure of addresses

(1) Nothing in these rules shall be construed as requiring any party to reveal the address of their private residence (or that of any child) except by order of the court.

(2) Where a party declines to reveal an address in reliance upon paragraph (1) he shall give notice of that address to the court in Form C8 and that address shall not be revealed to any person except by order of the court.][1]

NOTES

Amendments.[1] Rule inserted: SI 1994/3156.

[33B Setting aside on failure of service

Where an application has been sent to a respondent in accordance with rule 8(1) and, after an order has been made on the application, it appears to the court that the application did not come to the knowledge of the respondent in due time, the court may of its own motion set aside the order and may give such directions as it thinks fit for the rehearing of the application.][1]

NOTES

Amendments.[1] Rule inserted: SI 1997/1895.

34 Consequential and minor amendments, savings and transitionals

(1) Subject to paragraph (3) the consequential and minor amendments in Schedule 3 to these Rules shall have effect.

(2) Subject to paragraph (3), the provisions of the 1981 rules shall have effect subject to these Rules.

(3) Nothing in these Rules shall affect any proceedings which are pending (within the meaning of paragraph 1 of Schedule 14 to the Act of 1989) immediately before these Rules come into force.

****

SCHEDULE 1
FORMS

[C1	Application	[[Children Act 1989 except care and supervision orders, Section 8 orders and orders related to enforcement of a contact order][8]][6]
[C100	Application	under the Children Act 1989 for a residence, contact or other section 8 order][6]
[C110	Application	under the Children Act 1989 for a care order or supervision order][8]
[C1A		Supplemental Information Form][4]
C2	Application	for an order or directions in existing family proceedings
	Application	to be joined as, or cease to be, a party in existing family proceedings
	Application	for leave to commence proceedings
C3	Application	for an order authorising search for, taking charge of, and delivery of a child
C4	Application	for an order for disclosure of a child's whereabouts
C5	Application	concerning the registration of a child-minder or a provider of day care
C6	Notice	of proceedings [Hearing] [Directions Appointment] (*Notice to parties*)
C6A	Notice	of proceedings [Hearing] [Directions Appointment] (*Notice to non-parties*)
C7		Acknowledgement
C8		Confidential Address
C9	Statement	of Service
C10	Supplement	for an application for financial provision for a child or for variation of financial provision for a child
C10A	Statement	of Means
[C11	Supplement	for an application for an Emergency Protection Order][2]
C12	Supplement	for an application for a Warrant to assist a person authorised by an Emergency Protection Order
...[8]		
[C13A	Supplement	for an application for a Special Guardianship Order][5]

C14	Supplement	for an application for authority to refuse contact with a child in care
C15	Supplement	for an application for contact with a child in care
C16	Supplement	for an application for a Child Assessment Order
C17	Supplement	for an application for an Education Supervision Order
C17A	Supplement	for an application for an extension of an Education Supervision Order
C18	Supplement	for an application for a Recovery Order
C19	Supplement	for a Warrant of Assistance
C20	Supplement	for an application for an order to hold a child in Secure Accommodation
C21	Order or direction	Blank
C22	Record	of hearing
[C23	Order	Emergency Protection Order][2]
C24	Order	Variation of an Emergency Protection Order
		Extension of an Emergency Protection Order
		Discharge of an Emergency Protection Order
C25	Warrant	To assist a person authorised by an Emergency Protection Order
C26	Order	Authority to keep a child in Secure Accommodation
C27	Order	Authority to search for another child
C28	Warrant	To assist a person to gain access to a child or entry to premises
C29	Order	Recovery of a child
C30	Order	To disclose information about the whereabouts of a missing child
C31	Order	Authorising search for, taking charge of, and delivery of a child
C32	Order	Care Order
		Discharge of a Care Order
[C33	Order	Interim Care Order][2]
C34	Order	Contact with a child in care
		Authority to refuse contact with a child in care

Part II   Statutory Instruments

C35	Order	Supervision Order
		Interim Supervision Order
C36	Order	Substitution of a Supervision Order for a Care Order
		Discharge of a Supervision Order
		Variation of a Supervision Order
		Extension of a Supervision Order
C37	Order	Education Supervision Order
C38	Order	Discharge of an Education Supervision Order
		Extension of an Education Supervision Order
C39	Order	Child Assessment Order
C40	Direction	To undertake an investigation
C41	Order	Cancellation of the registration of a child-minder or a provider of day care
		Removal, Variation or Imposition of a requirement on a child-minder or a provider of day care
C42	Order	Family Assistance Order
C43	Order	Residence Order
		Contact Order
		Specific Issue Order
		Prohibited Steps Order
[C43A	Order	Special Guardianship Order][5]
C44	Order	Leave to change the surname by which a child is known
		Leave to remove a child from the United Kingdom
C45	Order	Parental Responsibility Order
		Termination of a Parental Responsibility Order
C46	Order	Appointment of a guardian
		Termination of the appointment of a guardian
C47	Order	Making or refusing the appointment of a [children's guardian][3]
		Termination of the appointment of a [children's guardian][3]
C48	Order	Appointment of a solicitor for a child
		Refusal of the appointment of a solicitor for a child
		Termination of the appointment of a solicitor for a child

C49	Order	Transfer of Proceedings to [the High Court] [a county court] [a family proceedings court]
C50	Certificate	Refusal to transfer proceedings
C51	Application	for a Parental Order
C52		Acknowledgement of an application for a Parental Order
C53	Order	Parental Order
C54	Notice	of Refusal of a Parental Order][1]
[A64A	Application	for a recovery order
A101A	Consent	to the making of a parental order][7]

NOTES

Amendments.[1] Forms substituted: SI 1994/3156.[2] Form substituted: SI 1997/1895.[3] Words substituted: SI 2001/818.[4] Entries inserted: SI 2004/3376.[5] Entries inserted: SI 2005/2930.[6] Words substituted and entry inserted: SI 2008/2858. [7] Entries inserted: SI 2010/1065. [8] Words substituted and entries inserted and revoked: SI 2010/787.

SCHEDULE 2
RESPONDENTS AND NOTICE

Rules 4 and 7

(i)	(ii)	(iii)	(iv)
Provision under which proceedings brought	*Minimum number of days prior to hearing or directions appointment for service under rule 4(1)(b)*	*Respondents*	*Persons to whom notice is to be given*
All applications.	See separate entries below.	Subject to separate entries below.	Subject to separate entries below,

Part II Statutory Instruments

(i)	(ii)	(iii)	(iv)
Provision under which proceedings brought	*Minimum number of days prior to hearing or directions appointment for service under rule 4(1)(b)*	Respondents	*Persons to whom notice is to be given*
		every person whom the applicant believes to have parental responsibility for the child; where the child is the subject of a care order, every person whom the applicant believes to have had parental responsibility immediately prior to the making of the care order;	the local authority providing accommodation for the child; persons who are caring for the child at the time when the proceedings are commenced; in the case of proceedings brought in respect of a child who is alleged to be staying in a refuge
		in the case of an application to extend, vary or discharge an order, the parties to the proceedings leading to the order which it is sought to have extended, varied or discharged;	which is certificated under section 51(1) or (2), the person who is providing the refuge.

(i)	(ii)	(iii)	(iv)
Provision under which proceedings brought	Minimum number of days prior to hearing or directions appointment for service under rule 4(1)(b)	Respondents	Persons to whom notice is to be given
...¹		in the case of specified proceedings, the child.	
Section [4(1)(c)]³, 4(3), [4ZA(1)(c), 4ZA(6),]⁸ [4A(1)(b), 4A(3),]⁴ 5(1), 6(7), [8,]¹ 13(1), [14A, 14C(3), 14D,]⁴ ...⁵, 33(7), 77(6), [Schedule 1,]¹ paragraph 19(1), 23(1) or 23(8) of Schedule 2, paragraph 8(1) of Schedule 8, or paragraph 11(3) or 16(5) of Schedule 14.	14 days.	Except for proceedings under section 77(6), Schedule 2, or paragraph 8(1) of Schedule 8, as for 'all applications' above, and – in the case of an application under paragraph 11(3)(b) or 16(5) of Schedule 14, any person, other than the child, named in the order or directions which it is sought to discharge or vary; [in the case of proceedings]¹ under section 77(6), the	As for 'all applications' above, and – in the case of an application under paragraph 19(1) of Schedule 2, the parties to the proceedings leading to the care order; in the case of an application under section 5(1), [the father or parent (being a woman who is a parent by virtue of section 43 of the Human Fertilisation and Embryology Act 2008) of the child if that person]⁸ does not have parental responsibility.

(i)	(ii)	(iii)	(iv)
Provision under which proceedings brought	*Minimum number of days prior to hearing or directions appointment for service under rule 4(1)(b)*	*Respondents*	*Persons to whom notice is to be given*
		local authority against whose decision the appeal is made; [in the case of proceedings under Schedule 1, those persons whom the applicant believes to be interested in or affected by the proceedings;]¹ in the case of an application under paragraph 23(1) of Schedule 2, the contributor; in the case of an application under paragraph 23(8) of Schedule 2 (i) if the applicant is the local authority, the contribu-tor, and	

(i)	(ii)	(iii)	(iv)
Provision under which proceedings brought	Minimum number of days prior to hearing or directions appointment for service under rule 4(1)(b)	Respondents	Persons to whom notice is to be given
		(ii) if the applicant is the contributor, the local authority. In the case of an application under paragraph 8(1) of Schedule 8, the local authority against whose decision the appeal is made. [in the case of an application for a section 8 order, every person whom the applicant believes – (i) to be named in a court order with respect to the same child, which has not ceased to have effect,	

Part II   Statutory Instruments

(i)	(ii)	(iii)	(iv)
Provision under which proceedings brought	*Minimum number of days prior to hearing or directions appointment for service under rule 4(1)(b)*	Respondents	*Persons to whom notice is to be given*
		(ii) to be a party to pending proceedings in respect of the same child, or	
		(iii) to be a person with whom the child has lived for at least three years prior to the application,	
		unless, in a case to which (i) or (ii) applies, the applicant believes that the court order or pending proceedings are not relevant to the application.]¹	

(i)	(ii)	(iii)	(iv)
Provision under which proceedings brought	*Minimum number of days prior to hearing or directions appointment for service under rule 4(1)(b)*	*Respondents*	*Persons to whom notice is to be given*
		[in the case of an application under section 14A, if a care order is in force with respect to the child, the child]	[in the case of an application under section 14A – (a) if the child is not being accommodated by the local authority, the local authority in whose area the applicant is ordinarily resident, and (b) every other person whom the applicant believes –

Part II Statutory Instruments

(i) Provision under which proceedings brought	(ii) Minimum number of days prior to hearing or directions appointment for service under rule 4(1)(b)	(iii) Respondents	(iv) Persons to whom notice is to be given
			(i) to be named in a court order with respect to that child which remains in force, (ii) to be a party to pending proceedings in respect of the same child, (iii) to be a person with whom the child has lived for at least 3 years prior to the application,

(i)	(ii)	(iii)	(iv)
Provision under which proceedings brought	*Minimum number of days prior to hearing or directions appointment for service under rule 4(1)(b)*	*Respondents*	*Persons to whom notice is to be given*
			unless, in a case to which (i) or (ii) applies, the applicant believes that the court order or pending proceedings are not relevant to the application;
			in the case of an application under section 14D –
			(a) as for applications under section 14A above, and
			(b) the local authority that prepared the report under section 14A(8) or (9) in the proceedings leading to the order which it is sought to have varied or discharged, if different from any local authority that will be otherwise be notified][4]

(i)	(ii)	(iii)	(iv)
Provision under which proceedings brought	*Minimum number of days prior to hearing or directions appointment for service under rule 4(1)(b)*	*Respondents*	*Persons to whom notice is to be given*
Section 36(1), 39(1), 39(2), 39(3), 39(4), 43(1), or paragraph 6(3), 15(2) or 17(1) of Schedule 3.	7 days.	As for 'all applications' above, and –	As for 'all applications' above, and –
		in the case of an application under section 39(2) or (3), the supervisor;	in the case of an application for an order under section 43(1) –
		in the case of proceedings under paragraph 17(1) of Schedule 3, the [local authority][10] concerned;	(i) every person whom the applicant believes to be a parent of the child,
		in the case of proceedings under section 36 or paragraph 15(2) or 17(1) of Schedule 3, the child.	(ii) every person whom the applicant believes to be caring for the child,

Family Proceedings Courts (Children Act 1989) Rules 1991, Sch 2

(i)	(ii)	(iii)	(iv)
Provision under which proceedings brought	*Minimum number of days prior to hearing or directions appointment for service under rule 4(1)(b)*	*Respondents*	*Persons to whom notice is to be given*
			(iii) every person in whose favour a contact order is in force with respect to the child, and
			(iv) every person who is allowed to have contact with the child by virtue of an order under section 34.
Section 31, 34(2), 34(3), 34(4), 34(9) or 38(8)(b).	3 days.	As for 'all applications' above, and – in the case of an application under section 34, the person whose contact with the child is the subject of the application.	As for 'all applications' above, and – in the case of application under section 31 –

Part II   Statutory Instruments

(i)	(ii)	(iii)	(iv)
Provision under which proceedings brought	*Minimum number of days prior to hearing or directions appointment for service under rule 4(1)(b)*	*Respondents*	*Persons to whom notice is to be given*
Section 43(12).	2 days.	As for 'all applications' above.	(i) every person whom the applicant believes to be a party to pending relevant proceedings in respect of the same child, and (ii) every person whom the applicant believes to be a parent without parental responsibility for the child. Those of the persons referred to in section 43(11)(a) to (e) who were not party to the application for the order which it is sought to have varied or discharged.

Family Proceedings Courts (Children Act 1989) Rules 1991, Sch 2

(i)	(ii)	(iii)	(iv)
Provision under which proceedings brought	*Minimum number of days prior to hearing or directions appointment for service under rule 4(1)(b)*	*Respondents*	*Persons to whom notice is to be given*
Section 25, 44(1), 44(9)(b), 45(4), 45(8), 46(7), 48(9), 50(1), ...[6] or 102(1).	1 day.	Except for applications under section ...[6] 102(1), as for 'all applications' above, and – in the case of an application under section 44(9)(b) – (i) the parties to the application for the order in respect of which it is sought to vary the directions;	As for 'all applications' above and – in the case of an application under section 44(1), every person whom the applicant believes to be a parent of the child; in the case of an application under section 44(9)(b) – (i) the local authority in whose area the child is living, and

PART II – Statutory Instruments

(i)	(ii)	(iii)	(iv)
Provision under which proceedings brought	*Minimum number of days prior to hearing or directions appointment for service under rule 4(1)(b)*	*Respondents*	*Persons to whom notice is to be given*
		(ii) any person who was caring for the child prior to the making of the order; and (iii) any person whose contact with the child is affected by the direction which it is sought to have varied; in the case of an application under section 50, the person whom the applicant alleges to have effected or to have been or to be responsible for the taking or keeping of the child;	(ii) any person whom the applicant believes to be affected by the direction which it is sought to have varied.

Family Proceedings Courts (Children Act 1989) Rules 1991, Sch 2

(i)	(ii)	(iii)	(iv)
Provision under which proceedings brought	*Minimum number of days prior to hearing or directions appointment for service under rule 4(1)(b)*	*Respondents*	*Persons to whom notice is to be given*
[...⁹]²		in the case of an application under section 75(1), the registered person; in the case of an application under section 102(1), the person referred to in section 102(1) and any person preventing or likely to prevent such a person from exercising powers under enactments mentioned in subsection (6) of that section.	

PART II – Statutory Instruments

Part II Statutory Instruments

(i)	(ii)	(iii)	(iv)
Provision under which proceedings brought	*Minimum number of days prior to hearing or directions appointment for service under rule 4(1)(b)*	*Respondents*	*Persons to whom notice is to be given*
Section 79 of the Childcare Act 2006	1 day	Any person preventing or likely to prevent Her Majesty's Chief Inspector of Education, Children's Services and Skills from exercising a power conferred on him by section 77][7]	

NOTES

Amendments.[1] Words substituted, revoked or inserted: SI 1992/2068. [2] Words inserted: SI 1994/2166. [3] Words substituted: SI 2003/2840. [4] Words inserted: SI 2005/2930. [5] Reference revoked: SI 2007/2188. [6] References and word revoked: SI 2009/637. [7] Entry inserted: SI 2009/637. [8] References and words inserted: SI 2009/2025. [9] Entry revoked: SI 2010/1065. [10] Words substituted: SI 2010/1172.

****

Part III
PRACTICE DIRECTIONS AND GUIDANCE

PRESIDENT'S DIRECTION
24 JULY 2000

Citations: [2000] 2 FLR 429

HUMAN RIGHTS ACT 1998

1 It is directed that the following practice shall apply as from 2 October 2000 in all family proceedings:

Citation of authorities

2 When an authority referred to in s 2 of the Human Rights Act 1998 ('the Act') is to be cited at a hearing:

(a) the authority to be cited shall be an authoritative and complete report;
(b) the court must be provided with a list of authorities it is intended to cite and copies of the reports:
  (i) in cases to which *Practice Direction (Family Proceedings: Court Bundles)* (10 March 2000) [2000] 1 FLR 536 applies, as part of the bundle;
  (ii) otherwise, not less than 2 clear days before the hearing; and
(c) copies of the complete original texts issued by the European Court and Commission, either paper based or from the Court's judgment database (HUDOC) which is available on the internet, may be used.

Allocation to judges

3(1) The hearing and determination of the following will be confined to a High Court judge:

(a) a claim for a declaration of incompatibility under s 4 of the Act; or
(b) an issue which may lead to the court considering making such a declaration.

(2) The hearing and determination of a claim made under the Act in respect of a judicial act shall be confined in the High Court to a High Court judge and in county courts to a circuit judge.

Issued with the concurrence and approval of the Lord Chancellor.

Dame Elizabeth Butler-Sloss
President

PRESIDENT'S DIRECTION
27 JULY 2006

Citations: [2006] 2 FLR 199

FAMILY PROCEEDINGS: COURT BUNDLES (UNIVERSAL PRACTICE TO BE APPLIED IN ALL COURTS OTHER THAN THE FAMILY PROCEEDINGS COURT)

1 The President of the Family Division has issued this practice direction to achieve consistency across the country in all family courts (other than the Family Proceedings Court) in the preparation of court bundles and in respect of other related matters.

Application of the practice direction

2.1 Except as specified in para 2.4, and subject to specific directions given in any particular case, the following practice applies to:

(a) all hearings of whatever nature (including but not limited to hearings in family proceedings, Civil Procedure Rules 1998 Part 7 and Part 8 claims and appeals) before a judge of the Family Division of the High Court wherever the court may be sitting;

(b) all hearings in family proceedings in the Royal Courts of Justice (RCJ);

(c) all hearings in the Principal Registry of the Family Division (PRFD) at First Avenue House; and

(d) all hearings in family proceedings in all other courts except for Family Proceedings Courts.

2.2 'Hearings' includes all appearances before a judge or district judge, whether with or without notice to other parties and whether for directions or for substantive relief.

2.3 This practice direction applies whether a bundle is being lodged for the first time or is being re-lodged for a further hearing (see para 9.2).

2.4 This practice direction does not apply to:

(a) cases listed for one hour or less at a court referred to in para 2.1(c) or 2.1(d); or

(b) the hearing of any urgent application if and to the extent that it is impossible to comply with it.

2.5 The designated family judge responsible for any court referred to in para 2.1(c) or 2.1(d) may, after such consultation as is appropriate (but in the case of hearings in the PRFD at First Avenue House only with the agreement of the Senior District Judge), direct that in that court this practice direction shall apply to all family proceedings irrespective of the length of hearing.

Responsibility for the preparation of the bundle

3.1 A bundle for the use of the court at the hearing shall be provided by the party in the position of applicant at the hearing (or, if there are cross-applications, by the party whose application was first in time) or, if that person is a litigant in person, by the first listed respondent who is not a litigant in person.

3.2 The party preparing the bundle shall paginate it. If possible the contents of the bundle shall be agreed by all parties.

Contents of the bundle

4.1 The bundle shall contain copies of all documents relevant to the hearing, in chronological order from the front of the bundle, paginated and indexed, and divided into separate sections (each section being separately paginated) as follows:

(a) preliminary documents (see para 4.2) and any other case management documents required by any other practice direction;
(b) applications and orders;
(c) statements and affidavits (which must be dated in the top right corner of the front page);
(d) care plans (where appropriate);
(e) experts' reports and other reports (including those of a guardian, children's guardian or litigation friend); and
(f) other documents, divided into further sections as may be appropriate.

Copies of notes of contact visits should normally not be included in the bundle unless directed by a judge.

4.2 At the commencement of the bundle there shall be inserted the following documents (the preliminary documents):

(i) an up to date summary of the background to the hearing confined to those matters which are relevant to the hearing and the management of the case and limited, if practicable, to one A4 page;
(ii) a statement of the issue or issues to be determined (1) at that hearing and (2) at the final hearing;
(iii) a position statement by each party including a summary of the order or directions sought by that party (1) at that hearing and (2) at the final hearing;
(iv) an up to date chronology, if it is a final hearing or if the summary under (i) is insufficient;
(v) skeleton arguments, if appropriate, with copies of all authorities relied on; and
(vi) a list of essential reading for that hearing.

4.3 Each of the preliminary documents shall state on the front page immediately below the heading the date when it was prepared and the date of the hearing for which it was prepared.

4.4 The summary of the background, statement of issues, chronology, position statement and any skeleton arguments shall be cross-referenced to the relevant pages of the bundle.

4.5 The summary of the background, statement of issues, chronology and reading list shall in the case of a final hearing, and shall so far as practicable in the case of any other hearing, each consist of a single document in a form agreed by all parties. Where the parties disagree as to the content the fact of their disagreement and their differing contentions shall be set out at the appropriate places in the document.

4.6 Where the nature of the hearing is such that a complete bundle of all documents is unnecessary, the bundle (which need not be repaginated) may comprise only those documents necessary for the hearing, but

(i) the summary (para 4.2(i)) must commence with a statement that the bundle is limited or incomplete; and
(ii) the bundle shall if reasonably practicable be in a form agreed by all parties.

4.7 Where the bundle is re-lodged in accordance with para 9.2, before it is re-lodged:

(a) the bundle shall be updated as appropriate; and
(b) all superseded documents (and in particular all outdated summaries, statements of issues, chronologies, skeleton arguments and similar documents) shall be removed from the bundle.

Format of the bundle

5.1 The bundle shall be contained in one or more A4 size ring binders or lever arch files (each lever arch file being limited to 350 pages).

5.2 All ring binders and lever arch files shall have clearly marked on the front and the spine:

(a) the title and number of the case;
(b) the court where the case has been listed;
(c) the hearing date and time;
(d) if known, the name of the judge hearing the case; and
(e) where there is more than one ring binder or lever arch file, a distinguishing letter (A, B, C etc).

Timetable for preparing and lodging the bundle

6.1 The party preparing the bundle shall, whether or not the bundle has been agreed, provide a paginated index to all other parties not less than 4 working days before the hearing (in relation to a case management conference to which the provisions of the *Protocol for Judicial Case Management in Public Law Children Act Cases* [2003] 2 FLR 719 apply, not less than 5 working days before the case management conference).

6.2 Where counsel is to be instructed at any hearing, a paginated bundle shall (if not already in counsel's possession) be delivered to counsel by the person instructing that counsel not less than 3 working days before the hearing.

6.3 The bundle (with the exception of the preliminary documents if and insofar as they are not then available) shall be lodged with the court not less than 2 working days before the hearing, or at such other time as may be specified by the judge.

6.4 The preliminary documents shall be lodged with the court no later than 11 am on the day before the hearing and, where the hearing is before a judge of the High Court and the name of the judge is known, shall at the same time be sent by email to the judge's clerk.

Lodging the bundle

7.1 The bundle shall be lodged at the appropriate office. If the bundle is lodged in the wrong place the judge may:

  (a) treat the bundle as having not been lodged; and
  (b) take the steps referred to in para 12.

7.2 Unless the judge has given some other direction as to where the bundle in any particular case is to be lodged (for example a direction that the bundle is to be lodged with the judge's clerk) the bundle shall be lodged:

  (a) for hearings in the RCJ, in the office of the Clerk of the Rules, Room TM 9.09, Royal Courts of Justice, Strand, London WC2A 2LL (DX 44450 Strand);
  (b) for hearings in the PRFD at First Avenue House, at the List Office counter, 3rd floor, First Avenue House, 42/49 High Holborn, London, WC1V 6NP (DX 396 Chancery Lane); and
  (c) for hearings at any other court, at such place as may be designated by the designated family judge or other judge at that court and in default of any such designation at the court office of the court where the hearing is to take place.

7.3 Any bundle sent to the court by post, DX or courier shall be clearly addressed to the appropriate office and shall show the date and place of the hearing on the outside of any packaging as well as on the bundle itself.

Lodging the bundle – additional requirements for cases being heard at First Avenue House or at the RCJ

8.1 In the case of hearings at the RCJ or First Avenue House, parties shall:

  (a) if the bundle or preliminary documents are delivered personally, ensure that they obtain a receipt from the clerk accepting it or them; and
  (b) if the bundle or preliminary documents are sent by post or DX, ensure that they obtain proof of posting or despatch.

The receipt (or proof of posting or despatch, as the case may be) shall be brought to court on the day of the hearing and must be produced to the court if requested. If the receipt (or proof of posting or despatch) cannot be produced to the court the judge may: (i) treat the bundle as having not been lodged; and (ii) take the steps referred to in para 12.

8.2 For hearings at the RCJ:

- (a) bundles or preliminary documents delivered after 11 am on the day before the hearing will not be accepted by the Clerk of the Rules and shall be delivered:
    - (i) in a case where the hearing is before a judge of the High Court, directly to the clerk of the judge hearing the case;
    - (ii) in a case where the hearing is before a Circuit Judge, Deputy High Court Judge or Recorder, directly to the messenger at the Judge's entrance to the Queen's Building (with telephone notification to the personal assistant to the Designated Family Judge, 020 7947 7155, that this has been done).
- (b) upon learning before which judge a hearing is to take place, the clerk to counsel, or other advocate, representing the party in the position of applicant shall no later than 3 pm the day before the hearing:
    - (i) in a case where the hearing is before a judge of the High Court, telephone the clerk of the judge hearing the case;
    - (ii) in a case where the hearing is before a circuit judge, deputy high court judge or recorder, telephone the personal assistant to the designated family judge;

to ascertain whether the judge has received the bundle (including the preliminary documents) and, if not, shall organise prompt delivery by the applicant's solicitor.

Removing and re-lodging the bundle

9.1 Following completion of the hearing the party responsible for the bundle shall retrieve it from the court immediately or, if that is not practicable, shall collect it from the court within 5 working days. Bundles which are not collected in due time may be destroyed.

9.2 The bundle shall be re-lodged for the next and any further hearings in accordance with the provisions of this practice direction and in a form which complies with para 4.7.

Time estimates

10.1 In every case a time estimate (which shall be inserted at the front of the bundle) shall be prepared which shall so far as practicable be agreed by all parties and shall:

(a) specify separately: (i) the time estimated to be required for judicial pre-reading; and (ii) the time required for hearing all evidence and submissions; and (iii) the time estimated to be required for preparing and delivering judgment; and

(b) be prepared on the basis that before they give evidence all witnesses will have read all relevant filed statements and reports.

10.2 Once a case has been listed, any change in time estimates shall be notified immediately by telephone (and then immediately confirmed in writing):

(a) in the case of hearings in the RCJ, to the Clerk of the Rules;

(b) in the case of hearings in the PRFD at First Avenue House, to the List Officer at First Avenue House; and

(c) in the case of hearings elsewhere, to the relevant listing officer.

Taking cases out of the list

11 As soon as it becomes known that a hearing will no longer be effective, whether as a result of the parties reaching agreement or for any other reason, the parties and their representatives shall immediately notify the court by telephone and by letter. The letter, which shall wherever possible be a joint letter sent on behalf of all parties with their signatures applied or appended, shall include:

(a) a short background summary of the case;

(b) the written consent of each party who consents and, where a party does not consent, details of the steps which have been taken to obtain that party's consent and, where known, an explanation of why that consent has not been given;

(c) a draft of the order being sought; and

(d) enough information to enable the court to decide (i) whether to take the case out of the list and (ii) whether to make the proposed order.

Penalties for failure to comply with the practice direction

12 Failure to comply with any part of this practice direction may result in the judge removing the case from the list or putting the case further back in the list and may also result in a 'wasted costs' order in accordance with CPR, Part 48.7 or some other adverse costs order.

Commencement of the practice direction and application of other practice directions

13 This practice direction replaces *Practice Direction (Family Proceedings: Court Bundles) (10 March 2000)* [2000] 1 WLR 737, [2000] 1 FLR 536 and shall have effect from 2 October 2006.

14 Any reference in any other practice direction to *Practice Direction (Family Proceedings: Court Bundles) (10 March 2000)* shall be read as if substituted by a reference to this practice direction.

15 This practice direction should where appropriate be read in conjunction with *Practice Direction (Family Proceedings: Human Rights)* [2000] 1 WLR 1782, [2000] 2 FLR 429 and with *Practice Direction (Care Cases: Judicial Continuity and Judicial Case Management)* appended to the *Protocol for Judicial Case Management in Public Law Children Act Cases*. In particular, nothing in this practice direction is to be read as removing or altering any obligation to comply with the requirements of the *Public Law Protocol*.

This Practice Direction is issued:

(i) in relation to family proceedings, by the President of the Family Division, as the nominee of the Lord Chief Justice, with the agreement of the Lord Chancellor; and

(ii) to the extent that it applies to proceedings to which s 5 of the Civil Procedure Act 1997 applies, by the Master of the Rolls as the nominee of the Lord Chief Justice, with the agreement of the Lord Chancellor.

The Right Honourable
Sir Mark Potter
President of the Family Division & Head of Family Justice

The Right Honourable
Sir Anthony Clarke
Master of the Rolls & Head of Civil Justice

Practice Direction of 1 April 2008

PRACTICE DIRECTION
1 APRIL 2008

EXPERTS IN FAMILY PROCEEDINGS RELATING TO CHILDREN

The Practice Direction below is made by the President of the Family Division under the powers delegated to him by the Lord Chief Justice under Schedule 2, Part 1, paragraph 2(2) of the Constitutional Reform Act 2005, and is approved by the Lord Chancellor.

1 Introduction

1.1 This Practice Direction deals with the use of expert evidence and the instruction of experts in family proceedings relating to children, and comes into force on 1st April 2008. The guidance supersedes, for such proceedings, that contained in Appendix C (*the Code of Guidance for Expert Witnesses in Family Proceedings*) to the Protocol of June 2003 (*Judicial Case Management in Public Law Children Act Cases*) and in the Practice Direction to Part 17 (Experts) of the Family Procedure (Adoption) Rules 2005[1] ('FP(AR) 2005') with effect on and from 1st April 2008.

Where the guidance refers to 'an expert' or 'the expert', this includes a reference to an expert team.

1   SI 2005/2795.

1.2 For the purposes of this guidance, the phrase 'family proceedings relating to children' is a convenient description. It is not a legal term of art and has no statutory force. In this guidance it means[1]-

- placement and adoption proceedings, or
- family proceedings held in private which
  - relate to the exercise of the inherent jurisdiction of the High Court with respect to children,
  - are brought under the Children Act 1989 in any family court, or
  - are brought in the High Court and county courts and 'otherwise relate wholly or mainly to the maintenance or upbringing of a minor'.

1   Following rule 10.20A(1) of the Family Proceedings Rules 1991, SI 1991/1247 ('FPR 1991') which defines the application of rule 10.20A (*Communication of information relating to proceedings*). Compare the definition of 'relevant proceedings' in section 93(3) of the Children Act 1989 (*Rules of court*), applied in the equivalent rule 23A (*Confidentiality of documents*) of the Family Proceedings Courts (Children Act 1989) Rules 1991, SI 1991/1395 ('FPC(ChA)R 1991').

Part III   Practice Directions and Guidance

Aims of the guidance

1.3 The guidance aims to provide the court in family proceedings relating to children with early information to determine whether an expert or expert evidence will assist the court to:

– identify, narrow and where possible agree the issues between the parties;
– provide an opinion about a question that is not within the skill and experience of the court;
– encourage the early identification of questions that need to be answered by an expert; and
– encourage disclosure of full and frank information between the parties, the court and any expert instructed.

1.4 The guidance does not aim to cover all possible eventualities. Thus it should be complied with so far as consistent in all the circumstances with the just disposal of the matter in accordance with the rules and guidance applying to the procedure in question.

Permission to instruct an expert or to use expert evidence

1.5 In family proceedings relating to children, the court's permission is required to instruct an expert. Such proceedings are confidential and, in the absence of the court's permission, disclosure of information and documents relating to such proceedings risks contravening the law of contempt of court or the various statutory provisions protecting this confidentiality. Thus, for the purposes of the law of contempt of court, information relating to such proceedings (whether or not contained in a document filed with the court or recorded in any form) may be communicated only to an expert whose instruction by a party has been permitted by the court.[1] Additionally, in proceedings under the Children Act 1989, the court's permission is required to cause the child to be medically or psychiatrically examined or otherwise assessed for the purpose of the preparation of expert evidence for use in the proceedings; and, where the court's permission has not been given, no evidence arising out of such an examination or assessment may be adduced without the court's permission.[2]

1 FPR 1991 rule 10.20A(2)(vii); FPC(ChA)R 1991 rule 23A(1)(c)(vii); FP(A)R 2005 rule 78(1)(c)(vii).
2 FPR 1991 rule 4.18(1) and (3); FPC(ChA)R 1991 rule 18(1) and (3).

1.6 In practice, the need to have the court's permission to disclose information or documents to an expert – and, in Children Act 1989 proceedings, to have the child examined or assessed – means that in proceedings relating to children the court strictly controls the number, fields of expertise and identity of the experts who may be first instructed and then called.

1.7 Before permission is obtained from the court to instruct an expert in family proceedings relating to children, it will be necessary for the party wishing to instruct an expert to make enquiries designed so as to provide the court with information about that expert which will enable the court to decide whether or not to give permission. In practice, enquiries may need to be made of more than one expert for this purpose. This will in turn require each expert to be given sufficient information about the case to enable that expert to decide whether or not he or she is in a position to accept instructions. Such preliminary enquiries, and the disclosure of anonymised information about the case which is a necessary part of such enquiries, will not require the court's permission and will not amount to a contempt of court: see sections 4.1 and 4.2 (*Preliminary Enquiries of the Expert* and *Expert's Response to Preliminary Enquiries*).

1.8 Section 4 (*Preparation for the relevant hearing*) gives guidance on applying for the court's permission to instruct an expert, and on instructing the expert, in family proceedings relating to children. The court, when granting permission to instruct an expert, will also give directions for the expert to be called to give evidence, or for the expert's report to be put in evidence: see section 4.4 (*Draft Order for the relevant hearing*).

When should the court be asked for permission?

1.9 The key event is 'the relevant hearing', which is any hearing at which the court's permission is sought to instruct an expert or to use expert evidence. Both expert issues should be raised with the court – and, where appropriate, with the other parties – as early as possible. This means:-

– in public law proceedings under the Children Act 1989, by or at the Case Management Conference: see the *Practice Direction: Guide to Case Management in Public Law Proceedings*, paragraphs 13.7, 14.3 and 25(29) which contains the definition of public law proceedings for the purposes of that practice direction;
– in private law proceedings under the Children Act 1989, by or at the First Hearing Dispute Resolution Appointment: see the *Private Law Programme* (9th November 2004), section 4 *(Process)*;
– in placement and adoption proceedings, by or at the First Directions Hearing: see FP(A)R 2005 rule 26 and the *President's Guidance: Adoption: the New Law and Procedure* (March 2006), paragraph 23.

2 General matters

Scope of the Guidance

2.1 This guidance does not apply to cases issued before 1st April 2008, but in such a case the court may direct that this guidance will apply either wholly or partly. This is subject to the overriding objective for the type of proceedings, and to the proviso that such a direction will neither cause further delay nor involve repetition of steps already taken or of decisions already made in the case.

2.2 This guidance applies to all experts who are or have been instructed to give or prepare evidence for the purpose of family proceedings relating to children in a court in England and Wales.

Pre-application instruction of experts

2.3 When experts' reports are commissioned before the commencement of proceedings, it should be made clear to the expert that he or she may in due course be reporting to the court and should therefore consider himself or herself bound by this guidance. A prospective party to family proceedings relating to children (for example, a local authority) should always write a letter of instruction when asking a potential witness for a report or an opinion, whether that request is within proceedings or pre-proceedings (for example, when commissioning specialist assessment materials, reports from a treating expert or other evidential materials); and the letter of instruction should conform to the principles set out in this guidance.

Emergency and urgent cases

2.4 In emergency or urgent cases – for example, where, before formal issue of proceedings, a without-notice application is made to the court during or out of business hours; or where, after proceedings have been issued, a previously unforeseen need for (further) expert evidence arises at short notice – a party may wish to call expert evidence without having complied with all or any part of this guidance. In such circumstances, the party wishing to call the expert evidence must apply forthwith to the court – where possible or appropriate, on notice to the other parties – for directions as to the future steps to be taken in respect of the expert evidence in question.

Orders

2.5 Where an order or direction requires an act to be done by an expert, or otherwise affects an expert, the party instructing that expert – or, in the case of a jointly instructed expert, the lead solicitor – must serve a copy of the order or direction on the expert forthwith upon receiving it.

Adults who may be protected parties

2.6 The court will investigate as soon as possible any issue as to whether an adult party or intended party to family proceedings relating to children lacks capacity (within the meaning of the Mental Capacity Act 2005) to conduct the proceedings. An adult who lacks capacity to act as a party to the proceedings is a protected party and must have a representative (a litigation friend, next friend or guardian ad litem) to conduct the proceedings on his or her behalf.

2.7 Any issue as to the capacity of an adult to conduct the proceedings must be determined before the court gives any directions relevant to that adult's role in the proceedings.

2.8 Where the adult is a protected party, his or her representative should be involved in any instruction of an expert, including the instruction of an expert to assess whether the adult, although a protected party, is competent to give evidence. The instruction of an expert is a significant step in the proceedings. The representative will wish to consider (and ask the expert to consider), if the protected party is competent to give evidence, their best interests in this regard.

The representative may wish to seek advice about 'special measures'. The representative may put forward an argument on behalf of the protected party that the protected party should not give evidence.

2.9 If at any time during the proceedings there is reason to believe that a party may lack capacity to conduct the proceedings, then the court must be notified and directions sought to ensure that this issue is investigated without delay.

Child likely to lack capacity to conduct the proceedings on when he or she reaches 18

2.10 Where it appears that a child is –

- a party to the proceedings and not the subject of them;
- nearing his or her 18th birthday, and
- considered likely to lack capacity to conduct the proceedings when he or she attains the age of 18,

the court will consider giving directions for the child's capacity in this respect to be investigated.

3 The Duties of Experts

Overriding Duty

3.1 An expert in family proceedings relating to children has an overriding duty to the court that takes precedence over any obligation to the person from whom the expert has received instructions or by whom the expert is paid.

Particular Duties

3.2 Among any other duties an expert may have, an expert shall have regard to the following duties:

1) to assist the court in accordance with the overriding duty;
2) to provide advice to the court that conforms to the best practice of the expert's profession;
3) to provide an opinion that is independent of the party or parties instructing the expert;
4) to confine the opinion to matters material to the issues between the parties and in relation only to questions that are within the expert's expertise (skill and experience);
5) where a question has been put which falls outside the expert's expertise, to state this at the earliest opportunity and to volunteer an opinion as to whether another expert is required to bring expertise not possessed by those already involved or, in the rare case, as to whether a second opinion is required on a key issue and, if possible, what questions should be asked of the second expert;
6) in expressing an opinion, to take into consideration all of the material facts including any relevant factors arising from ethnic, cultural, religious or linguistic contexts at the time the opinion is expressed;

7) to inform those instructing the expert without delay of any change in the opinion and of the reason for the change.

Content of the Expert's Report

3.3 The expert's report shall be addressed to the court and prepared and filed **in accordance with the court's timetable** and shall:

1) give details of the expert's qualifications and experience;
2) contain a statement setting out the substance of all material instructions (whether written or oral) summarising the facts stated and instructions given to the expert which are material to the conclusions and opinions expressed in the report;
3) identify materials that have not been produced either as original medical or other professional records or in response to an instruction from a party, as such materials may contain an assumption as to the standard of proof, the admissibility or otherwise of hearsay evidence, and other important procedural and substantive questions relating to the different purposes of other enquiries (for example, criminal or disciplinary proceedings);
4) identify all requests to third parties for disclosure and their responses in order to avoid partial disclosure which tends only to prove a case rather than give full and frank information;
5) make clear which of the facts stated in the report are within the expert's own knowledge;
6) state who carried out any test, examination or interview which the expert has used for the report and whether or not the test, examination or interview has been carried out under the expert's supervision;
7) give details of the qualifications of any person who carried out the test, examination or interview;
8) in expressing an opinion to the court:
    (a) take into consideration all of the material facts including any relevant factors arising from ethnic, cultural, religious or linguistic contexts at the time the opinion is expressed, identifying the facts, literature and any other material including research material that the expert has relied upon in forming an opinion;
    (b) describe their own professional risk assessment process and process of differential diagnosis, highlighting factual assumptions, deductions from the factual assumptions, and any unusual, contradictory or inconsistent features of the case;
    (c) highlight whether a proposition is an hypothesis (in particular a controversial hypothesis), or an opinion deduced in accordance with peer-reviewed and -tested technique, research and experience accepted as a consensus in the scientific community;
    (d) indicate whether the opinion is provisional (or qualified, as the case may be), stating the qualification and the reason for it, and identifying what further information is required to give an opinion without qualification;

9) where there is a range of opinion on any question to be answered by the expert:
   (a) summarise the range of opinion;
   (b) highlight and analyse within the range of opinion an 'unknown cause', whether on the facts of the case (for example, there is too little information to form a scientific opinion) or because of limited experience, lack of research, peer review or support in the field of expertise which the expert professes;
   (c) give reasons for any opinion expressed: the use of a balance sheet approach to the factors that support or undermine an opinion can be of great assistance to the court;
10) contain a summary of the expert's conclusions and opinions;
11) contain a statement that the expert understands his or her duty to the court and has complied and will continue to comply with that duty;
12) contain a statement that the expert:
   (a) has no conflict of interest of any kind, other than any conflict disclosed in his or her report;
   (b) does not consider that any interest disclosed affects his or her suitability as an expert witness on any issue on which he or she has given evidence;
   (c) will advise the instructing party if, between the date of the expert's report and the final hearing, there is any change in circumstances which affects the expert's answers to (a) or (b) above;
13) be verified by a statement of truth in the following form:

'I confirm that insofar as the facts stated in my report are within my own knowledge I have made clear which they are and I believe them to be true, and that the opinions I have expressed represent my true and complete professional opinion.'

4 Preparation for the relevant hearing

Preliminary Enquiries of the Expert

4.1 In good time for the information requested to be available for the relevant hearing or for the advocates' meeting or discussion where one takes place before the relevant hearing, the solicitor for the party proposing to instruct the expert (or lead solicitor or solicitor for the child if the instruction proposed is joint) shall approach the expert with the following information:

1) the nature of the proceedings and the issues likely to require determination by the court;
2) the questions about which the expert is to be asked to give an opinion (including any ethnic, cultural, religious or linguistic contexts);
3) the date when the court is to be asked to give permission for the instruction (or if – unusually – permission has already been given, the date and details of that permission);

4) whether permission is to be asked of the court for the instruction of another expert in the same or any related field (that is, to give an opinion on the same or related questions);
5) the volume of reading which the expert will need to undertake;
6) whether or not permission has been applied for or given for the expert to examine the child;
7) whether or not it will be necessary for the expert to conduct interviews – and, if so, with whom;
8) the likely timetable of legal and social work steps;
9) when the expert's report is likely to be required;
10) whether and, if so, what date has been fixed by the court for any hearing at which the expert may be required to give evidence (in particular the Final Hearing).

It is essential that there should be proper co-ordination between the court and the expert when drawing up the case management timetable: the needs of the court should be balanced with the needs of the expert whose forensic work is undertaken as an adjunct to his or her main professional duties, whether in the National Health Service or elsewhere.

The expert should be informed at this stage of the possibility of making, through his or her instructing solicitor, representations to the court about being named or otherwise identified in any public judgment given by the court.

Expert's Response to Preliminary Enquiries

4.2 In good time for the relevant hearing or for the advocates' meeting or discussion where one takes place before the relevant hearing, the solicitors intending to instruct the expert shall obtain confirmation from the expert:

1) that acceptance of the proposed instructions will not involve the expert in any conflict of interest;
2) that the work required is within the expert's expertise;
3) that the expert is available to do the relevant work within the suggested time scale;
4) when the expert is available to give evidence, of the dates and times to avoid and, where a hearing date has not been fixed, of the amount of notice the expert will require to make arrangements to come to court (or to give evidence by video link) without undue disruption to his or her normal professional routines;
5) of the cost, including hourly or other charging rates, and likely hours to be spent, attending experts' meetings, attending court and writing the report (to include any examinations and interviews);
6) of any representations which the expert wishes to make to the court about being named or otherwise identified in any public judgment given by the court.

Where parties have not agreed on the appointment of a single joint expert before the relevant hearing, they should obtain the above confirmations in respect of all experts whom they intend to put to the court as candidates for the appointment.

Practice Direction of 1 April 2008

The proposal to instruct an expert

4.3 Any party who proposes to ask the court for permission to instruct an expert shall, **by 11 a.m. on the business day before the relevant hearing**, file and serve a written proposal to instruct the expert in the following detail:

1) the name, discipline, qualifications and expertise of the expert (by way of C.V. where possible);
2) the expert's availability to undertake the work;
3) the relevance of the expert evidence sought to be adduced to the issues in the proceedings and the specific questions upon which it is proposed that the expert should give an opinion (including the relevance of any ethnic, cultural, religious or linguistic contexts);
4) the timetable for the report;
5) the responsibility for instruction;
6) whether or not the expert evidence can properly be obtained by the joint instruction of the expert by two or more of the parties;
7) whether the expert evidence can properly be obtained by only one party (for example, on behalf of the child);
8) why the expert evidence proposed cannot be given by social services undertaking a core assessment or by the Children's Guardian in accordance with their respective statutory duties;
9) the likely cost of the report on an hourly or other charging basis: where possible, the expert's terms of instruction should be made available to the court;
10) the proposed apportionment (at least in the first instance) of any jointly instructed expert's fee; when it is to be paid; and, if applicable, whether public funding has been approved.

Draft Order for the relevant hearing

4.4 Any party proposing to instruct an expert shall, **by 11 a.m. on the business day before the relevant hearing**, submit to the court a draft order for directions dealing in particular with:

1) the party who is to be responsible for drafting the letter of instruction and providing the documents to the expert;
2) the issues identified by the court and the questions about which the expert is to give an opinion;
3) the timetable within which the report is to be prepared, filed and served;
4) the disclosure of the report to the parties and to any other expert;
5) the organisation of, preparation for and conduct of an experts' discussion;
6) the preparation of a statement of agreement and disagreement by the experts following an experts' discussion;
7) making available to the court at an early opportunity the expert reports in electronic form;
8) the attendance of the expert at court to give oral evidence (alternatively, the expert giving his or her evidence in writing or

remotely by video link), whether at or for the Final Hearing or another hearing; unless agreement about the opinions given by the expert is reached at or before the Issues Resolution Hearing ('IRH') or, if no IRH is to be held, by a specified date prior to the hearing at which the expert is to give oral evidence ('the specified date').

5 *Letter of Instruction*

5.1 The solicitor instructing the expert shall, **within 5 business days after the relevant hearing**, prepare (in agreement with the other parties where appropriate), file and serve a letter of instruction to the expert which shall:

1) set out the context in which the expert's opinion is sought (including any ethnic, cultural, religious or linguistic contexts);
2) set out the specific questions which the expert is required to answer, ensuring that they:
   (a) are within the ambit of the expert's area of expertise;
   (b) do not contain unnecessary or irrelevant detail;
   (c) are kept to a manageable number and are clear, focused and direct; and
   (d) reflect what the expert has been requested to do by the court.
   The Annex to this guidance sets out suggested questions in letters of instruction to (1) child mental health professionals or paediatricians, and (2) adult psychiatrists and applied psychologists, in Children Act 1989 proceedings;
3) list the documentation provided, or provide for the expert an indexed and paginated bundle which shall include:
   (a) a copy of the order (or those parts of the order) which gives permission for the instruction of the expert, immediately the order becomes available;
   (b) an agreed list of essential reading; and
   (c) a copy of this guidance;
4) identify materials that have not been produced either as original medical (or other professional) records or in response to an instruction from a party, as such materials may contain an assumption as to the standard of proof, the admissibility or otherwise of hearsay evidence, and other important procedural and substantive questions relating to the different purposes of other enquiries (for example, criminal or disciplinary proceedings);
5) identify all requests to third parties for disclosure and their responses, to avoid partial disclosure, which tends only to prove a case rather than give full and frank information;
6) identify the relevant people concerned with the proceedings (for example, the treating clinicians) and inform the expert of his or her right to talk to them provided that an accurate record is made of the discussions;
7) identify any other expert instructed in the proceedings and advise the expert of his or her right to talk to the other experts provided that an accurate record is made of the discussions;

8) subject to any public funding requirement for prior authority, define the contractual basis upon which the expert is retained and in particular the funding mechanism including how much the expert will be paid (an hourly rate and overall estimate should already have been obtained), when the expert will be paid, and what limitation there might be on the amount the expert can charge for the work which he or she will have to do. In cases where the parties are publicly funded, there should also be a brief explanation of the costs and expenses excluded from public funding by Funding Code criterion 1.3 and the detailed assessment process.

Asking the court to settle the letter of instruction to a joint expert

5.2 Where the court has directed that the instructions to the expert are to be contained in a jointly agreed letter and the terms of the letter cannot be agreed, any instructing party may submit to the court a written request, which must be copied to the other instructing parties, that the court settle the letter of instruction. Where possible, the written request should be set out in an e-mail to the court, preferably sent directly to the judge dealing with the proceedings (or, in the Family Proceedings Court, to the legal adviser who will forward it to the appropriate judge or justices), and be copied by e-mail to the other instructing parties. The court will settle the letter of instruction, usually without a hearing to avoid delay; and will send (where practicable, by e-mail) the settled letter to the lead solicitor for transmission forthwith to the expert, and copy it to the other instructing parties for information.

Keeping the expert up to date with new documents

5.3 As often as may be necessary, the expert should be provided promptly with a copy of any new document filed at court, together with an updated document list or bundle index.

6 The Court's control of expert evidence: consequential issues

Written Questions

6.1 Any party wishing to put written questions to an expert for the purpose of clarifying the expert's report must put the questions to the expert **not later than 10 business days after receipt of the report**.

The court will specify the timetable according to which the expert is to answer the written questions.

Experts' Discussion or Meeting: Purpose

6.2 **By the specified date**, the court may – if it has not already given such a direction – direct that the experts are to meet or communicate:

1) to identify and narrow the issues in the case;
2) where possible, to reach agreement on the expert issues;

3) to identify the reasons for disagreement on any expert question and what, if any, action needs to be taken to resolve any outstanding disagreement or question;
4) to explain or add to the evidence in order to assist the court to determine the issues;
5) to limit, wherever possible, the need for the experts to attend court to give oral evidence.

Experts' Discussion or Meeting: Arrangements

6.3 In accordance with the directions given by the court, the solicitor or other professional who is given the responsibility by the court ('the nominated professional') shall – **within 15 business days after the experts' reports have been filed and copied to the other parties** – make arrangements for the experts to meet or communicate. Where applicable, the following matters should be considered:

1) where permission has been given for the instruction of experts from different disciplines, a global discussion may be held relating to those questions that concern all or most of them;
2) separate discussions may have to be held among experts from the same or related disciplines, but care should be taken to ensure that the discussions complement each other so that related questions are discussed by all relevant experts;
3) **5 business days prior to a discussion or meeting**, the nominated professional should formulate an agenda including a list of questions for consideration. The agenda should contain only those questions which are intended to clarify areas of agreement or disagreement. Questions which repeat questions asked in the letter of instruction or which seek to rehearse cross-examination in advance of the hearing should be rejected as likely to defeat the purpose of the meeting.

The agenda may usefully take the form of a list of questions to be circulated among the other parties in advance. The agenda should comprise all questions that each party wishes the experts to consider. The agenda and list of questions should be sent to each of the experts **not later than 2 clear business days before the discussion;**

4) the nominated professional may exercise his or her discretion to accept further questions after the agenda with list of questions has been circulated to the parties. **Only in exceptional circumstances should questions be added to the agenda within the 2-day period before the meeting. Under no circumstances should any question received on the day of or during the meeting be accepted.** Strictness in this regard is vital, for adequate notice of the questions enables the parties to identify and isolate the issues in the case before the meeting so that the experts' discussion at the meeting can concentrate on those issues;
5) the discussion should be chaired by the nominated professional. A minute must be taken of the questions answered by the experts, and a Statement of Agreement and Disagreement must be prepared which should be agreed and signed by each of the experts who participated in

the discussion. The statement should be served and filed **not later than 5 business days after the discussion has taken place;**
6) in each case, whether some or all of the experts participate by telephone conference or video link to ensure that minimum disruption is caused to professional schedules and that costs are minimised.

Meetings or conferences attended by a jointly instructed expert

6.4 Jointly instructed experts should not attend any meeting or conference which is not a joint one, unless all the parties have agreed in writing or the court has directed that such a meeting may be held, and it is agreed or directed who is to pay the expert's fees for the meeting or conference. Any meeting or conference attended by a jointly instructed expert should be proportionate to the case.

Court-directed meetings involving experts in public law Children Act cases

6.5 In public law Children Act proceedings, where the court gives a direction that a meeting shall take place between the local authority and any relevant named experts for the purpose of providing assistance to the local authority in the formulation of plans and proposals for the child, the meeting shall be arranged, chaired and minuted in accordance with the directions given by the court.

7 Positions of the Parties

7 Where a party refuses to be bound by an agreement that has been reached at an experts' discussion or meeting, that party must inform the court and the other parties in writing, **within 10 business days after the discussion or meeting or, where an IRH is to be held, not less than 5 business days before the IRH,** of his reasons for refusing to accept the agreement.

8 Arrangements for Experts to give evidence

Preparation

8.1 Where the court has directed the attendance of an expert witness, the party who is responsible for the instruction of the expert shall, **by the specified date or, where an IRH is to be held, by the IRH**, ensure that:

1) a date and time (if possible, convenient to the expert) are fixed for the court to hear the expert's evidence, substantially in advance of the hearing at which the expert is to give oral evidence and no later than a specified date prior to that hearing or, where an IRH is to be held, than the IRH;
2) if the expert's oral evidence is not required, the expert is notified as soon as possible;
3) the witness template accurately indicates how long the expert is likely to be giving evidence, in order to avoid the inconvenience of the expert being delayed at court;

4) consideration is given in each case to whether some or all of the experts participate by telephone conference or video link, or submit their evidence in writing, to ensure that minimum disruption is caused to professional schedules and that costs are minimised.

Experts attending Court

8.2 Where expert witnesses are to be called, all parties shall, **by the specified date or, where an IRH is to be held, by the IRH**, ensure that:

1) the parties' advocates have identified (whether at an advocates' meeting or by other means) the issues which the experts are to address;
2) wherever possible, a logical sequence to the evidence is arranged, with experts of the same discipline giving evidence on the same day;
3) the court is informed of any circumstance where all experts agree but a party nevertheless does not accept the agreed opinion, so that directions can be given for the proper consideration of the experts' evidence and of the party's reasons for not accepting the agreed opinion;
4) in the exceptional case the court is informed of the need for a witness summons.

9 Action after the Final Hearing

9.1 **Within 10 business days after the Final Hearing**, the solicitor instructing the expert shall inform the expert in writing of the outcome of the case, and of the use made by the court of the expert's opinion.

9.2 Where the court directs preparation of a transcript, it may also direct that the solicitor instructing the expert shall send a copy to the **expert within 10 business days after receiving the transcript.**

9.3 After a Final Hearing in the Family Proceedings Court, the (lead) solicitor instructing the expert shall send the expert a copy of the court's written reasons for its decision **within 10 business days after receiving the written reasons.**

ANNEX[1]
QUESTIONS IN LETTERS OF INSTRUCTION TO CHILD MENTAL HEALTH PROFESSIONAL OR PAEDIATRICIAN IN CHILDREN ACT 1989 PROCEEDINGS

1 Drafted by the Family Justice Council.

A The Child(ren)

1 Please describe the child(ren)'s current health, development and functioning (according to your area of expertise), and identify the nature of any significant changes which have occurred

- Behavioural
- Emotional

- Attachment organisation
- Social/peer/sibling relationships
- Cognitive/educational
- Physical
  - Growth, eating, sleep
  - Non-organic physical problems (including wetting and soiling)
  - Injuries
  - Paediatric conditions

2 Please comment on the likely explanation for/aetiology of the child(ren)'s problems/difficulties/injuries

- History/experiences (including intrauterine influences, and abuse and neglect)
- Genetic/innate/developmental difficulties
- Paediatric/psychiatric disorders

3 Please provide a prognosis and risk if difficulties not addressed above.

4 **Please describe the child(ren)'s needs in the light of the above**

- Nature of care-giving
- Education
- Treatment

in the short and long term (subject, where appropriate, to further assessment later).

B *The parents/primary care-givers*

5 Please describe the factors and mechanisms which would explain the parents' (or primary care-givers') harmful or neglectful interactions with the child(ren) (if relevant)

6 What interventions have been tried and what has been the result?

7 Please assess the ability of the parents or primary care-givers to fulfil the child(ren)'s identified needs now.

8 What other assessments of the parents or primary care-givers are indicated

- Adult mental health assessment
- Forensic risk assessment
- Physical assessment
- Cognitive assessment

9 **What, if anything, is needed to assist the parents or primary care-givers now, within the child(ren)'s time scales and what is the prognosis for change**

- Parenting work
- Support
- Treatment/therapy

C *Alternatives*

10 Please consider the alternative possibilities for the fulfilment of the child(ren)'s needs.

- What sort of placement
- Contact arrangements

Please consider the advantages, disadvantages and implications of each for the child(ren).

Questions in letters of instruction to adult psychiatrists and applied psychologists in Children Act 1989 proceedings

1 Does the parent/adult have – whether in his/her history or presentation – a mental illness/disorder (including substance abuse) or other psychological/emotional difficulty and, if so, what is the diagnosis?

2 How do any/all of the above (and their current treatment if applicable) affect his/her functioning, including interpersonal relationships?

3 If the answer to Q1 is yes, are there any features of either the mental illness or psychological/emotional difficulty or personality disorder which could be associated with risk to others, based on the available evidence base (whether published studies or evidence from clinical experience)?

1 What are the experiences/antecedents/aetiology which would explain his/her difficulties, if any, (taking into account any available evidence base or other clinical experience)?

5 What treatment is indicated, what is its nature and the likely duration?

6 What is his/her capacity to engage in/partake of the treatment/therapy?

7 Are you able to indicate the prognosis for, time scales for achieving, and likely durability of, change?

8 What other factors might indicate positive change?

(It is assumed that this opinion will be based on collateral information as well as interviewing the adult).

Editorial note—It is assumed that the second paragraph numbered 1, which appears between paragraphs 3 and 5 above, has been incorrectly numbered in *The Public Law Outline*.

The Right Honourable Sir Mark Potter
The President of the Family Division

The Lord Chancellor

PRACTICE DIRECTION
3 NOVEMBER 2008

Citation: [2009] 1 FLR 365

ALLOCATION AND TRANSFER OF PROCEEDINGS

1.1 This Practice Direction is given by the President of the Family Division under the powers delegated to him by the Lord Chief Justice under paragraph 2(2) of part 1 of Schedule 2 to the Constitutional Reform Act 2005 and is agreed by the Lord Chancellor.

1.2 The objective of this Practice Direction is to ensure that the criteria for the transfer of proceedings are applied in such a way that proceedings are heard at the appropriate level of court, that the capacity of magistrates' courts is properly utilised and that proceedings are only dealt with in the High Court if the relevant criteria are met.

1.3 This Practice Direction will come into effect on 25 November 2008. Where practicable, it applies to proceedings started before but not concluded by 25 November. The Practice Directions of 5 June 1992 (distribution of business) and 22 February 1993 (applications under the Children Act 1989 by children) are revoked except that they will continue to apply to any proceedings to which it is not practicable to apply this Practice Direction.

1.4 A reference to an article is a reference to the article so numbered in the Allocation and Transfer of Proceedings Order 2008.

Part 1

2 This Part of this Practice Direction applies to all family proceedings (whether or not the Allocation and Transfer of Proceedings Order 2008 applies to such proceedings).

Timing and continuing review of decision on appropriate venue

3.1 The issue as to which court is the most appropriate hearing venue must be addressed by the court speedily as soon as there is sufficient information to determine whether the case meets the criteria for hearing in that court. This information may come to light before, during or after the first hearing. It must then be kept under effective review at all times; it should not be assumed that proceedings will necessarily remain in the court in which they were started or to which they have been transferred. For example proceedings that have been transferred to a county court because one or more of the criteria in article 15 applies should be transferred back to the magistrates' court if the reason for transfer falls away. Conversely, an unforeseen late complication may require a transfer from a magistrates' court to a county court.

3.2 Where a court is determining where the proceedings ought to be heard it will consider all relevant information including that given by the applicant either in the application form or otherwise, for example in any request for proceedings to be transferred to another magistrates' court or to a county court under rule 6 of the Family Proceedings Courts (Children Act 1989) Rules 1991.

Timeliness

4.1 Article 13 and paragraph 12.1 require the court to have regard to delay. Therefore the listing availability of the court in which the proceedings have been started and in neighbouring magistrates' courts and county courts must always be ascertained before deciding where proceedings should be heard.

4.2 If a magistrates' court is considering transferring proceedings to a county court or a county court is considering transferring proceedings to the High Court but that decision is finely balanced, the proceedings should not be transferred if the transfer would lead to delay. Conversely, if the High Court is considering transferring proceedings to a county court or a county court is considering transferring proceedings to a magistrates' court but that decision is finely balanced, the proceedings should be transferred if retaining them would lead to delay.

4.3 Transferring proceedings may mean that there will be a short delay in the proceedings being heard since the papers may need to be sent to the court to which they are being transferred. The court will determine whether the delay is significant, taking into account the circumstances of the case and with reference to the interests of the child.

4.4 While there is no express reference in the Allocation and Transfer of Proceedings Order 2008 or in Part 3 of this Practice Direction to the length of the hearing or to judicial continuity such issues may be relevant.

Transfer of proceedings to or from the High Court

5.1 A court will take into account the following factors (which are not exhaustive) when considering whether the criteria in articles 7 or 18 or paragraph 11.2 or 12.3 apply, such that the proceedings ought to be heard in the High Court –

(1) there is alleged to be a risk that a child concerned in the proceedings will suffer serious physical or emotional harm in the light of –
   (a) the death of another child in the family, a parent or any other material person; or
   (b) the fact that a parent or other material person may have committed a grave crime, for example, murder, manslaughter or rape,

in particular where the essential factual framework is in dispute or there are issues over the causation of injuries or a material conflict of expert evidence;

(2) the application concerns medical treatment for a child which involves a risk to the child's physical or emotional health which goes beyond the normal risks of routine medical treatment;
(3) an adoption order is sought in relation to a child who has been adopted abroad in a country whose adoption orders are not recognised in England and Wales;
(4) an adoption order is sought in relation to a child who has been brought into the United Kingdom in circumstances where section 83 of the Adoption and Children Act 2002 applies and
   (a) the person bringing the child, or causing the child to be brought –
      (i) has not complied with any requirement imposed by regulations made under section 83(4); or
      (ii) has not met any condition required to be met by regulations made under section 83(5) within the required time; or
   (b) there are complicating features in relation to the application;
(5) it is likely that the proceedings will set a significant new precedent or alter existing principles of common law;
(6) where periodical payments, a lump sum or transfer of property are an issue –
   (a) the capital value of the assets involved and the extent to which they are available for, or susceptible to, distribution or adjustment;
   (b) any substantial allegations of fraud or deception or non-disclosure;
   (c) any substantial contested allegations of conduct.

5.2 The following proceedings are likely to fall within the criteria for hearing in the High Court unless the nature of the issues of fact or law raised in the proceedings may make them more suitable to be dealt with in a county court –

(1) proceedings involving a contested issue of domicile;
(2) applications to restrain a respondent from taking or continuing with foreign proceedings;
(3) suits in which the Queen's Proctor intervenes or shows cause and elects trial in the High Court;
(4) proceedings in which an application is opposed on the grounds of want of jurisdiction;
(5) proceedings in which there is a complex foreign element or where the court has invited submissions to be made under Article 11(7) of Council Regulation (EC) No 2201/2003 of 27 November 2003 concerning jurisdiction and the recognition and enforcement of judgments in matrimonial matters and the matters of parental responsibility;
(6) proceedings in which there is an application to remove a child permanently or temporarily from the jurisdiction to a non-Hague Convention country.
(7) interlocutory applications involving –

(a) search orders; or
(b) directions as to dealing with assets out of the jurisdiction.

5.3 Proceedings will not normally be suitable to be dealt with in the High Court merely because of any of the following –

(1) intractable problems with regard to contact;
(2) sexual abuse;
(3) injury to a child which is neither life-threatening nor permanently disabling;
(4) routine neglect, even if it spans many years and there is copious documentation;
(5) temporary or permanent removal to a Hague Convention country;
(6) standard human rights issues;
(7) uncertainty as to immigration status;
(8) the celebrity of the parties;
(9) the anticipated length of the hearing;
(10) the quantity of evidence;
(11) the number of experts;
(12) the possible availability of a speedier hearing.

5.4 A substantial reason for starting proceedings in the High Court will only exist where the nature of the proceedings or the issues raised are such that they ought to be heard in the High Court. Where proceedings have been started in the High Court under article 7(c) or paragraph 11.2(4) and the High Court considers that there is no substantial reason for them to have been started there, the High Court will transfer the proceedings to a county court or a magistrates' court and may make any orders about costs which it considers appropriate.

Part 2

6 This Part of this Practice Direction applies to family proceedings to which the Allocation and Transfer of Proceedings Order 2008 applies.

Transfer of proceedings from one magistrates' court to another or from one county court to another

7.1 Where a magistrates' court is considering transferring proceedings to another magistrates' court or a county court is considering transferring proceedings to another county court, the court will take into account the following factors (which are not exhaustive) when considering whether it would be more convenient for the parties for the proceedings to be dealt with by the other court –

(1) the fact that a party is ill or suffers a disability which could make it inconvenient to attend at a particular court;
(2) the fact that the child lives in the area of the other court;
(3) the need to avoid delay.

Practice Direction of 3 November 2008

Transfer of proceedings from a magistrates' court to a county court

8.1 Where a magistrates' court is considering whether one or more of the criteria in article 15(*1*) (except article 15(1)(*g*) and (*h*)) apply such that the proceedings ought to be heard in the county court, the magistrates' court will first consider whether another magistrates' court would have suitable experience to deal with the issues which have given rise to consideration of article 15. If so, the magistrates' court will then consider whether the proceedings could be dealt with more quickly or within the same time if they were transferred to the other magistrates' court rather than a county court. If so, the magistrates' court will transfer the proceedings to the other magistrates' court rather than a county court.

8.2 A magistrates' court may only transfer proceedings to a county court under article 15(1)(*a*) if it considers that the transfer will significantly accelerate the determination of the proceedings. Before considering a transfer on this ground, the magistrates' court must obtain information about the hearing dates available in other magistrates' courts and in the relevant county court. The fact that a hearing could be arranged in a county court at an earlier date than in any appropriate magistrates' court does not by itself justify the transfer of proceedings under article 15(1)(*a*); the question of whether the determination of the proceedings would be significantly accelerated must be considered in the light of all the circumstances.

Transfer of proceedings from a county court to a magistrates' court

9.1 A county court must transfer to a magistrates' court under article 16(1) proceedings that have previously been transferred under article 15(1) where the county court considers that none of the criteria in article 15(1) apply. In particular, proceedings transferred to a county court by a magistrates' court for resolution of a single issue, for example, use of the inherent powers of the High Court in respect of medical testing of a child or disclosure of information by HM Revenue and Customs, should be transferred back to the magistrates' court once the issue has been resolved.

9.2 Subject to articles 5(3), 6, 8 and 13 and paragraphs 4 and 12.1, straightforward proceedings for –

(1) a residence order;
(2) a contact order;
(3) a prohibited steps order;
(4) a specific issue order;
(5) a special guardianship order; or
(6) an order under Part 4 of the Family Law Act 1996

which are started in a county court should be transferred to a magistrates' court if the county court considers that none of the criteria in article 15(1)(*b*) to (*i*) apply to those proceedings.

Part 3

10 This Part of this Practice Direction applies to any family proceedings to which the Allocation and Transfer of Proceedings Order 2008 does not apply.

Starting proceedings

11.1 Subject to paragraph 11.2, family proceedings must be started in a county court.

11.2 Family proceedings may be started in the High Court only if –

  (1) the proceedings are exceptionally complex;
  (2) the outcome of the proceedings is important to the public in general;
  (3) an enactment or rule requires the proceedings to be started in the High Court; or
  (4) there is another substantial reason for starting the proceedings in the High Court.

Transferring proceedings

12.1 When making any decision about the transfer of proceedings the court must have regard to the need to avoid delay in the proceedings.

12.2 A county court will take into account the following factors (which are not exhaustive) when considering whether to transfer proceedings to another county court –

  (1) whether the transfer will significantly accelerate the determination of the proceedings;
  (2) whether it is more convenient for the parties for the proceedings to be dealt with by another county court; and
  (3) whether there is another good reason for the proceedings to be transferred.

12.3 A county court will take into account the following factors (which are not exhaustive) when considering whether to transfer proceedings to the High Court –

  (1) whether the proceedings are exceptionally complex;
  (2) whether the outcome of the proceedings is important to the public in general;
  (3) whether an enactment or rule requires the proceedings to be dealt with in the High Court; and
  (4) whether there is another substantial reason for the proceedings to be transferred.

12.4 The High Court will also take into account the factors in paragraph 12.3 when considering whether to transfer proceedings to a county court.

The Right Honourable
Sir Mark Potter
The President of the Family Division

Practice Direction of 3 November 2008

The Right Honourable
Jack Straw MP
The Lord Chancellor

PRACTICE DIRECTION
14 JANUARY 2009

Citation: [2008] 2 FLR 103 as amended in the light of *Re B (Care Proceedings: Standard of Proof)* [2008] 2 FLR 141

RESIDENCE AND CONTACT ORDERS: DOMESTIC VIOLENCE AND HARM

The Practice Direction issued on 9 May 2008 is re-issued in the following revised form to reflect the decision of the House of Lords in *Re B (Children)* [2008] UKHL 35, in which Baroness Hale confirmed (at [76]) that a fact-finding hearing is part of the process of trying a case and is not a separate exercise and that where the case is then adjourned for further hearing it remains part heard. This principle applies equally in private law and public law family cases. Paragraphs 15 and 23 of the Practice Direction have been amended to reinforce this principle.

1 This Practice Direction applies to any family proceedings in the High Court, a county court or a magistrates' court in which an application is made for a residence order or a contact order in respect of a child under the Children Act 1989 ("the 1989 Act") or the Adoption and Children Act 2002 ("the 2002 Act") or in which any question arises about residence or about contact between a child and a parent or other family member.

2 The practice set out in this Direction is to be followed in any case in which it is alleged, or there is otherwise reason to suppose, that the subject child or a party has experienced domestic violence perpetrated by another party or that there is a risk of such violence. For the purpose of this Direction, the term 'domestic violence' includes physical violence, threatening or intimidating behaviour and any other form of abuse which, directly or indirectly, may have caused harm to the other party or to the child or which may give rise to the risk of harm.

('Harm' in relation to a child means ill-treatment or the impairment of health or development, including, for example, impairment suffered from seeing or hearing the ill-treatment of another: Children Act 1989, ss 31(9),105(1))

General principles

3 The court must, at all stages of the proceedings, consider whether domestic violence is raised as an issue, either by the parties or otherwise, and if so must:

> identify at the earliest opportunity the factual and welfare issues involved;
> consider the nature of any allegation or admission of domestic violence and the extent to which any domestic violence which is admitted, or which may be proved, would be relevant in deciding whether to make an order about residence or contact and, if so, in what terms;

give directions to enable the relevant factual and welfare issues to be determined expeditiously and fairly.

4 In all cases it is for the court to decide whether an order for residence or contact accords with Section 1(1) of the 1989 Act or section 1(2) of the 2002 Act, as appropriate; any proposed residence or contact order, whether to be made by agreement between the parties or otherwise must be scrutinised by the court accordingly. The court shall not make a consent order for residence or contact or give permission for an application for a residence or contact order to be withdrawn, unless the parties are present in court, except where it is satisfied that there is no risk of harm to the child in so doing.

5 In considering, on an application for a consent order for residence or contact, whether there is any risk of harm to the child, the court shall consider all the evidence and information available. The court may direct a report under Section 7 of the 1989 Act either orally or in writing before it makes its determination; in such a case, the court may ask for information about any advice given by the officer preparing the report to the parties and whether they or the child have been referred to any other agency, including local authority children's services. If the report is not in writing, the court shall make a note of its substance on the court file.

Issue

6 Immediately on receipt of an application for a residence order or a contact order, or of the acknowledgement of the application, the court shall send a copy of it, together with any accompanying documents, to Cafcass or Cafcass Cymru, as appropriate, to enable Cafcass or Cafcass Cymru to undertake initial screening in accordance with their safeguarding policies.

Liaison

7 The Designated Family Judge, or in the magistrates' court the Justices' Clerk, shall take steps to ensure that arrangements are in place for:

the prompt delivery of documents to Cafcass or Cafcass Cymru in accordance with paragraph 6
any information obtained by Cafcass or Cafcass Cymru as a result of initial screening or otherwise and any risk assessments prepared by Cafcass or Cafcass Cymru under section 16A of the 1989 Act to be placed before the appropriate court for consideration and directions
a copy of any record of admissions or findings of fact made pursuant to paragraphs 12 & 21 below to be made available as soon as possible to any Officer of Cafcass or Welsh family proceedings officer or local authority officer preparing a report under section 7 of the 1989 Act.

Response of the court on receipt of information

8 Where any information provided to the court before the first hearing, whether as a result of initial screening by Cafcass or Cafcass Cymru or

otherwise, indicates that there are issues of domestic violence which may be relevant to the court's determination, the court may give directions about the conduct of the hearing and for written evidence to be filed by the parties before the hearing.

9 If at any stage the court is advised by Cafcass or Cafcass Cymru or otherwise that there is a need for special arrangements to secure the safety of any party or child attending any hearing, the court shall ensure that appropriate arrangements are made for the hearing and for all subsequent hearings in the case, unless it considers that these are no longer necessary.

First hearing

10 At the first hearing, the court shall inform the parties of the content of any screening report or other information which has been provided by Cafcass or Cafcass Cymru, unless it considers that to do so would create a risk of harm to a party or the child.

(Specific provision about service of a risk assessment under section 16A of the 1989 Act is made by the Family Proceedings Rules 1991, r 4.17AA and by the Family Proceedings Courts (Children Act 1989) Rules 1991, r 17AA.)

11 The court must ascertain at the earliest opportunity whether domestic violence is raised as an issue and must consider the likely impact of that issue on the conduct and outcome of the proceedings. In particular, the court should consider whether the nature and effect of the domestic violence alleged is such that, if proved, the decision of the court is likely to be affected.

Admissions

12 Where at any hearing an admission of domestic violence to another person or the child is made by a party, the admission should be recorded in writing and retained on the court file.

Directions for a fact-finding hearing

13 The court should determine as soon as possible whether it is necessary to conduct a fact-finding hearing in relation to any disputed allegation of domestic violence before it can proceed to consider any final order(s) for residence or contact. Where the court determines that a finding of fact hearing is not necessary, the order shall record the reasons for that decision.

14 Where the court considers that a fact-finding hearing is necessary, it must give directions to ensure that the matters in issue are determined expeditiously and fairly and in particular it should consider:

> directing the parties to file written statements giving particulars of the allegations made and of any response in such a way as to identify clearly the issues for determination;
> whether material is required from third parties such as the police or health services and may give directions accordingly;

whether any other evidence is required to enable the court to make findings of fact in relation to the allegations and may give directions accordingly.

15 Where the court fixes a fact-finding hearing, it must at the same time fix a further hearing for determination of the application. The hearings should be arranged in such a way that they are conducted by the same judge or, in the magistrates' court, by at least the same chairperson of the justices.

Reports under Section 7

16 In any case where domestic violence is raised as an issue, the court should consider directing that a report on the question of contact, or any other matters relating to the welfare of the child, be prepared under section 7 of the 1989 Act by an Officer of Cafcass or a Welsh family proceedings officer (or local authority officer if appropriate), unless the court is satisfied that it is not necessary to do so in order to safeguard the child's interests. If the court so directs, it should consider the extent of any enquiries which can properly be made at this stage and whether it is appropriate to seek information on the wishes and feelings of the child before findings of fact have been made.

Representation of the child

17 Subject to the seriousness of the allegations made and the difficulty of the case, the court shall consider whether it is appropriate for the child who is the subject of the application to be made a party to the proceedings and be separately represented. If the case is proceeding in the magistrates' court and the court considers that it may be appropriate for the child to be made a party to the proceedings, it may transfer the case to the relevant county court for determination of that issue and following such transfer the county court shall give such directions for the further conduct of the case as it considers appropriate.

Interim orders before determination of relevant facts

18 Where the court gives directions for a fact-finding hearing, the court should consider whether an interim order for residence or contact is in the interests of the child; and in particular whether the safety of the child and the residential parent can be secured before, during and after any contact.

19 In deciding any question of interim residence or contact pending a full hearing the court should: –

  (a) take into account the matters set out in section 1(3) of the 1989 Act or section 1(4) of the 2002 Act ('the welfare check-list'), as appropriate;
  (b) give particular consideration to the likely effect on the child of any contact and any risk of harm, whether physical, emotional or psychological, which the child is likely to suffer as a consequence of making or declining to make an order;

20 Where the court is considering whether to make an order for interim contact, it should in addition consider

(a) the arrangements required to ensure, as far as possible, that any risk of harm to the child is minimised and that the safety of the child and the parties is secured; and in particular:
   (i) whether the contact should be supervised or supported, and if so, where and by whom; and
   (ii) the availability of appropriate facilities for that purpose
(b) if direct contact is not appropriate, whether it is in the best interests of the child to make an order for indirect contact.

The fact-finding hearing

21 At the fact-finding hearing, the court should, wherever practicable, make findings of fact as to the nature and degree of any domestic violence which is established and its effect on the child, the child's parents and any other relevant person. The court shall record its findings in writing, and shall serve a copy on the parties. A copy of any record of findings of fact or of admissions must be sent to any officer preparing a report under Section 7 of the 1989 Act

22 At the conclusion of any fact-finding hearing, the court shall consider, notwithstanding any earlier direction for a section 7 report, whether it is in the best interests of the child for the court to give further directions about the preparation or scope of any report under section 7; where necessary, it may adjourn the proceedings for a brief period to enable the officer to make representations about the preparation or scope of any further enquiries. The court should also consider whether it would be assisted by any social work, psychiatric, psychological or other assessment of any party or the child and if so (subject to any necessary consent) make directions for such assessment to be undertaken and for the filing of any consequent report.

23 Where the court has made findings of fact on disputed allegations, any subsequent hearing in the proceedings should be conducted by the same judge or, in the magistrates' court, by at least the same chairperson of the justices. Exceptions may be made only where observing this requirement would result in delay to the planned timetable and the judge or chairperson is satisfied, for reasons recorded in writing, that the detriment to the welfare of the child would outweigh the detriment to the fair trial of the proceedings.

In all cases where domestic violence has occurred

24 The court should take steps to obtain (or direct the parties or an Officer of Cafcass or a Welsh family proceedings officer to obtain) information about the facilities available locally to assist any party or the child in cases where domestic violence has occurred.

25 Following any determination of the nature and extent of domestic violence, whether or not following a fact-finding hearing, the court should consider whether any party should seek advice or treatment as a precondition to an order for residence or contact being made or as a means of assisting the court

in ascertaining the likely risk of harm to the child from that person, and may (with the consent of that party) give directions for such attendance and the filing of any consequent report.

Factors to be taken into account when determining whether to make residence or contact orders in all cases where domestic violence has occurred

26 When deciding the issue of residence or contact the court should, in the light of any findings of fact, apply the individual matters in the welfare checklist with reference to those findings; in particular, where relevant findings of domestic violence have been made, the court should in every case consider any harm which the child has suffered as a consequence of that violence and any harm which the child is at risk of suffering if an order for residence or contact is made and should only make an order for contact if it can be satisfied that the physical and emotional safety of the child and the parent with whom the child is living can, as far as possible, be secured before during and after contact.

27 In every case where a finding of domestic violence is made, the court should consider the conduct of both parents towards each other and towards the child; in particular, the court should consider;

(a) the effect of the domestic violence which has been established on the child and on the parent with whom the child is living;

(b) the extent to which the parent seeking residence or contact is motivated by a desire to promote the best interests of the child or may be doing so as a means of continuing a process of violence, intimidation or harassment against the other parent;

(c) the likely behaviour during contact of the parent seeking contact and its effect on the child;

(d) the capacity of the parent seeking residence or contact to appreciate the effect of past violence and the potential for future violence on the other parent and the child;

(e) the attitude of the parent seeking residence or contact to past violent conduct by that parent; and in particular whether that parent has the capacity to change and to behave appropriately.

Directions as to how contact is to proceed

28 Where the court has made findings of domestic violence but, having applied the welfare checklist, nonetheless considers that direct contact is in the best interests of the child, the court should consider what if any directions or conditions are required to enable the order to be carried into effect and in particular should consider:

(a) whether or not contact should be supervised, and if so, where and by whom;

- (b) whether to impose any conditions to be complied with by the party in whose favour the order for contact has been made and if so, the nature of those conditions, for example by way of seeking advice or treatment (subject to any necessary consent);
- (c) whether such contact should be for a specified period or should contain provisions which are to have effect for a specified period;
- (d) whether or not the operation of the order needs to be reviewed; if so the court should set a date for the review and give directions to ensure that at the review the court has full information about the operation of the order.

29 Where the court does not consider direct contact to be appropriate, it shall consider whether it is in the best interests of the child to make an order for indirect contact.

The reasons of the court

30 In its judgment or reasons the court should always make clear how its findings on the issue of domestic violence have influenced its decision on the issue of residence or contact. In particular, where the court has found domestic violence proved but nonetheless makes an order, the court should always explain, whether by way of reference to the welfare check-list or otherwise, why it takes the view that the order which it has made is in the best interests of the child.

31 This Practice Direction is issued by the President of the Family Division, as the nominee of the Lord Chief Justice, with the agreement of the Lord Chancellor.

The Right Honourable Sir Mark Potter

President of the Family Division and Head of Family Justice

FAMILY PROCEEDINGS (ALLOCATION TO JUDICIARY) DIRECTIONS 2009

The President of the Family Division, in exercise of the powers conferred on him by section 9 of the Courts and Legal Services Act 1990 and having consulted the Lord Chancellor, gives the following Directions:

1 These Directions shall come into force on 16 February 2009.

2 In these Directions, in the absence of a contrary implication–

'adoption centre' means a court designated as an adoption centre by the Allocation and Transfer of Proceedings Order 2008;
'family proceedings' and 'judge' have the meanings assigned to them in section 9 of the Courts and Legal Services Act 1990;
'nominated' in relation to a judge means a judge who has been approved as one to whom family proceedings may be allocated by the President of the Family Division;
'Schedule' means the Schedule to these Directions.

3 Any reference in these Directions to the Allocation and Transfer of Proceedings Order 2008 ('the 2008 Order') is to be read as a reference to the Children (Allocation of Proceedings) Order 1991, the Children (Allocation of Proceedings) (Appeals) Order 1991 or the Family Law Act 1996 (Part IV) (Allocation of Proceedings) Order 1997, as appropriate, where any of those Orders applies as a result of Article 29 of the 2008 Order (transitional provisions).

4 These Directions apply to any family proceedings (except proceedings on appeal from an order or decision made by a magistrates' court) which are pending in a county court or which, by virtue of section 42 of the Matrimonial and Family Proceedings Act 1984 or of a provision of the Allocation and Transfer of Proceedings Order 2008, are treated as pending in a county court in the Principal Registry of the Family Division of the High Court.

5(1) These Directions apply, so far as practicable, to proceedings started before but not concluded by 16 February 2009.

(2) Where, by reason of paragraph (1), these Directions do not apply to particular proceedings which have been started but not concluded before 16 February 2009, the Family Proceedings (Allocation to Judiciary) Directions 1999 continue to apply to those proceedings.

6 Subject to the following paragraphs of these Directions, the proceedings described in the Schedule shall be allocated to a judge or to a specified description of judge in accordance with the following Table, by reference to the categories shown in column (b) of the Table and described in the Schedule and subject to the limitations specified in column (c) of the Table.

Part III Practice Directions and Guidance

(a) Judge or specified description of judge	(b) Categories of proceedings by reference to the Schedule	(c) Categories of proceedings by reference to the Schedule
A circuit judge, deputy circuit judge or recorder nominated for public family law proceedings	All categories of proceedings	
A circuit judge, deputy circuit judge or recorder nominated for private family law proceedings	B, D, E	
A district judge of the Principal Registry[1]	A, B, C, D	D Interlocutory matters only
A district judge nominated for public family law proceedings	A, B, C, D	D Interlocutory matters only
A district judge nominated for private family law proceedings	B, D	D Interlocutory matters only
A judge not referred to in any of the preceding entries in this table.	B(i), B(iii), B(vii)	B(i) Only: (1) proceedings in which an order under section 8 of the Children Act 1989 is sought at a without notice hearing where (a) no nominated judge is available to hear the proceedings; and (b) any order is limited in time until a hearing before a nominated judge; and (2) proceedings under section 15 of and Schedule 1 to the Children Act 1989. B(iii) In the case of a deputy district judge, all proceedings except enforcement

7 Without prejudice to the provisions of paragraph 6, any proceedings to which these Directions apply, including any appeal referred to in paragraph 10, may be allocated to–

(a) a judge of the Family Division of the High Court;
(b) a person acting as a judge of the Family Division of the High Court in pursuance of a request made under section 9(1) of the Supreme Court Act 1981 other than a former judge of the Court of Appeal or a former puisne judge of the High Court; but proceedings in categories A and C of the Schedule shall be allocated only to a judge who has been nominated for them;
(c) a person sitting as a recorder who has been authorised to act as a judge of the Family Division of the High Court under section 9(4) of the Supreme Court Act 1981;
(d) a person sitting as a recorder who is a District Judge (Magistrates' Courts) and is nominated for public family law proceedings in the County Court;
(e) a person sitting as a Recorder who is a District Judge of the Principal Registry of the Family Division.

8 When a person sitting as a recorder is also a district judge nominated for public family law proceedings, any proceedings may be allocated to him which, under these Directions, may be allocated to a district judge nominated for public family law proceedings.

9 A circuit judge or district judge nominated for private family law proceedings who is sitting at an adoption centre may, with the agreement of the Family Division Liaison Judge for the relevant region, hear proceedings in category C of the Schedule, limited in the case of a district judge to interlocutory matters only.

10 Where in any proceedings to which these Directions apply an appeal may be heard by a circuit judge, deputy circuit judge or recorder, it may be heard by any judge of that description who under these Directions would have been able to hear the proceedings at first instance.

The Right Honourable Sir Mark Potter

President of the Family Division and Head of Family Justice

SCHEDULE

Category	Description of proceedings
A	(i) Proceedings under section 25 of the Children Act 1989; (ii) Proceedings under Parts IV and V of the Children Act 1989; (iii) Proceedings under Schedules 2 and 3 to the Children Act 1989; (iv) Applications for leave under section 91(14),(15) or (17) of the Children Act 1989; (v) Proceedings under section 102 of the 1989 Act or section 79 of the Childcare Act 2006; (vi) Proceedings for a residence order under section 8 of the Children Act 1989 or for a special guardianship order under section 14A of the Children Act 1989 with respect to a child who is the subject of a care order.
B	(i) Proceedings under Parts I and II of the Children Act 1989, except where the proceedings come within Category A(vi), C(iii) or C(iv) of this Schedule; (ii) Proceedings under sections 33,34 and 37 of the Family Law Act 1986; (iii) Proceedings under Part 4 of the Family Law Act 1996; (iv) Proceedings under Part 4A of the Family Law Act 1996; (v) Proceedings under section 20 of the Child Support Act 1990; (vi) Proceedings under section 30 of the Human Fertilisation and Embryology Act 1990; (vii) Family proceedings for which no express provision is made in this Schedule.
C	(i) Proceedings under section 21 of the Adoption Act 1976; (ii) Proceedings under the Adoption and Children Act 2002; (iii) Proceedings for a residence order under section 8 of the Children Act 1989 where either section 28(1)(child placed for adoption) or 29(4)(placement order in force) of the Adoption and Children Act 2002 applies; (iv) Proceedings for a special guardianship order under section 14A of the Children Act 1989 where either section 28(1)(child placed for adoption) or section 29(5)(placement order in force) of the Adoption and Children Act 2002 applies.
D	Proceedings under sections 55,55A, 56 and 57 of the Family Law Act 1986

| E | The hearing of contested proceedings for
(i) a decree of divorce, nullity or judicial separation; or
(ii) an order for dissolution or nullity of civil partnership or a separation order. |

Practice Direction of 20 April 2009 (HClcc)

PRACTICE DIRECTION
20 APRIL 2009

ATTENDANCE OF MEDIA REPRESENTATIVES AT HEARINGS IN FAMILY PROCEEDINGS (HIGH COURT AND COUNTY COURTS)

This Practice Direction below is made by the President of the Family Division under the powers delegated to him by the Lord Chief Justice under Schedule 2, Part 1, paragraph 2(2) of the Constitutional Reform Act 2005, and is approved by Bridget Prentice, Parliamentary Under Secretary of State, by the authority of the Lord Chancellor.

1 Introduction

1.1 This Practice Direction supplements rule 10.28 of the Family Proceedings Rules 1991('FPR 1991') and deals with the right of representatives of news gathering and reporting organisations ('media representatives') to attend at hearings of family proceedings which take place in private subject to the discretion of the court to exclude such representatives from the whole or part of any hearing on specified grounds[1] It takes effect on 27 April 2009.

2 Matters unchanged by the rule

2.1 Rule 10.28(1) contains an express exception in respect of hearings which are conducted for the purpose of judicially assisted conciliation or negotiation and media representatives do not have a right to attend these hearings. Financial Dispute Resolution hearings will come within this exception. First Hearing Dispute Resolution appointments in private law Children Act cases will also come within this exception to the extent that the judge plays an active part in the conciliation process. Where the judge plays no part in the conciliation process or where the conciliation element of a hearing is complete and the judge is adjudicating upon the issues between the parties, media representatives should be permitted to attend, subject to the discretion of the court to exclude them on the specified grounds. Conciliation meetings or negotiation conducted between the parties with the assistance of an officer of the service or a Welsh Family Proceedings officer, and without the presence of the judge, are not 'hearings' within the meaning of this rule and media representatives have no right to attend such appointments.

The exception in rule 10.28(1) does not operate to exclude media representatives from:

- Hearings to consider applications brought under Parts IV and V of the Children Act 1989, including Case Management Conferences and Issues Resolution Hearings
- Hearings relating to findings of fact
- Interim hearings

- Final hearings.

The rights of media representatives to attend such hearings are limited only by the powers of the court to exclude such attendance on the limited grounds and subject to the procedures set out in paragraphs (4)–(6) of rule 10.28.

2.2 During any hearing, courts should consider whether the exception in rule 10.28(1) becomes applicable so that media representatives should be directed to withdraw.

2.3 The provisions of the rules permitting the attendance of media representatives and the disclosure to third parties of information relating to the proceedings do not entitle a media representative to receive or peruse court documents referred to in the course of evidence, submissions or judgment without the permission of the court or otherwise in accordance with Part 11 of the FPR 1991 (rules relating to disclosure to third parties). (This is in contrast to the position in civil proceedings, where the court sits in public and where members of the public are entitled to seek copies of certain documents[1]).

2.4 The question of attendance of media representatives at hearings in family proceedings to which rule 10.28 and this guidance apply must be distinguished from statutory restrictions on publication and disclosure of information relating to proceedings, which continue to apply and are unaffected by the rule and this guidance.

2.5 The prohibition in section 97(2) of the Children Act 1989, on publishing material intended to or likely to identify a child as being involved in proceedings or the address or school of any such child, is limited to the duration of the proceedings[1]. However, the limitations imposed by section 12 of the Administration of Justice Act 1960 on publication of information relating to certain proceedings in private[2] apply during and after the proceedings. In addition, in proceedings to which s 97(2) of the Children Act 1989 applies the court should continue to consider at the conclusion of the proceedings whether there are any outstanding welfare issues which require a continuation of the protection afforded during the course of the proceedings by that provision.

3 *Aims of the guidance*

3.1 This Practice Direction is intended to provide guidance regarding:

- the handling of applications to exclude media representatives from the whole or part of a hearing; and
- the exercise of the court's discretion to exclude media representatives whether upon the court's own motion or any such application.

3.2 While the guidance does not aim to cover all possible eventualities, it should be complied with so far as consistent in all the circumstances with the just determination of the proceedings.

4 Identification of media representatives as 'accredited'

4.1 Media representatives will be expected to carry with them identification sufficient to enable court staff, or if necessary the court itself, to verify that they are 'accredited' representatives of news gathering or reporting organisations within the meaning of the rule.

4.2 By virtue of paragraph (8) of the rule, it is for the Lord Chancellor to approve a scheme which will provide for accreditation. The Lord Chancellor has decided that the scheme operated by the UK Press Card Authority provides sufficient accreditation; a card issued under that scheme will be the expected form of identification, and production of the Card will be both necessary and sufficient to demonstrate accreditation.

4.3 A media representative unable to demonstrate accreditation in accordance with the UK Press Card Authority scheme, so as to be able to attend by virtue of paragraph (3)(f) of the rule, may nevertheless be permitted to attend at the court's discretion under paragraph (3)(g).

5 Exercise of the discretion to exclude media representatives from all or part of the proceedings

5.1 The rule anticipates and should be applied on the basis that media representatives have a right to attend family proceedings throughout save and to the extent that the court exercises its discretion to exclude them from the whole or part of any proceedings on one or more of the grounds set out in paragraph (4) of the rule.

5.2 When considering the question of exclusion on any of the grounds set out in paragraph (4) of the rule the court should –

- specifically identify whether the risk to which such ground is directed arises from the mere fact of media presence at the particular hearing or hearings the subject of the application or whether the risk identified can be adequately addressed by exclusion of media representatives from a part only of such hearing or hearings;
- consider whether the reporting or disclosure restrictions which apply by operation of law, or which the court otherwise has power to order will provide sufficient protection to the party on whose behalf the application is made or any of the persons referred to in paragraph (4)(a) of the rule;
- consider the safety of the parties in cases in which the court considers there are particular physical or health risks against which reporting restrictions may be inadequate to afford protection;
- in the case of any vulnerable adult or child who is unrepresented before the court, consider the extent to which the court should of its own motion take steps to protect the welfare of that adult or child.

5.3 Paragraph (4)(a)(iii) of the rule permits exclusion where necessary 'for the orderly conduct of proceedings'. This enables the court to address practical problems presented by media attendance. In particular, it may be difficult or even impossible physically to accommodate all (or indeed any) media representatives who wish to attend a particular hearing on the grounds of the restricted size or layout of the court room in which it is being heard. Court staff will use their best efforts to identify more suitable accommodation in advance of any hearing which appears likely to attract particular media attention, and to move hearings to larger court rooms where possible. However, the court should not be required to adjourn a hearing in order for larger accommodation to be sought where this will involve significant disruption or delay in the proceedings.

5.4 Paragraph (4)(b) of the rule permits exclusion where, unless the media are excluded, justice will be impeded or prejudiced for some reason other than those set out in sub-paragraph (a). Reasons of administrative inconvenience are not sufficient. Examples of circumstances where the impact on justice of continued attendance might be sufficient to necessitate exclusion may include:

- a hearing relating to the parties' finances where the information being considered includes price sensitive information (such as confidential information which could affect the share price of a publicly quoted company); or
- any hearing at which a witness (other than a party) states for credible reasons that he or she will not give evidence in front of media representatives, or where there appears to the court to be a significant risk that a witness will not give full or frank evidence in the presence of media representatives.

5.5 In the event of a decision to exclude media representatives, the court should state brief reasons for the decision.

6 Applications to exclude media representatives from all or part of proceedings

6.1 The court may exclude media representatives on the permitted grounds of its own motion or after hearing representations from the interested persons listed at paragraph (6) of the rule. Where exclusion is proposed, any media representatives who are present are entitled to make representations about that proposal. There is, however, no requirement to adjourn proceedings to enable media representatives who are not present to attend in order to make such representations, and in such a case the court should not adjourn unless satisfied of the necessity to do so having regard to the additional cost and delay which would thereby be caused.

6.2 Applications to exclude media representatives should normally be dealt with as they arise and by way of oral representations, unless the court directs otherwise.

6.3 When media representatives are expected to attend a particular hearing (for example, where a party is encouraging media interest and attendance) and a party intends to apply to the court for the exclusion of the media, that party should, if practicable, give advance notice to the court, to the other parties and (where appointed) any children's guardian, officer of the service or Welsh

Practice Direction of 20 April 2009 (HC/cc)

Family Proceedings officer, NYAS or other representative of the child of any intention to seek the exclusion of media representatives from all or part of the proceedings. Equally, legal representatives and parties should ensure that witnesses are aware of the right of media representatives to attend and should notify the court at an early stage of the intention of any witness to request the exclusion of media representatives

6.4 Prior notification by the court of a pending application for exclusion will not be given to media interests unless the court so directs. However, where such an application has been made, the applicant must where possible, notify the relevant media organisations.

Sir Mark Potter
President of the Family Division

Part III Practice Directions and Guidance

PRACTICE DIRECTION
20 APRIL 2009

ATTENDANCE OF MEDIA REPRESENTATIVES AT HEARINGS IN FAMILY PROCEEDINGS (FAMILY PROCEEDINGS COURT)

This Practice Direction below is made by the President of the Family Division under the powers delegated to him by the Lord Chief Justice under Schedule 2, Part 1, paragraph 2(2) of the Constitutional Reform Act 2005, and is approved by Bridget Prentice, Parliamentary Under Secretary of State, by the authority of the Lord Chancellor.

1 Introduction

1.1 This Practice Direction supplements rule 16A of the Family Proceedings Courts (Children Act 1989) Rules 1991 ('the Rules') and deals with the right of representatives of news gathering and reporting organisations ('media representatives') to attend at hearings of relevant proceedings[1] subject to the discretion of the court to exclude such representatives from the whole or part of any hearing on specified grounds.[2] It takes effect on 27th April 2009. References to a 'hearing' within this Practice Direction include reference to a directions appointment, whether conducted by the justices, a district judge or a justices' clerk.

2 Matters unchanged by the rule

2.1 Rule 16A(2) contains an express exception in respect of hearings which are conducted for the purpose of judicially assisted conciliation or negotiation and media representatives do not have a right to attend these hearings. First Hearing Dispute Resolution appointments in private law Children Act cases will come within this exception to the extent that the justices, a district judge or a justices' clerk play an active part in the conciliation process. Where the justices, a district judge or a justices' clerk play no part in the conciliation process or where the conciliation element of a hearing is complete and the court is adjudicating upon the issues between the parties, media representatives should be permitted to attend subject to the discretion of the court to exclude them on the specified grounds. Conciliation meetings or negotiation conducted between the parties with the assistance of an officer of the service or a Welsh Family Proceedings officer, and without the presence of the justices, a district judge or a justices' clerk, are not 'hearings' within the meaning of this rule and media representatives have no right to attend such appointments.

The exception in rule 16A(2) does not operate to exclude media representatives from:

- Hearings to consider applications brought under Parts IV and V of the Children Act 1989, including Case Management Conferences and Issues Resolution Hearings
- Hearings relating to findings of fact
- Interim hearings
- Final hearings.

The rights of media representatives to attend such hearings are limited only by the powers of the court to exclude such attendance on the limited grounds and subject to the procedures set out in paragraphs (3) to (5) of rule 16A.

2.2 During any hearing, the court should consider whether the exception in rule 16A(2) becomes applicable so that media representatives should be directed to withdraw.

2.3 The provisions of the rules permitting the attendance of media representatives and the disclosure to third parties of information relating to the proceedings do not entitle a media representative to receive or peruse court documents referred to in the course of evidence, submissions or decisions of the court (in particular, written reasons) without the permission of the court or otherwise in accordance with Part IIC (rules relating to disclosure to third parties).

2.4 The question of attendance of media representatives at hearings in family proceedings to which rule 16A and this guidance apply must be distinguished from statutory restrictions on publication and disclosure of information relating to proceedings, which continue to apply and are unaffected by the rule and this guidance.

2.5 The prohibition in section 97(2) of the Children Act 1989, on publishing material intended to or likely to identify a child as being involved in proceedings or the address or school of any such child, is limited to the duration of the proceedings[1]. However, the limitations imposed by section 12 of the Administration of Justice Act 1960 on publication of information relating to certain proceedings in private[2] apply during and after the proceedings. In addition, in the course of proceedings to which s 97(2) of the Children Act 1989 applies the court should consider whether at the conclusion of the proceedings there may be outstanding welfare issues which may require a continuation of the protection afforded during the course of the proceedings by s 97 (2) of the Children Act 1989 and which are not fully met by a direction under section 39 Children and Young Persons Act 1933,[3] so that any party seeking such protection has an opportunity to apply to the county court or High Court for the appropriate order before the proceedings are finally concluded.

3 Aims of the guidance

3.1 This Practice Direction is intended to provide guidance regarding:

- the handling of applications to exclude media representatives from the whole or part of a hearing: and

Part III   Practice Directions and Guidance

- the exercise of the court's discretion to exclude media representatives whether upon the court's own motion or any such application.

3.2 While the guidance does not aim to cover all possible eventualities, it should be complied with so far as consistent in all the circumstances with the just determination of the proceedings.

4 Identification of media representatives as 'accredited'

4.1 Media representatives will be expected to carry with them identification sufficient to enable court staff, or if necessary the court itself, to verify that they are 'accredited' representatives of news gathering or reporting organisations within the meaning of the rule.

4.2 By virtue of paragraph (7) of the rule, it is for the Lord Chancellor to approve a scheme which will provide for accreditation. The Lord Chancellor has decided that the scheme operated by the UK Press Card Authority provides sufficient accreditation: a card issued under that scheme will be the expected form of identification, and production of the Card will be both necessary and sufficient to demonstrate accreditation.

4.3 A media representative unable to demonstrate accreditation in accordance with the UK Press Card Authority scheme so as to be able to attend by virtue of paragraph (1)(*f*) of the rule may nevertheless be permitted to attend at the court's discretion under paragraph (1)(*g*).

5 Exercise of the discretion to exclude media representatives from all or part of the proceedings.

5.1 The rule anticipates and should be applied on the basis that media representatives have a right to attend family proceedings throughout save and to the extent that the court exercises its discretion to exclude them from the whole or part of any proceedings on one or more of the grounds set out in paragraph (3) of the rule.

5.2 When considering the question of exclusion on any of the grounds set out in paragraph (3) of the rule the court should –

- specifically identify whether the risk to which such ground is directed arises from the mere fact of media presence at the particular hearing or hearings the subject of the application or whether the risk identified can be adequately addressed by exclusion of media representatives from a part only of such hearing or hearings;
- consider whether the reporting or disclosure restrictions which apply by operation of law, or which the court otherwise has power to order will provide sufficient protection to the party on whose behalf the application is made or any of the persons referred to in paragraph (3)(a) of the rule;
- consider the safety of the parties in cases in which the court considers there are particular physical or health risks against which reporting restrictions may be inadequate to afford protection;

- in the case of any vulnerable adult or child who is unrepresented before the court, consider the extent to which the court should of its own motion take steps to protect the welfare of that adult or child.

5.3 Paragraph (3)(a)(iii) of the rule permits exclusion where necessary 'for the orderly conduct of proceedings'. This enables the court to address practical problems presented by media attendance. In particular, it may be difficult or even impossible physically to accommodate all (or indeed any) media representatives who wish to attend a particular hearing on the grounds of the restricted size or layout of the court room in which it is being heard. Court staff will use their best efforts to identify more suitable accommodation in advance of any hearing which appears likely to attract particular media attention, and to move hearings to larger court rooms where possible. However, the court should not be required to adjourn a hearing in order for larger accommodation to be sought where this will involve significant disruption or delay in the proceedings.

5.4 Paragraph (3)(b) of the rule permits exclusion where, unless the media are excluded, justice will be impeded or prejudiced for some reason other than those set out in sub-paragraph (a). Reasons of administrative inconvenience are not sufficient. An example of circumstances where the impact on justice of continued attendance might be sufficient to necessitate exclusion would be any hearing at which a witness (other than a party) states for credible reasons that he or she will not give evidence in front of media representatives, or where there appears to the court to be a significant risk that a witness will not give full or frank evidence in the presence of media representatives.

5.5 In the event of a decision to exclude media representatives, the court should state brief reasons for the decision.

6 Applications to exclude media representatives from all or part of proceedings.

6.1 The court may exclude media representatives on the permitted grounds of its own motion or after hearing representations from the interested persons listed at paragraph (5) of the rule. Where exclusion is proposed, any media representatives who are present are entitled to make representations about that proposal. There is, however, no requirement to adjourn proceedings to enable media representatives who are not present to attend in order to make such representations, and in such a case the court should not adjourn unless satisfied of the necessity to do so having regard to the additional cost and delay which would thereby be caused.

6.2 Applications to exclude media representatives should normally be dealt with as they arise and by way of oral representations, unless the court directs otherwise.

6.3 When media representatives are expected to attend a particular hearing (for example, where a party is encouraging media interest and attendance) and a party intends to apply to the court for the exclusion of the media, such party should, if practicable, give advance notice to the court, to the other parties and (where appointed) any children's guardian, officer of the service or Welsh Family Proceedings officer, NYAS or other representative of the child of any intention to seek the exclusion of media representatives from all or part of the proceedings. Equally, legal representatives and parties should ensure that witnesses are aware of the right of media representatives to attend and should notify the court at an early stage of the intention of any witness to request the exclusion of media representatives

6.4 Prior notification by the court of a pending application for exclusion will not be given to media interests unless the court so directs. However, where such an application has been made, the applicant must where possible, notify the relevant media organisations.

Sir Mark Potter
President of the Family Division

PRESIDENT'S GUIDANCE
22 APRIL 2009

APPLICATIONS CONSEQUENT UPON THE ATTENDANCE OF THE MEDIA IN FAMILY PROCEEDINGS

1 The Government's announcement about the attendance of the media at hearings in family proceedings (see *Family Justice in View* Cm 7502, December 2008) has been implemented by a change to the Family Proceedings Rules made by *The Family Proceedings (Amendment) (No 2) Rules 2009* SI 2009 No 857 (county court and High Court) and *The Family Proceedings Courts (Miscellaneous Amendments) Rules 2009* SI 2009 No 858 (magistrates' courts) and two Practice Directions *Attendance of Media Representatives at Hearings in Family Proceedings* dated 20th April 2009 made by the President to support the rule changes in the respective courts.

2 In the county court and High Court media attendance is implemented by the change to FPR Rule 10.28. (to which the Practice Direction applies). Change regarding media attendance in the family proceedings courts is introduced through amendment to the Family Proceedings Courts (Children Act 1989) Rules 1991, with the insertion of rule 16A.

3 In broad terms the changes for the county court and the High Court relating to media attendance permit duly accredited representatives of news gathering and reporting organisations, and any other unaccredited person whom the court permits, to be present at hearings of all family proceedings (defined by s 32 Matrimonial and Family Proceedings Act 1984) except hearings conducted for the purposes of judicially assisted conciliation or negotiation. They also provide that the court can exclude media representatives

4 For the county court and the High Court, the change relates to most of the proceedings which are for the time being heard in private. It therefore covers a wide range of proceedings including for example public and private law proceedings under the Children Act 1989 and claims for ancillary relief under the Matrimonial Causes Act 1973.

5 Representatives of newspapers or news agencies are admitted to the family proceedings courts under section 69 (2) Magistrates' Courts Act 1980. Media attendance will now be regulated by the insertion of rule '16A Restrictions on presence of persons at directions appointment and hearing'. Duly accredited representatives of news gathering and reporting organisations are not entitled to be present at hearings conducted for the purposes of judicially assisted conciliation or negotiation. They may also be excluded for reasons set out in rule 16A(3).

6 In respect of the county court and the High Court the new Part 11 of the FPR, and in respect of the family proceedings court the new Part 11C of the Family Proceedings Courts (Children Act 1989) Rules 1991 as amended, regarding communication of information only apply to proceedings concerning

children. In particular, they do not apply to proceedings for ancillary relief. Nor do they expressly cover communication of information to representatives of the media.

7 As appears from the Practice Direction governing the county court and High Court, it is a premise of the change for these courts that the proceedings remain proceedings held in private and that therefore the existing position relating to the publication of matters relating to proceedings which are so heard continues to apply, both whilst the proceedings continue and when they have ended (see the Practice Direction paras 2.4 and 2.5)

8 Useful summaries of the position relating to the publication of matters relating to proceedings heard in private can be found in: *Clayton v Clayton* [2006] EWCA Civ 878 [2007] 1 FLR 11 (in particular at paragraphs 23 to 60, 82 to 85, 92 to 104 and 118 to 136 and *Re B (A Child) (Disclosure)* [2004] EWHC 411 (Fam), [2004] 2 FLR 142 (in particular at paragraphs 62 to 82 (on s 12 AJA 1960) and 83 to 107 (on the jurisdiction to relax or increase the statutory restrictions on publication). Other useful cases are listed in the footnote to this paragraph.[1]

9 It is to be noted that the above decisions all concern the interests and welfare of children and that the approach in ancillary relief proceedings (which are also likely to be productive of media applications) has not been the subject of similar judicial consideration and guidance.

10 The new Rules and the Practice Directions include provisions relating to the exclusion of media representatives but are silent on the approach to be taken by the courts to the exercise of their discretion in respect of other issues which may well arise as a consequence of the attendance of media representatives at hearings in family proceedings. In this respect the Government declined to adopt the recommendation of the High Court judges to address the detail of such issues when introducing the change. It is therefore left to the courts to determine how such issues are to be approached and decided. It is clear that a principled approach to such issues should be applied by the courts and that this can only properly be developed by the courts with the benefit of full argument from the interested parties.

11 The change to admit media representatives to hearings in family proceedings in county courts and the High Court is likely to give rise to a number of issues relating to the exercise of discretion by all levels of court. In particular it is likely that courts will quickly be faced with applications for the provision of documents to media representatives present in court to enable them the better to follow the substance of the proceedings. If minded to grant such application, the court will need to consider the terms of any restriction relating to the use (and in particular the publication) of information contained in any such documents provided to media representatives as a condition of their being so provided.

12 In cases involving children, applications, whether by the media or the parties, are also likely to raise issues as to

(i) The proper application of the existing statutory provisions restricting the publication of the identity of children and information relating to proceedings heard in private;
(ii) the adequacy of the protection afforded in children cases by Section 12 of the Administration of Justice Act 1960 ('AJA 1960') which, inter alia, does not extend to the identity of the parties or witnesses;
(iii) the effect of the publication of any anonymised judgment;

and whether or not injunctive relief may be required upon a wider basis.

13 In relation to the need for injunctive relief in cases affecting children, particularly in local courts, it may be necessary to consider how far it is appropriate to protect from identification not only the children and the parties, but also witnesses and others whose identities will be known locally as associated with the child or his family.

14 Finally, there will be issues over the need on child welfare grounds for protection to extend beyond the end of the hearing (see paragraph 2.5 of the respective Practice Directions).

15 No doubt the basic opposing arguments in relation to the question of access to documents will be, on the one hand, that the Government has sought to retain the basic structure and rationale of the long standing policy of privacy in relation to children proceedings, while at the same time admitting the press, to avoid charges of 'secret justice' and to promote better understanding of the working of the family courts. For these purposes, however, access to court documents is not generally necessary or desirable having regard to their confidential nature.

16 On the other hand, the media may argue that, particularly in those cases where there is not a formal oral opening, they should be enabled to see statements and documents filed in order fully to understand the nature and progress of the proceedings, and so as to be able to publish articles, within appropriate reporting constraints, about the cases which they attend. In this connection, it is likely, if not inevitable, that in individual cases of high interest to the media, courts at all levels and all over the country will be faced with detailed legal argument relating to rival Convention Rights, public and private interests, the welfare of children, and the construction and application of the primary and secondary legislation.

17 Inconsistency of approach in children cases as to the principles to be applied to the determination of such issues on the part of the courts, parties, witnesses, other persons involved in the relevant events (eg social workers and doctors) and the media could well give rise to justified criticism on grounds of uncertainty. It would not promote the public interest in the proper administration of justice and could be damaging to children.

18 So far as ancillary relief proceedings are concerned, policy, privacy and Convention issues may also arise for decision, albeit the interests of children may not be engaged.

19 The purpose of this guidance is therefore to try to avoid, or at least to minimise, inconsistency by providing that decisions are made by the High Court (and the Appellate Courts) as soon as possible as to the principled approach to be taken. Its purpose is also to provide that, until that is done, delay in decision making in individual cases, (particularly those concerning children) should be avoided. It is to be hoped that the media will co-operate in these aims.

20 Pending the availability of formal judicial guidance from the High Court or Court of Appeal as to the principled approach to be adopted, all County Courts and Magistrates' Courts hearing family proceedings should carefully consider adopting the following course:

(i) The court should deal in accordance with the Rules and Practice Directions with any application made for exclusion of the media from the proceedings or any part of them on any of the grounds set out in the Practice Directions.

(ii) Where a representative of the media in attendance at the proceedings applies to be shown court documents, the court should seek the consent of the parties to such representative being permitted (subject to appropriate conditions as to anonymity and restrictions upon onward disclosure) to see such summaries, position statements and other documents as appear reasonably necessary to a broad understanding of the issues in the case.

(iii) If the objection of any of the parties is maintained, then in any case where the objecting party demonstrates reasonably arguable grounds for resisting disclosure of the document or documents sought, no order for disclosure should be made, but the following course of action should be considered.

(iv) If considered necessary or appropriate the court should transfer (or, in the case of a family proceedings court, take the first step to bring about an urgent transfer of) the proceedings to the High Court for the determination of any disclosure and/or reporting issues.

(v) Alternatively, in order to avoid delay in decision making on the substantive issues in the case, the court should adjourn determination of any disclosure and/or reporting issues pending a decision by the High Court (or the Appellate Courts) on the principled approach to be taken to them and should make any necessary interim orders in accordance with the argument mentioned in paragraph 15 above in order to secure the position meanwhile.

(vi) Similarly, if a representative of the media applies for reporting restrictions to be lifted during the currency of a case, in the absence of agreement between the parties the court should consider following one or the other of the alternative steps set out in sub-paragraphs (iv)–(v) above.

(vii) If injunctive relief is sought restraining publication based on Convention rights rather than statutory provisions, the matter should in any event be transferred to the High Court to be dealt with under the *President's Practice Direction (Applications for Reporting*

Restriction Orders) 18 March 2005 and the *Practice Note (Official Solicitor: Deputy Director of Legal Services CAFCASS: Applications for Reporting Restriction Orders* [2005] 2 FLR 111 and, if interim injunctive relief appears necessary under threat of publication before such application can be dealt with by a High Court judge, the county court should comply with s 12(2) of Human Rights Act 1998.

21 The underlying aim of this guidance is to seek to ensure that the principled approach to be taken is determined by the High Court (and the Appellate Courts) as soon as possible and that in the interim changes of practice do not take place which may not accord with that principled approach. Though this may result in delayed rulings on some early contested applications involving arguments such as those mentioned in paragraphs 15 and 16 above, it may be considered desirable, in the absence of legislative guidance, that such rulings should only be made on the basis of authoritative judicial guidance following proper determination, with the benefit of full argument, of the relevant principled approach for the longer term.

22 To assist in the early determination of the principled approach:

(i) Arrangements will be made in the High Court to identify appropriate test cases and for their early determination, and

(ii) Arrangements will be made to seek to ensure that directions are given as soon as is practicable in any proceedings that are transferred to the High Court because they raise substantial issues arising from the attendance of media representatives

(iii) Proceedings which are transferred to the High Court other than in the PRFD should be put before a family High Court Judge on circuit or, failing the presence on circuit of a High Court Judge, before the Family Division Liaison Judge as an urgent application for directions.

Sir Mark Potter
President of the Family Division

PRESIDENT'S GUIDANCE
1 APRIL 2010

THE REVISED PRIVATE LAW PROGRAMME

1 Introduction

1.1 The Private Law Programme has achieved marked success in enabling the resolution of the majority of cases by consent at the First Hearing Dispute Resolution Appointment ("FHDRA"). It has been revised to build on the successes of the initial programme and to take account of recent developments in the law and practice associated with private family law.

1.2 In particular, there have been several legislative changes affecting private family law. The Allocation and Transfer of Proceedings Order 2008 (the "Allocation Order"), requires the transfer of cases from the County Court to the Family Proceedings Court (FPC). Sections 1 to 5 and Schedule 1 of the Children and Adoption Act 2006 which came into force on 8th December 2008, amends the Children Act 1989 by introducing Contact Activity Directions, Contact Activity Conditions, Contact Monitoring Requirements, Financial Compensation Orders and Enforcement Orders.

1.3 There has been growing recognition of the impact of domestic violence and abuse, drug and alcohol misuse and mental illness, on the proper consideration of the issues in private family law; this includes the acceptance that Court orders, even those made by consent, must be scrutinised to ensure that they are safe and take account of any risk factors. Coupled with this is the need to take account of the duty on Cafcass, pursuant to s 16A Children Act 1989, to undertake risk assessments where an officer of the Service ("Cafcass Officer") suspects that a child is at risk of harm. (References to Cafcass include CAFCASS CYMRU and references to the Cafcass Officer include the Welsh family proceedings officer in Wales).

1.4 There is awareness of the importance of involving children where appropriate in the decision making process.

1.5 The Revised Programme incorporates these developments. It also retains the essential feature of the FHDRA as the forum for the parties to be helped to reach agreement as to, and understanding of, the issues that divide them. It recognises that having reached agreement parties may need assistance in putting it into effect in a co-operative way.

1.6 The Revised Programme is designed to provide a framework for the consistent national approach to the resolution of the issues in private family law whilst enabling local practices and initiatives to be operated in addition and within the framework.

1.7 The Revised Programme is designed to assist parties to reach safe agreements where possible, to provide a forum in which to find the best way to resolve issues in each individual case and to promote outcomes that are sustainable, that are in the best interests of children and that take account of their perspectives.

2 Principles

2.1 Where an application is made to a court under Part II of the Children Act 1989, the child's welfare is the court's paramount concern. The court will apply the principle of the "Overriding Objective" to enable it to deal with a case justly, having regard to the welfare principles involved. So far as practicable the Court will –

- (a) Deal expeditiously and fairly with every case;
- (b) Deal with a case in ways which are proportionate to the nature, importance and complexity of the issues;
- (c) Ensure that the parties are on an equal footing;
- (d) Save unnecessary expense;
- (e) Allot to each case an appropriate share of the court's resources, while taking account of the need to allot resources to other cases.

2.2 The court will give effect to the overriding objective when applying this programme and when exercising its powers to manage cases.

The parties are required to help the court further the overriding objective and promote the welfare of the child by the application of the welfare principle, pursuant to s 1(1) of the Children Act 1989.

This Programme provides that consideration and discussion of all issues will not take place until the FHDRA when parties are on an equal footing and can hear what is said to and by each other. This excludes the safety checks and enquiries carried out by Cafcass before the first hearing that are required for that hearing and deal only with safety issues.

At the **FHDRA** the Court shall consider in particular –

- (a) Whether and the extent to which the parties can safely resolve some or all of the issues with the assistance of the Cafcass Officer and any available mediator.
- (b) Risk identification followed by active case management including risk assessment, and compliance with the Practice Direction 14th January 2009: "Residence and Contact Orders: Domestic Violence and Harm".
- (c) Further dispute resolution.
- (d) The avoidance of delay through the early identification of issues and timetabling, subject to the Allocation Order.
- (e) Judicial scrutiny of the appropriateness of consent orders.
- (f) Judicial consideration of the way to involve the child.
- (g) Judicial continuity.

Part III   Practice Directions and Guidance

3 Practical arrangements before the FHDRA

3.1 Applications shall be issued on the day of receipt in accordance with the appropriate Rules of Procedure. It is important that the form C100 is fully completed, especially on pages 1, 2, 3, 10 and 11 otherwise delay may be caused by requests for information.

3.2 If possible at the time of issue, and in any event by no later than 24 hours after issue, or in courts where applications are first considered on paper, by no later than 48 hours after issue, the court shall

- (i) send or hand to the Applicant
- (ii) send to Cafcass

the following:

- (a) a copy of the Application Form C100, (together with Supplemental Information Form C1A) (if provided) (references to form C1A are to be read as form C100A following the introduction of this replacement form),
- (b) the Notice of Hearing,
- (c) the Acknowledgment Form C7,
- (d) a blank Form C1A,
- (e) the Certificate of Service Form C9,
- (f) information leaflets for the parties.

3.3 Save in urgent cases that require an earlier listing, the fully effective operation of this Practice Direction requires the FHDRA to take place within **4** weeks of the application. Where practicable, the first hearing must be listed to be heard in this period and in any event no later than within **6** weeks of the application. Where, at the time of introduction of this Programme, the Designated Family Judge/Justices' Clerk determines that it is not practicable to list the first hearing within 4 weeks, they should, in consultation with HMCS and Cafcass, formulate a timetable for revisiting the position and managing to list the FHDRA within 4 weeks.

3.4 Copies of each Application Form C100 and Notice of Hearing shall be sent by the court to Cafcass in accordance with 3.2 above.

3.5 The Respondent shall have at least 14 days notice of the hearing where practicable, but the court may abridge this time.

3.6 The Respondent should file a response on the Forms C7/C1A no later than 14 days before the hearing.

3.7 A copy of Forms C7/C1A shall be sent by the court to Cafcass on the day of receipt.

3.8 **NOTE:** This provision relates to cases that are placed in the FHDRA list for hearing other than by direct application in accordance with the procedure referred to in paragraph 3.1. Such listing may follow an application under the Family Law Act 1996, or a direction by the Court in other proceedings. In all such cases, or where the Court adjourns proceedings to a 'dispute resolution hearing' (sometimes called 'conciliation'), this will be treated as an adjournment to a FHDRA, and the documents referred to in para 3.2 must be filed and copied to parties and Cafcass for safety checks and enquiries, in the same way.

3.9 Before the FHDRA Cafcass shall identify any safety issues by the steps outlined below. Such steps shall be confined to matters of safety. Neither Cafcass nor a Cafcass Officer shall discuss with either party before the FHDRA any matter other than relates to safety. The Parties will not be invited to talk about other issues, for example relating to the substance of applications or replies or about issues concerning matters of welfare or the prospects of resolution. If such issues are raised by either party they will be advised that such matters will be deferred to the FHDRA when there is equality between the parties and full discussion can take place which will also be a time when any safety issues that have been identified also can be taken into account.

(a) In order to inform the court of possible risks of harm to the child in accordance with its safeguarding framework Cafcass will carry out safeguarding enquiries, including checks of local authorities and police, and telephone risk identification interviews with parties.
(b) If risks of harm are identified, Cafcass may invite parties to meet separately with the Cafcass Officer before the FHDRA to clarify any safety issue.
(c) Cafcass shall record and outline any safety issues for the court.
(d) The Cafcass Officer will not initiate contact with the child prior to the FHDRA. If contacted by a child, discussions relating to the issues in the case will be postponed to the day of the hearing or after when the Cafcass officer will have more knowledge of the issues.
(e) At least 3 days before the hearing the Cafcass Officer shall report the outcome of risk identification work to the court by completing the Form at Schedule 2.

4 The First Hearing Dispute Resolution Appointment.

4.1 The parties and Cafcass Officer shall attend this hearing. A mediator may attend where available.

4.2 At the hearing, which is not privileged, the court should have the following documents:

(a) C100 application, and C1A if any
(b) Notice of Hearing
(c) C7 response and C1A if any
(d) Schedule 2 safeguarding information

4.3 The detailed arrangements for the participation of mediators will be arranged locally. These will include:

(a) Arrangements for the mediator to ask the parties in a particular case to consent to the mediator seeing the papers in the case where it seems appropriate to do so.

(b) Arrangements for the mediator to ask the parties to waive privilege for the purpose of the first hearing where it seems to the mediator appropriate to do so in order to assist the work of the mediator and the outcome of the first hearing.
(c) In all cases it is important that such arrangements are put in place in a way that avoids any pressure being brought to bear in this connection on the parties that is inconsistent with general good mediation practice.

4.4 At the FHDRA the Court, in collaboration with the Cafcass Officer, and with the assistance of any mediator present, will seek to assist the parties in conciliation and in resolution of all or any of the issues between them. Any remaining issues will be identified, the Cafcass Officer will advise the court of any recommended means of resolving such issues and directions will be given for the future resolution of such issues. At all times the decisions of the Court and the work of the Cafcass Officer will take account of any risk or safeguarding issues that have been identified.

4.5 The Cafcass Officer shall, where practicable, speak separately to each party at court and before the hearing.

4.6 In the County Court, the Court shall have available a telephone contact to the Family Proceedings Court listing manager, diary dates for the appropriate Family Proceedings Court, or other means by which the County Court, at the time of the hearing, will be able to list subsequent hearings in the Family Proceedings Court.

5 Conduct of the Hearing. The following matters shall be considered

5.1 **Safeguarding:**

(a) The court shall inform the parties of the content of any screening report or other information which has been provided by Cafcass, unless it considers that to do so would create a risk of harm to a party or the child. The court may need to consider whether and how any information contained in the checks should be disclosed to the parties if Cafcass have not disclosed it.
(b) Whether a risk assessment is required and when.
(c) Whether a fact finding hearing is needed to determine allegations whose resolution is likely to affect the decision of the court.

5.2 **Dispute Resolution:**

(a) There will be at every FHDRA a period in which the Cafcass Officer, with the assistance of any Mediator and in collaboration with the Court, will seek to conciliate and explore with the parties the resolution of all or some of the issues between them. The procedure to be followed in this connection at the hearing will be determined by

local arrangements between the Cafcass manager, or equivalent in Wales, and the Designated Family Judge or the Justices' Clerk where appropriate.
(b) What is the result of any such meeting at Court?
(c) What other options there are for resolution e.g. may the case be suitable for further intervention by Cafcass; mediation by an external provider; collaborative law or use of a parenting plan?
(d) Would the parties be assisted by attendance at Parenting Information Programmes or other activities, whether by formal statutory provision under section 11 Children Act 1989 as amended by Children and Adoption Act 2006 or otherwise?

5.3 **Consent Orders:**

Where agreement is reached at any hearing or submitted in writing to the court, no order will be made without scrutiny by the court. Where safeguarding checks or risk assessment work remain outstanding, the making of a final order may be deferred for such work. In such circumstances the court shall adjourn the case for no longer than 28 days to a fixed date. A written notification of this work is to be provided by Cafcass in accordance with the timescale specified by the court. If satisfactory information is then available, the order may be made at the adjourned hearing in the agreed terms without the need for attendance by the parties. If satisfactory information is not available, the order will not be made, and the case will be adjourned for further consideration with an opportunity for the parties to make further representations.

5.4 **Reports:**

(a) Are there welfare issues or other specific considerations which should be addressed in a report by Cafcass or the Local Authority? Before a report is ordered, the court should consider alternative ways of working with the parties such as are referred to in paragraph 5.2 above. If a report is ordered in accordance with Section 7 of the Children Act 1989, it should be directed specifically towards and limited to those issues. General requests should be avoided and the Court should state in the Order the specific factual and other issues that are to be addressed in a focused report. In determining whether a request for a report should be directed to the relevant local authority or to Cafcass, the court should consider such information as Cafcass has provided about the extent and nature of the local authority's current or recent involvement with the subject of the application and the parties, and any relevant protocol between Cafcass and the Association of Directors of Children's Services.
(b) Is there a need for an investigation under S 37 Children Act 1989?
(c) A copy of the Order requesting the report and any relevant court documents are to be sent to Cafcass or, in the case of the Local Authority, to the Legal Adviser to the Director of the Local Authority Children's Services and, where known, to the allocated social worker by the court forthwith.

Part III Practice Directions and Guidance

(d) Is any expert evidence required in compliance with the Experts' Practice Direction?

5.5 **Wishes and feelings of the child:**

(a) Is the child aware of the proceedings?
How are the wishes and feelings of the child to be ascertained (if at all)?
(b) How is the child to be involved in the proceedings, if at all, and whether at or after the FHDRA?
(c) If consideration is given to the joining of the child as a party to the application, the court should consider the current Guidance from the President of the Family Division. Where the court is considering the appointment of a guardian ad litem, it should first seek to ensure that the appropriate Cafcass manager has been spoken to so as to consider any advice in connection with the prospective appointment and the timescale involved. In considering whether to make such an appointment the Court shall take account of the demands on the resources of Cafcass that such appointment would make.
(d) Who will inform the child of the outcome of the case where appropriate?

5.6 **Case Management:**

(a) What, if any, issues are agreed and what are the key issues to be determined?
(b) Are there any interim orders which can usefully be made (e.g. indirect, supported or supervised contact) pending final hearing?
(c) What directions are required to ensure the application is ready for final hearing – statements, reports etc?
(d) List for final hearing, consider the need for judicial continuity (especially if there has been or is to be a fact finding hearing or a contested interim hearing).

5.7 **Transfer to FPC:**

The case should be transferred to the FPC, pursuant to the Allocation and Transfer of Proceedings Order 2008 unless one of the specified exceptions applies. The date should be fixed at court and entered on the order.

6 The Order

6.1 **The Order shall set out in particular:**

(a) The issues about which the parties are agreed
(b) The issues that remain to be resolved
(c) The steps that are planned to resolve the issues
(d) Any interim arrangements pending such resolution, including arrangements for the involvement of children.
(e) The timetable for such steps and, where this involves further hearings, the date of such hearings.

(f) A statement as to any facts relating to risk or safety; in so far as they are resolved the result will be stated and, in so far as not resolved, the steps to be taken to resolve them will be stated.
(g) If it be the case, the fact of the transfer of the case to the Family Proceedings Court with the date and purpose of the next hearing
(h) If it be the case, the fact that the case cannot be transferred to the Family Proceedings Court and the reason for the decision.
(i) Whether in the event of an order, by consent or otherwise, or pending such an order, the parties are to be assisted by participation in mediation, Parenting Information Programmes, or other types of parenting intervention, and to detail any contact activity directions or conditions imposed by the court.

6.2 A suggested template order is available as set out in Schedule 1 below.

7 Commencement and Implementation

7.1 This Practice Direction will come into effect on April 1st 2010. So that procedural changes can be made by all agencies, the requirement for full implementation of the provisions is postponed, but in any event it should be effected by no later than October 4th 2010.

SCHEDULE 1

The suggested form of Order which courts may wish to use is PLP10 which is available from Her Majesty's Court Service.

SCHEDULE 2

Report Form on outcome of safeguarding enquiries. See version for Cafcass in England and for CAFCASS CYMRU in Wales.

Sir Mark Potter

President of the Family Division

THE PUBLIC LAW OUTLINE
APRIL 2010

PUBLIC LAW PROCEEDINGS GUIDE TO CASE MANAGEMENT

The Practice Direction below is made by the President of the Family Division under the powers delegated to him by the Lord Chief Justice under Schedule 2, Part 1, paragraph 2(2) of the Constitutional Reform Act 2005, and is approved by Bridget Prentice, Parliamentary Under Secretary of State, by authority of the Lord Chancellor.

Scope

1.1 This Practice Direction applies to care and supervision proceedings. In so far as practicable, it is to be applied to all other Public Law Proceedings.

1.2 This Practice Direction replaces Practice Direction Guide to Case Management in Public Law Proceedings dated April 2008.

1.3 This Practice Direction will come into effect on 6th April 2010. The new form of application for a care or supervision order (Form C110) only applies to proceedings commenced on or after 6th April 2010. Subject to this it is intended that this Practice Direction should apply in so far as practicable to applications made and not disposed of before 6th April 2010. In relation to these applications –

> (1) the Practice Direction Guide to Case Management in Public Law Proceedings dated April 2008 applies where it is not practicable to apply this Practice Direction; and
> (2) the court may give directions relating to the application of this Practice Direction or the April 2008 Practice Direction. This is subject to the overriding objective below and to the proviso that such a direction will neither cause further delay nor involve repetition of steps already taken or decisions already made in the case.

1.4 This Practice Direction is to be read with the rules and is subject to them.

1.5 A Glossary of terms is at paragraph 26.

The overriding objective

2.1 This Practice Direction has the overriding objective of enabling the court to deal with cases justly, having regard to the welfare issues involved. Dealing with a case justly includes, so far as is practicable –

- (1) ensuring that it is dealt with expeditiously and fairly;
- (2) dealing with the case in ways which are proportionate to the nature, importance and complexity of the issues;
- (3) ensuring that the parties are on an equal footing;

(4) saving expense; and
(5) allotting to it an appropriate share of the court's resources, while taking into account the need to allot resources to other cases.

Application by the court of the overriding objective

2.2 The court must seek to give effect to the overriding objective when it –

(1) exercises the case management powers referred to in this Practice Direction; or
(2) interprets any provision of this Practice Direction.

Duty of the parties

2.3 The parties are required to help the court further the overriding objective.

Court case management

The main principles

3.1 The main principles underlying court case management and the means of the court furthering the overriding objective in Public Law Proceedings are –

(1) **Timetable for the Child**: each case will have a timetable for the proceedings set by the court in accordance with the Timetable for the Child;
(2) **judicial continuity**: each case will be allocated to one or not more than two case management judges (in the case of magistrates' courts, case managers), who will be responsible for every case management stage in the proceedings through to the Final Hearing and, in relation to the High Court or county court, one of whom may be – and where possible should be – the judge who will conduct the Final Hearing;
(3) **main case management tools**: each case will be managed by the court by using the appropriate main case management tools;
(4) **active case management**: each case will be actively case managed by the court with a view at all times to furthering the overriding objective;
(5) **consistency**: each case will, so far as compatible with the overriding objective, be managed in a consistent way and using the standardised steps provided for in this Direction.

The main case management tools

The Timetable for the Child

3.2 The "Timetable for the Child" is defined by the rules as the timetable set by the court in accordance with its duties under section 1 and 32 of the 1989 Act and shall-

(1) take into account dates of the significant steps in the life of the child who is the subject of the proceedings; and
(2) be appropriate for that child. The court will set the timetable for the proceedings in accordance with the Timetable for the Child and review

this Timetable regularly. Where adjustments are made to the Timetable for the Child, the timetable for the proceedings will have to be reviewed. The Timetable for the Child is to be considered at every stage of the proceedings and whenever the court is asked to make directions whether at a hearing or otherwise.

3.3 The steps in the child's life which are to be taken into account by the court when setting the Timetable for the Child include not only legal steps but also social, care, health and education steps.

3.4 Examples of the dates the court will record and take into account when setting the Timetable for the Child are the dates of –

(1) any formal review by the Local Authority of the case of a looked after child (within the meaning of section 22(1) of the 1989 Act);
(2) the child taking up a place at a new school;
(3) any review by the Local Authority of any statement of the child's special educational needs;
(4) any assessment by a paediatrician or other specialist;
(5) the outcome of any review of Local Authority plans for the child, for example, any plans for permanence through adoption, Special Guardianship or placement with parents or relatives;
(6) any change or proposed change of the child's placement.

3.5 Due regard should be paid to the Timetable for the Child to ensure that the court remains child-focused throughout the progress of Public Law Proceedings and that any procedural steps proposed under the Public Law Outline are considered in the context of significant events in the child's life.

3.6 The applicant is required to provide the information needed about the significant steps in the child's life in the Application Form and to update this information regularly taking into account information received from others involved in the child's life such as other parties, members of the child's family, the person who is caring for the child, the children's guardian and the child's key social worker.

3.7 Before setting the timetable for the proceedings the factors which the court will consider will include the need to give effect to the overriding objective and the timescales in the Public Law Outline by which the steps in the Outline are to be taken. Where possible, the timetable for the proceedings should be in line with those timescales. However, there will be cases where the significant steps in the child's life demand that the steps in the proceedings be taken at times which are outside the timescales set out in the Outline. In those cases the timetable for the proceedings may not adhere to one or more of the timescales set out in the Outline.

3.8 Where more than one child is the subject of the proceedings, the court should consider and may set a Timetable for the Child for each child. The children may not all have the same Timetable, and the court will consider the appropriate progress of the proceedings in relation to each child.

3.9 Where there are parallel care proceedings and criminal proceedings against a person connected with the child for a serious offence against the child, linked directions hearings should where practicable take place as the case progresses. The timing of the proceedings in a linked care and criminal case should appear in the Timetable for the Child.

Case Management Documentation

3.10 Case Management Documentation includes the –

(1) Application Form and Annex Documents;
(2) Case Analysis and Recommendations provided by Cafcass or CAFCASS CYMRU;
(3) Local Authority Case Summary;
(4) Other Parties' Case Summaries.

3.11 The court will encourage the use of the Case Management Documentation which is not prescribed by the rules.

The Case Management Record

3.12 The court's filing system for the case will be known as the Case Management Record and will include the following main documents –

(1) the Case Management Documentation;
(2) Standard Directions on Issue and on First Appointment;
(3) Case Management Orders approved by the court.

3.13 Parties or their legal representatives will be expected to retain their own record containing copies of the documents on the court's Case Management Record.

The first appointment

3.14 The purpose of the First Appointment is to confirm allocation of the case and give initial case management directions.

The Case Management Order

3.15 The Case Management Order is an order which will be made by the court at the conclusion of the Case Management Conference, the Issues Resolution Hearing and any other case management hearing. It is designed to achieve active case management as defined in paragraph 3.20 below. The parties are required to prepare and submit to the court a draft of this order in accordance with paragraphs 5.8 to 5.10 below. The order will include such of the provisions referred to in the Glossary at paragraph 26(12) as are appropriate to the proceedings.

Advocates' meeting/discussion

3.16 The court will consider directing advocates to have discussions before the Case Management Conference and the Issues Resolution Hearing. Advocates may well find that the best way to have these discussions is to meet. Such discussion is intended to facilitate agreement and to narrow the issues for the court to consider. Advocates and litigants in person may take part in the Advocates' Meeting or discussions.

The Case Management Conference

3.17 In each case there will be a Case Management Conference to enable the case management judge or case manager, with the co-operation of the parties, actively to manage the case and, at the earliest practicable opportunity to –

- (1) identify the relevant and key issues; and
- (2) give full case management directions including confirming the Timetable for the Child.

The Issues Resolution Hearing

3.18 In each case there will be an Issues Resolution Hearing before the Final Hearing to –

- (1) identify any remaining key issues; and
- (2) as far as possible, resolve or narrow those issues.

Active case management

3.19 The court must further the overriding objective by actively managing cases.

3.20 Active case management includes –

- (1) identifying the Timetable for the Child;
- (2) identifying the appropriate court to conduct the proceedings and transferring the proceedings as early as possible to that court;
- (3) encouraging the parties to co-operate with each other in the conduct of the proceedings;
- (4) retaining the Case Management Record;
- (5) identifying all facts and matters that are in issue at the earliest stage in the proceedings and at each hearing;
- (6) deciding promptly which issues need full investigation and hearing and which do not and whether a fact finding hearing is required;
- (7) deciding the order in which issues are to be resolved;
- (8) identifying at an early stage who should be a party to the proceedings;
- (9) considering whether the likely benefits of taking a particular step justify any delay which will result and the cost of taking it;
- (10) directing discussion between advocates and litigants in person before the Case Management Conference and Issues Resolution Hearing;
- (11) requiring the use of the Case Management Order and directing advocates and litigants in person to prepare or adjust the draft of this Order where appropriate;
- (12) standardising, simplifying and regulating –
  - (a) the use of Case Management Documentation and forms;
  - (b) the court's orders and directions;
- (13) controlling –

(a) the use and cost of experts;
(b) the nature and extent of the documents which are to be disclosed to the parties and presented to the court;
(c) whether and, if so, in what manner the documents disclosed are to be presented to the court;
(d) the progress of the case;
(14) where it is demonstrated to be in the interests of the child, encouraging the parties to use an alternative dispute resolution procedure if the court considers such a procedure to be appropriate and facilitating the use of such procedure;
(15) helping the parties to reach agreement in relation to the whole or part of the case;
(16) fixing the dates for all appointments and hearings;
(17) dealing with as many aspects of the case as it can on the same occasion;
(18) where possible dealing with additional issues which may arise from time to time in the case without requiring the parties to attend at court;
(19) making use of technology; and
(20) giving directions to ensure that the case proceeds quickly and efficiently.

The Expectations

4.1 The expectations are that proceedings should be –

(1) conducted using the Case Management Tools and Case Management Documentation referred to in this Practice Direction in accordance with the Public Law Outline;
(2) finally determined within the timetable fixed by the court in accordance with the Timetable for the Child – the timescales in the Public Law Outline being adhered to and being taken as the maximum permissible time for the taking of the step referred to in the Outline unless the Timetable for the Child demands otherwise.

4.2 However, there may be cases where the court considers that the child's welfare requires a different approach from the one contained in the Public Law Outline. In those cases, the court will –

(1) determine the appropriate case management directions and timetable; and
(2) record on the face of the order the reasons for departing from the approach in the Public Law Outline.

Part III   Practice Directions and Guidance

How the parties should help court case management

Main methods of helping

Good case preparation

5.1 The applicant should prepare the case before proceedings are issued. In care and supervision proceedings the Local Authority should use the Pre-proceedings checklist.

The Timetable for the Child

5.2 The applicant must state in the Application Form all information concerning significant steps in the child's life that are likely to take place during the proceedings. The applicant is to be responsible for updating this information regularly and giving it to the court. The applicant will need to obtain information about these significant steps and any variations and additions to them from others involved in the child's life such as other parties, members of the child's family, the person who is caring for the child, the children's guardian and the child's key social worker. When the other persons involved in the child's life become aware of a significant step in the child's life or a variation of an existing one, that information should be given to the applicant as soon as possible.

5.3 The information about the significant steps in the child's life will enable the court to set the Timetable for the Child and to review that Timetable in the light of new information. The Timetable for the Child will be included or referred to in the draft of a Case Management Order, the Case Management Order, Standard Directions on Issue and on First Appointment and the directions given at the Case Management Conference and Issues Resolution Hearing.

Case Management Documentation

5.4 The parties must use the Case Management Documentation.

Co-operation

5.5 The parties and their representatives should co-operate with the court in case management, including the fixing of timetables to avoid unacceptable delay, and in the crystallisation and resolution of the issues on which the case turns.

Directions

5.6 The parties will –

(1)   monitor compliance with the court's directions; and
(2)   tell the court or court officer about any failure to comply with a direction of the court or any other delay in the proceedings.

The Case Management Record

5.7 The parties are expected to retain a record containing copies of the documents on the court's Case Management Record.

Drafting the Case Management Order

5.8 Parties should start to consider the content of the draft of the Case Management Order at the earliest opportunity either before or in the course of completing applications to the court or the response to the application. They should in any event consider the drafting of a Case Management Order after the First Appointment.

5.9 Only one draft of the Case Management Order should be filed with the court for each of the Case Management Conference and the Issues Resolution Hearing. It is the responsibility of the advocate for the applicant, which in care and supervision proceedings will ordinarily be the Local Authority, to prepare those drafts and be responsible for obtaining comments from the advocates and the parties.

5.10 There should be ongoing consideration of the Case Management Orders throughout the proceedings. The Case Management Orders should serve as an *aide memoire* to everyone involved in the proceedings of –

(1) the Timetable for the Child;
(2) the case management decisions;
(3) the identified issues.

5.11 In paragraphs 5.4, 5.6 to 5.9 "parties" includes parties' legal representatives.

Findings of fact hearings

6 In a case where the court decides that a fact finding hearing is necessary, the starting point is that the proceedings leading to that hearing are to be managed in accordance with the case management steps in this Practice Direction.

Ethnicity, language, religion and culture

7 At each case management stage of the proceedings, particularly at the First Appointment and Case Management Conference, the court will consider giving directions regarding the obtaining of evidence about the ethnicity, language, religion and culture of the child and other significant persons involved in the proceedings. The court will subsequently consider the implications of this evidence for the child in the context of the issues in the case.

Adults who may be protected parties

8.1 The applicant must give details in the Application Form of any referral to or assessment by the local authority's Adult Learning Disability team (or its equivalent). The Local Authority should tell the court about other referrals or assessments if known such as a referral to Community Mental Health.

8.2 The court will investigate as soon as possible any issue as to whether an adult party or intended party to the proceedings lacks capacity (within the meaning of the Mental Capacity Act 2005) to conduct the proceedings. A representative (a litigation friend, next friend or guardian ad litem) is needed to conduct the proceedings on behalf of an adult who lacks capacity to do so ("a protected party"). The expectation of the Official Solicitor is that the Official Solicitor will only be invited to act for a protected party as guardian ad litem or litigation friend if there is no other person suitable and willing to act.

8.3 Any issue as to the capacity of an adult to conduct the proceedings must be determined before the court gives any directions relevant to that adult's role within the proceedings.

8.4 Where the adult is a protected party, that party's representative should be involved in any instruction of an expert, including the instruction of an expert to assess whether the adult, although a protected party, is competent to give evidence. The instruction of an expert is a significant step in the proceedings. The representative will wish to consider (and ask the expert to consider), if the protected party is competent to give evidence, their best interests in this regard. The representative may wish to seek advice about 'special measures'. The representative may put forward an argument on behalf of the protected party that the protected party should not give evidence.

8.5 If at any time during the proceedings, there is reason to believe that a party may lack capacity to conduct the proceedings, then the court must be notified and directions sought to ensure that this issue is investigated without delay.

Child likely to lack capacity to conduct the proceedings when aged 18

9 Where it appears that a child is –

(1) a party to the proceedings and not the subject of them;
(2) nearing age 18; and
(3) considered likely to lack capacity to conduct the proceedings when 18, the court will consider giving directions relating to the investigation of a child's capacity in this respect.

Outline of the process and how to use the Main Case Management Tools

10.1 The Public Law Outline set out in the Table below contains an outline of –

(1) the order of the different stages of the process;
(2) the purposes of the main case management hearings and matters to be considered at them;
(3) the latest timescales within which the main stages of the process should take place.

10.2 In the Public Law Outline –

(1) "CMC" means the Case Management Conference;

The Public Law Outline of April 2010

(2) "FA" means the First Appointment;
(3) "IRH" means the Issues Resolution Hearing;
(4) "LA" means the Local Authority which is applying for a care or supervision order;
(5) "OS" means the Official Solicitor.

Public Law Outline

PRE-PROCEEDINGS	
PRE-PROCEEDINGS CHECKLIST	
Annex Documents (the documents specified in the Annex to the Application Form to be attached to that form where available):	**Other Checklist Documents which already exist on LA's files which are to be disclosed in the event of proceedings normally before the day of the FA:**
– Social Work Chronology	– Previous court orders & judgments/reasons
– Initial Social Work Statement	– Any relevant assessment materials
– Initial and Core Assessments	– Section 7 & 37 reports
– Letters Before Proceedings – Schedule of Proposed Findings	– Relatives & friends materials (e.g., a genogram)
– Care Plan	– Other relevant reports & records
	– Single, joint or inter-agency materials (e.g., health & education/Home Office & Immigration documents)
	– Records of discussions with the family
	– Key LA minutes & records for the child (including Strategy Discussion Record)
	– Pre-existing care plans (e.g., child in need plan, looked after child plan & child protection plan)

PART III – Practice Directions and Guidance

STAGE 1 – ISSUE AND THE FIRST APPOINTMENT	
ISSUE	FIRST APPOINTMENT
On DAY 1 and by DAY 3	By DAY 6
Objectives: To ensure compliance with pre-proceedings checklist; to allocate proceedings; to obtain the information necessary for initial case management at the FA	**Objectives:** To confirm allocation; to give initial case management directions
On Day 1: The LA files the Application Form and Annex Documents where available – Court officer issues application – Court nominates case manager(s) – Court gives Standard Directions on Issue including: – Pre-proceedings checklist compliance including preparation and service of any missing Annex Documents – Allocate and/or transfer – Appoint children's guardian – Appoint solicitor for the child – Case Analysis for FA – Appoint a guardian ad litem or litigation friend for a protected party or any non subject child who is a party, including the OS where appropriate – List FA by Day 6	– LA normally serves Other Checklist Documents on the parties – Parties notify LA & court of need for a contested hearing – Court makes arrangements for a contested hearing – Initial case management by court including: – Confirm Timetable for the Child – Confirm allocation or transfer – Identify additional parties & representation (including allocation of children's guardian) – Identify "Early Final Hearing" cases – Scrutinise Care Plan – Court gives Standard Directions on FA including: – Case Analysis and Recommendations for Stages 2 & 3 – Preparation and service of any missing Annex Documents – What Other Checklist Documents are to be filed

The Public Law Outline of April 2010

– Make arrangements for contested hearing (if necessary) By Day 3 – Cafcass/CAFCASS CYMRU expected to allocate case to children's guardian – LA serves the Application Form and Annex Documents, on parties	– LA Case Summary – Other Parties' Case Summaries – Parties' initial witness statements – For the Advocates' Meeting – List CMC or (if appropriate) an Early Final Hearing – Upon transfer

STAGE 2 – CASE MANAGEMENT CONFERENCE	
ADVOCATES' MEETING	**CMC**
No later than 2 days before CMC	**No later than day 45**
Objectives: To prepare the Draft Case Management Order; to identify experts and draft questions for them	**Objectives: To identify issue(s); to give full case management directions**
– Consider information on the Application Form, all Other Parties' Case Summaries and Case Analysis and Recommendations – Identify proposed experts and draft questions in accordance with Experts Practice Direction – Draft Case Management Order – Notify court of need for a contested hearing – File draft of the Case Management Order with the case manager/case management judge by 11am one working day before the CMC	– Detailed case management by the court – Scrutinise compliance with directions – Review and confirm Timetable for the Child – Identify key issue(s) – Confirm allocation or transfer – Consider case management directions in the draft of the Case Management Order – Scrutinise Care Plan – Check compliance with Experts Practice Direction – Court issues Case Management Order

PART III – Practice Directions and Guidance

	– Court lists IRH and, where necessary, a warned period for Final Hearing

STAGE 3 – ISSUES RESOLUTION HEARING	
ADVOCATES' MEETING	**IRH**
Between 2 and 7 days before the IRH	**Between 16 & 25 weeks**
Objective: To prepare or update the draft Case Management Order	**Objectives: To resolve and narrow issue(s); to identify any remaining key issues**

– Consider all other parties' Case Summaries and Case Analysis and Recommendations
 	
– Draft Case Management Order
 	
– Notify court of need for a contested hearing/time for oral evidence to be given
 	
– File Draft Case Management Order with the case manager/case management judge by 11am one working day before the IRH
	– Identification by the court of the key issue(s) (if any) to be determined
	
	– Final case management by the court:
	
	    – Scrutinise compliance with directions
	
	    – Review and confirm the Timetable for the Child
	
	    – Consider case management directions in the draft of the Case Management Order
	
	    – Scrutinise Care Plan
	
	    – Give directions for Hearing documents:
	
	        – Threshold agreement or facts/issues remaining to be determined
	
	        – Final Evidence & Care Plan
	
	        – Case Analysis and Recommendations
	
	        – Witness templates
	
	        – Skeleton arguments

The Public Law Outline of April 2010

	– Judicial reading list/reading time/judgment writing time
	– Time estimate
	– Bundles Practice Direction compliance
	– List or confirm Hearing
	– Court issues Case Management Order

STAGE 4	
HEARING	
Hearing set in accordance with the Timetable for the Child	
Objective: To determine remaining issues	
– All file & serve updated Case Management Documentation & bundle – Draft final order(s) in approved form	– Judgment/Reasons – Disclose documents as required after hearing

Starting the proceedings

Pre-proceedings Checklist

11.1 The Pre-proceedings Checklist is to be used by the applicant to help prepare for the start of the proceedings.

11.2 The Pre-proceedings Checklist contains the documents which are specified in the Annex to the Application Form. The rules require those documents which are known as the "Annex Documents" to be filed with the Application Form where available. The Annex Documents are –

(1) Social Work Chronology;
(2) Initial Social Work Statement;
(3) Initial and Core Assessments;
(4) Letters before Proceedings;
(5) Schedule of Proposed Findings; and
(6) Care Plan.

11.3 In addition, the Pre-proceedings Checklist contains examples of documents other than the Annex Documents which will normally be on the Local Authority file at the start of proceedings so that they can be served on parties in accordance with the Public Law Outline. These documents are known as the "Other Checklist Documents" and are not to be filed with the court at the start of the proceedings but are to be disclosed to the parties normally before the day of the First Appointment or in accordance with the court's directions and to be filed with the court only as directed by the court.

Compliance with Pre-proceedings Checklist

11.4 It is recognised that in some cases the circumstances are such that the safety and welfare of the child may be jeopardised if the start of proceedings is delayed until all of the documents appropriate to the case and referred to in the Pre-proceedings Checklist are available. The safety and welfare of the child should never be put in jeopardy because of lack of documentation. (Nothing in this Practice Direction affects an application for an emergency protection order under section 44 of the 1989 Act).

11.5 The court recognises that the preparation may need to be varied to suit the circumstances of the case. In cases where any of the Annex Documents required to be attached to the Application Form are not available at the time of issue of the application, the court will consider making directions on issue about when any missing documentation is to be filed. The expectation is that there will be a good reason why one or more of the documents are not available. Further directions relating to any missing documentation are likely to be made at the First Appointment. The court also recognises that some documents on the Pre-proceedings Checklist may not exist and may never exist, for example, the Section 37 report, and that in urgent proceedings no Letter Before Proceedings may have been sent.

What the court will do at the issue of proceedings

Objectives

12.1 The objectives at this stage are for the court –

    (1)   to identify the Timetable for the Child;
    (2)   in care and supervision proceedings, to ensure compliance with the Pre-proceedings Checklist;
    (3)   to allocate proceedings;
    (4)   to obtain the information necessary to enable initial case management at the First Appointment.

12.2 The steps which the court will take once proceedings have been issued include those set out in paragraphs 12.3 to 12.5 below.

Allocation

12.3 By reference to the Allocation Order, the court will consider allocation of the case and transfer to the appropriate level of court those cases which are obviously suitable for immediate transfer.

Other steps to be taken by the court

Directions

12.4 The court will –

(1) consider giving directions –
   (a) appropriate to the case including Standard Directions On Issue;
   (b) in care and supervision proceedings, relating to the preparation, filing and service of any missing Annex Documents and what Other Checklist Documents are to be filed and by when;
   (c) relating to the representation of any protected party or any child who is a party to, but is not the subject of, the proceedings by a guardian ad litem or litigation friend, including the Official Solicitor where appropriate;
(2) appoint a children's guardian in specified proceedings (in relation to care and supervision proceedings the court will expect that Cafcass or CAFCASS CYMRU will have received notice from the Local Authority that proceedings were going to be started);
(3) appoint a solicitor for the child under section 41(3) of the 1989 Act where appropriate;
(4) request the children's guardian or if appropriate another officer of the service or Welsh family proceedings officer to prepare a Case Analysis and Recommendations for the First Appointment;
(5) make arrangements for a contested hearing, if necessary.

(A suggested form for the drafting of Standard Directions on Issue is Form PLO 8 which is available from HMCS)

Setting a date for the First Appointment

12.5 The court will record the Timetable for the Child and set a date for the First Appointment normally no later than 6 days from the date of issue of the proceedings and in any event in line with the Timetable for the Child.

Case managers in the magistrates' courts

12.6 In the magistrates' courts, the justices' clerk may nominate one but not more than two case managers.

The First Appointment objectives

13.1 The First Appointment is the first hearing in the proceedings. The main objectives of the First Appointment are to –

(1) confirm allocation; and
(2) give initial case management directions having regard to the Public Law Outline.

13.2 The steps which the court will take at the First Appointment include those set out in paragraphs 13.3 to 13.6 below.

Part III Practice Directions and Guidance

Steps to be taken by the court

13.3 The court will –

(1) confirm the Timetable for the Child;
(2) make arrangements for any contested interim hearing such as an application for an interim care order;
(3) confirm in writing the allocation of the case or, if appropriate, transfer the case;
(4) request the children's guardian or if appropriate another officer of the service or Welsh family proceedings officer to prepare a Case Analysis and Recommendations for the Case Management Conference or Issues Resolution Hearing;
(5) scrutinise the Care Plan;
(6) consider giving directions relating to –
   (a) those matters in the Public Law Outline which remain to be considered including preparation, filing and service of any missing Annex Documents and what Other Checklist documents are to be filed and by when;
   (b) the joining of a person who would not otherwise be a respondent under the rules as a party to the proceedings;
   (c) where any person to be joined as a party may be a protected party, an investigation of that person's capacity to conduct the proceedings and the representation of that person by a guardian ad litem or litigation friend, including the Official Solicitor where appropriate;
   (d) the identification of family and friends as proposed carers and any overseas, immigration, jurisdiction and paternity issues;
   (e) any other documents to be filed with the court;
   (f) evidence to be obtained as to whether a parent who is a protected party is competent to make a statement.

(A suggested form for the drafting of Standard Directions on First Appointment is Form PLO 9 which is available from HMCS)

Early Final Hearing

13.4 Cases which are suitable for an early Final Hearing are those cases where all the evidence necessary to determine issues of fact and welfare is immediately or shortly available to be filed. Those cases are likely to include cases where the child has no parents, guardians, relatives who want to care for the child, or other carers. The court will –

(1) identify at the First Appointment whether the case is one which is suitable for an early Final Hearing; and
(2) set a date for that Final Hearing.

Setting a date for the Case Management Conference.

13.5 The court will set a date for the Case Management Conference normally no later than 45 days from the date of issue of the proceedings and in any event in line with the Timetable for the Child.

Advocates' Meeting/discussion and the drafting of the Case Management Order

13.6 The court will consider directing a discussion between the parties' advocates and any litigant in person and the preparation of a draft of the Case Management Order as outlined below.

Experts

13.7 A party who wishes to instruct an expert should comply with the Experts Practice Direction. Where the parties are agreed on any matter relating to experts or expert evidence, the draft agreement must be submitted for the court's approval as early as possible in the proceedings.

Advocates' Meeting/discussion and the drafting of the Case Management Order

14.1 The main objective of the Advocates' Meeting or discussion is to prepare a draft of the Case Management Order for approval by the court.

14.2 Where there is a litigant in person the court will consider the most effective way in which that person can be involved in the advocates discussions and give directions as appropriate including directions relating to the part to be played by any McKenzie Friend.

14.3 Timing of the discussions is of the utmost importance. Discussions of matters "outside the court room door", which could have taken place at an earlier time, are to be avoided. Discussions are to take place no later than 2 days before the Case Management Conference or the Issues Resolution Hearing whichever is appropriate. The discussions may take place earlier than 2 days before those hearings, for example, up to 7 days before them.

14.4 Following discussion the advocates should prepare or adjust the draft of the Case Management Order. In practice the intention is that the advocate for the applicant, which in care and supervision proceedings will ordinarily be the Local Authority, should take the lead in preparing and adjusting the draft of the Case Management Order following discussion with the other advocates. The aim is for the advocates to agree a draft of the Case Management Order which is to be submitted for the approval of the court.

14.5 Where it is not possible for the advocates to agree the terms of the draft of the Case Management Order, the advocates should specify on the draft, or on a separate document if more practicable –

(1) those provisions on which they agree; and
(2) those provisions on which they disagree.

14.6 Unless the court directs otherwise, the draft of the Case Management Order must be filed with the court no later than 11am on the day before the Case Management Conference or the Issues Resolution Hearing whichever may be appropriate.

14.7 At the Advocates' Meeting or discussion before the Case Management Conference, the advocates should also try to agree the questions to be put to any proposed expert (whether jointly instructed or not) if not previously agreed. Under the Experts Practice Direction the questions on which the proposed expert is to give an opinion are a crucial component of the expert directions which the court is required to consider at the Case Management Conference.

Case Management Conference objectives

15.1 The Case Management Conference is the main hearing at which the court manages the case. The main objectives of the Conference are to –

(1) identify key issues; and
(2) give full case management directions.

15.2 The steps which the court will take at the Case Management Conference include those steps set out in paragraphs 15.3 to 15.5 below.

Steps to be taken by the court

15.3 The court will –

(1) review and confirm the Timetable for the Child;
(2) confirm the allocation or the transfer of the case;
(3) scrutinise the Care Plan;
(4) identify the key issues;
(5) identify the remaining case management issues;
(6) resolve remaining case management issues set out in the draft of the Case Management Order;
(7) identify any special measures such as the need for access for the disabled or provision for vulnerable witnesses;
(8) scrutinise the Case Management Record to check whether directions have been complied with and if not, consider making further directions as appropriate;
(9) where expert evidence is required, check whether the parties have complied with the Experts Practice Direction, in particular the section on preparation for the relevant hearing and consider giving directions as appropriate.

Case Management Order

15.4 The court will issue the approved Case Management Order. Parties or their legal representatives will be expected to submit in electronic form the final approved draft of the Case Management Order on the conclusion of, and the same day as, the Case Management Conference.

Setting a date for the Issues Resolution Hearing/Final Hearing

15.5 The court will set –

(1) a date for the Issues Resolution Hearing normally at any time between 16 and 25 weeks from the date of issue of the proceedings and in any event in line with the Timetable for the Child; and
(2) if necessary, specify a period within which the Final Hearing of the application is to take place unless a date has already been set.

The Issues Resolution Hearing objectives

16.1 The objectives of this hearing are to –

(1) resolve and narrow issues;
(2) identify key remaining issues requiring resolution.

16.2 The Issues Resolution Hearing is likely to be the hearing before the Final Hearing. Final case management directions and other preparations for the Final Hearing will be made at this hearing.

Steps to be taken by the court

16.3 The court will –

(1) identify the key issues (if any) to be determined;
(2) review and confirm the Timetable for the Child;
(3) consider giving case management directions relating to –
   (a) any outstanding matter contained in the draft of the Case Management Order;
   (b) the preparation and filing of final evidence including the filing of witness templates;
   (c) skeleton arguments;
   (d) preparation and filing of bundles in accordance with the Bundles Practice Direction;
   (e) any agreement relating to the satisfaction of the threshold criteria under section 31 of the 1989 Act or facts and issues remaining to be determined in relation to it or to any welfare question which arises;
   (f) time estimates;
   (g) the judicial reading list and likely reading time and judgment writing time;
(4) issue the Case Management Order.

16.4 For the avoidance of doubt the purpose of an Issues Resolution Hearing is to –

(1) identify key issues which are not agreed;
(2) examine if those key issues can be agreed; and
(3) where those issues cannot be agreed, examine the most proportionate method of resolving those issues.

16.5 The expectation is that the method of resolving the key issues which cannot be agreed will be at a hearing (ordinarily the Final hearing) where there is an opportunity for the relevant oral evidence to be heard and challenged.

Attendance at the Case Management Conference and the Issues Resolution Hearing

17 An advocate who has conduct of the Final Hearing should ordinarily attend the Case Management Conference and the Issues Resolution Hearing. Where the attendance of this advocate is not possible, then an advocate who is familiar with the issues in the proceedings should attend.

Flexible powers of the court

18.1 Attention is drawn to the flexible powers of the court either following the issue of the application in that court, the transfer of the case to that court or at any other stage in the proceedings.

18.2 The court may give directions without a hearing including setting a date for the Final Hearing or a period within which the Final Hearing will take place. The steps, which the court will ordinarily take at the various stages of the proceedings provided for in the Public Law Outline, may be taken by the court at another stage in the proceedings if the circumstances of the case merit this approach.

18.3 The flexible powers of the court include the ability for the court to cancel or repeat a particular hearing. For example, if the issue on which the case turns can with reasonable practicability be crystallised and resolved by having an early Final Hearing, then in the fulfilment of the overriding objective, such a flexible approach must be taken to secure compliance with section 1(2) of the 1989 Act.

Alternative Dispute Resolution

19.1 The court will encourage the parties to use an alternative dispute resolution procedure and facilitate the use of such a procedure where it is –

- (1) readily available;
- (2) demonstrated to be in the interests of the child; and
- (3) reasonably practicable and safe.

19.2 At any stage in the proceedings, the parties can ask the court for advice about alternative dispute resolution.

19.3 At any stage in the proceedings the court itself will consider whether alternative dispute resolution is appropriate. If so, the court may direct that a hearing or proceedings be adjourned for such specified period as it considers appropriate –

- (1) to enable the parties to obtain information and advice about alternative dispute resolution; and

(2) where the parties agree, to enable alternative dispute resolution to take place.

Co-operation

20.1 Throughout the proceedings the parties and their representatives should cooperate wherever reasonably practicable to help towards securing the welfare of the child as the paramount consideration.

20.2 At each court appearance the court will ask the parties and their legal representatives –

(1) what steps they have taken to achieve co-operation and the extent to which they have been successful;
(2) if appropriate the reason why co-operation could not be achieved; and
(3) the steps needed to resolve any issues necessary to achieve co-operation.

Agreed directions

21.1 The parties, their advisers and the children's guardian, are encouraged to try to agree directions for the management of the proceedings.

21.2 To obtain the court's approval the agreed directions must –

(1) set out a Timetable for the Child by reference to calendar dates for the taking of steps for the preparation of the case;
(2) include a date when it is proposed that the next hearing will take place.

Variation of case management timetable

22 It is emphasised that a party or the children's guardian must apply to the court at the earliest opportunity if they wish to vary by extending the dates set by the court for –

(1) a directions appointment;
(2) a First Appointment;
(3) a Case Management Conference;
(4) an Issues Resolution Hearing;
(5) the Final Hearing;
(6) the period within which the Final Hearing of the application is to take place; or
(7) any Meeting/discussion between advocates or for the filing of the draft of the Case Management Orders.

Who performs the functions of the court

23.1 Where this Practice Direction provides for the court to perform case management functions, then except where any rule, practice direction, any other enactment or the Family Proceedings (Allocation to Judiciary) Directions ([2009] 2 FLR 51) provides otherwise, the functions may be performed –

(1) in relation to proceedings in the High Court or in a district registry, by any judge or district judge of that Court including a district judge of the principal registry;

(2) in relation to proceedings in the county court, by any judge or district judge including a district judge of the principal registry when the principal registry is treated as if it were a county court; and

(3) in relation to proceedings in a magistrates' court by –
   (a) any family proceedings court constituted in accordance with sections 66 and 67 of the 1980 Act;
   (b) a single justice; or
   (c) a justices' clerk.

23.2 The case management functions to be exercised by a justices' clerk may be exercised by an assistant justices' clerk provided that person has been specifically authorised by a justices' clerk to exercise case management functions. Any reference in this Practice Direction to a justices' clerk is to be taken to include an assistant justices' clerk so authorised. The justices' clerk may in particular appoint one but not more than two assistant justices' clerks as case managers for each case.

23.3 In proceedings in a magistrates' court, where a party considers that there are likely to be issues arising at a hearing (including the First Appointment, Case Management Conference and Issues Resolution Hearing) which need to be decided by a family proceedings court, rather than a justices' clerk, then that party should give the court written notice of that need at least 2 days before the hearing.

23.4 Family proceedings courts may consider making arrangements to ensure a court constituted in accordance with s 66 of the 1980 Act is available at the same time as Issues Resolution Hearings are being heard by a justices' clerk. Any delay as a result of the justices' clerk considering for whatever reason that it is inappropriate for a justices' clerk to perform a case management function on a particular matter and the justices' clerk's referring of that matter to the court should then be minimal.

Technology

24 Where the facilities are available to the court and the parties, the court will consider making full use of technology including electronic information exchange and video or telephone conferencing.

Other Practice Directions

25.1 This Practice Direction must be read with the Bundles Practice Direction.

25.2 The Bundles Practice Direction is applied to Public Law Proceedings in the High Court and county court with the following adjustments –

(1) add "except the First Appointment; Case Management Conference, and Issues Resolution Hearing referred to in the Practice Direction

Public Law Proceedings Guide to Case Management: April 2010 where there are no contested applications being heard at those hearings" to paragraph 2.2;

(2) the reference to –
  (a) the "Protocol for Judicial Case Management in Public law Children Act Cases [2003] 2 FLR 719" in paragraph 6.1;
  (b) the "Practice Direction: Care Cases: Judicial Continuity and Judicial Case Management" in paragraph 15; and
  (c) "the Public Law Protocol" in paragraph 15, shall be read as if it were a reference to this Practice Direction.

25.3 Paragraph 1.9 of the Practice Direction: Experts in Family Proceedings Relating to Children dated April 2008 should be read as if "Practice Direction: Guide to Case Management in Public law Proceedings, paragraphs 13.7, 14.3 and 25(29)" were a reference to "Practice Direction Public Law Proceedings Guide to Case Management: April 2010, paragraphs 14.7, 15.3 and 26(33)".

Glossary

26 In this Practice Direction –

(1) "the 1989 Act " means the Children Act 1989;
(2) "the 1980 Act" means the Magistrates' Courts Act 1980;
(3) "advocate" means a person exercising a right of audience as a representative of, or on behalf of, a party;
(4) "Allocation Order" means any order made by the Lord Chancellor under Part 1 of Schedule 11 to the 1989 Act;
(5) "alternative dispute resolution" means the methods of resolving a dispute other than through the normal court process;
(6) "Annex Documents" means the documents specified in the Annex to the Application Form;
(7) "Application Form" means Form C110 and Annex Documents;
(8) "assistant justices' clerk" has the meaning assigned to it by section 27(5) of the Courts Act 2003;
(9) "the Bundles Practice Direction" means the Practice Direction Family Proceedings: Court Bundles (Universal Practice to be Applied in all Courts other than Family Proceedings Court) of 27 July 2006;
(10) "Case Analysis and Recommendations" means a written or oral outline of the case from the child's perspective prepared by the children's guardian or other officer of the service or Welsh family proceedings officer at different stages of the proceedings requested by the court, to provide –
  (a) an analysis of the issues that need to be resolved in the case including-
    (i) any harm or risk of harm;
    (ii) the child's own views;
    (iii) the family context including advice relating to ethnicity, language, religion and culture of the child and other significant persons;

(iv) the Local Authority work and proposed care plan;
(v) advice about the court process including the Timetable for the Child; and
(vi) identification of work that remains to be done for the child in the short and longer term; and
(b) recommendations for outcomes, in order to safeguard and promote the best interests of the child in the proceedings;
(11) "Case Management Documentation" includes the documents referred to in paragraph 3.10;
(12) "Case Management Order" means an order made by the court which identifies the Timetable for the Child, any delay in the proceedings and the reason for such delay and the key issues in the proceedings and includes such of the following provisions as are appropriate to the proceedings –
(a) preliminary information:
(i) the names and dates of birth of the children who are the subject of the proceedings;
(ii) the names and legal representatives of the parties, and whether they attended the hearing;
(iii) any interim orders made in respect of the children and any provisions made for the renewal of those orders;
(b) any recitals that the court considers should be recorded in the order, including those relating to:
(i) any findings made by the court or agreed between the parties;
(ii) any other agreements or undertakings made by the parties;
(c) orders made at the hearing by way of case management relating to:
(i) the joinder of parties;
(ii) the determination of parentage of the children;
(iii) the appointment of a guardian ad litem or litigation friend (including the Official Solicitor where appropriate);
(iv) the transfer of the proceedings to a different court;
(v) the allocation of the proceedings to a case management judge;
(vi) the filing and service of threshold criteria documents;
(vii) the preparation and filing of assessments, including Core Assessments and parenting assessments;
(viii) in accordance with the Experts' Practice Direction, the preparation and filing of other expert evidence, and experts' meetings;
(ix) care planning and directions in any application for placement for adoption;
(x) the filing and service of evidence/further evidence on behalf of the local authority;
(xi) the filing and service of evidence/further evidence on behalf of the other parties;

(xii) the filing and service of the Case Analysis and Recommendations;
(xiii) the disclosure of documents into the proceedings held by third parties, including medical records, police records and Home Office information;
(xiv) the disclosure of documents and information relating to the proceedings to non-parties;
(xv) the listing of further hearings, and case management documentation to be prepared for those hearings;
(xvi) advocates' Meetings;
(xvii) the filing of bundles and other preparatory material for future hearings;
(xviii) technology/special measures;
(xix) media attendance and reporting;
(xx) linked or other proceedings;
(xxi) non-compliance with any court orders;
(xxii) such further or other directions as may be necessary for the purposes of case management;
(xxiii) attendance at court (including child/children's guardian);

(13) "Case Management Record" means the court's filing system for the case which includes the documents referred to at paragraph 3.12;
(14) "Case manager" means the justices' clerk or assistant justices' clerk who manages the case in the magistrates' courts;
(15) "Care Plan" means a "section 31A plan" referred to in section 31A of the 1989 Act;
(16) "Core Assessment" means the assessment undertaken by the Local Authority in accordance with The Framework for the Assessment of Children in Need and their Families (Department of Health et al, 2000);
(17) "court" means the High Court, county court or the magistrates' court;
(18) "court officer" means –
    (a) in the High Court or a county court, a member of court staff ; and
    (b) in a magistrates' court, the designated officer;
(19) "Experts Practice Direction" means the Practice Direction regarding Experts in Family Proceedings relating to Children;
(20) "genogram" means a family tree, setting out in diagrammatic form the family's background;
(21) "hearing" includes a directions appointment;
(22) "Initial Assessment" means the assessment undertaken by the Local Authority in accordance with The Framework for the Assessment of Children in Need and their Families (Department of Health et al, 2000);
(23) "Initial Social Work Statement" means a statement prepared by the Local Authority strictly limited to the following evidence –
    (a) the precipitating incident(s) and background circumstances relevant to the grounds and reasons for making the application

including a brief description of any referral and assessment processes that have already occurred;
(b) any facts and matters that are within the social worker's personal knowledge limited to the findings sought by the Local Authority;
(c) any emergency steps and previous court orders that are relevant to the application;
(d) any decisions made by the Local Authority that are relevant to the application;
(e) information relevant to the ethnicity, language, religion, culture, gender and vulnerability of the child and other significant persons in the form of a 'family profile' together with a narrative description and details of the social care and other services that are relevant to the same;
(f) where the Local Authority is applying for an interim order: the Local Authority's initial proposals for the child (which are also to be set out in the Care Plan) including placement, contact with parents and other significant persons and the social care services that are proposed;
(g) the Local Authority's initial proposals for the further assessment of the parties during the proceedings including twin track /concurrent planning (where more than one permanence option for the child is being explored by the Local Authority);

(24) "legal representative" means a –
(a) barrister,
(b) solicitor,
(c) solicitor's employee,
(d) manager of a body recognised under section 9 of the Administration of Justice Act 1985, or
(e) person who, for the purposes of the Legal Services Act 2007, is an authorised person in relation to an activity which constitutes the conduct of litigation (within the meaning of that Act), who has been instructed to act for a party in relation to the proceedings;

(25) "Letter Before Proceedings" means any letter from the Local Authority containing written notification to the parents and others with parental responsibility for the child of the Local Authority's plan to apply to court for a care or supervision order and any related subsequent correspondence confirming the Local Authority's position;

(26) "Local Authority Case Summary" means a document prepared by the Local Authority advocate for all case management hearings including –
(a) a recommended reading list and suggested reading time;
(b) the key issues in the case;
(c) any additional information relevant to the Timetable for the Child or for the conduct of the hearing or the proceedings;
(d) a summary of updating information;
(e) the issues and directions which the court will need to consider at the hearing in question, including any interim orders sought;

(f) any steps which have not been taken or directions not complied with, an explanation of the reasons for non–compliance and the effect, if any, on the Timetable for the Child;
(g) any relevant information relating to ethnicity, cultural or gender issues;

(27) "justices' clerk" has the meaning assigned to it by section 27(1) of the Courts Act 2003;

(28) "McKenzie Friend" means any person permitted by the court to sit beside an unrepresented litigant in court to assist the litigant by prompting, taking notes and giving advice to the litigant;

(29) "Other Checklist Documents" means the documents listed in the Pre-proceedings Checklist which will normally be on the local authority file prior to the start of proceedings but which are not –
(a) to be filed with the court on issue; or
(b) Annex Documents.

(30) "Other Parties' Case Summaries" means summaries by parties other than the Local Authority containing –
(a) the party's proposals for the long term future of the child (to include placement and contact);
(b) the party's reply to the Local Authority's Schedule of Proposed Findings;
(c) any proposal for assessment / expert evidence; and
(d) the names, addresses and contact details of any family or friends who it is suggested be approached in relation to long term care / contact or respite;

(31) "Pre-proceedings Checklist" means the Annex Documents and the Other Checklist Documents set out in the Public Law Outline;

(32) "Public Law Outline" means the Table contained in paragraph 10;

(33) "Public Law Proceedings" means proceedings for –
(a) a residence order under section 8 of the 1989 Act with respect to a child who is subject of a care order;
(b) a special guardianship order relating to a child who is subject of a care order;
(c) a secure accommodation order under section 25 of the 1989 Act;
(d) a care order under section 31(1)(*a*) of the 1989 Act or the discharge of such an order under section 39(1) of the 1989 Act;
(e) an order giving permission to change a child's surname or remove a child from the United Kingdom under section 33(7) of the 1989 Act;
(f) a supervision order under section 31(1)(*b*) of the 1989 Act, the discharge or variation of such an order under section 39(2) of that Act, or the extension or further extension of such an order under paragraph 6(3) of Schedule 3 to that Act;
(g) an order making provision for contact under section 34(2) to (4) of the 1989 Act or an order varying or discharging such an order under section 34(9) of that Act;
(h) an education supervision order, the extension of an education supervision order under paragraph 15(2) of Schedule 3 to the

1989 Act, or the discharge of such an order under paragraph 17(1) of Schedule 3 to that Act;
(i) an order varying directions made with an interim care order or interim supervision order under section 38(8)(*b*) of the 1989 Act;
(j) an order under section 39(3) of the 1989 Act varying a supervision order in so far as it affects a person with whom the child is living but who is not entitled to apply for the order to be discharged;
(k) an order under section 39(3A) of the 1989 Act varying or discharging an interim care order in so far as it imposes an exclusion requirement on a person who is not entitled to apply for the order to be discharged;
(l) an order under section 39(3B) of the 1989 Act varying or discharging an interim care order in so far as it confers a power of arrest attached to an exclusion requirement;
(m) the substitution of a supervision order for a care order under section 39(4) of the 1989 Act;
(n) a child assessment order or the variation or discharge of such an order under section 43(12) of the 1989 Act;
(o) an order permitting the Local Authority to arrange for any child in its care to live outside England and Wales under paragraph 19(1) of Schedule 2 to the 1989 Act;
(p) a contribution order, or the variation or revocation of such an order under paragraph 23(8), of Schedule 2 to the 1989 Act;
(q) an appeal under paragraph 8(1) of Schedule 8 to the 1989 Act.
(34) "rules" means rules of court governing the practice and procedure to be followed in Public Law Proceedings;
(35) "Schedule of Proposed Findings" means the schedule of findings of fact prepared by the Local Authority sufficient to satisfy the threshold criteria under section 31(2) of the 1989 Act and to inform the Care Plan;
(36) "section 7 report" means any report under section 7 of the 1989 Act;
(37) "section 37 report" means any report by the Local Authority to the court as a result of a direction under section 37 of the 1989 Act;
(38) "Social Work Chronology" means a schedule containing –
(a) a succinct summary of the significant dates and events in the child's life in chronological order- a running record to be updated during the proceedings;
(b) information under the following headings –
(i) serial number;
(ii) date;
(iii) event-detail;
(iv) witness or document reference (where applicable);
(39) "specified proceedings" has the meaning assigned to it by section 41(6) of the 1989 Act;
(40) "Standard Directions on Issue" mean directions made by the court which will include such of the directions set out in the Public Law Outline, Stage 1, column 1 as are appropriate to the proceedings;

(41) "Standard Directions on First Appointment" means directions made by the court which will include such of the directions set out in the Public Law Outline, Stage 1, column 2 and directions relating to the following as are appropriate to the proceedings –
  (a) the Timetable for the Child;
  (b) the joining of a party to the proceedings;
  (c) the appointment of a guardian ad litem or litigation friend including the Official Solicitor where appropriate for a protected party or non subject child;
  (d) allocation of the case to a case manager or case management judge;
  (e) experts in accordance with the Experts Practice Direction;
  (f) the interim care plan setting out details as to proposed placement and contact;
  (g) any other evidence(such as evidence relating to vulnerability, ethnicity, culture, language, religion or gender) and disclosure of evidence between the parties;
  (h) filing and service of the draft of the Case Management Order before the Case Management Conference;
  (i) listing the Issues Resolution Hearing and Final Hearing;
  (j) media attendance and reporting;
(42) "Strategy Discussion Record" means a note of the strategy discussion within the meaning of "Working Together to Safeguard Children" (2006);
(43) "Timetable for the Child" has the meaning assigned to it by the rules (see paragraph 3.2 of this Practice Direction).

Part IV
MISCELLANEOUS

2008

JANUARY
M	T	W	T	F	S	S
	1	2	3	4	5	6
7	8	9	10	11	12	13
14	15	16	17	18	19	20
21	22	23	24	25	26	27
28	29	30	31			

FEBRUARY
M	T	W	T	F	S	S
				1	2	3
4	5	6	7	8	9	10
11	12	13	14	15	16	17
18	19	20	21	22	23	24
25	26	27	28	29		

MARCH
M	T	W	T	F	S	S
					1	2
3	4	5	6	7	8	9
10	11	12	13	14	15	16
17	18	19	20	21	22	23
24	25	26	27	28	29	30
31						

APRIL
M	T	W	T	F	S	S
	1	2	3	4	5	6
7	8	9	10	11	12	13
14	15	16	17	18	19	20
21	22	23	24	25	26	27
28	29	30				

MAY
M	T	W	T	F	S	S
			1	2	3	4
5	6	7	8	9	10	11
12	13	14	15	16	17	18
19	20	21	22	23	24	25
26	27	28	29	30	31	

JUNE
M	T	W	T	F	S	S
						1
2	3	4	5	6	7	8
9	10	11	12	13	14	15
16	17	18	19	20	21	22
23	24	25	26	27	28	29
30						

JULY
M	T	W	T	F	S	S
	1	2	3	4	5	6
7	8	9	10	11	12	13
14	15	16	17	18	19	20
21	22	23	24	25	26	27
28	29	30	31			

AUGUST
M	T	W	T	F	S	S
				1	2	3
4	5	6	7	8	9	10
11	12	13	14	15	16	17
18	19	20	21	22	23	24
25	26	27	28	29	30	31

SEPTEMBER
M	T	W	T	F	S	S
1	2	3	4	5	6	7
8	9	10	11	12	13	14
15	16	17	18	19	20	21
22	23	24	25	26	27	28
29	30					

OCTOBER
M	T	W	T	F	S	S
		1	2	3	4	5
6	7	8	9	10	11	12
13	14	15	16	17	18	19
20	21	22	23	24	25	26
27	28	29	30	31		

NOVEMBER
M	T	W	T	F	S	S
					1	2
3	4	5	6	7	8	9
10	11	12	13	14	15	16
17	18	19	20	21	22	23
24	25	26	27	28	29	30

DECEMBER
M	T	W	T	F	S	S
1	2	3	4	5	6	7
8	9	10	11	12	13	14
15	16	17	18	19	20	21
22	23	24	25	26	27	28
29	30	31				

2009

JANUARY
M	T	W	T	F	S	S
			1	2	3	4
5	6	7	8	9	10	11
12	13	14	15	16	17	18
19	20	21	22	23	24	25
26	27	28	29	30	31	

FEBRUARY
M	T	W	T	F	S	S
						1
2	3	4	5	6	7	8
9	10	11	12	13	14	15
16	17	18	19	20	21	22
23	24	25	26	27	28	

MARCH
M	T	W	T	F	S	S
						1
2	3	4	5	6	7	8
9	10	11	12	13	14	15
16	17	18	19	20	21	22
23	24	25	26	27	28	29
30	31					

APRIL
M	T	W	T	F	S	S
		1	2	3	4	5
6	7	8	9	10	11	12
13	14	15	16	17	18	19
20	21	22	23	24	25	26
27	28	29	30			

MAY
M	T	W	T	F	S	S
				1	2	3
4	5	6	7	8	9	10
11	12	13	14	15	16	17
18	19	20	21	22	23	24
25	26	27	28	29	30	31

JUNE
M	T	W	T	F	S	S
1	2	3	4	5	6	7
8	9	10	11	12	13	14
15	16	17	18	19	20	21
22	23	24	25	26	27	28
29	30					

JULY
M	T	W	T	F	S	S
		1	2	3	4	5
6	7	8	9	10	11	12
13	14	15	16	17	18	19
20	21	22	23	24	25	26
27	28	29	30	31		

AUGUST
M	T	W	T	F	S	S
					1	2
3	4	5	6	7	8	9
10	11	12	13	14	15	16
17	18	19	20	21	22	23
24	25	26	27	28	29	30
31						

SEPTEMBER
M	T	W	T	F	S	S
	1	2	3	4	5	6
7	8	9	10	11	12	13
14	15	16	17	18	19	20
21	22	23	24	25	26	27
28	29	30				

OCTOBER
M	T	W	T	F	S	S
			1	2	3	4
5	6	7	8	9	10	11
12	13	14	15	16	17	18
19	20	21	22	23	24	25
26	27	28	29	30	31	

NOVEMBER
M	T	W	T	F	S	S
						1
2	3	4	5	6	7	8
9	10	11	12	13	14	15
16	17	18	19	20	21	22
23	24	25	26	27	28	29
30						

DECEMBER
M	T	W	T	F	S	S
	1	2	3	4	5	6
7	8	9	10	11	12	13
14	15	16	17	18	19	20
21	22	23	24	25	26	27
28	29	30	31			

PART 4 – Miscellaneous

Part IV Miscellaneous

2010

JANUARY
M	T	W	T	F	S	S
				1	2	3
4	5	6	7	8	9	10
11	12	13	14	15	16	17
18	19	20	21	22	23	24
25	26	27	28	29	30	31

FEBRUARY
M	T	W	T	F	S	S
1	2	3	4	5	6	7
8	9	10	11	12	13	14
15	16	17	18	19	20	21
22	23	24	25	26	27	28

MARCH
M	T	W	T	F	S	S
1	2	3	4	5	6	7
8	9	10	11	12	13	14
15	16	17	18	19	20	21
22	23	24	25	26	27	28
29	30	31				

APRIL
M	T	W	T	F	S	S
			1	2	3	4
5	6	7	8	9	10	11
12	13	14	15	16	17	18
19	20	21	22	23	24	25
26	27	28	29	30		

MAY
M	T	W	T	F	S	S
					1	2
3	4	5	6	7	8	9
10	11	12	13	14	15	16
17	18	19	20	21	22	23
24	25	26	27	28	29	30
31						

JUNE
M	T	W	T	F	S	S
	1	2	3	4	5	6
7	8	9	10	11	12	13
14	15	16	17	18	19	20
21	22	23	24	25	26	27
28	29	30				

JULY
M	T	W	T	F	S	S
			1	2	3	4
5	6	7	8	9	10	11
12	13	14	15	16	17	18
19	20	21	22	23	24	25
26	27	28	29	30	31	

AUGUST
M	T	W	T	F	S	S
						1
2	3	4	5	6	7	8
9	10	11	12	13	14	15
16	17	18	19	20	21	22
23	24	25	26	27	28	29
30	31					

SEPTEMBER
M	T	W	T	F	S	S
		1	2	3	4	5
6	7	8	9	10	11	12
13	14	15	16	17	18	19
20	21	22	23	24	25	26
27	28	29	30			

OCTOBER
M	T	W	T	F	S	S
				1	2	3
4	5	6	7	8	9	10
11	12	13	14	15	16	17
18	19	20	21	22	23	24
25	26	27	28	29	30	31

NOVEMBER
M	T	W	T	F	S	S
1	2	3	4	5	6	7
8	9	10	11	12	13	14
15	16	17	18	19	20	21
22	23	24	25	26	27	28
29	30					

DECEMBER
M	T	W	T	F	S	S
		1	2	3	4	5
6	7	8	9	10	11	12
13	14	15	16	17	18	19
20	21	22	23	24	25	26
27	28	29	30	31		

2011

JANUARY
M	T	W	T	F	S	S
					1	2
3	4	5	6	7	8	9
10	11	12	13	14	15	16
17	18	19	20	21	22	23
24	25	26	27	28	29	30
31						

FEBRUARY
M	T	W	T	F	S	S
	1	2	3	4	5	6
7	8	9	10	11	12	13
14	15	16	17	18	19	20
21	22	23	24	25	26	27
28						

MARCH
M	T	W	T	F	S	S
	1	2	3	4	5	6
7	8	9	10	11	12	13
14	15	16	17	18	19	20
21	22	23	24	25	26	27
28	29	30	31			

APRIL
M	T	W	T	F	S	S
				1	2	3
4	5	6	7	8	9	10
11	12	13	14	15	16	17
18	19	20	21	22	23	24
25	26	27	28	29	30	

MAY
M	T	W	T	F	S	S
						1
2	3	4	5	6	7	8
9	10	11	12	13	14	15
16	17	18	19	20	21	22
23	24	25	26	27	28	29
30	31					

JUNE
M	T	W	T	F	S	S
		1	2	3	4	5
6	7	8	9	10	11	12
13	14	15	16	17	18	19
20	21	22	23	24	25	26
27	28	29	30			

JULY
M	T	W	T	F	S	S
				1	2	3
4	5	6	7	8	9	10
11	12	13	14	15	16	17
18	19	20	21	22	23	24
25	26	27	28	*29	30	31

AUGUST
M	T	W	T	F	S	S
1	2	3	4	5	6	7
8	9	10	11	12	13	14
15	16	17	18	19	20	21
22	23	24	25	26	27	28
29	30	31				

SEPTEMBER
M	T	W	T	F	S	S
			1	2	3	4
5	6	7	8	9	10	11
12	13	14	15	16	17	18
19	20	21	22	23	24	25
26	27	28	29	30		

OCTOBER
M	T	W	T	F	S	S
					1	2
3	4	5	6	7	8	9
10	11	12	13	14	15	16
17	18	19	20	21	22	23
24	25	26	27	28	29	30
31						

NOVEMBER
M	T	W	T	F	S	S
	1	2	3	4	5	6
7	8	9	10	11	12	13
14	15	16	17	18	19	20
21	22	23	24	25	26	27
28	29	30				

DECEMBER
M	T	W	T	F	S	S
			1	2	3	4
5	6	7	8	9	10	11
12	13	14	15	16	17	18
19	20	21	22	23	24	25
26	27	28	29	30	31	

CONVERSION TABLES

Length

kilometres (km)	km or miles	miles
1.609	1	0.621
3.219	2	1.243
4.828	3	1.864
6.437	4	2.485
8.047	5	3.107
9.656	6	3.728
11.265	7	4.350
12.875	8	4.971
14.484	9	5.592
16.093	10	6.214
32.187	20	12.427
48.280	30	18.641
64.374	40	24.855
80.467	50	31.069
96.561	60	37.282
112.654	70	43.496
128.758	80	49.710
144.841	90	55.923
160.934	100	62.137

Area

hectares (ha)	ha or acres	acres
0.405	1	2.471
0.809	2	4.942
1.214	3	7.413
1.619	4	9.884
2.023	5	12.355
2.428	6	14.826
2.833	7	17.297
3.237	8	19.769
3.642	9	22.240
4.047	10	24.711

Part IV Miscellaneous

8.094	20	49.421
12.140	30	74.132
16.187	40	98.842
20.234	50	123.553
24.281	60	148.263
28.328	70	172.974
32.375	80	197.684
36.422	90	222.395
40.469	100	247.105

Capacity

litres	litres or UK gallons	UK gallons
4.546	1	0.220
9.092	2	0.440
13.638	3	0.660
18.184	4	0.880
22.730	5	1.100
27.276	6	1.320
31.822	7	1.540
36.368	8	1.760
40.914	9	1.980
45.460	10	2.200
90.919	20	4.399
136.379	30	6.599
181.839	40	8.799
227.298	50	10.998
272.758	60	13.198
318.217	70	15.398
363.677	80	17.598
409.137	90	19.797
454.596	100	21.997

Weight

kilograms (kg)	kg or lb	pounds (lb)
0.454	1	2.205
0.907	2	4.409
1.361	3	6.614
1.814	4	8.819
2.268	5	11.023
2.722	6	13.228
3.175	7	15.432
3.629	8	17.637
4.082	9	19.842
4.536	10	22.046
9.072	20	44.092
13.608	30	66.139
18.144	40	88.185
22.680	50	110.231
27.216	60	132.277
31.752	70	154.324
36.287	80	176.370
40.823	90	198.416
45.359	100	220.462